J. Bradford DeLong is a professor of economics at UC Berkeley and was a research associate at the NBER, 1990-2018. He was Deputy Assistant Secretary of the US Treasury, 1993-1995. Throughout his career and in his blog *Grasping for Reality* he has tried to straddle the fields of economics, history, and public education. Previous books include *Th~ F~~~~ ~luence* (Basic Books US, 2010) and *C~~~~~~~~ ~~~~~~~~ ~~~~~~ ~rvard Business School, 2016).

Praise for *Slou~~~~~~~ ~~~~~~~ ~~pia*

'A magisterial history . . . asks the right questions and teaches us a lot of crucial history along the way'
            Paul Krugman, winner of the Nobel Memorial Prize in
                                    Economic Sciences, 2008

'Like many people, I've been eagerly anticipating *Slouching Towards Utopia* and it doesn't disappoint . . . an unmissable book . . . The strength of the book – as well as its immense scope and depth . . . is that it's a work of political economy, braiding the different strands of ideas, Hayek, Polanyi and Keynes . . . In addition, there are plenty of pleasing asides and details. Definitely one to read'
                        Diane Coyle, host of *Enlightenment Economics*

'A brilliant and important book. It offers an original and penetrating analysis of what its author calls "the long twentieth century" . . . Material abundance poured upon humanity. Previous generations would have thought such wealth to be a guarantee of utopia. Yet the age of material progress has ended not in a utopia, but in recrimination and discord. No book has explained the successes and failures of this extraordinary period with comparable insight'
                Martin Wolf, chief economics commentator, *Financial Times*

'An intellectually exciting and entertaining gallop along the arc of twentieth-century economic history. DeLong puts together the puzzle of the past to tell a story of remarkable achievements as well as setbacks. A great way to understand the forces that have shaped the world today'

Minouche Shafik, Director, London School of Economics and Political Science

'DeLong learnedly and grippingly tells the story of how all the economic growth since 1870 has created a global economy that today satisfies no one's ideas of fairness. The long journey toward economic justice and more equal rights and opportunities for all shall and will continue'

Thomas Piketty, No.1 *New York Times* bestselling author of *Capital in the Twenty-First Century*

'An impressive achievement, written with wit and style and a formidable command of detail'

The Economist

'The period 1870-2010 – what DeLong calls the "long twentieth century" – saw the world break decisively free of its Malthusian chains, with levels of per capita economic growth without any parallel in human history. This wonderfully researched and written book explains the roots of this vertiginous ascent towards utopia, while also exposing the causes of the subsequent flat-lining in our economic fortunes and what action is now needed to ensure the long century is viewed by future historians as the historical rule, not the exception'

Andrew G. Haldane, Chief Executive of the RSA and former Chief Economist at the Bank of England

'History provides the only data we have for charting a course forward in these turbulent times. I have not seen a more revealing and illuminating book about economics and what it means in a very long time. *Slouching Towards Utopia* should be required reading for anybody who cares about the future of the global system, and that should be everyone'

Lawrence H. Summers, Harvard University

'DeLong explores the slice of history he has chosen – the "long twentieth century" from 1870 to 2010 – in depth, and he often writes with verve combined with thought-provoking detail'

Daily Telegraph

'What a joy to finally have DeLong's masterful interpretation of twentieth-century economic history down on paper. . . engaging, important, and awe-inspiring in its breadth and creativity'

Christina Romer, University of California, Berkeley

'DeLong manages brilliantly to combine detailed analysis of a huge sweep of global history with an accessible and engaging narrative. The result is a book full of well-founded and penetrating insights that will appeal to anyone interested in the causes and consequences of modern economic growth'

Robert C. Allen, Distinguished Professor of Economic History at New York University, Abu Dhabi, and a Senior Research Fellow of Nuffield College, Oxford

'Eloquent and clear . . . makes one sad for the utopian possibilities that might have been realized'

Emanuel Derman, author of *My Life as a Quant* and *The Volatility Smile*

'I've been waiting for Brad [DeLong]'s big economic history opus for a long time now'

Ezra Klein, journalist, political analyst and host of The Ezra Klein Show

'If you want to follow the conversation right now on global economic history, you should check out DeLong's *Slouching Towards Utopia*'

Adam Tooze, author of
Crashed, on The Ezra Klein Show

'A masterfully sweeping account . . . a joy to read. Few economic historians have as fluent a grasp of political or military history or, more important, write as lucidly and with such great flair about these subjects'

Liaquat Ahamed, author of *Lords of Finance*

'One of the most ambitious and admirable economic history books of the year . . . DeLong is a guide whose conclusions I cannot fault'

Strategy+Business

'Conveys a wealth of information in elegant, accessible prose, combining grand, epochal perspectives with fascinating discursions on everything from alternating-current electricity to the gender wage gap. The result is a cogent interpretation of economic modernity that illuminates both its nigh-miraculous achievements and its seething discontents'

Publishers Weekly

'Accessible and illuminating explanations of key historical shifts and the socio-economic forces driving them . . . A sprawling but carefully argued, edifying account of modern economic history and its impact on global well-being'

Kirkus Reviews

'This volume, partly an economic history but mostly a thorough record of the global economy's connection with politics, is destined to become a classic in its category'

Library Journal

'A masterpiece'

Zachary D. Carter, *Dissent*

'A fantastic read . . . you don't have to be an economist or historian to enjoy this book or reach for the smelling salts to revive you from boredom'

Patrick Luciani, *The Hub*

'Deeply engaging . . . a work of strikingly expansive breadth and scope'

Benjamin M. Friedman, *Harvard Magazine*

'DeLong has written the most entertaining End Times narrative since *The Late Great Planet Earth*'

Steve Donoghue, *Open Letters Review*

'Worries that the future will be worse than the present are an excellent reason to read economic histories such as DeLong's new book, *Slouching Towards Utopia*'

Joshua Kim, *Inside Higher Ed*

'A magisterial new economic history'

Michael Hiltzik, *Los Angeles Times*

'Comprehensive, beautifully written, and fun to read'

Andrew Koppelman, *Los Angeles Review of Books*

'It does what all the best nonfiction books do: it changes the way you understand the world around you'

Nathan Baschez, *Every*

SLOUCHING
TOWARDS UTOPIA

SLOUCHING TOWARDS UTOPIA

An Economic History of the Twentieth Century

J. Bradford DeLong

BASIC BOOKS

LONDON

First published in Great Britain in 2022 by Basic Books UK
An imprint of John Murray Press
An Hachette UK company

This paperback edition published in 2023

1

Text design by Jeff Williams

A CIP catalogue record for this title is available from the British Library

Paperback ISBN 9781399803434
eBook ISBN 9781399803441

Typeset in HBG Adobe Garamond

Printed and bound in Great Britain by Clays Ltd, Elcograf S.p.A.

John Murray Press policy is to use papers that are natural, renewable and recyclable
products and made from wood grown in sustainable forests. The logging and manufacturing processes are expected to conform to the environmental regulations of the
country of origin.

Basic Books UK
Carmelite House
50 Victoria Embankment
London EC4Y 0DZ

www.basicbooks.uk

To the next generation:
Michael, Gianna, Brendan, Mary Paty, Matthew,
Courtney, Brian, Barbara, Nicholas, Maria, Alexis, and Alex.

Contents

Introduction: My Grand Narrative   1

1. Globalizing the World   27

2. Revving Up the Engine of Technology-Driven Growth   59

3. Democratizing the Global North   85

4. Global Empires   115

5. World War I   141

6. Roaring Twenties   165

7. The Great Depression   205

8. Really-Existing Socialism   235

9. Fascism and Nazism   259

10. World War II   283

11. The Cold War of Hostile Yet Coexisting Systems   311

12. False (and True) Starts to Economic Development
    in the Global South   339

13. Inclusion   373

14. Thirty Glorious Years of Social Democracy   395

Contents

15. The Neoliberal Turn   427

16. Reglobalization, Information Technology,
    and Hyperglobalization   461

17. Great Recession and Anemic Recovery   485

Conclusion: Are We Still Slouching Towards Utopia?   519

Acknowledgments   537

Notes   539

Index   579

INTRODUCTION

My Grand Narrative

What I call the "long twentieth century" started with the watershed-crossing events of around 1870—the triple emergence of globalization, the industrial research lab, and the modern corporation—which ushered in changes that began to pull the world out of the dire poverty that had been humanity's lot for the previous ten thousand years, since the discovery of agriculture.[1] And what I call the "long twentieth century" ended in 2010, with the world's leading economic edge, the countries of the North Atlantic, still reeling from the Great Recession that had begun in 2008, and thereafter unable to resume economic growth at anything near the average pace that had been the rule since 1870. The years following 2010 were to bring large system-destabilizing waves of political and cultural anger from masses of citizens, all upset in different ways and for different reasons at the failure of the system of the twentieth century to work for them as they thought that it should.

In between, things were marvelous and terrible, but by the standards of all of the rest of human history, much more marvelous than terrible. The 140 years from 1870 to 2010 of the long twentieth century were, I strongly believe, the most consequential years of all humanity's centuries. And it was the first century in which the most important historical thread was what anyone would call the economic one, for it was the century that saw us end our near-universal dire material poverty.

My strong belief that history should focus on the long twentieth century stands in contrast to what others—most notably the Marxist British historian Eric Hobsbawm—have focused on and called the "short twentieth century," which lasted from the start of World War I in 1914 to the fall of the Soviet Union in 1991.[2] Such others tend to see the nineteenth century as the long rise of democracy and capitalism, from 1776 to 1914, and the short twentieth century as one in which really-existing socialism and fascism shook the world.

Histories of centuries, long or short, are by definition grand narrative histories, built to tell the author's desired story. Setting these years, 1914–1991, apart as a century makes it easy for Hobsbawm to tell the story he wants to tell. But it does so at the price of missing much of what I strongly believe is the bigger, more important story. It is the one that runs from about 1870 to 2010, from humanity's success in unlocking the gate that had kept it in dire poverty up to its failure to maintain the pace of the rapid upward trajectory in human wealth that the earlier success had set in motion.[3]

What follows is my grand narrative, my version of what is the most important story to tell of the history of the twentieth century. It is a primarily economic story. It naturally starts in 1870. I believe it naturally stops in 2010.

As the genius, Dr. Jekyll–like, Austro-English-Chicagoan moral philosopher Friedrich August von Hayek observed, the market economy crowdsources—incentivizes and coordinates at the grassroots—solutions to the problems it sets.[4] Back before 1870 humanity did not have the technologies or the organizations to allow a market economy to pose the problem of how to make the economy rich. So even though humanity had had market economies, or at least market sectors within its economies, for thousands of years before 1870, all that markets could do was to find customers for producers of luxuries and conveniences, and make the lives of the rich luxurious and of the middle class convenient and comfortable.

Things changed starting around 1870. Then we got the institutions for organization and research and the technologies—we got full globalization, the industrial research laboratory, and the modern corporation. These were the keys. These unlocked the gate that had previously kept humanity in dire poverty. The problem of making humanity rich could now be posed to the market economy, because it now had a solution. On the other side of the gate, the trail to utopia came into view. And everything else good should have followed from that.

Much good did follow from that.

My estimate—or perhaps my very crude personal guess—of the average worldwide pace of what is at the core of humanity's economic growth, the proportional rate of growth of my index of the value of the stock of useful ideas about manipulating nature and organizing humans that were discovered, developed, and deployed into the world economy, shot up from about 0.45 percent per year before 1870 to 2.1 percent per year afterward, truly a watershed boundary-crossing difference. A 2.1 percent average growth for the 140 years from 1870 to 2010 is a multiplication by a factor of 21.5. That was very good: the growing power to create wealth and earn an income allowed humans to have more of the good things, the necessities, conveniences, and luxuries of life, and to better provide for themselves and their families. This does not mean that humanity in 2010 was 21.5 times as rich in material-welfare terms as it had been in 1870: there were six times as many people in 2010 as there were in 1870, and the resulting increase in resource scarcity would take away from human living standards and labor-productivity levels. As a rough guess, average world income per capita in 2010 would be 8.8 times what it was in 1870, meaning an average income per capita in 2010 of perhaps $11,000 per year. (To get the figure of 8.8, you divide 21.5 by the square root of 6.) Hold these figures in your head as a very rough guide to the amount by which humanity was richer in 2010 than it was in 1870—and never forget that the riches were vastly more unequally distributed around the globe in 2010 than they were in 1870.[5]

A 2.1 percent per year growth rate is a doubling every thirty-three years. That meant that the technological and productivity economic underpinnings of human society in 1903 were profoundly different from those of 1870—underpinnings of industry and globalization as opposed to agrarian and landlord-dominated. The mass-production underpinnings of 1936, at least in the industrial core of the global north, were profoundly different also. But the change to the mass consumption and suburbanization underpinnings of 1969 was as profound, and that was followed by the shift to the information-age microelectronic-based underpinnings of 2002. A revolutionized economy every generation cannot but revolutionize society and politics, and a government trying to cope with such repeated revolutions cannot help but be greatly stressed in its attempts to manage and provide for its people in the storms.

Much good, but also much ill, flowed: people can and do use technologies—both the harder ones, for manipulating nature, and the softer ones, for organizing humans—to exploit, to dominate, and to tyrannize. And the long twentieth century saw the worst and most bloodthirsty tyrannies that we know of.

And much that was mixed, both for good and for ill, also flowed. All that was solid melted into air—or rather, all established orders and patterns were steamed away.[6] Only a small proportion of economic life could be carried out, and was carried out, in 2010 the same way it had been in 1870. And even the portion that was the same was different: even if you were doing the same tasks that your predecessors had done back in 1870, and doing them in the same places, others would pay much less of the worth of their labor-time for what you did or made. As nearly everything economic was transformed and transformed again—as the economy was revolutionized in every generation, at least in those places on the earth that were lucky enough to be the growth poles—those changes shaped and transformed nearly everything sociological, political, and cultural.

Suppose we could go back in time to 1870 and tell people then how rich, relative to them, humanity would become by 2010. How would they react? They would almost surely think that the world of 2010 would be a paradise, a utopia. People would have 8.8 times the wealth? Surely that would mean enough power to manipulate nature and organize humans that all but the most trivial of problems and obstacles hobbling humanity could be resolved.

But not so. It has now been 150 years. We did not run to the trail's end and reach utopia. We are still on the trail—maybe, for we can no longer see clearly to the end of the trail or even to wherever the trail is going to lead.

What went wrong?

Well, Hayek may have been a genius, but only the Dr. Jekyll side of him was a genius. He and his followers were extraordinary idiots as well. They also thought the market alone could do the whole job—or at least all the job that could be done—and commanded humanity to believe in the workings of a system with a logic of its own that mere humans could never fully understand: "The market giveth, the market taketh away; blessed be the name of the market." They thought that what salvation was possible for humanity would come not through St. Paul of Tarsus's *solo fide* but through Hayek's *solo mercato*.[7]

But humanity objected. The market economy solved the problems that it set itself, but then society did not want those solutions—it wanted solutions to other problems, problems that the market economy did not set itself, and for which the crowd-sourced solutions it offered were inadequate.

It was, perhaps, Hungarian-Jewish-Torontonian moral philosopher Karl Polanyi who best described the issue. The market economy recognizes property rights. It sets itself the problem of giving those who own property—or, rather, the pieces of property that it decides are valuable—what they think they want. If you have no property, you have no rights. And if the property you have is not valuable, the rights you have are very thin.

But people think they have other rights—they think that those who do not own valuable property should have the social power to be listened to, and that societies should take their needs and desires into account.[8] Now the market economy might in fact satisfy their needs and desires. But if it does so, it does so only by accident: only if satisfying them happens to conform to a maximum-profitability test performed by a market economy that is solving the problem of getting the owners of valuable pieces of property as much of what the rich want as possible.[9]

So throughout the long twentieth century, communities and people looked at what the market economy was delivering to them and said: "Did we order that?" And society demanded something else. The idiot Mr. Hyde side of Friedrich von Hayek called it "social justice," and decreed that people should forget about it: the market economy could never deliver social justice, and to try to rejigger society so that social justice could be delivered would destroy the market economy's ability to deliver what it could deliver—increasing wealth, distributed to those who owned valuable property rights.[10]

Do note that in this context "social justice" was always only "justice" relative to what particular groups desired: not anything justified by any consensus transcendental principles. Do note that it was rarely egalitarian: it is unjust if those unequal to you are treated equally. But the only conception of "justice" that the market economy could deliver was what the rich might think was just, for the property owners were the only people it cared for. Plus, the market economy, while powerful, is not perfect: it cannot by itself deliver enough research and development, for example, or environmental quality, or, indeed, full and stable employment.[11]

No: "The market giveth, the market taketh away; blessed be the name of the market" was not a stable principle around which to organize society and political economy. The only stable principle had to be some version of "The market was made for man, not man for the market." But who were the men who counted, for whom the market should be made? And what version would be the best making? And how to resolve the squabbles over the answers to those questions?

Throughout the long twentieth century, many others—Karl Polanyi, Theodore Roosevelt, John Maynard Keynes, Benito Mussolini, Franklin Delano Roosevelt, Vladimir Lenin, and Margaret Thatcher serve as good markers for many of the currents of thought, activism, and action—tried to think up solutions. They dissented from the pseudo-classical (for the order of society, economy, and polity as it stood in the years after 1870 was in fact quite new), semi-liberal (for it rested upon ascribed and inherited authority as much as on freedom) order that Hayek and his ilk advocated and worked to create and maintain. They did so constructively and destructively, demanding that the market do less, or do something different, and that other institutions do more. Perhaps the closest humanity got was the shotgun marriage of Hayek and Polanyi blessed by Keynes in the form of post–World War II North Atlantic developmental social democracy. But that institutional setup failed its own sustainability test. And so we are still on the path, not at its end. And we are still, at best, slouching toward utopia.

RETURN TO MY CLAIM above that the long twentieth century was the first century in which the most important historical thread was the economic one. That is a claim worth pausing over. The century saw, among much else, two world wars, the Holocaust, the rise and fall of the Soviet Union, the zenith of American influence, and the rise of modernized China. How dare I say that these are all aspects of one primarily economic story? Indeed, how dare I say that there is one single most consequential thread?

I do so because we have to tell grand narratives if we are to think at all. Grand narratives are, in the words of that bellwether twentieth-century philosopher Ludwig Wittgenstein, "nonsense." But, in a sense, all human thought is nonsense: fuzzy, prone to confusions, and capable of leading us astray. And our fuzzy thoughts are the only ways we can think—the only ways we have to progress. If we are lucky, Wittgenstein said, we can "recognize . . . them as nonsensical," and use them as steps "to climb beyond them . . . [and then] throw away the ladder"—for, perhaps, we will have learned to transcend "these propositions" and gained the ability to "see the world aright."[12]

It is in hopes of transcending the nonsense to glimpse the world aright that I've written this grand narrative. It is in that spirit that I declare unhesitatingly that the most consequent thread through all this history was economic.

Before 1870, over and over again, technology lost its race with human fecundity, with the speed at which we reproduce. Greater numbers, coupled with resource scarcity and a slow pace of technological innovation, produced a situation in which most people, most of the time, could not be confident that in a year they and their family members would have enough to eat and a roof over their heads.[13] Before 1870, those able to attain such comforts had to do so by taking from others, rather than by finding ways to make more for everyone (especially because those specializing in producing, rather than taking, thereby become very soft and attractive targets to the specializers in taking).

The ice was breaking before 1870. Between 1770 and 1870 technology and organization gained a step or two on fecundity. But only a step or two. In the early 1870s that British establishment economist, moral philosopher, and bureaucrat John Stuart

Mill claimed, with some justification, that "it is questionable if all the mechanical inventions yet made have lightened the day's toil of any human being."[14] You have to go forward a generation after 1870 before general material progress becomes unquestionable. The ice could then have resolidified—the nineteenth-century technologies of steam, iron, rails, and textiles were approaching their culmination point; moreover, they all depended on hyper-cheap coal, and the hyper-cheap coal was being exhausted.

But tell anyone from before the long twentieth century about the wealth, productivity, technology, and sophisticated productive organizations of the world today, and their likely response, as noted above, would be that with such enormous power and wealth in our collective hands we must have built a utopia.

That is in fact what they did tell us. Perhaps the third best-selling novel in the United States in the nineteenth century was *Looking Backward, 2000–1887*, by Edward Bellamy. Bellamy was a populist and—although he rejected the name—a socialist: he dreamed of a utopia created by government ownership of industry, the elimination of destructive competition, and the altruistic mobilization of human energies. Technological and organizational abundance, he believed, would generate a society of abundance. His novel, therefore, was a "literary fantasy, a fairy tale of social felicity," in which he imagined "hanging in mid-air, far out of reach of the sordid and material world of the present . . . [a] cloud-palace for an ideal humanity."[15]

He throws his narrator-protagonist forward in time, from 1887 to 2000, to marvel at a rich, well-functioning society. At one point the narrator-protagonist is asked if he would like to hear some music. He expects his hostess to play the piano. This alone would be testament to a vast leap forward. To listen to music on demand in around 1900 you had to have—in your house or nearby—an instrument, and someone trained to play it. It would have cost the average worker some 2,400 hours, roughly a year at a 50-hour workweek, to earn the money to buy a high-quality piano. Then there would be the expense and the time committed to piano lessons.

But Bellamy's narrator-protagonist is awed when his hostess does not sit down at the pianoforte to amuse him. Instead, she "merely touched one or two screws," and immediately the room was "filled with music; filled, not flooded, for, by some means, the volume of melody had been perfectly graduated to the size of the apartment. 'Grand!' I cried. 'Bach must be at the keys of that organ; but where is the organ?'"

He learns that his host has dialed up, on her telephone landline, a live orchestra, and she has put it on the speakerphone. In Bellamy's utopia, you see, you can dial up a local orchestra and listen to it play live. But wait. It gets more impressive. He further learns he has a choice. His hostess could dial up one of four orchestras currently playing.

The narrator's reaction? "If we [in the 1800s] could have devised an arrangement for providing everybody with music in their homes, perfect in quality, unlimited in quantity, suited to every mood, and beginning and ceasing at will, we should have considered the limit of human felicity already attained."[16] Think of that: the limit of human felicity.

Utopias are, by definition, the be-all and end-all. "An imagined place or state of things in which everyone is perfect": so says Oxford Reference.[17] Much of human history has been spent in disastrous flirtations with ideals of perfection of many varieties. Utopian imaginings during the long twentieth century were responsible for its most shocking grotesqueries.

Citing a quotation from the eighteenth-century philosopher Immanuel Kant—"Out of the crooked timber of humanity no straight thing was ever made"—the philosopher-historian Isaiah Berlin concluded, "And for that reason no perfect solution is, not merely in practice, but in principle, possible in human affairs."[18]

Berlin went on to write, "Any determined attempt to produce it is likely to lead to suffering, disillusionment, and failure." This observation also points to why I see the long twentieth century as most fundamentally economic. For all its uneven benefits, for all its expanding human felicity without ever reaching its limit, for all its manifest imperfections, economics during the twentieth century has worked just shy of miracles.

The consequences of the long twentieth century have been enormous: Today, less than 9 percent of humanity lives at or below the roughly $2-a-day living standard we think of as "extreme poverty," down from approximately 70 percent in 1870. And even among that 9 percent, many have access to public health and mobile phone communication technologies of vast worth and power. Today, the luckier economies of the world have achieved levels of per capita prosperity at least twenty times those of 1870, and at least twenty-five times those of 1770—and there is every reason to believe prosperity will continue to grow at an exponential rate in the centuries to come. Today, the typical citizens of these economies can wield powers—of mobility, of communication, of creation, and of destruction—that approach those attributed to sorcerers and gods in ages past. Even the majority of those living in unlucky economies and in the "global south" confront not the $2- to $3-a-day living standard of those economies in 1800 or 1870, but an average closer to $15 a day.

Many technological inventions of the past century have transformed experiences that were rare and valued luxuries—available only to a rich few at great expense—into features of modern life that we take so much for granted that they would not make the top twenty or even the top one hundred in an ordered list of what we think our wealth consists of. So many of us have grown so accustomed to our daily level of felicity that we utterly overlook something astounding. We today—even the richest of us—rarely see ourselves as so extraordinarily lucky and fortunate and happy, even though, for the first time in human history, there is more than enough.

There are more than enough calories produced in the world, so it is not necessary for anybody to be hungry.

There is more than enough shelter on the globe, so it is not necessary for anybody to be wet.

There is more than enough clothing in our warehouses, so it is not necessary for anybody to be cold.

And there is more than enough stuff lying around and being produced daily, so nobody need feel the lack of something necessary.

In short, we are no longer in anything that we could call "the realm of necessity." And, as G. W. F. Hegel said, "Seek food and clothing first, and then the Kingdom of God shall be added unto you."[19] So, one would think, we humans ought to be in something recognizably utopian. That we cannot accept this is another consequence of living our lives fully in the stream of economic history. While history fueled by utopian aspirations is an all or nothing proposition, economic history's successes and failures are most often experienced in the margins.

Which is partly why no full-throated triumphalism over the long twentieth century can survive even a brief look at the political economy of the 2010s: the stepping back of the United States from its role of good-guy world leader and of Britain from its role as a key piece of Europe; and the rise in North America and Europe of political movements that reject democratic representative consensus politics—movements that former US secretary of state Madeleine Albright has called "fascist" (and who am I to tell her she is wrong?).[20] Indeed, any triumphalist narrative would collapse in the face of the conspicuous failures over the previous decade by the stewards of the global economy.

Yes, during the years between 1870 and 2010, technology and organization repeatedly lapped fecundity. Yes, a newly richer humanity resoundingly triumphed over tendencies for population to expand and so for greater resource scarcity to offset more knowledge and better technology. But material prosperity is unevenly distributed around the globe to a gross, even criminal, extent. And material wealth does not make people happy in a world where politicians and others prosper mightily from finding new ways to make and keep people unhappy. The history of the long twentieth century cannot be told as a triumphal gallop, or a march, or even a walk of progress along the road that brings us closer to utopia. It is, rather, a slouch. At best.

One reason why human progress toward utopia has been but a slouch is that so much of it has been and still is mediated by the market economy: that Mammon of Unrighteousness. The market economy enables the astonishing coordination and cooperation of by now nearly eight billion humans in a highly productive division of labor. The market economy also recognizes no rights of humans other than the rights that come with the property their governments say they possess. And those property rights are worth something only if they help produce things that the rich want to buy. That cannot be just.

As I noted above, Friedrich von Hayek always cautioned against listening to the siren song that we should seek justice rather than mere productivity and abundance. We needed to bind ourselves to the mast. Interference in the market, no matter how well-intentioned when it started, would send us into a downward spiral. It would put us on a road to, well, some industrial-age variant of serfdom. But Karl Polanyi responded that such an attitude was inhuman and impossible: People firmly believed, above all else, that they had other rights more important than and prior to the property rights that energized the market economy. They had rights to a community that gave them support, to an income that gave them the resources they deserved, to economic stability that gave them consistent work. And when the market economy tried to dissolve all rights other than property rights? Watch out![21]

Slouching, however, is better than standing still, let alone going backward. That is a truism no generation of humanity has ever disputed. Humans have always been inventive. Technological advance has rarely stopped. The windmills, dikes, fields, crops, and animals of Holland in 1700 made the economy of its countryside very different from the thinly farmed marshes of 700. The ships that docked at the Chinese port of Canton had much greater range, and the commodities loaded on and off of them had much greater value, in 1700 than in 800. And both commerce and agriculture in 800 were far more technologically advanced than they were in the first literate civilizations of 3000 BCE or so.

But before our age, back in the preindustrial Agrarian Age, technological progress led to little visible change over one or even several lifetimes, and little growth in typical living standards even over centuries or millennia.

Recall my very crude index that tracks the value of humanity's useful ideas about manipulating nature and organizing collective efforts—an index of our "technology," as economists call it. To calculate it, assume that each 1 percent increase in typical human standards of living worldwide tells us that the value of our useful ideas has risen by 1 percent. That is simply a normalization: I want the index to scale with real income, and not with something else, such as the square root of or the square of income. Also assume that each 1 percent increase in the human population at a constant typical living standard tells us that the value of useful ideas has risen by 0.5 percent—for such an increase is necessary to hold living standards constant in the face of resource scarcities that emerge from a higher population. This is a way of taking account of the fact that, since our natural resources are not unlimited, we depend on as much added human ingenuity to support a larger population at the same standard of living as we would depend on to support the same population at a higher standard of living.[22]

Set this quantitative index of the global value of useful human knowledge equal to a value of 1 in 1870, at the start of the long twentieth century. Back in the year 8000 BCE, when we discovered agriculture and developed herding, the index stood at 0.04: roughly, and on average across the globe, with the same materials and on the same-size farms, it would take twenty-five workers in 8000 BCE to do what one worker could do in 1870. By the year 1, eight thousand years later, this index was 0.25: with the same resources, better "technologies" meant that the typical worker was now more than six times as productive as the typical worker had been back at the beginning of the Agrarian Age—but only one-quarter as productive as the typical worker of 1870. By the year 1500, the index stood at 0.43, more than 70 percent above the year 1 and a little less than half the value of the year 1870.

These are impressive changes in an index number. They summarize, from the standpoint of those who lived eight thousand years ago, truly miraculous and impressive enlargements of the human empire. Technologies of the year 1500, the Ming pottery or the Portuguese caravel or the wet cultivation of rice seedlings, would have seemed miraculous. But this growth, and the pace of invention, took place over an enormous span of time: technology crawled ahead at only 0.036 percent per year for the entire period between 1 and 1500—that is only 0.9 percent over an average twenty-five-year lifetime of that age.

And did greater knowledge about technology and human organization cause the life in 1500 of a typical person to be much sweeter than it had been in 8000 BCE? It turns out not. The human population grew at an average rate of 0.07 percent per year from year 1 to 1500, and this 0.07 percent per year decrease in average farm size and other available natural resources per worker meant that more skillful work produced little, if any, additional net product on average. While the elite lived far better in 1500 than they had in 8000 BCE or the year 1, ordinary people —peasants and craftsmen—lived little or no better than their predecessors.

Agrarian Age humans were desperately poor: it was a subsistence-level society. On average, 2.03 children per mother survived to reproduce. A typical woman (who was not among the one in seven who died in childbirth, or the additional one in five who died before her children were grown, sometimes from the same contagious diseases to which her children succumbed) would have spent perhaps twenty years eating for two: she would have had perhaps nine pregnancies, six live births, and three or four children surviving to age five, and the life expectancy of her children remained under, and perhaps well under, thirty.[23]

Keeping your children from dying is the first and highest goal of every parent. Humanity in the Agrarian Age could not do so at all reliably. That is an index of how much pressure from material want humanity found itself under.

Over the millennia, 1.5 percent average population growth per generation added up, however. In 1500 there were about three times as many people as there had been in year 1—500 million rather than 170 million. Additional humans did not translate to less individual material want. As of 1500, advances in technological and organizational knowledge went to compensate for fewer natural resources per capita. Thus economic history remained a slowly changing background in front of which cultural, political, and social history took place.

The ice started to groan and shift after 1500. Or perhaps a better metaphor is crossing a divide and entering a new watershed—you are now going downhill, and things are flowing in a new direction. Call this shift the coming of the age of the "Imperial-Commercial Revolution." The pace of inventions and innovation sped up. And then, in around 1770, the ice was cracking as we crossed into yet a different watershed, as far as the level of worldwide prosperity and the pace of global economic growth was concerned: call the century after 1770 the coming of the age of the "Industrial Revolution." By 1870 the index of the value of knowledge stood at 1, more than twice as large as in 1500. It had taken 9,500 years to get the tenfold jump from 0.04 to 0.43—an average time-to-double of some 2,800 years—and then the next doubling took less than 370 years.

But did this mean a richer, more comfortable humanity in 1870? Not very much. There were then in 1870 1.3 billion people alive, 2.6 times as many as there had been in 1500. Farm sizes were only two-fifths as large, on average, as they had been in 1500, canceling out the overwhelming bulk of technological improvement, as far as typical human living standards were concerned.

Around 1870 we crossed over another divide into yet another new watershed: the age Simon Kuznets called an era of "modern economic growth."[24] During the period that would follow, the long twentieth century, there came an explosion.

The approximately seven billion people in 2010 had a global value of knowledge index of 21. Pause to marvel. The value of knowledge about technology and organization had grown at an average rate of 2.1 percent per year. Since 1870, the technological capability and material wealth of humankind had exploded beyond previous imagining. By 2010, the typical human family no longer faced as its most urgent and important problem the task of acquiring enough food, shelter, and clothing for the next year—or the next week.

From the techno-economic point of view, 1870–2010 was the age of the industrial research lab and the bureaucratic corporation. One gathered communities of engineering practice to supercharge economic growth, the other organized communities of competence to deploy the fruits of invention. It was only slightly less the age of globalization: cheap ocean and rail transport that destroyed distance as a cost factor and allowed humans in enormous numbers to seek better lives, along with communications links that allowed us to talk across the world in real time.

The research laboratory, the corporation, and globalization powered the wave of discovery, invention, innovation, deployment, and global economic integration that have so boosted our global useful-economic-knowledge index. Marvel still. In 1870 the daily wages of an unskilled male worker in London, the city then at the forefront of world economic growth and development, would buy him and his family about 5,000 calories worth of bread. That was progress: in 1800, his daily wages would have bought him and his family perhaps 4,000 coarser-bread calories, and in 1600, some 3,000 calories, coarser still. (But isn't coarser, more fiber-heavy bread better for you? For us, yes—but only for those of us who are getting enough calories, and so have the energy to do our daily work and then worry about things like fiber intake. In the old days, you were desperate to absorb as many calories as possible, and for that, whiter and finer bread was better.) Today, the daily wages of an unskilled male worker in London would buy him 2.4 million wheat calories that they could then straightforwardly bake into bread at home: nearly five hundred times as much as in 1870.

From the biosociological point of view, this material progress meant that the typical woman no longer needed to spend twenty years eating for two—pregnant or breastfeeding. By 2010, it was more like four years. And it was also during this century that we became able, for the first time, to prevent more than half our babies from dying in miscarriages, stillbirths, and infancy—and to prevent more than a tenth of mothers from dying in childbirth.[25]

From the nation-and-polity point of view, the wealth creation and distribution drove four things, of which the first was by far the most important: 1870–2010 was the century when the United States became a superpower. Second, it was during this period that the world came to be composed primarily of nations rather than empires. Third, the economy's center of gravity came to consist of large oligopolistic firms ringmastering value chains. Finally, it made a world in which political orders would be primarily legitimated, at least notionally, by elections with universal suffrage—rather than the claims of plutocracy, tradition, "fitness," leadership charisma, or knowledge of a secret key to historical destiny.

Much that our predecessors would have called "utopian" has been attained step by step, via economic improvements year by year, each of which is marginal, but which compound.

Yet, as of 1870, such an explosion was not foreseen, or not foreseen by many. Yes, 1770–1870 did see, for the first time, productive capability begin to outrun population growth and natural resource scarcity. By the last quarter of the nineteenth century, the average inhabitant of a leading economy—a Briton, a Belgian, a Dutchman, an American, a Canadian, or an Australian—had perhaps twice the material wealth and standard of living of the typical inhabitant of a preindustrial economy.

Was that enough to be a true watershed?

Back in the early 1870s, John Stuart Mill put the finishing touches on the final edition of the book that people seeking to understand economics then looked to: *Principles of Political Economy, with Some of Their Applications to Social Philosophy*. His book gave due attention and place to the 1770–1870 era of the British Industrial Revolution. But he looked out on what he saw around him and saw the world still poor and miserable. Far from lightening humanity's daily toil, the era's technology merely "enabled a greater population to live the same life of drudgery and imprisonment, and an increased number of manufacturers and others to make fortunes."[26]

One word of Mill's stands out to me: "imprisonment."

Yes, Mill saw a world with more and richer plutocrats and a larger middle class. But he also saw the world of 1871 as not just a world of drudgery—a world in which humans had to work long and tiring hours. He saw it as not just a world in which most people were close to the edge of being desperately hungry, not just a world of low literacy—where most could only access the collective human store of knowledge, ideas, and entertainments partially and slowly. The world Mill saw was a world in which humanity was imprisoned: in a dungeon, chained and fettered.[27] And Mill saw only one way out: if the government were to take control of human fecundity and require child licenses, prohibiting those who could not properly support and educate their children from reproducing, only then—or was he thinking "if"?—would mechanical inventions wreak the "great changes in human destiny, which it is in their nature and in their futurity to accomplish."[28]

And there were others who were much more pessimistic than even Mill. In 1865, then thirty-year-old British economist William Stanley Jevons made his reputation by prophesying doom for the British economy: it needed to immediately cut back on industrial production in order to economize on scarce and increasingly valuable coal.[29]

With so much pessimism circulating, the coming explosion in economic growth was far from expected—but it would also be dangerously misconstrued by some.

Karl Marx and Friedrich Engels had in 1848 already seen science and technology as Promethean forces that would allow humanity to overthrow its (mythical) old gods and give humanity itself the power of a god. Science, technology, and the profit-seeking entrepreneurial business class that deployed them had, they said,

> during its rule of scarce one hundred years, . . . created more massive and more colossal productive forces than have all preceding generations together. Subjection of Nature's forces to man, machinery, application of chemistry to industry and agriculture, steam-navigation, railways, electric telegraphs, clearing of whole continents for cultivation, canalisation of rivers, whole populations conjured out of the ground—what earlier century had even a presentiment that such productive forces slumbered in the lap of social labour?[30]

ENGELS SNARKED THAT IN overlooking the power of science, technology, and engineering, mere economists (such as Mill) had demonstrated that they were little more than the paid hacks of the rich.[31]

But Marx and Engels's promise was not that there would someday be enough to eat, or enough shelter, or enough clothing for the masses, let alone an exponential increase in the value of global knowledge, or even a nearly unlimited choice of music to listen to. Slouching, galloping economic growth was but a necessary paroxysm on the way to utopia. *Their promise was utopia.* In Marx's few and thin descriptions of life after the socialist revolution, in works such as his *Critique of the Gotha Program*, the utopian life he foresaw echoed—deliberately, but with what authorial intent?—the descriptions in the Acts of the Apostles of how people who had attained the Kingdom of Heaven behaved: each contributed "according to his ability" (Acts 11:29), and each drew on the common, abundant store "according to his needs" (4:35).[32] Perhaps he kept these descriptions rare and without detail because they differed so little from what Mill envisioned: an end to the imprisonment and drudgery of poverty, a society in which all people could be truly free.

However, economic improvement, attained by slouch or gallop, matters.

How many of us today could usefully find our way around a kitchen of a century ago? Before the coming of the electric current and the automatic washing machine, doing the laundry was not an annoying, minor chore but instead a major part of the household's—or rather the household's women's—week. Today few among us are gatherers, or hunters, or farmers. Hunting, gathering, farming, along with herding, spinning and weaving, cleaning, digging, smelting metal, and shaping wood—indeed, assembling structures by hand—have become the occupations of a small and dwindling proportion of humans. And where we do have farmers, herdsmen, manufacturing workers, construction workers, and miners, they are overwhelmingly controllers of machines and increasingly programmers of robots. They are no longer people who manufacture, who make or shape things with their hands.

What do modern people do instead? Increasingly, we push forward the body of technological and scientific knowledge. We educate each other. We doctor and nurse each other. We care for our young and our old. We entertain each other. We provide other services for each other so that we can all take advantage of the benefits of specialization. And we engage in complicated symbolic interactions that have the emergent effect of distributing status and power and coordinating the division of labor of today's economy, which encompassed seven billion people in 2010.

Over the course of the long century we have crossed a great divide, between what we used to do in all of previous human history and what we do now. Utopia, it is true, this is not. I imagine Bellamy would be at once impressed and disappointed.

The economic historian Richard Easterlin helps explain why. The history of the ends humans pursue, he suggests, demonstrates that we are ill-suited for utopia. With our increasing wealth, what used to be necessities become matters of little concern—perhaps even beyond our notice. But conveniences turn into necessities. Luxuries turn into conveniences. And we humans envision and then create new luxuries.[33]

Easterlin, bemused, puzzled over how "material concerns in the wealthiest nations today are as pressing as ever, and the pursuit of material needs as intense." He saw humanity on a hedonic treadmill: "Generation after generation thinks it needs only another ten or twenty percent more income to be perfectly happy. . . . In the end, the triumph of economic growth is not a triumph of humanity over material wants; rather, it is the triumph of material wants over humanity."[34] We do not use our wealth to overmaster our wants. Rather, our wants use our wealth to continue to overmaster us. And this hedonic treadmill is one powerful reason why, even when all went very well, we only slouched rather than galloped toward utopia.

Nevertheless, getting off the treadmill looks grim. Only a fool would wittingly or ignorantly slouch or gallop backward to near-universal dire global poverty.

LET ME REMIND YOU, again, that what follows is a grand narrative. Of a necessity, I spend chapters on what others have spent books, indeed multiple volumes, describing. In pursuit of big themes, details necessarily suffer. Moreover, I will, as needed—which will be often—"pull up the roots" and jump far back in time to identify and quickly trace an influential origin story, for we cannot do other than think in narrative terms. What happened in 1500, say, had consequences for what happened in 1900. Details, gray areas, controversies, historical uncertainties—they suffer, they suffer greatly, but they suffer for a purpose. To date, we humans have failed to see the long twentieth century as fundamentally economic in its significance—and consequently we have failed to take from it all the lessons we must. We have drawn lessons aplenty from the myriad political, military, social, cultural, and diplomatic histories of these decades. But the economic lessons are no less pressing, and, in fact, are more pressing.

The source from which all else flows was the explosion of material wealth that surpassed all precedent: the long twentieth century saw those of us who belong to the upper-middle class, and who live in the industrial core of the world economy, become far richer than the theorists of previous centuries' utopias could imagine. From this explosion flowed five important processes and sets of forces that will constitute the major themes of this book:

History became economic: Because of the explosion of wealth, the long twentieth century was the first century ever in which history was predominantly a matter of economics: the economy was the dominant arena of events and change, and economic changes were the driving force behind other changes, in a way never seen before.

The world globalized: As had never been the case before, things happening on other continents became not just minor fringe factors but among the central determinants of what happened in every single place human beings lived.

The technological cornucopia was the driver: Enabling the enormous increase in material wealth—its essential prerequisite, in fact—was the explosion in human technological knowledge. This required not just a culture and educational system that created large numbers of scientists and engineers, and means of communication and memory, so that they could build on previous discoveries, but also a market economy structured in such a way that it was worth people's while to funnel resources to scientists and engineers so that they could do their jobs.

Governments mismanaged, creating insecurity and dissatisfaction: The governments of the long twentieth century had little clue as to how to regulate the un-self-regulating market to maintain prosperity, to ensure opportunity, or to produce substantial equality.

Tyrannies intensified: The long twentieth century's tyrannies were more brutal and more barbaric than those of any previous century—and were, in strange, complicated, and confused ways, closely related to the forces that made the explosion of wealth so great.

I write this book to engrave these lessons on our collective memories. The only way I know how is to tell you the story, and the substories.

The place to start is in the year 1870, with humanity still en-sorcelled, so that better technology meant not higher living standards for the typical human but rather more people and more resource scarcity that ate up nearly all, if not all, of the potential for material human betterment. Humanity was then still under the spell of a Devil: the Devil of Thomas Robert Malthus.[35]

1

Globalizing the World

He was annoyed by the disquisitions in favor of democracy, reason, feminism, enlightenment, and revolution that crossed his desk. So, just before 1800, English scholar and cleric Thomas Robert Malthus wrote a counterblast, his *Essay on the Principle of Population*. His objective? To demonstrate that his explicit target, William Godwin (the father of *Frankenstein* author Mary Wollstonecraft Shelley)—and all of Godwin's ilk—were, however good their intentions, shortsighted and deluded enemies of the public welfare. Rather than revolution to bring about democracy, reason, feminism, and enlightenment, what humanity needed was religious orthodoxy, political monarchy, and familial patriarchy.[1]

Why? Because human sexuality was a nearly irresistible force. Unless it was somehow checked—unless women were kept religious, the world stayed patriarchal, and governmental sanctions were in place to keep people from making love except under certain approved and stringent conditions—the population would always expand until it reached the limit imposed by the "positive check": that is, population would only stop growing when women became so skinny that ovulation became hit-or-miss, and when children became so malnourished that their immune systems were compromised and ineffective. The good alternative Malthus saw was the "preventative check": a society in which paternal authority kept women virgins until the age of twenty-eight or so, and in which, even after the age of twenty-eight, government restrictions kept women without the blessing of a current marriage from making love, and in which religion-induced fear of damnation kept women from evading those restrictions. Then, and only then, could a population settle at a stable equilibrium in which people were (relatively) well nourished and prosperous.

What Malthus wrote was, from his point of view, not false, at least for his day and for earlier days as well. The world in the year 6000 BCE was a world with perhaps 7 million people on it and a technological index of 0.051. The standard of living was about what the United Nations and academic development economists might peg at an average of $2.50 per day, or about $900 a year. Fast-forward to the year 1, and we see a world with a great deal of accumulated invention, innovation, and technological development compared to 6000 BCE. Technology had advanced far, with my index having now reached 0.25, but the approximate standard of living was still about $900 per year. Why no change? Because human sexuality was indeed a nearly irresistible force, as Malthus knew, and the world human population had grown from about 7 million in 6000 BCE to perhaps 170 million in the year 1. The economist Greg Clark has estimated English construction-worker real wages over time, and this data tells us that, on an index that sets these wages in 1800 at 100, construction-worker real wages had also been at a value of 100 in 1650, in 1340, in 1260, and in 1230. The highest they had reached was a value of 150 in 1450, after the Black Plague of 1346–1348 had carried off perhaps one-third of the population of Europe, and after subsequent waves of plague, generation by generation, plus peasant revolts, had severely limited the power of aristocrats to maintain serfdom. From 1450 to 1600, real wages fell back to what would be their 1800 level.[2]

Malthus's proposed cures—orthodoxy, monarchy, and patri-archy—did not help much to raise this inevitably grim Agrarian Age typical human standard of living. By 1870 there had been some improvement, at least in England. (But remember that England in 1870 was by a substantial margin the richest in-dustrial nation and by far the most industrial economy in the world.) In 1870 Clark's English construction-worker real-wage series stood at 170. But there were some who were not impressed: Remember John Stuart Mill? Smart money still bet that there had not yet been any decisive watershed boundary crossing in human destiny.

John Stuart Mill and company did have a point. Had the Industrial Revolution of 1770–1870 lightened the toil of the overwhelming majority of humanity—even in Britain, the coun-try at the leading edge? Doubtful. Had it materially raised the living standards of the overwhelming majority—even in Brit-ain? By a little. Compared to how mankind had lived before the revolution, it was unquestionably a big deal: steam power and iron making and power looms and telegraph wires had provided comforts for many and fortunes for a few. But how humans lived had not been transformed. And there were legitimate fears. As late as 1919 British economist John Maynard Keynes wrote that while Malthus's Devil had been "chained up and out of sight," with the catastrophe of World War I, "perhaps we have loosed him again."[3]

A fixation on food makes compelling sense to the hun-gry. From the year 1000 BCE to 1500 CE, human populations, checked by a shortage of available calories, had grown at a snail's pace, at a rate of 0.09 percent per year, increasing from perhaps fifty million to perhaps five hundred million. There were lots of children, but they were too malnourished for enough of them to survive long enough to boost the overall population. Over these millennia the typical standards of living of peasants and craft-workers changed little: they consistently spent half or more of their available energy and cash securing the bare minimum of essential calories and nutrients.

It could hardly have been otherwise. Malthus's Devil made certain of that. Population growth ate the benefits of invention and innovation in technology and organization, leaving only the exploitative upper class noticeably better off. And the average pace of invention and innovation in technology and organization was anemic: perhaps 0.04 percent per year. (Recall, for context, that the average pace starting in around 1870 was 2.1 percent per year.)

That was life up to 1500, when there came a crossing of a watershed boundary: the Industrial-Commercial Revolution. The rate of growth of humanity's technological and organizational capabilities took a fourfold upward leap: from the 0.04 percent per year rate following year 1 to 0.15 percent per year. The oceangoing caravels, new horse breeds, cattle and sheep breeds (the Merino sheep, especially), invention of printing presses, recognition of the importance of restoring nitrogen to the soil for staple crop growth, canals, carriages, cannons, and clocks that had emerged by 1650 were technological marvels and were—with the exception of cannons, and for some people caravels—great blessings for humanity. But this growth was not fast enough to break the Devil of Malthus's spell trapping humanity in near-universal poverty. Population expansion, by and large, kept pace with greater knowledge and offset it. Globally, the rich began to live better.[4] But the typical person saw little benefit—or perhaps suffered a substantial loss. Better technology and organization brought increases in production of all types—including the production of more effective and brutal forms of killing, conquest, and slavery.

In 1770, a generation before Malthus wrote his *Essay on the Principle of Population*, there came another watershed boundary crossing: the coming of the British Industrial Revolution. The rate of growth of humanity's technological and organizational capabilities took another upward leap, roughly threefold, from 0.15 percent to around 0.45 percent per year, and perhaps twice that in the heartland of the original Industrial Revolution: a charmed circle with a radius of about three hundred miles around the white cliffs of Dover at the southeastern corner of the island of Britain (plus offshoots in northeastern North America). At this more rapid pace, from 1770 to 1870 more technological marvels became commonplace in the North Atlantic and visible throughout much of the rest of the world. Global population growth accelerated to about 0.5 percent per year, and for the first time global production may have exceeded the equivalent of $3 a day per head (in today's money).

The numbers are important: indeed, they are key. As the economic historian Robert Fogel once said—echoing my great-great-uncle, the economic historian Abbott Payson Usher—the secret weapon of the economist is the ability to count.[5] Remember, we humans are narrative-loving animals. Stories with an exciting plot and an appropriate end of comeuppances and rewards fascinate us. They are how we think. They are how we remember. But individual stories are only important if they concern individuals at a crossroads whose actions end up shaping humanity's path, or if they concern individuals who are especially representative of the great swath of humanity. It is only by counting that we can tell which stories are at all representative and which decisions truly matter. The individual technologies are important. But more important is their weight: counting up the overall extent to which people were becoming more productive at making old things and more capable at making new things.

The causes of the Industrial Revolution were not foreordained. The revolution was not inevitable. But tracing its causes and the lack of necessity in history is outside the scope of my book. Theorists of the multiverse assure me that there are other worlds out there like ours, worlds that we cannot hear or see or touch in much the same way as a radio tuned to one station cannot pick up all the others. And knowing what we know about our world leaves me utterly confident that in most of those other worlds there was no British Industrial Revolution. That growth would more likely than not have leveled out at the Commercial Revolution–era level of 0.15 percent per year or the medieval level of 0.04 percent per year. These seem like far more likely scenarios: worlds of semipermanent gunpowder empires and sail-driven global commerce.[6]

But that is not our world. And even in our world I do not think that the Imperial-Commercial and British Industrial Revolutions were decisive.

Consider that the 0.45 percent per year global rate of growth of deployed human technological and organizational capabilities typical of the Industrial Revolution era would have been eaten up by global population growth of 0.9 percent per year, or a hair under 25 percent per generation. Instead of four average couples having eight children survive to reproduce among them, the four couples together have fewer than ten. But with even moderately well-fed people, human sexuality can and does do much more: British settler populations in North America in the yellow-fever-free zone north of the Mason-Dixon Line quadrupled by natural increase along every one hundred years, without any of the advantages of modern public health. Consider well-fed but poor people facing high infant mortality and desperate to have some descendants survive to care for them in their old age. Four such couples could easily have had not ten, but fourteen children. A growth of 0.45 percent per year in human technological capabilities was not enough to even start drawing a sorcerous pentagram to contain the Malthusian Devil. And so the world of 1870 was a desperately poor world. In 1870, more than four-fifths of humans still by the sweat of their brow tilled the earth to grow the bulk of the food their families ate. Life expectancy was little higher than it had ever been, if any. In 1870, 5 ounces of copper were mined per person worldwide; by 2016, we mined 5 pounds per person. In 1870,

1 pound of steel was produced per person worldwide; by 2016, we produced 350 pounds per person.

And would the growth of technological ideas continue at that 0.45 percent per year global pace of 1770–1870? All of humanity's previous efflorescences had exhausted themselves and ended in renewed economic stagnation, or worse, a Dark Age of conquest. Delhi had been sacked by foreign invaders in 1803—Beijing in 1644, Constantinople in 1453, Baghdad in 1258, Rome in 410, Persepolis in 330 BCE, and Nineveh in 612 BCE.

Why should people expect the growth of 1770–1870 not to similarly exhaust itself? Why should people expect imperial London to confront a different fate?

Economist William Stanley Jevons made his reputation in 1865 when he was still a young whippersnapper of thirty-three years old with *The Coal Question*: arguing that Britain at least would within a generation run out of easily accessible coal, and then the factories would just . . . stop.[7] There was nobody who was a bigger believer in the British Empire than Rudyard Kipling. The British Empire was very good to Rudyard Kipling—until September 27, 1915, when, during World War I, it devoured his son John by killing him in the bloody fields outside the French city of Lille. Yet his reaction to the sixtieth anniversary of Queen-Empress Victoria Hanover's accession to the throne, in 1897, was a poem about London's destiny being the same as Nineveh's, closing: "For frantic boast and foolish word—/ Thy mercy on Thy People, Lord!"[8]

Thus without a further acceleration—a bigger than Industrial Revolution acceleration—of the underlying drivers of economic growth, today's world might indeed have been a permanent steampunk world. It might in 2010 have had a global population of the then current seven billion. But, even if invention had maintained its 1770–1870 average global pace, the vast majority of people would have remained at little more than the 1800–1870 typical global standard of living. With global technology and organization today at about the level of 1910, the airplane might still be an infant technological novelty, and the disposal of horse manure our principal urban transportation-management problem. We might have not 9 percent but, rather, more like 50 percent of the world living on $2 per day, and 90 percent living below $5. Average farm sizes would be one-sixth of what they had been in 1800, and only the uppermost of the upper classes would have what we today regard as a global-north middle-class standard of living.

This, of course, is not what happened. What did happen was post-1870 innovation growth acceleration: a third watershed boundary crossing.

Around 1870 the proportional rate of growth of humanity's technological and organizational capabilities took a further four-fold upward leap to our current 2.1 percent per year or so. Thereafter, technology far outran population growth. And thereafter, population growth in the richest economies began to decline: humans became rich enough and long-lived enough that limiting fertility became a desirable option.

The period from 1870 to 1914 was, in the perspective of all previous eras, "economic El Dorado," or "economic Utopia," as John Maynard Keynes put it, looking back from 1919.[9]

The resulting world of 1914 was an odd mix of modernity and antiquity. Britain burned 194 million tons of coal in 1914. The total coal-equivalent energy consumption of Britain today is only 2.5 times that. US railroads carried passengers some 350 miles per citizen, on average, in 1914. Today US airlines carry passengers 3,000 miles per citizen. Yet in 1914, all of Europe save France still saw the powerful political and social dominance of agrarian landlords, who still mostly saw themselves as descendants of knights who had fought for their kings with their swords.

Compared to the past, it was almost utopia. Globally, the real wages of unskilled workers in 1914 were half again above their levels of 1870. Such a standard of living hadn't been attained since before we'd moved to the farm.

Why has every year since 1870 seen as much technological and organizational progress as was realized every four years from 1770 to 1870? (Or as much progress as was realized every twelve years from 1500 to 1770? Or every sixty years before 1500?) And how did what was originally a geographically concentrated surge in and around parts of Europe become a global (albeit unevenly so) phenomenon?

To foreshadow a more thorough discussion in Chapter 2, I think the answers lie in the coming of the industrial research laboratory, the large modern corporation, and globalization, which made the world one global market economy, all of which then proceeded to solve the problems that the economy set itself. And the biggest of those problems turned out to be finding a way to ratchet up the pace of economic growth. The lab and the corporation are what allowed the likes of Thomas Edison and Nikola Tesla to become inventors. They did not have to fulfill the ten other roles that their predecessors had had to fill, from impresario to human resource manager. That work was left to the corporation. This made a huge difference. Invented technologies could be rationally, routinely, and professionally developed; and then they could be rationally, routinely, and professionally deployed.

Was their development around 1870 necessary and inevitable? We can see how many things in history are neither inevitable nor necessary—how we are as much the product of what didn't happen as we are of what did. Our history is littered with such might-have-beens. Here's just one: Lillian Cross does not hit assassin Giuseppe Zangara with her purse on February 15, 1933, and so his bullet finds the brain of president-elect Franklin Delano Roosevelt rather than the lung of Chicago mayor Anton Čermák; Roosevelt dies and Čermák lives—and America's history in the Great Depression years of the 1930s is very different. But the creation of the industrial research lab was not the action of one, or of even only a few, humans. It took many working together, often at cross-purposes, over a course of years. Inevitable? No, but many people working together over time does make a particular outcome increasingly likely.

We feel that that process could have worked out differently, but we have no good way to conceptualize how that might have happened, or what the plausible range of different outcomes is. As the historian Anton Howes has pointed out, nearly any weaver for five thousand years before 1773 could have made his or her life much easier by inventing the flying shuttle. None did until John Kay, who had no deep knowledge and used no advanced materials, just, as Howes marveled, "two wooden boxes on either side to catch the shuttle . . . [and] a string, with a little handle called a picker." Thus, he added, "Kay's innovation was extraordinary in its simplicity." By comparison, the research lab and the corporation were complex, and could have perhaps escaped humanity's conceptual grasp.[10]

The labs and corporations needed accelerants if they were to spread and transform the world. The biggest accelerant is clear: globalization.

Back before 1700, what we would call "international trade" was a trade of high-valued preciosities for precious-metal cash—spices, silks, psychoactives (opium, for example), fine manufactures (steel swords, porcelains, and so forth), important and scarce raw materials such as tin (essential for making bronze), occasional staples transported by ship between and within empires (wheat from Egypt and Tunisia to Rome, rice from the Yangtze Delta to Beijing)—and slaves: pull humans out of their social context and enforce a zero-status hierarchical role on them, and you can get a lot of work out of them for a little food. It mattered. It mattered a lot as far as the comfort and sophistication of elites were concerned. But it was not an essential force shaping economic life (except, of course, for those whom the pre–Industrial Revolution trade networks enslaved). What we would call "international trade" was at most 6 percent of global economic life: about 3 percent of what a typical region consumed was imported from elsewhere, and about 3 percent of what a typical region produced was exported elsewhere. This began to change after 1700. Between 1700 and 1800 the guns-slaves-sugar triangle trade in the North Atlantic did become an essential force, powerfully shaping Africa and the Caribbean for great evil, and playing a still-debated role in concentrating and transferring to Britain the wealth of a global seaborne empire, and in setting Britain on its path to a market economy, limited government, the Industrial Revolution, and world domination. But international trade in 1800 was still, at most, just 6 percent of global economic life.

After 1800, cotton and textiles became important additions to the list of key commodities in world trade. The cotton was imported to the manufacturing heartlands of the British Industrial Revolution—Britain itself; the regions immediately across the English Channel, inside a rough circle with a radius of three hundred miles, with its center at Dover in the southeastern corner of England; plus New England in the United States—and textiles and other manufactures were exported from those same regions to the rest of the world. But world trade in 1865 was still only 7 percent of global economic activity.[11]

There was the globalization of transport, too, in the form of the iron-hulled, screw-propellered oceangoing steamship, linked to the railroad network. There was the globalization of communication, in the form of the global submarine telegraph network, linked to landlines. By 1870 you could communicate at near–light-speed from London to Bombay and back, by 1876 from London to New Zealand and back.

Yet another aspect of globalization was a lack of barriers. Of the consequences arising from open borders, the most influential was migration—with the very important caveat that the poorest migrants, those from China, India, and so on, were not allowed into the temperate settlements. Those were reserved for

Europeans (and sometimes Middle Easterners). Caveat aside, a vast population of people moved: between 1870 and 1914, one in fourteen humans—one hundred million people—changed their continent of residence.[12]

The embrace of openness by world governments also meant the absence of legal barriers to trade, investment, and communication. As people moved, finance, machines, railroads, steamships, and the telegraph nerves of production and distribution networks followed, chasing abundant natural, physical, and biological resources. The proportion of global economic activity that was traded across today's national borders rose from perhaps 9 percent in 1870 to perhaps 15 percent in 1914, as the revolutionary decreases in the cost of transport massively outstripped what were also that era's revolutionary decreases and differentials in costs of production. Thus transportation made a huge difference.

Consider the railroad.

The metallurgy to cheaply make rails and engines made transport over land, at least wherever the rails ran, as cheap as travel up navigable watercourses or across the oceans, and made it faster.

Some groused. The mid-nineteenth-century Massachusetts transcendentalist author and activist Henry David Thoreau's response to the railroad was: "Get off my lawn!"

Men have an indistinct notion that if they keep up this activity of joint stocks and spades long enough all will at length ride somewhere in next to no time and for nothing, but though a crowd rushes to the depot and the conductor shouts "All aboard!" when the smoke is blown away and the vapor condensed, it will be perceived that a few are riding, but the rest are run over—and it will be called, and will be, "a melancholy accident."[13]

My ancestors, and most of humanity, had a very different view.

Before the railroad, as a general rule you simply could not transport agricultural goods more than one hundred miles by land. By that mile marker, the horses or oxen would have eaten as much as they could pull. Either you found a navigable watercourse—ideally much, much closer than one hundred miles away—or you were stuck in bare self-sufficiency for all your staples. This also meant that, overwhelmingly, what you wore, ate, and used to pass your hours was made within your local township, or dearly bought.

For Thoreau, the fact that it took him a day to walk or ride into Boston was a benefit—part of living deliberately. But his was the point of view of a rich guy, or at least of a guy without a family to care for, and for whom Ralph Waldo Emerson's second wife, Lidian Jackson, was willing to bake pies.

The laboratory, the corporation, global transportation, global communications, and falling barriers—together, these factors were more than enough to trigger the decisive watershed and carry humanity out of Malthusian poverty. They also made the story of the world's economies one story in a way that had never been true before.

Given our global propensity to live close to navigable water, perhaps the biggest revolution in transportation came not in the 1830s, with the railroad, but later, with the iron-hulled oceangoing coal-fired steamship. In 1870 the Harland and Wolff shipyard of Belfast launched the iron-hulled, steam-powered, screw-propellered passenger steamship RMS *Oceanic*. It promised to take nine days to go from Liverpool to New York, a journey that in 1800 would have taken more like a month.

The *Oceanic*'s crew of 150 supported 1,000 third-class passengers at a cost of £3 each—the rough equivalent of a month and a half's wages for an unskilled worker—and 150 first-class passengers at £15 each.[14] In today's dollars, the same share of average income for the first-class seats comes to $17,000. But the more relevant context is to the 1870s' recent past. A generation earlier, a third-class berth on the (slower and less safe) equivalent of the *Oceanic* cost twice as much, and that berth cost four times as much in 1800. After 1870, sending a family member across the ocean to work became a possibility open to all save the very poorest of European households.

And humans responded by the millions. The production and trade globalization of the late 1800s was fueled by one hundred million people leaving their continent of origin to live and work elsewhere. Never before or since have we seen such a rapid proportional redistribution of humanity around the globe.

Some fifty million people left the settled areas of Europe, mainly for the Americas and Australasia, but also for South Africa, the highlands of Kenya, the black-earth western regions of the Pontic-Caspian steppe, and elsewhere. It was an extraordinary age, 1870–1914, in which working-class people could repeatedly cross oceans in search of better lives.

If I have my family history right, all of my ancestors had made it to the United States by 1800, back in the days when cross-ocean migration was for people who had been enslaved, were indentured, or were middle class. The last that I know of was Edmund Edward Gallagher (born in Watmeath, Ireland, in 1772). He and Lydia McGinnis (born in New Hampshire in 1780) were living at the start of the 1800s in Chester, Pennsylvania, where they recorded the birth of their son John. But all of my wife's ancestors came here during the post-1870 great wave of global migration. One was Maria Rosa Silva, born in 1873 in Portugal. She arrived in 1892. In 1893, in Lowell, Massachusetts, she married José F. Gill, born in 1872, not in Portugal but on the Portuguese-speaking island of Madeira. He had arrived in 1891—not on a ship to Boston, but to Savannah.

Perhaps he knew sugarcane, and heard that Savannah had it, but decided that he was too Black in Savannah, and so decamped to Lowell. We do not know. We do know that they and their children, Mary, John Francis, and Carrie, went back across the

Atlantic from Boston to Madeira soon after 1900. And we know that he died in South Africa in 1903. We find Maria Rosa and four children—a newborn Joseph added—going back across that Atlantic and, in the 1910 census, in Fall River, Massachusetts, where she is recorded as a widowed weaver renting a house, with five children born and four living.

The migrations were not always one way. As we have seen with José Gill and Maria Rosa Silva, some people crossed the Atlantic multiple times. One person who made the reverse journey permanently—born in America, moved to England—was Jennie Jerome, born in 1854, the daughter of New York financier Leonard Jerome and Clara Hall. The occasion was her marriage to Lord Randolph Spencer-Churchill, younger son of the 7th Duke of Marlborough. The couple became engaged in 1873, just three days after their first meeting at a sailing regatta off the Isle of Wight in the English Channel. Their marriage was then delayed for seven months, while Jennie's father, Leonard, and the groom's father, the Duke, John Winston Spencer-Churchill, argued over how much money she would bring to the marriage and how it would be safeguarded. Their son Winston was born eight months after their marriage. They had another son, John, six years later.[15]

Randolph died about two decades later, in 1895, at the age of forty-five, perhaps of syphilis, certainly of something with a pronounced neurological character. The diagnosis on the death certificate is "general paralysis of the insane." Jennie was thereafter "much admired by the Prince of Wales" and others, as they put it in those days. In 1900 she married George Cornwallis-West, who was a month older than Winston.

Winston Spencer Churchill—he dropped the hyphen and turned the first half of his last name into a middle name—would be the *enfant terrible* of British politics when young, a disastrous British chancellor of the exchequer—the equivalent of finance minister or treasury secretary—when middle-aged, and a decisive factor in defeating the Nazis as British prime minister during World War II. And not least of Winston's excellences as a wartime prime minister was that he was half American, and so knew how to talk to America, and particularly how to talk to then American president Franklin Delano Roosevelt.

Though the redwood forests of northern California contain shrines to the Boddhisatva Guan-Yin, migration from China to European-settled California and to the rest of the temperate-climate settler colonies and ex-colonies was quickly shut down. Plutocrats such as Leland Stanford (the railroad baron and governor of California who founded and endowed Stanford University in memory of his son) might have favored immigration, but the populists favored exclusion. For the most part, they were unable to staunch the flow of Europeans and Eastern Europeans, but they were largely able to enforce "Chinaman go home." People from the Indian subcontinent fell into the same category in this respect.

Mohandas Karamchand Gandhi was born in 1869, the son of Karamchand Uttamchand Gandhi, the prime minister of the small British-allied and British-subject principality of Porbandar on the peninsula of Kathiawar, and of Karamchand's fourth wife, Putlibai.[16] When he was fourteen their families married him and Kasturbai. In 1888, at the age of eighteen, he sailed from Mumbai to England to study law. Three years later, at the age of twenty-two, he was a lawyer, and sailed back to India. He did not do well in his career. In 1893 he ran across a merchant who needed a lawyer to try to collect a £40,000 debt in South Africa. Gandhi volunteered for the job and again crossed the ocean. He thought he was going for a year. But he decided to stay. In 1897 he went back to India to collect his family and bring them to South Africa. He would remain in South Africa for twenty-two years. And it was there that he became an anti-imperialist, a politician, and an activist, for in South Africa people from the Indian south continent were not treated as badly as indigenous African peoples, but they were at most only one step higher.

Another participant in these great migrations was Deng Xiao-ping, born in 1904 as the son of a middling-rich landlord whose income was perhaps five times the Chinese average at the time.[17] In December 1920 he arrived in France to work and study: World War I, from 1914 to 1918, had pulled huge numbers of workers into the army and left them dead and maimed. The French government was eager to allow anyone who wanted to replace them in, both during and after the war. Deng took advantage of the postwar part of the program. He worked as a fitter—a metal-parts fabricator—in the suburbs of Paris at a Le Creusot factory. There he became a communist and met many other future leaders of the Chinese Communist Party, including Zhou Enlai. In 1926 he studied in Moscow at its Sun Yat-sen University, and in 1927 he returned to China to become first a cadre and then a high official in the Chinese Communist Party. During the Mao era, he was twice purged, the first time as the "number-two person in authority taking the capitalist road," and yet he became China's paramount leader as the country finally stood up in the 1980s, and may well have been the most consequential single figure in the history of the long twentieth century.

Throughout the temperate-zone lands settled from Europe, local populists were overwhelmingly successful in keeping the United States, Canada, Argentina, Chile, Uruguay, Australia, and New Zealand "European." The flow of migrants out of China and India was directed elsewhere, to the tea plantations of Ceylon or the rubber plantations of Malaya. Still, fifty million Chinese and Indians migrated, going instead to South Asia, Africa, the Caribbean, and the highlands of Peru.

Resource-rich settlement areas such as Canada and Argentina with Europe-like climates provided a further boost to European living standards. The one-third who migrated and then returned home did so, in most cases, with resources that made them solid members of their home economies' middle classes. The two-thirds who migrated and stayed found their living standards and their children's living standards higher by a factor of between 1.5 and 3. Those left behind also benefited. Ultimately, these decades of migration raised wages in Europe, as workers at home faced less competition for jobs and could buy cheap imports from the New World.[18]

Plutocrat and populist alike benefited. Indeed, there is no sign that workers already on the labor-scarce western, peripheral side of the Atlantic lost out as their shores absorbed the migration wave from labor-abundant Europe. Real wages in America, Canada, and Argentina appear to have grown at 1.0, 1.7, and 1.7 percent per year, respectively, in the years leading up to 1914—compared to growth rates that averaged 0.9 percent per year in northwestern Europe. Only in Australia, where real wages seemed to stagnate in the half century before 1914, does increased trade appear to have played any role in eroding the relative wages of workers in a labor-scarce economy. Regardless, migration to temperate-zone countries meant people carried capital with them, which built out the scale of the recipient economies.[19]

Did migration lower relative wages in tropical-zone recipient economies? Yes—and such was the case in economies that never saw a migrant. British capital, Brazilian-stock rubber plants, and labor imported from China to Malaya could and did put heavy downward pressure on the wages of workers in Brazil who did not know there was such a place as Malaya. Economic underdevelopment was a process, something that itself developed over 1870–1914.

And migration did not raise wages much in the migration-source economies of China and India. Both had such substantial populations that emigration was a drop in the bucket.

Through misfortune and bad government, India and China had failed to escape the shackles of the Malthusian Devil. Technology had advanced, but improvements in productive potential had been absorbed by rising populations, and not in rising living standards. The population of China in the late nineteenth century was three times what it had been at the start of the second millennium in the year 1000. So potential migrants from China and India were willing to move for what to Europeans seemed to be starvation wages.

Thus, the large populations and low levels of material wealth and agricultural productivity in China and India checked the growth of wages in any of the areas—Malaya, Indonesia, the Caribbean, or East Africa—open to Asian migration. Workers could be cheaply imported and employed at wages not that far above the level of physical subsistence. Nevertheless, these workers sought out these jobs: their opportunities and living standards in Malaya or on African plantations were significantly above what they could expect if they returned to India or China. Low wage costs meant that commodities produced in countries open to Asian immigration were relatively cheap. And competition from the Malayan rubber plantations checked growth and even pushed down wages in the Brazilian rubber plantations. The result: living standards and wage rates during the late nineteenth century remained low, albeit higher than in China and India, throughout the regions that would come to be called the global south.

For ill and good, the world was now an integrated unit, with one story.

Part of this global story was the emergence of a sharp division of international labor: "Tropical" regions supplied rubber, coffee, sugar, vegetable oil, cotton, and other relatively low-value agricultural products to Europe. Temperate-zone regions of expanding European settlement—the United States, Canada, Australia, New Zealand, Argentina, Chile, Uruguay, Ukraine, and perhaps South Africa—produced and shipped staple grains, meats, and wool to Europe. German farmers found themselves with new competitors, and not just from the Americas: as much came in the form of Russian grain shipped from Odessa. Western Europe paid for its imports by exporting manufactured goods. As did the northeastern United States, where industrial supplies and materials would rise to be fully half of US exports by 1910.

And as wages in economies that were to become the global periphery diminished, so, too, did the possibility that this periphery would develop a rich enough middle class to provide demand for a strong domestic industrial sector.

To understand why, consider the British Empire.

Wherever the British went they built a fort, some docks, and a botanical garden—the latter to discover what valuable plants grown elsewhere might flourish under the guns of their fort as well. During the nineteenth century it was the British Empire that brought the rubber plant from Brazil to Kew Gardens, and then to Malaya, and that brought the tea shrub directly from China to Ceylon. Although rubber was not introduced into Malaya, Indonesia, and Indochina until the last quarter of the nineteenth century, by the end of World War I these three regions had become the principal sources of the world's natural rubber supply. Most of this process was mediated by the British Empire, but not all. The Portuguese brought the coffee bush from Yemen to Brazil. The comparative advantages of the regions that were to become the periphery of the late nineteenth-century global economy were not so much given as made.[20]

The United States was the most prominent long-run beneficiary. Casting our glance, briefly, out into the future, these decades of migration in the 1800s and early 1900s were crucial steps on the path that turned the long twentieth century into an era of US predominance. Consider that in 1860 the United States had a population of full citizens, with women and children included—that is, "Caucasian" English speakers whom the government regarded as worth educating—of 25 million, while Britain and its Dominions had a full-citizen population of 32 million. By the midpoint between 1870 and 2010, 1940, things had massively changed: the United States had 116 million full citizens, and Britain and its Dominions had 75 million. Natural increase had multiplied both populations, and so it was immigrants, welcomed and assimilated, who gave the United States greater heft than the British Empire by 1940.

The decades between 1870 and 1914 were a time of technological advance, population growth, and migration, and with transportation and communication advances came a concomitant rise in trade and investment. The cost of transporting people fell alongside the cost of transporting goods: flour that cost 1.5 cents per pound in Chicago and 3 cents per pound in London in 1850 cost only 2 cents per pound in London in 1890. Indeed, every commodity that was neither exceptionally fragile nor spoilable could, after 1870, be carried from port to port across oceans for less than it cost to move it within any country.[21] As long as there were docks and railroads, every place in the world became cheek by jowl with every other place. Everyone's opportunities and constraints depended on what was going on in every other piece of the world economy.

This mattered: between 1870 and 1914, exports as a share of national product doubled in India and in Indonesia and more than tripled in China. And in Japan—which was forced out of two and a half centuries of Tokugawa isolationism by US gunboats—exports rose from practically zero to 7 percent of the national product in just two pre–World War I generations. In 1500, international trade as a proportion of total world production had been around 1.5 percent. By 1700, it had risen to around 3 percent. By 1850, to about 4 percent. In 1880, it was 11 percent, and by 1913, 17 percent. Today it is 30 percent.[22]

The story of this rise from 1870 to 1914 is what international economist Richard Baldwin has called the "first unbundling": the mammoth fall in shipping costs that substantially meant that the use and consumption of goods no longer had to be "bundled" in the same region as their production. You could produce goods where it was cheapest, transport them inexpensively, and

have use and consumption take place where the wealth to purchase them was located.[23]

But this did not "make the world flat" in any sense. If you were
doing anything more complicated than buying a simple, well-
understood, known-quality good, you had to communicate—
they had to learn what you wanted, you had to learn what their
production capabilities were, and you had to reach a meeting of
the minds about how both of you should best adjust. You also had
to look them in the eye, face-to-face, to understand with what and
how far they could be trusted. Baldwin's "first unbundling" meant
that production could and did move away from use and consumption, but it did not just move to that point on the transport network where resources were most available. It moved together, into
industrial districts, so that producers could economize on the costs
associated with communications and meetings of the minds, and
with face-to-face negotiations and trust.

The factories came to be located near each other. This meant
that the industrial research labs and the new ideas were concentrated as well—and the still-high costs of communications meant
that the ideas tended to stick in one place. The goods could be
carried and used anywhere on the transport network. But they
could only be most cheaply and efficiently produced in a few
places worldwide. Thus the world boomed in its pre-1914 economic El Dorado. And the global north industrialized. The serpent in the garden was that the world diverged in relative income
levels: as the market giveth (in this case, to the global north), so
it may taketh away (as it did in what was to become the global
south, which industrialized far less, in many places industrialized
not at all, and in important places deindustrialized).[24]

Northwestern Europe gained an enormous comparative advantage in making manufactured goods. And natural resources
out on the periphery became more valuable as well: copper, coal,
coffee, and all mineral and agricultural products could be shipped
by rail to the ports where the iron-hulled, steam-powered,

oceangoing cargo ships lay. The market economy responded as knowledge sped along copper wires. The industrializing core specialized in the manufactures because of its superior access to industrial technologies. The periphery specialized in the primary products that its newly improving infrastructure allowed it to export. The ability for both to specialize was of great economic value.

The social returns on the investments in technology and infrastructure that created this late nineteenth-century world economy were enormous. Consider just one example: economic historian Robert Fogel calculated that the social rate of return on the Union Pacific's transcontinental railroad was some 30 percent per year.[25]

The growth of trade meant that the logic of comparative advantage could be deployed to its limit. Wherever there was a difference across two countries in the value of textiles relative to ironmongery—or any other two nonspoilable goods—there was profit to be made and societal well-being to be enhanced by exporting the good that was relatively cheap in your country and importing the good that was relatively dear. Once established, a comparative advantage tended to stick for a long time. There was nothing about British-invented automated textile machinery that made it work better in Britain than elsewhere. Yet Britain's cotton textile exports rose decade after decade from 1800 to 1910, peaking at 1.1 billion pounds a year in the years before World War I.[26]

The reach of comparative advantage was also broad. A country near-hapless in growing food but even less capable of making machine tools could improve its lot by exporting food and importing machine tools. A country that was best in class at making automobiles, but even better, in relative terms, at making airplanes, could get ahead by exporting airplanes and importing cars. Such was the power of expanding world trade. Whether one's comparative advantage came from innovative entrepreneurs, a deeper community of engineering practice, a well-educated workforce, abundant natural resources, or just poverty that made your labor cheap, business could profit and society grow richer. And so the surge in real wages was worldwide, not confined to where industrial technologies were then being deployed.

This was the consequence of finance and trade following labor. The 1870–1914 world economy was a high-investment economy—in historical comparative perspective. The industrialization of Western Europe and of the East and Midwest of North America provided enough workers to make the industrial products to satisfy global demands, and also to build the railways, ships, ports, cranes, telegraph lines, and other pieces of transport and communications infrastructure to make the first global economy a reality. There were twenty thousand miles of railways in the world when the American Civil War ended in 1865. There were three hundred thousand miles in 1914. (There are a million miles of rails worldwide today.)

Workers in Hamburg, Germany, ate cheap bread made from North Dakotan or Ukrainian wheat. Investors in London financed copper mines in Montana and railroads in California. (And railroad baron Leland Stanford diverted a large tranche into his own pockets.) State-funded entrepreneurs in Tokyo bought electrical machinery made by the workers of Hamburg. And the telegraph wires that connected all were made of copper from Montana and insulated by rubber gathered by Chinese workers in Malaya and Indian workers in Bengal.

As John Maynard Keynes would write in 1919, the upshot was that, for the globe's middle and upper classes, by 1914 "life offered, at a low cost and with the least trouble, conveniences, comforts, and amenities beyond the compass of the richest and most powerful monarchs of other ages."[27]

And the upshot for the working classes of the globe—at least those touched by ships and railroads and by international commerce—was an increasing margin between living standards and bare subsistence. Malthusian forces responded: as of 1914 there were five people where there had been four a generation before. Half a century saw more population growth than had taken place over half a millennium back in the Agrarian Age. Yet there was no sign of downward pressure on nutrition standards. Investment and technology meant that, for the first time ever, as population grew, available resources, including nutrition, more than kept pace. Malthus's Devil was chained.

Consider the ability to communicate.

Around 1800, Arthur Wellesley, a fourth son of a financially shaky Anglo Irish aristocratic family, a man whose only obvious talent was as a not incompetent but definitely amateur-class violin player, sought to make his fortune and reputation. He had bought himself a post as a major in the British Army's 33rd Regiment of Foot. (The British government believed that an officer corps overwhelmingly staffed by the relatives of rich, established landlords would never repeat the quasi-military dictatorship of 1650–1660, hence the rule was that officers had to buy their posts, and so the only men who could become officers were those with close landlord relatives willing to lend or give them the money.) His elder brother Richard then loaned him the money to buy the step-up to lieutenant colonel. Richard was then appointed viceroy of India, and so Arthur, the future Duke of Wellington, went along for the ride, banking correctly that nepotism would lead his brother to make him a general. His brother did. Ever after, Arthur Wellesley, the only general ever to command an army that overwhelmed an army commanded by Napoleon Bonaparte, would say that the battle where he had been at his best as a general was the first one he ever commanded: Assaye in Maharashtra, the battle that won the Second Anglo-Maratha War.[28]

It took Arthur Wellesley seven months to get to India from Britain. It would take him six months to get back. That time lag meant, among other things, that whatever questions, instructions, and orders the British imperial cabinet and the directors of the

East India Company asked him to convey to their proconsuls in India would be a year stale by the time they even reached Fort William in Calcutta, Fort St. George in Chennai, or Bombay Castle. A conversation where a single question-and-answer interchange takes a year is not a dialogue: it is two overlapping monologues. And conveying attitudes, practices, capabilities, and goals across such a gulf is haphazard to the point of being hazardous.

The electric telegraph allowed a conversation. It connected points on the globe as messages sped through copper at nearly the speed of light.

Not everyone was welcoming. Henry David Thoreau, again, groused: "We are in great haste to construct a magnetic telegraph from Maine to Texas, but Maine and Texas, it may be, have nothing important to communicate."[29]

While Texas may not have had much important to learn from Maine, in the summer of 1860 Texas had a great deal to learn from Chicago: the Republican Party National Convention meeting at the Wigwam nominated Abraham Lincoln as its candidate for president. So started a chain of events that would kill twenty-five thousand white adult Texans and maim twenty-five thousand more, and that would free all two hundred thousand enslaved Black Texans within five years. Maine may not have had much to learn from Texas, but telegraphs reporting relative prices of Grand Bank codfish in Boston, Providence, New York, and Philadelphia were of great importance to Maine fishermen slipping their moorings.

Knowing the price of codfish is valuable, the freeing of hundreds of thousands of Americans is profound, and both only hint at the shift that came with telegraphed intelligence. Ever since the development of language, one of humanity's great powers has been that our drive to talk and gossip truly turns us into an anthology intelligence. What one of us in the group knows, if it is useful, pretty quickly everyone in the group knows, and often those well beyond the group, too. The telegraph enlarged the relevant group from the village or township or guild to, potentially, the entire world.

Spanning the globe with telegraphs was difficult. Particularly difficult to set up were the submarine telegraph cables. The year 1870 saw the English engineer Isambard Kingdom Brunel's SS *Great Eastern*—then the largest ship ever built (nothing larger was to be built until 1901)—lay the submarine telegraph cable from Yemen to Mumbai, completing the undersea line from London. Future dukes of Wellington, and millions besides, no longer took months conveying news and commands from London to Bombay and back. It took only minutes. After 1870 you could find out in the morning how your investments overseas had done the previous day, and wire instructions and questions to your bankers overseas before lunch.

This mattered for three reasons:

First, this process brought not just more information with which to make decisions; it also improved trust and security. Consider that 1871 saw thirty-four-year-old American financier J. Pierpont Morgan join forty-five-year-old American financier Anthony Drexel in an investment banking partnership to guide and profit from the flow of investment funds from capital-rich Britain to the resource- and land-abundant United States. Today's J. P. Morgan Chase and Morgan Stanley are the children of that partnership.[30] Second, this greatly aided technology transfer—the ability in one corner of the globe to use technologies and methods invented or in use in another corner of the globe. Third, this process was a handmaiden of empire. Where you could cheaply and reliably communicate and move goods and people, you could also command and move and supply armies. Thus conquest, or at least invasion and devastation, became things that any European great power could undertake in nearly any corner of the world. And the European powers did.

Before 1870 European imperialism was—with the very notable exception of the British Raj in India—largely a matter of ports and their hinterlands. By 1914 only Morocco, Ethiopia, Iran, Afghanistan, Nepal, Thailand, Tibet, China, and Japan had escaped European (or, in the case of Taiwan and Korea, Japanese) conquest or domination.

BY THE END OF the 1800s, with the greatly increased speed of transmitting information, the greatly lowered cost of transporting people, and the greatly lowered cost of transporting machines, it seemed as though, for the first time in history, it ought to have been possible to apply any productive technology known to humanity in any corner of the world.

There were textile factories in places such as Mumbai, Calcutta, Shanghai, Cape Town, and Tokyo, as well as in Manchester, in Fall River, Massachusetts, and in Brussels. The North Atlantic economic core supported these endeavors with capital, labor, organization, and demand, which is to say its need for and willingness to buy products from the periphery. Before 1870 Western Europe's staple imports were limited to cotton, tobacco, sugar, and wool—with small quantities of palm oil, furs, hides, tea, and coffee as well: luxuries, not necessities or even conveniences. After 1870, however, technology demanded oil for diesel and gasoline engines, nitrate for fertilizing fields, copper wiring, and rubber tires. And even without new technologies, the much richer post-1870 North Atlantic core's demand for cocoa, tea, coffee, silk, jute, palm oil, and other tropical products skyrocketed. Commodity demand and industrial technology transfer ought to have begun to draw the world together. But they didn't.

As Saint Lucia–born trade and development economist W. Arthur Lewis put it, the net effect of the coming of a single economic world was to enable a great many countries and regions to jump on an "escalator" of modern economic growth that would raise them "to ever higher levels of output per head." Yet Lewis judged that as of 1870, only six countries were fully on the escalator.[31]

We glimpse why there were so few of them in the story of the khedive, or viceroy, of Egypt from 1805 to 1848, Muhammed Ali. His foremost desire was to transform his country so his grand-children would not be the puppets of French bankers and British proconsuls. One way in which he set out to achieve this dream was by seeking to turn Egypt into a center of textile manufacture. The problem was that keeping the machines working proved unachievable. His textile factories stopped. And his grandson, Is-mail, who became khedive in 1863, indeed became the puppet of French bankers and British proconsuls.[32]

It is understandable that China, India, and the other regions of what would become the post–World War II global south did not produce and export the relatively high-value commodities, such as wheat and wool, that were exported by temperate settler economies: agricultural productivity was too low, and the climate was unfavorable. It is understandable why—with heavy down-ward pressure put on wages in Malaya, Kenya, and Colombia by migration and threatened migration from China and India—the prices of the export commodities that they did produce started out and remained relatively low.

What is more puzzling is why industrialization did not spread much more rapidly to the future global south in the years before World War I. After all, the example of the North Atlantic indus-trial core seemed easy to follow. Inventing the technologies of the original British Industrial Revolution—steam power, spin-ning mills, automatic looms, iron refining and steelmaking, and railroad building—had required many independent strokes of genius. But copying those technologies did not, especially when you could buy and cheaply ship the same industrial equipment that supplied the industries of England and the United States.

If Henry Ford could redesign production so that unskilled assembly-line workers could do what skilled craftsmen used to do, why couldn't Ford—or someone else—also redesign produc-tion so that unskilled and even lower-wage Peruvians or Poles or

Kenyans could do what Americans were then doing? After all, even by 1914, Americans were extraordinarily expensive labor by world standards.

Did the difficulty lie in political risks? Was the decisive factor the relative advantage afforded by being near your machine suppliers and other factories making similar products? Was it the need to have specialists close at hand to fix the many things that can go wrong?

It remains a great puzzle to me. And not just to me, but to other economic historians as well. We understand far too little about why the pace of technological diffusion outside of the industrial core was so slow before World War I.

"Peripheral" economies did a superb job at specializing in plantation agriculture for export. They did a bad job at creating modern manufacturing industries that could have also turned their low relative wages into a durable source of comparative advantage.

When I am asked why this happened, I say that the initial cost advantage enjoyed by Britain (and then the United States, and then Germany) was so huge that it would have required staggeringly high tariffs in order to nurture "infant industries" in other locations. I say that colonial rulers refused to let the colonized try. I say that the ideological dominance of free trade kept many others from even considering the possibility. Few even thought of taking a few steps away from the ideology of free trade as the be-all and end-all toward the practical political economy of Alexander Hamilton and company. Yet a Hamiltonian "developmental state" approach might have mightily benefited their economies in the long run.[33]

Unmanaged, a market economy will strive to its utmost to satisfy the desires of those who hold the valuable property rights. But valuable property owners seek a high standard of living for themselves boosted by purchase of foreign luxuries. They are not patient people who wish to enable and accelerate long-run growth, let alone encourage the trickling down of wealth and opportunity to the working class. Moreover, while the market economy sees the profits from establishing plantations, and from the revenues that can be charged for the use of infrastructure such as railroads and docks, it does not see and cannot take account of the knowledge that workers and engineers gain from being part of a community of practice. Watching what goes wrong and right with pioneers and competitors, and listening to them boast when things go right and commiserating with them when things go wrong with their enterprises, is a powerful social channel for productivity growth. Yet there was no money flow associated with conversations at Silicon Valley's Wagon Wheel bar.[34] And so the market cannot see the benefits to the economy.

Such "acquired skill and experience," John Stuart Mill wrote, can create a "superiority of one country over another in a branch of production . . . aris[ing] only from having begun it sooner . . . [with] no inherent advantage." But—unless managed—the market economy's maximum-profitability test would keep that skill and experience from ever being acquired. And so 1870–1950 saw the most profitable and the most innovation-supporting parts of economic activity becoming more and more concentrated in what we now call the global north.[35]

The economic historian Robert Allen thinks the dominant factor was imperialism: colonial governments were uninterested in adopting a "standard package"—ports, railroads, schools, banks, plus "infant industry" tariffs in sectors just beyond currently profitable export industries—of policy measures that would have enabled industrialization. W. Arthur Lewis thought that the most important issue was migration and global commodity trade: industrialization required a prosperous domestic middle class to buy the products of the factories, and tropical economies could not develop one. Economic historian Joel Mokyr thinks that it was the habits of thought and intellectual exchange developed during the European Enlightenment that laid the groundwork for the communities of engineering practice upon which the North Atlantic core's industrial power was based. And development economist Raul Prebisch thought that what mattered most were the landlord aristocracies notionally descended from Castilian conquistadores, who thought their dominance over society could best be maintained if the factories that produced the luxuries they craved were kept oceans away.[36]

I do not know enough to judge. The answer lies somewhere in the causal mix of individuals reaching individual decisions and larger cultural and political forces. What I know that we cannot know is what might have happened if the twentieth century hadn't happened the way it did.

2

Revving Up the Engine of Technology-Driven Growth

The world that emerged after 1870 was globalized in a way that it had never been before. But what exactly did that mean? Globalization was clearly something more than just the planet-crossing lines of communication and transportation that were beginning to move ideas and people faster than ever before. To get a better sense of what globalization meant, we might begin by examining the story of Herbert Hoover.[1]

Hoover was born in 1874 in Iowa. His father, a blacksmith, died in 1880, and his mother died in 1884. Herbert was therefore orphaned at the age of ten. In 1885 he started moving west—first to Oregon to live with an aunt and uncle; then, in 1891, to California—as he always claimed, to be the first student to attend Stanford University (he arrived before opening day, and the staff let him sleep on campus). There he studied to become a mining engineer, graduating in 1895 in the distressed aftermath of the Panic of 1893.

Hoover's first job was as a mine laborer in Grass Valley, California, earning $600 a year. His next was as an intern and special assistant to a mining engineer, for which he earned $2,400 a year. He kept moving west. In 1897 he crossed the Pacific—first to Australia, where he worked for the mining company Bewick Moreing, earning a salary of $7,000 a year, and then to China, where he earned $20,000 a year. It was in China that Hoover made the first major tranche of his fortune, albeit in ways he sometimes found hard to explain later on.[2]

From 1901 until 1917, he lived in London, working as a consulting engineer and investor, with jobs and investments in Australia, China, Russia, Burma, Italy, and Central America in addition to the United States. In 1917 he moved back to America, where he was appointed secretary of commerce in 1925 and elected president in 1928. From son of the town blacksmith to college graduate to multimillionaire mining consultant to president of the United States—had anyone else ascended so far and so fast, even in America? It was an exceptional country. And the fact that it was exceptional was a significant shaper of how the long twentieth century was exceptional.

Hoover, however, did not make the bulk of his fortune from globalization. He made it, rather, through his mastery of the application of mining technologies, and through his skills as a manager and organizer. Globalization was not the most consequential development contributing to the watershed of 1870. Between 1870 and 1914, technology and organization improved at a rate of 2 percent per year—more than quadruple the pace of progress during the previous century, from 1770 to 1870. The global economic leaders—initially the United States, Germany, and Britain, with Britain rapidly falling off—had been growing faster than the rest of the world even before 1870, perhaps 0.9 percent per year faster.[3] Now, they picked up the pace and maintained their lead in growth of perhaps 2.5 percent per year, nearly three times as rapid a pace relative to what it had been before 1870.

Before 1870, inventions and innovations had by and large been singular discoveries and adaptations. They produced new and better ways of doing old things: of making thread, of weaving cloth, of carrying goods about, of making iron, of raising coal, and of growing wheat and rice and corn. Having pioneered these improvements, their inventors then set about finding ways to exploit them. It was a process that required inventors to be not just researchers but development engineers, maintenance technicians, human resource managers, bosses, cheerleaders, marketers, impresarios, and financiers as well.

That pre-1870 system was good enough as long as the confluence of circumstances was just right. Consider the invention of the steam engine in the eighteenth century. It needed a cheap source of fuel, it needed something important and profitable to do, and it needed societal competence at the metalworking technological frontier. Fuel was found at the bottom of the coal mines. With the steam engine, cheap, plantation-grown cotton, ideally suited for machine spinning, quickly reached factories that produced sought-after goods. And with practical metallurgy to make iron rails and iron wheels cheaply, the fuse that was the Industrial Revolution was lit. Steam power propelled the automatic spindles, looms, metal presses, and railroad locomotives of the nineteenth century.

But the fuse might well have sputtered out. That, after all, is what the pre-1870 track record would lead one to expect. Printing, the windmill, the musket, the seagoing caravel, the water mill, and before that the horse collar, the heavy plow, the 3,600-soldier legion—each of these did revolutionize a piece of the economies and societies of their day. Yet none of them lit anything like the rocket of economic growth we have ridden since 1870. Ancient Mediterranean civilization was followed by what is rightly called a Dark Age. Printing revolutionized the dissemination of information, but books were always a small part of total spending, and the printing press was one revolutionary invention, not a series of them. The windmill and the water mill meant women no longer had to spend so much time nose to grindstone, but their fathers and husbands found other things for them to do instead.

The musket and the caravel made the Imperial-Commercial Age and the gunpowder empires, but that, again, was a discrete jump rather than a takeoff into sustained growth. The horse collar and the heavy plow shifted the center of European settlement and commerce northward, but did not drastically improve the lot of Europe's working class. The legion was essential for the making of the Roman Empire, but it then reached the limits of its expansion, and eventually fell.[4] What changed after 1870 was that the most advanced North Atlantic economies had *invented invention*. They had invented not just textile machinery and railroads, but also the industrial research lab and the forms of bureaucracy that gave rise to the large corporation. Thereafter, what was invented in the industrial research labs could be deployed at national or continental scale. Perhaps most importantly, these economies discovered that there was a great deal of money to be made and satisfaction to be earned by not just inventing better ways of making old things, but inventing brand-new things.

Not just inventions, but the systematic invention of how to invent. Not just individual large-scale organizations, but organizing how to organize. Both were essential to the arrival of the integrated, command-and-control central planning of modern corporations. Every year between 1870 and 1914 the newer and better industrial technologies that emerged from the first industrial research laboratories were deployed, sometimes as they were sold to already established producers, but more often as they spurred the emergence and expansion of large corporations.

As W. Arthur Lewis observed, a rich man in 1870 possessed the same things that a rich man in 1770 possessed.[5] The 1870 rich might well have had more of those things—more houses, more clothes, more horses and carriages, more furniture. But displaying wealth was a matter of displaying the number of servants one employed, rather than the commodities one personally enjoyed. After the 1870s, that changed. The making of new commodities added a new twist, granting the rich access to, as Lewis put it, "telephones, gramophones, typewriters, cameras, automobiles, and so on, a seemingly endless process whose latest twentieth-century additions include æroplanes, radios, refrigerators, washing machines, television sets, and pleasure boats." Four percent of Americans had flush toilets at home in 1870; 20 percent had them in 1920, 71 percent in 1950, and 96 percent in 1970. No American had a landline telephone in 1880; 28 percent had one in 1914, 62 percent in 1950, and 87 percent in 1970. Eighteen percent of Americans had electric power in 1913; 94 percent had it by 1950.[6]

The arrival of these wonders of convenience and consumption is often called a "second industrial revolution." The economist Robert Gordon wrote of "one big wave" consisting of everything from flush toilets to microwave ovens, after which the low- and even the moderate-hanging fruit of organic chemicals, internal combustion engines, and electric power had been picked and technology was bound to slow. For him, the steady progress of science happened to suddenly bring us to a place extraordinarily rich in technological potential. But that, I think, misses much of the point: we associate these with a single "second industrial revolution" because they came in quick succession: instead of being spread out over a century and a half, as they would have been at the previous British Industrial Revolution–era pace, they arrived in a generation. What is most important is never so much the arrival of any particular technology as it is a burgeoning understanding that there is a broad and deep range of new technologies to be discovered, developed, and deployed.

Consider steel. What would be the fundamental building material of the twentieth century and the master metal of industrial civilization was effectively invented anew in the second half of the 1800s. Steel is composed of 90 to 95 percent iron mixed with carbon. You can make carbon-free wrought iron in your furnace if you keep its temperature below the melting point of iron and hammer it as the slag, or the various impurities in the iron, melt and run out, and then do this over and over again. But wrought iron is too soft for industrial purposes. If you heat your furnace with coke, a pure form of coal, and keep it high enough to melt the iron, the carbon from the coke alloys with it and you get pig or cast iron. But it is too brittle for industrial purposes.

Creating steel requires getting the details just right—but doing so is not easy.

For thousands of years steel was made by skilled craftsmen heating and hammering wrought iron in the presence of charcoal and then quenching it in water or oil. In the centuries before the nineteenth, making high-quality steel was a process limited to the most skilled blacksmiths of Edo or Damascus or Milan or Birmingham. It seemed, to outsiders—and often to insiders—like magic. In the Germanic legends as modernized in Wagner's *Ring* cycle operas, the doomed hero Siegfried acquires a sword made by a skilled smith. Its maker, the dwarf Mime, is in no respect a materials-science engineer. His brother, Alberich, is a full magician.[7]

That changed in 1855–1856, when Henry Bessemer and Robert Mushet developed the Bessemer-Mushet process. It forced air through the molten cast iron to burn off all non-iron impurities, and then added back just enough carbon (and manganese) to make the steel needed for industry. The price of a ton of steel dropped by a factor of seven, from £45 down to £6, at a time when £70 per year was the average wage in Britain. The Thomas-Gilchrist and Siemens-Martin processes followed, offering further improvements. Worldwide steel production would rise from trivial amounts—enough for swords, some cutlery, and a few tools that needed the sharpest attainable edge—to some 70 million tons a year by 1914.[8] By 1950 this would grow to 170 million tons, and as of 2020 it is 1.5 billion tons a year. As of 2016, steel cost about $500 per ton, and the average North Atlantic full-time wage was nearly $50,000 per year.

But it was not just steel. Robert Gordon was 100 percent right when he wrote that the year 1870 was the dawn of something new in the world, for over the next several decades, "every aspect of life experienced a revolution. By 1929, urban America [had] electricity, natural gas, [the] telephone, [and] clean running water[,] . . . the horse had almost vanished from urban streets[,] . . . [and] the household . . . enjoy[ed] entertainment[s] . . . beyond the 1870 imagination."[9] From the railroad and the steel mill as the high-tech edge of the economy in 1870, to the dynamo and the motor car as the high-tech edge in 1903, to the assembly line and the aircraft of 1936, to the television set and rocket (both moon and military) of 1969, to the microprocessor and World Wide Web of 2002—technological revolution, with its economic and then its sociological and political consequences, problems, and adjustments, came faster and more furiously than in any previous age.

Many of these changes came long before 1929. And they were not confined to the United States. On the 1889 centennial of the French Revolution's storming of the Bastille, France held a universal exposition. At the center of it was not some tableau of revolutionary martyrs, but a tower designed by and named after Gustave Eiffel. As historian Donald Sassoon wrote, the French exposition became a "consecrat[ion of] . . . commerce and trade, modernity, and the wonders of technology exhibited in the Galerie des Machines. . . . Under the banner of modernity, progress, and the peaceful pursuit of wealth, the French people would regain national pride and unity."[10]

Eiffel's steel-built tower, saved from dismantling at the end of the universal exposition by a public outcry, has dominated the Paris skyline ever since. Across the Atlantic Ocean from Paris, in New York City's harbor, stood another of Gustave Eiffel's designs. But this steel framework was clothed in copper and called the Statue of Liberty.

Life was still hard and dirty. America, rapidly becoming the world's growth center as the year 1900 passed, was still poor. And it was very unequal. Indeed, but for those Americans held in bondage just a few decades earlier, it was more unequal than it had ever been before, or than it would be again for the remainder of the 1900s.[11] Yet the United States in the first decade of the 1900s was also a very attractive place compared to every single other place in the rest of the world. In spite of the long hours and the risk of death or injury at the hands of corporations that cared little or not at all for worker safety, US jobs were very good ones by international standards.[12] They were jobs worth moving five thousand miles for, from, say, Hungary or Lithuania to suburban Pittsburgh or New Jersey.

It is traditional at this point in any economic history to talk about Thomas Alva Edison—the most famous inventor in the world, "the wizard of Menlo Park," New Jersey, who would register more than a thousand patents and found fifteen companies, including what is now called General Electric. But Edison's story is already widely known and in fact obscures the global reach of the revolution.

Let's talk instead about another migrant, who, like Herbert Hoover, moved west—but in this case someone who moved west from Croatia to America: Nikola Tesla.[13]

Tesla was born on July 10, 1856, in the town of Smiljan, in the Krajina region of the province of Croatia in the Habsburg Empire—then ruled by the young emperor Franz Joseph in Vienna. Tesla was the fourth of five children. His father was literate—a priest in the Serbian Orthodox Church—but his mother was not. His parents wanted him to become a priest. He wanted to become an electrical engineer.

Tesla studied electrical engineering in Graz, Austria, for two years, and then dropped out of school. He broke off relations with his family and friends, worked as an engineer for two years, and apparently suffered a nervous breakdown. His father urged him to return to college at Prague's Karl-Ferdinand University. Perhaps Nikola did, but if so only for one summer. Around which time his father died.

The year 1881 finds Nikola Tesla working in Budapest for a startup, the National Telephone Company of Hungary, as chief electrician and engineer. But he would not stay for long. In the very next year he moved to Paris, where he worked to improve and adapt American technology, and two years after that, in June 1884, he arrived in New York, New York, with nothing in his pockets save a letter of recommendation from engineer Charles Batchelor to Thomas Edison: "I know of two great men," Batchelor had written. "You are one of them. This young man is the other." And so Edison hired Tesla.

In America Tesla went to work for Edison Machine Works. He would later claim that Edison promised him $50,000—the entire net worth at the time of the Edison Machine Works—to improve and redesign Edison's direct current generators. Whatever was or wasn't agreed to, in 1885 Edison refused to pay that sum. Tesla quit and found himself digging ditches for a living for a couple of years.

By his own estimations, Tesla was a difficult man who found other men difficult. The day after Edison died, for example, Tesla seemed to demonstrate an extraordinary lack of any social intelligence whatsoever as he sketched, for the newspapers, his onetime employer and world-renowned inventor thusly: Edison, he said,

had no hobby, cared for no sort of amusement of any kind and lived in utter disregard of the most elementary rules of hygiene. . . . His method was inefficient in the extreme, for an immense ground had to be covered to get anything at all unless blind chance intervened and, at first, I was almost a sorry witness of his doings, knowing that just a little theory and calculation would have saved him 90 percent of the labor. But he had a veritable contempt for book learning and mathematical knowledge, trusting himself entirely to his inventor's instinct and practical American sense.[14]

Of his own personality, Tesla wrote:

I had a violent aversion against the earrings of women . . . bracelets pleased me more or less according to design. The sight of a pearl would almost give me a fit but I was fascinated with the glitter of crystals. . . . I would get a fever by looking at a peach. . . . I counted the steps in my walks and calculated the cubical contents of soup plates, coffee cups and pieces of food—otherwise my meal was unenjoyable. All repeated acts or operations I performed had to be divisible by three and if I missed I felt impelled to do it all over again, even if it took hours.[15]

Tesla coupled his eccentricities with bizarre and utopian claims about the future course of science and technology. He was, as much as Mary Wollstonecraft Shelley's fictional Dr. Viktor von Frankenstein, the very model of the mad scientist. Unsurprisingly, he found it difficult to maintain either financial backers or a supporting engineering staff. Yet Tesla and his allies beat Thomas Edison in the struggle over whether electricity was going to have an alternating or direct current.

Direct vs. alternating current—what does that mean? Back up to the 1770s, and to Alessandro Volta's discovery of the effects produced by a zinc atom's property that it can step itself down to a preferred, lower-energy quantum state by giving up an electron. Moreover, a silver atom can step itself down to a preferred, lower-energy quantum state by accepting an extra electron. Connect an anode to a piece of zinc, and electrons released from the zinc will pile up in it. Connect a cathode to a piece of silver, and the silver will grab electrons from it. Now run a conducting wire from the anode to the cathode. Then a direct current—actual electrons—will flow from the anode to the cathode until this "electrical battery" has run down, which happens when the zinc as a whole acquires enough of a positive charge that that charge's attracting electrons offset the strength of the chemical-reaction tendency of electrons to leave the zinc. And as the electrons flow in a direct current from the anode to the cathode, the energy of their motion can be tapped to do work. That is DC—direct current—electricity: intuitive and sensible. But its range is small: as an electron travels from the anode to the cathode, it bumps and jiggles and loses energy to heat with each inch it travels.

Suppose that, instead, you spun a wire near a magnet so that it made one revolution sixty times a second. A stationary electron does not notice that it is near a magnet. A moving one does: it gets pushed by the magnet with a force proportional to the electron's velocity. So as the wire is spun near the magnet, the electrons in it get pushed first one way and then another: shaken sixty times a second. Since the wire is a conductor, this shaking gets transmitted to pieces of the wire not near the magnet. By wrapping the wire many times around a cylinder, you can turn the wire into a very powerful magnet—which can then shake another wire extremely vigorously in this alternating-current (AC) pattern, and this is then a transformer. The more vigorously an electron is shaken, the greater the efficiency with which the power is transmitted—a lower current carries the same energy, and fewer electrons means less in the way of heat loss.

Edison's DC systems therefore required lots of power plants: one per neighborhood. Tesla's AC systems therefore required only a few large power plants, placed where they were most convenient, with the power then transmitted via vigorous shaking—high AC voltage—through long- and short-distance power lines, and the degree of the shaking stepped up and stepped down via transformers. Economies of scale are thus on Tesla's side. And they are powerful indeed. But this was witchcraft. There was no flow of electrons to carry the energy. There was just shaking back and forth, first one way, then the other. How could shaking with no actual movement of electrons from place to place produce useful power? And so there was great resistance, as even trained engineers had a hard time seeing how this could work.[16]

There was a time, perhaps, when Nikola Tesla was the only electrical engineer who understood that power transmission via AC was more than a theoretical curiosity, that it would and could work much more efficiently, hence much more cheaply, than Edison's method.

He was right. Our entire electrical power grid and everything that draws off of it are Tesla's much more than they are Edison's. The world viewed from space at night, illuminated by the electric power grid, is Tesla's world. His ideas about how to make electrons dance in an efficient and powerful way were correct, even though they struck nearly all of his contemporaries as highly speculative, unlikely to be practical, and borderline or over-the-borderline insane.

Tesla did much, much more. In 1894 he staged perhaps the first, or at least one of the first, demonstrations of radio. Many of his ideas panned out. Many of his ideas were too many years ahead of their time. Many of his ideas were simply mad: death rays and broadcast power, for two. He made a huge difference—perhaps five to ten years' worth of difference—in advancing electricity in the economy, and may have permanently shifted the economy into a somewhat different direction from the one in which it had been heading. How could the mad scientist Tesla make such a difference? Because he could work in *industrial research labs* and his ideas could be developed and applied by corporations. He could work for George Westinghouse. And General Electric could copy what he had done.

Tesla was first, foremost, and finally an inventor. In 1887, he founded Tesla Electric Light and Manufacturing, but his financial backers fired him from his own company. The next year, he staged a demonstration of an AC induction motor—the ancestor of all our current AC motors—at the American Institute of Electrical Engineers meeting. And the year after that, he found at last a permanent financial backer, George Westinghouse and his Westinghouse Electric and Manufacturing Company. Tesla soon began working at the company's laboratory in Pittsburg. In 1891, at the age of thirty-five, Tesla was back in New York establishing his own laboratory with money he'd made by selling his patents to Westinghouse under a patent-sharing agreement. In 1892 he became vice president of the American Institute of Electrical Engineers and received patents for the polyphase AC electric power system he invented. In 1893 he and George Westinghouse used AC power to illuminate the Chicago World's Fair—the first World's Fair ever to have a building for electricity and its applications.

The late 1880s and 1890s saw Westinghouse and Tesla and their backers struggle against Edison and his backers in the so-called "war of the currents." Edison had bet on a DC electrical grid. Direct current worked very well with incandescent lamps and with the motors of the day. It worked well with storage batteries, which meant that you only had to build the expensive generating capacity for average loads rather than peak loads. And Edison had not fully comprehended what Tesla was getting at when Tesla worked for him: "[Tesla's] ideas are splendid," he said. "But they are utterly impractical."[17]

The AC systems of Tesla and Westinghouse allowed the efficient transmission of electrical power over long distances through high-voltage power lines. Once the energy got where you wanted it to go, it could then be reduced, via step-down transformers, to a voltage that wasn't immediately fatal. Edison's DC system was far less risky, though it required low voltage to be pushed across long distances, incurring extremely large resistance power losses. On the one hand, Tesla's system, with all its attendant risks, got more energy where you wanted it. On the other, it was not obvious how alternating current could be used to power anything useful. Until, that is, Tesla invented the induction motor.

Both Westinghouse and Edison nearly bankrupted themselves as each struggled to build out an electrical power grid fast enough to become the dominant standard. Westinghouse and Tesla won.

The reach of Tesla's ideas was vastly expanded by the wealth and organizational intelligence of others and continued to expand even after Tesla, in 1899, moved from New York to Colorado Springs to conduct experiments in high-voltage power distribution—both through wires and wireless. His wireless power distribution experiments soon turned into radio, an outcome in which he had limited interest. Tesla was instead captivated with the idea of distributing electric power throughout the world without having to build power lines, and in distributing electric power for free. His was a kind of open-source electric power movement that antedated the open-source software movement by ninety years.

Dominant financiers J. P. Morgan and George F. Baker decided in 1907, when that year's financial panic, plus George Westinghouse's having unwisely borrowed too much money from them, gave them the opportunity, that the heroic age of electricity was over. It was time, Morgan decided, to rationalize operations and replace visionary inventors like Tesla (and wild-eyed, charismatic entrepreneurs like George Westinghouse, who would back him) with sober, flannel-suited executives, such as Robert Mather and Edwin F. Atkins, who would routinize the business. They focused on the bottom line: spend less on blue-sky experiments, pay workers less, and channel free cash flow not into overseas expansion or (horrors!) into competing with banker favorite General Electric, but into dividends. Tesla gave Westinghouse a perpetual royalty-free license to use all his inventions, and so impoverished himself. Morgan and Baker pushed Westinghouse out anyway, and kept the license.[18]

Tesla was not alone in straddling the end of the short nineteenth century and the start of the long twentieth. As a creative, inventive genius he kept rare company, but as a post-Westinghouse charity case of the Waldorf-Astoria in New York

City, his impoverishment meant he kept vast company, for the world then was still a poor one.

In 1914 perhaps two-thirds of nearly all humans still tilled the earth to grow the bulk of the food their families ate. Most humans could not read; nor had they seen a steam engine up close, traveled on a railway train, spoken on a telephone, or lived in a city. Life expectancy was still little higher than it had been in the Agrarian Age. And in 1914, even in the United States, more than one-third of the labor force worked in agriculture. At the time, the United States was a beacon to the world's toiling millions, who were often willing to move continents to improve their lot. Of all the countries of the world, only Britain and Belgium were moving their workers out of agriculture and into the cities faster than America was. Consider that early in the first decade of the 1900s Germany became the world's third superpower, more powerful and more industrialized than any other nation save Britain and the United States. But by the time Adolf Hitler's Nazi Germany went to war in 1939, four-fifths of the wheeled and tracked vehicles in his army were still powered by horses and mules.[19]

To get a better sense of not just how poor but how unequal a society the United States was at the beginning of the twentieth century, consider the case of an anonymous college professor, who in 1902 was the subject of a four-page article for the *Atlantic Monthly* under the byline of G.H.M.[20] The professor, claiming to be vastly underpaid, asserted, with pique, that the "average college professor's salary" was "about $2,000." He saw this as clearly inadequate and unfairly low. Yet, at the time, $2,000 was roughly four times the average American worker's gross production and six times his annual wage. For comparison's sake, in 2020 a professor earning four times the national average would command an annual salary of $500,000.[21]

But G.H.M. saw himself as a "reasonable man." He did not ask for "a large [salary], commensurate with what equal ability would bring in other lines of work ($10,000 to $50,000)"—or twenty to one hundred times the nation's then current average income per worker.

Yet the *Atlantic Monthly* did not give this ordinary professor four pages for parody. As G.H.M. went through his budget, readers nodded in agreement that his family was indeed strapped for cash. The first large expense he listed was for personal services. With no consumer durables—refrigerators, washers and dryers, oven ranges powered by an electric grid or municipal gas, not to mention cars and home appliances—"we must pay $25 a month for even a passable servant," the prof wrote. Add to that $10 a month for laundry, for the regular servants would "do no laundry work," he complained. And then $1 a month for haircuts, and $2 a month for a gardener. On personal services alone we are up to $445 a year—roughly the average level of US gross domestic product (GDP) per worker in 1900. And the individuals hired to help did so without benefit of a gasoline-powered lawnmower, electric hedge clippers, a vacuum cleaner, or a dishwasher.

Professor G.H.M. could not afford to live within walking distance of campus, and could not afford to keep a horse and carriage, so he had to use that newfangled high-tech invention—the bicycle—to commute. That an ordinary professor could feel, along with a reading public, that his talents should command such an enormous multiple of the average income, and worry about its insufficiency, is a sign of the deeply stratified economy in which he found himself.

That inequality comes into sharp relief when we turn our attention from this average professor to the average working-class family at the start of the twentieth century.

Perhaps a third of American households in 1900 had boarders, almost always male and unrelated, sleeping and eating in the house. It was the only way for the housewife to bring income directly into the household. It also multiplied the amount of labor she had to do. Much of it was manual. For example, few households had running water or a hot water heater. Instead, water came in by the bucket from a common faucet that was, hopefully, near the house, and for washing it was then heated on a wood- or coal-burning stove. The same absence of durable goods that cursed our professor damned our housewife, from heating that stove to cleaning a shirt.[22]

Those who could afford the resources to maintain bourgeois styles of cleanliness flaunted it. White shirts, white dresses, and white gloves were all powerful indications of wealth in turn-of-the-twentieth-century America. They said, "I don't have to do my own laundry," and they said it loudly.

The relatively prosperous steel factory town of Homestead, Pennsylvania, provides further insight into the vast disparities of wealth at the time. In 1910, only one in six working-class households had indoor bathrooms. Half of "Slav" and "Negro" families lived in one- or two-room houses. Most white families lived in four-room houses—and many groups that would be called "white" today were not considered to be so then, including "Slavs," "Latins," and "Hebrews." But even in the relative comfort of a four-room house, few could afford to heat more than one room through a Pennsylvania winter. And how many ways can you think of to cook potatoes on an antique cast-iron stove? Meal preparation was not a one-hour-a-day but a four-hour-a-day task.

Infant mortality was still high. One in five babies in Homestead, Pennsylvania, died before reaching his or her first birthday. Adult women faced substantial risks in childbirth. And adult men died, too, like flies. Accident rates in the Homestead factory left 260 injured per year and 30 dead. This out of a total population of 25,000 and a steel mill working population of 5,000. Each year, 5 percent of those 5,000 workers were injured sufficiently in factory accidents to miss work, 1 percent were permanently disabled, and half a percent were killed.

We can do the math. If you had started to work for U.S. Steel when you were twenty, there was then a chance of one in seven that the factory would have killed you before you reached fifty, and of almost one in three that it would have disabled you. Is it any wonder that life insurance and disability insurance provided by local lodges and organizations (because the company provided few) loomed so large in American working-class consciousness at the turn of the century? Is it any wonder that Homestead was home to some of the most violent and brutal labor disputes of the late nineteenth century, exceeded in viciousness only by the mines of the Rocky Mountains and the railroad marshaling yards of Chicago? And is it any wonder that the first component of the welfare state put into place in many parts of the United States was workmen's compensation?

Most of the Homestead workforce only worked six days a week. That "only" was hard won, for U.S. Steel viewed shutting most of the mill on Sundays as a major concession on their part, one its principals hoped would produce large public relations benefits. As long as they could find workers willing to work the night shift, the Homestead mill (depressions and recessions apart) stayed open twenty-four hours a day on weekdays. And when things changed, they changed all at once—from two twelve-hour shifts, before and during World War I, to two (or three) eight-hour shifts during the 1920s, World War II, and thereafter.

Yet Homestead jobs—at least Homestead jobs taken by people born in the United States—were good jobs for the time, even by the elevated standards of the United States. Most who held those jobs were grateful. "Their expectations were not ours," historian Ray Ginger explained. "A man who grew up on a Southern farm did not think it cruel that his sons had to work as bobbin boys [collecting spun thread in a textile mill]. An immigrant living in a tenement and working in a sweatshop yet knew that for the first time in his life he was wearing shoes seven days a week."[23] White households in Homestead could make around $900 a year, which placed them well within the upper third of the US population in terms of income per household, in the richest country in the world save for Australia.

Relative to what could be earned by people of similar skill levels anywhere else in the world, a job in the Homestead mill was a very attractive job. And so people came to America, and people in America sought out the places like Homestead where the economy bustled.

The sources of America's exceptional wealth were many.

By 1870 the focus of economic growth crossed the Atlantic from Britain to America, where, on a continent-wide scale, a flood of immigration, vast resources, and an open society made inventors and entrepreneurs cultural heroes.

Some have noted that the country's vast size and population induced industries that could embrace mass production and modern management. Some have noted the great tide of immigrants who turned to America, bringing with them labor, talent, and a willingness to work and consume. Still others have stressed the crucial role played by natural resources in America's industrial supremacy: in a world in which transport costs were still significant, a comparative advantage in natural resources became a comparative advantage in manufacturing. Others have stressed the links between a resource-rich economy and the "American system" of manufactures, relying on standardization, attempts to make interchangeable parts, heavy use of machinery—and wasteful use of natural resources, including both materials and energy. Finally, some have stressed the openness of American society, the ease with which individuals, ideas, capital, and initiative moved across the continent, and across other continents and back again.[24]

It was a system of opportunities in which a Hoover and a Tesla, not to mention a Westinghouse, an Edison, a professor going by the initials G.H.M., and a Homestead laborer, could feel hopeful and be ambitious. But calling it a "system" is too grandiose, suggesting some farsighted process. In the twentieth century these collective sources of exceptional wealth led to possibilities of mass production not because of any deliberative, planned process of industrial development, but through myopic choices that generated further technological externalities. The invention of inventing, it turns out, produces yet more inventions.

To which we can add two additional sources of American wealth: education and peace, though we must note that these were largely unavailable to both the Indigenous peoples—First Nations, descendants of earlier immigrants by land rather than later ones by sea—who were then being exposed to diseases via "gifts" of blankets and herded onto reservations, and Blacks, against whom white society was then waging a campaign of terror.

In America in 1914, even in rural America, children went to school. The years before World War I saw a large increase in education, as at least elementary school became the rule for children in leading-edge economies. And the number of years that a typical student attended school grew as well.[25]

The United States made the creation of a literate, numerate citizenry a high priority. And that encouraged those with richer backgrounds, better preparations, and quicker or better-trained minds to go on to ever-higher education. Industrialists and others soon found the higher quality of their workforce more than making up for the taxes levied to support mass secondary and higher education. This was not a unique American advantage. While the United States' strong educational system provided an edge in productivity, Britain's Dominions, and even more so Germany, also had a strong commitment to education and enjoyed a similar advantage in industrial competitiveness.

American exceptionalism was very real, but can blur a point: the country was exceptional compared to the rest of the developed Western world only by degrees. Cumulatively, the differences by degree, however, added up to something that to many appearances was a difference in kind. And the end result was a United States that enjoyed a remarkable extent of technological and industrial dominance over the rest of the world for much of the twentieth century. It also captured much of the world's imagination.

Because it was in relative terms so prosperous, and because its gradient of technological advance in the pre–World War I period was so much faster than that of Western Europe, the United States was where people looked to see the shape of the dawning twentieth century. In the seventeenth century, much of Europe had looked to Holland; in the nineteenth, much of the world had looked to Britain. As the long twentieth century began, almost the entire world, and certainly all of Europe, looked to America. To observers it appeared to be a qualitatively different civilization. The United States lacked the burden of the past that constrained the politics and oppressed the peoples of Europe, and, freed from that burden, it could look boldly toward the future.

The unique American advantage was greatly reinforced by the fact that in the United States, the period of explosive prosperity set in motion around 1870 (also called the Belle Époque, the Gilded Age, or the economic El Dorado) lasted without interruption longer than elsewhere in the world. China collapsed into revolution in 1911. Europe descended into the hell of World War I in 1914. In the United States, the period of progress and industrial development lasted from 1865, when the guns fell silent at Appomattox at the end of the Civil War, until the start of the Great Depression in the summer of 1929.

We can see some of the admiration and wonder that turn-of-the-century America triggered by gazing at the country through the eyes of yet another migrant: Lev Davidovich Bronstein.

Lev's parents had also been migrants: his father, David, and mother, Anna, crossed the greatest river they had ever seen to move hundreds of miles out of the forest and into the grasslands—lands where the horse nomads had roamed within recent historical memory before their suppression by the army. There they lived on what were among the richest agricultural soils in the world, and very thinly settled. It was fifteen miles from the Bronsteins' farm to the nearest post office.

But this is not Laura Ingalls Wilder's *Little House on the Prairie*, a story of the European settlement of the wheatlands of America. The Bronstein farm was in Yanovka, in Ukraine. The languages they spoke were Russian and Yiddish, not English. When they sent their son Lev to school by sending him to the nearest big city, it was not the Lake Michigan port city of Chicago, but the Black Sea port city of Odessa.

There he became a communist. And midway through his career he found himself feared by czars and policemen, and hunted and exiled because he was feared. In January 1917 he began a ten-week stay in New York City with his family (his second wife and their children). Unlike most of the people who had left the Old World for the New and wound up in New York in the 1910s, the communist Lev did not want to be there. But he and his family made the best of it, and he later wrote about their life in the city:

> We rented an apartment in a workers' district, and furnished it on the installment plan. That apartment, at eighteen dollars a month, was equipped with all sorts of conveniences that we Europeans were quite unused to: electric lights, gas cooking-range, bath, telephone, automatic service-elevator, and even a chute for the garbage. These things completely won the boys over to New York. For a time the telephone was their main interest; we had not had this mysterious instrument either in Vienna or Paris.

They—particularly the children—were overwhelmed by the prosperity of the United States and by the technological marvels that they saw in everyday use:

> The children had new friends. The closest was the chauffeur of Dr. M. The doctor's wife took my wife and the boys out driving[;] . . . the chauffeur was a magician, a titan, a super-man! With a wave of his hand, he made the machine obey

his slightest command. To sit beside him was the supreme delight.

When the Russian Revolution came, Lev returned to St. Petersburg, a city that would change its name several times over the long twentieth century, first to Petrograd, then to Leningrad, and finally back to St. Petersburg. Fittingly, Lev would change his name, too. He took an alias from one of his former czarist jailers in Odessa: Lev Bronstein became Leon Trotsky.

Trotsky was never allowed back into the United States. He was, after all, a dangerous subversive, with a long-run plan that included the overthrow of the government of the United States by force and violence. He became Lenin's right hand, the organizer of Bolshevik victory in the Russian Civil War, the first of the losers to Joseph Stalin in the subsequent power struggle, and finally the victim of the Soviet secret police, assassinated with an ice pick in his head outside Mexico City in 1940.

Before his murder, while in exile, Trotsky would recall his departure from New York City. And in doing so he would capture what much of the world believed. In leaving New York for Europe, Trotsky felt, he was leaving the future for the past: "I was leaving for Europe, with the feeling of a man who has had only a peek into the furnace where the future is being forged."[26]

Utopia was being built, Trotsky thought. But it was not being built in the Russian Empire to which he was returning to try to take advantage of the political moment opened by the abdication of Czar Nicholas II Romanov. It was the United States that was holding high the banner of utopia, and promising to be the world's leader and guide along the path.

The heat for this forge came from recurring waves of technological advance that kept coming at an unprecedented pace. These waves were created by the industrial research lab and the modern corporation, and though they were America centered, they diffused outward, first to the rest of the global north and then, slowly, throughout the world: remember, there was more proportional techno-economic progress and change in a single year over the 1870–2010 period than in fifty years before 1500, and more than in twelve years over the period from 1500 to 1770, or more than in four years over 1770–1870. This progress created much, and it also destroyed much. This is a market economy we are talking about: the financing to keep your job existing requires that it be part of a value chain that satisfies some maximum-probability test carried out by some financier who may be thousands of miles away; your ability to earn the income you think you deserve depends on your potential employers scrutinizing the value of what you can do by the same metric. As technological capabilities grow, the ability of those whose work relies on old technologies to pass such tests declines. "Capitalism," economist Joseph Schumpeter wrote in 1942, "never can be stationary. . . . The fundamental impulse that sets and keeps the capitalist engine in motion comes from the new consumers' goods, the new methods of production or transportation, the new markets, the new forms of industrial organization that capitalist enterprise creates. . . . Industrial mutation . . . incessantly revolutionizes the economic structure *from within*, incessantly destroying the old one. . . . This process of creative destruction is the essential fact about capitalism."[27] Great wealth is created by the creation. Poverty is imposed by the destruction. And uncertainty and anxiety are created by the threat. Someone had to manage this process, to contain rebellions against the consequences of the "destruction" part if the future of technological possibilities was in fact to be forged.

After 2006, the pace of measured economic growth in the United States was to plummet. In 2010, our ending date, many thought this was a flash in the pan because 2010 came just after the nadir of the Great Recession that had begun in 2008. But over the entire decade of 2006–2016, measured real GDP per capita grew at a pace of only 0.6 percent per year—a shocking falloff from anything that had been seen earlier in the long twentieth century. Over the 1996–2006 decade, the pace had been 2.3 percent per year. Over the two decades before that, 1976–1996, the pace had been 2 percent per year, and in the "Thirty Glorious Years" after World War II it had been 3.4 percent per year. After 2006, exceptional America's furnace's fires were rapidly cooling, if not out, or not yet out.

3

Democratizing
the Global North

There is a big difference between the *economic* and the *political economic*. The latter term refers to the methods by which people collectively decide how they are going to organize the rules of the game within which economic life takes place. It therefore relates to how people collectively decide to establish the rules by which they make decisions about organization and institutions. To see how political economy works in practice, let's jump back in time, to the start of the story of the federal government of the United States.

James Madison was never enthusiastic about democracy. He wrote, in the *Federalist Papers* in 1787, "Democracies have ever been spectacles of turbulence and contention; have ever been found incompatible with personal security or the rights of property; and have been . . . as short in their lives as . . . violent in their deaths."[1]

Then again, in the late 1700s next to nobody among the rich and powerful was enthusiastic about democracy.

What James Madison was enthusiastic about was a *republic*, a system of government in which a certain subset of people who counted—consisting, for the most part, of those already endowed with healthy amounts of security and property—would choose a small, select group of the wise, thoughtful, and energetic to represent them. These representatives would share the values of the people and advance their well-being but, it was hoped, would do so disinterestedly: seeking not their own profit but rather to demonstrate their virtue as citizens.

Madison fervently wanted to avoid the "turbulence and contention" of democracy. Recall that under the Constitution Madison and his peers drew up, states could restrict the franchise as much as they wished, as long as they preserved "a republican form of government."

America's Founding Fathers had their work cut out for them convincing anyone that even their limited-franchise republic was a good idea. At the time, feudal webs, monarchies, and empires seemed to be the more durable and quite likely the better forms of government. As of 1787, Madison and Alexander Hamilton, in the *Federalist Papers*, were reduced to arguing that establishing a republic was worth risking, in spite of its sorry historical past, because of "advances in the science of government" since classical antiquity. But Thomas Jefferson, for one, thought Hamilton at least was just "talking his book" because he had committed himself out of ambition to the revolutionary republican cause—that privately Hamilton wished for a monarchical form of government for America.[2] Back then, democracy's superiority wasn't so obvious.

Yet from 1776 to 1965, democracy—at least in the form of one male, of the right age and race, one vote—made huge strides in the North Atlantic. The feudal and monarchical systems of government fell into ever-greater disrepute.

For a while, *prosperity* was seen as the most important qualification for political participation. Up until the end of World War I, in the Prussian provincial legislature of the German Empire, those who paid the top one-third of taxes got to elect one-third of the representatives. In the early 1840s, François Guizot, a slightly left-of-center prime minister in France's constitutional monarchy, responded to demands for a broader electoral franchise with the words *enrichessez vous*: if you want to vote, get rich enough to qualify. It did not work. On February 23, 1848, King Louis-Philippe, of France's Orleanist dynasty—the only king of the Orleanist dynasty—threw Guizot under the proverbial horse cart in the hope of avoiding revolution and dethronement. Too little, too late. Louis-Philippe abdicated the following day.[3]

Over the period 1870–1914, expanding democracy proved to be the political principle that caused the least offense to the greatest number, and it consequently gained general acceptance. Political society would be a realm in which some or most of the male individuals' preferences would count equally in choosing the government, and government would then curb and control the economy somewhat. It would limit but not extinguish the extra influence of those whom Theodore Roosevelt called the "malefactors of great wealth."

But even this was not enough to satisfy everyone—indeed, there would be ongoing pressure to expand the franchise.

When liberals were in power, they tried to extend the suffrage on the principle that new, poorer voters would be less conservative and would support them. When conservatives were in power, they (more rarely and reluctantly) tried to extend the suffrage in the belief that workers, loyal to king and country, would support them. Allowing more people to vote would "dish the [liberal] Whigs," for the workers would remember who had and who had not succeeded in giving them the franchise.[4] And when revolution threatened, governments, fearing armed mobs in the streets, would extend the franchise to divide the potentially revolutionary opposition. "The principle," then prime minister Earl Grey said in an 1831 debate over Britain's franchise-extension reform bill, "is to prevent . . . revolution," and on the basis of that expectation he declared, "I am reforming to preserve, not to overthrow."[5]

By such means did the suffrage creep forward, step by step, under liberal and conservative regimes. Up until 1914, at least in the increasingly prosperous North Atlantic industrial core of the world economy, the prospects for spreading broad prosperity and stabilizing democracy looked good. The politico-economic system seemed to be working: the rising prosperity made aristocrats and plutocrats feel that the slow erosion of their relative social position was a price worth paying for the good things they received, and made those lower down feel that their continued toleration of upper-class dominance was a price worth paying for societal progress. Finally, conservatives and liberals saw wide-enough paths to political victory to make both confident that the current trajectory of history was on their side.

While suffrage expanded quickly in many respects, it came in fits and starts, and a much longer time passed before it was extended to women.

In 1792, France became the first country to grant universal male suffrage—although effective suffrage of any kind was gone by the time of Napoleon's coronation in 1804, and universal male suffrage did not return, save for a brief interval in 1848–1851, until 1871. In the United States the fight for the franchise for white men had been won around 1830. The first European state to offer universal suffrage—for both men and women—was Finland in 1906. In Great Britain (near) universal suffrage came in 1918, when the suffrage was extended to all men twenty-one and older and to women thirty and older. Adult women under thirty had to wait until 1928.

American suffragettes fought the good fight for decades. By the early 1900s it was ongoing. In their ranks was my great-grandmother, Florence Wyman Richardson, who, with others, chained herself to the statehouse fence in Missouri's capital, and as a consequence reportedly got herself expelled from the St. Louis Veiled Prophet debutante ball. The Nineteenth Amendment to the Constitution extending the vote to all women passed in 1920.

France, having led in the late 1800s, was the laggard. Not until the expulsion of the Vichy Nazi collaborationist regime in 1944 did it extend the vote to women.

It took even longer for the extension of the franchise to cross the race line, especially in the United States.

Events involving heroic sacrifices of every sort played out over more than a century during the fight for the right of Blacks to vote. Among these were the Colfax Massacre in Louisiana in 1873, during which approximately one hundred Blacks were murdered. At a much less heroic end of the spectrum, when my great-grandmother Florence joined others to launch the Urban League in St. Louis in the 1920s, she became the scandal of her neighborhood by inviting Black people to dinner.

The enfranchisement of Blacks would not truly come in the United States until 1965, with passage of the Voting Rights Act—and even thereafter, it remained tenuous. As I write this paragraph, one-third of US states have recently crafted bureaucratic and legal obstacles aimed at differentially disenfranchising up to one-fourth of Black voters. As august, at least institutionally, a person as the late Supreme Court chief justice William Rehnquist won his spurs by running "ballot security" efforts in the early 1960s, in which "every Black or Mexican[-looking] person was being challenged." Why did he do this? As one witness reported: "[As] a deliberate effort to slow down the voting . . . to cause people awaiting their turn to vote to grow tired of waiting, and leave . . . handbills were distributed warning persons that if they were not properly qualified to vote they would be prosecuted."[6]

FROM MADISON TO REHNQUIST and beyond, it has ever been the case that for some segment of humanity, democracy—and the right to vote, and the consequent exercise of influence and power—raised more questions than it solved. Of this richly braided material Gordian knots were tied, repeatedly, and efforts to sever them commanded the spilling of gallons of ink, and of even more of blood.

The history of these conflicts over democracy has intersected in important ways with economic history. To understand how, let us turn again to two Vienna-born thinkers whom I have already mentioned: the Austrian-British-Chicagoan right-wing economist Friedrich August von Hayek (1899–1992) and the slightly older Hungarian-Jewish-Torontonian moral philosopher Karl Polanyi (1886–1964).

We first give the floor to Hayek, driven always to teacheth the lesson that "the market giveth, the market taketh away; blessed be the name of the market."

In Hayek's view, to inquire whether a market economy's distribution of income and wealth was "fair" or "just" was to commit a fatal intellectual blunder. "Justice" and "fairness" of any form require that you receive what you deserve. A market economy gives not to those who deserve but to those who happen to be in the right place at the right time. Who controls the resources that are valuable for future production is not a matter of fairness. Once you step into the morass of "social justice," Hayek believed, you would not be able to stop chasing a "just" and "fair" outcome "until the whole of society was organized . . . in all essential respects . . . [as] the opposite of a free society."[7]

Note that this did not mean you were morally obligated to watch the poor starve and the injured bleed out and die in the street. Society should make "some provision for those threatened by the extremes of indigence or starvation due to circumstances beyond their control," Hayek said, if only as the cheapest way to protect hardworking and successful folks "against acts of desperation on the part of the needy." But beyond that you should not interfere with the market. The market was, or would lead us to, utopia—or as close to utopia as humans could attain. Interference was therefore worse than inexpedient.[8]

That a market economy can produce a highly unequal distribution of income and wealth just as it can produce a less unequal distribution of income and wealth was beside the point. To even raise the question of what the distribution of wealth should be was to presume—falsely, Hayek believed—that people had rights other than property rights, and obligations to others beyond those they freely assumed through contract.

Besides, rectifying inequality was awful because it was chimerical. Hayek believed we lacked and would always lack the knowledge to create a better society. Centralization always led to misinformation and bad decisions. Top-down was a disaster. Only bottom-up "spontaneous order," which emerged from everyone pursuing their own self-interest in what might seem to be a chaotic process, could possibly lead to progress.

To that end, what humanity had was market capitalism, the only system that could possibly be even moderately efficient and productive, for "prices are an instrument of communication and guidance which embody more information than we directly have," Hayek wrote, and so "the whole idea that you can bring about the same order based on the division of labor by simple direction falls to the ground." Any attempts to reorder the market distribution of income in order to reward the deserving at the expense of the undeserving would erode market capitalism: "The idea [that] you can arrange for distributions of incomes . . . correspond[ing] to . . . merit or need," he said, does not fit with your "need [for] prices, including the prices of labor, to direct people to go where they are needed." And once you start top-down planning, you are on what he called "the road to serfdom," and "the detailed scale of values which must guide the planning makes it impossible that it should be determined by anything like democratic means."[9] Hayek's was a "this-is-as-good-as-it-is-ever-going-to-get" sort of utopianism.

Hayek understood, however, that this better method of organizing society that cared not a whit for fairness and justice was unlikely to be accepted with universal cries of "huzzah!" That the only rights the market economy recognizes are property rights—and indeed, only those property rights that are valuable—predictably didn't inspire the multitudes. It was clear that people thought they had other rights beyond those that accrued to the property they happened to hold. And this feeling posed an enormous problem for Hayek. To his credit, he didn't shy away from the direction his arguments led. He identified two substantive enemies to a good (or at least as good as it is likely to get) society: *egalitarianism* and *permissiveness*. Too much democracy—democracy that made people feel that they should be able to do what they wanted and not be lorded over by those with more property—was, in short, bad.

Indeed, for Hayek, egalitarianism was "a product of the necessity under unlimited democracy to solicit the support even of the worst." In other words, democracy essentially meant conceding, as he put it, "'a right to equal concern and respect' to those who break the code"—which, he warned, was no way to maintain a civilization.[10]

The fearsome result for Hayek would then be *permissiveness*, which, "assisted by a scientistic psychology," he wrote, "has come to the support of those who claim a share in the wealth of our society without submitting to the discipline to which it is due." The lesson was clear. A prosperous market economy could only flourish if it was protected by authority.

For Hayek, overly democratic, egalitarian, and permissive societies would probably need at some point someone to seize power and reorder the society in an authoritarian mode that would respect the market economy. Such an interruption would be a temporary "Lykourgan moment," as he called it—using a term harking back to the mythical ordainer of the laws of the classical Greek city of Sparta—and afterward, the music could restart and the normal dance of ordered individual liberty and market-driven prosperity resume. Hayek, standing on the shoulders of giants and tyrants alike, articulated a position about the market economy that throughout the twentieth century would turn the political right against democracy again and again, leading a great many to view the institution not just as a lesser good but as a genuine evil. These views did not lose strength as World War I drew near.

Now the paragraphs above have cast a harsh light on Hayek's thought as a moral philosopher and political activist. And, later on, I will make even harsher judgments of Hayek's thought as a macroeconomist. Why, then, should we not ignore him? There are three main reasons.

First, he serves as a marker for an extremely influential current of thought and action, influential not least because it found itself congenial to and backed by the rich and powerful.

Second, Hayek's political economy is not completely wrong. The democratic political sphere can turn into one in which the logic is not cooperation and growth but rather confiscation and redistribution—with "deserving" and "undeserving" standing in, respectively, for the friends and enemies of the powerful. Hayek is not wrong that keeping your head down, concentrating on win-win production for market exchange, and ignoring appeals to "social justice" as chimerical can be vastly better than such a scenario.

Third, Hayek was a farsighted genius Dr. Jekyll in one crucially important aspect of his thinking—he was a hedgehog who knew one very good trick, as Isaiah Berlin quoted Arkhilokhos as saying, rather than a fox who knew many tricks.[11] He was the thinker who grasped most thoroughly and profoundly what the market system could do for human benefit. All societies in solving their economic problems face profound difficulties in getting reliable information to the deciders and then incentivizing the deciders to act for the public good. The market order of property, contract, and exchange can—if property rights are handled properly—push decision-making out to the decentralized periphery where the reliable information already exists, solving the information problem. And by rewarding those who bring resources to valuable uses, it automatically solves the incentivization problem. (There remain the macrocoordination problem and the distribution problem, and most of the flaws in Hayek's thinking come from his inability to recognize the nature of those problems at all. But absolutely nailing two out of four ain't bad.)

Overall, what Hayek got right is absolutely essential in making sense of the long twentieth century's economic history. His reasoning not only is cited by decision makers of varying influence throughout these decades, but aspects of what his reasoning elucidates were unquestionably at play.

We give the floor now to Karl Polanyi, who teacheth the lesson that "the market is made for man, not man for the market."[12]

Friedrich von Hayek loved that the market turned everything into a commodity, and he feared those who damned the market because it did not make everybody materially equal. Polanyi disagreed emphatically. In *The Great Transformation*, Polanyi explained that land, labor, and finance were "fictitious commodities." They could not be governed by the logic of profit and loss but needed to be *embedded* in society and managed by the community, taking into account religious and moral dimensions. The result, Polanyi wrote, was a tension, a contest, a *double movement*. Ideologues of the market and the market itself attempted to remove land, labor, and finance from society's moral and religious governance. In reaction, society struck back by restricting the domain of the market and putting its thumb on the scales where market outcomes seemed "unfair." As a consequence, a market society will face a backlash—it can be a left-wing backlash, it can be a right-wing backlash, but there will be a backlash—and it will be powerful.

Now these were—are—brilliant insights. As expressed by Polanyi in the original, they are also, sadly, incomprehensible to an overwhelming proportion of those who try to read him. With deference to comprehension, my summary of what Polanyi was really saying follows:

The market economy believes that the only rights that matter are property rights, and the only property rights that matter are those that produce things for which the rich have high demand. But people believe that they have other rights.

With respect to *land*, people believe they have rights to a stable community. This includes the belief that the natural and built environment in which they grew up or that they made with their hands is *theirs*, whether or not market logic says it would be more profitable if it were different—say a highway ran through it—or more lucrative if somebody else lived there.

With respect to *labor*, people believe they have a right to a suitable income. After all, they prepared for their profession, played by the rules, and so believe society owes them a fair income, something commensurate with their preparation. And this holds whether or not the logic of the world market says otherwise.

With respect to *finance*, people believe that as long as they do their job of working diligently, the flow of purchasing power through the economy should be such as to give them the wherewithal to buy. And "rootless cosmopolite" financiers—powerful people with no connection to the community, and yes, this often shades, and more than shades, over into antisemitism, as what is for Polanyi a critique of the operation of a system turns into a condemnation of Jewish and Jew-like people who fill a particular role in it—who may be thousands of miles away should have no commensurate right to decide that this or that flow of purchasing power through the economy is no longer sufficiently profitable, and so should be shut off. They should not be able to make your job dry up and blow away.[13]

People have not just property rights, Polanyi declared, but these other economic rights as well—rights that a pure market economy will not respect. A pure market economy will lay down that highway, ignore years of preparation when doling out an income, and allow your purchasing power to dry up and blow away along with your job if someone thousands of miles away decides better returns on investments are to be found elsewhere. Hence society—by government decree or by mass action, left-wing or right-wing, for good or ill—*will* intervene, and re-embed the economy in its moral and religious logic so that these rights are satisfied. The process is one of double movement: the economy moves to remove the embedding of production, transactions, and consumption from the network of relationships that is society, and then society moves—somehow—to reassert itself.[14]

Note that these rights that society will attempt to validate do not—or might not—be rights to anything like an *equal* distribution of the fruits of industry and agriculture. And it is probably wrong to describe them as *fair*: they are what people expect, given a certain social order. Equals should be treated equally, yes; but unequals should be treated unequally. And societies do not have to and almost never do presume that people are of equal significance.

What can we do with these insights? Hayek and Polanyi were theoreticians and academicians—brilliant ones. But their insights and their doctrines are important only because they capture deep broad currents of thought that sparked through the brains of millions and drove actions. Not Hayek but Hayekians, and not Polanyi but Polanyians, and those acting on the motives identified by Polanyi, made history. So to get a glimpse of how this played out in practice, let us take a look at economics and politics interacting at the bleeding edge—at the most rapidly growing and industrializing place on the pre–World War I earth, in that era's counterpart to the twenty-first century's Shenzhen: Chicago.[15]

In 1840, when the Illinois and Michigan Canal opened connecting the Mississippi River with the Great Lakes, Chicago had a population of four thousand. In 1871, Mrs. O'Leary's cow burned down a third, perhaps, of the city. Chicago built the world's first steel-framed skyscraper in 1885, the city had a population of two million by 1900, and at that point 70 percent of its citizens had been born outside the United States.

On May 1, 1886, the American Federation of Labor declared a general strike to fight for an eight-hour workday. A front line of that conflict formed at the gates of the McCormick Harvesting Machine Company in Chicago. There, hundreds of police, backed up by private Pinkerton agency security guards, protected hundreds of strikebreakers who passed an angry crowd. On May 3, police officers opened fire on the crowd, killing six. The next day in Haymarket Square eight police officers were murdered by an anarchist bomb during a rally in protest of police violence and in support of the striking workers. The police opened fire and killed perhaps twenty civilians (nobody seems to have counted), largely immigrants, largely non-English-speaking ones. A kangaroo court convicted eight innocent (we now believe) left-wing politicians and labor organizers of murdering the eight policemen. Five were hanged.[16]

In 1889 Samuel Gompers, president of the American Federation of Labor, asked the world socialist movement—the "Second International"—to set aside May 1 every year as the day for a great annual international demonstration in support of the eight-hour workday and in memory of the victims of police violence in Chicago in 1886.

In the summer of 1894 President Grover Cleveland, in the fine tradition of triangulating politicians, persuaded Congress to establish a national holiday in recognition of the place of labor in American society. But not on the International Workers' Day, May 1, which commemorated Chicago's slain workers— rather, the new holiday would be observed on the first Monday in September.

Not all American politicians were so timid. In 1893 the new Democratic governor of Illinois, John Peter Altgeld—the state's first Democratic governor since 1856, the first Chicago resident to become governor ever, and the first foreign-born governor ever—pardoned the three still-living so-called Haymarket Bombers. His reasons were unambiguous. Those convicted of the bombing had likely been innocent. The real reason for the bombing, in Altgeld's view, had been the out-of-control violence by the Pinkerton guards hired by McCormick and others.

Who was this Altgeld who pardoned convicted anarchists and blamed violence on the manufacturing princes of the Midwest and their hired armed goons? And how did he become governor of Illinois?

Altgeld was born in Germany. His parents moved him to Ohio in 1848, when he was three months old. He fought in the Union Army during the Civil War, and at Fort Monroe, in the Virginia tidewater country, he caught a lifelong case of malaria. After the war he finished high school, became a roving railroad worker, found work as a schoolteacher, and somewhere in there read the law sufficiently to become a lawyer. By 1872 he was the city attorney of Savannah, Missouri. By 1874 he was county prosecutor. In 1875 he showed up in Chicago as the author of *Our Penal Machinery and Its Victims*.[17] By 1884 he was an unsuccessful Democratic candidate for Congress—and a strong supporter of Democratic presidential candidate Grover Cleveland.

He won election as a judge on Cook County's Superior Court in 1886. And somewhere in there he became rich. He was a real estate speculator and a builder: his biggest holding was the tallest building in Chicago in 1891, the sixteen-story Unity Building, at 127 N. Dearborn Street.

An immigrant in a city of immigrants, he was also a Progressive. As governor, Altgeld supported and persuaded the legislature to enact what became the most stringent child labor and workplace safety laws in the nation up to that point, increased state funding for education, and appointed women to senior state government positions. And he pardoned anarchists.

The largely Republican and Republican-funded press condemned Governor Altgeld for his Haymarket pardons. For the rest of his life, to middle-class newspaper readers nationwide, especially on the East Coast, who were the middle tranche of those who managed to vote, Altgeld was the foreign-born alien anarchist, socialist, murderous governor of Illinois. Even when they brought themselves to consider reforms, they looked to the likes of President Cleveland to deliver them. To see the consequences, consider the Pullman Strike.

On May 11, 1894, workers of the Pullman Company, manufacturer of sleeping railcars and equipment, went on strike rather than accept wage cuts. Altgeld's friend and fellow attorney Clarence Darrow explained in his autobiography how he wound up as the lawyer of the strikers, the American Railway Union, and their leader Eugene V. Debs. Darrow had been a railroad lawyer for the Chicago and North Western, with a wife and a ten-year-old. He quit his job to defend strike leader Debs.

About the nature of the contest he had no doubts:

> Industrial contests take on the attitudes and psychology of war, and both parties do many things that they should never dream of doing in times of peace. . . . As I stood on the prairie watching the burning [railroad] cars I had no feeling of enmity toward either side, I was only sad to realize how little pressure man could stand before he reverted to the primitive. This I have thought many times since that eventful night.[18]

Yet with no feelings of enmity, and even after watching striker violence and arson, Darrow sided with the strikers. What won Darrow over to their cause was watching the railroads' blatant efforts to bring the force of the government in on their side. "I did not regard this as fair," Darrow later wrote. So when Debs and others asked him to take on the case, he agreed to do so, later writing, "I saw poor men giving up their livelihood."

The railroads were successful in bringing in the government. The ever-triangulating President Cleveland—the only

Democrat elected president between James Buchanan and Woodrow Wilson—decided to grant their request. He attached a mail car to every train, making blocking any train an interference with the US mail, and thus a federal crime. The US attorney general, Richard Olney, got the courts to enjoin the strikers, forbidding the obstruction of trains. Cleveland then ordered the US Army to deploy in Chicago.

Governor Altgeld protested. In two telegraphs to the president, he pointed out that the Constitution gave the president power to use troops against domestic violence *only* "on application of the [state] legislature, or the executive (when the legislature cannot be convened)."[19] Altgeld protested that neither he nor the Illinois legislature had applied. Cleveland's response was dismissive. It was more important to protect property against rioters, anarchists, and socialists, he declared: "If it takes the entire army and navy of the United States to deliver a postcard in Chicago, that card will be delivered!"[20]

On July 7, Debs and the other union leaders were arrested for violating the terms of the injunction, and the strike collapsed.

This was a breaking point for Altgeld and for many others, who subsequently decided that it was time for the Democratic Party's presidential nominee to be a truly Democratic candidate, not a centrist like Cleveland. Altgeld and his supporters wanted their rights as Polanyi would later express them: they wanted the fairness and justice that Hayek would decry. They also wanted the United States to abandon the gold standard and permit the free coinage of silver, at a ratio of sixteen ounces of silver to one ounce of gold.

Cleveland and his supporters, many of them businessmen and bankers, favored adherence to a strict gold standard in order to maintain the value of the dollar. Altgeld and his supporters, many of them laborers or farmers, wanted an expansionary money policy—unlimited coinage of silver—because they felt it would ease their credit burdens and raise prices for their crops.

What the "Free Silver" proponents wanted was, in short, the opposite of what Cleveland and his supporters wanted. Both views were reactions in part to the Panic of 1893.

At the 1896 Democratic National Convention, Altgeld seized control of the platform and changed it to condemn the gold standard, denounce the government's interventions against labor unions, support federalism, and call for an income tax amendment or a Supreme Court that would declare an income tax constitutional to allow the government to gradually redistribute wealth and to raise the resources to carry out the Progressive platform. The platform also supported the right to unionize and called for expanded personal and civil liberties.

To advance the cause, Altgeld sought to get the Democratic Party to nominate former US senator Richard P. Bland. The young William Jennings Bryan, politician from Nebraska, however, had other ideas. In a speech that damned the gold standard and a parade of moneyed interests, Bryan wowed the convention. He headed a presidential ticket, with the unprepossessing Arthur Sewall as his running mate.

In response, President Cleveland and his supporters abandoned the Democratic Party and formed the National Democratic Party, which ran the ex–Republican Illinois governor and ex–Union general John M. Palmer alongside ex–Kentucky governor and ex–Confederate general Simon Bolivar Buckner, in hopes of syphoning votes from Bryan and Sewall.

The Republican ticket of William McKinley and Garret Hobart won.

Popular vote totals in presidential elections in the decades before 1896 had been narrow. The political mythology might have led people to think that, by nominating a populist like Bryan, the Democrats could enjoy an overwhelming victory in 1896. But it was not to be so. Bryan lost, and lost by much more than Democrats had lost in the presidential elections of recent previous decades. William McKinley won in an electoral landslide, with a final electoral count of 271–176, and a popular-vote semilandslide. It was not so much that crucial swing voters in the US electorate swung to the Republican side. It was, rather, a huge countermobilization against William Jennings Bryan and a turnout increase that determined the outcome of the election. There were many voters, it turned out, who were formerly on the fence and insufficiently interested to take the trouble to show up at the polls who did show up in 1896, and they definitely did not want the sort of Democratic candidate that Altgeld and his allies favored. (Not, mind you, that the Democratic Party in 1896 could be properly characterized as *egalitarian*: of Bryan's 176 electoral votes, 129 came from states that, had Blacks been allowed to vote, would have swung to the Republican side because Lincoln had freed the slaves.)

When the crucial center of the white males who had the vote and exercised it was asked to choose between protecting property, on the one hand, and promoting opportunity through means convincingly portrayed as threatening property and order, on the other, they chose property—because they had it, or thought they would have it—and because they feared that too many of those who would benefit from redistribution were in some sense unworthy of it. Even the very weak-tea leveling associated with pardoning those railroaded after Haymarket and supporting the Pullman strikers was too much for start-of-twentieth-century America to bear.

Altgeld lost his governorship, lost a bid to be mayor of Chicago in 1899, and died, at the age of fifty-four, in 1902. Clarence Darrow lived longer and more successfully, in part because he was willing to defend large corporations, among other groups and ideas, in the remainder of his legal career—including evolution and high school teachers, murderers, and trade union officials. Whatever affinities he had for the notions of Polanyi, he was mindful of the influence of Hayek's ideas on the society in which he lived. "Conflicted" is the word, as he noted in a letter to his friend Jane Addams in the mid-1890s: "I came [to Chicago] without friends or money. Society provides no fund out of which such people can live while preaching heresy. It compels us to get our living out of society as it is or die. I do not choose yet to die, although perhaps it would be the best."[21] Among those idealistic workers who passed through Jane Addams's private social-welfare agency, Hull-House, was the young Frances Perkins, who was to become President Franklin Delano Roosevelt's secretary of labor and the principal author of America's social security system.

For all of his personal concessions, Darrow shared Altgeld's opinion of the Democratic politicians. They were not proper standard-bearers for the causes that he thought would bring the United States closer to utopia, as his 1932 memoirs explained: "I had always admired Woodrow Wilson and distrusted [his successor] Republican President [Warren] Harding. Doubtless my opinions about both in relation to affairs of government were measurably correct; still, Mr. Wilson, a scholar and an idealist, and Mr. Palmer, a Quaker, kept [Eugene V.] Debs in prison; and Mr. Harding and Mr. Dougherty unlocked the door."[22]

Darrow spent the 1920s defending the teaching of evolution (in the Scopes Monkey Trial) and attacking social Darwinist eugenicists. (Of one such, he said, "By what psychological hocus-pocus he reaches the conclusion that the ability to read intelligently denotes a good germ-plasm and [produces] desirable citizens I cannot say."[23]) Darrow died in 1938 at the age of eighty-one. In the mid-1920s Scopes Trial, he had faced off against his old political ally, William Jennings Bryan. Bryan had added anti-evolutionism and tolerance of the Ku Klux Klan to his 1920s causes of an equal rights amendment for women, agricultural subsidies, a federal minimum wage, public financing of political campaigns, and Florida real estate.

The Democratic Party of 1900 or so was against plutocrats, bankers, and monopolists. It was for a rough equality. But it was a strange kind of rough equality among the right sort of people. Socialist-pacifists—such as Eugene V. Debs, who besides being involved with the Pullman strikers opposed US entry into World War I—did not belong. And neither did Blacks. Woodrow Wilson was a Progressive, and well respected on the left. He also segregated the US federal government's civil service.

W. E. B. Du Bois was born in 1868 in Great Barrington, Massachusetts. He was raised by his mother, Mary, and her parents, Othello and Sarah Lampman Burghardt. Othello's grandfather, Tom, had been the first Black person to move to Great Barrington, where he died in around 1787 at the age of fifty. W. E. B. Du Bois's white neighbors took up a collection to pay for him to go to Fisk University, a historically Black university in Nashville. He then went from Fisk to Harvard (earning a bachelor's degree in history and graduating *cum laude* in 1890). He went from Harvard to the University of Berlin, where, as he later said, his peers did not see him "as a curiosity, or something sub-human," but as "a man of the somewhat privileged student rank, with whom they were glad to meet and talk over the world; particularly, the part of the world whence I came." He found himself "on the outside of the American world, looking in." He then returned to Harvard, where he earned a PhD—the first Black man to do so—in 1895 at the age of twenty-seven.[24]

In 1895 there was a Cotton States and International Exposition held in Atlanta, Georgia, to show the world that the ex-Confederate states of the US South were back—with technology, with agriculture, ready to produce and trade with the world. But at the same time, there were all the lynchings of Blacks—at least 113 of them in 1895. President Ulysses S. Grant had attempted to make it the US Army's mission to protect Black people from the white supremacists' guerrilla-terror campaign, and at his urging, Congress had passed bills attempting to stop the violence. These attempts, however, ended when Grant left the White House. His successor, Rutherford B. Hayes, traded that cause away—along with the power of one million Black men in the South to vote—in return for electoral votes.

At the exposition, the Black leader Booker T. Washington gave a speech proposing what became known as his "Atlanta compromise": Blacks, he said, should not seek the vote—or integration, or, indeed, equal treatment; instead, they, and white northerners seeking their uplift, should focus their attention on education and employment. "The opportunity to earn a dollar in a factory just now is worth infinitely more than the opportunity to spend a dollar in an opera house," he said. Blacks should get a "basic" education. In return for this submission, they should receive the protection of the rule of law and the guerrilla-terror campaign should end. "Cast down your bucket where you are," was Washington's watchword. That was the best he thought Blacks could do at the time. They should concentrate on education—seeking an overwhelmingly vocational education—and then work, save, and let the wheel of history turn.[25]

Du Bois disagreed with Booker T. Washington and took the leadership of those arguing and agitating for full equality—social, political, economic—now. Yes, there had been progress since the days of slavery.[26] No, the progress was not sufficient. Meanwhile, he noted, the white supremacist campaign of terror was not ending.

Four years after Washington's speech, in the same city, a Black man, Sam Hose, was accused of killing his white employer, Alfred Cranford, a farmer, who had gotten out his gun and threatened to shoot Hose when Hose had asked for time off to visit his mother. White supremacist agitators, lying, claimed that Hose had also tried to rape Alfred's wife, Mattie Cranford. A mob of at least five hundred took Hose away from the sheriff; cut off his testicles, penis, fingers, and ears; chained him to a pine tree; and then lit the pine tree on fire. The members of the mob did not wear masks or refuse to give their names. It took Hose more than thirty minutes to die. Members of the mob then cut off more of his body parts, including bones, and sold them as souvenirs.

Du Bois later said that when he saw Hose's burned knuckles in a storefront display, he knew he had to break with Booker T. Washington. Blacks needed to make demands for equal rights, equal treatment, integration, and parity.

Du Bois believed in the promise of education to solve the problem, but not just technical and trade education, like Washington. For Du Bois, the answer lay in a full liberal arts college education for the potential meritocratic elite he called the "Talented Tenth": "Education must not simply teach work—it must teach Life. The Talented Tenth of the Negro race must be made leaders of thought and missionaries of culture among their people. No others can do this and Negro colleges must train men for it."[27]

The community needed to support the Talented Tenth, who would show the world what educated and entrepreneurial Blacks could and would do, and the Talented Tenth needed to repay the community by going into politics. Otherwise, white supremacy would grind Black people down and then justify itself by pointing to the small numbers of accomplished Blacks: "For three long centuries this people lynched Negroes who dared to be brave, raped black women who dared to be virtuous, crushed dark-hued youth who dared to be ambitious, and encouraged and made to flourish servility and lewdness and apathy," he wrote. And yet "a saving remnant continually survives and persists," demonstrating "the capability of Negro blood, the promise of black men."

But Du Bois and company were rowing against a very strong current. From 1875 to 1925 or so, rising segregation and discrimination continued to stomp down the Talented Tenth wherever they appeared. Politicians and interest groups, fearing white populism, sensed the possibility of anger directed at rich urban eastern plutocrats and worked hard to redirect it into anger at lazy Negroes. Those who stuck to the goal of a relatively egalitarian income distribution in the face of social Darwinism redefined the "fitness" that was to survive and flourish as an ethnoracial attribute. Thus Woodrow Wilson sought to raise up the white middle class and degrade the Black population, and Wilson's Progressive coalition did not say "boo."

WHATEVER ELSE CONSTITUTED AMERICAN exceptionalism, marked caution toward "utopian" overhauls of social relations and social hierarchies—whether race or class based—was very high on that list. And the United States was not alone. Once European society was no longer a contest of a closed aristocracy of wealth, honor, and blood against everybody else, once upward mobility was possible, anything that was or could be misrepresented as full-fledged leveling socialism proved broadly unattractive.

We can see this at work well before our starting date of 1870. Consider France in June 1848. That year a wave of political discontent washed across Europe, encouraging many to embrace liberal reforms. But those who thought a truly just, equitable utopia beckoned were to be disappointed. What Alexis de Tocqueville discovered, along with all of Europe, was that the overwhelming majority of Frenchmen did not want to be taxed to provide full employment for urban craftsmen. It turned out they valued their property more than they valued opportunity for the unemployed.

In 1848 the farmers of Tocqueville's France sided against the socialists when, as Tocqueville put it, the socialists—that is, the workers—rose in "a blind and rude, but powerful, effort . . . to escape from the necessities of their condition, which had been depicted to them as one of unlawful oppression."[28] He was referring to the June Days uprising, a reaction against the government's decision to close the Second Republic's National Workshops, which had provided work for the unemployed. The workshops had been funded by taxing farmers, who did not want to pay for a burgeoning program for urban workers. In the heated conflict, an estimated 4,500 died, and thousands more were injured.

The politicians of the French Second Republic were terrified and abandoned the worker movement. The lesson of French politics since 1789 had been that, unless there was a Napoleon (or someone similar) on hand to send in a disciplined military—with orders to shoot down the mob and blow up the barricades—mobs in Paris unmade governments. But the Paris June Days were different. Tocqueville, who opposed the worker movement, later wrote that he saw "thousands . . . hastening to our aid from every part of France." He noted that peasants, shopkeepers, landlords, and nobles "rushed into Paris with unequalled ardour," partly via rail travel, making for a "strange and unprecedented" spectacle: "The insurgents received no reinforcements, whereas we had all France for reserves."

The same principle was at work in the United States in 1896 as in France in 1848.

Yet back in the days of the French Revolution of 1789, order had much less appeal to those not at the top of the social pyramid: "Let's strangle the last king with the guts of the last priest!" said philosopher and critic Denis Diderot.[29] Diderot died before the revolution—which might well have been a blessing for Diderot: the revolutionaries came within a hair of executing American democracy activist Thomas Paine, who had traveled to France to help them, just because. Yes, the French did manage to murder King Louis XVI. Yes, they did wind up with an egalitarian distribution of land parceled out to families of small farmers. But they did not wind up with a stable political democracy.

In succession after 1791, France experienced the terrorist dictatorship of the Jacobins; the corrupt and gerrymandered five-man Directory; a dictatorship under Napoleon Bonaparte as "first consul"; a monarchy until 1848; a First Republic; a Second

Republic; a shadow of an empire under Napoleon Bonaparte's nephew Louis Napoleon; a socialist commune (in Paris at least); a Third Republic, which suppressed the commune and elevated a royalist to president; and, peaking in 1889, the efforts of an aspirant dictator and ex-minister of war, Georges Ernest Jean-Marie Boulanger, with his promise of *Revanche, Révision, Restauration* (revenge on Germany, revision of the constitution, and restoration of the monarchy).[30]

And yet land reform stuck. Dreams of past and hopes of future military glory stuck. And for those on the left of politics, the dream of a transformational, piratical political revolution—the urban people marching in arms (or not in arms) to overthrow corruption and establish justice, liberty, and utopia—stuck as well. Regime stability did not, and "normal politics" between 1870 and 1914 always proceeded under revolutionary threat, or were colored by revolutionary dreams.

This was true elsewhere in Europe as well. The continent's nationalities grew to want unity, independence, autonomy, and safety—which first and foremost, especially in the case of the German states, meant safety from invasion by France. Achieving any portion of these outcomes generally entailed, rather than wholesale redistribution, a curbing of privileges, and then an attempt to grab onto and ride the waves of globalization and technological advance. Those waves, however, wrenched society out of its established orders. As class and ethnic cleavages reinforced themselves, the avoidance of civil war and ethnic cleansing became more difficult, especially when your aristocrats spoke a foreign language and your rabble-rousers declared that they were the ones who could satisfy peasant and worker demands for "peace, land, and bread." Increasingly, in those parts of the world without colonial masters, politics became a game without rules—except those the players made up on whim and opportunity. Nearly everywhere and at nearly any moment, the structure of a regime, and the modes of political action, might suddenly shift, perhaps in a very bad way. Representative institutions were shaky, and partial. Promises by rulers of new constitutions that would resolve legitimate grievances were usually empty promises.

In the end, the regimes held until World War I. The games went on. Outside the Balkans, the only regime change in Europe between 1871 and 1913 was the low-casualty proclamation of the Portuguese Republic in November 1910.

The expectation and fear that revolutions were on the agenda proved to be wrong. One reason was that always, in the moment, left-wing—even socialist—parties in pre–World War I Europe wanted parliamentary representation, but once they had that, they pressed immediately for only relatively weak tea. Consider the Socialist Party of Germany, which sought to rally the radical edge of the nation's voters with the following:

 universal male and female suffrage
 the secret ballot, proportional representation, and an end
  to gerrymandering
 holidays for elections
 two-year legislative terms
 the right to propose and vote on referendums
 elected local administrators and judges
 a referendum requirement for declarations of war
 international courts to settle international disputes
 equal rights for women
 freedom of speech, association, and religion
 a prohibition against spending public funds for religious
  purposes
 free public schools and colleges
 free legal assistance
 abolition of the death penalty
 free medical care, including midwifery

progressive income and property taxes

a progressive inheritance tax

an end to regressive indirect taxes

an eight-hour working day

child labor laws

a national takeover of unemployment and disability
   insurance "with decisive participation by the workers"[31]

Rather white bread, no?

But they also sought in the long run not incremental advance but the complete reordering of society and economy into a real utopia. The Socialist Party of Germany's platforms also called for:

> By every lawful means to bring about a free state and a social-istic society, to effect the destruction of the iron law of wages by doing away with the system of wage labor . . .
>
> The transformation of the capitalist private ownership of the means of production—land and soil, pits and mines, raw materials, tools, machines, means of transportation—into social property and the transformation of the production of goods into socialist production carried on by and for society . . .
>
> Emancipation . . . of the entire human race. . . . But it can only be the work of the working class, because all other classes . . . have as their common goal the preservation of the foundations of contemporary society.

The demands seem contradictory. Were the German social-ists revolutionary overthrowers of a rotten system or improvers of a going concern? They could not decide, and so found themselves falling between the two stools.

We now come to one of the inflection points in this long century's history. The tensions were already there between two camps, broadly speaking: those who fell under the banner of Hayek's "blessed be the name of the market" and those who fell under the banner of Polanyi's "the market is made for man." Broadly. Things get messy. What was held in common by all was a faith, of varying sorts, in the market. And some of these faiths were more utopian than others.

Karl Marx, Friedrich Engels, and those who drew inspiration from them had no illusions about what the market taketh, but they had a grand illusion as to what the market would eventually giveth, or transcend itself to become—the revolution of the proletariat. Earl Grey, Benjamin Disraeli, and other right-wingers understood that the market is made for some men, but not all—and, likewise, that some men, but not all, would benefit. Finally, centrists attempted to hold the tensions at bay with many reforms and a few bayonets. It mostly worked—until 1914.

While the center was holding, and the left was falling between two stools, the right was thinking up new justifications for its basic principle: "What I have, I hold!" English naturalist Charles Darwin's *On the Origin of Species* had set intellectual waves in motion: ideas that turned into *social Darwinism*. The social Darwinists justified economic inequality not by looking to the past, to the descent of the rich from the henchmen of William the Conqueror, but by looking to the present and the future, by claiming that inherent racial traits both accounted for their economic success and justified existing economic inequalities. One step further, and they were proposing that the superior races should be encouraged to breed, and others should not. As John Maynard Keynes was to remark a generation later, in the eyes of the social Darwinists, "socialist interferences became . . . impious, as calculated to retard the onward movement of the mighty process by which we ourselves had risen like Aphrodite out of the primeval slime of ocean."[32]

Ideologies are not like streetcars, in that you can pull the cord and get off at the next stop whenever you wish. But they are like streetcars in a different respect: they have tracks that they must follow. Social Darwinists justified economic inequality within societies as part of a progressive struggle for existence that, via evolution, improved the gene pool.[33] Why not, then, take the next step and see relationships between nations as a similar struggle for existence that, again via evolution, improved the gene pool? "I am better than you" became, all too easily, "We are better than they." And "we" had to have the weapons to prove it, should it come to a fight.

Jennie Jerome's son, Winston S. Churchill, was in the cabinet of the British Liberal government in the 1900s. Alarm at the growing size of the German battle fleet was mounting, and Britain needed control of the seas to tie its empire together. Moreover, Britain imported half its food. A German battle fleet that controlled the seas around Britain could starve half of Britain to death. As Churchill told the story, the Liberal Party government, to appease the navy and the press, offered to fund four new dreadnought-class battleships a year to defend against the growing German fleet. The navy demanded six. And, Churchill said, "We compromised at eight."[34]

Sir Arthur Conan Doyle had his detective character Sherlock Holmes comment on rising international tensions as World War I approached: "There's an east wind coming all the same," Holmes says. "It will be cold and bitter, Watson, and a good many of us may wither before its blast. But . . . a cleaner, better, stronger land will lie in the sunshine when the storm has cleared."[35]

Doyle wrote those words in 1917, when World War I was more than half done. But he placed them in the mouth of a pre-1914 Holmes. He had Holmes prophesy that, in spite of all the blood, global war should not be avoided, for it would, in the end, turn out to have been worthwhile. The political, social, cultural, and economic barometer was dropping. The warning signs were abundant: a right-wing upper class had, by and large, lost its social role; politicians were increasingly anxious to paper over class divisions with appeals to national unity; a social Darwinist ideological current advocating struggle—even or especially military struggle by peoples-in-arms—over not what language a province would be administered in but whose grandchildren would live there, was growing. These issues were storing up trouble as 1914 approached. The unleashing of unprecedented economic growth had shaken the world and transformed politics. And at the end of that transformation was a pronounced imperial and militaristic turn.

In 1919, John Maynard Keynes would write, bitterly, that he, his peers, and his elders among the well-thinking, self-confident establishment had all shrugged off the warning signs and passively sat by. They had regarded "the projects and politics of militarism and imperialism, of racial and cultural rivalries, of monopolies, restrictions, and exclusion, which were to play the serpent to this [pre-1914 economic growth] paradise . . . [as] little more than the amusements of [the] daily newspaper." To him and his ilk, Keynes would say, looking back through the rearview mirror, the idea that the progressive system of increasing prosperity might break down was "aberrant [and] scandalous"—and easily avoidable.[36]

As 1914 approached, there was no intellectual or organizational antimilitarist countermobilization to speak of to try to head off catastrophe.

4

Global Empires

I n 1870, at the start of the long twentieth century, one of the greatest empires the world has ever seen—the British Empire, the only potential peer of which was the Mongol Empire—was approaching its zenith. Part of what made it the greatest is that this empire had both formal and informal manifestations—it came in the form of standing armies, colonial offices staffed by bureaucrats, and jails to enforce deference, but exercised its will in all sorts of other, less tangible ways as well. Because we all know how this particular story ends, I feel no guilt in flashing forward. The year 1945 saw the completion of the supersession of Britain by the United States as the world's leading industrial, commercial, and imperial power. What's interesting is that once the United States established itself as the world's preeminent power, it set about building an American empire that was, unlike its predecessor's, almost entirely informal.

Right here I have a narrative problem. The big-picture story of the "global north," or the North Atlantic region, from 1870 to 1914 can be pounded (with some violence) into the framework of one narrative thread. What would become known as the "global south"—that is, countries generally south of, but more importantly, on the economic periphery of, the global north—cannot. And my space and your attention are limited. What is more, a century most defined by its economic history is a century centered on the global north. This, of course, says nothing about cultures or civilizations, or even the relative merits of global north or south in general, or nations in particular. It is merely to assert that the economic activity and advances of the one region of the world causally led the economic activity and advances of the other.

Given this background, what I offer you here are four important vignettes: India, Egypt, China, and Japan. To situate ourselves in these national histories, understand that while 1870 is the watershed year of the global north's economic growth spurt, it is (not coincidentally) the middle of the story of imperialism for the global south. Perhaps not the exact middle, for the imperialism project starts in 1500 and, as a project, ends in the later 1900s. As I said, the interpretive ground here gets slippery. And for purchase we can recall our two-person chorus, Friedrich August von Hayek and Karl Polanyi, watching, waiting, and whispering.

Europe—or, rather, Spain and Portugal—started building empires in the 1500s. It was not that they had unique technological or organizational powers compared to the rest of the world. Rather, they had interlocking systems—religious, political, administrative, and commercial—that together reinforced the reasons to seek power in the form of imperial conquest. Empire building made political-military, ideological-religious, and economic sense. Spain's conquistadores set out to serve the king, to spread the word of God, and to get rich.[1] Other adventurers and wannabe imperialists from elsewhere on the globe did not have such a strong set of interlocking incentives and capabilities.

When the Portuguese arrived in what is now Malaysia in the 1500s, they met political-military opposition from local rulers, ideological-religious opposition from Islamic communities, and economic opposition from Chinese traders who did not want to be displaced. But Chinese merchants had no political backing from their Ming rulers. Local sultans could not summon religious-ideological energy for crusades to expel the Portuguese.

And these local Islamic communities were not profitable enough for faraway sultans and allies to generate sustained intervention. The Portuguese—and the Spanish, and later the Dutch, French, and British—had it all, gold, guns, God, and kings, working together.[2]

So the European overseas empires took root and grew in the 1500s and thereafter. The period from 1500 to 1770 was an Imperial-Commercial Age, with imperialism and globalization advancing along all their dimensions: military, political, economic, and cultural, for great good and great ill.

These early empires were, however, limited. Outside of the Americas, the sea became European, but the land did not. Sea control, however, meant a great deal. In the 1500s and 1600s, control over the high-value, low-weight luxury goods of East Asia, or over the precious metals of Latin America, made individuals' fortunes, provided healthy boosts to early modern European royal treasuries, and channeled the energies of potentially disruptive young men and enthusiastic missionaries bent on pleasing their God.

This dynamic also produced the tobacco, sugar, and slave trades, and made West Indian empires both the focus of high politics and a driver of what was then slow economic growth. The slave trade, meanwhile, devastated Africa and plausibly created the conditions that today keep it the planet's poorest continent.[3]

But by 1870 the logic of empire appeared to be ebbing. There was little in the way of luxuries that could not be made more cheaply in the industrial core. Plus, it became more expensive to conquer than to trade. But empires are not built on logic alone, and even after 1870 they continued to grow. Conquering, controlling, exploiting, and with these a general debasing, continued.

Imperialism was perhaps lamentable, but inevitable, one-half of our chorus whispers. There was so much money to be made by bringing the world into a single marketplace, and to function, marketplaces have to be governed by something. The market giveth, the market taketh away; blessed be the name of the market. It was largely intentional, and explicable, if still lamentable, the other half of our chorus whispers. The market was made for man, not man for the market.

By 1870 the difference in power between imperial metropole and subjected colony had become immense—in technological, organizational, and political terms. The improvements in transport and communications made war and conquest and occupation vastly easier. There was no part of the world in which Western Europeans could not—if they wished—impose their will by armed force at moderate cost. And proconsuls were rarely focused on just what resources would flow back to the imperial metropolis from their particular outpost of empire. After all, the outposts were populated, and often led, by disruptive young men with things to prove, or enthusiastic missionaries with souls to save. Whether it might not be cheaper in the long run to simply trade and pay for those resources was for many a tertiary concern.

These enterprising young men and zealous missionaries not only had means but also method.

Consider the 1898 Battle of Omdurman in the Sudan, during which ten thousand soldiers of the Mahdist Sudanese regime died. Only forty-eight British and Egyptian soldiers died. The difference was not entirely due to superior European military technology. The Mahdist regime had proto-machine-guns, telegraphs, and mines—all bought from European suppliers. What it did not have was the organizational capacity and discipline to make effective use of them.[4]

The consequence of a disciplined global north more organizationally capable was a globe integrated into the European-dominated world economy, much of it ruled or swayed by European proconsuls, and the spread of European languages and European preferences: European-style schools, European culture, and European methods of administration, science, and technology.

Harbors, railroads, factories, and plantations sprung up, from Bali, in what is now Indonesia, to Accra, in what is now Ghana.

And everywhere peoples were told that they were dirt under the feet of their European rulers.

Consider India. In early 1756, the newly installed Nawab of Bengal, Mirza Mohammad Siraj ud-Dowla, wished to show the British in Calcutta who was master of Bengal. He borrowed some gunners and artillery pieces from the French and attacked and captured Calcutta and its Fort William. He expected negotiations, and that the subsequent peace would produce a grateful France, much higher taxes paid to him by trading Europeans, and much less tax evasion via smuggling by the chastened British.

Big mistake.

The British sent 3,000 soldiers—800 British, 2,200 Indian—north by sea from Madras to Calcutta. Siraj ud-Dowla mobilized for the battle. British commander Robert Clive bribed the Nawab's three subordinates. And in the aftermath the British East India Company acquired the taste for conquering, ruling, and taxing India rather than merely trading with it.

By 1772 Calcutta was the capital of British India. Warren Hastings was its first governor-general. The British East India Company had entered the sweepstakes in the succession wars over the territories of the Mogul Empire. Each generation saw formerly independent principalities become subservient allies. Each generation saw former allies become puppets. And each generation saw former puppets become territories ruled by London. Nearly a century after Clive and Siraj ud-Dowla came the great Sepoy Mutiny (also known as the Indian Mutiny, the Sipahi Rebellion, or the Great Rebellion of 1857). It was defeated. And on May 1, 1876, the British government proclaimed Queen Victoria I Hanover to be *Kaiser-i-Hind*: Empress of India.[5]

Back in 1853 Karl Marx had halted work on his magnum opus to try to get enough money together to keep from having to pawn his wife's silver (again). He had written an essay titled

"The Future Results of British Rule in India" in which he prophesied that the British imperial conquest was India's greatest short-run curse and greatest long-run blessing: "England has to fulfill a double mission in India: one destructive, the other . . . laying the material foundations of Western society in Asia. . . . The political unity of India . . . imposed by the British sword, will now be strengthened and perpetuated by the electric telegraph. The native army, organized and trained by the British drill-sergeant, [will be] the sine qua non of Indian self-emancipation."[6]

If you listen carefully, you'll hear an echo of half our chorus, albeit with very different intonations. Blessed be the market. Yes, Marx would have it that the bourgeoisie effects progress by "dragging individuals and people through blood and dirt, through misery and degradation." But while it takes, on the one hand, it gives most lavishly—full emancipation, human emancipation, by setting the stage for and providing the overwhelming incentives to pull the trigger to create Full Communism—with the other.

Yet as of 1914, the great economic and social changes that Karl Marx had confidently predicted sixty years before had not advanced very far. The drawing of a net of railways over India? Check. The introduction to India of those industries necessary to support the railroads? Check. The spread of other branches of modern industry across India? Not so much. The spread of modern education across India? Not so much. Improvements in agricultural productivity, resulting from the creation of effective private property in land? Not at all. Overthrow of the caste system? Not at all. The overthrow of British colonialism, the restoration of self-government, and the creation of subcontinental political unity by virtue of a revolt by the British-trained army? They had come remarkably close in 1857, but only close.

The failure of the British Raj to transform India poses an enormous problem for all of us economists. We are all, even the Marxist economists, the intellectual children of the Adam Smith who was reported by Dugald Stewart to have said, "Little else is requisite to carry a state to the highest degree of opulence from the lowest barbarism, but peace, easy taxes, and a tolerable administration of justice: all the rest being brought about by the natural course of things."[7] Under the British Raj in the late nineteenth and early twentieth centuries India had a remarkable degree of internal and external peace, a tolerable administration of justice, and easy taxes. Yet no sign of progress "to the highest degree of opulence" had occurred.[8]

Whether deemed natural or unnatural, the course of things had yielded different results.

Egypt provides another insightful example. Muhammed Ali (1769–1849), an Albanian orphan, son of shipping merchant Ibrahim Agha and his wife, Zeynep, was bored being a tax collector in the Ottoman-ruled Greek port of Kavala. In 1801 he enlisted as a mercenary in the Ottoman army sent to reoccupy Egypt, the French expeditionary army under Napoleon having wiped out the old Mamluke regime, before itself surrendering to the British navy. By 1803 Muhammed Ali commanded a regiment of his ethnically Albanian fellow countrymen. The Ottoman governor of Egypt ran short of cash. No longer able to afford them, he dismissed his Albanian troops. They mutinied and took over the government, and a scramble ensued.

Somehow Muhammed Ali wound up on top. He retained the loyalty of his Albanians and managed to suppress both Turkish and Egyptian fighters. He then received at least the temporary blessing of the Ottoman sultan, Selim III the Reformer (who shortly thereafter was deposed, imprisoned, and murdered by his own janissary guardsmen). Muhammed Ali looked northwest at Europe and east to India. He ruled a prosperous kingdom—but he saw that Europeans might do to his or his children's kingdom what they had done to India.

So Muhammed Ali strove to make Egypt great, introducing new crops, land reform, a modern military, a focus on exporting cotton, and the construction of state-owned textile factories to jump-start Egyptian industry. He understood that unless he could keep the machines working, his great-grandchildren would become the puppets of French bankers and British proconsuls. But the machines could not be kept working. Was it because Egypt did not train enough engineers? Was it because the bosses were state employees? Was it because the policy was not pursued long enough, and when Egypt's military came under pressure it became irresistibly attractive in the short run to buy weapons, ammunition, and uniforms from abroad?[9]

Muhammed Ali died in 1849. Had his progeny shared his worries, they might have reformed sufficiently to educate Egyptians capable of fixing those machines. But in Egypt it was Muhammed Ali's personal project, not an intergenerational, nationalist one.[10]

In 1863, six years before the completion of the Suez Canal, Muhammed Ali's grandson Ismail took the throne of Egypt as khedive at the age of thirty-three. Educated in France, open to European influences, and eager to modernize his country, he was also lucky. He became ruler of Egypt in the middle of the "cotton famine" created by the American Civil War. The temporary disappearance of the American South from the world's cotton supply resulted in a cotton boom everywhere else. The working textile factories of the Industrial Revolution needed cotton, and their owners were willing to pay almost any price for it. Egypt grew cotton. And so for a few years it seemed as though Egypt's economic resources and wealth were inexhaustible.

They weren't.

The Egyptian government declared bankruptcy in 1876. The creditors of the khedive became Egypt's rulers. Ismail abdicated. Two financial controllers—one British, one French—were appointed with substantial control over taxes and expenditures. Their task was to make sure that Egypt, now governed by Ismail's son, kept up revenue and paid off its debt. The heavily taxed Egyptians wondered why they were being made to pay off debts run up by their extravagant ex-khedive. British troops restored order in 1882, and thereafter the khedive was a British puppet. On varying pretexts, British troops stayed in Egypt until 1956.

So Muhammed Ali's great-grandchildren did become puppets of French bankers and British proconsuls.[11]

China, too, offers important insight.

Poor and disorganized in 1870, imperial China was a country where the government and the economy were in crisis. Over more than two centuries of rule, the government of the ethnically Manchu Qing dynasty had trained its ethnically Han Confucian landlord-bureaucrat-scholar aristocracy to be incapable of taking effective action. After all, effective action might be directed against the Central Government Security Perimeter (which is, perhaps, how we ought to translate what was back then translated as "Forbidden City").

One such, born in 1823 to a scholar-gentry family in a village about 150 miles west of Shanghai, was Li Hongzhang. The grind of studying the Confucian-school literary classics and passing the examinations was a hard and grueling one. In 1847, after intensive study under a tutor from Hunan, Zeng Guofan, Li succeeded. Filial piety required Zeng to return to Hunan to mourn his mother in 1851, just as the Taiping Rebellion broke out. The bureaucrat-commanded army was useless, the supposedly elite Manchu "banners" of the dynasty equally so. Zeng, desperate to save the situation he found himself in the middle of, turned out to have a great talent for military organization. He recruited, trained, and commanded a volunteer army—the Xiang Army—to resist the Taiping rebels. Li Hongzhang went along and became one of the dynasty's few competent generals.

By 1864 the Taiping Rebellion was suppressed, and Li was sent on to suppress another group of rebels, the Nian. By 1870, he was a diplomat trying to calm the French after the murder in a riot of sixty Catholic priests, nuns, and congregation members, along with the French consul in Tianjin. In 1875 he led the muscle in a military semicoup upon the death of Emperor Tongzhi, to make sure that the four-year-old Guangxu, nephew of Empress Dowager Cixi, ascended the throne. Li had been trained to be a bureaucrat, applying two-thousand-year-old philosophical principles to questions of governance. But he found that the skills that mattered were (a) generalship, and (b) being able to turn away the wrath of and procure the aid of European imperial powers.

Many Western China specialists see and can almost touch an alternative history—one in which late nineteenth-century China stood up economically, politically, and organizationally. Japan, after all, won its short war against Russia in 1905, negotiated as an equal with Britain and the United States over warship construction in 1921, and was perhaps the eighth industrial power in the world by 1929.[12]

We economists are much more skeptical. We note the corrupt and incompetent bureaucracies that failed to manage the Yellow River dikes and the Grand Canal. We note that the Qing could not get their local officials to collect the salt tax. We note that when, in the mid-1880s, the Qing dynasty, having bought foreign metalworking machinery and built a navy, arsenals, and docks, thought it was strong enough to oppose the French conquest of Vietnam, its fleet was destroyed in an hour. And we note that when, in 1895, the Qing dynasty thought it was strong enough to oppose the Japanese extension of their sphere of influence to Korea, it was, again, wrong. The Treaty of Shimonoseki added Taiwan, Korea, and southern Manchuria to Japan's sphere of influence.

Furthermore, we economists note that even as late as 1929 China produced only 20,000 tons of steel, less than 2 ounces per person, and 400,000 tons of iron, or 1.6 pounds per person. Meanwhile, it mined 27 million tons of coal, or 100 pounds per person. Compare this to America's 700 pounds of steel per capita in the same year or 200 pounds in 1900, or to America's 8,000 pounds of coal per capita in 1929 or 5,000 pounds of coal per capita in 1900.

Narrow the scope to one mine, the Kaiping coal mine in northern China. There we see general, diplomat, and governor Li Hongzhang at work in the 1880s. He saw that China needed industrial muscle. And so he became the prime bureaucratic mover behind the coal mine, as well as behind a number of China's other "self-strengthening efforts," such as the 1878 cotton mills in Shanghai, the Tianjin arsenal, the telegraph between Tianjin and Peking, and more. Men who were as focused as Li was on economic development could make things happen.[13]

But they could not work through the bureaucracy and get anything done. Li had commissioned a wealthy Hong Kong merchant, Tang Tingshu, to build the Kaiping mine. What he had sought was a large, modern, industrial mine that could help modernize the nation. But they faced unusual forms of opposition. A vice president of the Board of Civil Offices, Chi Shihehang, declared that "mining methods angered the earth dragon . . . [and so] the late empress could not rest quietly in her grave." Li had to choose between abandoning his idea of building a modern coal mine—and with it the fuel to power steam engines—or accepting blame for any deaths or diseases that might strike the imperial family. Very bravely—considering the large size of the imperial family and the high death rate of the time—he chose modernity.

Production began in 1881. By 1889, three thousand workers in three shifts were producing seven hundred tons of coal a day. By 1900, nine thousand workers were producing, but only a quarter of what was expected of miners in the United States or Australia. The mine was both a public governmental project and a private capitalist enterprise. The mine director was both an employee of the company's Hong Kong shareholders and an official of the Qing administrative bureaucracy.

The mine's director-general, Tang Tingshu, died in 1892. His replacement, Chang Li—called "Yenmao" in virtually all

English-language sources—was neither a merchant, nor an industrialist, nor an engineer, nor a manager. Chang was a political fixer—another key mover in the semicoup of 1875—for the Empress Cixi. But Chang was arguably the wealthiest man in Tianjin by 1900. Maintaining the favor and patronage network that supported the Qing court was a higher priority than effective management. The mine had become a source of income for the well connected, rather than an important piece of an industrialization program. Li Hongzhang died in 1901, after one last round of diplomatic fencing with the European imperial powers, who wanted to be paid handsomely for suppressing the "Boxer"—"Fighters United for Justice" would be a better translation—Rebellion.

In 1901, twenty-six-year-old expatriate mining engineer and future US president Herbert Hoover took over the mine. Hoover claimed that the nine thousand-worker payroll had been padded by six thousand names, and that the director of personnel doing the padding (and collecting the wages) had bribed Chang Li handsomely for the post.

"Wait," you say. "Herbert Hoover took over?"

Yes. Hoover arrived in Tientsin in 1900 just in time to be besieged in the city by the Boxer Rebellion. There Chang Li had fled, rightly fearing that the Boxers would execute him as a corrupt puppet of the Europeans, and that the besieged Europeans wanted to imprison him for passing intelligence to the Boxers.

From this point forward things become cloudy, as nearly all narrators become unreliable, desperate in various ways to appear in a good light. Somehow Hoover got Chang released from prison. Somehow Chang gave Hoover a power of attorney to reincorporate the Kaiping mine as a British-flag enterprise controlled completely by Herbert Hoover. The historian Ellsworth Carlson reported that the local British chargé d'affaires was disgusted. Hoover and company had "made a pretty pile at the expense of the Chinese," he said, and while "legally the Board of Directors were unassailable . . . morally they were in the wrong."

Britain shouldn't countenance "a financial transaction which had fleeced Chinese shareholders," the chargé d'affaires continued, and "lined the pockets of an Anglo-Belgian gang," all under the orchestration of "a Yankee man of straw."

None of which Herbert Hoover would have agreed with. More than a century later we can try to read Hoover's mind. Perhaps he thought the old shareholders should be grateful that he and his partners had only charged them 62.5 percent of the company; after all, the alternative was for the Russians to have confiscated the entire mine as war reparations, leaving the old shareholders with zero. Perhaps he thought that Chang Li was a corrupt thief, while Hoover would make the mine run productively and profitably. Indeed, Hoover managed to nearly triple the value of the old stockholders' shares: the 37.5 percent he left them was worth more than the 100 percent the old stockholders had owned before.

We again hear echoes of our whispering chorus. The impersonal market had taken from some, given to others, and greatly increased the total; blessed be the market. But the local chargé d'affaires heard something else: Man—in this case one Herbert Hoover—took and gave, not the market. Some—especially the new European stockholders who now owned the majority of the mine, and who now received the profits that Li Hongzhang had intended as part of the basis for a great economic leap forward for China and all its people—might bless the man; but others—say, the Boxers who had rebelled, and the Qing dynasty officials who found their room to maneuver against imperialist would-be conquerors diminished—would curse him.

And, by extension, the unhappy and rebellious would also curse a social-economic structure that could not find and promote competent executives but instead advanced corrupt political fixers; a political-ritual culture that required one of the few modernizing regional governors to focus his attention constantly on the enterprise to keep it on track, and to run interference in order to protect it from reactionaries; and an educational system that churned out literati instead of engineers, and that meant the country required foreign technical personnel for everything. But their curses changed little in the world around them. Outside of the charmed circles near ports created by the extraterritorial foreign concessions, and to a slight degree in regions within the control of the few modernizing governors, modern industries simply did not develop and modern technologies simply were not applied in late imperial China.

Visionary reforming politician Sun Yat-sen, who had offered his services to Li Hongzhang in 1894 only to be rebuffed, built up a financial and propaganda network among Chinese emigrants beyond the reach of the government. Military politicians, such as Yuan Shikai, concluded that working with the Manchu court was useless. In 1912, Sun Yat-sen launched a rebellion, which Yuan Shikai and his peers refused to suppress, and the Qing dynasty fell.

The six-year-old emperor abdicated. Yuan Shikai declared himself president of the subsequent republic and tried to seize control of the country. China descended into near anarchy.

There are many, many more stories I could tell of Europe's empires in the late 1800s and of how the colonized and the nearly colonized tried to respond. But India, Egypt, and China convey much of the picture. The power, real and threatened, of the formal empires of the North Atlantic, with all their wealth and influence, meant that at the start of the long twentieth century, even those who were not formally colonized were nevertheless dominated by informal empire—overwhelmingly by the British. It was a world in which offers were made that could not, realistically or prudently, be refused.

Perhaps the offers could not be refused because the consequences of accepting them were so good. Perhaps they could not be refused because the consequences of not accepting them were so bad. As the twentieth-century socialist economist Joan Robinson liked to say, the only thing worse than being exploited by the capitalists was not being exploited by the capitalists— being ignored by them, and placed outside the circuits of production and exchange.

There was also, of course, the question of who exactly bore the consequences of refusing a particular offer. Would it be the country's ruling elite, its current citizens, or their descendants? Generally, attitudes split along Hayekian and Polanyian lines: those who found that the market gaveth, blessed be the market (and some percent of imperialism); and those who found that the market tooketh, cursed be the men who deprived the people of bread, shelter, or dignity.

It was easier to decide who to bless and who to curse when it came to the formal mode of empire. In the first decades of the long twentieth century, however, making such distinctions became increasingly difficult as the informal mode of the British Empire—and to a lesser extent of other European empires— gained power. Such are the benefits of hegemony, which had four important aspects: free trade, concentrated industry, free migration, and freedom of investment.

It was technically possible, of course, to resist the advances of informal empire. But to refuse an offer often meant calling down upon yourself your own people's retribution. Afghanistan may indeed be where empires go to die, but it has also proved a grave for social progress, technological advancements, and longevity. Most of the nation-states that were extended offers they couldn't refuse ultimately agreed to play by Britain's rules—broadly, for three reasons.

First, playing by those rules was what Britain was doing, and Britain was clearly worth emulating. The hope was that by adopting the policies of an obviously successful economy, you— that is, the government—could make your economy successful, too. Second, trying to play by other rules—say, protecting your handmade textile sector—was very expensive. Britain and company could supply commodities and industrial goods cheaply as well as luxuries that were unattainable elsewhere. And Britain and company would pay handsomely for primary product exports. Finally, even if you sought to play by other rules, your control over what was going on in your country was limited. And there was a great deal of money to be made.

Playing by the rules of the international economic game had consequences.

The first, an aspect of globalization and free trade, was that steam-driven machinery provided a competitive advantage that handicrafts could not match, no matter how low workers' wages. And with very few exceptions, steam-driven machinery worked reliably only in the global north. Manufacturing declined outside the industrial core, and peripheral labor was shifted into agriculture and other primary products. And as a consequence, the global periphery was "underdeveloped." Gaining in the short run from advantageous terms of trade, the peripheral states were unable to build communities of engineering practice that might provide a path to greater, industrial riches.

An essential secondary consequence was that steam-driven machinery worked reliably and steadily enough to be *profitable* only in the global north. The "reliably" and the "profitable" parts required three things: a community of engineering practice, a literate labor force that could be trained to use industrial technology, and sufficient finances to provide the necessary maintenance, repair, and support services.[14]

Another consequence was the mostly free system of migration in the early years of the long twentieth century (save for Asians seeking to migrate to temperate-zone economies). Finally, free trade and free migration made possible by Europe's informal imperial domination helped to enrich the world greatly in the generations before World War I. Free capital flows, through the freedom of investment, greased the wheels.

You could lend to whomever you wished. You could borrow from whomever you wished. But, before World War I, it was understood that you would at least try to pay it back. Certainly those economies that received inflows of capital before World War I benefited enormously *if they had the labor, the skill, and the organizational resources to take advantage of them.* For the United States, Canada, Australia, Argentina, and perhaps others, such as India, the availability of large amounts of capital—largely British-financed capital—to speed development of industry and infrastructure was a godsend.

It is not clear that the free flow of capital benefited those exporting it. France subsidized the pre–World War I industrialization of czarist Russia in the belief that someday it would fight another war with Germany (correct) and that victory depended on a large, active, allied Russian army forcing Germany to fight a two-front war (not so correct). Before World War I, buying Russian bonds became a test of French patriotism. But after the war, there was no czar ruling from Moscow—there was only Vladimir Ilyich Lenin, who had no interest in repaying the czar's creditors.

One other way that informal empire exercised its influence was by providing the rest of the world with an example to emulate. This was most notably the case with the British Empire. British institutions and practices appeared to be—had in fact been—stunningly successful. Emulating them, at least on a trial basis, made compelling sense, whether that meant wearing business suits, translating Latin verse in school, establishing strong property rights, or investing in railroads and ports. Most of this was of substantial use elsewhere in the world. Some of it was not. And it would turn out that what had fit British circumstances in the mid-1800s fit the governments and economies of the periphery less and less successfully as the long century unfolded.

So stood most of the periphery to the North Atlantic economic core during the years of formal and informal empire. The pattern, which played out in India, Egypt, China, and elsewhere, seemed so common as to be declared the stuff of providence and nature. But there was one exception.

Alone among the non-European world before 1913, Japan managed to deal with the imperialists, prosper, industrialize, and join them.

To understand exactly what happened in Japan, we must look at least as far back as an early seventeenth-century daimyo warrior prince, Tokugawa Ieyasu, who was granted the title of shogun, that is, viceroy for the priest-emperor in all civil and military matters, in 1603. His son Hidetaka and grandson Iemitsu consolidated the new regime. From its capital, Edo—later Tokyo—the Tokugawa Shogunate ruled Japan for two and a half centuries.[15]

From the start, the shogunate looked with caution south to the Philippines. Only a century before, the Philippines had been made up of independent kingdoms. Then the Europeans landed. Merchants had been followed by missionaries. Converts had proved an effective base of popular support for European influence. Missionaries had been followed by soldiers. And by 1600, Spain ruled the Philippines.

The Tokugawa Shogunate was confident that it could control its potential rivals and subjects in Japan. It was not confident that it could resist the technology, military, and religious power of the Europeans. And so the country was closed: trade was restricted to a very small number of ships, and these were allowed access to the Port of Nagasaki only. Japanese subjects returning from abroad were executed; foreigners discovered outside of the restricted zone were executed; and Christianity was violently suppressed. For centuries formal empire struggled, and failed, to gain a foothold.

Another factor differentiating Japan was that one in six Japanese were urban. As of 1868, Kyoto, Osaka, and Tokyo together had two million people. Half of adult men were literate: in 1868, there were more than six hundred bookshops in Tokyo. And literacy and urbanization laid the groundwork for technological competence.

The historian Robert Allen tells the story of the Lord of Nagasaki, Nabeshima Naomasa, and his cannon foundry. His workers acquired and then translated a Dutch description of a foundry. They then set out to copy it: "In 1850, they succeeded in building a reverberatory furnace, and three years later were casting cannon. In 1854, the Nagasaki group imported state-of-the-art, breech-loading Armstrong guns from Britain and manufactured copies. By 1868, Japan had eleven furnaces casting iron."[16]

But the Tokugawa era came to an end in 1868 with the Meiji Restoration. Rule was grasped by a shifting coalition of notables—most prominently, at first, the "Meiji Six"—Mori Arinori, Ōkubo Toshimichi, Saigō Takamori, Itō Hirobumi, Yamagata Aritomo, and Kido Takayoshi—who were interested in absorbing European technology while maintaining Japanese civilization and independence.[17] The ambition was transparent. In the four-character slogans that the Meiji Restorers used to communicate with the country as a whole, *Wakon yosai* (Western learning with Japanese spirit) would be adopted in the interest of creating *Fukoku kyōhei* (a rich country with a strong army).

There followed the rapid adoption of Western organization: prefects, bureaucratic jobs, newspapers, language standardization on Tokyo samurai dialect, an education ministry, compulsory school attendance, military conscription, railways built by the government, the abolition of internal customs barriers to a national market, fixed-length hours of the working day to improve coordination, and the Gregorian calendar, all in place by 1873. Representative local government was in place by 1879. A bicameral parliament (with a newly created peerage) and a constitutional monarchy were in place by 1889. By 1890, 80 percent of school-age children were at least enrolled.

In China, Li Hongzhang had been one of the few able to swim against the institutional and cultural tide to push modernization and industrialization forward. In Japan there were many such men. One of the Meiji Six was Itō Hirobumi. In 1863, the Choshu clan elders decided they desperately needed to learn more about European organization and technology, so—illegally—they smuggled five of their promising young students out of Japan to travel and study in Europe. Itō worked for 130 days as a deckhand on the sailing ship *Pegasus* before arriving in England, where he studied at University College in London. He cut his studies short after only six months and returned to Choshu to argue stridently against a policy of confronting the imperial powers: Japan was too weak, he said, and the organizational and technological gap too large.

By 1870, Itō was in the United States, studying money and banking. The next year, he went back to Japan, where he wrote the regulations for the commutation of feudal dues and their replacement by a general system of national taxation. By 1873, he had become minister of industry, tasked with reverse-engineering as much European technology as possible and building telegraph lines, streetlights, textile mills, railroads, shipyards, lighthouses, mines, steel foundries, glassworks, the Imperial College of Engineering, and more.[18] In 1881, he muscled his contemporary Ōkuma Shigenobu out of the government and in so doing became the informal prime minister of Japan; four years later, he became the first formal prime minister of Japan, under a constitution he had written based on the model of Prussia's in 1850.

Itō launched the First Sino-Japanese War in 1895. With eleven European-built and two Japanese-built warships, and with an army trained by a Prussian major, Jakob Meckel, Japan quickly won. The major Chinese base and fort of Dalian in Liaoning—Port

Arthur—fell to a frontal Japanese assault in one day. Korea and Taiwan were grabbed as Japanese protectorates.

In 1902, Japan allied itself with Britain, seeking the role of Britain's viceroy in the North Pacific. Three years later, Japan again went to war, this time with Russia, a conflict the Japanese won decisively, bringing Manchuria into their sphere of influence.

In 1909, Itō Hirobumi met his end, assassinated by Korean nationalist An Jung-geun. In response, Japan formally annexed Korea in 1910.

It was not just the Meiji Six. There were many others who played important roles in shaping a more modern Japan. Takahashi Korekiyo, for example, born in 1854 as the illegitimate son of a Tokugawa court artist, sailed to Oakland, California, in 1867 to work as a laborer and learn English. He returned and began to work his way up the bureaucracy (while also temporarily crossing the Pacific again, this time to Peru, to fail at mining silver), becoming vice president of the Bank of Japan, selling bonds to finance the Russo-Japanese War of 1905, becoming president of the Bank of Japan, and then, in 1921, becoming prime minister. Upward mobility was a powerful possibility in Meiji Restoration–era Japan. Takahashi acquired knowledge of the levers of modern finance without having been inculcated into the cult of financial orthodoxy. This was to matter later on, for when the Great Depression of the 1930s started, Takahashi was finance minister, and was able to look at the situation with unblinkered eyes and set Japan on a course that allowed it to escape the Great Depression almost entirely.[19]

How did Japan manage it?

Economic historian Robert Allen believes the industrial economies that developed successfully before 1900 focused the power of government on creating four, and only four, institutional prerequisites: railways and ports, education, banks, and a shielding tariff on industries where their future comparative advantage would lie—if they could get there.

Imperial powers prohibited Meiji Japan from imposing tariffs on imports of greater than 5 percent. But the Japanese government, then and after, was willing to substitute. It did not so much "pick winners" as recognize winners—successful exporters—and subsidize them. When the Ministry of Industry established Japan's railway and telegraph systems, it also established a school to train Japanese engineers. And it relied as much as possible on domestic suppliers. Meiji Japan did not have large-scale banks. But it did have some very wealthy merchant clans willing to move into industry: Mitsui, Mitsubishi, Sumitomo, Yasuda. Lastly, Meiji military politicians focused on preparing the logistical trail to defend Japan and to conquer an empire in the age of steel and steam. Even before cotton-textile industrialization began, military industrialization was underway: shipyards, arsenals, and their linkages employed perhaps ten thousand industrial workers by the early 1880s.[20]

It was a near thing, however. Outlier Japan was an outlier by luck as much as by determination. In 1910, manufacturing was still only one-fifth of the nation's GDP, and in the preceding decade, Japan was only a semi-industrial civilization. It had, however, accomplished something unique: it had transferred a significant amount of industrial technology outside of the charmed circles of the North Atlantic and had the expertise necessary to keep it running and profitable.

EMPIRES, FORMAL AND INFORMAL, both accelerated and retarded economic growth and development throughout the global south. But on balance, empire did more to retard than to advance. After all, the business of empire was not economic development. The business of empire was . . . empire.

Within the industrial core, the conservative view was that empires were ordained by God—or at least were morally required. Let us give the mic to Rudyard Kipling:

> *Take up the White Man's burden—*
> *Send forth the best ye breed—*
> *Go send your sons to exile*
> *To serve your captives' need*
> *To wait in heavy harness*
> *On fluttered folk and wild—*
> *Your new-caught, sullen peoples*
> *Half devil and half child.*[21]

Those "sullen" "captives" you were being sent off to civilize might not like it. "Half devil and half child," these "wild . . . new-caught people" were definitely not your equals. And what you were being sent off to do wasn't any fun but rather "exile," "burden," and "heavy harness." But still, for some reason, you needed to do it.

The enlightened liberal belief in the early 1900s was that this made little sense. The belief was that the then-existing empires were little but confidence games, and that they were on their last legs.

The Austrian economist Joseph Schumpeter thought the people were being conned—diverted to cheering for victories so they would not notice that the landlord-aristocratic political power structure made no sense.[22] He thought the landlord-aristocrats were being conned, too: sent to die of dysentery, wound-caused infection, or shot and shell, when they could, instead, be drinking cappuccinos with whipped cream at the Café Central at Herrengasse 14 in Vienna.

Empire was the equivalent of a modern-day sports team, whose victories kicked off celebrations—such as the immense Mafeking Night party in Britain, which was kicked off by good news about British progress in the South African Boer War. The military aristocracy loved to play, and the people loved to watch.

Schumpeter hated this. And he thought that it was on the way out—that as people became richer and more prosperous, the bourgeois virtues would win, and the drive for empire would die. Schumpeter expected the con to end, and a peaceful, less aristocratic, less imperial, less bloodthirsty twentieth century.

He was wrong.

The British activist John Hobson had a different take on the driver of imperialism—that it was economics, rather than culture and sociology, that was the primary factor.[23] Hobson thought that having the government spend money putting people to work building weapons, and then using the weapons to conquer colonies that could be forced to buy exports, was a way of avoiding mass unemployment, and so keeping domestic political peace—albeit a highly suboptimal way.

As Hobson saw it, a government's main task was to keep its people working and prosperous and happy. And its main obstacles in doing this were disruptive business cycles, which could cause mass unemployment. Empire managed to overcome these obstacles in two ways: first, by equipping the military needed to maintain the empire, which put people to work; and second, by taking advantage of the fact that empire is a good source of consumers for the products of domestic factories. European governments that pursued empire, Hobson thought, were less likely to face economic distress, and so more likely to hang on to power. The solution to empire, he thought, would be more equality at home. This would translate into smaller business cycles, less unemployment, and less need for empire.

And Hobson thought that a pro-democratic, pro-equality political shift was coming, and that in its aftermath war and empire would lose their purpose, giving way to a peaceful, more egalitarian, more democratic, less imperial, less bloodthirsty twentieth century.

He, too, was wrong.

The British public intellectual Norman Angell thought that empire and war—except, perhaps, for wars of national liberation to give people self-government—were already pointless and ob-solete.[24] And he firmly believed that governments could not be so inept or so shortsighted not to realize that.

He was wrong as well.

The same forces that propelled European powers to empire would propel them to destructive industrial war, and in 1914 those forces would turn Europe into a truly dark continent. The history of the long twentieth century took its very sharp mili-taristic turn. The question was: Would that turn negate all the progress in world civilization since 1870?

5

World War I

Perhaps the saddest book on my bookshelf is Norman Angell's *The Great Illusion*—the retitled version of *Europe's Optical Illusion*, first published in 1909. It could well take pride of place within the "they didn't see it coming" genre. What draws forth tears in the twenty-first century is that we know all too well what in fact came to pass and the profound wish that the many, many readers of Angell's book had acted on its wisdom rather than only marveling at it.

The illusion that gave Angell's book its title was that war and territorial conquest were the two main means of moral and material progress: "If a nation's wealth is really subject to military confiscation," he wrote in his follow-up volume, *Peace Theories and the Balkan War*, then "small states should be insecure indeed," and "the Austrian should be better off than the Switzer." But this wasn't the case. For one example, Angell noted that "Belgian national [government bonds] stand 20 points higher than the German," despite Belgium's much smaller size and negligible global military power. "It is such quite simple questions as these, and the quite plain facts which underlie them which will lead to sounder conceptions in this matter [of conquest for gain] on the part of the peoples."[1]

If sound conceptions were arrived at by attention to plain facts, he would have had a point.

It was, Angell rightly argued, much cheaper to make and trade for what you want than to build military power and spill the blood of your own people in order to extract it from others. Using war and empire to obtain a greater domain for the king to rule was, Angell thought, no longer a viable strategy for anyone—and was in fact profoundly stupid in the age of destructive industrial warfare. And using empire to make people worship the right God the right way was, Angell thought, another habit that humanity had outgrown.

He was right in his belief that war could no longer make any form of economic sense. But in his belief that therefore humanity had outgrown it, he was totally, disastrously wrong.

STORIES HAVE PROTAGONISTS. THEY make most of the decisions and take most of the actions. Telling protagonist-led stories is how we think. A prime minister like Otto von Bismarck—a protagonist—maneuvers to retain power. The working class—another kind of protagonist—decides to give him the votes of their parliamentary representatives in return for national health insurance. And Germany—a third kind of protagonist—chooses, precociously, to march down the road of social insurance and social democracy.[2] Often this is pure metaphor: the ocean seeks to climb closer to the moon and so we feel the tides, or the lightning chooses to follow the path of least resistance to the ground. But we find it easiest to think this way. Perhaps this is the only way to think.

So at one level the history of the long twentieth century has two battling ideas as its protagonists. One is best associated with Friedrich August von Hayek—the market giveth, the market taketh; blessed be the market. The other is best associated with Karl Polanyi—the market is made for man, not man for the market. In the long twentieth century in which the *economic* and its repeated revolutionary transformations are dominant, nearly all of our other protagonists in all of our stories are profoundly shaped by at least one, perhaps both, of these ideas. This is as true for humanity as it is for Nikola Tesla or Bismarck or the German working class. What key substory protagonists made of Hayek's and Polanyi's notions, how they contorted them and imposed policies in light of them, made the difference.

Much of the time, the processes and factors of history can seem almost inevitable to us—the actions and decisions of particular individuals mostly offset one another, and if an opportunity was not seized by one person at one date it was soon enough seized by another. Or we have a sense that things could have turned out very differently, but we cannot point to a single moment when some individual decided to turn right instead of left, and so made *the* difference. Even as decisive and important an individual as Tesla simply turned one—very important—technological clock forward by a decade. Herbert Hoover and Li Hongzhang and company are important as individuals, but they are historically decisive only to the extent that they stand for thousands, if not more, whose actions made imperialism, failed to put China on the road to rapid industrialization, and so on. But there are moments when particular individuals really do matter, and where choice and chance come to the front of the stage.

Two chapters ago we shifted our focus from economics to political economy: we needed to look not just at technology, production, organization, and exchange, but also at how people governing themselves and others tried to regulate the economy to preserve or produce a good society—or at least a society that would be good for them. In the previous chapter, we shifted our focus to imperial politics: we needed to look not just at how peoples and their elites governed themselves, but at how they governed others. Each of these shifts narrowed our narrative focus. The protagonist humanity became the protagonist nation-states, which in turn became the protagonists of the North Atlantic industrial core and the southern periphery. In this chapter we take a further step. We move to where choice and chance are dominant, into war, governance, and high politics. In this chapter, individuals matter.

The world at the start of 1914 was growing at an unprecedented pace; it was substantially peaceful, and it was more prosperous than ever before—with problems, but prosperous. It was a world in which it was not irrational to be optimistic about human civilization. After World War I, the world, especially Europe, was different. For one thing, much of it was rubble and ashes. And we cannot attribute the difference to structures evolving in a logical and predictable way.

So how are we to grasp this illogical evolution of events, this upsetting of what we economic historians want to see as the natural pattern of human progress? I think a good place to start is a decade before Angell wrote *The Great Illusion*. Beginning in 1899, Britain waged a war of choice in South Africa, the Boer War.[3]

That it was a war of choice is clear from the British pattern of choosing otherwise in the preceding decades. From the 1860s, the expansion of European empires was coupled with a willingness to hand over power to locals—to white locals, that is: Canada in 1867, Australia in 1901, New Zealand in 1907. Indeed, that would be the choice with South Africa in 1910. But ten years earlier, in 1900, a different choice was made, one that eventually required Britain to send more than 250,000 soldiers to South Africa to convince 200,000 Boers that they did not want to govern themselves but rather to be ruled from London.

The Dutch were the first European settlers to colonize southern Africa, starting in 1652. The Boers were the descendants of these Dutch colonizers in the region. They came under British governance at the dawn of the nineteenth century, and, unhappy about it, founded their own republics, the Province of the

Transvaal and the Orange Free State. This was acceptable to the British for decades until it wasn't.

The British colonial secretary, Joseph Chamberlain—father of 1930s prime minister Neville Chamberlain—preached the annexation of the Transvaal and the Orange Free State. And in 1899, he sent an ultimatum: equal rights for British citizens in the Transvaal (with consequences for resource extraction) or war.

What, after all, did the mightiest empire the world had ever seen have to fear from two small republics populated by unindustrialized farmers, whose prosperity had been based largely on their power to exploit the land's earlier inhabitants, no matter their discovery of gold and mineral wealth? More than you would think. The Boer army attacked, besieging British garrisons in towns named Mafeking, Ladysmith, and Kimberley, and defeating British relief columns in battles at places named Spion Kop, Vaal Kranz, Magersfontein, Stormberg, and the Tugela River. Six hundred of Sir William Gatacre's 3,000 troops were captured at Stormberg as British troops fled, after being ordered up a near cliff against entrenched Boers with rifles. And 1,400 of Lord Methuen's 14,000 men were killed or wounded at Magersfontein, as they assaulted the Boer trench line. Redvers Buller's 21,000 suffered 1,200 killed and wounded to the Boers' 50 in a failed attempt to cross the Tugela River.

Short and victorious Joseph Chamberlain's war was not.

Any calculation of costs and benefits would have told the British cabinet to talk peace: it was time to stand down, in return for promises from the Boers to treat British miners and prospectors as white people should be treated.

Instead, a quarter of a million British soldiers were sent to South Africa starting in February 1900. It was a vast number. Were the United States in 2021 to commit the proportional equivalent, it would come to two million soldiers. The choice to send over such a force gave the British overwhelming superiority: a five-to-one edge even over the entire Boer people-in-arms. And in addition the British sent a competent general—Field Marshal Lord Roberts. The Orange Free State capital, Bloemfontein, fell on March 13, 1900; Johannesburg fell on May 31; and Transvaal's capital, Pretoria, fell on June 5.

But the war was not over. Defeated in open battle, the Boers turned to guerrilla warfare, waging an insurgency against the British for a year and a half—and at one point they captured the British second-in-command, Lord Methuen.

What does an invading military superpower do when its troops are faced with a guerrilla insurgency in a land where they do not speak the language? The British Empire invented the modern concentration camp. Are guerrillas active in an area? Round up everyone—men, women, and children—and stick them behind barbed wire. Don't feed them too well, and don't spend too much time worrying about sanitation. Then build small forts and construct wire fences to reduce the guerrillas' mobility.

Roughly 30,000 Boers, most of them children under sixteen, died in the concentration camps. Nearly 100,000 people died in the Boer War. In addition to the 30,000 Boer civilians who died, perhaps 8,000 British soldiers died in battle, another 14,000 died of disease, and 10,000 Boer soldiers died. On top of that, perhaps 30,000 indigenous Africans died—which, grotesquely, nobody counted at the time.

All in all, Britain mobilized 2.5 percent of its adult male population for the war, and about one in ten of those men died.

Would it not have been better if all this could have been avoided? We might think so. Most of Britain didn't.

The 1900 British general election was a huge political victory for the warmongering Conservatives, who were led by Lord Salisbury: it was called a "khaki election" because of the army's uniforms, and the term has stuck to denote any election heavily influenced by war. A peace treaty was signed in 1902 annexing the two Boer republics to the British Empire. But by 1910, when South Africa became a white self-governing dominion, with Afrikaans and English both named as official languages, it was inhabited with a voting population about as well disposed toward Westminster as, well, the population of Ireland was in 1910.[4]

What was wrong with all those voting British? Why didn't the people on the ground think a negotiated peace to a white self-governing dominion wouldn't have been better? Because they were nationalists.

What is a nationalist? Well, the venerated German social scientist and (for his day) *liberal* Max Weber, for one. In his inaugural lecture as professor at Frieburg university in 1895, "The National State and Economic Policy," Weber, a German sociologist, summarized the worldview that he shared with many others:

> We all consider the German character of the East as something that should be protected. . . . The German peasants and day-labourers of the East are not being pushed off the land in an open conflict by politically-superior opponents. Instead, they are getting the worst of it in the silent and dreary struggle of everyday economic existence, they are abandoning their homeland to a race which stands on a lower level, and moving towards a dark future in which they will sink without trace. . . . Our successors will not hold us responsible before history for the kind of economic organization we hand over to them, but rather for the amount of elbow-room we conquer for them in the world.[5]

Weber was a dark-haired and square-headed Caucasian male who spoke German. He greatly feared dark-haired, square-headed Caucasian males who spoke Polish. In the transparent code of nationalism, this fear led him to write, "The economic policy of a German state, and that standard of value adopted by a German economic theorist, can therefore be nothing other than a German policy and a German standard."

We know what all this points to. We will spend chapters on the consequences. But we can and should flash forward. No individuals ever make their decisions in a vacuum. No individuals ever make their decisions impelled mechanically by obvious material incentives or consequences. "Material interests may drive the trains down the tracks," Weber liked to say, "but ideas are the switchmen," the ones who throw the switches that determine which track the train follows.[6] When one individual decides he would like to turn right, not left, toward some war of choice, say, it matters if a large portion of the individuals surrounding that decision maker are enmeshed in, if not in thrall to, the same notions underlying the choice. Nationalism was a notion that could not just swamp competing beliefs but pervert them.

We see this at the level of the individual. Forty-eight years after Weber's speech, the largest single military command of German speakers ever—Adolf Hitler's *Heeresgruppe Sud*, Army Group South—would be fighting even larger formations of the Red Army in Ukraine in a war seeking to win "elbow-room" for the German *Volk*. Its commander would be a man who had, at birth, been named Fritz Erich Georg Eduard von Lewinski.[7]

The "von" signifies that the name is a German noble name. But "Lewinski" (Levi-ski)—is not a name that springs from the Germanic branch of the Indo-European language tree. The suffix "-ski" is Slavic: it signifies that the name is a Polish noble name— it's the Polish analog to the German "von." And then there is what is in between the "von" and the "ski": "Levi."

There is not a more Jewish surname in the world than "Levi."

Yet Fritz Erich Georg Eduard worked diligently and enthusiastically for Adolf Hitler, skillfully and tirelessly commanding soldiers who fought fanatically for a regime most focused on killing as many Jews (and almost as focused on killing enough Poles, Russians, and other Slavic peoples to gain "elbow-room" for German farmers) as possible. The histories call him not von Lewinsky but "von Manstein." This was because he was his mother Helene von Sperling's tenth child and fifth son, and his mother's sister Hedwig was childless, so Helene gave Fritz Erich Georg Eduard to Hedwig, and she and her husband von Manstein adopted him. It was under that name that he made his career in the Imperial, Weimar Republic, and Nazi armies.

Fritz Erich Georg Eduard von Manstein né von Lewinski was a nationalist. To him, just as for Max Weber and many others, the prospect of the "silent and dreary struggle" in the mixed borderlands—where some people spoke German and others looking much the same spoke Polish—was unacceptable. He, and millions like him, believed this to such an extent that both Hayekian and Polanyian notions of any sort of peaceful market path toward utopia shrank to near invisibility. The path to his becoming a soldier was well greased: the von Lewinskys, von Sperlings, and von Mansteins had five Prussian generals among them, including both of Erich's grandparents. Helene and Hedwig's sister Gertrude married Paul von Hindenberg, which made that field marshal and right-wing Weimar Republic president Erich's uncle.

In technologically advanced German cities such as Hamburg and Essen, industrialists and merchants desperate for workers found that many potential workers were already engaged in agricultural employment in Pomerania and Prussia. The industrialists and merchants therefore offered them higher wages and a better life if they would move to the seaports and to the Rhineland, and many did exactly that. The choices of industrialists and merchants translated to choices for agricultural workers, which translated to choices for the landlords of the German East. Rather than matching the wage offers made by the iron lords of the Rhineland, but needing to replace their agricultural workers, they pulled Polish workers from the Vistula valley farther east. Win-win-win-win, no?

The Polish-speaking population remaining in the Vistula was happy: they had larger farms. The Polish-speaking population who moved to Germany was happy: they had higher wages and a better life. The German-speaking landlords were happy: they could sell their grain at a higher price to the booming German West without having to match the wages of the German West. The German-speaking workers who moved west were happy: they had higher wages and a better life. The German-speaking iron lords and other industrialists and merchants were happy: they had an expanded labor force. The aristocrats who ran the German national state were happy: they had a stronger economy, more tax revenue, less poverty, and consequently a lower level of democratic-egalitarian-socialist agitation.

Who was left to be unhappy? Max Weber, and every other blinkered German nationalist, is who.

Note that Weber was, in pre–World War I Germany, solidly in the center-left. He was no socialist, but he was otherwise a friend to political democracy, to mass education, and to economic prosperity, and a foe to parasitic aristocracies and rigid social orders.

The scary thing is that German nationalism was not exceptional in pre–World War I Europe. Rather, if not quite the norm, it was close to it. Usually manifest, nationalism was understood as destiny in a winner-take-most (maybe all) contest in which war was viewed not as a catastrophe but as an opportunity: an opportunity for national assertion, national mobilization, and the creation of a stronger national identity—as well as an opportunity to win the spoils of war, whatever those might be.

However, suppose you refuse to fall under the spell of some particular nationalism. Suppose you do not buy into its encouragements for assertion, for mobilization, for identity, and for spoils. Then it becomes clear that all of the politicians and military officers near the apex of early decision-making were at best badly mistaken and at worst criminally insane. For it all ended badly. While the kings of the monarchies joining the "winning" Anglo-French side retained their thrones, all of the continental European emperors whose ministers made war would lose theirs.

But the ironic quote marks around "winning": those belong there. Nearly ten million people died in World War I. If we believe that the Spanish flu epidemic of 1918–1919 was made an order of magnitude greater than it would otherwise have been by the travel, disruption, and famine of the war, then the death toll approaches fifty million.

Consider that the rulers of Austria-Hungary had for a long time been worried about Serbian nationalism, or rather, the extension of Serbian nationalism northward as ideologues argued that Serbs, Bosnians, Croats, Slovenes, and others were really one nation—"Yugoslavs"—and that only alien rule by Turks from Istanbul and by Germans from Vienna had prevented the previous emergence of a glorious south-Slav nation.

Consider that eighty years separate 1914, when Serbs and Croats were blood brothers (so much so that the Serbs would risk bloody war with Europe's great powers to rescue the Croats from oppressive foreign despotism), from 1994 (when Serbs and Croats could not live in the same village or province without the political leaders of at least one side calling for the extermination and exile of the other). And, as happened eighty years earlier, what leaders called for, their followers undertook. To fight one set of wars at the start of the twentieth century to unify Serbs and Croats, and another set of wars at the end of that century to "ethnically cleanse" Serbs of Croats, and Croats of Serbs, seems among the sickest jokes history ever played on humans, or, more causally accurate, humans ever played on history.

A semidemocratic, constitutional monarchy like that of the Habsburg-ruled Austro-Hungarian Empire, which while ruling over various nationalities respected (most) local customs, kept the peace, and allowed freedom of commerce, belief, and speech (within limits), seems much more than halfway up the list of desirable regimes. But not to the blood-brother forebears of their genocidal Serb and Croat offspring.

In the summer of 1914, a Bosnian terrorist seeking Bosnian independence from the Austro-Hungarian Empire and union with Serbia assassinated the heir to the throne of the Austro-Hungarian Empire, the Archduke Franz Ferdinand, and his wife, Sophie. The terrorist had received some assistance from the secret police of the Kingdom of Serbia—although almost surely not with the active knowledge of the King of Serbia.[8]

For the old emperor Franz Joseph in Vienna and his advisers, the outrageous murder of his nephew (and his wife) seemed to call for action. And it would take the form of punishing the guilty, humbling Serbia, and making it plain that Austria was the great power in the Balkans. To establish this seemed worth a small risk of a large war. After all, the Balkan Wars of the early twentieth century, the Russo-Japanese War of 1905, the Franco-Prussian War of 1870, the Austro-Prussian War of 1866, the Prusso-Austro-Danish War of 1864, and the Franco-Austrian War of 1859 had all been very short. The Crimean War of 1853–1856 had been longer, but it had been a limited war: neither set of combatants had thought the stakes high enough to make it worthwhile to derange civilian society. And the American Civil War of 1861–1865, which had killed one in five and maimed another one in five of the white adult males in the arc of coastal states from Texas to Virginia—that was not seen as relevant.

It was not the only missed relevant fact.

For the not-so-old czar in St. Petersburg, Nicholas II, and his ministers, the most important priority was to demonstrate that czarist Russia was the great power in the Balkans. And this required that small Slavic-speaking nations understand that they could count on it to protect them from Viennese hegemony.

For the not-so-old German emperor in Berlin, Wilhelm II, and his ministers, the possibility of a quick, decisive victory over both France and Russia promised to secure for Germany a dominant "place in the sun" among the great powers of Europe. The decision to back Austria to the hilt, in whatever action it chose to take in response to the assassination of Franz Ferdinand, was nearly automatic. And how could it conceivably be otherwise? During the 1800s, the standing and power of the German Empire had been radically enhanced by short, victorious wars provoked and managed by the so-called Iron Chancellor, Otto von Bismarck, a German politician who had earned thunderous applause by declaring, "It is not by speeches and debates that the great issues of the day will be decided, but by Blood and Iron."

For the politicians of the French Third Republic, a war with Germany needed to be fought someday in order to recover Alsace and Lorraine, which had been stolen by Germany in 1870. And it was, to politicians and populace alike, self-evidently worth killing a lot of people to make sure that the city of Strasbourg was not called "Strassburg," and that its mayor spoke French, not German. For the politicians of the British Empire in London, risks of war were worth running to show that the British Empire could not be pushed around. What was more, Germany before World War I had built a battle fleet that Britain saw as an existential threat, and Britain found itself forced to spend a fortune to outmatch it. Recall Winston Churchill's joke about the pace of pre–World War I British dreadnought battleship construction: the Liberal government was willing to budget for four new battleships a year, the navy admirals demanded six, and the press and public opinion, with their fear of imperial Germany coming to the fore, pushed them to compromise at eight.

All those who thought that war would be good, even if just for them, were wrong. The old Emperor Franz Joseph's Habsburg dynasty would lose its throne and his empire. To uncertainly clarify the pronunciation of "Strasbourg," the French would lose a generation of young men. The British would also lose a generation of young men on the way to a much weaker post–World War I empire, with which it would confront, again, a German-dominated Europe. The Russian czar lost his throne, his life, and his country, with his entire family slaughtered as well. Russia, too, lost a generation of young men, as well as its chance to have a less-than-totally-unhappy twentieth century.

World War I did not secure for Germany a dominant "place in the sun" among the great powers of Europe. Wilhelm lost his throne. His country lost its political and military autonomy and a generation of young men, and took the first steps along the road to Hitler's Third Reich, a regime that would blacken the name of Germany for millennia. And it would take more than thirty years before French politicians would realize that trying to contain Germany by using their army simply did not work, and that perhaps a better way to try to contain German power would be to integrate it economically into a wider Europe.

So why did they do it? First, there was nationalism. There was also the political logic that winning this war made it less likely that you would lose a future one, and therefore less likely that you would suffer the consequences.

But there was more. There was aristocracy. The Europe of 1914 was a Europe of national populations, of industrialists and socialists, of factory workers and technicians. But Europe's governments in 1914—especially the defense and foreign affairs ministries—were largely populated by aristocrats, ex-aristocrats, and would-be aristocrats. This meant that the aristocratic, land-lord, military elites had control of many of the levers of propaganda and power. Moreover, the aristocrats had help from industrialists and entrepreneurs who were eager to secure economic benefits, as happened with the 1879 German "marriage of iron and rye": the imposition of tariffs on imports of British steel (to protect the positions of German manufacturers) and on imports of American grain (to protect the positions of German landlords).[9]

On the eve of World War I, these elites increasingly found themselves members of a social caste with no societal function. They could look forward only to the erosion of their influence and status, the erosion of their relative wealth, and the erosion of their self-respect. In the world of win-win-win economics, these aristocrats and wannabe aristocrats, in all their thousands, would inevitably lose. Or, to avoid that fate, they could lead their nations into war.

Power and propaganda were reinforced by ideology. Each nation decided that it had a strong interest in ensuring that its people left the most enduring imprint on all future civilizations. Enlightenment and Christian values of peace, fraternity, and charity, meanwhile, fell out of favor.

The aristocrats of Europe were at most half-conscious of how much they had to lose when they rolled the dice in 1914. But roll the dice they did. They rallied mass support by creating a powerful echo chamber, in which propaganda and ideology reinforced each other. And the civilized masses of the West, more learned and better fed and clothed and housed than any previous generation, rallied behind them enthusiastically.

Causation and metaphors matter. That the nations of Europe fell like dominoes is one sort of explanation, encouraging one set of understandings. Because a butterfly beat its wings, a tornado touched down a continent away. Because the zeitgeist, the dialectic unfolding of History, the finger of Providence—take your pick—set one domino in motion, the rest fell.

The archduke had been killed. Serbia had rejected Austria's ultimatum. Austria had declared war on Serbia. Germany sought to convince Austria that, to demonstrate it was serious, it should attack, but then "halt in Belgrade" and negotiate. Russia began to mobilize. At that point Germany attacked Belgium. It was August 4, 1914. It was that stupid.

The laughter of the guns began as Germany's heavy artillery began destroying Belgian forts and killing Belgian soldiers and civilians. Begin a war with a surprise attack on an uninvolved, neutral power, in a way that may well add the world's preeminent superpower to your enemies when you are already outproduced, outgunned, and outnumbered. Why would it make sense for a military bureaucracy to do such a thing?

I have long thought that a large component of the answer was "Prussia."[10] The German Empire on the eve of World War I was dominated by its component Kingdom of Prussia. And Prussia was dominated by its army—it was not so much a state with an army, as an army with a state, was the French witticism for centuries. Prussia's army had a dominant military tradition of attacking first, by surprise, from an unexpected direction. Why? Because it was in a region without natural defenses and surrounded by more populous and often richer potential adversaries. Any state in such a situation was very likely to lose any war it did not quickly win. So if there was going to be a strong state in the region, it would have to be one that did win wars quickly—hence the Prussian way of war. And Prussia then, by historical accident upon accident, became the nucleus around which the circa-1900 German imperial nation was formed.

Indeed, it almost worked. Had Britain stayed out of the war, the odds are that the Germans would have conquered Paris in August 1914, after which a peace of the diplomats could have been within immediate reach. But Britain entered the war, first for the sake of its treaty commitment to Belgium, but probably more important, to prevent the creation of a hegemonic Germany on the European continent that could then easily afford to build a battle fleet that would leave Britain with no strategic options.[11]

And so the trigger was pulled. The war would be fought by the mass-conscripted eighteen- to twenty-one-year-old boys of Europe, augmented by older reserves who had received their military training in the previous decades. These armies marched off enthusiastically, singing and taking the causes of the emperors, aristocrats, and generals for their own, and all sides expected a short, victorious war.

World War I would have been bad, but not an utterly and unutterably intolerable catastrophic disaster if it had been a short war. But the initial combatants were so evenly matched at the start that there would be no quick victory or short war. It was a long war. British assistance to France kept it from being overrun in the fall of 1914. German assistance on the eastern front kept Austria from being overrun in the fall of 1914. And then they all dug trenches. Ultimately, it became a total war, a resource-mobilization-based war of attrition that dragged on for more than four years.

Generals called for greater and greater commitments of resources to the front: if battles could not be won by strategy, perhaps they could be won by the sheer weight of men, metal, and explosives. In Britain—which attained the highest degree of mobilization—the government was sucking up more than one-third of national product (plus the time of conscripted soldiers) for the war effort by 1916.

Mobilizing economic resources for total war was not something anybody had planned for. Military plans had all assumed a short war, one that would be decisively won or lost in a matter of months, in a single battle or two. When reality set in, governments and armies turned to frantic expedients to resupply their troops and ramp up war production. Production became dictated by the representatives of industry's largest customer, the military, rather than by market forces. Yet the army could not simply pay through the nose what the industrialists wanted to charge. And so the market needed to be substantially replaced by rationing and command-and-control.[12]

Was that possible? Yes. In all cases, those who ran the industrial-materials-allocation directorates succeeded. Such success turned out to be surprisingly easy, even though running them efficiently would have been surprisingly difficult. Nevertheless, the example of the German war economy made some, such as Vladimir Lenin, believe that a "command economy" was possible. You could run a socialist economy not through the market but by using the government as a command-and-control bureaucracy—and not just during a national emergency, but as a matter of course. The evidence was there in the example of a war that made total mobilization necessary.

There were other, better lessons to be learned: for example, the importance of the military research laboratory, combined with a bureaucracy that could exploit it at scale. As the United States was to prove throughout the twentieth century, the winners of wars tended to be those with the biggest factories.

Once German dreams of a swift victory were dashed, and everyone went to their trenches, the logic of the Prussian way of war—if you fail to win quickly, sue for peace—fell out of favor. The German officer corps' adherence to *Totenritt*—a willingness to undertake a "death ride"—held sway, so that carrying out senseless orders to the best of one's ability substituted for logic.

But even then, hunkering down would have been to no avail without the genius of German scientists and administrators. The scientists were men such as Fritz Haber, winner of the Nobel Prize in 1918 for his creation of the power to extract useful nitrogen compounds literally out of thin air. (Carl Bosch, who managed the operation to scale up Haber's process to industrial size, received his prize in 1931.) This discovery was an enormous boon to those who needed fertilizers to grow crops. It was also essential to Germany's ability to fight anything other than a very short war: without nitrogen pulled from the air by the Haber-Bosch process, Germany would have run out of explosives and ammunition within six months, and nearly ten million people would not have died. On the one hand, Haber-Bosch prevented mass starvation: factory production of fertilizers on a large scale would have been impossible had it required finding and exploiting the very limited natural deposits of ammonia available. On the other hand, Fritz Haber is sometimes called the father of chemical weapons. He traveled from his laboratory to the trench line of the western front to watch his chlorine gas deployed for the first time at the Second Battle of Ypres in 1915.

A German Jew, Haber fled Germany when Adolf Hitler took power in 1933. He died in January 1934 in Basel, Switzerland.

The administrators were people such as Walther Rathenau, who established the industrial-materials priority command-and-control system that Germany used to keep its value chains functioning, at least for the production of war matériel, after the British naval blockade had cut off international trade. "I am a German of Jewish origin. My people are the German people, my home is Germany, my faith is German faith, which stands above all denominations," wrote Rathenau.[13]

He was assassinated by right-wing antisemitic German terrorists in 1922.

Another lesson comes courtesy of the Social Democratic Party of Germany (SPD). Founded in 1875, and promptly outlawed by Bismarck, by 1914 it had a million dues-paying members. The SPD was the largest political party in the world and held 34 percent of the seats in the German Reichstag. It had been founded to bring about the overthrow of capitalism and oversee the rise of a just socialist society. Whether that would be created by revolution, evolve naturally as the contradictions of capitalism manifested themselves, or evolve and then have to be defended in the streets against a reactionary coup was left ambiguous. The SPD, indeed, had been founded to advance the international brotherhood of workers, and with that in mind, had promised to oppose militarism in all of its forms.

So what did the SPD do when Emperor Wilhelm II's ministers asked for money to fight World War I? When the SPD's caucus met on August 3, 1914, cochair Hugo Haase, leader of the pacifist faction, was incredulous. "You want to approve war credits for the Germany of the Hohenzollern [Emperor] and the Prussian [landlord-aristocrat-officer-bureaucrat]

Junkers?" Haase asked. "No," said his fellow cochair, Friedrich Ebert. "Not for that Germany, but for the Germany of productive labor, the Germany of the social and cultural ascent of the masses. It is a matter of saving that Germany! We cannot abandon the fatherland in its moment of need. It is a matter of protecting women and children." Only 13 of the 110 SPD Reichstag deputies joined Haase's position in the internal caucus vote to determine the party line.[14]

What were they protecting women and children from? In August it was clear. They were protecting them from the czarist tyranny that would follow a Russian victory in the war that Germany had started by attacking Belgium. The efficiency of the innovative industrial research lab paired to modern corporations grasping for economies of scale and to well-ordered administration was immense. But that could be thrown away when principles and ideals told you that survival, or at least identity, was at risk. Economic growth is a measurable metric. Nationalism, not so much. Confronted by the powers of nationalist wars of choice, ideals such as utopia and principles of market over man, or vice versa, bend if they do not break. Yet, do the nationalist replacements truly have efficacy, utility, or value?

It would have been much better for the German people had the SPD stuck to its prewar pacifist guns and then been successful in hobbling the imperial German war effort, leading to an early peace. For Germany lost. In the end, the weight of men and metal arranged against Germany and its allies did tell. It was France, Belgium, Russia, the United Kingdom, Italy (from 1915), Romania, and the United States (from 1917) against the Austro-Hungarian, German, and Ottoman Empires and Bulgaria, and at the end of 1918, the Austro-Hungarian Empire's army collapsed. The generals announced that the German army in France was facing defeat. With foodstuffs stopped by British blockade, the German population at home was over the edge of starvation. And Germany sought an armistice.

If you want to know more about what happened during the war—about the battles and leaders and campaigns and casualties—you'd do well to read another book.[15] I don't have the heart to write it down. There were ten million dead, ten million maimed, and ten million lightly injured out of a population of some one hundred million adult men from the major belligerents. The overwhelming share of war casualties were soldiers, not civilians. A full year's worth of the full production powers of every belligerent power was wasted. The imperial-authoritarian political orders in the Russian, Ottoman, Austro-Hungarian, and German Empires had collapsed. The political order in Italy was at the point of collapse. Confidence that the world was run by farsighted statesmen in a way that supported progress was gone.

From 1870 to 1914, we can see global economic history as following a logic that was, if not inevitable, at least probable, or at least explicable after the fact. Luck and probability gave humanity an opening around 1870 in the form of a quintuple breakthrough: the ideology and policy of an open world, new forms of transportation, faster communications, and—most important—the beginnings of the research laboratory and the large corporation, which together would more than double the pace of invention and greatly speed the deployment of new technologies. From 1870 to 1914, the economic logic rolled forward: inventors became more specialized and prolific, corporations deployed more technology. An international division of labor developed, and global growth continued apace, while also spurring the creation of a low-wage periphery, as well as the concentration of industrialization and wealth in what is still the global north. Humanity, meanwhile, began to escape from the Malthusian dilemma, as the tendency for technological progress gained ground on ever-greater population numbers, and work shifted increasingly from farm to factory. All in all, the period saw the coming of sufficient (if ill-distributed) prosperity—and with it, the possibility that someday, not that far away, humanity, in the rich economies of the global north, at least, might attain something that previous eras would have judged to be a genuine utopia.

From 1870 to 1914 we can see global political-economic history as by and large following a possible, if not an overwhelmingly likely or near-necessary, path. We see the threading of the needle in the creation and maintenance of an increasingly liberal order within the economies and polities of the global north. We see expanding suffrage, growing rights, increasing prosperity, increasing inequality (accompanied by political movements to curb such inequalities), and an absence of large-scale revolution. We see the conquest of the rest of the world into formal and informal empires as the difference in power between the North Atlantic and the rest became overwhelmingly huge.

All of this could have been otherwise. But that events from 1870 to 1914 followed the course that they did is not surprising given where the world was in 1870.

This sense of history having a broad and nearly irresistible structural logic vanishes with World War I. It did not have to happen—the 1914 Bosnian crisis might have been finessed, or the war might have ended with a quick, decisive victory for one side or the other, or governments and elites might have come to their senses. Was some such catastrophe like World War I probable? Was humanity just unlucky?

History did not, after 1918, return to its structural pattern of broad forces and tides in which individual quirks and choices averaged out. History was still one damned thing after another. Individuals' visions, choices, and actions continued to matter. And not just the individuals who became dictators of great powers.

John Maynard Keynes saw the war as a previously unimaginable horror. He saw his own participation in its planning, from his desk at the British Treasury, as contemptible. Keynes, retrospectively, scorned the naïveté of the upper-middle-class pre–World War I inhabitants of London "for whom life offered, at a low cost and with the least trouble, conveniences, comforts, and amenities beyond the compass of the richest and most powerful monarchs of other ages." These Londoners had seen "this state of affairs," he said, "as normal, certain, and permanent, except in the direction of further improvement," and they had seen "any deviation from it . . . as aberrant, scandalous, and avoidable."

He was, of course, speaking of himself. As I already quoted 50 pages ago, Keynes and his had seen "the projects and politics of militarism and imperialism, of racial and cultural rivalries, of monopolies, restrictions, and exclusion, which were to play the serpent to this paradise," as "little more than the amusements of [the] daily newspaper." And "they appeared to exercise almost no influence at all on the ordinary course of economic and social life."[16]

They had been wrong, with awful consequences for the world. Keynes saw that he was one of the ones who had been so blind and so wrong. And so, for the rest of his life, he took on responsibility. Responsibility for what? For—don't laugh—saving the world. The curious thing is the extent to which he succeeded, especially for someone who was only a pitiful, isolated individual, and who never held any high political office.[17]

6

Roaring Twenties

Was the interruption of the patterns of 1870–1914 occasioned by World War I permanent? Or was there a fork in humanity's possible road after the guns stopped their laughter on November 11, 1918? Could history have treated World War I almost as if it had just been a bad dream? Could humanity have pursued a win-win logic of progress and prosperity after World War I, as it had broadly been doing before it—with large groups of people, acting both individually and collectively, trading, forming alliances, and making positive-sum decisions about how to rebuild, reform, and regulate their economies?

The pre–World War I pattern could not be restored completely, of course. Emperors were gone, much had been broken, and many were dead. But couldn't humanity in some sense wind back the clock four and a half years, adjust things, and fix the flaws so that the demons of militarism, imperialism, anarchism, and nationalism would not push the world forward into a similar immediate and dire catastrophe, and resume its march, or slouch, toward utopia?

The period from 1870 to 1914 had indeed been economic El Dorado, reaching both a level and a rate of growth of world prosperity previously unseen. The proportional advance in technologies for manipulating nature and organizing humanity deployed into the world economy had proportionally been roughly as great a leap forward as the combined progress over the period from 1500 to 1870. And that was as great a leap, in turn, as all the advances in technology from 1200 BCE to 1500 CE, from the era of the biblical Exodus and the Trojan War and the end of the Bronze Age to the beginning of the Imperial-Commercial Age.

In 1914, things had never before been so good. And it was not just the power to produce. The world in the first half of that year was much kinder and gentler than in previous ages: proportionately, there were many fewer slaves, and many more votes. Surely full consensus in favor of a rewind, and then a do-over, with the militarist-nationalists cowed by the memory of the abattoir of 1914–1918, was a complete no-brainer?

The political task of keeping the general peace, and of restoring the international division of labor, even deepening it, and deploying productive technologies ought, in some sense, to have been easy—in the wake of World War I, surely not even those of dubious sanity would want to do *that* again. Nationalism had proven a disaster. Surely its opposite, cosmopolitanism, a recognition that the nations shared a "common home" and should treat each other as housemates treat each other, was the obvious alternative?[1]

Plus, there was great opportunity: one-third of the belligerents' production—two-ninths of world production—no longer needed to be devoted to killing people, maiming people, and blowing things up. It could be turned instead to accomplish all kinds of wonderful things. The world, after all, had roughly three times the technological capability in the 1920s that it had had back in 1870. Even with a population half again as large as it had been in 1870, and even with a rising concentration of wealth at the between-country and within-country levels, that meant that the bulk of humanity had something their predecessors had never had: confidence that next year food, clothing, and shelter would be there, so that their families would not be overwhelmingly hungry, cold, and wet. The system that people were to look back on and call "classical liberalism," although it was so recent as to be only pseudo-classical, and so built on authority inherited and ascribed as to be only semi-liberal, had been a good one, the best one the world had hitherto seen.

So wasn't the process and system that had led the world to a better place in terms of potential material productivity in 1920 relative to 1870 worth restoring and continuing, in spite of its many and grievous flaws? Or, if it needed to be altered, surely people of goodwill could have reached rough consensus as to how.

Two currents of thought emerged after World War I that sought not just alteration but fundamental transformation of the pseudo-classical semi-liberal order. They were to gain flesh and rule, bloodily and destructively. They were Vladimir Lenin's version of really-existing socialism and Benito Mussolini's fascism, both of which you will see later at great length.

But there were others thinking hard and trying to work to find and implement a better system. If I may digress for a moment: If my editor would allow this book to be twice as long, I would trace many of these currents of thought and the actions that flowed from them. I would trace the current for which Joseph Schumpeter, born in 1882 one hundred miles away from Vienna in the primarily Czech-speaking part of the Austro-Hungarian Empire, is a convenient marker: society needing to be altered to elevate the role of the entrepreneur and provide space for the "creative destruction" of economic and other patterns of organization he set in motion to counterbalance growing bureaucratization brought about by the increasing scale of capital intensity needed to deploy technological advances.[2] I would trace the current for which Karl Popper, born in Vienna in 1902, is a convenient marker: society needing to double down on liberalism and freedom in all their forms to create a truly "open society."[3] I would trace the current for which Peter Drucker, born in Vienna in 1909, is a convenient marker: how freedom, entrepreneurship, cooperation, and organization could never be reconciled by either the laissez-faire market or the really-existing socialist plan, but instead required persuasion, in the form of *managers* and *management*, to reconcile points of view and actually get humans to, you know, work cooperatively semiefficiently.[4]

Moreover, I would trace the current for which Michael Polanyi, born in 1891 in Budapest, is a convenient marker: society needing not just the decentralized mercenary institution of the market, and definitely not needing comprehensive central planning, which can never be more than a fiction, but also needing decentralized fiduciary institutions focused on advancing knowledge about theory and practice, in which status is gained by teaching others—such as in modern science, communities of engineering practice, communities of legal interpretation, honorable journalism, evidence-based politics, and others—and in which people follow rules that have been half-constructed and that half emerged to advance not just the private interests and liberties of the participants but the broader public interest and public liberties as well.[5]

But as there is neither time nor space for all of that, in this book I can trace only two currents of thought and action: first, the current we have seen before, for which Friedrich von Hayek (born in Vienna in 1899) is a convenient marker (that all that needed to be altered was that market-economic institutions had to be purified and perfected, and supported by an antipermissive social and cultural order) and the current we have seen before for which Michael Polanyi's older brother Karl, born in Vienna in 1886, is the convenient marker (that the market presumes people only have property rights; but society is made up of humans who insist they have more rights; and society would react—left or right, sensibly or stupidly, but powerfully—against the market presumption). And I will trace how they could be shotgun married to each other, with the blesser of the wedding being John Maynard Keynes. That, I believe, is the principal grand narrative, or at least it is mine.

Could the clock have been turned back to 1914 and then set to ticking again as if World War I had just been a bad dream? Was the restoration of the pseudo-classical semi-liberal order, and a post-1918 that went again like 1870–1914, a road humanity could have taken in 1919, had just a few key decisions gone differently?

Whether or not there was a fork, and a better path that realistically could have been taken, the history of the post–World War I era tells us that it was not taken at all.

One big reason was that after 1918 the world lacked a single power to serve as what the economic historian (and my teacher) Charlie Kindleberger called the *hegemon*. General prosperity, stable financial calm, and rapid and balanced growth are what economists call *public goods*—everyone benefits from them with no one having to take individual steps to provide them. A large majority of countries tend to believe that some other country (or countries) will take care of the system as a whole. This belief allows them to concentrate on achieving their own national advantage. The state whose citizens play the largest role in the world economy—who ship the most exports, consume the most imports, and lend and borrow the most capital—winds up playing the leading role in the management of the international economy. It becomes the hegemon, often at its own citizens' encouragement. After all, its citizens have the most at stake in the successful management of the global economy. The other states "free-ride" on the hegemon. The world economy always needs a hegemon. In 1919, however, the United States, the world's new potential hegemon, demurred. Before 1914, Britain could play this role, and it did. After 1919, "the British couldn't and the United States wouldn't," wrote Kindleberger. "When every country turned to protect its national private interest, the world public interest went down the drain, and with it the private interests of all."[6]

World War I had not left the United States unscarred—it suffered 300,000 casualties, of which 110,000 were deaths, of which half were from combat (the other half were from the Spanish flu). But World War I had not been to Americans the civilization-disrupting shock it was to Europeans. In the United States, what people afterward were to call the Belle Époque did not end in 1914 but continued in various forms—the Prohibition experiment, the Jazz Age, and Florida land speculation; the build-out of mass production factories; new high-tech industrial sectors such as radio; and stock market castles in the air built on hopes of rapid technological revolution. In other words, humanity's utopian aspirations were made flesh—or rather, steel—in the 1920s United States. So, having been among the world's free-riders, the United States shied away from becoming the hegemon. Instead, it turned inward.

Rather than take up the role of world leader, its people and politicians opted for isolationism. Though President Woodrow Wilson was in a uniquely strong position at the end of hostilities—he had moral authority as the only belligerent not to have entered the war for territorial or political advantage, and he had the only effective army—he made next to nothing of the opportunity. Instead, he accepted the lead of Britain's David Lloyd George and France's Georges Clemenceau to a degree that outran even Lloyd George's calculations, and frightened him. Wilson did try to get one thing out of the Treaty of Versailles: the League of Nations, a forum in which international agreements could be reached, and in which arguments for revisions and readjustments to those agreements could be made. But Senator Henry Cabot Lodge of Massachusetts and his Republican peers, who ruled America in the 1920s, refused to even think about committing the country in any way to an internationalist foreign policy. The League would come into being without the United States as a member.[7]

In addition to refusing to join an international body that existed for the purpose of encouraging communication among countries, the United States in the aftermath of World War I added new restrictions on the flow of immigrants and raised tariffs. The increases were nowhere near the avowedly protectionist levels of the early 1800s, or even the revenue-raising-cum-protectionist levels of the late nineteenth century. But they were large enough to give pause to producers outside the United States who doubted if they could rely on uninterrupted access to the US market. There was no return to normalcy. There was no lifting the locomotives of economic growth, prosperity, and human flourishing back onto their pre–World War I tracks. While structural factors and underlying trends made their influence felt, they did so very much not for the better.

At the same time, the globalization fairy had turned evil, and brought a poisoned gift.

Humanity should have been expecting it. In May 1889, people had begun dying of influenza—the Asiatic flu—in Bokhara, Uzbekistan. There was then a trans-Caspian railway, and so the disease spread to the Caspian Sea, and then via the Russian Empire's river and rail network to Moscow, Kiev, and St. Petersburg, all by November. Half the population of Stockholm caught the flu by the end of the year. In the United States the *Evening World* newspaper in New York reported, "It is not deadly, not even necessarily dangerous, but it will afford a grand opportunity for the dealers to work off their surplus of bandanas." Deaths in the United States peaked in January 1890.

Globalization would continue to bring plagues, and the plagues spread rapidly throughout the world. More than 1 million people each were killed by the Asian flu of 1957–1958 and the Hong Kong flu of 1968–1970. The COVID-19 pandemic that began in 2020 has so far killed an estimated 4.5 million, as of this writing, and the slow-moving plague of HIV/AIDS has to date killed around 35 million. But by far the most deadly plague in modern history remains the Spanish flu of 1918–1920, which killed perhaps 50 million people out of a world population then approaching 1.9 billion—about 2.5 percent.[8]

It was not, actually, a Spanish flu. Wartime censorship among the Allied powers suppressed flu news out of a fear that it would be bad for morale, so the newspapers focused on the flu in neutral countries where they had correspondents, which meant, mostly, Spain, where patients included King Alfonso XIII. The greatest boost to the flu's spread may well have come from the French base and hospital of Étaples, through which tens of thousands of soldiers passed each day. It killed not just the young and the old but also the middle-aged and the healthy. Nearly half of those who died were adults between the ages of twenty and forty. The Lord branch of my ancestral family tree fled Boston and went to rural Maine. Many of their cousins who remained in Boston did not survive.

As the plague raged, European governments tried frantically to start winding back the clock to the spring of 1914. But they could not. The first reason they could not was that, while there might have been consensus that World War I should not have been, there was no consensus about how all the losing empires were to be governed. The post–World War I settlement would give a mandate to the victorious allies Britain and France to take over and rule former German colonies and former non-Turkish Ottoman dependencies—but Turkey itself, and the territories of the former Russian, Austro-Hungarian, and German Empires, were left to their own devices, which meant "voting" with some combination of weapons and ballots how they should be governed. For after World War I all the emperors (with the exception of the British king, George V, in his persona as Kaiser-i-Hind, Emperor of India) were gone. And with them went their camarillas and their dependent aristocrats.

The Russian czar, Nicholas II Romanov, abdicated in March 1917. Vladimir I. Lenin and his Bolsheviks shot him and his family—Nicholas, Alexandra, and their five children—along with family retainers, in mid-1918. The semisocialist government of Aleksandr Kerensky that followed organized an election for a Constituent Assembly to write a constitution. Lenin sent the assembly home at bayonet point. With no claim to legitimacy by election, Lenin and his faction then had to confront the others within the country who also hoped to base their rule on the barrels of guns. The Russian Civil War ran from 1917 to 1920.[9]

The German Kaiser, Wilhelm II, abdicated in November 1918. The Social Democratic Party leader Friedrich Ebert became provisional president of a democratic republic. He did so with the support of the German army high command because he agreed to suppress revolutionaries who wanted to expropriate and nationalize property and redistribute wealth. When the German socialist leaders Karl Liebknecht and Rosa Luxemburg called for not just a political but a socialist revolution, their Spartacus League demonstrations were quickly suppressed by soldiers and ex-soldiers. Luxemburg and Liebknecht were summarily shot and dumped into a canal—without even the pretense that they were trying to escape. The left wing of the Social Democratic Party of Germany split off, never forgave, and never forgot. From then on, their principal adversary was not the monarchists, not the plutocrats, not the center-right, not the fascists, but rather Ebert's party, the Social Democrats.

The Austro-Hungarian emperor, Karl I, likewise abdicated in November 1918. His regime was carved into individual nation-states very, very roughly following extremely blurry ethnolinguistic borders.

The last to fall was the Ottoman Empire's Mehmed VI Vahideddin (Revelation of Faith), sultan, successor of Muhammed, Commander of the Faithful, Caesar of Rome, and Custodian of the Two Holy Places, the last wielder of the sword of imperial dynasty founder Osman (1299–1324). Power in Turkey was taken up by Mustafa Kemal Atatürk in the spring of 1920.

But even among the victorious and politically stable Allied powers, simple winding back did not work. The politicians did not want to be voted out of office as incompetents who had led their peoples into a pointless, destructive bloodbath. So they fell over themselves to tell their people that they had "won" World War I, and that their triumph meant they were now free to harvest the fruits of victory.

For the citizens of the Allied nations—those who survived—the prospect of extracting resources from the defeated Central Powers promised to make life even better than it had been before the war, to make the war and its sacrifices somehow worthwhile. President Woodrow Wilson, however, struck a very different tone, announcing that the peace would be "a peace without victory," a peace that would have to be "accepted in humiliation, under duress." Claims of victory, he continued, "would leave . . . a bitter memory upon which terms of peace would rest, not permanently but only as upon quicksand." Wilson added, "Only a peace between equals can last."[10] But he let himself be ignored—"bamboozled" was John Maynard Keynes's word for it—as he was outmaneuvered by the French and British premiers, Clemenceau and Lloyd George.[11] They did not seek "indemnities." They merely demanded that Germany "repair" the damage done. But how was Germany to do this? It might be asked to ship goods to Britain and France. But the goods that Germany could ship would substitute for the heavy industrial productions of Britain and France. Britain and France did not want them. Accepting them would cause mass unemployment, and so was a nonstarter.

There was a third reason that post–World War I Europe did not draw away from nationalism but instead doubled down on it. Woodrow Wilson had proclaimed that postwar borders should be drawn "along historically established lines of allegiance and nationality," in order to enable the autonomous development of the resulting nations. The problem was that peoples were not divided along such lines. Every European state was left with a discontented minority. Many states' dominant ethnicities had previously been discontented minorities. They now saw themselves as having the power and the right to do as they had been done by.

Had the politicians of the Allied nations been wise and far-sighted, they would have sought to lower expectations at home. They would have sought to draw a firm line between the war-mongers in the defeated Central Powers—the emperors and the army officers and the warrior-aristocrats who were now gone—and the people of the Central Powers. Those who had started the war had been, as John Maynard Keynes put it, "moved by insane delusion and reckless self-regard" when they set things in motion that "overturned the foundations on which we all lived and built." And with their defeat, oppressed peoples could now join the Allies and build their own democracies.[12]

Keynes's characterization of the "insane delusion" comes from the very first paragraph of his 1919 book *The Economic Consequences of the Peace*. But he was not describing militarists, warrior-aristocrats, or emperors; he was referring to "the German people." Such was the attitude of even those sympathetic to the Germans among the Allies.

Though Keynes blamed "the German people" for the war and for all the destruction and death it brought, he believed that it was nevertheless essential for the Allies to immediately forget all of that. They must, he wrote at the end of the very same paragraph, let bygones be bygones. For if the spokesmen for the Allied powers sought to make Germany pay for any component of war damage and tried to keep Germany poor, "the spokesmen of the French and British peoples [would] run the risk of completing the ruin," he said, through a peace that would "impair yet further, when it might have restored, the delicate, complicated organization, already shaken and broken by war, through which alone the European peoples can employ themselves and live."[13]

In this Keynes sharply diverged from both popular opinion and the overwhelming consensus of elites among the victorious

Allied powers. He had been among the staff advising leaders at the Paris Peace Conference in Versailles and had watched in horror as it became clear that the object was to extract as much from Germany as possible. In his mind, this was likely to throw the whole project of post–World War I reconstruction off the rails.

South African prime minister Jan Christian Smuts was at the Versailles conference too, as leader of one of the dominions of the British Empire. He wrote a letter to his friend M. C. Gillett about what the conference was like:

> Poor Keynes often sits with me at night after a good dinner and we rail against the world and the coming flood. And I tell him this is the time for the Griqua prayer (the Lord to come himself and not send his Son, as this is not a time for children). And then we laugh, and behind the laughter is Hoover's terrible picture of 30 million people who must die unless there is some great intervention. But then again we think things are never really as bad as that; and something will turn up, and the worst will never be. And somehow all these phases of feeling are true and right in some sense. And in it all I do miss you, miss you greatly. How you and Arthur and I would talk things over if we were together.[14]

Herbert Hoover, again? Yes. When World War I broke out, he soon became aware that famine threatened Belgium. Britain was blockading Germany and not allowing food imports. The Germans had conquered Belgium and wrecked a good deal of it on their march through. The Germans, short of food themselves because of the blockade, put feeding Belgium at the bottom of their priorities. Somehow Hoover convinced the British that if they let him send grain ships to Belgium, it would strengthen Belgian attachment to the Allies without feeding the German army.

And somehow Hoover also convinced the Germans that if they allowed the grain ships into Belgium, Germany could stop sending any grain to Belgium and so feed its army, and this would mollify Belgians by making the consequences of German occupation less dire. Hoover was very persuasive.

After the war was over, Hoover continued in the famine-fighting business. He continued in his new career—that of "the Great Humanitarian."[15] And he did warn of thirty million famine deaths in the war's aftermath if nothing was done in the way of relief, and he did move heaven and earth to raise money for and ship food to Europe, from Russia to France.

Hoover's solution was to ship foodstuffs. Keynes's attempt was to take up the pen to try to change minds. When Keynes returned to England, he exploded with the publication of *The Economic Consequences of the Peace*, in which he excoriated short-sighted politicians who were, he felt, more interested in victory than in peace. He outlined alternative proposals. And he prophesied doom: "If we aim deliberately at the impoverishment of Central Europe, vengeance, I dare predict, will not limp. Nothing can then delay for long that final civil war between the forces of reaction and the despairing convulsions of revolution, before which the horrors of the late German war will fade into nothing, and which will destroy . . . the civilization and progress of our generation."[16]

If anything, he undersold what was to come.

The postwar trouble started with inflation. Market economies run off of the signals that prices give to economic decision makers about what it would be profitable to do, and if the prices are right, then what is profitable is also what advances societal well-being. But if decision makers do not understand what prices are, or if prices are systematically wrong, then accurate economic calculation becomes very difficult and growth suffers. We are not, here, talking about inflation as an upward creep of prices—1 or

2 or 5 percent per year, on average. That does not cause much trouble or confusion. But 10, 20, or 100 percent or more? Keynes commented on this very question in 1924:

> Lenin is said to have declared that the best way to destroy the capitalist system was to debauch the currency. By a continuing process of inflation, governments can confiscate, secretly and unobserved, an important part of the wealth . . . arbitrarily. . . . Those to whom the system brings windfalls, beyond their deserts and even beyond their expectations or desires, become "profiteers," who are the object of the hatred of the bourgeoisie, whom the inflationism has impoverished. . . . All permanent relations between debtors and creditors, which form the ultimate foundation of capitalism, become so utterly disordered as to be almost meaningless; and the process of wealth-getting degenerates into a gamble and a lottery. Lenin was certainly right. There is no subtler, no surer means of overturning the existing basis of society than to debauch the currency. The process engages all the hidden forces of economic law on the side of destruction, and does it in a manner which not one man in a million is able to diagnose.[17]

SO WHY THEN WOULD any government—except Lenin's— resort to a policy of high inflation?

Suppose that a government has made big promises, telling people they will have incomes that will allow them to purchase good things in life substantially exceeding what the government can finance through its taxes, or indeed, what the economy can produce. How can it then square that circle? One road is for the government to borrow by issuing bonds. By borrowing, it asks some to forgo purchasing the good things in life, and in return promises that they will have more social power over the good things—more money—in the future. When there is a gap between the goods and services citizens want the government to pay for, on the one hand, and, on the other, the taxes that the largely rich are willing to pay, governments have to fill that gap—and printing interest-paying bonds and selling them for cash is the obvious way.

Whether and how this works depends on the expectations of the individuals—mostly financiers—who buy and hold the bonds. How patient would they be? What kind of reward would they demand for holding and not selling the bonds? How trusting of the government would they be? And how long would their trust last? In the aftermath of World War I, financiers had limited patience and demanded healthy returns. When that is the psychology of financiers—as it was after World War I—the most likely outcome of resorting to large-scale debt finance is provided by the one-equation model that economists call the *fiscal theory of the price level*:

Price Level = (Nominal Debt) × (Interest Rate) /
(Real Debt Service Limit)

Take France in 1919 as an example. In June 1919, one French franc (F) was worth US$0.15. In 1919, France had a nominal national debt of F200 billion, on which it owed interest at a rate of 4 percent per year, so that the annual interest France paid on its national debt was F8 billion. If France's real debt service limit—the real resources the French government and electorate could mobilize to pay the interest on its debt—were equal to F8 billion per year at average 1919 prices, the equation would have balanced and France would not have experienced inflation in the 1920s:

1.00 = (nominal F200 billion × 4 percent per year) /
(real F8 billion / year)

But it turned out that the real resources the French government and electorate could mobilize to pay the interest on its debt amounted to only F3.2 billon (at average 1919 prices). And financiers did not have sufficient confidence to accept an interest rate of 4 percent per year—instead, they demanded 6 percent. So the *fiscal theory of the price level* equation was instead

3.75 = (nominal F200 billion × 6 percent per year) / (real F3.2 billion / year)

Equilibrium required that the average level of prices in France be 3.75 times their average level in 1919. And that would mean a value of the French franc of not F1 = US$0.15 but rather of F1 = US$0.04. Guess where the French franc ultimately stabilized in 1926? Yep: US$0.04. And that meant that France would have 20 percent average inflation for seven years—enough debauching of the currency to significantly distort economic planning and hinder real growth throughout the 1920s.

Worse outcomes came when financiers' trust broke down completely. That is the limit of *hyperinflation*, in which "worth less" becomes "worthless": the money printed and the bonds sold by the government turn out to have no value at all. The first post–World War I hyperinflations took place in the successor states to the old Austro-Hungarian Empire. After the war, the former empire, which had been a single economic unit, was split among seven countries, each with its own currency and its own high tariffs. The regional division of labor unwound.

Before the war ended, Joseph Schumpeter, just thirty-four years old at the time, had set out the resulting problem: "The material goods needed by the armies," he said, had been provided and would continue to be provided. "After the war, we will be left . . . with a 'monetary problem.'" He used an analogy, saying that countries paying for the war would be "in the position of an entrepreneur whose factory burnt down and now has to enter the losses in his books."[18]

Joseph Schumpeter was finance minister of the new Austrian Republic by 1919. He favored an immediate and substantial wealth tax on all real, industrial, commercial, residential, and financial property to pay off the debt. The rest of the cabinet, including Minister of Foreign Affairs Otto Bauer, said yes to the wealth tax. But they wanted the proceeds to be used for "socialization": buying up large Austrian companies, making them more efficient, and then using the profits from higher efficiency to first raise workers' wages and only second to pay off the debt. Schumpeter parried that if socialization was "efficient," then it did not need to be financed by the wealth tax. It would be what we now call an LBO, a leveraged buyout, and efficient LBOs finance themselves.

Schumpeter was fired. The cabinet dissolved into squabbling. The wealth tax was never levied.

Instead, money printing presses went: "brrrrrr . . ." Before World War I, the Austrian crown had been worth a little less than 20 US cents. By the late summer of 1922 the crown was worth 0.01 of a cent. The League of Nations—the international organization established at the end of World War I—provided a hard-currency loan on the condition that the Austrian government surrender control over its own currency and finances. The budget was balanced by severe cuts in expenditures and higher taxes, and Austria remained depressed, with high unemployment, for half a decade.

In Germany prices rose a trillionfold: what had cost 4 Reichsmarks in 1914 cost 4 trillion by the end of 1923. After the war, with respect to Germany, financiers had next to no patience and demanded exorbitant returns. The problem was the reparations that the Allies had imposed on Germany at the Treaty of Versailles, and the fact that it was absolute electoral poison for any German politician wanting to work out a plan to actually pay them. The German situation was not helped by the fact that it was also electoral poison for French or British politicians to work out a feasible plan to actually make substantial reparations deliveries, for then they would be assisting German workers in stealing jobs from British and French workers, who were then crowded out of their own domestic markets.[19]

The problem could perhaps have been finessed. France and Britain could have bought ownership shares of German companies with their reparations monies and then been satisfied with the resulting income. German leaders could have induced their wealthy citizens to sell their ownership shares by levying higher taxes. But that would have required Allied governments willing to accept such a postponement, as well as transformation of short-term demands for reparations payments now into long-term ownership shares, along with a German government strong enough to levy the taxes. The German government preferred to resist over figuring out a way to pay.

And so the bulk of the reparations burden was never paid. What was paid was financed by American investors. They made loans to Germany that Germany then turned around and transferred to the Allies. The American loans were a speculation on the success of Germany's postwar Weimar Republic government. That speculation was not wise ex post. The German reparations burden was forgiven during the Great Depression.

The imposition of those reparations in the first place turned out to be a very costly political decision, for it set off a chain of events that ultimately led to the Depression. The weaknesses the reparations created did not lead directly to the rise of Adolf Hitler—that came later. But they were key to the destabilization of the Weimar Republic and to its pre-Hitler collapse from a parliamentary democracy into a regime of Caesarist rule by presidential decree.

How big and important was this German hyperinflation? Back in 1914, the German currency, the Reichsmark, had been worth 25 US cents. By the end of 1919, the Reichsmark was worth just 1 cent. It then recovered somewhat, reaching a value of 2 cents by the end of 1920. But the government kept spending and printing, and by the end of 1921, the mark was back down to 0.33 of a cent, an inflation rate of 500 percent per year, 16 percent per month, 0.5 percent per day. By the end of 1922 the mark was worth only 0.0025 cents, an inflation rate of 13,000 percent per year, 50 percent per month, 1.35 percent per day.

For a while the government welcomed the inflation: it was easier to finance spending by printing money than by trying to collect taxes. Industrial and mercantile interests also benefited: they borrowed from banks and repaid them in badly depreciated marks. For a while, labor benefited too: unemployment almost vanished, and in the early stages of the inflation, at least real wages and workers' purchasing power did not fall. But in January 1923 the French government, to score domestic political points, sent in its army to occupy the Ruhr Valley and collect commodities at gunpoint. The German government and people responded with passive resistance. The inhabitants of the Ruhr went on strike. And the German government printed even more money to try to maintain the incomes of the passive resisters. By the end of 1923, the mark was worth 0.000000000025 of a cent, an inflation rate of 9,999,999,900 percent per year, averaging 364 percent per month, or 5 percent per day.

Of the countries that experienced post–World War I inflation, Germany was hit the worst, with prices increasing, as mentioned above, by a trillionfold. But a number of other countries also saw inflation climb to devastating levels. In Russia prices rose four billionfold. In Poland they rose two and a half millionfold. In Austria, prices rose two thousandfold. In France, inflation was only sevenfold, which, as we noted, meant that investors in French government debt from 1918 could, in 1927, purchase only one-seventh as much with their bonds as they could have had they spent rather than invested their money in 1918.

Driving this massive wave of inflation was the European focus on somehow appeasing those who had just lived through World War I: the maimed, the starved, and those grieving for lost brothers, fathers, husbands, and sons—in the minds of many, the fallen needed to have died for something. So political leaders tried to create a "land fit for heroes." In practice, this meant a government commitment to social welfare and infrastructure programs to make life better, plus extension of voting rights to the male working class, and even to women. This had consequences. In Britain, for example, less than half of adult males could vote before World War I. In the election of 1918, the socialist Labour Party multiplied its vote sevenfold.

There followed disability insurance for war veterans, unemployment insurance (so that returning soldiers did not have to beg in the street), mammoth government expenditures (to repair war damage), more mammoth government expenditures (to make up for all the infrastructure and other investments not made during the war), plus even more mammoth government expenditures (to pay off the war debts). Voters and heroes demanded that governments compensate them for their property that had been destroyed or that had lost its value from war-induced dislocations. And voters and heroes demanded anew their Polanyian rights. Old-age pensions, public housing, and public health insurance moved onto the agenda. Satisfying these demands would take vast resources. The world's governments, with their national economies, were all poorer than they had been in 1914, but the urge to spend was strong. The right did not dare resist it. The left did not have enough of an electoral mandate to make the rich pay. Financiers did not have the confidence to fill the gap by holding the resulting debt at low interest rates. The result was that the fiscal theory of the price level came into play—and inflation.

From a narrow economists' perspective, inflation is simply a tax, a rearrangement, and a confusion. It is a tax on cash, because your cash becomes worth less between when you acquire it and when you spend it. It is a rearrangement, as those who have borrowed pay back their loans in depreciated currency, while those who have lent have to accept the depreciated currency. And it is a source of confusion, because it is difficult to calculate whether what you—as a company, a household, or an individual—are doing makes economic sense when the numbers entered into your account books at different dates correspond to different amounts of real purchasing power.

All of these elements of inflation, and especially hyper-inflation—the tax, the rearrangement, and the confusion—are destroyers of trust. Trust in the economy, in society, in governments. And this destruction of trust, according to Keynes, was "fast rendering impossible a continuation of the social and economic order of the nineteenth century. But [European leaders had] no plan for replacing it." People who were not rich but were well-off pillars of their community, who generally saw no great need to move to the political right, even as they feared the redistributionist plans of the left, were disturbed by inflation's erosion of nominal forms of wealth. They felt cheated, and those who held government bonds felt cheated by the government. It was impossible for them to see that the market took just as it gave—and that it should, in fact, be blessed, not cursed. And no wonder—they were in the midst of seeing the abrupt revocation of their Polanyian right to stable finances and a certain standard of living.

NEARLY EVERYONE WITH POWER or property sought a return to what US president Warren G. Harding called "normalcy." Whatever had gotten broken during World War I needed to be fixed. And for many, that meant fixing the gold standard: the half-century-long general commitment of all the largest trading countries to buy and sell their currencies for gold at a fixed price. In the immediate aftermath of World War I, countries agreed that they had to peg their currencies back to gold—and eventually they did.[20]

That pleased the rich because it would guard against further inflation. In other words, any tendency toward inflation would generate, through capital flight or high import demand, a line of bankers at the central bank trying to turn currency into gold, unwinding inflationary pressures. Only Britain, with the Bank of England as the conductor of the international gold-standard order, got to raise and lower interest rates at home. This seemed a good system both for Britain and for world trade. After all, the pre–World War I gold standard had supported the fastest and broadest half century of economic growth of any era up until then.

During World War I, European finance ministers discovered the benefits of inflation—indeed, given governments' unwillingness to raise taxes sufficiently to fight the Great War, they found it to be a necessity. But you could not inflate if you kept your promise to buy and sell your currency for its fixed gold parity. So countries had dropped the gold standard during the war. And afterward, countries seeking normalcy sought to return to it.

Much easier sought than done. Wartime and postwar inflation had, roughly, tripled prices worldwide. Banks and governments made sure that their transactions stayed greased by holding a roughly constant fraction of their payments flow in the form of gold assets, gold as reserves. Triple prices and you triple the nominal value of transactions. Triple the nominal value of transactions, and you triple the gold you need to hold—unless you are willing to change the equivalency scale between gold bars and your currency.

After wartime and postwar inflations and hyperinflations, the interwar gold standard was attempting to run itself with only one-third of the gold-as-reserves ratio of asset holdings to transaction amounts that had been needed for even semismooth functioning before the war. It simply could not be expected to work.

One place where it did not work was Britain. Even though wartime and postwar inflation was smallest in Britain, Britain found itself facing a fraught situation. It had seen a currency depreciation. Instead of the pegged value of GB£1 = $4.86 that had existed in July 1914, the market seemed to want to settle the value of the British pound at slightly less than $4.00. In advising British officials on how to respond, the financiers assured them that the government would win a great deal of long-term market trust by enacting austerity measures to restore the £1 = $4.86 pre–World War I parity. The result, the financiers said, would be increased stability, lower interest rates, and faster growth. All the financiers sounded confident and credible.

The ruling politicians chose to follow their financiers' advice. But in an economy where the market wanted a pound to be valued at $3.80, the austerity measures needed to follow through on their plan required a 30 percent reduction in the average value of all wages and prices. In other words, deflation, which quickly led to high unemployment, bankruptcy driven by foreign competition, and an unrealistic exchange rate.

The decider in Britain in the mid-1920s was the finance minister—chancellor of the exchequer—Winston Churchill. His private secretary, P. J. Grigg, reports a dinner in 1924 hosted by Churchill at which supporters and opponents of returning the pound to its prewar peg argued. One diner painted a grim picture of hobbled exports, unemployment, substantial downward pressure on wages, and waves of strikes. The guest was John Maynard Keynes.

But hadn't John Maynard Keynes burned his bridges with the British establishment by denouncing the British government's negotiating position after the war in the strongest possible terms?

Yes and no. By this time, he had attained a stature that meant he floated across even burned bridges.[21]

The Economic Consequences of the Peace had made Keynes famous. In the words of biographer Robert Skidelsky, the economist spoke "like an angel with the knowledge of an expert." Keynes was propelled by "passion and despair" and showed an extraordinary mastery not just of economics but also of the words that were needed to make economics persuasive. He became a power to be conciliated—and at least listened to.

For after World War I, Keynes felt compelled to use what power he could command to restore civilization. Before the war, the world had been in a good place: economically, socially, culturally, and politically. Then the ruling elites had broken it. Now a road back had to be found. But simply winding back the clock to the 1914 exchange-rate parity of GB£1 = US$4.86 would not do the job. Fundamentals had changed profoundly. Smart adaptation was needed. Keynes's influence, however, while sufficient to be invited to Churchill's historic dinner, was not sufficient to nudge history, or, more precisely, politicians—or, more precisely still, Churchill.[22]

In 1919 the economic risks of returning to the prewar parity of pound to gold and dollar seemed vague, distant, and uncertain. The benefits of setting out on a path of further experimentation seemed unnecessary. The political risks of postponing the return, of continuing the experimentation, seemed large and immediate. The political risks of returning were the same as the economic risks: vague, distant, and uncertain. The decision was made to return Britain to the gold standard.[23]

Great Britain returned to the gold standard in 1925. British industries, from coal mining to textiles to chemical and steel manufacturers, found themselves facing severe competitive difficulties. This resulted in unemployment in export industries and a push for wage reductions to make domestic industry more competitive. Moreover, sterling speculators could see what the Bank of England could not: that returning to the gold standard at an overvalued parity weakened the pound sterling, creating a vulnerability. They began to pull their money out of Britain. In order to balance its payments, the Bank of England had to keep British interest rates above American interest rates. Higher interest rates depressed investment, further increasing unemployment.

Social conflict broke out in Britain over the distribution of the adjustment burden, ultimately leading to a general strike in 1926. As a result, the British government began to subsidize its declining and uncompetitive industries. But this response simply allowed the economy not to adjust to its changed circumstances—How would it ever boom?

At the end of the 1920s, citizens and voters in Western Europe at least could look back on not one but two low and dishonest decades. Because of World War I, the 1910s had been the last gasp of the age in which emperors, aristocrats, generals, politicians, and soldiers had been in the saddle—and the result had been a near-complete human catastrophe. Then, in the aftermath of the war, came the 1920s, a decade in which calculators, economists, and politicians were in the saddle. While their policies had not killed ten million people, they had failed to bring rapid growth, stable incomes, stable prices, and full-enough employment.

AMERICAN ISOLATIONISM IN THE 1920s was not limited to avoiding foreign diplomatic and military entanglements. Commercial globalization went into reverse—and not just in the United States, either. Up until 1950, globalization went into recession and retreat worldwide.

Some of it was that in times of unemployment nations jealously guarded their markets, reserving them for their own production. Some of it was that nations and their rulers feared that interdependence could be weaponized—too interdependent an economy, that could be hobbled or crippled by an embargo, was now seen as a political and perhaps a security risk. More of it was that interests that were being outcompeted and impoverished by globalization gained a greater political voice in polities that were increasingly democratic or demagogic. But most of it was that domestic manufacturing productivity levels themselves leaped ahead so rapidly without diverging substantially across countries. Whether it pays to trade something across oceans depends on (a) how high its production cost is relative to how much it costs to transport it, and (b) how large the proportional gaps in costs of production and demand for products are in different parts of the world that fuel potential gains from the trade.[24] The coming of mass production and the assembly line caused (a) to shrink and did not increase (b). All of this meant that come 1950 international trade was back to the 9 percent of global economic activity that it had been in 1800. The globalization cycle had been fully reversed.[25]

Furthermore, many influential Americans felt that curbing immigration should be an urgent priority.

There had been resistance to free immigration and open borders long before World War I. US senator Henry Cabot Lodge—a nativist, WASPy Boston Brahmin and a Republican—had long beaten the drum, as had Progressive Woodrow Wilson, seeking to avoid social Darwinist corruption of the American race, by which they meant white people, a category they defined very narrowly.[26] Most Italian immigrants, Lodge had said, were good, hardworking people. But some were members of the Mafia, and so it was necessary to exclude them. Most Polish immigrants, Lodge said, were good, hardworking people, too. But there were terrorists among them—after all, it had been a second-generation Polish immigrant anarchist, Leon Czolgosz, who had murdered President McKinley. And so it was necessary to exclude Poles as well.

Most Irish, Lodge had argued, were also good people—including many who had already been in America for generations, especially those who were voters in Massachusetts, and who had elected the state representatives who had elected Lodge to the US Senate. But among the more recent immigrants were those socialist-anarchist bomb-placing Molly McGuires. And so it was no less necessary to exclude the Irish.

Anarchists were a danger—and while few Jews were anarchists, many anarchists were Jews. And Jews were generally a problem, and specifically, a political problem. The Democrats were courting the Jewish vote—witness Woodrow Wilson's nomination to the Supreme Court of Louis Brandeis, a man Lodge declared underqualified and dangerously radical—and this would distort American politics in ways awful and conspiratorial. White people of British, German, Dutch, French, and Scandinavian descent were assets to America, in their view. Irish were on the borderline—and were quickly assimilated to "British" by politicians who had to run in districts where the Irish diaspora cast substantial votes. Others were more trouble than they were worth.

Setting aside the occasional self-serving specific instance, many voting Americans were of Lodge's way of thinking—or worse. Between 1900 and 1930 the economic and social position of America's Black middle class—W. E. B. Du Bois's "Talented Tenth"—was reduced to rubble. Hollywood reinvigorated the Ku Klux Klan. It was the left-of-center president Woodrow Wilson, too, who segregated the federal civil service and set personnel management to downgrading Black workers. Progressive Republican president Theodore Roosevelt had invited Booker T. Washington to lunch at the White House. His cousin, Democrat Franklin D. Roosevelt, had during World War I signed and transmitted the order segregating the bathrooms of what was then the State, War, and Navy building in the White House complex.[27]

And by the mid-1920s, immigration restrictions against eastern and southern Europeans took hold. Back in 1914, more than 1.2 million immigrants had come to the United States. By the mid-1920s, however, the immigration restrictions had fixed the number of immigrants allowed in each year at only 160,000 or so. Moreover, there were fixed quotas for each nation. The quotas for northern and western Europe were more than sufficient for the demand. The far lower quotas for immigrants from southern and eastern Europe were decidedly not. By 1930, there were 7 million missing Americans—people who would have immigrated were it not for Henry Cabot Lodge and company's legislative success in 1924. But America had kept building houses as though those 7 million had arrived and were living in them. And it was valuing houses and apartment buildings as though those 7 million were purchasing them or paying rent.

Truth be told, many Americans were not alarmed by the turn inward. The United States of the 1920s had plenty to do, very much including becoming a middle-class economy of radios, consumer appliances, automobiles, and suburbs. The utopian qualities of the Jazz Age weren't even sobered by the prohibition of the sale of alcohol. Nearly thirty million motor vehicles, one for every five Americans, were on the road by 1929. Assembly lines powered by electric motors in factories arranged for the convenience of workers made the post–World War I United States the richest society the world had ever seen. The world took notice.

In the middle of the 1800s, English engineers had spied some regularities in the way Americans seemed to do things. American manufacturing industries made simpler and rougher goods. American manufactures used much less skilled labor. American manufactures used up—the British would say "wasted"—lots of raw materials. American manufacturers paid their workers—even their unskilled workers—much better than did the British. And American manufacturers seemed to run the process of production relying on machines and organizations rather than on workers' brains and hands.

This "American system of manufactures" was the brainchild of Eli Whitney, an inventor-promotor famous for inventing the cotton gin, which made American short-staple cotton practical as an input for textile spinning. Truth be told, Eli Whitney was one-quarter inventor, one-quarter salesman, one-quarter maniac, and one-quarter fraud. The idea born of this combination was that American manufacturers could make the pieces of their goods to better, tighter specifications in order to make parts *interchangeable*—the barrel of one firearm would fit the trigger mechanism of another. It was an idea that Eli Whitney could never quite make work, but it remained a very compelling idea.

The diffusion of American-system techniques played a substantial part in the late nineteenth-century growth of American manufacturing. Through the intermediation of the machine tool industry, companies such as Singer (making sewing machines), McCormick (making reapers and other agricultural machinery), and the Western Wheel Works (making bicycles) all adopted the strategy of trying to make their parts interchangeable, and so economize on the handling, fitting, and finishing costs that took up so much of skilled workers' time.[28]

Economizing costs, certainly, held the attention of nineteenth-century manufacturers. But more was needed: they aimed at also producing a higher-quality (though, note, not the highest-quality) product than would otherwise be possible, which they could then sell for a premium price.

The key difference between Henry Ford and his predecessors in using the "American system" for metalworking—and between Ford and his competitors abroad—was that Ford's focus was not always on making a superior product (to sell to rich men with chauffeurs) but rather on making a low-priced product he could sell to as many people as possible.

How? Ford minimized his costs by building a capital-intensive plant that was very good at building automobiles, but not at building anything else. This capital intensity carried risk. The productivity and profitability of the Ford plant depended on a high rate of production. This was achieved in part by "moving the work to the men" by means of the assembly line (which became another fundamental tenet of mass production). Ford engineers had found a method to speed up slow men. The pace of work could be increased. The monitoring of the worker could be increased. Unskilled workers could be substituted for skilled ones. The task of management was made much simpler than it had ever been before: the assembly line forced the pace of the slower workers and made it obvious where bottlenecks were occurring. Fixed overhead costs were spread out over larger and larger volumes of production, and thus lower and lower prices became possible.[29]

Henry Ford would have been happy if he could have found qualified workers for his assembly lines at low rates of pay. But he could not. Work on Ford's emerging assembly line was brutal. Workers paid the standard wages for unskilled labor at Ford's Detroit factory—a little less than $2 a day—quit at astonishing rates. In one year, 1913, Ford had an average annual labor force of 13,600, and yet 50,400 people quit or were fired. Ford's workers—sped up, automated, short term, alienated, and about to quit—seemed like obvious fodder for recruitment into the Industrial Workers of the World, and Ford's profits were very vulnerable to IWW-style wildcat strikes.

Ford's solution was a massive increase in wages: to $5 a day for unskilled workers, so long as their family circumstances and deportment satisfied Ford. By 1915, annual turnover was down from 370 percent to 16 percent. Many men who had found a Ford factory job not worth keeping at $1.75 a day found it more than bearable for $5 a day. Many more lined up outside the Ford factory for the chance to work at what appeared to them to be (and, for those who did not mind the pace of the assembly line much, was) an incredible boondoggle of a job.[30]

In the highly unequal, highly stratified America of the 1910s and 1920s, the idea that a high-paid, blue-collar, semiskilled worker could be well in the upper half of the income distribution seemed radical. Yet it was happening in Detroit. And social commentators, and Ford's imitators, envisioned the spread of mass production to the rest of the economy, making Detroit the rule rather than the exception. For all of this Ford became a celebrity, and a symbol. The extraordinary productivity of mass production, as some nameless publicist began to call it, offered the prospect of a ride to utopia via technology alone. Between the world wars, Henry Ford was—as Aldous Huxley made him out to be in his ambiguously dystopian novel *Brave New World*—a legend, a mythical figure, a near-Moses to the world.

Not everyone was convinced, and a few were outright suspicious. The boogiemen of Lodge's dire warnings, the anarchists and the socialists, were real, even if much of their influence over events wasn't. And however ambiguous, Huxley's *Brave New World* was still clearly dystopian. Fordism as fictionalized by Huxley gave rise to a world not everyone would, or should, wish to live in.

Like many of the long century's most prominent figures, Ford managed to retain much of the world's regard even as his ideas became wilder, crankier, crueler, and more prejudiced. His brave new world of mass production was certainly a shock to all who thought, as Polanyi had, that they deserved stability. But it brought wonderful new, visible, and tangible things, including radios, cars, and square footage. A little instability could then be dealt with, and some of the wild and cranky and cruel could then be overlooked. All in all, America's mass-produced future looked bright.

Increasingly, America's decision makers believed that the key to the modern business enterprise lay in creating enormous economies of scale that could be realized by a large, vertically integrated organization able to plan the flow of raw materials into the factory and the flow of finished goods out into distribution channels. The realization of these economies of scale required the highest output, as well as the lowest practicable prices to make sure that the output could be sold. But corporations like

Ford's were proving this formula to be practical, or at least practical enough.

Theodore N. Vail, president of American Telephone and Telegraph in the early twentieth century, distinguished two different strategies for generating net revenue: "by a large percentage of profit on a small business, or a small percentage of profit on a large business." And in America, the second was best.[31]

Manufacturers of mass-produced items, however, faced a problem literally of their own creation. Once the market had been saturated, replacement demand of the same product dropped considerably. Producers needed consumers who would not simply "replace" but would "upgrade." This was a big problem for Ford. He had adhered to changelessness for ideological as well as production-based reasons. It became an especially knotty problem because, it turned out, consumers, unlike Ford, wanted novelty. They were (and are) willing to pay a premium to have not only a car but a car different from some, even most, of their neighbors.[32]

Aldous Huxley had believed that it would require sophisticated psychological manipulation to persuade people to buy what mass production could produce, which is exactly what he depicts in *Brave New World*.[33] The real world proved much simpler: make it, and tell people you've made it (with some pictures of people using it, having more fun than you will ever have in your lifetime), and the public will buy it.

What Ford wrestled with, Alfred P. Sloan, at General Motors, embraced. Make the guts of the cars the same, so as to take full advantage of economies of scale, put the guts in differently colored boxes, and rely on advertising to create different auras surrounding different lines of cars. Some psychology was certainly involved, but sophisticated? No.

It is natural to be of two minds about this surge of product differentiation. It seems wasteful and deceptive. Yet product differentiation, monopolistic competition, and even advertising are all genuinely popular. Mass production plus mass consumption is

what made the creation of America as a middle-class society possible—a middle-class society made up increasingly of people living in suburban houses and using automobiles to commute and
shop, with washing machines, refrigerators, electric irons, electric
and gas stoves, and much more. A whole host of inventions and
technologies that greatly transformed the part of economic life
that takes place within the household became interwoven with
the public's understanding of Polanyian rights.

Back before World War I, the United States had had the most
virulent business cycle in the industrialized part of the world. A
huge crash and depression occurred after the 1873 bankruptcy of
Jay Cooke and Company, then the largest investment bank in the
nation, when the public subsidies for the Northern Pacific Railway that it had counted on failed to materialize. Another major
railroad-crash depression started in 1884. Another depression ensued in the early 1890s, when fears that the United States might
abandon the gold standard set British and urban eastern capital
fleeing the country—though J. P. Morgan profited handsomely
from betting that Grover Cleveland would stay the gold-standard
course, and lending him the cash to allow him to do so. Then
there was the Panic of 1901, generated as a byproduct of a fight
between E. H. Harriman and J. P. Morgan over control of the
Northern Pacific Railway. The Panic of 1907 came next, and was
only kept from turning into a Great Depression–like event when
J. P. Morgan decided to do what the Bank of England had been
doing since the 1820s—backing banks that were in trouble until
the crisis passed. The Bank of England could do so by printing banknotes that were legal tender. Morgan did so by printing
"clearing house certificates" and telling everyone that if they did
not accept them as if they were cash, he would ruin them after the
crisis was over—and he had a good memory.[34]

Afterward, however, politicians and bankers alike thought it
was not for the best that central-banking panic-fighting functions
could be carried out in the private sector by a ruthless and greedy,

if highly competent, financier. The United States had not had anything like a central bank since Andrew Jackson had vetoed the Second Bank of the United States' recharter as a threat to liberty in the 1830s. The United States got a central bank in 1913, the Federal Reserve, tasked with keeping the financial system sound and liquid so that the wheels of commerce and industry could turn smoothly. And so, after World War I, for about a decade, for most Americans, the market gaveth and rarely tooketh, so blessed be the market. And all this was achieved without the bother of taking on hegemonic responsibility for stabilizing the world as a whole. It was enough to stabilize the United States.

One substantial cheerleader and bridge builder for the rapid buildout of American industrialization in the 1920s was Herbert Hoover. Woodrow Wilson had pulled Hoover off of his Belgian relief projects and set him up as the "food czar" of America. Congress in 1919 gave Hoover $100 million to spend—and he raised another $100 million—to pay for postwar food relief. With the change of administration from Democrats back to Republicans in 1921, President Warren Harding made a concession to bipartisanship, or rather progressivism, and to the idea of a can-do government, by naming Hoover secretary of commerce, a job he held from 1921 to 1928.[35]

Hoover thought the secretary of commerce ought to be the management consultant for every single company in America, and the person who drove the other departments to cooperate and aid American industry. He promoted aviation. He promoted radio. He was ringmaster for the federal aid response to the Great Mississippi Flood of 1927. And he ran for and got the Republican presidential nomination in the summer of 1928, and then beat Democrat Al Smith in the 1928 presidential election.

At the end of 1928, in his last State of the Union message to Congress, President Calvin Coolidge began with, "No Congress of the United States ever assembled, on surveying the state of the

Union, has met with a more pleasing prospect than that which appears at the present time." All, the outgoing president declared, should "regard the present with satisfaction and anticipate the future with optimism." And indeed, nearly everyone in America in the 1920s had good reasons to be optimistic: the United States appeared to be riding a wave of innovation and invention that was carrying the country toward higher prosperity more rapidly than any previous generation would have believed.[36]

Automobiles and other consumer durables, especially radios, became leading sectors. The electric motor and electricity became prime movers in industrial production. The growth of the utilities sector was interlinked with these. With electrification, potential demand for the services provided by utilities was immense, rapidly growing, and predictable. Their plant costs were fixed. And nearly all utilities had near monopolies.

The clear utilities strategy was to use the underlying soundness of the industry as collateral to borrow money from banks, use that money to purchase more utilities, take advantage of engineering economies of scale to lower costs, reap the profits, and make sure the profits were shared with the right people, in order to keep potential regulators sweet on the industry. Samuel Insull, a utilities magnate based in Chicago, became a prince of infrastructure with this strategy, and he might well have dominated midcentury American capitalism had not the jealousy and greed of investment bankers led them to withdraw their support for him.

Not that there was no malcontent. In the United States the rising concentration of wealth provoked a widespread feeling that something had gone wrong. Explaining exactly what, however, was difficult, and no faction or group was able to effectively turn that malcontent into political energy. The Populists had been broken in the 1890s by a combination of anti-Black prejudice and an increased sense that inequality was regional and poverty was rural. And the Progressive tide ebbed as moderates embraced only moderate reforms. Voters, meanwhile, continued to elect Republican presidents who were more or less satisfied with American economic and social developments, and who believed that "the business of America is business."[37]

Still, the managers who ran America's firms and the politicians who got elected were not oblivious to the Progressive challenge. Scared of what unionization or a shift to left-wing politics might bring, and concerned about the welfare of their workers, American business leaders in the 1920s developed "welfare capitalism." Social-work professionals employed by the firm provided counseling and visited workers' homes. The businesses offered stock-purchase plans, to help workers save for retirement, and sickness, accident, and life insurance.[38]

With welfare capitalism unevenly distributed, socialism and social democracy were deemed moot, unnecessary, and un-American. The long-run interest of American companies was to take care of their workers, a fact as obvious as Henry Ford's $5-a-day wage and the Pullman Company's worker housing.

As the 1920s proceeded, Americans forgot about the deep recessions of the pre–World War I period and began to accept that they were living in a "new era" of faster economic growth and general prosperity. The recently established Federal Reserve had the tools to calm the business cycle. The systematic application of science to technology in research laboratories was generating an ever-accelerating stream of new inventions. This world was, if you looked selectively at the facts, brave and new and ambiguously utopian. Why shouldn't people in America in the 1920s have expected prosperity to continue, and economic growth to accelerate?

One consequence of this seemingly permanent "new era" was that financial asset prices went up.

To properly value any given financial asset, first we need to take the rate of return the market requires on safe assets—for example, the bonds of the world's most trustworthy government. Second, we add on an appropriate adjustment for the risk of the asset. Third, subtract from that adjusted rate of return the rate at which you expect the payments from the asset to grow (for a constant-coupon bond, that rate will be zero; for a stock, it will be the expected rate of earnings growth). Call this the "adjusted yield factor." Fourth, divide the current payout of the asset—its bond coupon or stock dividend payment—by the adjusted yield factor. This gives the price the asset should sell for. Americans in the 1920s who bothered to do all four steps did so with presumptions that told them the asset's price had to go up.

The result was widespread faith in the permanent "new era" of low risks, low-interest rates produced by successful macroeconomic stabilization, rapid growth produced by new technology, and confidence that in the future, depressions would be few and small. Concretely, this meant very high prices for financial assets, especially stocks, and especially stock in high-tech companies. Monetary economist (and Prohibition enthusiast) Irving Fisher ruined his reputation as an economic forecaster for all time with his late-1929 declaration that "stock prices have reached what looks like a permanently high plateau." True, he declared this to a near-universal sea of heads nodding in agreement.[39]

That the US stock market did go off its rails is clear. A host of anomalies in stock market values indicate that those who were paying for stocks in the summer and early fall of 1929 had not the slightest rational clue of what they were doing.

Consider the closed-end investment fund. A closed-end investment fund is a pure holding company. Investors were supposed to pool their resources and limit their risk by buying stock in this holding company, this closed-end investment fund, which would then buy and hold for them the stock of one hundred or more individual operating companies. The theory was that the management of the fund would be better able to pick stocks and manage risk than individual investors.

In practice, this meant that the only assets of a closed-end investment fund were its financial assets: the stocks and bonds that it held. By elementary principles of rational finance, therefore, the fundamental value of a closed-end investment fund was nothing more than the current value of the stocks and bonds that made up its portfolio. Yet by the fall of 1929 closed-end investment funds were selling at a 40 percent premium relative to their net asset values.[40]

According to the "rules of the game" of the gold standard, a country that receives an inflow of gold is supposed to use it to back an expansion of its money stock, which in turn triggers inflation. That inflation then encourages the country to import more and export less so trade rebalances. But neither the United States nor France was willing to tolerate domestic inflation. They squirreled the gold away in their government vaults. Both began to view their gold reserves not as shock absorbers but rather as national treasures, to be defended and hoarded—and any outward flow would be viewed a defeat.

The United States and France held more than 60 percent of the world's monetary gold by 1929. The global price level was twice what it had been in 1914. Outside the United States and France, countries undertaking to trade did so with only a fraction of the world's gold. As a consequence, a single gold coin or gold bar had to do more than five times the work that it normally would have of cushioning shocks, providing liquidity, and creating trust.[41]

After the fact, economists Friedrich von Hayek and Lionel Robbins blamed the Great Depression that started in 1929 on the Federal Reserve's unwillingness to raise interest rates earlier. They pointed to the Fed's decision (at the request of the Reichsbank and the Bank of England) to cut the discount rate at which it lent to banks from 4 to 3.5 percent in the spring of 1927. They claimed that this shift in the rate was clearly inflationary, that it made money too inexpensively available to the economy, and that it ultimately drove the inflationary boom that led to the speculative mania of 1929.[42]

We know today that this is wrong because we have the benefit of knowing what excessively inflationary monetary policy looks like: it looks like the United States between 1965 and 1973. The late 1920s were nothing of the sort: overall prices remained constant. The goods and product markets showed no sign of too much money chasing too few goods.

Economists such as Milton Friedman make a more convincing case, claiming that the Federal Reserve was not too expansionary but too contractionary in the run-up to the 1929 stock market crash. From 1928 on, Federal Reserve officials began to worry that gold might start flowing out if they did not raise interest rates. They also worried that stock prices were too high, that they might end in a crash, and that such a crash might bring on a depression. So they took measures to try to choke off both gold outflows and stock market speculation by making it more expensive to borrow money. They succeeded in the first. They failed in the second.[43]

It seems as though the Federal Reserve's attempts to keep stock market overvaluation from growing large enough to trigger a crash were counterproductive. In fact, they triggered a crash—and then a recession—all by themselves. The US economy entered a cyclical downturn in June 1929. By that time, the German economy had already been in recession for almost a year. The Great Depression had begun.

7

The Great Depression

Understanding the Great Depression begins by looking back at the first economists' debates early in the 1800s. Economists then saw the market economy emerging. They worried that things would not necessarily fit together smoothly. Might not the farmers be unable to sell the crops they grew to the artisans, because the artisans could not sell the products they made to the merchants, who would be unable to make money carrying artisans' products to the farmers, because the farmers would not purchase anything?

The French economist Jean-Baptiste Say wrote in 1803 that there was no cause for worry. Such a "general glut"—economy-wide "overproduction" or "under demand," and consequent mass unemployment—was incoherent. Nobody, Say argued, would ever produce anything for sale unless they expected to use the money they earned in order to buy something else.[1] And so "by a metaphysical necessity," as subsequent-generation economist John Stuart Mill wrote in 1829, summarizing Say's 1803 argument, there could be no imbalance between the aggregate value of planned production for sale, the aggregate value of planned sales, and the aggregate value of planned purchases. This is "Say's Law."[2]

Now Say stressed that this equality only applied to economy-wide totals. Individual commodities could be and often were in excess demand, with buyers unsatisfied and rapidly increasing the prices they were willing to pay—or excess supply, with sellers rapidly cutting the prices at which they had planned to sell. The idea that you could have excess demand for (and therefore high profits in) scarce commodities, or excess supply of (and therefore losses in) overabundant commodities—this was not a bug but a feature. The market provided incentives to quickly shift resources to erase such imbalances. But a deficiency of demand relative to production of well-nigh everything? That, Say said, was impossible.

Other economists questioned Say's conclusion. What if you wanted to buy before you had sold—if the artisan wanted to buy food before the merchant had come around to buy the textiles? That, said Say, was what banks and trade credit were for: "Merchants know well enough how to find substitutes for the product serving as the medium of exchange." Karl Marx dismissed this as the "childish babble of a Say."[3] One did not just sell in order to buy: one might be forced to sell in order to pay off an old debt, if credit that had been extended by some bank was withdrawn. In that case, the demand for goods was in the past and could not in the present balance out your supply. If everyone was trying to sell in order to pay off old debts, there would indeed be a "general glut." And if those who were calling in loans saw businesses collapsing into bankruptcy around them, they would be unlikely to provide "substitutes for the product serving as the medium of exchange."

Say was wrong. As economist Thomas Robert Malthus had vaguely intuited in 1819, and as the young John Stuart Mill had nailed it in 1829, there can be an excess demand for money along with an excess supply of pretty much everything else.[4]

If a manufacturer has excess demand for a good, he can respond by raising its price. If it is a good you want, you can respond by being willing to pay more for it. And this, in turn, may well cause you to want to have more money with which to buy more of this good and others like it. Something similar happens when there is an excess demand for money. People who are demanding it can "buy" more money by working longer and harder. But because money is special, you can do something else as well. You can stop your spending. And when you stop spending, your counterparties lose their markets, their income, and their work.[5]

If money is in excess demand and so an increasing number of goods and services swing into excess supply, factories will be shut and workers will be jobless. That shareholders then have no dividends, lenders have no interest payments, and workers have no wages will only further widen the gap between the aggregate-supply productive potential of the economy and the current level of aggregate demand.

Say came to recognize the point that Marx and Mill (and others) would make after the British Canal Panic of 1825.[6] The banks and merchants of England decided in late 1825 that they had made too many loans to too many counterparties whose investments were not turning out well. So they stopped advancing cash in return for merchants' promised future earnings from customers. Thus, Say wrote, "commerce found itself deprived at a stroke of the advances on which it had counted," which ultimately led to financial and economic collapse, a true "general glut." Money and credit are, after all, liquid trust. And if there is not trust that your counterparty is solvent, the money and credit will not be there.

However, there is one organization that is almost always trusted to be good for the money. The government accepts as payment for taxes the money that it issues itself. Because of this, everybody who owes taxes will be willing to sell what they have in return for the government-issued money. Whenever the economy freezes up due to a shortage of demand and income, the government can fix it—as long as its own finances are trusted over the long term—by increasing the amount of government-issued cash in the public's hands. People then will be able to buy. Their purchases then become extra income for others. Those others will then be able to scale up their purchases. And so the economy will unwedge itself—if the government acts properly to enable it to do so.

There are a number of ways the government can get extra purchasing power into the hands of the public to cure a depression:

It can have its functionaries throw bundles of cash out of helicopters—an arresting idea first proposed by Milton Friedman (a reference to which earned former US Federal Reserve chair Ben Bernanke his nickname of "Helicopter Ben").

It can hire people, set them to work, and pay them.

It can simply buy useful stuff, and so provide the extra demand to make it profitable for employers to hire more people, set them to work, and pay them.

It can have an arm—a central bank—that trades financial assets for cash.

The last of these options is the one most favored by governments in recent history. In response to the Canal Crisis of 1825, the Bank of England took major steps to boost the cash holdings—and the spending—of the banks, businesses, and individuals of England.[7] As Jeremiah Harman, then one of the directors of the Bank of England, wrote, "We lent [cash] by every possible means and in modes we had never adopted before; we took in stock on security, we purchased Exchequer bills, we made advances on Exchequer bills, we not only discounted outright, but we made advances on the deposit of bills of exchange to an immense amount, in short, by every possible means consistent with the safety of the Bank, and we were not on some occasions over-nice. Seeing the dreadful state in which the public were, we rendered every assistance in our power."[8]

Despite these efforts, there was a depression: 16 percent less cotton was spun into yarn in England in 1826 than had been spun in 1825. But the depression was short: 1827 saw 30 percent more cotton spun into yarn than 1826 had. Could it have been worse? Absolutely. Indeed, there is good reason to think that the downturn would have been considerably worse had the Bank of England behaved the same way the US Treasury and Federal Reserve did in the early 1930s.

AS THE WORLD SLID into the Great Depression from 1929 to 1933, central banks did *not* take large-scale emergency steps to put cash into the hands of the public. It is straightforward to narrate the slide. It is more complicated, however, to understand why these central banks sat on their hands.

The 1920s had seen a stock market boom in the United States that was the result of general optimism. Businessmen and economists believed that the newly born Federal Reserve would stabilize the economy, and that the pace of technological progress guaranteed rapidly rising living standards and expanding markets. The Federal Reserve feared that continued stock speculation would produce a huge number of overleveraged financial institutions that would go bankrupt at the slightest touch of an asset price drop. Such a wave of bankruptcies would then produce an enormous increase in fear, a huge flight to cash, and the excess demand for cash that is the flip side of a "general glut." The Federal Reserve decided that it needed to curb the stock market bubble to prevent such speculation. And so it came to pass that its attempt to head off a depression in the future brought one on in the present.[9]

Previous depressions had been—and future depressions would be—far smaller than the Great Depression. In the United States, the most recent economic downturns had inflicted significantly less damage: in 1894, the unemployment rate had peaked at 12 percent; in 1908, at 6 percent; and in 1921, at 11 percent. The highest unemployment rate reached between World War II and the COVID-19 pandemic of 2020 was 11 percent. In the Great Depression, the US unemployment rate peaked at 23 percent—and at 28 percent for nonfarm workers (in the family-farm sector, "unemployment" is harder to measure). Some of the greatness of the Great Depression was a result of the relative expansion of the nonfarm sector at the expense of the family-farm sector: working from the best available data, I estimate that the nonfarm unemployment rate peaked at 14 percent in 1921, and working backward in time, at 8 percent in 1908, 20 percent in 1894, and 11 percent in 1884. Depressions with large-scale unemployment are a disease of the nonfarm economy of workers and businesses, not of a yeoman farmer or even an independent craftsman economy.

But even taking the growing relative size of the industrial and nonfarm sectors into account, the Great Depression was greater and longer by far than any previous depressions or any since. Others had produced one big shock that threw people out of work and shuttered factories and businesses, after which recovery began, sometimes rapidly and sometimes slowly, as people picked themselves up, confidence returned, the excess demand for money ebbed, and people no longer wished to hoard as much cash against future emergencies.

The Great Depression was different. The start of the recession in mid-1929 was the first shock to confidence. The stock market crash of late 1929 was a consequence of both that shock and of overleverage, and was itself a second, major confidence shock that quickly reverberated around the entire world. Then, a year later, came a banking crisis in the United States. The thought that the money you had been depositing in the bank might get locked away and become inaccessible—or vanish completely—caused a run on banks. Bank deposits ceased to be fully "money" because you could not be confident they would still be there when you needed them. So people demanded more money, this time insisting that it be in the particular form of visible cash, further boosting the excess demand for money. March 1931 saw a second banking crisis. The summer and fall of 1931 saw panics in other countries, which made the Great Depression great worldwide—and greatest in Germany.[10]

Up until late 1930, people continued clamoring for cash. With the Roaring Twenties over and the stock market in a pronounced bear market, demand for cash was high. But shortly thereafter, banks began to get scared and to restrict the amount of cash they were willing to provide to their customers. They called in loans and canceled lines of credit as they sought to raise the ratio of their own reserves held against the deposits they owed their customers. And households began to want to raise their currency-to-deposits ratio: to hold more cash under the mattress than in the bank.

From late 1930 into 1933, month by month, these reserves-to-deposits and currency-to-deposits ratios grew as confidence fell, and so month by month the money supply shrank. During that period, 1931 had been a year of banking and international financial crises; 1932 saw no large extra crises, but it also saw no recovery, as the situation had become so dire and so unprecedented that there was no recovery of confidence.

Conventional anti-Keynesian economic thinking would hold that any depression will be cured faster if wages and prices are encouraged—or forced—to fall in nominal terms. The same amount of spending in dollars will then buy more stuff and provide demand for more people to work. The problem is that when wages and prices fall, debts do not fall along with them. Thus, a decline in prices—deflation—during the Depression caused bankruptcies—companies unable to pay their debts—which led to further contractions in production, which triggered additional falls in prices, bankruptcies, and so on.

Banking panics and the collapse of the world monetary system cast doubt on everyone's credit and reinforced the belief that the early 1930s was a time to watch and wait. Demand for cash went up, and the excess supply of goods and services grew. And with prices falling at 10 percent per year, investors had compelling reasons to sit on the sidelines. Investing now would earn them less profit than if they waited to invest next year, when their dollars would stretch 10 percent further. The slide into the Depression, with increasing unemployment, falling production, and falling prices, continued throughout then newly elected Herbert Hoover's presidential term.

At its nadir, the Depression was collective insanity. Workers were idle because firms would not hire them to work their machines; firms would not hire workers to work their machines because they saw no market for goods; and there was no market for goods because idle workers had no incomes to spend. Journalist and novelist George Orwell's 1936 account of the Great Depression in Britain, *The Road to Wigan Pier*, speaks of "several hundred men risk[ing] their lives and several hundred women scrabbl[ing] in the mud for hours . . . searching eagerly for tiny chips of coal" in slag heaps so they could heat their homes. For them, this "free" coal was "more important almost than food." While they risked and scrabbled, all around them the machinery they had previously used to mine in five minutes more coal than they could now gather in a day stood idle.[11]

There is no fully satisfactory explanation for why the Great Depression happened just when it did, and why there was only one. If such huge depressions were always a possibility in an unregulated capitalist economy, why weren't there two, three, or more of them in the years before World War II? Milton Friedman and Anna Schwartz would later argue that the Depression resulted from an incredible sequence of blunders in monetary policy. But those controlling policy during the early 1930s thought they were following the same gold-standard rules that their predecessors had used. Were they wrong? If they were not wrong, why was *the* Great Depression the *only* Great Depression?

A number of pieces of bad luck did all come together. In the United States, the decision to cut immigration in 1924 meant that a great deal of construction undertaken in the mid-1920s was undertaken for people who, it turned out, did not exist—or, rather, existed elsewhere. The rapid expansion of financial markets, and broader participation in them, made them more vulnerable than usual to overspeculation and panic. The shortage of monetary gold to act as a shock absorber, due to France and the United States deciding to lock it in their vaults, played a role. The international monetary system's reliance not just on gold but on other assets—assets also subject to runs—played a role as well.

When I first started writing this book, I felt, as many others did, that 1929–1933 was a uniquely vulnerable time, and planned to devote considerable space to explaining why. But in 2008, we skated to the edge of another Great Depression (which we'll explore in more detail in Chapter 17), which made it painfully clear that the years 1929–1933 were not so uniquely vulnerable after all. Rather, we had been remarkably lucky before 1929, and we had been remarkably lucky after 1929.

In the lead-up to the Great Depression, policy elites doubled down on the austerity measures to which they had committed themselves in the late 1920s. Faced with the gathering depression, the first instinct of governments and central banks was to do, well, nothing. Businessmen, economists, and politicians expected the recession of 1929–1930 to be self-limiting. They expected workers with idle hands and capitalists with idle machines to try to undersell their still at-work peers. Prices would fall. When prices fell enough, entrepreneurs would gamble that even with slack demand, production would be profitable at the new, lower wages. Production would then resume. This is how earlier recessions had come to an end.

Throughout the decline—which saw the unemployment rate rise to nearly a quarter of the US workforce, and production per worker fall to a level 40 percent below where it had been in 1929—the government did not try to prop up aggregate demand. The Federal Reserve did not use open-market operations to keep the money supply from falling. Instead, the only significant systematic use of open-market operations was in the other direction. After the United Kingdom abandoned the gold standard in the fall of 1931, the Fed raised interest rates to discourage gold outflows.[12]

The Federal Reserve thought it knew what it was doing: it was letting the private sector handle the Depression in its own fashion. And it feared that expansionary monetary policy or fiscal spending and the resulting deficits would impede the necessary private-sector process of readjustment.

The Fed's do-little-to-nothing approach was backed by a large chorus, which included some of the most eminent economists of the era.

For example, Harvard's Joseph Schumpeter argued that "depressions are not simply evils, which we might attempt to suppress, but forms of something which has to be done, namely, adjustment to change."[13] Friedrich von Hayek wrote, "The only way permanently to mobilize all available resources is, therefore, to leave it to time to effect a permanent cure by the slow process of adapting the structure of production."[14]

Hayek and company believed that enterprises were gambles that sometimes failed. The best that could be done in such circumstances was to shut down those that turned out to have been based on faulty assumptions about future demands. The liquidation of such investments and businesses released factors of production from unprofitable uses so that they could be redeployed. Depressions, said Hayek, were this process of liquidation and preparation for the redeployment of resources.

Schumpeter put it this way: "Any revival which is merely due to artificial stimulus leaves part of the work of depressions undone and adds, to an undigested remnant of maladjustment, new maladjustment of its own which has to be liquidated in turn, thus threatening business with another [worse] crisis ahead."[15] The market giveth, the market taketh away, and—in this case—blessed be the name of the market through gritted teeth. Except many didn't just grit their teeth, they also cursed loudly and repeatedly.

Herbert Hoover moved from commerce secretary to president on March 4, 1929, three months before the recession began and half a year before the 1929 stock market crash. He kept Andrew Mellon on as treasury secretary. Mellon had been nominated by Warren G. Harding and confirmed on March 9, 1921, five days after Harding's term began. Mellon stayed in his post when Harding died of a heart attack in 1923 and was succeeded by Calvin Coolidge. Mellon stayed in his post when Coolidge won a term in his own right and was inaugurated in 1925. Mellon stayed in his post when Hoover took over in 1929. Only Albert Gallatin—treasury secretary for Jefferson, Madison, and Monroe—served longer. Tax, budget, and monetary policy (for the treasury secretary was in those days the chair of the Federal Reserve Board)—all those were within Mellon's purview. Hoover was an expert mining engineer and a manager who believed in experts. And Mellon was his expert on how to deal with the Great Depression.

Looking back from the 1950s and contemplating the wreck of his country's economy and his own political career, Hoover cursed Mellon and his supporters in his administration who had advised inaction during the downslide:

The "leave-it-alone liquidationists" headed by Secretary of the Treasury Mellon felt that government must keep its hands off and let the slump liquidate itself. Mr. Mellon had only one formula: "Liquidate labor, liquidate stocks, liquidate the farmers, liquidate real estate." He held that even panic was not altogether a bad thing. He said: "It will purge the rottenness out of the system. High costs of living and high living will come down. People will work harder, live a more moral life. Values will be adjusted, and enterprising people will pick up the wrecks from less competent people."[16]

In his memoirs, Hoover wrote as though he had wanted to pursue more activist policies: do more than simply hand out relief and assure people that prosperity was, if not just around the corner, nearby. Hoover wrote as though Mellon had overruled him and he had no choice but to comply. But, of Hoover and Mellon, which of them was head of the executive branch? And which was merely head of one of its departments?

This ruling doctrine—that, in the long run, the Great Depression would turn out to have been good medicine for the economy, and that proponents of stimulative policies were shortsighted enemies of the public welfare—was, to put it bluntly, completely bats, simply insane. John Stuart Mill had nailed the analytical point back in 1829: an excess demand for money was what produced a "general glut," and if the economy's money supply were matched to money demand there would be no depression.[17] Practical central bankers had developed a playbook for what to do.[18] Yet it was not followed.

Why? Perhaps because in previous downturns the excess demand for money had triggered a scramble for *liquidity*: people desperate for cash immediately dumped other assets, including the government bonds they held. As government bonds fell in price, the interest rates they paid rose. Central bankers saw such sharp spikes in government bond interest rates as a signal that the economy needed more cash.

But the Great Depression was not like previous downturns.

In this downturn the excess demand for money was so broad and fear was so great that it triggered a scramble for *safety*. Yes, people were desperate for more cash, but they were also desperate for assets that they could easily turn into cash. Believing the troubles would last for quite a while, they dumped other assets on the market—speculative stocks, industrial stocks, utility stocks, bonds of all kinds, even secure railroad stocks and things like their ancestors' furniture and their summer homes. The scramble was on for both cash and government bonds. Along with furniture left curbside, there was also no government-bond interest-rate spike, leaving central bankers unsure as to what was going on.

For their part, governments everywhere strained their every nerve and muscle to restore competitiveness and balance their budgets, which meant, in practice, further depressing demand, and in turn reducing wages and prices. In Germany, the chancellor—the prime minister—Heinrich Brüning, decreed a 10 percent cut in prices and a 10 to 15 percent cut in wages. But every step taken in pursuit of financial orthodoxy made matters worse.

When you look at interest rates during the Great Depression you see a steadily widening gap between safe interest rates on government securities and the interest rates that companies able to borrow had to pay. Even though credit, understood as liquidity, was ample—in the sense that borrowers with perfect and unimpaired collateral could obtain loans at extremely low interest rates—the vast majority of businesses struggling to stay afloat—namely, businesses with imperfect, impaired collateral—found it next to impossible to obtain capital to finance investment because new investment expenditures on plants and equipment were risky, and the financial economy was desperately short of safety.

The banking system froze up. It no longer performed its social function of channeling purchasing power from savers to investors. Private investment collapsed; falling investment produced more unemployment, excess capacity, further falls in prices, and more deflation; and further deflation rendered investors less willing to invest and the banking system even more insolvent, deepening the freeze.

The spiral of deflation would continue to depress the economy until something was done to restore solvency to the banking system in a way that broke the expectation of further falls in prices. During the Great Depression, few economists understood this process. None of them who did walked the corridors of power.

So it was that the ruling "liquidationist" doctrine overrode the anguished cries of dissent from those less hindered by their theoretical blinders (as well as the anguished cries of the unemployed, the hungry, and the uncertainly housed, if housed at all). As the British monetary economist R. G. Hawtrey wrote, "Fantastic fears of inflation were expressed. That was to cry, Fire, Fire, in Noah's Flood."[19] The Great Depression was the twentieth century's greatest case of self-inflicted economic catastrophe. As John Maynard Keynes wrote at its very start, in 1930, the world was "as capable as before of affording for every one a high standard of life." But the outlook was nevertheless ominous: "Today," he said, "we have involved ourselves in a colossal muddle, having blundered in the control of a delicate machine, the working of which we do not understand." Keynes feared that "the slump" of 1930 might "pass over into a depression, accompanied by a sagging price level, which might last for years with untold damage to the material wealth and to the social stability of every country alike." He called for resolute, coordinated monetary expansion by the major industrial economies "to restore confidence in the international long-term bond market . . . and to restore [raise] prices and profits, so that in due course the wheels of the world's commerce would go round again."[20] His was the croaking of a Cassandra.

But such action never emerges from committees, or from international meetings, unless it has been well prepared beforehand. It emerges, rather, from the actions of a hegemon. Such is required for a well-functioning global economy. Before World War I, everybody knew that Britain was the hegemon and adjusted their behavior to conform with the rules of the game laid down in London. After World War II, everyone would similarly know that the United States was the hegemon. America had the power to take effective action to shape the patterns of international finance all by itself, had it wished. But, during the interwar period, it didn't. The necessary action was not forthcoming.

And so Keynes's fears came to pass.

During World War I and after, the main belligerents, he said, had shaken "the delicate, complicated organization . . . through which alone the European peoples can employ themselves and live." Broken by war, the system was shattered by the Depression. Recall what Keynes had written: that this destruction of trust was "fast rendering impossible a continuation of the social and economic order of the nineteenth century. But [European leaders had] no plan for replacing it." Keynes warned that the consequences could be dire: "Vengeance, I dare predict, will not limp." And he was right. For once the Great Depression began, "nothing can then delay for long that final civil war between the forces of Reaction and the despairing convulsions of Revolution, before which the horrors of the late German war [World War I] will fade into nothing, and which will destroy, whoever is victor, the civilization and progress of our generation."[21] Keynes was pessimistic. As it came to pass, civilization would not be "destroyed" but rather "maimed."

A large part of what made the Great Depression so painful was that it was not only deep but also long. There were many reasons for this. Let me pick out three:

A first reason it stretched on for so long was workers' unwillingness to take risks. With so much instability, most were content to settle for what manner of living they could find that was most secure. The experience of long and high unemployment casts a large and deep shadow on the labor market. Risky but profitable enterprises had a difficult time attracting the workers they needed, and so investment remained depressed.

A second reason it was long was the memory of the gold standard and the belief that economies needed to get back to it. This belief dissuaded governments in the 1930s from taking many of the steps to boost production and employment that they otherwise might have pursued: the gold standard was dead by 1931, but its ghost continued to haunt the world economy. Few of these much-needed measures were undertaken. The only one that governments did take up was currency depreciation: stimulating net exports by switching demand to domestic-made goods and away from foreign-made goods. Commentators disparaged currency depreciation as "beggar-thy-neighbor." It was. But it was the only thing generally undertaken that was effective.[22]

A third reason was that the lack of a hegemon to guide coordinated action in international monetary affairs not only prevented anticipatory reforms but also blocked coordinated global policy responses. The major monetary powers of the world passed up their chances to do anything constructive together. Recovery, where it came, was national only, not global.

In general, the sooner countries went off the gold standard, and the less constrained they were thereafter by the orthodoxy of gold-standard habits, the better they fared. Thus, the Scandinavian countries that bailed first from the gold standard did best. Japan was second. Britain also abandoned the gold standard, in 1931, but Japan embraced expansionary policies more thoroughly. The United States and Germany abandoned the gold standard in 1933, but Hitler had a clearer view that success required putting people to work than FDR did with the try-everything-expediency of his New Deal.

But all of the opinions of the great and good blocked action toward "reflation," that is, adopting policies to restore the level of prices and the flow of spending to pre-Depression 1929 levels. The consensus opinion of the powerful—the "money changers . . . in their high seats in the temple of our civilization," as President Franklin Roosevelt called them in his 1933 Inaugural Address—was that what was needed was, instead, "austerity": sound money, government spending cuts, and balanced budgets.[23] Those who proposed doing something were denounced from the right as con artists, for, as Churchill's private secretary, P. J. Grigg, put it, "an economy could not forever by government financial legerdemain live beyond its means on its wits."[24]

The most incisive, if not the shrewdest, contemporary critic of Keynes, the University of Chicago's Jacob Viner, said that such policies could work only if the "volume of employment, irrespective of quality, is considered important." He added that the economy could avoid inflationary self-destruction only as long as "the printing press could maintain a constant lead" in an inevitable race with "the business agents of the trade unions."[25]

Again, it is impossible not to note the history of the Great Depression rhyming with the history of the Great Recession. "Austerity" went into eclipse after World War II, but it continued to burble underground, and would resurface to vengeful and disastrous effect in 2008. That year saw a revival of the Schumpeterian claim that mass unemployment was an essential part of the process of economic growth, and that attempts to artificially keep the unproductive from experiencing it would only store up more trouble for the future. The University of Chicago's John Cochrane claimed in November 2009 that he welcomed the prospect of a recession because "people pounding nails in Nevada need to find something else to do": he thought recession unemployment would be a welcome spur.

Keynes snarked back. While policies of government activism and reflation certainly violated orthodox canons of laissez-faire economics, the system would be judged on whether it managed to get people jobs. Activism and reflation were nevertheless "the only practicable means of avoiding the destruction of existing economic forms in their entirety."[26]

Moreover, Keynes snarked further, if his critics were even half-smart, they would have understood that successful capitalism needed the support of an activist government ensuring full employment, for without that, only the lucky innovators would survive, and only the mad would attempt to become innovators. Growth would therefore be much slower than necessary: "If effective demand is deficient," he said, the entrepreneur was "operating with the odds loaded against him." The "world's wealth" had "fallen short of . . . individual savings; and the difference has been made up by the losses of those whose courage and initiative have not been supplemented by exceptional skill or unusual good fortune." Austerity and orthodoxy and laissez-faire were, in the conditions of the world after 1914, deadly destructive mistakes. And the persistence of the Great Depression, no matter how big the budget cuts, showed that Keynes was right.

In one region of the North Atlantic alone was the Great Depression shallow, short, and followed by a decade of strong economic growth: Scandinavia. In the interwar period the socialists of the Scandinavian countries won enough votes to exercise power. In sharp contrast to their counterparts in Britain and France (who had no idea of what a left-wing exercise of political power would be), these socialists pursued housing subsidies, paid holiday and maternity benefits, expanded public-sector employment, government loans to the newly married, and the like—all made possible by a monetary policy that cut loose from the gold standard earlier than other countries. Thus socialists turned into social democrats: they lost their commitment to the apocalyptic doctrines of socialism, lost their belief that all private property was inherently evil, lost their belief that only a great and sudden revolutionary transformation could bring about a better society. Democracy became a goal rather than a tactic.[27]

Close behind Scandinavia in having a mild Great Depression was Japan, which abandoned fiscal orthodoxy and budget balancing in 1931. The Great Depression in Japan was not deep, and it was over by 1932.[28] This was largely thanks to Takahashi Korekiyo, not one of the "Meiji Six" but in the next rank of Japanese modernizers. In 1931, at the age of seventy-two, he became minister of finance for the third time, and he had little tolerance for European models of "sound finance." Japan devalued its currency in order to boost demand by making its export industries hypercompetitive and generating an export boom. It also embarked on a massive program of armaments manufacturing. Industrial production in Japan in 1936 was half again what it had been in 1928. This proved an effective short-run economic policy, but turned out to be a bad long-run strategy: the armaments boom and the loss of civilian control over the military led to Japan getting involved in a land war in Asia, and then, ultimately, to its attacks on the world's two superpowers, Britain and the United States.

Takahashi would not live to see the horrors and tragedies of World War II. He was one of three senior politicians who were assassinated on February 26, 1936, when the Imperial Way faction of the army attempted to seize power. He had not pushed the military budget high enough to please the coup plotters.

Elsewhere, the Great Depression was a long disaster. It was worst in Germany, where it brought to power Adolf Hitler—his mass support came not in the 1920s as a consequence of inflation but in the 1930s as a consequence of mass unemployment.

Once Hitler had taken power and broken adherence to monetary and fiscal orthodoxy, his Nazi Germany was able to recover. With the Gestapo in the background, and with strong demand from the government for public works and military programs, unemployment fell rapidly in Germany in the 1930s.[29] Hitler appears to have been focused on employment and weapons, not adding to industrial capacity and increasing national wealth. Political effectiveness and military capacity were the priorities.[30]

Political effectiveness we understand. But weapons? Armies? Hadn't World War I taught the Germans, and even the Nazis, and even Hitler, not to do *that* again? No, it had not.[31]

Overall, the major monetary powers of the world regularly passed up their chances to do something constructive and coordinated to help the world monetary system recover. In 1933, the last chance, the London Economic Conference, collapsed in disagreement. The French believed they should try to maintain the gold standard. The British, who had long since abandoned it, were unwilling to, in economist Barry J. Eichengreen's words, "tie their policies to those of a foreign partner [the United States] of whose intentions they were unsure."[32] Coordinated reflation was the first obvious strategy. But it was never tried. Fiscal expansion was the next obvious thing to try. But it was not attempted until the very end of the decade, when the threat of war made governments realize that spending public money to build weapons was more important than trying, yet again, to balance the budget.[33]

Close to bringing up the rear in the race for recovery was Britain. Great Britain had been forced off the gold standard in September 1931. But its abandonment of the gold standard was not followed by large-scale reflation. The Bank of England did its part, cutting back on its short-term discount rate. The National-Conservative government, however, did not do its part. In October, the Conservative Party swept the general election, winning 78 percent of seats in the House of Commons. Britain's recovery from the Great Depression would be slow and painful.[34]

France, which stuck it out on the gold standard until 1937, did worst of all. Its undervalued exchange rate parity chosen after its sevenfold inflation in the 1920s made France, temporarily, an export powerhouse. So when the Great Depression began, it had little effect on France at first. But as exports dropped, country after country devalued to try to regain some foreign demand. Increasingly, countries that had not devalued found their industries uncompetitive, their payments in deficit, and their maintenance of convertibility a source of domestic unemployment, because they had to maintain higher interest rates and apply further deflation to keep foreign exchange speculators' greed in balance with their fear. A fragmented electorate produced unstable coalition governments. From the crash of 1929 to 1936, the French prime ministers were, in succession, Aristide Briand, André Tardieu, Camille Chautemps, Tardieu again, Théodore Steeg, Pierre Laval, Tardieu yet again, Édouard Herriot, Joseph Paul-Boncour, Édouard Daladier, Albert Sarraut, Chautemps again, Daladier again, Gaston Doumergue, Pierre-Étienne Flandin, Fernand Bouisson, Laval again, Sarraut again, and finally Léon Blum, the Popular Front prime minister who grasped the nettle. Finally, France and the other holdouts—the Netherlands, Switzerland—abandoned their gold parity in 1936.[35]

Blum promised to restore pensions and public-sector wages to where they had been before the budget cuts. He also promised to greatly increase unemployment benefits, to defend the franc, to balance the budget, to cut back on military spending, and to share the work and the wealth by cutting back on working hours and supporting strikes.

It did not add up.

Blum abandoned the gold standard. But that did not mean substantial expansion of aggregate demand: the government's belief that the government *should* be trying to balance the budget led it to scale back its nonmilitary spending programs. The investing public's fear of socialism more than offset the positive, stimulative effects of a late devaluation. France entered 1938, the last year before the beginning of World War II in Europe, with its level of industrial production still less than it had been in 1929.

That the Great Depression was long meant that the reaction to it shaped countries' politics and societies for a long time to come. George Orwell was one of the most eloquent in expressing how the system that had produced the Great Depression had failed humanity: "The thing that horrified and amazed me was to find that many were *ashamed* of being unemployed. I was very ignorant, but not so ignorant as to imagine that when the loss of foreign markets pushes two million men out of work, those two million are any more to blame than the people who draw blanks in the Calcutta Sweep."[36]

But once unemployment is no longer seen as the fault of the unemployed, any belief that the unpleasantness of work is the result of personal responsibility becomes vulnerable as well. And so someone like Orwell could reframe coal miners not as unskilled workers with a union who were probably overpaid, but as benefactors whom the rest of us had not properly acknowledged:

> Practically everything we do, from eating an ice to crossing the Atlantic, and from baking a loaf to writing a novel, involves the use of coal. . . . It is only because miners sweat their guts out that superior persons can remain superior. You and I and the editor of the *Times Lit. Supp.*, and the Nancy Poets and the Archbishop of Canterbury and Comrade X, author of *Marxism for Infants*—all of us really owe the comparative decency of our lives to poor drudges underground, blackened to the eyes, with their throats full of coal dust, driving their shovels forward with arms and belly muscles of steel.[37]

Orwell's touchstone for judging a social system was a combination of honesty, decency, prosperity, and liberty, but with the accent on decency. The social and economic system had a moral obligation to treat these men well. It was not decent that they should be without work. And since the system did not live up to the obligations it had undertaken, it did not deserve to.

With the coming of the Depression, it was impossible not to conclude that the old order was bankrupt. And as it fell, it took representative democracy down with it. By 1939, representative democracy was to be found only in Great Britain and its Dominions, in the United States, in France, and in an arc of small northwestern European countries: Switzerland, Luxembourg, Belgium, the Netherlands, Denmark, Norway, Sweden, and Finland.

IN SCANDINAVIA, THE SUCCESS of social democratic parties in navigating through the Great Depression would put them in power for the succeeding half century. In much of continental Europe, the Depression reinforced reaction—which is to say, it reinforced the sense that Mussolini in Italy had it right, and that fascism was the way of the future and the best way to organize industrial societies. Thus, one of the gifts that the Great Depression gave the world was the victory in the Spanish Civil War of the 1930s of the man who became one of the world's longest-living fascist dictators, Generalissimo Francisco Franco. A second such gift was Germany's Adolf Hitler. Where it did not reinforce reaction, the Depression reinforced allegiance to the belief that the old system was irremediably broken and that a revolutionary change was needed—perhaps one based on people's fantasies of what was then going on in that part of the world ruled absolutely by Joseph Stalin from Moscow's Kremlin.

More important than that the United States was going to be a laggard in recovery from the Great Depression was that the United States, under left-of-center Franklin Roosevelt, who was elected president in a landslide at the end of 1932, did learn this first principal rule about recovery—spend money and buy things—and then applied it. Roosevelt's policies worked well enough to gain him durable majority support.

That was enormously consequential. First, he was willing enough to break political norms that he is the only US president to have been elected four times. He ruled for twelve years, and his designated successor, Harry S Truman, for eight. Second, he was a conservative radical: he wanted to save what was good about America by throwing overboard everything that he saw as blocking it.

Before the 1930s, US presidential candidates had simply not appeared at the national political conventions. Candidates were supposed to remain at their homes, tending to their private affairs, until party officials informed them (a week or so after the convention) that they had been chosen. They were supposed to emulate the Roman politician Cincinnatus, who mythically remained on his small farm plowing his fields until he was told that he had been elected commander-in-chief of the Roman army and dictator of Rome. The conventional pretense was that the man did not seek the office: the office sought the man.

But in 1932, Roosevelt, who was then governor of New York, broke tradition and flew to Chicago—in part, historian William Leuchtenburg says, to disprove whispers that a polio victim with paralyzed legs was too frail to undertake a full-scale presidential campaign. Roosevelt spoke to the delegates:

> I have started out . . . by breaking the absurd traditions that the candidate should remain in professed ignorance of what has happened for weeks. . . .
>
> . . . You have nominated me and I know it, and I am here to thank you for the honor.
>
> . . . In so doing I broke traditions. Let it be from now on the task of our Party to break foolish traditions. . . .
>
> . . .
>
> I pledge you, I pledge myself, to a New Deal for the American people.[38]

And, indeed, the cards were thrown into the center, picked up, and redealt. Franklin Roosevelt meant what he said about a "New Deal." In the United States, by striking contrast with so much else of the global north, the Great Depression did not empower reaction but rather far-reaching liberal and social democratic experimentation.

This is somewhat of a surprise: Why did the Great Depression not push the United States to the right, into reaction, or protofascism, or fascism, as it did in so many other countries, but instead to the left? My guess is that it was sheer luck—Herbert Hoover and the Republicans were in power when the

Great Depression started, and they were thrown out of office in 1932. That Franklin Roosevelt was center-left rather than center-right, that the length of the Great Depression meant that institutions were shaped by it in a durable sense, and that the United States was the world's rising superpower, and the only major power not crippled to some degree by World War II—all these factors made a huge difference. After World War II, the United States had the power and the will to shape the world outside the Iron Curtain. It did so. And that meant much of the world was to be reshaped in a New Deal rather than a reactionary or fascist mode.

Usually US politics is the politics of near gridlock. The elections of the 1930s would be different. Roosevelt won 59 percent of the vote in 1932—an 18 percentage-point margin over Herbert Hoover. Congress swung heavily Democratic in both houses. To an extent not seen since the Civil War, the president and his party had unshakable working majorities. But Roosevelt had little idea what he was going to do. He did have a conviction that he could do something important. And he was certain that Herbert Hoover had gotten pretty much everything wrong. What Hoover had been doing was blocking attempts to start employment-promoting public works, acting aggressively to balance the budget, raising tariffs, and maintaining the gold standard. Roosevelt decided to do the opposite. What else? If you had a half-plausible thing, you had a good chance of persuading Roosevelt to try to do it. After trying it, he would take a look and then drop and abandon things that did not seem to be working, while pushing hard the things that did.

The First New Deal was therefore made up of many things: a strong "corporatist" program of joint government-industry planning, collusive regulation, and cooperation; the entire farm sector on the federal dole indefinitely, with strong regulation of commodity prices; a program of building and operating utilities; huge

SLOUCHING TOWARDS UTOPIA

amounts of public works spending; meaningful federal regulation of financial markets; insurance for small depositors' bank deposits; mortgage relief; unemployment relief; plus promises to lower tariffs, lower working hours, and raise wages.[39]

Some of it was very good indeed: the devaluation of the dollar and the shock effect of the National Industrial Recovery Act (NIRA) of 1933 did break the back of expectations of future deflation. The creation of deposit insurance and the reform of the banking system did make savers willing to trust their money to the banks again and began the re-expansion of the money supply. Corporatism and farm subsidies did spread the pain. Taking budget balancing off the agenda helped. Promising unemployment and mortgage relief helped. Promising public works spending helped. All these policy moves kept things from getting worse. They certainly made things somewhat better. And things became substantially better immediately. But aside from devaluation, monetary expansion, and an end to expectations of deflation and pressure for more fiscal contraction, what was the effect of Roosevelt's "Hundred Days"? It is not clear whether the balance sheet of the rest of the First New Deal was positive or negative. Certainly it did not bring complete recovery.

Therefore Roosevelt kept trying. He launched a Second New Deal.

The Roosevelt lieutenant who had the most influence on the Second New Deal—for once again Roosevelt was calling for bold action, but did not have very strong prior beliefs about the direction that action should take—was his labor secretary, Frances Perkins. Despite the burdens she carried—being the first-ever female US cabinet member; caring for her frequently hospitalized bipolar husband, Paul Wilson; being distrusted by both unions and managers for not being fully on their respective sides; and being denounced by the right for being a communist because she did everything she could to delay and block deportation proceedings against communist West Coast longshoreman union leader Harry Bridges—she served for twelve years in the post and was one of the most effective cabinet members ever.

The most enduring and powerful accomplishment of the Second New Deal was to be her Social Security Act, which provided federal cash assistance for widows, orphans, children without fathers in the home, and the disabled, and which also set up a near-universal system of federally funded old-age pensions. And if pushing up the dollar price of gold did not work well enough, perhaps strengthening the union movement would: the Wagner Act of 1935, which set down a new set of rules for labor-management conflict, massively strengthened the union movement, so that large-scale private unionization in the United States survived for half a century after the 1930s. In the end, the programs of the Second New Deal probably did little to cure the Great Depression in the United States. But they did turn the United States into a modest European-style social democracy.

The New Deal Order—with its near-total rejection of the idea of laissez-faire—lasted. Truth be told, laissez-faire had never been economists' consensus: it was, rather, what other people thought and wrote that governments had applied and economists had taught. Nevertheless, it had been a very powerful doctrine—up until and then well into the Great Depression.

But afterward, for a while, laissez-faire and its cousin, "austerity," were greatly diminished. The US economy did recover from the nadir of 1933 under Roosevelt's New Deal, albeit incompletely. By 1941, 82 percent of US households had a radio; 63 percent had a refrigerator; 55 percent had an automobile; and 49 percent had a vacuum cleaner. Nobody had had any of these back in 1914.[40]

It was, in the 1950s, a Republican, President Dwight D. Eisenhower, who wrote, in a letter to his brother Edgar, that the workings of the market should not be accepted as in any way "blessed," that laissez-faire was (or ought to be) dead, and that attempts to resurrect it were simply "stupid":

> The Federal government cannot avoid or escape responsibilities which the mass of the people firmly believe should be undertaken by it. . . . If a rule of reason is not applied in this effort, we will lose everything—even to a possible and drastic change in the Constitution. This is what I mean by my constant insistence upon "moderation" in government. Should any political party attempt to abolish social security, unemployment insurance, and eliminate labor laws and farm programs, you would not hear of that party again in our political history. There is a tiny splinter group, of course, that believes you can do these things. . . . Their number is negligible and they are stupid.[41]

In 1930, as the Great Depression started, John Maynard Keynes distracted an audience one evening with a talk on "Economic Possibilities for Our Grandchildren." Suppose the problems of managing the economy to maintain full employment; of providing incentives for technological discovery, development, and deployment; of providing incentives for savings and investment; and of keeping people confident that society was working, in the sense that equals were not being treated too unequally and that unequals were not being treated too equally, could be solved. What, then, would be the economic problems—or rather possibilities—for humanity, or at least for the global north, come 2030?

Keynes's conclusion was that science and technology and compound interest would within a century deliver sufficient material abundance that "the economic problem" would prove not to be "the permanent problem of the human race." Although "the struggle for subsistence" had "always . . . been hitherto the primary, most pressing problem," once the economic problems were solved, humankind would "be deprived of its traditional purpose," and instead would face the "real, . . . permanent problem—how to use . . . freedom from pressing economic cares . . . to live wisely and agreeably and well."[42]

That was indeed a very hopeful and entrancing vision. Even in the distress of the arriving Great Depression, Keynes saw an end to the tunnel and much light there.

8

Really-Existing Socialism

To most living through it, the Great Depression reinforced a conviction that had been building since the shock of World War I, or perhaps even earlier—a growing sense that both the global economic order and individual countries' political orders had failed. They had failed to restore the rapid upward march of prosperity. They had failed to provide a land fit for heroes. They had failed to generate a stable and high level of employment. And by the Depression's midpoint, the political-economic orders had clearly failed to vindicate citizens' Polanyian rights.

They had manifestly failed to provide people with a secure place in a stable community. They had failed to provide them with a sense of job security. They had failed patently to ensure incomes that corresponded to what individuals felt that they deserved. The political-economic orders had even failed to provide the rights that a market society is supposed to protect above all: that ownership of property gives you security, prosperity, and power.

Rather, the opposite seemed true. The Great Depression had demonstrated that even property rights can become strained in a dysfunctional economy. The political insurgencies of the postwar years had demonstrated that property rights themselves could be up for grabs. And the coming of truly mass politics—reinforced by radio and the gutter press—had shown that deference to secure, prosperous elites and respect for authority were in tatters, along with the formation of societal consensus. In short, the old system did not work.

What was this old system, this Old Order—this thing that had managed the explosion of economic growth and the expansion of human freedom from 1870 to 1914? It was, at best, pseudo-classical, for it was not old and time honored but rather newly invented by those who had held power over society before 1870, who wanted to continue to hold it, and who recognized that, as Prince Tancredi Falconeri, the nephew of the Prince of Salina, says in Lampedusa's novel *Il Gattopardo*: "If we want things to stay as they are, things will have to change! Do you understand?"[1]

It was only semi-liberal, for pressure to allow market forces a freer rein was resisted, and every "liberalization" of economic life from regulation was a brutal, prolonged, and only half-won struggle if such a change would adversely affect the wealth of the rich and the noble. Yes, there was pressure to judge people as equals differing only by the weight of their purses, but what this meant was that wealth could gain you entry into a hierarchical elite of social networks and superior status.

This pseudo-classical semi-liberalism remained an ideal for many in the 1920s and for a few well into the 1930s. Rolling back the changes of the World War I era and the Great Depression, and returning to this Old Order, was the express desire of a large but waning political and governmental coalition in the global north. To his last day in office, Herbert Hoover kept trying to bind his successor to balancing the budget and maintaining the gold standard.

But by the middle of the 1930s, the numbers and confidence of those who were committed to rollback had dwindled considerably. In the middle of the Great Depression, few believed that liberalizing markets could deliver enough economic growth and enough redistribution to keep society's most powerful groups from concluding that it was time to overthrow the political game board. Better, in the view of many, to get in on the winning side than to go down supporting attempts to reconstruct a system that manifestly did not work.

What were the alternatives? There was, on the one hand, fascism—freshly coined from the brains of its inventors—and, on the other, socialism—distantly descended from the idea of Marx, Engels, and company. Fascism was something visible and tangible: by its fruits you could judge it. Socialism, however, was the interpretation of a dream. All agreed that the reality as implemented on the ground fell vastly short of what ought to be—and what someday might be.

Lenin's regime was the first seizure of power by latter-day disciples of Marx who were eager to bring Marx's dream kingdom down to earth: really-existing socialism, implemented via something called the "dictatorship of the proletariat." That first word, "dictatorship," meant, for the phrase's coiner, Joseph Weydemeyer—as it meant for Marx and Engels—the temporary suspension of checks and balances, procedural impediments, and established powers so the government could make the needed changes and actually govern—violently, when necessary, to overcome reactionary opposition.[2] Originally it meant the same nonpermanent thing for Lenin.[3]

But in whose interest would it govern?

In Lenin's mind, that concentrated power would be administered for the proletariat. Why not just have a dictatorship of the people—a democracy? Because, Lenin believed, all society's nonproletariat classes had selfish interests. To allow them any political power during the initial postrevolutionary dictatorship would only retard the inevitable progress of history. Which was toward utopia. Which was true socialism.

I trust I give little away when I tell you, really-existing socialism was, in the hands of its disciples, to become the most murderous of the totalitarian ideologies of the twentieth century. Admitting this now can, and should, help focus our attention.

Until it really existed, "socialism" could mean many things—things other than the system Lenin created and Stalin solidified. In Western Europe and North America during the World War I era, most who called themselves any flavor of "socialist" held that in a good society there ought to be enormous scope for individual initiative, for diversity, for the decentralization of decision-making, for liberal values, and even for non-commanding-heights private property. True freedom was, after all, the point. Eliminating the unequal distribution of income under capitalism that kept the bulk of the formally free imprisoned in the same life of drudgery was the goal.

In price regulation and in public ownership, the question was an empirical one: private where private belongs, public where it was needed. And most people trusted representative democracy and rational argument to settle things case by case. But others took a more radical view, pushing for something beyond even a reformed, well-managed, and gentler market economy. It wasn't until Lenin began to exercise power that people began to discover the tradeoffs that would be involved in a really-existing socialism focused on destroying the power of the market.

Lenin, his followers, and his successors began with a general article of faith: Karl Marx was right. In everything. If properly interpreted.

Marx had mocked the sober businessmen of his time. They claimed to view revolution with horror. Yet, Marx asserted, they were themselves, in a sense, the most ruthless revolutionaries the world had ever seen. The business class—what Marx called the *bourgeoisie*—was responsible for the (up to then) greatest of all revolutions, and that revolution had changed the human condition. For the better. After all, it was the business class of entrepreneurs and investors, together with the market economy that pitted them against one another, that was responsible for bringing an end to the scarcity, want, and oppression that had been human destiny theretofore.

But Marx also saw an inescapable danger: the economic system that the bourgeoisie had created would inevitably become the main obstacle to human happiness. It could, Marx thought, create wealth, but it could not distribute wealth evenly. Alongside prosperity would inevitably come increasing disparities of wealth. The rich would become richer. The poor would become poorer, and they would be kept in a poverty made all the more unbearable for being needless. The only solution was to utterly destroy the power of the market system to boss people around.

My use of "inescapable" and "inevitable" is not for dramatic effect. Inevitability was for Marx and the inheritors of his ideas the fix to a fatal flaw. Marx spent his entire life trying to make his argument simple, comprehensible, and watertight. He failed. He failed because he was wrong. It is simply not the case that market economies necessarily produce ever-rising inequality and ever-increasing immiseration in the company of ever-increasing wealth. Sometimes they do. Sometimes they do not. And whether they do or do not is within the control of the government, which has sufficiently powerful tools to narrow and widen the income and wealth distribution to fit its purposes.

But utopian, and for that matter dystopian, thinking does poorly with sometimes this and sometimes that, better or worse outcomes dependent on governments and their decisions. Inevitable was the patch for the flaw of contingent uncertainty. So Marx decided to prove that the existing system guaranteed dystopia: "The more productive capital grows, the more the division of labor and the application of machinery expands. The more the division of labor and the application of machinery expands, the more competition among the workers expands and the more their wages contract. The forest of uplifted arms demanding work becomes thicker and thicker, while the arms themselves become thinner and thinner."[4] Marx was also certain that his dystopian vision of late capitalism would not be the end state of human history. For this bleak capitalist system was to be overthrown by one that nationalized and socialized the means of production. The rule of the business class, after creating a truly prosperous society, would "produce . . . above all . . . its own gravediggers."

What would society be like after the revolution? Instead of private property, there would be "individual property based on . . . cooperation and the possession in common of the land and of the means of production." And this would happen easily, for socialist revolution would simply require "the expropriation of a few usurpers by the mass of the people," who would then democratically decide upon a common plan for "extension of factories and instruments of production owned by the State; the bringing into cultivation of waste-lands, and the improvement of the soil generally." Voilà, utopia.[5]

Except, of course, Marx was wrong.

This inequality-increasing immiseration-inevitable socialist revolution simply did not happen. For one thing, immiseration did not happen, in Britain at least, beyond 1850. Inequality had increased up to a peak of 1914 in Western Europe and 1929 in North America. But the upward leap in economic growth after 1870 meant that working classes all over the globe were also becoming richer and richer than their predecessors.

That Marx got it wrong is not surprising. The fact is he was a theorist with only one example of industrialization to draw on, Britain. And in Britain, large and visible sections of the working class were worse off in 1840 than in 1790. Technological unemployment was a powerful thing. The construction of dark satanic mills in Lancashire left rural weaving skills useless and populations impoverished. There was a window of time when some of, even much of, Marx's dark brooding seemed plausible. In 1848 the belief that market capitalism necessarily produced a distribution of income that was unbearable was not reasonable.[6] By 1883, when Marx died, such a belief was indefensible. By 1914, the doctrine of inevitable immiseration was indeed a *doctrine*: a matter not of human reason but of pure transcendent faith alone.

But if Marx was so wrong, why, then, spill so much ink on him? Because he became a prophet, and his writings became the sacred texts of a Major World Religion. It is hard (for me, at least) to read Marx without being reminded of the Great Voice heard by John the Theologian, inspired by the magic mushrooms of the Island of Patmos, saying, "I shall wipe away all tears from their eyes; and there shall be no more death, neither sorrow, nor crying, neither shall there be any more pain: for the former things are passed away." Socialism after the revolution was supposed to be Heaven here and now: the New Jerusalem brought down to earth.

Among Marx's adherents were a small cadre of individuals, including Lenin, Leon Trotsky, and Joseph Stalin. There were others—rounding out the Soviet Union's first Politburo were Lev Kamenev and Nikolai Krestinsky—but it is a small-enough group that it is plausible to wonder what would have happened if different people with differing characters and different views had shaken out on top. They didn't, and perhaps it was because these men were not just scholars and journalists, not just the inept and hopeful, but also sufficiently capable, timely, and ruthless.

Lenin and his successors, all the way down to 1990, took the doctrines of Marx the prophet seriously. And they tried to make them real. But they were not gods. While they said, "Let there be true socialism," what they made was, instead, *really-existing socialism*. It was *socialism* in that it claimed to have gotten as close to the hopes of Marx and other socialists as could be realized—but it was also enacted in reality, on the ground, in regimes that at their peak ruled perhaps one-third of the world's population. It was not an intellectual utopian fantasy but a necessary compromise with the messiness of this world. Really-existing socialism was, its propagandists and apparatchiks claimed, as close to utopia as it was possible to get.

Throughout most of really-existing socialism's career, Marx would probably have regarded it with dismay and perhaps disdain—a frequent fate of prophets. To really exist, socialism had to depart in significant ways from the predictions (and the instructions) of the prophet. For, it turns out, not only do you have to break eggs to make an omelet, but the omelet you end up making—indeed, whether what you make can be called an omelet at all—depends a good bit on the eggs you have at hand. This matters, because Russia in the early twentieth century was not where any of the early theorists of what became really-existing socialism ever thought socialism would first really exist. And for good reason.

In 1914, Russia was perhaps half as rich as the United States and two-thirds as rich as Germany, and more unequal than both: figure $4 a day as a typical standard of living. Life expectancy at birth was barely thirty years at a time when in Western Europe it was fifty, and in the United States fifty-five. Russia's wealthy, educated classes were dominated by aristocratic landlords who had no functional societal role. The feudal rules of lordship and vassalage governed the vast majority, rather than those of private property, proletariat, and bourgeoisie.

While sharing little of the Industrial Revolution of the West, Russia did absorb Western ideas about equality before the law, governments deriving their just powers from the consent of the governed, and meritocracy and the end of caste-status privileges. These had been flowing into Russia through St. Petersburg, the window on the West and the Baltic Sea port capital that Peter the Great had built centuries before. Included in this flow of ideas were those of Marx and Engels.

In February 1917 the czar fell. In October the provisional government was overthrown in Lenin's coup. In December Lenin dissolved the constituent assembly that was to write a democratic constitution. That left the Communist Party of the Soviet Union and its political bureau in charge. And being in charge was their only asset. As British historian Eric Hobsbawm has written: "Lenin recognized [that] . . . all it had going for it was the fact that it was . . . the established government of the country. It had nothing else."[7]

A brutal civil war followed. It involved "White" supporters of the czar; local autocrats seeking effective independence; Lenin's "Red" followers; and stray other forces—including Japanese regiments, an American expeditionary force, and a Czech army of ex-prisoners of war that for a while found itself effectively in charge of Siberia. For three years the contestants, mostly White and Red—fought back and forth over much of Russia.

To stay in this fight, and to have any hope of prevailing, the communist government needed to draw on the skills of the old czarist army officers. But could they be trusted? Leon Trotsky, commissar for war, came up with the answer: draft the officers and shadow each one with an ideologically pure political commissar who needed to sign each order and would indoctrinate the soldiers in socialism. This system of "dual administration" could be—and was—applied to everything. It was the origin of the pattern of administration that was to be common throughout Soviet society: the party watches over the technocrats to ensure their obedience (at least to the formulas of communist rule). And if the technocrats do not behave, the Gulag awaits.[8]

The first imperative Lenin's regime faced was survival. But the first imperative the regime *thought* it faced was the elimination of capitalism by way of nationalizing private property and removing business owners from management. How, though, do you run industry and economic life in the absence of business owners—in the absence of people whose incomes and social standing depend directly on the prosperity of individual enterprises, and who have the incentives and the power to try to make and keep individual pieces of the economy productive and functioning? Lenin's answer was that you organize the economy like an army: top down, planned, hierarchical, with under managers promoted, fired, or shot depending on how well they attained the missions that the high economic command assigned them.

It was against the desperate background of the Russian Civil War that Lenin attempted "war communism," an effort to match the degree of military mobilization of the economy that he believed World War I–era Germany had attained.

Lenin had been impressed by what he saw of the German centrally directed war economy. He judged that the war had shown that capitalism had "fully matured for the transition to socialism." If Germany could "direct the economic life of 66 million people from a single, central institution," then the "nonpropertied masses" could do something similar if they were "directed by the class-conscious workers": "Expropriate the banks and, relying on the masses, carry out in their interests the very same thing" the German wartime machine was doing.[9] But how did this work, exactly? How could you run an economy without private property and without a market economy?

The World War I–era German war economy, as run by Walther Rathenau and company in the War Ministry's Raw Materials Section, started with the government selling bonds or printing money and buying things it needed for the war effort at whatever prices the market demanded. This pleased producers: they got profits.

As prices rose and as worries about debt financing burdens grew, the German government began to impose price controls: we will pay you what we paid you last month but no more. But then materials that the government wanted to buy began to be diverted to the civilian economy. So the German government imposed rationing. It prohibited the use of "strategic" materials for nonmilitary or nonpriority products and began keeping track of material balances. Analysts matched production capabilities to uses, with the money flows for purchases becoming simply an accounting device, and then had the planning authorities decide which military uses certain materials should go toward.

In Germany, war matériel, especially ammunition, especially explosives—which meant nitrogen compounds—were the first to come under the aegis of government planning. Foodstuffs followed. War expenditures rose from one-sixth of the national income to two-thirds. Soon, the government was not just managing the movement of key raw materials to and through the factories, and then off to the front in the form of finished products, but also commanding that factories be expanded and built to provide for additional war production.

So it was that Germany of World War I became an inspiration for war communism in the Soviet Union.

War communism in the Soviet Union started with the government nationalizing industries; it next commanded that the nationalized industries be supplied with raw materials at fixed prices; and then it started rationing the use of scarce materials for nonpriority projects. And with that, the Soviet Union's centrally planned economy was launched. A few key commodities were controlled by material balances from the center, demands were issued to factory managers from the center, and the factory managers then had to make do—beg, borrow, barter, buy, and steal the resources over and above those directed to them to fulfill as much of the plan as possible. It was highly inefficient.

It was also highly corrupt. But it did focus attention on producing those commodities on which the center placed the highest priority and to which, via material balances, it devoted the key resources.

War communism was an agricultural disaster—the first of many. The do-it-yourself redistribution of land that the peasants accomplished (and the Bolshevik Party blessed) was very popular. But the government needed food for cities and towns, and, it turned out, peasant farmers living in the countryside were much less interested in delivering grain in exchange for urban luxuries than the now deposed or dead noble landlords had been. The government tried to requisition food. The peasants hid the grain. Hungry urban workers returned to their relatives' family farms, where they could get fed. Urban factories struggled with the remaining underfed workers.

It may have been inefficient, corrupt, and even disastrous, yet war communism managed to produce and control enough resources—and the Leon Trotsky–led Red Army managed to find enough weapons and win enough battles—that the Bolsheviks won the Russian Civil War.

Individual people at particular places of decision-making proved influential.

Lenin and the communists won the Civil War in part because of Trotsky's skill at organizing the Red Army; in part because, although the peasants hated the Reds (who confiscated their grain), they hated the Whites (who would bring back the landlords) even more; and in part because of Feliks Dzerzhinsky's skill at organizing the secret police. Finally, the communists won because during the Civil War their party adopted a ruthlessness that would be exercised not only against society at large but also against activists within the party itself. A "command economy" turned out to require a "command polity."

Lenin was uniquely suited to enacting this ethos of ruthlessness. The writer Maxim Gorky reported him to have said that he liked Beethoven's music, especially the Appassionata Sonata: "I'd like to listen to it every day. . . . What marvelous things human beings can do!" However, music "makes you want to say stupid nice things, and stroke the heads of people who could create such beauty while living in this vile hell. And now you must not stroke anyone's head: you might get your hand bitten off. You have to strike them on the head, without any mercy, although our ideal is not to use force against anyone. Hm, hm, our duty is infernally hard."[10]

Perhaps 10 million out of the 165 million people in the Russian Empire died during the Russian Civil War: roughly 1 million Red soldiers, 2 million White ones, and 7 million civilians. These casualties were on top of the perhaps 7 million dead from the Spanish flu, 2 million dead from World War I, and 100,000 dead from the Russo-Polish War. By 1921, Russian levels of prosperity had fallen by two-thirds, industrial production was down by four-fifths, and life expectancy was down to twenty. Additionally, a large chunk of what had been the western fringe of the czarist empire had broken off. A great many of the czarist generals and officers were dead or in exile. And any liberal democratic or social democratic center had been purged, by both the Whites and the Reds. The bulk of the pre–World War I czarist empire was now Lenin's, becoming the Union of Soviet Socialist Republics, or USSR.

The relatively small group of socialist agitators that had gathered under Lenin's banner before the revolution and cut their teeth during the years of civil war now found itself with the problem of running a country and building a utopia by way of really-existing socialism.

They began the task with a faith-based expectation of help. Because the Marxist-Engelsian sciences of dialectical and historical materialism had told them so, Lenin and his comrades confidently expected their revolution in Russia to be followed by other, similar communist revolutions in the more advanced, industrial countries of Western Europe. Once they were communist, they believed, these countries would provide aid to poor, agrarian Russia, and so make it possible for Lenin to stay in power as he guided his country to a stage of industrial development where socialism might function the way Marx had promised it would. Lenin pinned his hopes on the most industrialized country in Europe, with the largest and most active socialist political party: Germany.

A communist republic briefly held power in Hungary. Another one briefly held power in Bavaria, in southern Germany. But, in the end, the Russian Revolution was the only one that stuck. Really-existing socialism at the end of World War I found itself under the leadership of Vladimir Lenin and confined to one country—albeit a very large country—in which few had ever imagined that any form of socialism might be attempted.

Initially, the attempt required stepping back from war communism and into the "New Economic Policy," which required letting prices rise and fall, letting people buy and sell and get richer, letting managers of government factories make profits (or be sacked), and letting a class of merchants and middlemen grow, as what Keynes called "tolerated outlaws." It was an expediency. Capitalism, but subject to state control; socialized state enterprises, but run on a profit basis. And while the leash was rarely tugged, it remained.

Part of the expedience was due to the fact that the centralized Soviet government had limited grasp. Even by the mid-1930s, the planners could only track material balances for about one hundred commodities. The movements of these were indeed centrally planned. Nationwide, producers of these commodities who did not fulfill their goals according to the plan were sanctioned. Otherwise, commodities were exchanged between businesses and shipped out to users either through standard market cash-on-the-barrelhead transactions or via *blat*: connections. Who you knew mattered.

When *blat*, market exchange, or central planning failed to obtain the raw materials an enterprise needed, there was another option: the *tolkachi*, or barter agents. *Tolkachi* would find out who had the goods you needed, what they were valued, and what goods you might be able to acquire given what you had to barter with.[11]

If this sounds degrees familiar, it should.

One hidden secret of capitalist business is that most companies' internal organizations are a lot like the crude material balance calculations of the Soviet planners. Inside the firm, commodities and time are not allocated through any kind of market access process. Individuals want to accomplish the mission of the organization, please their bosses so they get promoted, or at least so they don't get fired, and assist others. They swap favors, formally or informally. They note that particular goals and benchmarks are high priorities, and that the top bosses will be displeased if they are not accomplished. They use social engineering and arm-twisting skills. They ask for permission to outsource, or dig into their own pockets for incidentals. Market, barter, *blat*, and plan—this last understood as the organization's primary purposes and people's allegiance to it—always rule, albeit in different proportions.

The key difference, perhaps, is that a standard business firm is embedded in a much larger market economy, and so is always facing the make-or-buy decision: Can this resource be acquired most efficiently from elsewhere within the firm, via social engineering or arm-twisting or *blat*, or is it better to seek budgetary authority to purchase it from outside? That make-or-buy decision is a powerful factor keeping businesses in capitalist market economies on their toes, and more efficient. And in capitalist market economies, factory-owning firms are surrounded by clouds of middlemen. In the Soviet Union, the broad market interfaces of individual factories and the clouds of middlemen were absent. As a consequence, its economy was grossly wasteful.

Though wasteful, material balance control is an expedient that pretty much all societies adopt during wartime. Then hitting a small number of specific targets for production becomes the highest priority. In times of total mobilization, command-and-control seems the best we can do. But do we wish a society in which all times are times of total mobilization?

Lenin lived for only half a decade after his revolution. In May 1922 he suffered a stroke, but he was back on his feet and in his office by July. In December he suffered a second stroke. In March 1923 he suffered a third stroke, which temporarily affected his ability to speak. In January 1924 he fell into a coma and died. But he had had time to think about his succession—what committee or individual should follow him in guiding the dictatorship of the proletariat.

During his illness, in what is now called "Lenin's Testament," he wrote out what he thought of his probable successors:[12]

Joseph Stalin, he said, had "unlimited authority over personnel . . . which he may not be capable of always using with sufficient caution."

Leon Trotsky was "personally perhaps the most capable man" but had "excessive self-assurance" and had "shown excessive preoccupation with the purely administrative side."

Feliks Dzerzhinsky, Sergo Ordzhonikidze, and Joseph Stalin had all displayed "Great Russian chauvinism."

Nikolai Bukharin's "theoretical views," he said, "can be classified as fully Marxist only with . . . great reserve, for there is something scholastic"—that is, medieval and obscurantist—"about him."

Georgy Pyatakov "show[ed] far too much zeal for administrating and the administrative side of the work to be relied upon in a serious political matter."

And he added a postscript, saying that Stalin was "too coarse," which would be "intolerable in a General Secretary." Some, he wrote, had even tried to figure out how to remove Stalin from his current post as the general secretary of the Communist Party in favor of someone "more tolerant, more loyal, more polite and more considerate to the comrades, less capricious, etc." This "detail," Lenin said, was of "decisive importance."

Lenin had named Stalin general secretary after the Civil War. It was seen, by both Lenin and his inner circle, as a boring job, a simple job, a job for someone with a good work ethic who was committed to the party but otherwise without great gifts. Stalin's control of personnel was a more powerful weapon than Lenin or any of the others had realized.

Among Lenin's failings was that his late-in-life scribbled warnings were insufficient. In the end, Lenin failed to use his prestige to anoint a successor. He refused to set up mechanisms by which the will of the people, or even of the industrial proletariat, could be ascertained. He failed to attend to this "detail," which would indeed prove to be of "decisive importance."

So the party would choose Lenin's successor. And who was the party? The party was people. And who had chosen the people? Stalin. Recruitment drives brought the party membership up to one million. It was the general secretary—Stalin—who appointed local committee secretaries. Local secretaries appointed those who screened incoming members and who chose the delegates to the Communist Party congresses—who would then do as their patron's patron suggested.

And their patron's patron was Stalin.

After Lenin's death and a three-year interregnum, the party fell into line and accepted Joseph Stalin in the driver's seat in 1927.

Before considering his character and the consequences of his decisions, let's pause briefly to consider the state of the Soviet Union in those years. By 1927, the Soviet Union had recovered to where it had been in 1914—in terms of life expectancy, population, industrial production, and standards of living. The imperative of survival had been met. And there was no longer the deadweight of the czarist aristocracy consuming resources and thinking and behaving feudally. As long as Lenin's successors could avoid destroying the country through their own mistakes, and as long as they could keep encouraging people to judge their management of things against a baseline of war and chaos, it would be hard for them to fall out of favor.

The recovered Soviet Union remained subject to existential threats, to be sure. Those in the upper echelons of Soviet government greatly feared that the capitalist powers of the industrial core would decide to overthrow their regime. Someday soon, their thinking went, the really-existing socialist regime might have to fight yet another war to survive. They remembered that they had already fought two: a civil war, in which Britain and Japan had at least thought about making a serious effort to support their enemies; and a war against Poland to the west. They were desperately aware of the Soviet Union's economic and political weaknesses. To meet external threats, the Soviet leaders had ideology, a small cadre of ruthless adherents, and a bureaucracy that sort of ran an economy recovered to its 1914 level. What they didn't have was time.

They were not wrong.

I again give little away by acknowledging that on June 22, 1941, Adolf Hitler's Nazi Germany attacked the Soviet Union. Its aims were twofold: first, to exterminate Jewish Bolshevism as an idea, a political movement, and a regime; and second, to herd onto reservations, enslave, or exterminate the bulk of the inhabitants of the Soviet Union. The land they occupied was needed to provide larger farms for German farmers and more "living space"—*Lebensraum*—for the German nation.[13]

There might have been another path. It was not foreordained that the Soviet Union would turn into a terror-ridden prison camp. But Lenin's refusal to plan for succession or create mechanisms for any form of normal politics within the Communist Party meant that Russia was likely to fall back into an old political pattern. It meant that Soviet Russia was likely to acquire a czar. And in a time of turmoil and troubles, a czar was likely to behave like the Rurik dynasty's Dread Ivan IV—in modern English, "the Terrible" misses the mark. The czar they got was the Dread Joseph Stalin, born Ioseb Dzhugashvili: a paranoid psychopath, and one of the leading candidates for the greatest mass-murderer in human history.

Stalin had turned to revolutionary politics after being expelled from an Orthodox seminary. He was exiled to Siberia four times. All four times he escaped and returned to Georgia. To some this seemed suspicious. How did he escape so easily? And why was he not afterward afraid to return to his old stomping grounds? Trotsky and others would later come to claim that Stalin had spent his time before World War I as an agent provocateur who spied on the communists for the Okhrana, the czar's secret political police.

No matter. In 1912 Lenin needed somebody to stir up agitation at the fringes of the empire, and he chose Stalin. Stalin was the first major Bolshevik to return to what was then the capital—St. Petersburg or Petrograd—after the fall of the czar in 1917. Lenin gave Stalin the post of editor of the party newspaper, *Pravda*. During the Civil War he was responsible for trying to cement the revolution among the same ethnic minorities he had agitated earlier that decade. As party general secretary, Stalin determined who would be in the party, which meant who and what would be the party. After World War II, East German playwright Bertolt Brecht observed that the ideal of his really-existing socialist masters would be if they could "dissolve the people, and elect another." As far as the party membership was concerned, their ideal was Stalin's reality.[14] It is no surprise then that Stalin came out on top, though he acquired many enemies in the process. Nor is it surprising that a paranoid personality like Stalin with many enemies, including powerful ones, took the next steps he did.

Dzerzhinsky died of a heart attack in 1926, before Stalin had consolidated power. Stalin shot all the others whom Lenin had mentioned in his testament, save for Leon Trotsky and perhaps Sergo Ordzhonikidze. Trotsky was exiled. He was then killed by Soviet secret police in Mexico City in 1940—with an icepick. Perhaps Ordzhonikidze managed to shoot himself before the secret police could. We do not know. But, in short, Stalin silenced, and then executed, all of his former peers. And he promoted to the second rank of power people who were utterly dependent on him, and who served—and kept their lives—at his whim.

The Bolsheviks thought they were viewed by the nonsocialist powers as an existential threat. And all the Bolsheviks agreed that to survive, Russia needed to industrialize rapidly. But how were they to persuade the peasants to boost agricultural production if they had no factory-made consumer goods to trade for their grain?

Marx had interpreted the economic history of Britain as one of "primitive accumulation." Landlords had used the political system to steal land from the peasantry and squeeze their standard of living. This forced some of the peasantry to migrate to the cities, where they became a penniless urban working class. There, manufacturers and owners of means of production used the political system to force them to build and work in factories.

For Marx, this awful outcome was one of the things that made capitalism an obstacle to human development and flourishing. The Bolsheviks took Marx's critique of British modernization and made it their business model. Not just Stalin, but Trotsky, Yevgeni Preobrazhensky, and others among the elite had concluded that rapid industrialization was possible only if the ruling communists first waged economic war against Russia's peasants. They would squeeze their standard of living as much as possible in order to feed and populate the growing industrial cities. They would keep urban wages high enough to provide a steady stream of migrants to city jobs but no higher. This strategy was the first of what would ultimately become a series of Five-Year Plans.

The "goods famine" this policy generated shifted urban production from consumer goods to capital goods, and from light industry to heavy industry—ultimately bringing about a "grain famine." The result was a "scissors crisis": As the price of industrial goods manufactured in cities continued to rise to meet the government's investment targets, the price of farm goods fell, and on the graph, the widening gap looked like a pair of scissors. Peasants unable to buy manufactures (and increasingly uninterested in doing so) were also unable to sell farm goods. The cities struggled to be fed, threatening the Five-Year Plan and Russia's ability to industrialize, which Bolsheviks believed would determine its ability to survive.

Stalin claimed that the scissors crisis had been caused by a few bad apples: the kulaks, rich peasants who he thought were holding back their grain in order to extort unfairly high prices. The kulaks, he said, were the problem.

No kulaks, no problem.

The government determined that it would have to do something about these peasants—the ones they believed were producing a surplus of agricultural products and yet were unwilling to deliver it up to the party. The solution? Confiscate their land and animals and force them onto collective farms along with other peasants. Tighten down their standard of living, though, so it would be a little bit worse than the others. The other peasants would be happy, the party thought: only the kulaks would be upset—and their resistance could be handled. Thereafter, the entire agricultural surplus could be taken to the cities, with no need to supply the countryside with any consumer goods at all.

The government was wrong.

Some 94 percent of the Soviet Union's twenty-five million peasant households were gathered into state and collective farms, averaging some fifty peasants per farm. Many peasants were shot; others died of famine. During the 1930s, millions were exiled to Siberian prison labor camps. Perhaps fifteen million died. Agricultural production dropped by a third. The number of farm animals in the Soviet Union dropped by half.[15]

Were there any benefits to the policy? Not likely. Food for the cities could have been obtained—more food on better terms—by devoting a share of urban industrial production to consumer goods that farmers would find useful and buy. Serfdom is not a very efficient way of squeezing food out of the countryside—especially if the peasants see the serfdom coming and slaughter their animals and eat them before the government bureaucrats arrive to take them. It would have been far more efficient to have kept millions of people who were killed alive (was it two million? five? fifteen?) and engaged them in trading their agricultural goods for consumer products.

That there was a better way to have obtained results doesn't mean the Bolsheviks didn't obtain results. During the First and Second Five-Year Plans, Soviet statisticians claimed that industrial production—which had stood 11 percent above its 1913 level in 1928—was some 181 percent higher by 1933, and some 558 percent higher by 1938. Heavy industry had the highest priority: coal, steel, chemicals, and electricity. Consumer goods were to come later, if at all.

The plans consisted of a series of selected objectives— finish this dam, build so many blast furnaces, open so many coal mines—to be achieved whatever the cost. The aim was to build up heavy metallurgy. The task was to acquire—by buying from abroad or making at home—the technology that American heavy industry deployed. In this spirit, a "steel city" was to be built in the Urals, at Magnitogorsk, and supplied with coal from the Chinese border. Without Magnitogorsk, it is hard to see how Stalin could have won World War II, for the factories of western Russia were under German occupation from July 1941 until late 1943. Similarly, dams, automobile factories, and tractor (or tank) factories were all built far to the east of Moscow. That there were far fewer people east of Moscow was a solvable problem.

How was Stalin to get workers to man the new heavy industrial plants—especially since he couldn't pay them much? The answer was by drafting the population. Internal passports destroyed your freedom of movement. Access to housing and ration books depended on you keeping your job (and satisfying your employer). Satisfying your employer also helped safeguard your life. For there was always the threat of Siberian exile to a concentration camp or a bullet in the neck for those whose bosses accused them of "sabotage." At the start of the industrialization drive, there were show trials of engineers accused of being "plan-wreckers."

Squeezing the rural standard of living further produced a mass exodus: as unhealthy and low paid as living in the cities was, for an adult male, being a semiserf on the collective farm was worse. More than twenty-five million people moved to the cities and the factories during the 1930s. And it worked, in its way. The Soviet Union would go on to outpace Germany and Britain in war weapons production during World War II—and many of the weapons were of acceptable quality. Acceptable, however, was set to a low bar. The Soviet T-34C tank was designed to last for six months and for only twenty-four hours of intensive combat.

The claims of nearly sevenfold growth in industrial production from 1913 to 1940 were significantly exaggerated. Perhaps industrial production in 1940 was (measured using standard techniques) 3.5 times industrial production in 1913. As best as one scholar could estimate, Soviet real national product grew at some 4.5 percent per year, on average, from 1928 to 1958, which was impressive. But the butcher's bill was immense.

Factory workers were shot or exiled to labor camps for failing to meet production targets assigned from above. Intellectuals were shot or exiled to labor camps for being insufficiently pro-Stalin, or for not keeping up. Being in favor of the policies that Stalin had advocated in the previous year, but not in the current year, could also get you killed.

Communist activists, bureaucrats, and secret policemen fared no better. More than five million government officials and party members were killed or exiled in the Great Purge of the 1930s. It is a grim historical irony that the most dangerous place to be in the Soviet Union in the 1930s was among the high cadres of the Communist Party. Of the 1,800 delegates to the party's 17th Congress in 1934, fewer than one in ten went on to become delegates to the 18th Congress in 1939. The rest were dead, in prison, or in Siberian exile. The most prominent generals of the Red Army were shot as well. The Communist Party at the start of World War II was more than half made up of those who had been recruited in the late 1930s, and all of them were keenly aware that they owed their jobs—and their status in Soviet society—to Stalin, Stalin's protégés, and Stalin's protégés' protégés.

Because of the poor records kept, we really do not know the full butcher's bill. We know more about how many cows and sheep died in the 1930s than about how many of Stalin's opponents, imagined enemies, and bystanders were killed. We do know that the Siberian concentration camps were filled by the millions, again and again and again. The "Gulag Archipelago" grew to encompass millions with the deportation of the kulaks during the collectivization of agriculture. It was filled again by the purges of the late 1930s. It was filled yet again by Poles, Lithuanians, Estonians, Latvians, and Moldavians when the Soviet Union annexed those territories on the eve of World War II. Soldiers being disciplined, those critical of Stalin's wartime leadership, and members of ethnic groups thought to be pro-German were deported during World War II. After the war, perhaps four million Soviet soldiers who had been captured by the Germans and survived Hitler were sent to the Gulag. There they rotted and died.

9

Fascism and Nazism

The Russian novelist Alexander Solzhenitsyn wrote:

> Macbeth's self-justifications were feeble. . . . Iago was a little lamb. . . . The imagination and the spiritual strength of Shakespeare's evildoers stopped short at a dozen corpses. Because they had no *ideology*. Ideology—that is what gives evildoing its long-sought justification and gives the evildoer the necessary steadfastness and determination. That is the social theory which helps to make his acts seem good instead of bad in his own and others' eyes, so that he won't hear reproaches and curses but will receive praise and honors. . . . Thanks to ideology, the twentieth century was fated to experience evildoing on a scale calculated in the millions. This cannot be denied, nor passed over, nor suppressed.[1]

His examples included the Inquisition, which justified its crimes by "invoking Christianity"; conquerors, who did the same by calling upon "the grandeur of the Motherland"; and then "colonizers, by civilization; the Nazis, by race"; and the Jacobins, the most radical of the French Revolutionaries, "by equality, brotherhood, and the happiness of future generations." To see a utopian future in your mind's eye and think that it is almost within your grasp, and that your actions, even if severe, even if cruel and brutal, can bring it closer, out of the realm of fantasy, as a reality down here on earth—that is the curse of ideology.

Economic history is not immune to ideology. In large part, this is because economic historians aren't immune to ideology. Numbers and indicators can support many interpretive stories. But, as Solzhenitsyn pointed out, there are limits. Intentional murder on the scale of tens of millions cannot be denied, passed over, or suppressed. Economic failures of catastrophic proportions that result in tens of millions of dead, by, say, famine, cannot be denied, passed over, or suppressed. The decades of grotesque ideologies that fall in the middle of the long twentieth century make for difficult but necessary reading. They puncture political and economic ideology—though, I am always shocked to encounter, not fatally. And in the period between the world wars, three great ideologies confronted each other, demanding fundamental reworking of economy and society.

We met one of the three overwhelming, totalizing ideologies of the twentieth century—by far the tamest of them—even before World War I: the market giveth, the market taketh away; blessed be the name of the market. And so major alterations were needed to purify the pre–World War I order so that it could be strong. Ideology rests in that word "blessed." Crossing that word with social Darwinism has proven particularly pernicious. The words of American steelmaster and philanthropist Andrew Carnegie are telling: "The price which society pays for the law of competition . . . is also great," he acknowledged. But, he added, "we cannot evade it; . . . and while the law may be sometimes hard for the individual, it is best for the race, because it insures the survival of the fittest."[2] Even the bad about what the laissez-faire market economy would grind out had to be seen as good.

We met the second of the ideologies in the preceding chapter: the really-existing socialism of Lenin and Stalin. It, too, was an ideology that prescribed pouring immense effort into reconfiguring the *economy*—in this case, to eliminate the market as a system, for that was what, ideology told them, was the root of all future evil, in that it blocked using the material abundance of industrialization to build a utopia that would really exist, and exist soon.

That Lenin and Stalin's really-existing socialism was to accumulate the largest butcher's bill of any ideology was certainly not obvious at the start of the twentieth century. Nor was it obvious by the end of World War I. And it still was not obvious during the years leading up to the start of World War II.

A great many thoughtful, observant, passionate individuals would have without hesitation put their money on the third horseman: fascism. They had good cause to do so. It indeed looked to be the most terrible and most destructive ideology. In truth, had not all others—pragmatists, socialists, market worshipers, true liberals—gathered together to stop it, it would have won that race of terror. The fifty million or so killed by fascist movements were just an appetizer-sized portion of the full meal that fascists wished to serve the world.

And fascism was also, at its root, an ideology that prescribed expending great effort to reconfigure the *economy*. The pre-fascist economy organized people into classes. It created a politics of interest-group bargaining and conflict. But, fascism said, what was needed was a unified national people and a politics of solidarity and common purpose. The market economy of rich bosses bargaining with organized groups of workers could not produce that unity. Moreover, the world economy needed a redistribution of global resources. The big problem was not that there were proletarian—poor, working, overburdened—*classes*, but rather that there were proletarian—resource- and colony- and land-deprived—*nations*. One major purpose of a fascist leader was to make the world economy work for the benefit of the people of his nation—and not for some transnational global elite of "rootless cosmopolites."

Benito Mussolini of Italy was, up until the start of World War II in Europe, the leader of world fascism. He had started out as the editor of an Italian socialist newspaper: *Avanti!*. He had agitated Italian workers in Switzerland to start a general strike. He was arrested and deported. He had been an agitator for socialism in the mostly Italian-speaking alpine regions of the Austro-Hungarian Empire. He had protested Italy's imperial adventure conquering Libya. By the eve of World War I he had become one of Italy's most prominent socialist journalist-politicians.[3]

On July 29, 1914, the day after the Austro-Hungarian Empire declared war on Serbia, while the armies were mobilizing for World War I, Europe's socialist leaders were mobilizing too. They came to Brussels for a meeting of the world's Second International. At previous meetings, in 1912 and 1907, all had agreed on the following: the working class knew no country; a threat of war should be met by a general strike; workers would put down their tools, bring the machines to a halt, stop the railroads literally on their tracks, and force war munitions factories to shutter their doors—then diplomats could do their work and maintain the peace.

But that day in Brussels, Austrian socialist leader Victor Adler announced that the workers of Vienna were in the streets not demonstrating for peace but chanting for war. It had long been Adler's maxim that "it is better to be wrong with the working classes than right against them."[4] The Austrian socialists would support their kaiser. In France, the president of the Council of Ministers, René Viviani, was a socialist. Viviani called on French workers to defend their country against those whom socialism decreed were their primary comrades. Only a handful of socialist leaders in belligerent nations stood against the war: Hugo Haase, Rosa Luxemburg, and Karl Liebknecht from Germany, and Vladimir Lenin from Russia.

The socialists of Italy were not subject to this dilemma. They did not then have to choose between their pacifist principles and a government urging war for the sake of the nation. In 1882 Italy had formed a *defensive* military alliance with Germany and Austria. The Italian government announced that Germany and Austria were not defenders but aggressors. Consequently, Italy would stay neutral. The Italian socialists applauded the government.

Mussolini, however, was profoundly shaken by what had happened in Brussels, and by what he saw in the countries around him. The Second International had come up against the forces of nationalism and had collapsed. "I see no parties, only Germans," declared the German kaiser, Wilhelm II. And he was, for that moment, right. What did it mean that, when push came to shove, the international working class dissolved, and what crystallized instead were nations within whom class divisions receded in importance?

The Italian socialists Mussolini knew and liked landed on the side of nationalism. They began to clamor to enter the war on the Allied side, with the aim of conquering Austria's Italian-speaking regions. "Cardi, Corridoni, la Rygier," Mussolini called them out by name. "Apologists for war! It is a contagion that spares no one! But I want to hold the rampart to the end."[5] But even more, Mussolini wanted to be a leader of a mass movement. Mussolini was no George Orwell, who thought that one had a duty to go against the crowd when it was wrong, even when "to see what is in front of one's nose needs a constant struggle."[6]

And so, in the third month of the war, Mussolini abandoned the rampart. If the Italian workers he wanted to lead were going to be nationalists first and socialists second, he would join them. By the late fall of 1914, Mussolini had drawn a lesson from the collapse of the Second International and the mass enthusiasm of the working classes for war. Class had shattered under moderate pressure, and so could not carry the weight needed for a strong and durable mass movement. By contrast, the ethno-nation might well be strong enough.

Benito Mussolini had become convinced of the psychological inadequacy of Marxian socialism. It inspired nothing like the enormous outpouring of nationalist enthusiasm that he saw during the war. Socialism's leaders seemed incapable of fully recognizing the fact that solidarity was associated with one's national community—not with one's international class or with humanity in general.

Being a socialist seemed inconsistent with leading a mass *nationalist* movement, and that seemed to be the only kind of movement there could be. So Mussolini started his own new newspaper, *Il Popolo d'Italia*, calling for intervention on the side of France and Britain. His ex-comrades denounced him as having been bribed by the French intelligence service. (He probably had not been before his change; he almost surely was after—just what they were backing mattered less to the French than that they were backing a nascent Italian movement that wanted Italy to come into the war on France's side.) On November 24, 1914, Mussolini was expelled from the Italian Socialist Party. The bridges had been burned. He had become an ex-socialist. He had become the leader of a movement that would be different, and stronger.

But what might that movement be?

Originally, Mussolini had just a placeholder, the word "fascism." Originally, he had just an observation: that while the working classes were hard to mobilize for a largely economic internal struggle of protests, demonstrations, strikes, and votes to obtain respect and an end to poverty, they were easy to mobilize for a bloody and destructive war to reclaim, or rather claim, Alto Adige, Trentino, Friuli, Udine, and the city of Trieste. Appeals to an ethno-nation rooted in blood and soil drove masses to act in ways that appeals to abstract ideals, moral principles, and universalist solidarity did not. Mussolini therefore felt his way forward into his doctrine. And many have followed him since.[7]

At the core of fascism as a *movement* was a contempt for limits, especially those imposed by reason-based arguments; a belief that reality could be altered by the will; and an exaltation of the violent assertion of that will as the ultimate argument—indeed, the only kind of argument that mattered. At the core of fascism as an *ideology* was a critique: semi-liberal industrial capitalism and parliamentary government had had its chance, and had failed. The failures had become manifest in several different ways, but all were linked together. The ideology was secondary, but it was not important. Why should someone choose to submit their will to that of some fascist leader? The ideology had to resonate with them for that to happen. So let us look at the failures that fascism ascribed to the pseudo-classical semi-liberal order that establishment politicians were attempting to rebuild after World War I. And make no mistake: the failures were real.

The first was a macroeconomic failure: semi-liberal capitalism had failed to guarantee high employment and rapid economic growth.

The second was a distributional failure: either semi-liberal capitalism made the rich richer while everyone else stayed poor, or it failed to preserve an adequate income differential between the more-educated, more-respectable lower middle class and the unskilled industrial proletariat. It could not win. Depending on which aspect of income distribution was highlighted, either industrial capitalism produced an income distribution that was too unequal (rich get richer, the rest stay poor) or not unequal enough (respected lower middle classes slip into joining the unskilled proletariat). That the charge of not-unequal-enough carried an implied or explicit ethno-racial-religious distinction—too much equality with Jews, or Poles, or Slavs, or any other minority—lent it an even greater ability to inspire the national masses.

The third failure was a moral failure: the market economy reduced all human relationships—or in any event many human relationships—to arms-length market transactions—you do this for me, and I will pay you. But people are not comfortable dealing with each other as nothing but machines for transforming your money into useful commodities, or, vice versa, your labor into money. Contests and gift exchanges have more psychological resonance. It is more satisfying to receive (or give) a present, or to win a prize, than to buy the exact same thing. It is more satisfying to receive genuine applause for your performance than to pay a claque. It is more inspiring to follow a leader than to be paid to join a crowd. By ignoring and trying to suppress these dimensions—to require that everything pass through a *cash nexus*—the market society dehumanizes much of life.

Fourth was a solidarity-recognition failure: the pseudo-classical semi-liberal order failed to acknowledge that everyone (that is, all citizens bound together by a given culture and contained within given geographical borders) was in this together—that inhabitants of an ethnic nation had common interests that were much more powerful than any one individual's interest. Thus, economic policy needed to be made in a "syndicalist" or "corporatist" mode. This meant that the state needed to mediate between employers and unions, and the state needed to crack heads when necessary to make sure that employers and unions did the right thing. Not market forces, but government regulation, would set the price of labor and the quantity of employment, for those were too important for the health of society to be determined by the distribution of property and the workings of the market.

The fifth failure was governmental: not only was the semi-liberal economy flawed—so, too, was the semi-liberal government. Parliaments were incompetent. Cretinous. They were composed either of timeservers with no initiative, corrupt distributors of favors to special interests, or ideological champions who focused not on the public interest but on what made their own narrow slice of supporters feel good. What the country needed was a strong leader who would say what he thought and do what was needed without paying attention to norms or niceties.

Many of these real and declared shortcomings resulted in simmering to boiling discontent. Giving this discontent form and direction helped decide the first two planks of fascism's platform.

Nationalist assertion became Mussolini's first plank. He demanded that Italy be "respected." He demanded that the Italian border be moved north into the Alps and east into what would become Yugoslavia. Moved how far? As far as possible. Anti-socialism became his second plank: that is, recruiting groups of young thugs and sending them out into the streets to beat up socialists and disrupt working-class organizations.

"Corporatism," or the replacement of the anarchy of the market by some form of government-administered planning, at least of wage levels and incomes, became his third plank. Fascism would embrace the dignity of work and of occupations, and not value every form of work and every worker solely by what the market wanted to pay them.

And to make people sit up and behave—that is, subordinate their class interests to their ethno-national interests—there needed to be a strong leader: Mussolini. This was less plank than precondition. People did not have interests that politicians existed to satisfy. Instead, people needed to be led and given a sense of national purpose by having their leader tell them what their interests were. Rulers should not listen and obey, but speak and command.

Was this thing called "fascism" real, or was this just a con game?

Perhaps it was just a confidence trick. A normal political movement is based on interest groups who see their well-being as part of a good society, who have a view of how the world works that suggests certain policies to advance that well-being, and who then attempt to assemble coalitions to implement those policies. Fascism certainly was not a normal political movement.

To seize power, Mussolini needed to present himself as the prophet of a new ideology; he needed a doctrine in which to cloak his personal despotism; and he needed to keep his opponents divided and off balance. Fascism was opportunistic, and the leadership principle could paper over contradictions. By this point of view, fascism was always a confidence game run by con artists. The goal of the one promoting fascism was to become a leader in order to gain status, wealth, and power. In order to do that, Mussolini needed to find people who wanted to be led. And then he had to undertake a delicate psychological negotiation with them to figure out where they wanted to be led to. Only then could he enthrall them, and then pick their pockets.

It is tempting to declare that the greatest trick Mussolini ever pulled was convincing the world, or at least much of Italy, that he and fascism were the real deal. Unquestionably he succeeded for a time. Initially, Italy's elected politicians tried alternately to suppress and to ally with fascism. In 1922, after winning some electoral successes, Mussolini threatened to make Italy ungovernable through large-scale political violence—unless he was named prime minister. The king named him prime minister. From there he became dictator of Italy: Il Duce, or "The Leader." By judicious murders, imprisonments, and political wheeling and dealing, he remained at the top of Italy until the Western allied armies of Britain and the United States came knocking in 1943.

But while it is certainly true that "fascism" was disorganized, self-contradictory, confused, and vague, most political movements embody these qualities. In forming a coalition or a party, the goal is to maintain friendships and alliances by blurring differences and avoiding conceptual clarity. Both tend to drive wedges among your followers.

Fascism's claim to be something real rests on another, incontrovertible fact: in the twentieth century, it had too many adherents to be only an illusionary confidence trick, even if most fascists most of the time were clearer on what they were against than what they were for. I count six elements usually found in regimes that called themselves "fascist": a leadership commanding rather than representing; a unified community based on ties of blood and soil (and rejecting and degrading those who are not of the community); coordination and propaganda; support for at least some traditional hierarchies; hatred of socialists and liberals; and—almost always—hatred of "rootless cosmopolites," which, in their antisemitic worldview, meant Jews and people who acted like Jews, in some form or another.

Fascism was also often considered to be the only game in town. This is certainly true if you do not approve of liberal democracy, or if you fear socialism and believe that liberal democracy will inevitably lead to socialism, once the working class realizes its voting strength. For many after World War I, it seemed clear that restoring the Old Order was impossible. For many anti-socialists, therefore, fascism appeared to them to be the only choice left standing. Monarchy was out. An aristocracy of birth and rank was out. Theocracy was out. Plutocracy had difficulties keeping a mass base. Fascism was it. And a lot of people were (and are) willing to endorse and support it.

Indeed, someone living between the world wars looking at European and Latin American governments could easily become convinced that fascism was the wave of the future. Nearly everywhere, democracy was in retreat, unable to provide answers to the economic problems of the Great Depression or to resolve social conflicts. On the eve of World War II, democracies in the world were few and far between: Great Britain and its Dominions (Australia, New Zealand, Canada, and perhaps South Africa), the United States (if you were white), Ireland, France, the Low Countries (Belgium, Holland, and Luxembourg), and Scandinavia (Finland, Sweden, Norway, and Denmark). That was it. Everywhere else you had authoritarian, nondemocratic, or antidemocratic governments of the left or the right.

IN GERMANY AFTER WORLD War I, supporters of the German Socialist Party were called *Sozis*—the first two syllables of *Sozialist*. For some reason, urban Bavarians made fun of people named Ignatz. The name was a stand-in for a what in English is a country bumpkin: someone rural, foolish, and awkward. There was a diminutive nickname for Ignatz: Nazi. Hence the political enemies of Adolf Hitler and his National Socialist German Workers' Party in Bavaria in the 1920s began calling them a mash-up of these terms, "Nazis." The name stuck.

Once Adolf Hitler seized power in 1933 and consolidated it in 1934, he was, with reason, popular.[8] Germany had recovered from the Great Depression relatively rapidly once Hitler had taken power and broken adherence to monetary and fiscal orthodoxy. With the Gestapo in the background to suppress agitation for higher wages, better working conditions, or the right to strike, and with strong demand from the government for public works and military programs, unemployment fell during the 1930s. The Great Depression in Germany had been the deepest in the world save for the United States. Recovery in Germany was fastest, save for Japan and Scandinavia.

Hitler in power during peacetime appears to have been focused on boosting employment and building weapons, not adding to industrial capacity and increasing national wealth. Build national highways, yes—but build them not by building individual city-to-city or resources-to-industry links but by building first where it would be seen by as many as possible. Political effectiveness and military capacity were the priorities.

Political effectiveness we understand: The Nazi movement was still a minority movement. Even at its high point it could command a majority in the Reichstag, the legislature, only with the socialist and communist deputies excluded from the room. And even then, this rump legislature was only willing to vote to give Hitler emergency and dictatorial powers in the panic that followed the "mysterious" burning of the Reichstag's building. In part because of their minority-majority, Hitler and his party did see building more and stronger political support as a priority—hence jobs, and at least the appearance of a government that was building large infrastructure projects.

But weapons? Armies? How do we understand these as priorities? One could order up one world war from the menu by mistake. But why in the Holy Name of the One Who Is would anyone ever, ever order up two?

Hitler disagreed. Hitler had actually rather liked World War I.

Hitler's experiences during World War I do not seem to add up to what a normal person would regard as a "good war." But he thought they did.[9]

He enlisted—untrained—in the Bavarian Army in August 1914, after having been rejected by his Austrian homeland as unfit for military service. In October he joined the 16th Bavarian Reserve Regiment, or List Regiment (named after its first commander), part of nine new and largely untrained infantry divisions that were thrown immediately into combat on an emergency basis. The 16th was sent to the First Battle of Ypres, where the Germans faced the British, and it was the first mauling that the 16th Bavarian Reserve Regiment underwent.

The Germans called this the *Kindermord*, the child death. That is an explicit reference to the biblical massacre of the innocent babies of Bethlehem by King Herod of Judea following the birth of Christ. Perhaps the analogy is apt: in all, 40,000 of 90,000 Germans were killed or wounded in twenty days. By the end of the battle, of the 16th's original company of 250, only 42 men were alive, out of the hospital, and able to present for further duty.

The List Regiment, like so many others during World War I, followed a predictable pattern: inexperienced, they were sent into the fight, where they were chewed up, a decent percent were thrown away, a modest percent were regrouped, repeat. The List Regiment was sacrificed over and over again, in the Battles of the

Somme (1916), Fromelles (1916), Arras (1917), and Passchendaele (1917). The casualties were horrifying—in the hundreds of thousands—in each battle. Hitler was wounded in the thigh in 1916 by a shell exploding at his dugout entrance. He was hospitalized for two months. He was then ordered to the reserves behind the line in Munich. He could not stand it. With his comrades under fire, he begged to be recalled back to the front. His wish was granted. He was then (temporarily) blinded and struck dumb by a British gas attack in October 1918. He spent the last twenty-five days of the war in the hospital.

Yet these experiences did not put him off war.

Hitler was then demobilized and set adrift. No matter his dedication, his conduct had not been such that he was one of those soldiers the General Staff wanted to keep for the peacetime army. But Major Karl Mayr of the army's Intelligence Division picked him up as an undercover operative in mid-1919. Mayr sent him to spy on socialists. One small socialist group he was sent to spy on was Anton Drexler's German Workers' Party. Drexler found Hitler to be "an absurd little man." But he was also impressed with Hitler's ability to speak. Drexler invited Hitler to join his party in September 1919.

Drexler's party became the Nazi Party five months later, when "National" and "Socialist" were added at the front of its name, "National" with Hitler's enthusiastic support, and "Socialist" over his objection. The idea seems to have been that the full name change might lure Germans looking for a socialist meeting to wander in. Since the Nazis were, like the socialists, recruiting from the groups for whom the system was not working, such wanderers-in might stay. Later it was too late to change the name of the party. And by that point it had become the party of Hitler first and foremost, mooting the name.

A sliver, albeit a highly telling sliver, of what the party of Hitler stood for can be glimpsed in how it treated the men who gave Hitler his first legs up into it.

In 1921, Hitler would ultimately push the man who invited him into the party, and who thereafter mentored him, Anton Drexler, out of the Nazi leadership. Drexler resigned from the party in 1923. In *Mein Kampf*, published in 1925, years after Drexler had done all that he could for his mentee, Hitler described Drexler as "a simple worker, as speaker not very gifted, moreover no soldier." He added that he was "weak and uncertain"; "not a real leader"; and "not cut out to be fanatical enough to carry the movement in [his heart]" or "to use brutal means to overcome the opposition to a new idea."[10] Drexler died of natural causes in the Bavarian city of Munich in 1942. He got off relatively easy.

The man who recruited Hitler to spy on Drexler's party, Karl Mayr, started out on the German right and steadily moved left. In 1925 he joined the Socialist Party, where he led some of the socialist left-wing paramilitary street bullies. In 1933, after Hitler assumed dictatorial power, Mayr fled to France. When the Nazis conquered France in 1940, he was on the Gestapo's list. He was sent first to the Sachsenhausen and then to the Buchenwald concentration camp. There he was murdered on February 9, 1945.

Most of what Nazism stood for can be grasped by understanding Adolf Hitler's deadly serious appreciation for the work of economist Thomas Robert Malthus from the turn of the nineteenth century.

It has been chapters since we last crossed paths with Malthus, the pessimist who gloomily predicted that human populations would outrun their food supply. When people and food got out of balance, too much of the former given not enough of the latter, Malthus argued, nature or mankind would provide a corrective. It would come in the forms, one or all, of war, famine, disease, and death; or (a better alternative) "moral restraint." This would be evidenced by late marriages and infrequent sex supported by strong religious faith, practices Malthus believed allowed a small gap between the edge of starvation and average living standards.

From those earlier chapters we know Malthus as someone whose doctrines provided a good description of life before he wrote but were a bad guide to subsequent history. When looking backward, the lesson he drew was less a lesson than a trap, and an inevitable one at that: population growth checked by insufficient foodstuffs would produce poverty. But in post-Malthus history the rationalization and routinization of scientific discovery, technological innovation, and mass-scale deployment had banished the Malthusian Devil.

Hitler, however, drew different lessons from Malthus. The Malthusian trap, with more than a dash of social Darwinism, was, he argued, useful for thinking about foreign policy. "Germany," he wrote in *Mein Kampf*, "has an annual increase in population of nearly nine hundred thousand souls. The difficulty of feeding this army of new citizens must grow greater from year to year and ultimately end in catastrophe."[11]

Hitler saw four options. One was birth control to reduce population growth. But Hitler saw any check on the number of Germans as weakening the German race. A second was to increase agricultural productivity, but he saw this endeavor as doomed for the same reason that Malthus did: diminishing returns. A third was to purchase food from abroad by "produc[ing] for foreign needs through industry and commerce." Hitler deemed this option "unhealthy." Moreover, he saw it as unrealistic: Britain would never allow Germany to become the dominant industrial and mercantile power without a fight, and if it could wield the hunger weapon again—as it had with the World War I blockade—Britain would win.

What was left? The fourth way: territorial expansion. Hitler went on to write:

> We must . . . coolly and objectively, adopt the standpoint that it can certainly not be the intention of Heaven to give one people fifty times as much land and soil in this world

as another. . . . [W]e must not let political boundaries obscure for us the boundaries of internal justice. . . . The law of self-preservation goes into effect; and what is refused to amicable methods it is up to the fist to take. . . . If land was desired in Europe, it could be obtained by and large only at the expense of Russia, and this meant that the new Reich must again set itself on the march along the road of the Teutonic knights of old, to obtain by the German sword sod for the German plow and daily bread for the nation.[12]

Standing atop historical inaccuracies and mystical justifications, Hitler concluded that Germany must continue that barbaric, bloody quest: "We take up where we broke off six hundred years ago. We stop the endless German movement to the south and west, and turn our gaze toward the land in the east. At long last we break off the colonial and commercial policy of the pre-War period and shift to the soil policy of the future"[13]

But how could Germany expand to the east? Here he was certain that fate (or Heaven, or cosmic justice, or the laws of self-preservation) had already intervened on Germany's behalf. "By handing Russia to Bolshevism, it robbed the Russian nation" of the "Germanic nucleus of its upper leading strata." That group, he said, had been "replaced by the [Bolshevik] Jew." Drawing upon thousands of years of antisemitic hate, fear, and loathing, now cloaked in scientific-sounding social Darwinism, Hitler declared that it was "impossible for the Jew to maintain the mighty [Russian] empire forever." Therefore, "the giant empire in the east is ripe for collapse."

All Germany had to do was make sure that it had an army large enough to be prepared when the collapse would come. Be prepared, but also be impatient. As Hitler said in June 1941, when he launched the Nazi armies into Russia, "You only have to kick in the door and the whole rotten structure will come crashing down."

Now we see the four braided assumptions at Nazism's center. First, a strong dose of German antisemitism. Second, a belief in the German nation and the "Aryan" German race as an entity with a special, heroic destiny. Third, the understanding that war was the ultimate test of national and racial strength and worth. And, fourth, the idea that conquest, which explicitly required the extermination or removal of populations, was necessary to create more "living space" for Germans, especially German farmers, who would oversee large fields yielding the agricultural production necessary to feed Germans.

Essential to this braided core were three presumptions: First, the leadership principle. This was not just the belief that an inspired leader was essential to a good political order; rather, it was an active disdain—even hatred—of any obstacle to that leader's ambitions, including, especially, parliamentary institutions, which Hitler believed engaged in ineffectual and disgraceful bargaining practices on behalf of interest groups. Second, the use of terror to obtain obedience. And third, the desire to make sure that all of society, from its citizens to its organizations, served the national cause.

There you have Nazism. Whereas really-existing socialism in the Soviet Union started with utopian expectations, only to end up mired in dystopian horrors, Nazism began with dystopian expectations, looking forward to inevitable violent contests of races and nations—and fully realized the sought-out dystopian horrors.

Hitler tested his Malthusian economics–based Aryan-racial-domination ideology, Nazism, on March 15, 1939, when he gambled by ordering German tanks to roll (unopposed) into Prague, thereby annexing Czechoslovakia. He took it more seriously yet on September 1, 1939, when he ordered German tanks to roll across the Polish border, this time meeting resistance but easily crushing the Polish army (in less than three weeks), and beginning the European phase of World War II. He then pursued his new ideology with existential earnestness on June 22,

1941, when German tanks rolled (opposed) across the Soviet border and Germany—still engaged in a brutal war with the British Empire—took on the Soviet Union as well. The entire point of Hitler's foreign policy, after all, was the drive to the east, to win by the sword bread for the German nation and sod for the German plow. In so doing, he sought to exterminate, expel, or enslave all the Slavic peoples across Germany's eastern border.

And he took the braided logics of Nazism in genocidal earnestness by implementing, with millions of abettors, the Final Solution to the "Jewish Problem."[14]

Perhaps fifty million people died because of Hitler's wars. But if the Nazis had won their war—conquered Europe up to the Urals and filled the land with ethnic German landlord-farmer estates—that number would have more than tripled. And afterward, what would race-maddened victorious Nazis have done in Africa? And in Asia east and south of the Urals?

It is a question history and ideology provides an answer to.

HAVE I COMMITTED AN error by lumping fascists in with Nazis?

A great many people did (and some still do) applaud fascists, after all.

The political philosopher Leo Strauss, who had been born in Germany in 1899 to German Jewish parents, emigrated to Paris in 1932 and to the United States in 1937, where he became a professor at the University of Chicago. Teacher of some and darling of many on America's intellectual political right, he proudly stated in 1933 that even though the Nazis were misapplying them, he remained a believer in "fascist, authoritarian and imperial" principles.[15]

Economist and darling of the far right Ludwig von Mises, born to Jewish parents in Austria-Hungary, in what is now Ukraine, wrote of fascism in 1927, "Fascism and similar movements aiming at the establishment of dictatorships are full of the best intentions . . . [and] their intervention has, for the moment, saved European civilization. The merit that Fascism has thereby won for itself will live on eternally in history."[16] True, in the same work he called it an "emergency makeshift" arrangement; warned that "view[ing] it as something more would be a fatal error"; and denounced it for "its complete faith in the decisive power of violence"—for, in his view, ideas rather than fists and clubs were needed to decisively scotch socialism. In 1940, the Jewish-born Mises, too, emigrated to the United States (via Switzerland in 1934), acknowledging that fists trump intentions.

At the start of the 1980s, libertarian darling Friedrich von Hayek wrote a letter to Margaret Thatcher suggesting that the British hew more closely to the methods of fascistic Augusto Pinochet, whose 1973 Cold War coup overthrowing and murdering President Salvador Allende Hayek had greatly applauded as rescuing Chile from the road to serfdom. We catch his urged sympathies in her politely worded reply. Thatcher wrote, "Some of the measures adopted in Chile are quite unacceptable. . . . We shall achieve our reforms in our own way and in our own time."[17] All of these—save Thatcher—at least flirted with a temporary and tactical alliance with and allegiance to fascism, and some of them did much, much more: believing that representative democracy could not summon the strength to resist really-existing socialism, and believing that that disastrous threat to civilization called for desperate measures and alliances in response.

In seeing history's fascists, as they have cropped up across continents and over decades, as part of the same species as Hitler and his company of genocidal madmen, am I illegitimately tarring their views? It is certainly true that if fascists are all of the same species, many were much tamer versions than the Nazis. Most fascists' economic doctrines were largely negative: they were not socialists, and they did not believe that the Marxist platform of the nationalization of industry and the expropriation of the capitalist class was the right way to run an economy. But neither did they buy into the "national living space" doctrines of Hitler. They were less antisemitic, and they were less murderous than the Nazis.

But other fascists were identifiably of the same ideological genus as the Nazis. They recognized each other. It is no accident that Hitler wrote of his "profoundest admiration for the great man south of the Alps," Benito Mussolini, the founder of fascism.[18] It is also no accident that Mussolini allied with Hitler during World War II, or that both Hitler and Mussolini sent aid to Francisco Franco's Royalist rebels in the Spanish Civil War of the late 1930s. No more accidental, in any case, than the fact that Nazis fleeing Europe after the collapse of Hitler's Third Reich found a welcome in Juan Perón's Argentina.

Have I committed an error by not lumping fascists in with really-existing socialists? After all, how much light really shines between the fascist and the really-existing socialist?

A distressing number of people, starting with Mussolini himself, seem to have transited from one to the other directly. That suggests not a left-right political spectrum but rather a horseshoe, or even a color wheel. Red and blue are as far apart in terms of visual wavelengths as colors can be. Yet if you take magenta paint and add a little bit of cyan you get blue; if you take magenta and add a little bit of yellow you get red. George Orwell famously asked, "But aren't we all socialists?"[19] He was in Barcelona, it was 1937, and the Stalinist-backed socialists were exterminating the Spanish Marxist faction that he had joined when he arrived in the city (the Workers' Party of Marxist Unification). All the while, Franco's fascists waited outside the city.

There were important policy differences.

As Hermann Rauschning claimed Hitler had said to him, "Why need we trouble to socialize banks and factories? We socialize human beings!"[20] That is to say, really-existing socialism focuses first on control over institutions and commodity flows and only secondarily on control over what people think, say, and do—but we focus first on what people think, say, and do. How profound a difference was this really? And while status inequality was important to really-existing socialists, material inequality and ruling-class luxury was . . . embarrassing. By contrast, for fascists, if material inequality and ruling-class luxury bothered you, it only demonstrated that you were not really with the program.

But do these constitute a difference in species, or just variation within a species properly called "totalitarian"?

Let us bring in as a reference British socialist historian Eric Hobsbawm—a card-carrying communist from before World War II until 1956, thereafter becoming more moderate—who had a couple of asides in his histories that strike me as revealing. The first comes in his 1994 book *The Age of Extremes*, a history of what he called the short twentieth century, or the period from the start of World War I in 1914 to the fall of the Soviet Union in 1991. Hobsbawm, writing in his old age, still believed that joining a "Moscow-aligned Communist party" was, for those who desired global revolution, "the only game in town": "Lenin's 'party of a new type' . . . gave even small organizations disproportionate effectiveness, because the party could command extraordinary devotion and self-sacrifice from its members, more than military discipline and cohesiveness, and a total concentration on carrying out party decisions at all costs," he wrote. "This impressed even hostile observers profoundly."[21]

Is there a hair's breadth of difference between the fascists' worship of a heroic leader and Hobsbawm's belief that unthinking obedience to the dictator in Moscow—whoever he might be—who had murdered nearly all of his peers—was praiseworthy, and profoundly impressive? To accept that being a follower meant devotion and self-sacrifice at all costs would absolutely have earned Mussolini's and Hitler's approval. "This is a fascist coup" were perhaps the last words of Stalin's peer Bolshevik Gregory Zinoviev, as Stalin's henchmen shot him.[22]

BEFORE THE TWENTIETH CENTURY, *ideology*—as opposed to religion—did not kill people by the millions and tens of millions. The stakes were not thought to be worth it. Such enthusiasm for mass murder awaited the combination of aristocratic militarism, really-existing socialism, and fascism. Thus it was only in the twentieth century that utopian aspirations about how the economy should be organized led nations and global movements to build dystopias to try to bring the utopian future closer. And then they turned around and justified the dystopia: compromises must be made, and this is as good as it is going to get.

My view is that too much mental and historical energy has been spent parsing differences between movements that are justly classified as dystopian, and even totalitarian, in aspiration. Time spent on such a task is time wasted, given their commonalities— if not in formal doctrine, then at least in modes of operation. The guards of Auschwitz, Majdanek, Treblinka, Dachau, and the rest were very like the guards of the Gulag Archipelago.

Rather, mental and historical energy should be focused on where these movements got their energy. Why was the world unable to offer people a society in which they could live good lives? Why was a total reconfiguration necessary? Karl Polanyi saw fascism and socialism as reactions against the market society's inability or unwillingness to satisfy people's Polanyian rights. It could not guarantee them a comfortable community in which to live because the use to which land was put had to pass a profitability test. It could not offer them an income commensurate with what they deserved because the wage paid to their occupation had to pass a profitability test. And it could not offer them stable employment because the financing to support whatever value chain they were embedded in also had to pass a profitability test. These failures all gave energy to the thought that there needed to be a fundamental reconfiguration of economy and society that would respect people's Polanyian rights. And the hope of millions was that fascism and really-existing socialism would do so.

Instead, both turned out to erase, in brutal and absolute ways, people's rights, and people's lives, by the millions. So why were people so gullible? The German socialist Rosa Luxemburg in 1919 could see the path Lenin was embarked upon and called it "a brutalization of public life: attempted assassinations, shooting of hostages, etc."[23] The German liberal Max Weber, writing in 1918, could also foresee what would become of Lenin's sociological experiment, saying it would end in "a laboratory with heaps of human corpses."[24] Similarly, the British diplomat Eric Phipps wrote in 1935 that if Britain were to take Hitler's *Mein Kampf* seriously and literally, "we should logically be bound to adopt the policy of a 'preventive' war."[25]

The dangers of a fascist turn were clear. The unlikelihood of success at even slouching toward a good society of those who took that turn ought to have been obvious.

Utopian faith is a helluva drug.

10

World War II

During the 1930s, while most other countries continued to stagnate in the Great Depression, Germany recovered rapidly. But Nazi ideology made plain that a recovery fueled by peaceful spending was not what Hitler's regime was about.

In March 1935, Hitler announced that Germany was breaking the shackles of the Treaty of Versailles and rearming.[1] The victorious allies of World War I faced a knotty foreign policy problem. The isolationist United States was uninterested in sending soldiers and garrisons to Europe. The British and French electorates definitely did not want to do World War I again. And Hitler's program of rearmament and national self-assertion demanded that Britain and France make a choice.

The diplomatic jostling of the 1930s was unequal, and not because Britain and France were well armed and less affected by the Great Depression, while Germany was disarmed and deeply depressed. The jostling was unequal because Britain and France did not want to get close to war, and were certain nobody else wanted to, either, as they then might fall into another one as horrible as the last. The jostling was unequal because Hitler did not share their view. Nor did the German power structure share it.

The policies of Britain and France can rightly be called strategies of *appeasement*: Give Hitler diplomatic victories. Dribble them out. Get him invested in small successes so he would honor the commitments he had made to gain them. As British ambassador Eric Phipps wrote in his diary in 1935, if they could "bind him . . . by an agreement bearing his signature," he might "honour it": "Agreement only partially agreeable to Great Britain and France and not too distasteful to Italy might prevent for a time any further German shots among the International ducks," he wrote. "Years might then pass and even Hitler might grow old."[2]

If that was the strategy, it did not work.

When Hitler began his diplomatic campaign, he had a powerful array of arguments on his side. The Versailles Treaty that had ended World War I had restricted the German army to one hundred thousand soldiers. But the other nations of the world had never cut back their own armies. Was Germany to be the only great power to fear invasion from Denmark or Yugoslavia? That was not fair. And the response that Nazi Germany was a pariah nation—ruled by a cruel, oppressive dictatorship—was not a statement that made sense in the language of European diplomacy. The idea that what a duly recognized government did within its borders was of no concern to the world's other governments was deeply ingrained.

What did make sense in the language of European diplomacy was language: the language that a majority of people in any given village spoke. The Versailles Treaty, and the other aspects of the post–World War I settlement, had tried, imperfectly, but as much as was possible, to redraw national borders along linguistic lines. Except for Germany's. Linguistic German speakers were ruled not just from Berlin but from Rome, Vienna, Budapest, Prague, Warsaw, Vilnius, Paris, and even Bucharest.

As long as Hitler limited his foreign policy goals to removing the restrictions on German armaments that made Germany a less-than-equal nation, and to trying to "settle" national minority problems by redrawing borders to more closely match linguistic lines, it was hard for Britain, France, and others to say no.

After all, did Britain and France want to invade Germany, depose Hitler, and set up an unstable puppet government bound to further inflame German nationalism? Well yes, they did, but pretty much only Winston Churchill had the foresight to recognize that such a step was the least-bad option.[3] And he was regarded as harebrained: he had been wrong in wishing to make no compromise with Indians seeking self-government, wrong in his aggressive embrace of deflation as Britain's finance minister in 1925, wrong in his support of King Edward VII in his desire to marry the twice-divorced, social-climbing Wallis Warfield Spencer Simpson, and (they said) wrong in his plans for winning World War I not in France and Belgium but in Turkey.[4] Why should anyone think he was right in his fearmongering about a German threat?

In the middle of the Great Depression, French and British political leaders believed that they had bigger problems than enforcing every jot and tittle provision of the Treaty of Versailles. And some wished actively to see Germany rejoin the community of Western European nations. With Germany effectively disarmed, there was a power vacuum between the border of the Soviet Union and the Rhine River. Poland and the Soviet Union had fought one war in the early 1920s that had seen the Red Army approach Warsaw before being turned back. Wise men said a strong German army could serve as a buffer against communist Russia. In the 1930s, as the German army, navy, and air force demonstrably grew past treaty limits, Britain and France did effectively nothing.

Hitler broke yet another provision of the Treaty of Versailles in March 1936: he moved token military forces into the Rhineland, the province of Germany west of the Rhine that had been demilitarized after 1918. Britain and France faced the same choice again. And once again it seemed pointless to act. No other European country had demilitarized zones within its borders. To require that Germany maintain a demilitarized zone seemed only apt to inflame German nationalism. And, once again, to enforce the provision would presumably require an invasion of Germany, the deposition of Hitler, and the installation of a puppet government.

Hitler annexed Austria in March 1938. Austria was inhabited overwhelmingly by ethnic Germans who all spoke German. In annexing Austria, Hitler declared, he was simply gathering the German people into their proper one nation and reversing a political error committed in the late nineteenth century, when the Austrian Germans were excluded from the political boundaries of Germany. Had but the Allies applied the same national self-determination principles to the Germans that they had applied to themselves and to the rest of Europe, there would have been no error to correct. And to his point, Germany's armies crossed into Austria unopposed and were greeted, in at least some places, enthusiastically.

After the annexation of Austria, Hitler turned his attention to a second of the anomalous boundaries of post–World War I Europe: the "Sudetenland." The northern and western boundaries of Czechoslovakia followed the boundaries of the medieval Kingdom of Bohemia, and included a mountainous region that was the location of all the Czech frontier defenses. It was also heavily populated by German speakers. A percentage of them cried oppression and demanded annexation by Germany, which funded their campaign of complaints.

The British government had commitments to defend France; the French government had commitments to defend the territorial integrity of Czechoslovakia; Czechoslovakia had no desire to surrender its mountain territories—and its frontier defenses. And yet the British and French governments had no desire to go to war to prevent the people of the Sudetenland from becoming part of Germany. The Western democracies' military advisers feared that World War II would bring the horrors of the World War I trench line to civilians located far from the front.

They would be proven right.

To avoid war, on September 29–30, 1938, British prime minister Neville Chamberlain and French prime minister Édouard Daladier went to Munich and reached an agreement with Hitler: Hitler would annex the Sudetenland and pledge to respect the independence of the rest of Czechoslovakia, and Britain and France would guarantee the independence of Czechoslovakia. The Czech representatives were not even allowed in the room where the negotiations took place.[5]

A cheering crowd applauded Chamberlain on his return to Britain. War had been averted. Irretrievably blackening his reputation for all time, Chamberlain declared he had secured "peace with honour. I believe it is peace for our time."[6] Churchill—shunned by the other conservative members of the British House of Commons—had a very different view: "I think we shall have to choose in the next few weeks between war and shame, and I have very little doubt what the decision will be," he had written to ex–prime minister David Lloyd George in advance of Chamberlain's visit to Munich.[7]

Hitler annexed all of Czechoslovakia, after first having sponsored a secessionist movement in the "Slovakia" part of the country, on March 15, 1939. Britain and France took no action. Chamberlain stated, "The effect of this declaration [of independence by the Hitler-sponsored secessionist movement] put an end by internal disruption to the state whose frontiers we had proposed to guarantee [at Munich]. His Majesty's government cannot accordingly hold themselves any longer bound by this obligation."[8]

But within two days, Chamberlain reversed himself. Not as regards Czechoslovakia, but as regards appeasement.

Chamberlain and company extended security guarantees to Poland and Romania. German attacks on Poland or Romania, he publicly declared, would cause declarations of war against Germany by Britain and France. Chamberlain appeared to believe that this commitment would deter Hitler from further adventures.

But why should it? How could British troops and warships help Poland in a war with the nation, Nazi Germany, that separated the two? Hitler concluded that the British and French were bluffing. And he wanted to get himself ready for the attack east to do to the Slavic populations of European Russia what the United States had done to the Indigenous peoples who lived in North America. Just as had happened in America, Hitler's hope was that Germany would come into ownership of a huge breadbasket, in this case Ukraine, which, after many different trails of tears, would be populated by ethnic Germans managing large, mechanized farms.

In the spring of 1939 Hitler again demanded the redrawing of borders, this time to reclaim ethnolinguistic Germans trapped in a "Polish corridor" dividing Germany and the province of East Prussia.

Had the British and French diplomatic policy makers been flint-eyed realists, they would have shrugged their shoulders: Hitler wants to go east? Let him go east. They would have concluded that a Hitler fighting a series of wars to his east was unlikely to cause them trouble, at least for a while. And that if Hitler at some point turned west, then that would be the time to deal with him.

But they did not do this. They had guaranteed Poland and Romania. They doubled down, betting on deterrence.

Chamberlain and his foreign minister, Lord Halifax, appear to have given little thought to what would happen if deterrence failed. They knew they did not want war. They were sure Hitler felt similarly. Which meant Hitler must be bluffing too, mustn't he? Nobody wanted a repeat of World War I, right?

On one side were participants who were willing to come close to war, but who still held to the belief that nobody wanted one. They had, they thought, given Hitler enough diplomatic victories. Drawing a line would prevent a war from actually starting. On the other side were participants confident that war was inevitable, preferable to the status quo, and necessary to secure manifestly destined "living space." Moreover, the British and French politicians had folded when their cards were strong. Why should they not fold when their cards were weak? Neither was in a position to help Poland militarily.

If they didn't, however, Germany might face a war on its western border, and it was for this reason that Hitler became interested in a—temporary—alliance with Stalin and the Soviet Union.

Over the years, even while pursuing a "Popular Front" and "collective security" among nonfascist states to counter fascism in the mid-1930s, Stalin had put out feelers to Hitler. Hitler was not interested. Hitler became interested in a deal with Stalin only in 1939, when he recognized how useful Soviet neutrality would be for his conquest of Poland. Or at least half of it, for now. He and Stalin agreed to split Poland down the middle at the Bug River. Additionally, the Soviet Union got a green light from Germany to annex the three Baltic republics of Lithuania, Latvia, and Estonia.

Stalin had made the mother of all miscalculations. The pact allowed Hitler to fight three one-front wars in succession—one against Poland, one against Britain and France, and then one against the Soviet Union. Only by the skin of its teeth did the Soviet Union survive until the United States entered the war. US factories and logistical support kept the Soviet Red Army fed, fueled, wheeled, and moving, and the US Army and Air Force made it possible for an Anglo-American force to reenter the main theaters of the war. Much better for the Soviet Union to have fought Germany in 1939 with powerful British and French allies fielding armies on the continent than to face Germany's undivided attention in 1941, 1942, and the first half of 1943.

It is always difficult to understand Stalin, or indeed anything about the Stalin-ruled Soviet Union. "A riddle wrapped in a mystery inside an enigma," Churchill called it.[9] It is possible, however, to guess at what the thinking inside Moscow's Kremlin palace-fortress was:

Q: What is Hitler, comrade?
A: Hitler is a tool of the capitalists, comrade.

Q: Why might Hitler wish to wage an aggressive war against the Soviet Union, comrade?
A: To gain cheap access to our raw materials, comrade, so that his big-business capitalist backers can earn higher profits.

Q: So what happens if we offer him as many of our raw materials as possible at an incredibly cheap price, comrade?
A: Then he will not seek to invade, comrade. He will have no reason to do so.

Q: What will happen then, comrade?
A: What always happens in the highest stage of capitalism, comrade. The big capitalist powers become imperialists, and then they fight terrible wars over markets.

Q: Correct. And after the war is over?
A: We will do what we did at the end of World War I, comrade. We move in and expand the socialist camp.

Q: Therefore our goal, comrade, is?
A: To appease Hitler by providing him with all the raw materials he wants. And then wait for our moment, comrade.

Perhaps Stalin wrongly anticipated a replay of World War I: trench warfare that would lead to a prolonged stalemate on the Franco-German border, during which another generation of young men would be slaughtered, another set of bourgeois countries would exhaust themselves, and another group of countries would become ripe for a Moscow-led communist revolution. What is certain is that Stalin did not recognize the danger of even a temporary alliance with Hitler.

On one side were participants convinced that market-capitalist nations were doomed to violently compete among themselves and fail, ultimately hastening the arrival of a proletarian paradise; on the other side were participants convinced that a Jewish-Bolshevik conspiracy was an existential threat standing between them and the land destined to become their breadbasket.

In September 1939, Hitler and Stalin moved their armies in and partitioned Poland.

And it turned out that Britain and France were not bluffing.

They carried out their commitments. Hitler and the Nazi army attacked the Poles at dawn on September 1. That afternoon, the British prime minister, Neville Chamberlain, invited his principal critic, Winston Churchill, to join the War Cabinet. He then ignored Churchill for two full days. I do not think anyone alive knows the decision-making process, but fifty hours after the Nazi attack—at 9:00 a.m. on September 3—the British government demanded that the German army withdraw from Poland. And at 11:00 a.m., Britain declared war. France followed. But their forces were not ready and were far from Poland, which fell to Hitler and Stalin in a month.

And while they had not been bluffing, they had not precisely been preparing, either. They had no plans for waging a war against Germany. And they did not develop any. And so for eight months after the fall of Poland all was quiet on the western front.

It is conventional to damn Chamberlain and Daladier and the other politicians who ruled Britain and France in the 1930s for their actions and inactions. They had not destroyed Hitler when he was weak. They had not prepared their countries to fight Hitler when he was strong. They had not even constructed a grand alliance, calling on the United States and the Soviet Union in an antifascist coalition. That all evidence suggests that neither country's decision makers wished to be so enlisted doesn't moot the failure of not bothering to try.

But there is another point of view. Only one country with a land border with Nazi Germany, Daladier's France, declared war on it. Everybody else waited until Hitler declared war on them—or, more often, just attacked. In the case of Stalin's Russia, being attacked had been preceded by the Soviet's signing, and mostly adhering to, a nonaggression pact. Only one other country in the 1930s, albeit one without a land border with Nazi Germany, ever declared war on it. That country was Chamberlain's Britain. Admittedly, the British declared war only when they saw no other option, and thought (correctly) that their political survival was at stake. And they had no idea how to fight the war that they declared. But they were willing to put their empire and its people in harm's way in an attempt to stamp out the greatest tyranny the world had ever seen. Spare a moment for the limited virtue that Édouard Daladier and Neville Chamberlain exhibited: it was more than anybody else.

Their virtue was not rewarded.

In six weeks starting on May 10, 1940, France fell.[10] The Nazis then enforced the surrender of France and chased the British army off the continent at the port of Dunkirk, where it left all its equipment behind. To everyone's surprise, however, Britain—by then led by Winston Churchill—did not then negotiate a peace. It kept fighting, daring Hitler to try an invasion across the English Channel. Hitler did not try. He sent fleets of bombers by day in 1940, and afterward sent fleets of bombers by night. He aggressively funded Wernher von Braun's rocket-building program, producing the "V" series of terror-vengeance weapons in 1944.[11]

But after the fall of France he turned his armies east, as he had always intended he would. On June 22, 1941, Hitler launched the Nazi army against the Soviet Union. But he had not fully mobilized the economy and society for a total war. He attacked with what he had on hand.

Stalin's first instinct was to tell his troops not to fire back, for fear of "provoking" the Nazis. As a result, the Soviet air force was destroyed on the ground in the first day of the war. And the Soviet armies on the border died (or were taken prisoner) where they stood. Stalin's vices proved costly.

Stalin had purged and repurged the army of anyone he thought might be a threat. He had built a system in which it was a career- and often a life-threatening move to be the bearer of disappointing tidings. When the Nazis attacked, the Red Army deployed out of the defenses it had constructed before 1939. It had not yet fully deployed its defenses for the border after the partition of Poland. And so the USSR lost an entire army, as large as and as well equipped (but not nearly as well trained or capable) as the army the Nazis had attacked with in late June, July, and early August 1941 in battles around Riga, Brest-Litovsk, Lvov, and elsewhere near the border.

By August 1941, however, the Nazis had outrun their supply lines and paused their advance. Stalin and the USSR's high command (the *Stavka*) misjudged the situation and lost a second army, as large and as well equipped (but not nearly as well trained or capable) as the army the Nazis had attacked with in late August, September, and early October in the battles around Smolensk and Kiev, as they tried to push forward in counterattacks, refusing to withdraw. Thus, in the four months after the Nazi invasion of Russia, nearly four million Soviet troops were captured. And the Nazis attacked again. By December 7, 1941, coinciding with America's entry into World War II, Nazi armies were at the gates of the cities of Leningrad, Moscow, Kharkov, and Rostov, an average of 620 miles east of the 1941 Nazi-Soviet border.

But the USSR had a third army, as large as, but this time not as well equipped as, the one the Nazis had attacked with. This army held, and counterattacked, and fought the battles of the fall and winter of 1941–1942.[12]

WHEN THE UNITED STATES entered World War II—rather, when it was pushed into it (for, remember, no countries save Daladier's France and Chamberlain's Britain deliberately entered the war against Hitler), on December 7, 1941, by the Imperial Japanese Navy's *Kido Butai*, its six large-carrier mobile strike force, and its attack on Pearl Harbor on the Hawaiian island of Oahu— the War in the Pacific was already in its fifth year. It had commenced with Japan's 1937 invasion of China.

World War II in Europe is hard to imagine without World War I. This is so at the macro level: World War I's economic, political, and human devastation rent the fabric of European stability and prosperity. It is also so at the micro level: the normal peacetime course of human events would never have given a Stalin and a Hitler the opportunities they seized. The same was true for the other side of the globe. World War I and the Great Depression gave powerful nudges to Japan in its turn to imperialism.

World War I was a powerful indirect stimulus to Japanese industrialization. During hostilities, exports from Europe to Asia effectively ceased. Where were the countries of Asia to purchase the manufactures they had previously received from Europe? The growing and industrializing Japanese Empire was an obvious source. Industrial production and manufactured exports from Japan nearly quadrupled during World War I. Strong demand for Japanese goods provoked inflation: prices more than doubled during the European conflict.

After the war, European economies once again began to export to Asia, and the newly expanded Japanese industries faced heavy competition. The Japanese economy was also badly affected by the disastrous 1923 Tokyo earthquake, in which between fifty thousand and one hundred thousand people died. But despite all this, Japanese industrialization continued. In the 1920s, manufacturing surpassed agriculture in value-added products.

Japanese manufacturing originally relied—as had manufacturing in other countries—on unmarried young women. From the employers' point of view, the main problem with this workforce was its relative lack of experience and high rate of turnover. So, over the first half of the twentieth century, Japanese manufacturers worked to balance their short-term labor pool of unmarried female workers with a longer-term cadre of experienced male workers.

What evolved was what is now called the "permanent employment system." Japanese male workers were recruited on leaving school, or as apprentices, and promised lifetime employment, with wage increases, medical care, and pension benefits, in return for loyal service to the company. It is possible that this permanent employment system flourished in Japan because it fitted Japanese society well. It is also possible that by avoiding deep recessions, the Japanese economy avoided conditions that might have given manufacturing firms cause to fire workers.

Cotton textiles, furniture manufacturing, apparel, and a relatively small heavy industrial sector were the heart of the Japanese economy by the 1930s. This modern manufacturing sector was dominated by the *zaibatsu*: associations of businesses that exchanged executives, cooperated, owned each other's stock, and relied on the same banking and insurance companies for finance. Japan's form of financial capitalism seemed to mimic Germany's to a large degree.

The Great Depression came to Japan in an attenuated form in 1930. Its exports, especially of silk, fell dramatically. Adhering to the gold standard applied pressure that deflated the Japanese economy. Japan responded by cutting loose from the gold standard and by expanding government spending—especially military spending. The Great Depression touched but did not stun the Japanese economy. More important, perhaps, the Great Depression revealed that the European imperialist powers were in crisis.

So, in 1931, the Japanese government turned expansionist. The extension of Japanese influence into Manchuria was followed by a Manchurian declaration of "independence" as the Japanese client state of Manchukuo. Expansion was followed by rearmament. Rearmament was followed by a full-scale attack on China in 1937. Government orders for war material and for capital goods to construct infrastructure in Manchuria provided a strong boost to Japanese industrial production. Japan embraced a war economy from 1937 on, building warships, airplanes, engines, radios, tanks, and machine guns.

But in order to continue its war against China, it needed oil, which would have to come either from the United States or from what was to become Indonesia (it was then the Dutch East Indies). President Franklin Roosevelt was anxious to exert what pressure he could to contain the expanding Japanese Empire. So, on July 25, 1941, the day after the Japanese army occupied the southern half of Indochina, Roosevelt directed that all known Japanese financial assets in the United States be frozen.

The Japanese government obtained bureaucratic licenses to buy oil in the United States and ship it to Japan. But how were they to pay? Their assets were blocked by the freeze. Requests from the Japanese government for the release of funds to pay for the oil went into Assistant Secretary of State Dean Acheson's office, but nothing ever came out. Bureaucracy? Policy? And, if policy, whose? It is unclear whether Roosevelt or the Army and Navy Departments were ever told before December 7 that the asset freeze had turned into a de facto oil embargo—one that extended to oil from what is now Indonesia as well, as the Dutch colonial authorities insisted on being paid in dollars.

So the United States, with its asset freeze, had essentially embargoed exports of oil to Japan—all oil, not just oil from the United States. Without imports of oil Japan's military machine could not run. The embargo offered Japan a choice between acquiescing to the United States' demands or starting a war to, at the very least, seize the oil fields of the Dutch East Indies. That was predictable, and should have been predicted, and then responded to. The response should have been a much higher level of alert in the Pacific than was in fact adopted by the US Army and Navy.

Faced with a choice that its leaders perceived as no choice at all, the Japanese military elected to strike first and strike hard. On December 7, 1941, attacks began on British, Dutch, and US forces and possessions in the Pacific. Most famous was the Japanese attack on Pearl Harbor sinking the battleships of the US Pacific Fleet. But most damaging was the attack on the US air base of Clark Field in the Philippines, which destroyed the B-17 bomber force that might have blocked Japanese seaborne invasions.

If not for the Imperial Japanese attack on Pearl Harbor, followed immediately by Adolf Hitler's declaration of war against the United States, it is very difficult to see how the United States would have entered World War II. US public opinion in late 1941 favored giving Britain and the Soviets enough weapons to fight Hitler to the last man but keeping American boys out of the fray. If that opinion had continued to take precedence in US policy, history might have turned out very differently indeed,

The range of World War II belligerents expanded and contracted. In Europe the war began as France, Britain, and Poland against Nazi Germany. Nazi Germany and Soviet Russia conquered Poland by the end of September 1939. The Soviets attacked Finland, which in the winter and spring of 1940 fought it to a draw and a peace. The spring of 1940 also saw Germany attack and occupy Norway, Denmark, Belgium, the Netherlands, Luxembourg, and France, with Italy joining in on Germany's side. By the summer of 1940 only Britain was fighting Nazi Germany. In late 1940 and early 1941 Britain acquired Greece and Yugoslavia as allies. But they were conquered by Nazi Germany by the spring of 1941. In the summer of 1941 Nazi Germany attacked Soviet Russia. And on December 7, 1941, the Japanese navy attacked a wide range of US, British, and Dutch territories in the Pacific. Nazi Germany declared war on the United States a day later. (But, curiously enough, Japan remained at peace with Soviet Russia.) At that point, the war was truly global.

It was a "total war." At its peak, some 40 percent of the US gross domestic product was being devoted to the war. Some 60 percent of British GDP was devoted to the war. Some sixty million—plus or minus ten million—people died in, during, and as a result of the war.

How are we to understand World War II?

Consider death only.

When World War II ended, perhaps forty-five million in Europe and fifteen million in Asia were dead by violence or starvation. More than half of that number were inhabitants of the Soviet Union. But even west of the post–World War II Soviet border, perhaps one in twenty were killed. In Central Europe that number was close to one in twelve. During World War I, the overwhelming proportion of those killed had been soldiers. During World War II, well under half of those killed were soldiers. Raw numbers do no justice, but carry the point with the following tally of deaths:

European Jews: 6 million (70 percent) (one-third of them Poles)
Poland: 6 million (16 percent) (one-third of them Jews)
Soviet Union: 26 million (13 percent)
Germany: 8 million (10 percent)
Japan: 2.7 million (4 percent)
China: 10 million (2 percent)
France: 600,000 (1 percent)
Italy: 500,000 (1 percent)
Britain: 400,000 (1 percent)
United States: 400,000 (0.3 percent)

To help explain the course of the war, we can first look at it tactically and operationally. Consider the first three major campaigns—the Polish campaign of September 1939, the French campaign of May and June 1940, and the first six months of the Russian campaign, from June 22 to the end of 1941.

In the 1939 Polish campaign, the Nazis lost 40,000 soldiers killed and wounded. The Poles lost 200,000 killed and wounded. The Poles also lost about 1 million taken prisoner. In the 1940 French campaign, the Nazis lost 160,000 soldiers killed and wounded. The Allies lost 360,000 soldiers killed and wounded. And the Allies also lost 2 million soldiers taken prisoner. In the first six months of the 1941 Russian campaign, the Nazis lost 1 million soldiers killed and wounded. The Russians lost 4 million soldiers killed and wounded. And the Russians lost 4 million soldiers taken prisoner.

The Nazis were simply better, tactically, at the business of war than any of their enemies. They understood dive bombers, they understood tank columns, and they understood surprise and flank attacks and digging in. The interwar German army on which the Nazis had built had had only 100,000 soldiers. But those 100,000 soldiers had learned and developed their business to a terrifying degree of tactical superiority. That is the first lesson of World War II: fight the Nazis and expect to be tactically outclassed. Expect to lose between two and five times as many soldiers on the battlefield as the Nazi armies do. That was true for everyone at the start of the war, and it was still true remarkably late into the war—even though the Allies did learn.

Moreover, the Nazis' opponents were operationally outclassed. Hence the second lesson of World War II: fight the Nazis and expect periodically to find large groups of your soldiers overwhelmed, surrounded, cut off, out of supplies, fleeing in panic, and forced to surrender in large numbers. The last such episode took place in December 1944, less than five months before the collapse of the Nazi regime, when the Nazi Fifth Panzer Army surrounded nearly the entire 106th Infantry Division of the US Army in the Snowy Mountains of the Ardennes Forest on the Belgian-German border, forcing it to surrender.

Simply put, tactical and operational superiority matters immensely.

Consider again the French campaign of 1940. The French were expecting the Nazis to attack through Belgium north of the Ardennes Forest. Instead, the Nazis made their main attack through the Ardennes Forest itself, against the weak French Ninth Army—weak because the French command thought that the forest, the poor road network, and the Meuse River would be sufficient additional defenses.

Three days into the 1940 battle it was clear that a major Nazi attack was coming through the Ardennes, and the French began to respond. According to Ernest May's *Strange Victory*, they did so robustly. He reported that at 3:00 p.m. on May 12, the French general Charles Huntziger ordered "strong reinforcements to repel a prospective German attack." What May called "three of the strongest elements in the general reserve" then joined Huntziger's Second Army: the Third Armored, the Third Motorized Infantry, and the Fourteenth Infantry Divisions. "The infantry division was a crack unit," May wrote.[13]

By May 15, these three divisions had been further reinforced: The French First Armored Division had been switched from the Belgian plain to the Ninth Army sector to its south; infantry formations had been ordered to assemble behind the Ninth Army to form a new Sixth Army; and the Second Armored Division had been ordered to assemble behind the Ninth Army as well. Charles de Gaulle, placed in command of the newly formed Fourth Armored Division, was ordered to attack the southern flank of the incipient Nazi German breakthrough.

So what happened to all these forces—four heavy armored divisions, with perhaps eight hundred tanks between them, plus a large chunk of the sixteen infantry divisions that were in the

French strategic reserve? Before hearing the answer, consider that the French had as many tanks in their four armored divisions as the Nazis had in the seven panzer divisions that were in the Nazi main thrust.

Here's what happened.

The French First Armored Division simply ran out of gas. While it was waiting for the fuel trucks to replenish its tanks, General Erwin Rommel's Seventh Panzer Division came down the road. Seizing the opportunity, Rommel attacked and destroyed the French First Armored. For want of fuel, it was wiped off the board as a fighting unit.

The French Second Armored Division was ineffective because its assembly areas had been overrun by the Nazis before it could even begin to fight. According to William L. Shirer's *The Collapse of the Third Republic*, "orders for the [Second Armored] Division to move . . . did not come until noon of May 13," and "the trains with the tanks and artillery were not able to start until the afternoon of the 14th." Then, "the wheeled vehicles with the supplies ran into the panzers" and had to withdraw, as they had "no combat elements." By the time the tanks and tracked artillery were ready, "between Saint Quentin and Hirson," they were "hopelessly dispersed over a large triangle."[14]

Huntziger ordered the French Third Armored Division to retreat to the south, judging that its principal task should be to guard the left flank against an attack if the Nazis turned south after crossing the Meuse River. The infantry formations of the French Sixth Army, like the French Second Armored Division, were overrun by General Georg-Hans Reinhardt's Sixth Panzer Division on May 15 and 16 while they were trying to organize themselves.

By May 16, as Shirer put it, France's three heavy armored divisions, "all of which on May 10 had been stationed . . . within 50 miles of the Meuse at Sedan and Mezieres, which they could have reached by road overnight, had thus been squandered. . . .

Not one had been properly deployed." They were now out of the action.

When the Nazis had attacked on May 10, the French had had only three armored divisions. On May 11, the French high command ordered an annoying and arrogant colonel, Charles de Gaulle, to form and take command of the Fourth Armored Division. On May 17 he led what troops he had in an attack that at least caused the Nazi spearheads some hours of uncertainty. De Gaulle's Fourth Armored Division did make its weight felt on the battlefield. But, as Shirer noted, that division "was below strength and without divisional training."[15] When France fell, de Gaulle did not surrender, but instead declared that he himself was the leader of France—Free France: "The flame of French resistance must not be extinguished and will not be extinguished."[16] Somehow, he made it stick, and the "Free French," armed with American weapons, fought with the Allies until 1945.

The French failed in tactics—the comparative battlefield casualties make that clear. The French failed in strategy—by opposing the main Nazi attack with the weak Ninth Army while leaving the stronger formations to the north, where they were vulnerable to encirclement. And the French failed in operations.

On May 10, Churchill had left his job as First Lord of the Admiralty, kissed the hands of the king, and taken over as First Lord of the Treasury, replacing Chamberlain as leader of the British Empire. Five days later he received a phone call from the French prime minister, Paul Reynaud: "We have been defeated. We are beaten. We have lost the battle. The road to Paris is open. We are defeated," Reynaud told him.

On May 16, Churchill crossed the English Channel. The flight to the Paris airport took just over an hour. It became immediately clear that the situation was dire, far more dire than he had understood before boarding the flight. The French general Maurice Gamelin explained the situation in simple, stark terms, which Churchill recorded in his memoir:

North and south of Sedan, on a front of fifty or sixty miles, the Germans had broken through. The French army in front of them was destroyed or scattered. A heavy onrush of armoured vehicles was advancing with unheard-of speed. . . . Behind the armour, he said, eight or ten German divisions, all motorized, were driving onwards, making flanks for themselves as they advanced against the two disconnected French armies on either side.[17]

The Germans, General Gamelin stated, were expected in Paris in a few days. Gobsmacked, Churchill asked, in clear English and poor French, about the French Army's strategic reserve:

General Gamelin turned to me and, with a shake of the head and a shrug, said "Aucune" [None]. . . . I was dumbfounded. What were we to think of the great French Army and its highest chiefs? . . . One can have, one must always have, a mass of divisions which marches up in vehement counter-attack at the moment when the first fury of the offensive has spent its force. . . . I admit this was one of the greatest surprises I have had in my life. . . . Presently I asked General Gamelin when and where he proposed to attack. . . . His reply was "Inferiority of numbers, inferiority of equipment, inferiority of method"—and then a hopeless shrug of the shoulders.[18]

Churchill was wrong: the French had possessed a strategic reserve. It had been committed, and it had been ground up in a week. Systemic failures in tactics, strategy, and operations had rendered it ineffective in combat, dooming France.

Before we scorn the French army of 1940 as cheese-eating surrender monkeys, remember what happened to the US 106th Infantry Division when Hitler's Third Reich was on its very last legs. The same had happened to Major General Lloyd Fredendall's US II Corps at Kasserine Pass in Tunisia, in the US forces' first encounter with the Nazi army on the attack. Everybody—the Poles, the Dutch, the Belgians, the French, the Yugoslavs, the Greeks, the British, the Americans, and the Russians—who faced the Nazis failed more or less equally, both tactically and operationally, at least in their initial encounters, and in no small number of subsequent encounters.

The tactical and operational superiority of the Nazi armies was a powerful force multiplier. Fortunately for the world and for the Allies, it was offset by equally large strategic deficits. Consider the high-water mark of Nazi conquest in Europe, November 1942. The Nazis had thirteen of their field army formations in Russia, between the Baltic Sea to the northwest and the Black and Caspian Seas to the south and southeast. Eight of those were spread out in a line extending from what was then Leningrad on the Baltic Sea south-southeast to the city of Voronezh on the Don, the middle one of European Russia's three great southern rivers, three-fifths of the way from the Baltic Sea (on which Leningrad sat) to the Caspian Sea. Then there was a gap. Then there were two armies where the Don and Volga Rivers nearly touched, halfway from Voronezh to the Caspian. That is where the city then called Stalingrad was located. And there were three more armies much farther to the southeast, in the Caucasus Mountains.

Why were those five armies in the southeast—the two grinding the city of Stalingrad to rubble and the three in the Caucasus—extended so far from the rest? What were they doing? And what was the gap between them and the rest of the Nazi German army? The answer for the three southernmost is that they were trying to conquer the Caucasus oil fields. Hitler and his staff were convinced that Nazi Germany could not continue the war unless they controlled more oil fields than the Romanian ones around Ploesti.

As it happens, they were wrong. Subordinates were lying to superiors about how much fuel they had and how much they were using. One of the defects of command-and-control central planning is that you are increasingly beholden to the honesty of subordinates, who are increasingly encouraged to fall on the side of conservative speculation, rather than being called out for failing to plan adequately. In any case, Hitler was convinced that everything must be risked to conquer the oil fields.

The two armies, the German Sixth Army and the German Fourth Panzer Army, near the banks of the Don and Volga Rivers, were guarding the left flank of the three armies committed to the Caucasus. Both were also expending men and materials and precious time trying to capture the bombed-out wreckage that had been the city of Stalingrad.

It's unclear why—other than that the city was named after the Soviet Russian dictator. Capture of Stalingrad and the Volga River banks on which it sat would not provide better flank protection for the armies farther south than a position back at Kalach on the Don River. And the Sixth Army and Fourth Panzer Army ought to have been worrying about their own flanks, for between them and Voronezh were only badly trained and poorly equipped soldiers from Italy and Germany's less-than-enthusiastic allies in the Balkans.

The USSR had avoided losing the third tranche of the Red Army—that which had fought in the late fall and winter of 1941–1942, plus reinforcements—in the summer and fall of 1942. They had been mauled. They had fallen back—unwillingly—in front of the Nazi offensive. They had, however, avoided destruction via mass encirclements and surrenders, like those of 1941. And, meanwhile, scraping the bottom of their manpower barrel—and relying on a combination of Lend-Lease supplies and the armaments factories that Aleksei Kosygin's team had evacuated from in front of the Nazi advance and moved to safety in the east[19]—they had built a fourth tranche of their army with which to launch winter offensives.

The Soviets attempted two great offensives in the winter of 1942–1943. Operation Mars was directed against the center of the Nazi line, near Moscow. It was a failure, with heavy casualties. Operation Uranus was directed against the long exposed Nazi flanks near Stalingrad. It was a total and overwhelming success, pulling off a grand encirclement and a grand surrender by surrounding and capturing the entire German Sixth Army (and large chunks of the Fourth Panzer Army as well) and forcing a precipitous withdrawal of the Nazi forces farther south away from the oil fields and back toward Germany. It was an extraordinary victory, and one made possible only by the extraordinary strategic lapses that had ordered the Nazi eastern front forces to their dispersed positions in late 1942.

The Red Army might thus have grasped the last chance for the Allies to win a victory in World War II that did not require reducing Germany to a radioactive wasteland. If Operation Uranus at Stalingrad had failed as did Operation Mars in front of Moscow, and if the fourth tranche of the Red Army had, like its three predecessors, also been ground up into ineffectiveness in the months after its deployment, would Stalin have been able to raise a fifth? Or would that have been the end of the Soviet Union?

Whereas the Allies could afford strategic lapses, in the sense of paying the butcher's bill and keeping in the fight, the Nazis could not. Not while they were fighting a total war on several fronts across an entire continent (and to varying degrees across several of the planet's oceans). Consider the number of German troops killed or missing month by month from the start of 1941 to the end of 1944. From the start of Russian theater operations in June 1941 on, with occasional pauses, the Nazis lost, killed or missing, about 50,000 German soldiers every month. At the start of the war, Nazi Germany had an ethnic German population of about 60 million, with perhaps 15 million men of military age. Half of those could be mobilized. The other half were needed for war work, though these men could have been moved to various fronts if the Nazis had been willing to go against their ideology and mobilize women on a large scale, which they were not. With a maximum potential army strength of only 7.5 million, steadily losing 50,000 each month is a heavy drain.

Then comes a 250,000 spike in December 1942 through February 1943. This mass loss of manpower caused the surrender of the Sixth Army at Stalingrad. A smaller spike in late spring followed, causing the surrender of the Nazi army group in Tunisia. A year later, in the summer of 1944, there was a 1-million-soldier spike during the collapse and surrender of the Nazi Army Group Center under the impact of Soviet Russia's offensive Operation Bagration.

Better Nazi strategy that did not undermine Germany's tactical and operational edge would have prolonged the war. Perhaps it would have allowed Germany to win it: a Germany that picked its enemies sequentially and fought each until it was defeated would have been much more dangerous than a Germany that attacked Soviet Russia while still fighting a war with Britain, and that then declared war on the United States on December 8, 1941.

But Germany probably would still not have won the war. Even the best strategy, coupled with Germany's operational and tactical advantages, would have been unlikely to make up for the logistical and productivity differentials. They were just too great.

Set war production of the United States in 1944 equal to 100. By this metric, in 1940 Britain's production was 7 and Nazi Germany's and Japan's were 11. In 1942, all the Allies together were producing 92, and Germany and Japan were producing 16. And by 1944, it was 150 to 24.

From 1942 on, once the war had become truly global, Hitler's defeat was nearly inevitable. Even Britain alone was matching Nazi Germany and Nazi-occupied Europe in war production. Throw in the United States and the Soviet Union, and Nazi Germany was outproduced more than eight to one. Nazi Germany and Japan together were outproduced more than six to one.

A three-to-one tactical-operational advantage in casualties does not help when you are outnumbered in tanks and aircraft eight to one and outnumbered in potential military manpower ten to one. Starting in the fall of 1942, a large number of important battles went against Nazi Germany and Imperial Japan: The Battle of Midway northwest of Hawaii. The Battle of Guadalcanal. The Battle of El Alamein in Egypt. The years-long Battle of the Atlantic. And most of all, the Battle of Stalingrad and Operation Uranus. By the end of all this it was very clear who would win the war, if the Nazis elected to keep on fighting. Ideology dictated that they must, so they did. It was not, said Churchill in November 1942, the end. It was not even, said Churchill, the beginning of the end. But it was the end of the beginning. He was right.

In the spring of 1945, US, British, and Russian forces met in the rubble that had been Germany. In his bunker in Berlin Adolf Hitler committed suicide as the Russians closed in on his command post. And even if the armies of these nations had not proven victorious on the battlefield, there was the Manhattan Project and the atomic bomb. Japan, atom bombed, firebombed, blockaded, and threatened with invasion, surrendered in the summer of 1945.

Might science have offered the Nazis an escape hatch? No. When Hitler took power, Germany had the best atomic physicists in the world. But what they did was dismissed as "Jewish science." The lucky were able to flee into exile, some making their way to the United States and England, where they lent their knowledge to defeating the Nazis.

The Nazis had no atom bombs; nor did they know how to build any. In contrast, starting in August 1945, the United States had the power to turn cities, starting at two for the first month, into radioactive wastelands. And the United States would have used that power until unconditional surrender was offered. We know this because that is what it did.

World War II was, in an utterly insufficient word, horrid. A number of scholars have observed that it was all avoidable. Had the British and French governments been willing to use force to remove Hitler when he occupied the Rhineland in 1936, or when he threatened Czechoslovakia in 1938, there would have been no World War II in Europe. Had Stalin allied with Britain and France and declared war on Nazi Germany when Hitler invaded Poland in 1939, in all probability Hitler would have been crushed much sooner, and World War II in Europe would have ended by the end of 1941.

Perhaps. Such speculation turns more on individuals than underlying facts, either of ideology or of economy.

Or suppose Franklin D. Roosevelt had decided, in the spring of 1941, that with Europe ablaze it was unwise to try to use an economic embargo of militarily necessary oil to pressure Japan to withdraw from China. Perhaps even by 1945 the United States and Japan would have been at peace, the coastal provinces of China would have been Japanese-occupied colonies, anarchy would have reigned in China's interior, and the Japanese military would have enjoyed great prestige for establishing this co-prosperity.

Had anyone other than Winston Churchill become British prime minister in 1940—had Neville Chamberlain remained, or had Lord Halifax assumed the post—then the British government would almost surely have negotiated a separate peace with Nazi Germany in 1940. When Nazi Germany attacked Soviet Russia in 1941, it would have done so with its full strength. Stalin's regime might well have collapsed, and European Russia up to the Urals (and perhaps beyond) could have become a Nazi German territory, colony, or puppet state.

It is not likely that Hitler would have refrained from attacking Russia in any possible universe. The need to do so was buried too deeply in his ideological worldview. It is only slightly more plausible to think that Hitler might not have declared war on the United States in 1941.

Except Roosevelt, and Churchill, and Stalin, and Hitler, and Emperor Hirohito, were who they were, and that made a difference—perhaps *the* difference.

We do know that most of the alternative ways that World War II might have gone would trade a postwar period with a communist evil empire, centered in Moscow and dominant over Eastern Europe, for a postwar period with a Nazi evil empire, centered in Berlin and dominant over all of Europe, or perhaps Eurasia. Not an improvement.

What the world confronted after the surrenders were accepted was very different from those alternatives: a defeated, ruined Germany; a victorious, ruined Russia; a defeated, ruined, and in places radioactive Japan; various paths of destruction crisscrossing Europe; a victorious, but exhausted, British Empire; and a victorious, territorially unscathed, economically dominant, and newly confident United States. The world was thus very different from what anyone could have forecast back in 1933, or even 1938.

11

The Cold War of Hostile
Yet Coexisting Systems

Militarism and imperialism, racial and cultural rivalries—those had played the serpent to the pre-1914 Belle Époque era of largely peaceful progressive prosperity. After World War II these serpents were still out there slithering, and they soon took huge and nightmarish shape in the form of the US-Soviet Cold War.

Yet, paradoxically, the Cold War did not block or even hobble human progress toward prosperity and utopia. Rather, the Cold War seems more likely to have accelerated it.

Why isn't obvious. Indeed, on several occasions the Cold War veered toward a decidedly worse outcome. It teetered and tottered toward various brinks, including *the* brink. The Cold War blossomed violently on occasion. It expended vast resources on developing means of annihilation and extinction. It could have gone very badly.[1]

But it also kept other sources of conflict from themselves hobbling growth and progress.

The surreal character of the Cold War is neatly captured in the fact that, in one sense, Nikita Sergeyevich Khrushchev, one of

Stalin's more bloody-handed henchmen in the 1930s and 1940s, who ran the Soviet Union from 1956 to 1964, could be declared among its *winners*. In 1959 he wrote about competition and the need for peaceful coexistence, central themes of US-Soviet rivalries:

> Peaceful coexistence does not mean merely living side by side . . . with the constantly remaining threat of [war] break-ing out in the future. Peaceful coexistence can and should develop into peaceful competition for the purpose of satisfy-ing man's needs in the best possible way. . . . Let us try out in practice whose system is better, let us compete without war. This is much better than competing in who will pro-duce more arms and who will smash whom. We stand and always will stand for such competition as will help to raise the well-being of the people to a higher level. . . . We may argue, we may disagree with one another. The main thing is to keep to the positions of ideological struggle, without resorting to arms in order to prove that one is right. . . . Ultimately that system will be victorious on the globe which will offer the na-tions greater opportunities for improving their material and spiritual life.[2]

Khrushchev—who had also been quoted as declaring that Soviet Russia would "bury" the world's capitalist states—would have been surprised that, by 1990, it was clear even to his suc-cessors sitting in the Kremlin that really-existing socialism was a dead end for humanity.[3] It wasn't the case that the capitalist states had managed to bury the socialist states; they hadn't. While the Cold War briefly flared hot—for example, in Korea and Viet-nam—it was kept from becoming a global conflagration. What was more, the Cold War ended sort of the way Khrushchev had hoped: with one system offering clearly greater opportunities for improving material and spiritual life.

There was not supposed to be a Cold War.[4] The Allied powers—they called themselves the United Nations—had cooperated to destroy the greatest and most dangerous tyranny the world had ever seen. Why could they not continue to cooperate to build a better world? The post–World War II world was a great place for new global cooperative organizations. Chief among them was the broadening of this wartime United Nations alliance into the UNO—the United Nations Organization—with its Security Council, its General Assembly, and all of its branches.

And again, there was not supposed to be a Cold War. Marxist-Leninist theory was very clear on what was to come if World War II was followed by a genuine peace. Capitalism, in Lenin's view, needed imperialism.[5] Imperialism produced militarization, with its enormous demand for weapons and colonies, which offered captive markets. These were essential to preserve near-full employment, and so stave off the catastrophic economic crises— like the Great Depression—that would otherwise produce communist revolution. But imperialism also produced war. Thus, capitalism was staving off revolution due to economic catastrophe by courting revolution due to political-military catastrophe. And in Lenin's opinion, such staving off could only last so long.

As Lenin's successors saw it, the capitalist-imperialist powers had successfully delayed revolution from the late 1890s though imperialism and militarism, but they had then fallen into the catastrophe of World War I. And that brought Lenin to power in Russia and led to the creation of the first really-existing socialist country: the USSR. The revolution had greatly marched forward because of and in the aftermath of World War I.

After World War I, Lenin's successors believed, the capitalists had concluded that representative institutions were no longer compatible with their continued rule, so they swung their support behind fascists: Mussolini in Italy, Hitler in Germany, Franco in Spain, Philippe Pétain in France, Hideki Tojo in Japan. This did not remove the need for imperialism and militarism but rather sharpened it. The second great imperialist war, World War II, had been worse than the first.

Stalin and his subordinates saw, after the post–World War II consolidation, that there were five tasks they needed to carry out:

First, they had to build the USSR up militarily to defend the territories of really-existing socialism because the fascist-militarist capitalists might well try once again to destroy world socialism by military means. That was a reasonable notion, given that there were American generals—George Patton most prominent among them—who had wanted to start World War III the day after World War II ended, and ex-president Hoover thought that the United States had quite possibly fought on the wrong side in World War II. Although Hoover deeply regretted that the war had advanced the development of weapons of unbearable power, a president who thought like him might well use those weapons. From the Soviet point of view, more war in the not-so-distant future was a legitimate worry.

Second, Stalin and his followers thought, they had to extend the really-existing socialist order to new territories.

Third, the USSR had to advance economically, so as to realize the promise of socialism and demonstrate to the capitalist world how good life could be.

Fourth, they should stand ready to assist socialist movements in capitalist countries when they decided they were strong enough to attempt a revolution.

Fifth, they should lie low.

If they accomplished those tasks, then, they thought—and their faith assured them—that the logic of imperialist-militarist capitalism would do the rest of the work. The capitalist powers would clash again, in another catastrophic world war. And, provided the really-existing socialist bloc could keep its head down and survive, in the aftermath it would expand again. That was the Soviet Union's strategy: defend, rebuild, and wait, for history was on their side. Waging a cold war was not part of the plan.

Generals like Patton and ex-presidents like Hoover aside, there was little appetite for confrontation in the West, either. Isolationist currents in the United States were not as strong as they had been after World War I, but they were strong. Western Europe was exhausted. Rather than wishing to roll back really-existing socialism, Britain was seeking to find a role for its diminished (and diminishing) empire. General George Patton in the United States might muse about taking his Third Army's tanks and driving to Moscow, but that was far beyond the pale for any sane politician (and most others) in the North Atlantic. After four years of bloodshed and sacrifice (for Americans, that is—it had been years longer for the populations of Europe and Asia), the prospect of sending millions more to die at the front was in bad odor.

The whiff of which was even detectable by Joseph Stalin. Stalin did have a very strong taste for brutally snatching up territory when he thought it could be taken cheaply—starting with the suppression of the Mensheviks in Georgia at the end of the Russian Civil War. But after World War II, he curbed his appetite. He did not impose a really-existing socialist government on Finland but let it remain democratic, as long as it was disarmed and joined to no potentially anti-Soviet alliances—and as long as its government was riddled with Soviet agents. He cut off support to the Communist Party of Greece—largely. He counseled Mao Zedong in China to join a coalition with Chiang Kai-shek and wait. Marx had promised and prophesied that the *internal* contradictions of capitalism would destroy it. So there was no need for immediate action, and, indeed, action before the time was ripe might well be counterproductive.

Remember: the memory of the Great Depression was very fresh. It was not just communists who thought that countries relying on the market were likely to lapse into a period of underemployment and stagnation. A not uncommon judgment was that history would dramatically reveal the superiority of central planning. The feeling, as Marxist economist Paul Sweezy wrote in 1942, was that "the socialist sector of the world would [after World War II] quickly stabilize itself and push forward to higher standards of living, while the imperialist sector would flounder in difficulties."[6] Likewise, the British historian A. J. P. Taylor spoke in 1945 of how "nobody in Europe believes in the American way of life—that is, in private enterprise; or rather those who believe in it are a defeated party and a party which seems to have no more future."[7]

But Stalin could not resist grabbing the marshmallow. In 1948, he snatched up Czechoslovakia in a coup d'état. Moreover, Mao Zedong ignored Josef Stalin's cautions, defeated Chiang Kai-shek, and chased him and his Kuomintang to Taiwan. No doubt Stalin heard whispers that he was being overly cautious, perhaps that he had lost his nerve as a result of the shocks of World War II. West of what was to become the Iron Curtain, really-existing socialism was viewed with concern, disdain, and animus. Cadres had been decimated at the start of World War II by the departure of all those who could not stomach the Hitler-Stalin Pact. Really-existing socialism became more unattractive the more outsiders were able to scrutinize it closely. Plus it ran into the buzzsaw of nationalism, again. Rather than any universalizing creed binding the proletariat regardless of borders, it became clearer and clearer that allegiance to really-existing socialism required submission to or absorption into the latest incarnation of Russian Empire. Waiting for the contradictions of capitalism to emerge did not seem to be working, at least not quickly.

And so the post–World War II Soviet Union began to march toward further expansion rather than consolidation. And the United States felt compelled to respond. The Truman administration, which came into power in 1945 after Franklin Roosevelt's death, believed—as many members of Congress did—that the US withdrawal from international engagement after World War I had been one of the major triggers of World War II. Both the Truman administration and Congress wanted to make different mistakes, their own mistakes, rather than duplicate those of the past.

The view from Washington, DC, saw a Western Europe that might well run into the arms of really-existing socialism. In the aftermath of World War II, it was not clear that Western Europe would utilize market mechanisms to coordinate economic activity to any significant degree. Belief in the market had been severely shaken by the Great Depression. Wartime controls and plans, while implemented as extraordinary measures for extraordinary times, had created a governmental habit of control and regulation. Seduced by the very high economic growth rates reported by Stalin's Soviet Union, and awed by its war effort, many expected centrally planned economies to reconstruct faster and grow more rapidly than market economies.

Had European political economy taken a different turn, post–World War II European recovery might have been stagnant. Governments might have been slow to dismantle wartime allocation controls, and so have severely constrained the market mechanism. Europe after World War II was in worse economic shape than it had been after World War I. Another episode of financial and political chaos like that which had plagued the continent following World War I appeared likely. Politicians were predisposed toward intervention and regulation: no matter how damaging "government failure" might be to the economy, it had to be better than the "market failure" of the Depression.

One can imagine an alternative scenario in which European governments maintained and expanded wartime controls in order to guard against substantial shifts in income distribution. In such a case, the late 1940s and early 1950s might have seen the creation in Western Europe of allocative bureaucracies to ration scarce foreign exchange. It might have seen the imposition of price controls on exports to keep some of home production in the country, in order to protect the living standards of the urban working classes—as happened in various countries of Latin America, which nearly stagnated in the two decades after World War II. Consider Argentina, for example. In 1913, Buenos Aires was among the top twenty cities of the world in telephones per capita. In 1929 Argentina had been perhaps fourth in density of motor vehicles per capita, with approximately the same number of vehicles per person as France or Germany. Yet after World War II it rapidly fell from the ranks of the First World to the Third, with politics no more poisonous than Western European politics had typically been before World War II. From the perspective of 1947, the political economy of Western Europe would lead one to think that it was at least as vulnerable as Argentina.[8]

Indeed, in 1946–1947, US State Department officials wondered whether Europe might be dying—like a wounded soldier who bleeds to death after the fighting. State Department memoranda presented an apocalyptic vision of a complete breakdown in Europe of the division of labor—between city and country, industry and agriculture, and different industries themselves. The war had given Europe more experience than Argentina with economic planning and rationing. Militant urban working classes calling for wealth redistribution voted in such numbers as to make communists plausibly part of a permanent ruling political coalition in France and Italy. Economic nationalism had been nurtured by a decade and a half of depression, autarky, and war. European political parties had been divided brutally along economic class lines for two generations.

Certainly after World War I Western European growth had proceeded poorly—even more poorly than Argentinian growth after World War II. The recovery of coal production after World War I was erratic, and actually declined from 1920 to 1921, falling to 72 percent of 1913's level. This drop was a result of the deflation imposed on the European economy by central banks, which sought the restoration of pre–World War I gold-standard parities. Coal production fell again in 1923–1924, when the French army occupied Germany's Ruhr Valley because reparations were not being delivered fast enough. And coal production fell once more in 1925–1926, when austerity's pressure to lower wages on Britain's coal producers triggered first a coal and then a brief general strike.

Post–World War I Europe had seen the recovery of output repeatedly interrupted by political and economic "wars of attrition" between different classes and interests. So after World War II, European political leaders were intently focused on the question of how these difficulties could be avoided and political compromise attained. Indeed, if it had happened that such difficulties proved unavoidable, it seemed likely that Western Europe would vote to join Stalin's empire.

Yet Europe avoided these traps. By 1949, national income per capita in Britain, France, and Germany had recovered to within a hair of prewar levels. By 1951, six years after the war, as the US-led Marshall Plan to offer foreign aid to Europe came to an end, national incomes per capita were more than 10 percent above prewar levels. Measured by the admittedly imperfect yardstick of the national product estimates, the three major economies of Western Europe had achieved a degree of recovery that post–World War I Europe had not reached in the eleven years between World War I and the Great Depression.

Western Europe's mixed economies built substantial systems for redistribution. But they built these systems on top of—and not as replacements for—market allocations of consumer and producer goods and the factors of production. Though there was support for the restoration of a market economy in Western Europe, it was far from universal. Wartime controls were viewed as exceptional policies for exceptional times, but it was not clear what was to replace them. Communist and some socialist ministers opposed a return to the market. It was not clear when, or even if, the transition would take place. Yet it did.

Post–World War II Europe was very far indeed from laissez-faire. Government ownership of utilities and heavy industry was substantial. Government redistributions of income were large. The magnitude of the "safety nets" and social insurance programs provided by the post–World War II welfare states were far beyond anything that had been thought possible before World War I. But these large welfare states were accompanied by financial stability and by substantial reliance on market processes for allocation and exchange.

Why did things go so well for Western Europe after World War II?

It is easy to conclude that Western Europe's success came thanks to the US administrations of Franklin D. Roosevelt and Harry S Truman. Hobbled inside the United States by a sometimes recalcitrant Congress, the US executive branch from 1945 to 1952 somewhat strangely found itself with more power outside. First, it ran the occupations of Japan and the bulk of West Germany. It also extended a wide array of assistance—direct relief, offers of military support against potential Soviet expansion, large-scale loans, and access to US markets—to Western European countries, and these programs shaped their post–World War II policies in ways that gave the US administration confidence.

Within two years of the end of the war, it became US policy to build up Western Europe politically, economically, and militarily. The Truman Doctrine inaugurated the policy of "containment" of the Soviet Union. Included was a declaration that containment required steps to quickly regenerate economic prosperity in Western Europe. And as columnist Richard Strout wrote, "One way of combating Communism is to give western Europe a full dinner pail."[9]

Outflanking isolationist and antispending opposition, the Truman administration maneuvered the Truman Doctrine, the Marshall Plan, and then the North Atlantic Treaty Organization

(NATO) for the defense of Europe through Congress. To do so, it employed every weapon at its disposal, including Secretary of State George C. Marshall's reputation as the architect of military victory in World War II, conservative fears of the further extension of Stalin's empire, and a political alliance with influential Republican senator Arthur Vandenberg of Michigan.

Why was the plan named not for the US president, Truman, but for his secretary of state, Marshall? Truman put it best: "Can you imagine [the plan's] chances of passage in an election year in a Republican [majority] congress if it is named for Truman and not Marshall?"[10]

The Marshall Plan was a large multiyear commitment. From 1948 to 1951, the United States contributed $13.2 billion to European recovery. Of this total, $3.2 billion went to the United Kingdom, $2.7 billion to France, $1.5 billion to Italy, and $1.4 billion to the Western-occupied zones of Germany that would become the post–World War II *Bundesrepublik*. Figure 1 percent of the US national income over the years the program ran. Figure 3 percent of Western European national income.

Marshall Plan dollars did affect the level of investment: countries that received large amounts of Marshall Plan aid invested more. Barry Eichengreen and Marc Uzan calculated that out of each dollar of Marshall Plan aid some 65 cents went to increased consumption and 35 cents to increased investment. The returns to new investment were high: an extra dollar of investment raised national product by 50 cents in the subsequent year. Another way that Marshall Plan aid stimulated growth was by relaxing foreign exchange constraints. Marshall Plan funds were hard currency in a dollar-scarce world. After the war, coal, cotton, petroleum, and other materials were in short supply.[11]

But these direct effects were small potatoes. Marshall Plan aid plausibly boosted investment by only 1 percent of GDP. Even if it was concentrated on relieving the tightest bottleneck, such a commitment over three years can hardly be thought to have boosted Western Europe's productive potential by more than 1 percent. Yet Western Europe's post–World War II growth exceeded expectations by at least ten times that, and did so for three decades in a row.

It is most likely that the political-economic effects dominated, for after World War II the United States enthusiastically stepped into its role as the hegemon. Here the game theory matters: simply having an acknowledged hegemon made some things possible, made other things more possible, and amplified still other things that were accomplished because everyone understood how to coordinate and fell into line. Marshall Plan aid was preconditioned on successful financial stabilization. Each recipient had to sign a bilateral pact with the United States. Countries had to agree to balance government budgets, restore internal financial stability, and stabilize exchange rates at realistic levels.

Financial stabilization required balanced budgets. Balanced budgets required successful resolution of distributional conflicts. Here the Marshall Plan provided a very strong incentive. It gave European countries a pool of resources that could be used to cushion the wealth losses sustained in restructuring—and to soothe disappointed expectations from groups of labor and capitalists and landlords who thought they were not getting their proper shares of the pie. Marshall Plan administrators with one hand pressured European governments and interest groups to compromise, and to liberalize their economies in a more "American" mold. With the other hand they offered resources.

The resources did not obviate the need for sacrifice. But they increased the size of the pie available for division among interest groups.

And there were other institutions as well, besides the Marshall Plan's Economic Cooperation Administration, pushing in a positive and positive-sum direction. In the mid-1950s Western

Europe created its own European Coal and Steel Community for free trade in those commodities, an initiative that grew into today's European Union. The dominant United States had bet heavily on international trade as an enabler of international peace as well as of domestic prosperity. At the 1944 Bretton Woods Conference, US Treasury Department official Harry Dexter White and John Maynard Keynes from Britain had designed a system to try to make increased globalization work for good. There was to be a World Bank—an International Bank for Reconstruction and Development—to finance, via loans (on nonusurious terms), the reconstruction of those parts of the world that had been ruined by war and to develop those parts of the world that had not yet grasped the productive opportunities of modern machine and industrial technologies. There was also to be an International Monetary Fund (IMF), to manage the values of currencies and the net flow of financial resources across borders, to help countries to reset the terms on which they traded to do so, and to be the bad guy to urge, and perhaps command, countries to live up to their obligations, and reorient how they managed their economies in order to do so. The fact that Western Europe and the United States were together tied into alliance by the Cold War gave these institutions life and energy. Plus, the post–World War II global north was very lucky in its statesmen.

There was supposed to be an International Trade Organization (ITO) as well, to negotiate mutually beneficial reductions in tariffs to low or zero levels and to referee trading disputes. But although the Truman administration had pushed the United Nations, the World Bank, and the IMF through Congress, it decided at the end of 1950 that the ITO was too heavy a lift to even submit to Congress, given that by the end of that year the administration needed Congress to fund the Korean War and build out the long-run Cold War military structure. By 1950, too, openhanded international benevolent cooperation was out, and cash-on-the-barrelhead demands for assistance in the long twilight struggle between the free world and global communism were in. Instead of an organization with at least some teeth to enforce its judgments, there was to be an agreement—a General Agreement on Tariffs and Trade (GATT)—under the aegis of which multiple rounds of multilateral tariff reductions were to be gradually negotiated over decades.

And so a sizable part of the credit for Europe's successful post–World War II reconstruction belongs to these acts of cooperative international statesmanship: the Marshall Plan and other initiatives that sped Western European growth by altering the environment in which political and economic policy was made. The Marshall Plan era saw the creation of the social democratic "mixed economy": the restoration of price freedom and exchange rate stability, reliance on market forces within the context of a large social insurance state, some public ownership of industry and utilities, and a great deal of public demand management.

There was one additional very important factor making for post–World War II social democracy. The totalitarian threat from Stalin's Soviet Union across the Iron Curtain became very real. Many observers, such as the historian A. J. P. Taylor, simply did not believe "in the American way of life—that is, in private enterprise." But on close inspection, really-existing socialism was something they could believe in even less. The higher standards of living in the really-existing socialist Eastern Bloc did not emerge. The Great Depression did not return to Western Europe. Western Europeans came to fear a Soviet takeover. They wanted a US presence in Europe to deter such aggression. Hence they created the North Atlantic alliance and were willing to follow America's lead, and to drag America into leadership if necessary. What America wanted, they were eager to provide.

There is a story that when the Belgian statesman Paul-Henri Spaak was asked if it wouldn't be a good idea to set up a bunch of statues to the founders of the European Union, he answered:

"What a wonderful idea! We should erect a 50-foot tall statue in front of the Berlaymont [Palace in Brussels]! Of Joseph Stalin!"[12] It was the group of Soviet forces in Germany and the presence of the tanks of the Red Army at the Fulda Gap that most concentrated everyone's mind on how much they wanted NATO, the Coal and Steel Community, the European Economic Community, and then the European Union to succeed.

BY 1948, THE US government had drawn up plans to wage a real cold war: plans for boosting defense spending to 10 percent of national income and deploying US armies all across the globe. But those plans remained fantasies for unimaginable contingencies—until the Korean War.

In 1950, the strongman Kim Il-Sung, whom Stalin had installed in North Korea at the end of World War II, begged him for tanks and support to take over the south. Split at the 38th parallel, a somewhat arbitrary line of latitude, Korea was divided between the Soviet-overseen north and the US-overseen south.

But when Kim Il-Sung put his request to Stalin, there were no US garrisons in the south. At the start of 1950, Dean Acheson—now secretary of state for President Truman—announced that the day of "old relationships between east and west are gone." "At their worst," he said, they had been "exploitation," and "at their best . . . paternalism." Now those relationships had come to an end, and the United States had a "defense perimeter" in the Pacific that ran from "the Aleutians to Japan and then . . . to the Ryukyus [south of Japan]," and finally to the Philippines. Defense outside that perimeter was for "the entire civilized world under the Charter of the United Nations." For the United States to guarantee that it would come to the aid of any country outside of that area was "hardly sensible." Moreover, even within the defense perimeter in the Pacific, US strategists concluded, it made most sense to wield US power by air and sea rather than by land.[13]

Moreover, the United States was in favor of decolonization—getting the British out of India, the Dutch out of Indonesia, and other global powers out of the territories they had held for years. While the United States was happy to provide logistical support to the French, who were fighting a war against the communist Vietminh in Southeast Asia, it wanted the French to promise independence rather than further colonial rule as the end point.

Acheson's speech, however, did not specifically mention Korea or say how it fit into the defense perimeter in the Pacific. Did this omission tip the balance in Stalin's mind? It may have. In June 1950, Stalin let slip the dog of war that was Kim Il-Sung and his Soviet-trained and supplied army. The Korean War began. The United States surprised Kim Il-Sung, Stalin, Mao, and itself by rallying the United Nations to send an army. That army was largely made up of US troops but formally was a force of the United Nations, and its mission was to defend the order that had been established in the US-controlled zone of occupation that was to become South Korea—and perhaps to create a single unified Korea as well.

Fighting raged all across the Korean Peninsula, from near the Yalu River in the north to the Port of Pusan in the south. South Koreans and North Koreans fought on land; Americans fought on land, in the sea, and in the air; Chinese fought on land; Russians fought in the air (350 of their planes were shot down). In three years, somewhere between 1 million and 2 million Korean civilians died, 5 to 10 percent of the population, and perhaps 400,000 South Koreans were abducted from their homes and taken to North Korea. The military dead and missing amounted to roughly 500,000 Chinese, 300,000 North Koreans, 150,000 South Koreans, 50,000 Americans, and 4,400 others who fought to defend South Korea. The US Air Force dropped half a million tons of bombs during the war, which works out to 40 pounds for every North Korean then alive.

The United States did not use its nuclear weapons. It was a war, but it was a limited war. US theater of operations commander General Douglas MacArthur asked for their use at the end of 1950, when the Chinese People's Liberation Army forced the United Nations' army to retreat from near the Yalu River back to south of Seoul. The Pentagon and President Harry Truman refused.

Nonnuclear arms proved sufficient, and starting in March 1951, the battlefront stabilized near the 38th parallel, the original divide between north and south. The Pentagon and Truman began to seek a cease-fire and a return to the *status quo ante*—leaving neither victor nor vanquished.

On March 5, 1953, as the war dragged on, Joseph Stalin died of a stroke. Stalin's heirs decided that the Korean War was pointless and should end. Mao's negotiators accepted the United Nations' prisoner-of-war position: repatriation would not be forced. As a consequence, 10,000 of 15,000 Chinese prisoners of war decided not to return to China; 5,000 of 70,000 North Korean prisoners of war decided not to return to North Korea; and 327 South Korean prisoners of war decided to stay in North Korea, as did 21 Americans and 1 Briton. (Eventually, 18 of these 22 returned to the Western Bloc.)[14]

And so began the state of affairs that would continue for decades, even past the end of the long twentieth century—with North Korea still under the autocratic rule of the Kim dynasty, which presided over one of the worst famines of the post–World War II period, and with South Korea independent—a rich industrial power and a democracy.

But the Korean War was important not just for Korea. The Korean War was one of those butterfly-wing flaps that changed the world, for it turned the United States and its national security apparatus onto a new path, one defined by spending five times the previous level of annual military expenditure and by establishing a truly global reach. Put succinctly, in the aftermath of the Korean War the United States took up a new role.

To start with, Germany looked analogous to Korea—a country divided by what had been intended to be a temporary, postwar military occupation boundary.

Stalin's successors were largely unknown. The only certain thing about them was that they had flourished—which often meant managed to survive—under Stalin, and that they proved willing to shoot a couple of their own number in the struggle that followed Stalin's death.

Thus, by the middle of the 1950s, there was a full US army sitting in West Germany waiting for Stalin's successors to attempt in Germany what Stalin, Mao, and Kim Il-Sung had attempted in Korea: the reunification by force of a country that had been divided by the armistice that ended World War II.

What had before June 1950 been the fantasies of national security staffers and planners became reality: they were able to push US national security spending up to 10 percent of national income. The weapons were, by and large, not used. But the fact that the government was buying them made a return of anything like the Great Depression all but impossible. It provided a strong floor to demand and employment in the United States—for the government bought, and those it bought from put people to work and had the revenue to buy other things, and so to put still other people to work.

This spending was in large part intended as a way of allowing the United States to project its Cold War military might far beyond its borders. The United States deployed troops and established permanent military bases on every continent save Antarctica. Roughly three-quarters of a percent of the US national product in the mid-1950s was "net military transactions"—expenditures abroad by the US military that generated no dollar inflow. In Europe, the increase in net US military transactions did much to offset the winding-down of the Marshall Plan. In short, NATO provided more than shock troops to thwart a Soviet invasion. It also provided one more secure source of demand for European production during Europe's booms in the 1950s and 1960s.

Which brings us to nuclear weaponry.

From 1956, the formal policy of the Soviet Union was "peaceful coexistence." The Russians would, of course, continue to support just revolts against colonialism and capitalism. But war between the superpowers? Off the table. The United States and the USSR would coexist. The priority would be to lie low and demonstrate really-existing socialism's advantages—which would lead to triumph in the end, of course.

From 1954, the US policy became one of "massive retaliation." In a speech that year, Secretary of State Allen Dulles made clear that the strategy would be to "contain the mighty landpower of the Communist world": "The way to deter aggression," he said, was for "the free community to be willing and able to respond vigorously at places and with means of its own choosing."[15] This policy, pointedly, did not take a nuclear-weapon response to a conventional provocation off the table; nor did it restrict retaliation and deterrence to the particular theater of conflict.

Each side viewed the other as a potential existential threat, which led to both sides becoming existential threats in fact.

Nuclear forces that US planners regarded as perhaps inadequate to deter a Russian nuclear strike or conventional-force invasion of Western Europe struck Russian planners as dangerously close to a level of force that could devastate the Soviet Union and support a conventional occupation of their territory. They remembered the burning of Moscow by the Crimean Tartars in 1571, the occupation of Moscow by the Poles in 1610, the invasion by the Swedes in 1709, the occupation of Moscow by the French in 1812, the German-dictated Peace of Brest-Litovsk in 1918, and Hitler's invasion in 1941.

But the key word in Dulles's 1954 speech detailing America's strategy of massive resistance was "contain": the US policy, and indeed the NATO alliance's policy, for the Cold War was one of *containment*. As US diplomat George Kennan put it, the right strategy was one of "holding the line and hoping for the best." Because "ideology convinces the rulers of Russia that truth is on their side and they can therefore afford to wait," he went on, "Soviet pressure" could be "contained by the adroit and vigilant application of counter-force at a series of constantly shifting geographical and political points."

And there was more: "The issue of Soviet-American relations is in essence a test of the overall worth of the United States as a nation among nations," Kennan wrote:

> The thoughtful observer of Russian-American relations will find no cause for complaint in the Kremlin's challenge to American society. He will rather experience a certain gratitude to a Providence which, by providing the American people with this implacable challenge, has made their entire security as a nation dependent on their pulling themselves together and accepting the responsibilities of moral and political leadership that history plainly intended them to bear.[16]

It was American Exceptionalism with a capital "E" taken to the max. If only the United States could, Kennan believed, truly be a City upon a Hill—if only it could, as John Winthrop had preached back in 1630, "follow the counsel of Micah, to do justly, to love mercy, to walk humbly with our God," so that "he shall make us a praise and glory that men shall say of succeeding plantations, 'may the Lord make it like that of New-England'"—if only it could behave thusly, then the United States and the NATO alliance would have nothing to fear from the Cold War.

The Americans who ran foreign policy overwhelmingly agreed. Nevertheless, the menace of totalitarianism loomed large. It was true that one, the greater, totalitarian power had been scotched—Nazi

Germany. But another, if lesser, version—Stalin's and Mao's systems of really-existing socialism—was growing. The nations that it comprised were materially weak, and poor. But they were populous. And their governments had a disturbing ability to get people to endorse and fight for their cause by telling implausible lies.

For the majority of the United States' political leaders and their military and diplomatic staffs, however, there was no reason to panic. Deterrence would control the nuclear threat. The Kremlin was run by colorless apparatchiks who liked their standard of living and position. Bureaucratic ossification was the destiny of really-existing socialism, if only it could be contained and outwaited. They were right to think so.

Soviet leader Nikita Khrushchev also saw no reason to panic, and every reason to wait for the verdict of history. "Whether you like it or not, history is on our side," he said in 1956.[17] More ominously, he added, "We will bury you." But this translation could use further explanation. Probably the Russian, "Мы вас похороним," meant something like "We will outlast you." Later on, Khrushchev clarified what he had meant: "I once said, 'We will bury you,' and I got into trouble with it. Of course, we will not bury you with a shovel. Your own working class will bury you." Russia had lost twenty-seven million people in World War II—including those who starved to death. Nobody in Russia wanted World War III.

And so the world entered a stable, well-shy-of-utopia equilibrium, though you had to squint hard to see it.

There were reasons for Khrushchev to have confidence, reasons derivable not from the excellences of really-existing socialism's central-planning mechanisms but from the deficiencies of market economies. After all, market economies can and do go horribly wrong. Markets carry out their implicitly assigned tasks with ruthless efficiency. The key to managing systems of markets is to determine what instructions the market is being implicitly given and how to alter those instructions. A market economy can only produce good results if it defines the general welfare appropriately—if it weights the material well-being and utility of each individual in an appropriate manner as it adds up and makes tradeoffs. And the problem is that the value that a market economy gives an individual depends on his or her wealth.

Suppose each doubling of material consumption adds an equal amount to individual utility—that the first dollar of income is more valuable than the second, the second more valuable than the third, and so on. Then theoretical economists' formulas and theorems take on a particularly simple form: the market maximizes the general welfare if and only if the general welfare weights each person's well-being by the market value of his or her wealth. With unequal distribution, a market economy will generate extraordinarily cruel outcomes. If my wealth consists entirely of my ability to work with my hands in someone else's field, and if the rains do not come, so that my ability to work with my hands has no productive market value, then the market will starve me to death—as it did to millions of people in Bengal in 1942 and 1943.

The market could fail.

And central planning could succeed. The Soviet economy had, after all, proven itself very effective in building the most cost-effective tanks of World War II, the T-34C and the T-34/85. American tank production was more efficient. But the centrally planned economy mobilized more resources. And as long as there is just one overwhelming goal, or a few, to be accomplished, inefficiencies from overenthusiastic and overrigid plans are of second-order importance.

A centrally planned economy has an easier time persuading those who would otherwise divert resources from investment to consumption not to do so. US economists in the 1950s and 1960s speculated about a future in which the USSR's higher share of national income devoted to investment would give it, in the long run, a much greater capital intensity. The added production from that capital intensity might then outweigh the inefficiencies of central planning and provide Soviet citizens with a high material standard of living in spite of planned inefficiency.

And there was never any terribly good reason to believe that market economies were by any theoretical necessity superior in the discovery, development, and deployment of technology. The Soviet Union's launch of Sputnik, the first satellite, was an especially loud wake-up call to any who did not see Kennan's call to fight the Cold War by making America into its best self as a serious challenge requiring serious effort.

WAS THIS NONUTOPIA STABLE? The post–World War II world stood under the shadow of nuclear war. The nuclear weapons strategists embraced "MAD" strategies, which seemed to be not just an acronym for "mutual assured destruction" but also accurate shorthand for "insane."

And the world was not free from other serpents in the garden—other forms of militarism and imperialism, of national, cultural, and economic rivalries.

For example, in the same letter in which Truman's successor, President Dwight Eisenhower, admonished his brother Edgar for imagining that his administration could, or should, roll back the New Deal, he boasted about how the CIA under his administration had led the coup that had entrenched Mohammed Reza Pahlavi as shah and dictator in Iran, thus keeping the oil-rich states of the Middle East from going commie. Eisenhower was certain that the Truman administration would have allowed just that—and so he believed he had largely removed the greatest "threat that has in recent years overhung the free world."[18] But no rational person saw the Iranian prime minister, Mohammad Mosaddegh, as a little Stalin, or even a Lenin.

Two decades later, rational believers in peaceful coexistence would have watched the elected Chilean president, Salvador

Allende, with interest, though perhaps not enthusiasm. If his attempts to manage a peaceful transition to a more attractive form of really-existing socialism failed to produce prosperity and liberty, it would be a useful warning to other nations, as something it would be better not to do. If Allende succeeded, it might be a model that other countries could draw on to make themselves better. But that was not the logic of Cold Warriors: they sought the military coup by general-turned-dictator Augusto Pinochet, along with mass executions, and right-wing ideologues proclaimed the necessity of Pinochet taking on a role analogous to that of the mythical classical Greek lawmaker Lykourgos of Sparta. On the other side of the Iron Curtain, rational believers in peaceful coexistence would have welcomed the attempts of Czechoslovakia's Alexander Dubček to build "socialism with a human face," but instead, the reaction of Leonid Brezhnev in the Kremlin was to send in the tanks: really-existing socialism did not and could not be allowed to have a human face.

And yet, for some other colonized nations during the first post–World War II generation, the Cold War might be a blessing. Before independence, they could push for decolonization by arguing that if it was delayed, the Russians and the Chinese would use the grievances justly felt by the colonized to build support for insurgencies, which would risk that nation joining the communist bloc. After independence, they could declare themselves "nonaligned," taking their cue from the movement that started at the Bandung Conference in Indonesia, spearheaded by Indonesian strongman Sukarno and Indian prime minister Jawaharlal Nehru. Nonaligned nations could then call for bids of support from both sides in the Cold War. The more important the nonaligned state was to the Cold War's dueling contestants, the more both sides would be willing to spend to support a nonaligned government that was trying to decide what its political and economic system, or at least its allegiances, should be.

Of course, the hotter the Cold War became, the more likely it was that a government or a popular movement trying to steer its own course would be pulled up short by the choke chain of one of the superpowers, and that people would die. Yugoslavia and Finland managed to pursue their own paths—but the Red Army stepped in to enforce the party line and discipline in East Germany in 1953, in Hungary in 1956, in Czechoslovakia in 1968, and in Afghanistan in 1978. The United States sponsored coups or sent troops to overthrow governments in Iran and Guatemala in 1954, Cuba in 1961, Chile in 1973, the Dominican Republic and Nicaragua in 1981, and Grenada in 1983. And there were the cases where the Cold War turned genuinely hot: Korea (5 million dead), Vietnam (2.5 million dead), Ethiopia (1.5 million dead), Angola (500,000 dead), and more.

There were governments as well that attacked their own societies: somewhere between 100,000 and 500,000 of Indonesia's population of 100 million were murdered in 1965, "the year of living dangerously." Strongman Indonesian leader Suharto used an attempted communist coup as a pretext to sideline the previous strongman leader, Sukarno, and then slaughter every Indonesian whom anyone said might be a communist. The Khmer Rouge in 1975–1979 killed perhaps 2 million of Cambodia's 8 million people for no reason whatsoever—and still China and the United States backed the Khmer Rouge against the Cambodian government that the Vietnamese installed in 1979. There were more—many more—such instances.

As bad as these large-scale butcheries were, there was always the potential for even more disastrous outcomes, and every now and then, the stability of this nonutopia teetered toward Armageddon.

For example, humanity perched on the edge of thermonuclear war during the Cuban missile crisis of October 1962. Nikita Khrushchev was somewhat surprised by the bellicose reaction of

US president John F. Kennedy to Russia's deployment in Cuba of missiles like those the United States had previously deployed in Turkey, next to Russia's border. In the end, the United States promised not to overthrow the Cuban communist dictator, Fidel Castro, by force, and Russia withdrew its missiles from Cuba. More quietly, the United States withdrew its missiles from Turkey.

It has gone down in American political historical lore that, eyeball to eyeball, Russia blinked. Perhaps. But it should also be noted that Russia was the reasonable one, willing to lose "face," for both sides agreed to keep the US withdrawal from Turkey a secret. A lot of grossly misleading histories were written over the next two decades based on those bad-faith reports—some by Kennedy administration insiders—before that secret was revealed.

There were other teeters.

In 1960, the moonrise was mistaken by NATO radar for a nuclear attack—and the United States went on high alert, even though Khrushchev was in New York City at the United Nations at the time. In 1967, the North American Aerospace Defense Command (NORAD) thought a solar flare was Soviet radar jamming, and nearly launched its bombers. In 1979, the loading of a training scenario onto an operational computer led NORAD to call the White House, claiming that the USSR had launched 250 missiles against the United States, and that the president had only between three and seven minutes to decide whether to retaliate. In 1983, the Soviet Union's Lieutenant Colonel Stanislav Petrov refused to classify an early warning system missile sighting as an attack, dismissing it (correctly) as an error, and thereby preventing a worse error.

That same year, the Soviet air force mistook an off-course Korean airliner carrying 100 people for one of the United States' RC-135 spy planes that routinely violated Russian air space and shot it down. In 1988, the US Navy cruiser *Vincennes*—at the time in Iranian territorial waters without Iran's permission—shot down an Iranian airliner carrying 290 people.

Sometimes, the Cold War went badly. Sometimes very badly. And sometimes it threatened to go very, very badly indeed.

It is salutary to admit that the Cold War could have ended otherwise. It could have ended horribly. It could have ended with an Eastern Bloc victory, or a more permanent stasis that might still be going on. Why didn't it? People could and did make a difference. Those who made the greatest difference, I think, were those who kept the Cold War from getting hot, those who persuaded many who wanted to keep fighting it that it was over, and those who worked hardest to make the social democratic Western alliance its best self.

There was, after all, a deadly serious underlying contest. Two systems were purporting to have their people's interests, perhaps even their best interests, in mind. And in 1990 it was unambiguously the case that one of those two was better, or perhaps just less bad. But be not proud: in many ways, it is less the case that the "West" categorically proved its system to be the best than that it categorically proved its system not to be worse. Not more utopian so much as less dystopian. For by that time, the Soviet Union had set a rather low bar by which to judge better and worse.

12

False (and True) Starts
to Economic Development
in the Global South

For many, many pages now the focus has been on the global north. That is fair. It, for the most part, led the world in the causal dance of economic history. And the struggle over systems was—China a very important aside—carried out in and near the global north. But now it is time to survey what was happening in the meantime in the poorer and less industrialized and deindustrialized parts of the world, addressing the era between the fall of China's Qing dynasty in 1911 and the end of the Cold War in 1990.

As economist W. Arthur Lewis warned in 1978, the history of the global south is so varied that you can find in it at least one example of any interpretive position you might wish to assert.[1] For my purposes, this means acknowledging that it is where grand narratives risk running aground, again and again and again. Still, I hold to their virtue—that is, to the ability of grand narratives to help us think—and it is in that spirit that I undertake this grand narrative. The five themes—economic history, the technological cornucopia, government mismanagement, world globalization, and intensive tyranny—remain the same in my analysis of the global south as they were for the global north. And it is with these in mind that I freely admit, with scholarly wincing, that my plan for this chapter is to briefly give an overview and then zoom in to particular vignettes.

In 1870, when the long twentieth century began, British industry stood at the leading edge of economic and technological progress, and the nation's real income per capita had reached perhaps $6,000 a year. However, that was already at least double what was found anywhere outside the charmed area of Britain (in the circle centered on Dover), its overseas settler colonies, and the United States, its ex-colony. Outside this nascent global north, our standard estimates show annual income per capita levels with a spread of a factor of five, ranging from $600 in the poorer parts of Africa to $3,000 in those European economies about to join the global north. The curve is heavily weighted toward the lower end, because China and India were then in the down-phase of the Malthusian cycle. The average per capita annual income level within the global south alone was perhaps $1,300.

By 1911 the world had grown—largely together. Global-south incomes were now spread by a factor of almost six, ranging from $700 to $4,000—with Russia, fueled by French loan capital to build its railways, in the lead. The global-south center of gravity had inched up to perhaps $1,500. That's not bad growth measured against previous eras. But the technological frontier of the global north was growing at a much faster pace.

Then, over the years when the global north writhed—world war, Great Depression, world war, Cold War—the global south diverged even more substantially, falling further behind. As the end of the Cold War neared in 1990, the United States (which by that time had replaced Britain as the leading edge of technological and economic progress) reached an average per capita income level of $35,000. That was still twice the high end of the average income range in the global south, which now stretched from $600 to $17,000, a factor of about twenty-eight. And the center of gravity of the global south was at perhaps $2,500, largely because China and India were still desperately poor. Many global-south economies had managed to take some advantage of technologies from the global north in their domestic production. Others had benefited substantially from enhanced and richer markets for their exports. But the results were strikingly at variance with the expectations of neoclassical, neoliberal, and neoliberal-adjacent economists like myself, who hold that discovery is—or should be—more difficult than development, that development is more difficult than deployment, and so that the world economy should "converge" over time. Between 1911 and 1990 that did not happen. The opposite did: the world economy *diverged* to a stunning degree.[2]

How to make sense of this? Economic historian Robert Allen had a checklist that countries needed to work through in order to step onto the escalator to prosperity that was post-1870 economic growth. It included having a stable, market-promoting government; building railroads, canals, and ports; chartering banks for commerce and investment; establishing systems of mass education; and imposing tariffs to protect industries and the communities of engineering practice that support them, and in which their long-run comparative advantage lay. Then, in addition, there needed to be a "Big Push" to set all the virtuous circles of economic development in motion.[3]

For most of the economies in the global south, it simply did not happen. They did not catch up to, or even keep pace with, the fast runners of economic growth and development. The reason? The pre–World War II colonial masters did next to nothing to prepare the colonized nations of Asia and Africa for independent prosperity. Before World War II, these colonizers had little interest in bringing about a Big Push to jumpstart the economies and aid the populations of their colonial subjects. Compounding their problems, the workers of the colonized nations of Asia and Africa faced stiff competition from the workers of extremely low-wage India and China, which hindered their ability to build the sort of middle class that could have driven demand and spurred industry.

Similar patterns held elsewhere in the global south. Consider Latin America, which had achieved independence from Spain and Portugal early in the 1800s. Mexico, Colombia, Peru, Brazil, and the others suffered, by and large, from what one might call "internal colonialists": a landed elite privileged by property ownership and Iberian descent that feared an educated proletariat, loved foreign-made manufactures, and had Iberian-derived legal systems that did not mesh well with the needs of commerce and industry.[4]

After World War II, the now dominant United States would not bless the aging colonial empires. The "winds of change" would bring independence to Asia and Africa.[5] And in one of the more bitter ironies of colonization, the false claim of a civilizing mission that had justified empires was dropped right when acting on it in fact would have made a difference. After generations of providing to the colonizers, the ex-colonized needed help. Yet back in the colonial masters' home offices there was little appetite for meeting the needs of reconstruction and financing. Instead, Britain, France, and the others withdrew bit by bit.

Newly decolonized nations tried to follow the plan the wise men of the global north had laid out for them. Many of them began with bureaucracies and structures of government typical of the industrial north: representative parliamentary institutions, independent judiciaries, laws establishing freedom of speech and of assembly, and a formally apolitical civil service bureaucracy. The goal was to achieve typical liberal democratic politics. Power would alternate among parties somewhat to the left and somewhat to the right of some sober median voter center. And, it was presumed, economic prosperity would follow.

But it was not to be. These ex-colonized nations could build the railroads, canals, and ports. They could charter the banks for commerce and investment. They could establish educational systems and impose tariffs to nurture modern industries and the communities of engineering practice in which their long-run comparative advantage lay. But taking these steps did not automatically put them onto the escalator to prosperity. Something else, the Big Push, was necessary.

In much of the global south, the political aftermath of decolonization turned out to be a long-run disappointment. The hoped-for liberal democratic politics became rare exceptions rather than the norm. This was a problem for economic development because so much of the checklist of prosperity was predicated on Westminster-style parliamentary politics, independent judiciaries, and the like—but these took root rarely and shallowly. The important exception was India.[6] Elsewhere, regimes emerged that derived their authority not from electoral competition among different groups, but from the army and the police, whose authority came from suppressing dissent with varying levels of brutality, or—in the best case—from populist attachment to a charismatic nation-symbolizing reforming leader. Throughout much of the newly decolonized third world, political democracy collapsed with disheartening speed. One of the very first democratically-elected decolonized African political leaders to fall victim—to be assassinated by members of his own army—was the first prime minister of independent Nigeria, Abubakar Tafawa Balewa.

The disheartened had been, quite likely, delusional in their optimism. There was no historical reason to suppose that representative democracy and liberal freedom would be durable in the global south, or, for that matter, in the global north. Indeed, there was recent history to suggest the opposite was true. The country of Goethe and Schiller could not maintain them, after all. The "mother of parliaments" in Britain's Palace of Westminster took centuries to grow its procedures, gain its powers, and work its way toward a workable approximation of representative democracy.

And the democratizing phase of the great French Revolution had lasted for less than four years. Why should anyone expect it to be different elsewhere?

Still, even if the recently decolonized countries were unsuccessful in implementing political democracy and freedom, it seemed inevitable that they would reap some economic benefits. After all, the storehouse of industrial technologies that had been developed since the beginning of the Industrial Revolution was open to all. The forms of knowledge and technologies that made the global north so rich were public goods. The benefits from tapping this storehouse were enormous and had the potential to multiply the wealth of all social groups and classes—property owners and nonproperty owners, politically powerful and politically powerless alike—manyfold. It stands to reason that all developing economies ought to have experienced not just substantial growth in absolute living standards and productivity levels in the years following their independence, but ought to have closed some of the prosperity gap vis-à-vis the world's industrial leaders.

The global south did grow, by and large. But it did not catch up. Latin America lost a decade of development in the 1980s. As of the early 2020s, Chile and Panama are the only Latin American countries that are better off than China, while Mexico, Costa Rica, and Brazil are China's rough equals. In Africa, only Botswana. In Asia, only Japan, the Four Tigers (South Korea, Taiwan, Hong Kong, and Singapore), Malaysia, and Thailand. The gap between China and the global north is still a factor of about 3.5 to 1. It was not all disappointing: progress in education and health was rapid and extremely heartening. But that did not hide the disappointing growth in material production.

And Africa has fallen way, way behind: South Africa, Kenya, Zambia, Ghana, and Nigeria—all those for which in the 1960s there were great expectations for economic development—have fallen well short of their promise. Perhaps most discouraging, during the generation after independence, was the fall in the production and export of crops that had been the staples of African exports. As scholar Robert Bates wrote as early as the start of the 1980s, "Palm oil in Nigeria, groundnuts in Senegal, cotton in Uganda, and cocoa in Ghana were once among the most prosperous industries in Africa. But in recent years, farmers of these crops have produced less, exported less, and earned less." The only continent in which farmers still made up a plurality of the workforce was spending an ever-increasing portion of its export earnings on imported food.[7]

In 1950, more than half the world's population still lived in extreme poverty: at the living standard of our typical preindustrial ancestors. By 1990 it was down to a quarter. By 2010 it would be less than 12 percent. And in 1950, most of this extreme poverty was spread throughout the global south. Thereafter it would become concentrated in Africa, where, by 2010, some three-fifths of the world's extreme poor would reside. This concentration came as a surprise: there had been few signs back in the late colonial days of palm oil, groundnuts, cotton, and cocoa exports—the days when Zambia was more industrialized than, and almost as rich as, Portugal—that Africa south of the Sahara would fall further and further behind, and not just behind the global north, but behind the rest of the global south as well. From 1950 to 2000, Egypt and the other countries of North Africa grew along with the world at about 2 percent per year in average incomes. But—to pick three countries from south of the Sahara—Ethiopia, Ghana, and Zambia grew at only 0.3 percent per year.

Thinkers like Nathan Nunn grappled with this data and concluded that this retardation had something to do with the massive slave trades that had afflicted Africa in previous years.[8] There had been other massive slave trades: the armies and elite citizens of classical Greece and Rome had stolen 30 million people over the span of a millennium and moved them around the Mediterranean. The Vikings had stolen perhaps 1 million—moving

345

slaves from Russia to western Europe or down to the Aegean, and moving Irish and Britons to Russia. Over the millennium before 1800, perhaps 1.5 million Europeans were kidnapped and taken as slaves to North Africa. Between 1400 and 1800, some 3 million people were enslaved in what is now southern Russia and Ukraine and sold south of the Black Sea.

But the African slave trades were bigger, by most estimates: 13 million were carried across the Atlantic over the period from 1600 to 1850; 5 million were carried across the Indian Ocean between 1000 and 1900; 3 million were carried north across the Sahara from 1200 to 1900, and an unknown number were taken in internal African slave trades—which did not stop when the transoceanic trades did: even if Europeans and Middle Easterners would no longer buy slaves, the slaves could be put to work on plantations producing crops that they would buy. Compare these numbers to a population in Africa in 1700 of perhaps 60 million, and to perhaps 360 million people born in Africa and surviving to age five over the years from 1500 to 1800.

Being subjected to millennium-spanning slave raiding as a major part of life created a long-lasting durable culture of social distrust. In a well-functioning market economy you begin nearly every meeting you have with a stranger thinking that this person might become a counterpart in some form of win-win economic, social, or cultural exchange. This is not the case if you think there is even a small chance that the stranger is in fact a scout for people with weapons over the next hill who will seek to enslave you, and perhaps kill you or your family in the process. This background assumption of distrust did not matter much as long as the trading and commercial infrastructure of the colonizers governed economic activity. But after the colonizers left, the distrust came to the forefront, and it led people to grab for weapons more quickly and more often than they would have in a more trusting society.

Remember assassinated Nigerian prime minister Abubakar Tafawa Balewa? He had been born in the north of the British colony of Nigeria in 1912 and had been sent to boarding school at Katsina College. There, he was student number 145, to be slotted into the imperial bureaucracy as a teacher of English. He did very well. By 1941 he was a headmaster. In 1944 he was sent to University College London to be trained to become a schools inspector for the colonial administration.

But earlier, back when he was twenty-two, in 1934, a colonial official named Rupert East had commissioned five novellas, to be written in Hausa, in an attempt to spread literacy. East had wanted to build up an "indigenous literature" that was more or less secular—that would not be "purely religious or written with a strong religious motive." Abubakar Tafawa Balewa contributed, and he chose to write about slavery.

In his short novel *Shaihu Umar* (Elder Umar), the protagonist's students distract him from teaching them the Quran by asking him how he came to be a teacher. The story that follows is of his enslavement and its consequences: large-scale slave raids, kidnappings, adoptions by childless slavers, and more kidnappings. The protagonist finally meets up with his mother (she has been kidnapped and enslaved too, by the guards she had hired) in Tripoli. She sees that he is pious and prosperous, and then she promptly dies. The vibe is that "people really will do terrible things for money" and that "the world is a Hobbesian war of all against all, but if you read the Quran really well, then you'll probably prosper, maybe."[9]

Balewa used his post as a traveling schools inspector to enter politics in Nigeria in the 1940s. He was one of the founders of the Northern People's Congress. By 1952 he was colonial Nigeria's minister of works. By 1957 he was prime minister. In 1960 he became prime minister of an independent and sovereign Nigeria. He was reelected in 1964. And then in January 1966 he was murdered in the military coup led by the Young Majors—Chukwuma

Kaduna Nzeogwu and company—whose troops slaughtered senior politicians and their generals and their wives, and then were themselves suppressed by a countercoup led by army commander Johnson Aguiyi-Ironsi.

Aguiyi-Ironsi was assassinated six months later in a July counter-countercoup led by Yakuba Gowon. A year later the Igbo people declared the independent republic of Biafra, which was suppressed after a three-year war causing some four million deaths (out of a population of about fifty-five million), the overwhelming majority of them Igbo dead of starvation. Yakuba Gowon was overthrown by Murtala Muhammed in July 1975. And Murtala was then assassinated in February 1976. A return to civilian rule in 1979 lasted only until 1983, when the next military coup took place in Nigeria.

WAS THE GLOBAL SOUTH richer in the 1990s than it had been in 1911? Yes, much richer. Was the world more integrated in terms of trade, technology, and communication? Yes, by impressive degrees. But was the world more unequal? Yes, vastly so.

Who, or what, is to blame?

Some insights emerge. Low savings rates and the high cost of capital investment meant that the yield from a given savings effort in the global south was low. Because poor countries are by definition those in which labor is cheap and machines are expensive, and all the more so when governments made foreign-produced machines hard to obtain, prices on most manufactured goods remained high. An incomplete demographic transition to low fertility (because fear of poverty translates into more children, in the hopes that some of them will look after the aged) meant high rates of population growth, which meant, in turn, that investment went to equip a growing labor force with all the basic tools they needed, rather than to the higher-quality tools that would make a shrinking labor force productive. All of this brought about a general lack of education and entrepreneurship.

Vicious cycles abounded and were easily triggered. Virtuous cycles were rare and difficult to set in motion. Economic growth was held back by what the economist Michael Kremer has called the "O-ring theory": the more modern and the more potentially productive the division of labor and the value chain, the more nearly everything had to go right for things to work. And if everything didn't go right, substantial amounts of capital, resources, and labor would be idle.

But what triggered the vicious cycles that opened and then widened the gap between the global north and the global south?

One short and too-simple answer is that the fault lies with governments—specifically, with governmental institutions that were "extractive" rather than "developmental," in the currently fashionable jargon of growth economists. We are talking here about kleptocracy: government not by one ruler (monarchy), or by the self-proclaimed best (aristocracy), or by the people (democracy), or by the rich (plutocracy)—but, rather, rule by thieves.

Yet kleptocracy is nothing new. Perhaps the major drawback to the invention of agriculture was that you had to be around to harvest the fields that you planted. This meant that you could not run away when thugs with spears came by to demand the lion's share of your crops. And as this practice became general, people got into the business of supplying spears for the thugs, and the thugs began to organize hierarchically: we call the people at the top of the thug hierarchies "kings." Thus, to fault the governments of the global south ignores history. Most governments at most times in most places have followed policies that show little interest in nurturing sustained increases in productivity.

After all, the first priority of governments must be to prevent food riots in the capital. Regimes rule peacefully in part because they control the visible centers of sovereignty: those buildings in the capital from which members of the bureaucracy expect to receive their orders, and the centrally located radio and television broadcast sites through which rulers speak to their nations. If an urban riot overruns the president's palace, the ministries, or the television stations, the government's rule is in serious danger. Conversely, bread, circuses, and a well-supplied and compliant police force keep riots at bay. The second priority of governments is to keep the army well fed, well paid, and equipped with lots of new weapons to play with. Rulers can only rule so long as the army tolerates them. The third priority is to keep the bureaucrats and the political operatives content, and any potential opposition quiet or disorganized.

For insecure rulers, pursuing these aims almost always takes precedence over policy. All rulers believe they are the best people for the job. Their rivals are at best incompetent, most likely wrongheaded and corrupt, and at worst amoral and destructive. As these insecure rulers see it, nothing good will be achieved for the country or the people unless they maintain their grip on power. Only after the government's seat is secure will debates about development policy take place. But the pursuit of a secure hold on power almost always takes up all the rulers' time, energy, and resources. The life span of the average government is often too short for any reasonable historian-critic to expect it to focus on long-run economic development.

And, as Niccolò Machiavelli wrote in his little book about new princes back in the early 1500s, things are even worse with a new regime, in which the first task is currying supporters, who are unlikely to remain supporters unless they benefit.[10] So, job number one in building a state is to seize control of and redirect benefits, tangible and otherwise, to the most influential of one's supporters. And that process of seizure and redirection follows a different logic—a very different logic—than that of channeling resources to produce rapid economic growth.

When we wonder over the vast inequality between global north and global south, perhaps the most pressing question isn't who is to blame, or even what is to blame. It is more pragmatic: What needs to happen for growth to take place? For selfish and selfless reasons, most rulers would be benevolent if they thought they could be. Believing they could be requires stability and security, and increasing prosperity can be a powerful source of increased stability and security.

But why don't potential entrepreneurs—those who would benefit most from prodevelopment policies, and whose enterprises would in turn benefit many others—work to overthrow an antidevelopment ruling regime? Political scientist Robert Bates asked this question of a cocoa farmer in Ghana. Bates was seeking to learn why farmers did not agitate for a reduction in the huge gap between the (very low) price the government paid them for cocoa and the (higher) price at which the government sold the cocoa on the world market. The farmer "went to his strongbox," Bates reported, "and produced a packet of documents: licenses for his vehicles, import permits for spare parts, titles to his real property and improvements, and the articles of incorporation that exempted him from a major portion of his income taxes. 'If I tried to organize resistance to the government's policies on farm prices,' he said while exhibiting these documents, 'I would be called an enemy of the state, and would lose all these.'"[11]

This isn't always or only an accident of "overregulation." From an economic development perspective, potential future entrants into industries produce the most social benefit. Yet because they have no existing businesses or clients, they also have no resources with which to lobby the influential. Therefore, from the perspective of those in power who wish to remain so, restricting future entrants into industries is a way of doing existing businesses a favor at a very low political cost. Since the overvalued exchange rate has made foreign currency a scarce good, competition from manufacturers abroad can also be easily strangled in select sectors as a favor to key existing businesses.

There is so much in addition that has driven the divergence between the global north and the global south that the responsibility-attributing answers to "why?" and "what?" questions can only be unsatisfactory: strait is the gate, and narrow is the way, which leadeth unto prosperity in the global south. The "who?" question has a more straightforward answer: the global north, collectively, had the wealth and power to take steps to arrange things more favorably for the global south, and it did not do so.

Successful economic development depends on a strong but limited government. Strong in the sense that its judgments of property rights are obeyed, that its functionaries obey instructions from the center, and that the infrastructure it pays for is built. And limited in the sense that it can do relatively little to help or hurt individual enterprises, and that political power does not become the only effective road to wealth and status.

Vignettes tell parts of a very few of the tales.

ONE OF THE MORE heartbreaking cases in the global south over the period from 1911 to 1990 is Argentina. In a very strong sense, Argentina has no business being a member of the global south today. In 1913 Buenos Aires was in the top twenty cities of the world in the likelihood that a typical resident had a telephone. In 1929 Argentina was in the top five economies in the world in the likelihood that a typical citizen owned an automobile. Of the countries that were its peers in the 1930s, most were overrun by or caught up in the turmoil of World War II. Argentinian politics in the 1930s was rough-and-tumble, with strong antidemocratic currents. But it was no worse than politics almost anywhere else, and better than politics in most other places. Strait was the gate.

Argentina's leaders responded to the social and economic upheavals by adopting new policies aimed at stimulating demand

and redistributing wealth. At the same time, Argentina's leaders became more distrustful of foreign trade and capital, and more inclined to use controls instead of prices as mechanisms to allocate goods.[12] What followed were spurts of growth that ended in monetary chaos and deep depression. Politics was nasty—"nasty" not in the sense of people arrested but in the sense of people simply "disappeared," and "disappeared" in the sense of some of them murdered by being thrown out of helicopters.[13]

Such was the persistent environment in which charismatic leaders could gain mass political support. One such, at the end of World War II, was Juan Perón. Perón's policies were broadly popular: his government increased taxes, created agricultural marketing boards, supported unions, and regulated international trade. Perón sought to generate rapid growth and full employment through government spending; he wanted to twist terms of trade against exporters, agricultural oligarchs, foreigners, and entrepreneurs; and he wanted to redistribute wealth to urban workers, his most ardent supporters. After all, Argentina was a rich country: it could afford to treat its urban working class well.

Perón's program produced almost half a decade of rapid growth. Then exports fell sharply. The international business cycle has ups and downs, and it hit Argentina heavily, with a fall in demand for its exports. Reductions in prices of rural exportables then made themselves felt in reduced supply. Agricultural production fell because of low prices offered by the government for agricultural goods. Domestic consumption rose. The rural sector found itself short of fertilizer and tractors. By the first half of the 1950s, the real value of Argentine exports dropped to only 60 percent of the already low levels they had reached during the Depression, and only 40 percent of 1920s levels. And because Perón had twisted the terms of trade so drastically against agriculture and exportables, when the network of world trade was put back together in the 1950s, Argentina was no longer thickly connected.

The consequent foreign exchange shortage presented Perón with unattractive options. First, he could attempt to balance foreign payments by devaluing to bring imports and exports back into balance in the long run (and in the short run by borrowing from abroad). But effective devaluation would have entailed raising the real price of imported goods, and therefore cutting the living standards of the urban workers who made up his political base. Foreign borrowing would have meant a betrayal of his strong nationalist position. Second, he could contract the economy, raising unemployment and reducing consumption, and expand incentives to produce for export by easing controls on agricultural prices. But, once again, this would have required a reversal of the distributional shifts that had been his central aim.

The remaining option was one of controlling and rationing imports by government command. Not surprisingly, Perón and his advisers believed that a dash for growth and a reduction in dependence on the world economy was good for Argentina. It wasn't. It wasn't even good for Perón, who was deposed by the army (although he did retain high popularity among many, and did return as president in the years before his death in 1974). Subsequent governments did not fully reverse these policies, for the political forces that Perón had mobilized still had to be appeased. Post–World War II Argentina saw foreign exchange allocated by the central government in order to, first, keep existing factories running and, second, keep home consumption high. Its third and last priority went to imports of capital goods for investment and capacity expansion.

One way to think about early post–World War II Argentina is that its mixed economy was poorly oriented: the government allocated goods, especially imports, among alternative uses; the controlled market redistributed income. Neither the private nor the public sector was used to its comparative advantage. As a result, the early 1950s saw a huge rise in the price of capital goods. Each percentage point of total product saved led to less than half a percentage point's worth of investment. Unable to invest at scale, the Argentine economy fell behind the countries of Western Europe. As the economy fell behind, discontent grew, and the government oscillated between overpromising politicians and undercompetent, murderous generals.

But could it be the case that Argentina's slow-growth path was not an exception but the natural course? Could it be that Europe should view Argentina in the spirit of, "There but for the grace of America and the Marshall Plan go we?" With a non-internationalist United States not so interested in fighting the Cold War, in restructuring Western Europe in general, or in a program of sustained support like the Marshall Plan, might Western Europe have followed a post–World War II trajectory similar to Argentina's?[14]

Conversely, much of the global south would be justified in asking: What about us? In the presence of a global-north foreign-aid effort on the scale of the Marshall Plan, might the same virtuous circles that lifted Western Europe likewise give life to the global economy's periphery?

THE EXTREME DIFFICULTY OF mounting any substantial catch-up to the global north is reinforced by the case of Reza Shah Pahlavi and the Iranian Revolution.[15] From the 1950s through the 1970s, Iran and Reza Shah were the darling of many who thought they were playing the Great Game of international politics: Reza Shah was strongly anticommunist and anti-Russian and eager to "modernize" Iran; he listened to global-north experts, especially with respect to the importance of land reform and engineers; and although he spent some of his oil revenues on luxuries, and more on the military, he channeled an even more substantial portion back into the economy of Iran.

Yes, pre-1979, the imperial Iranian government was, to put it bluntly, a tyranny. Yes, it had a fierce and justifiably dreaded secret police. But what precipitated the Iranian Revolution and led to the overthrow of the shah was not so much opposition to police or military strength. Religious ideology played a role, but not as large a role as many have assumed: afterward, most Iranians were quite surprised at the fundamentalist religious-ideological revolution they had helped make. The causes of the revolution had much more to do with the wealth and poverty created by the oil- and land-reform-based economic transformations that were put into place, who that wealth flowed to, who the poverty was inflicted upon, and the obstacles to successful economic development that followed from those stresses.

In 1973, world oil prices tripled, and with the revenue from the bonanza, Reza Shah hoped to turn Iran into an industrial country in one generation. This meant, first, land reform: distributing land to turn tenants and sharecroppers into independent farmers, and compensating landlords with government oil revenues. But rapid population growth and a desire not to offend rich landlords *too* much meant that the plots distributed were small. At the same time, the boom in oil exports and the rise in oil prices together pushed up Iran's exchange rate by a wide margin, and with an overvalued exchange rate it became profitable to import food. So newly propertied peasant farmers found themselves with small plots selling their crops for declining prices.

They were supposed to become bulwarks of the regime, grateful to it for distributing land. Instead, they scratched what they saw as an inadequate living off of too-small plots, or moved to the cities. While many Iranians saw their incomes growing rapidly in the years leading up to 1979, many others did not. Karl Polanyi would not have been surprised that the latter—those for whom things had not worked out as they had expected—were angrier than those who benefited from the windfalls, who were pleased by the changes that Reza Shah's "White Revolution" had wrought. Certainly few in the street were willing to demonstrate or fight for it, however, or for him.

Moreover, as the world became smaller through advances in transportation and communications, the people of Iran could see further into what was happening in other countries. For one thing, rich and arrogant Russians and Britons and Americans were showing up to walk their streets and their corridors of power and influence. Iranians had been used to seeing themselves at the center of an Islamic civilization that had been preeminent among world civilizations. They were now exposed to daily reminders that this was no longer the case. How were people to make sense of such a world?

Reza Shah Pahlavi's answer was to try to turn Iranians into Europeans—that is, to follow an authoritarian state-led development road reminiscent of pre–World War I Imperial Germany. But this left scant place for Islam. And the state that resulted was highly corrupt. Reza Shah's reforms quickly proved problematic. Steps to emancipate women were unpopular among influential traditionalists. And although the shah was truly committed to turning Iran into a literate, educated, technologically proficient country, steps to boost education had the unintended consequence of producing a large body of students and intellectuals attracted to revolutionary politics.

From exile, the Ayatollah Ruhollah Khomeini—a former opponent of land reform, who had thought it was un-Islamic to dispossess landlords and free peasants from debt bondage—lit the fuse, calling on the Islamic clergy and the people to seize power from the despot and carry out an Islamic revolution. A forty-day cycle of demonstrations began, during which young religious activists would be shot by the police, triggering another demonstration to mourn their deaths.

In January 1979 Reza Shah Pahlavi fled into exile.

Thereafter, Iran's economy stagnated. First a catastrophic decade-long war with Iraq—not started by Iran's ayatollahs but continued by them, as they believed God was on their side, that their cause was just, and that they could not but prevail—absorbed tremendous resources. And the newly dominant religious government had little interest in economic development: its leaders were interested in paradise in heaven, not utopia here on earth. The Iranian people had not made the Islamic Revolution to lower the price of watermelons—which was what Ayatollah Khomeini was reputed to have said in dismissal of the concerns of those of his advisers who wanted policies to bring material prosperity to Iran.

IF ALL THESE OBSTACLES to rapid and successful catch-up growth were not enough, there were also the pitfalls produced by *ideology*: those seeking to create a utopia in a relatively short time by means of a complete societal transformation. The lure of such a transformation led many newly independent decolonized governments in the 1950s and 1960s to follow the advice of intellectuals from the global north's left—ultimately leading to prolonged difficulties.

This was only natural: the left had been, to its great credit, anticolonial, while the center and the right, before World War II, and even today, have been imperialist. This had a very large influence on global-south development policy in the first post–World War II generation. Marx had looked forward to a utopia of free speech, democratic governments with equal political voice for all, great freedom of occupational and residential choice, and immense material wealth. The really-existing socialist governments that the political left found itself associated with, the products of the Bolshevik revolution, had relatively little of any of these. Intellectuals on the left in the global north kept finding excuses to throw them over the side, one by one. And governments in the global south found themselves being told that the absence of these was a virtue: No freedom of speech? You could not mobilize the population to achieve the national purpose of development with conflicted caterwauling confusing the people, could you?

The core freedoms of Western society were always promised in the abstract. There would be free speech, government with equal political voice, freedom to choose your job and your residence, and great wealth—someday. But those commitments were easily delayed because of the exigencies of the moment. There was a need to shed the last vestiges of old colonial orders. There was a need for stability first. There was a need for authoritarian command for national mobilization. And the delays became permanent. The era of transition was never-ending. There was a constant emergency.

Until an educated and informed socialist electorate could be created, a centralized party was necessary in its place. It was—mistakenly—thought by many in the newly decolonized nations, and by those who wished them well, that to rank representative institutions high on any list of the criteria of a good society was implicitly to attack decolonization and to defend the late colonial order. Nation building required unity, and in new nations that unity could be fragile. If politicians and newspapers could whistle different tunes and criticize the government, this would disrupt that fragile unity. Then advocacy of private economic freedoms would disappear: all of the resources of society had to be mobilized according to a single plan for rapid industrialization. Eggs would be broken. And as time pressed on, the habit of breaking them on whim grew. But no omelet appeared.

We see this dynamic most strikingly, most powerfully, and most destructively at work in the years after World War II in the really-existing socialist regimes of Asia, led by Maoist China.

Mao Zedong's Chinese Communist Party (CCP) had unexpectedly won the Chinese Civil War in 1949. Its plan had been simple: arrive at a village, shoot the landlords, distribute the land. The peasants would then be richer than they had ever imagined—and would support the CCP. The victory of the CCP then looks not inevitable but understandable: the promise of release from dire material poverty and from landlord tyranny was attractive, and in its initial years the People's Republic of China made good on this promise.

By the mid-1950s, however, a downward spiral had begun. Mao and company were predisposed to take advice from their Soviet comrades. And so it was that as Stalin had reenserfed the Russian peasants by collectivizing agriculture, Mao did the same. When Stalin brutally suppressed dissent and discussion within and without the party, Mao quickly followed suit. However, when Stalin made heavy industrialization a priority by hiring technical advisers from outside and copying plans from US and German factories, Mao took a slightly different route. Being more suspicious of foreigners and less patient, he decreed that there would be a "Great Leap Forward." To address China's underdeveloped industrial and human resources, the party would replace the "material" factor with a "spiritual" one. What technocratic "experts" said could not be done, citing material limitations, the "Red" revolutionaries would do by force of conviction. China would industrialize village by village, without imports of foreign capital goods or the advice of foreign engineers.[16]

Of course it was a disaster. To command—from the center— that peasant farmers go out and build backyard blast furnaces to produce steel guarantees that you will get little steel and less grain. Worse, when the command comes directly from the dictator, you are guaranteed not to learn the truth. Because it was Mao himself who set out this policy, everyone reported back to him that the Great Leap Forward was proceeding magnificently. In reality, perhaps forty million people died in the ensuing famine.

This was, note, an even worse disaster than the standard disaster that really-existing socialism turned out to be. If you walked along the edge of the Iron Curtain and then the Bamboo Curtain from Leningrad to Odessa, along the Caucasus, and then from Yunnan up to the Sea of Japan—or if you looked from really-existing socialist Cuba across the Caribbean to Costa Rica or Mexico—you would see that those countries where the armies of Stalin or Mao or Kim Il-Sung or Ho Chi Minh or (shudder) Pol Pot had marched were, on average, only one-fifth as well-off when 1990 came and the curtains were raised as those that had been just beyond those armies' reach. But Maoist China in the throes of the Great Leap Forward was worse than average.

As the extent of the disaster became known, Mao's principal lieutenants moved slowly and cautiously against him. In December 1958, Mao was replaced by Liu Shaoqi as head of state, with Deng Xiaoping at Liu's right hand. At a conference in July 1959, Peng Dehuai, minister of defense, criticized Mao's policies, and Mao threatened to split the party. The majority of the party members remained "loyal" to Mao. Peng Dehuai was condemned and dismissed from the party and the government. But Mao Zedong was also sidelined: the near-consensus of his deputies and their deputies was that Mao's role should thereafter be ceremonial and symbolic. Mao did not agree.

Nevertheless, it took six years before Mao could arrange a counterstrike. Eventually he managed to use his power as a symbol of the regime, particularly with lower-level cadres and the young, to return to command. His political counteroffensive was a call to "bombard the headquarters"—that is, to destroy anyone whose loyalty or revolutionary commitment he doubted within the leadership of the Communist Party, to wage a Cultural Revolution.[17] Liu Shaoqi, now the second-ranking member of the Politburo Standing Committee, was killed. Deng Xiaoping was purged from the party and lost his leadership post for the heresy of claiming that it was more important to be competent than to be politically correct—"A good cat is not a cat that is black or white, a good cat is a cat that catches mice" (Mao feared that Deng meant his listeners to hear not "black" but "red"—revolutionary—and "white"—counterrevolutionary). Perhaps Deng Xiaoping escaped with his life by sheer luck. Mao's Red Guards threw Deng Xiaoping's son, Deng Pufang, out of a window, and his back was broken, causing permanent paraplegia. During the Cultural

Revolution, universities were closed so that curricula could be revised to better reflect Mao Zedong's ideology. Engineers were sent to the countryside so they could learn how to perform agricultural labor. Technocrats of all kinds were dismissed from their jobs for similar reasons. The Cultural Revolution followed a strongly anti-intellectual ideology. Mao turned on his own tools next, purging the leftist ideologue-intellectuals. In 1971, the new second-ranking member of the Chinese Communist Party's Politburo Standing Committee, Lin Biao, fled before Mao could purge him, dying in a plane crash.

Mao's Cultural Revolution, much like his Great Leap Forward, continued until his death in 1976. We do not know its human cost—perhaps as many as 1.5 or 2 million people were killed, and perhaps tens of millions of others were purged and/or imprisoned. We can also estimate that in 1970—after the first phase of the Cultural Revolution—China's level of material prosperity was perhaps half that of India's, having become the rough equivalent of today's level of material well-being in the very poorest countries on earth. In the end, Deng Xiaoping returned from his purge and exile to take up the reins. He was the only person able to govern with credibility among both the bureaucratic cadres and the military, for many of them still knew him well.[18] Only then he was purged again. And this time, his only shield against the wrath of the Gang of Four, the Maoist political faction that implemented his policies, was either his military allies or Mao himself, before their overthrow after Mao's death.

Only two things ultimately rescued China and its economy. The first was twofold: the failure of Mao's armies to conquer Taiwan, and his unwillingness in 1949 to pick a fight with Great Britain to attack Hong Kong. Taiwan and Hong Kong subsequently provided China with the entrepreneurs and the mobilizers of finance for industrial development that it needed to grow after 1978. The second was Deng Xiaoping. Deng had certainly not been an advocate of a return to the market economy when he was purged in 1966—indeed, he was not at all what Mao's Red Guards called him: the "number 2 person in authority taking the capitalist road." But he certainly was the number-one person in authority taking the capitalist road after his accession to paramountcy in 1978. And that was to make a huge difference. Once in power, he gave the baton to Hu Yaobang, Zhao Ziyang, Xi Zhongzun, and other reformers to find a way forward to restore and then develop China's economy. And so the government of China found its way forward after Mao's death. Mao claimed that he had made China stand up, but that was false. It was Deng who did the job.

FROM A CYNICAL PERSPECTIVE, perhaps the most interesting question about emerging economies is not why they have so frequently stagnated or experienced precipitous declines, but why they have sometimes experienced rapid growth. Chile, Mexico, southern Brazil, and Panama in Latin America; Algeria in Saharan and Botswana in sub-Saharan Africa; and Hong Kong, Malaysia, Singapore, South Korea, Taiwan, Thailand, and now, of course, post-Mao China in Asia have all made impressive strides toward closing the relative material prosperity gap vis-à-vis the global north in the post–World War II era. How have they managed to do this? What have been the key factors separating successful from unsuccessful episodes of economic development?

So we now turn in a more hopeful and positive direction. There were two groups of countries that did manage to catch up to global-north norms in the years after 1950. The first comprised the countries that were the original members of the Organisation for Economic Co-operation and Development (OECD), now thought of as a rich-country club but not so much at its beginning—the member countries were largely Marshall Plan aid recipients and British settler dominions, along with Japan and the United States. The other group comprised the countries of the East Asian Pacific Rim. It is on these that we'll now focus our attention.

The speed of Japan's recovery after 1950 surprised many.[19] Immediately after World War II, it remained unclear whether its economy would successfully surmount the shock of defeat. With its factories leveled, without oil or iron, starting from ground zero and having to purchase from abroad nearly every input needed for industrial civilization, save rice and coal, what were Japan's chances? Things changed when the Korean War, starting in 1950, made Japanese industry a valuable hot-war resource, which in turn made Japanese economic success an important Cold War goal. It became a keystone of US policy that Japan become a prosperous, democratic, and unsinkable ally in the troubled regions of East Asia. By 1955, the Japanese economy was as strong as it had been on December 7, 1941. And growth thereafter was the fastest the world had hitherto seen.

From 1960 to 1973, the Japanese economy grew at an average rate of 10 percent annually, quadrupling the economy in a short sprint and raising GDP per capita from the equivalent of 25 percent of the US economy to 57 percent. In the next period, 1973 to 1990, the country's GDP grew at an average rate of 4.5 percent annually, doubling the economy again and bringing Japanese per capita GDP up to the equivalent of 78 percent of the US economy.

How did Japan achieve such a stunning period of sustained growth? A significant part of the plan was a policy of strong domestic protectionism through an intricate network of non-tariff economic and social network barriers. Economists generally oppose protectionism because it hurts consumers (by increasing prices) while benefiting producers (who have done nothing productive to earn it). An economy of protectionism produces firms that are good at getting what they want out of the capital but inefficient and often bad at developing new technologies. It is true that Japan's protectionism did have some such elements— but Japanese protection was, it seemed, smart policy. Over time it appears that producers gained enough to offset the static losses. Overpaying, they grew rich.

After the fact, global-north observers rationalized continuance of the policy. Japan, they thought, was very special: it had entered the modern age with a strong, functional government, an elite that rapidly saw the need for westernization, a population expanding at a modest-enough rate that it was not in danger of going hungry, a deep respect for commerce and industry, and an enthusiasm for mass education. But Japan seemed to be the only East Asian country where all of these conditions were present. The societal transformation undertaken during the Meiji Restoration of the mid-1800s had no parallel elsewhere in what the global north saw as a culturally static and bureaucratically and hierarchically ossified region.

Back in 1945, most outside observers regarded East Asia, with the exception of Japan, the way observers today regard Africa: as the part of the globe facing the biggest development challenges, and most likely to stay poor. The rest of the region seemed to face incredibly long odds. So the Pacific Rim's rapid economic growth in the latter half of the long twentieth century was nothing short of miraculous. Many countries have attempted to grow their economies rapidly under the aegis of a "developmental state." Yet, most of the time, these efforts have failed.

Why were East Asian countries any different? One reason is that other "developmental states," including those in Latin America, and to some extent those in the Soviet bloc, were designed, above all else, to achieve independence and self-sufficiency. They walled their economies off from world market prices and, indeed, from prices altogether. East Asia started with the assumption that it would have to export—and export big-time—if only because its resources were thin and scarce.

The goal was not to forge a new economic path; the goal was simply to catch up. The global north believed it possessed the secret sauce to running an efficient, growing, and innovative technological frontier economy, but there is no a priori reason to think that the economic organization best suited to inventing the industrial future should be the same as the one best suited to catching up to a known target.

The king of England did not call a meeting of barons, bishops, bankers, and a few mechanics and say, "Let's have an Industrial Revolution." But that is pretty much what Japan did at the beginning of the long twentieth century with its reforms under the Meiji Restoration. This strategy succeeded. And Japan then provided a model for how its ex-colonies, South Korea and Taiwan, should attempt to play catch-up under their dictators (Park Chung-Hee and Chiang Kai-shek, respectively), which then provided models for Malaysia, Thailand, and others. The verdict is very clear: for catch-up development, whatever it is that the "Pacific Rim development model" is, it works.

What defines this model? First, trade, but managed trade. Undervalue the exchange rate, so that you can export manufactures that are not, initially at least, up to global-north quality standards. And then channel subsidies to companies that have successfully exported—the ones to which global-north middle-class consumers award the prizes. Those same Japanese firms that were protected against imports from abroad were, in international markets, forced to hone their competitive abilities and match international standards of innovation, quality, and price. Very patient cheap capital helped. And by the 1980s it was clear that protectionism had yielded incredible results. Indeed, something remarkable was going on with Kawasaki and Nippon in steel; Toyota, Nissan, and Honda in automobiles; eventually Bridgestone in tires; Komatsu in construction equipment; and Toshiba, Matsushita (Panasonic), and Nikon, Fujitsu, Sharp, Sony, and Canon in electronics.

In Latin America, an overvalued exchange rate would see a lot of society's wealth spent on the purchase of foreign luxuries, as the upper class preferred to live well rather than channel its resources into national development. In these instances, the strategy that Latin American leaders chose was to use high tariffs and nontariff barriers to restrict imports of intermediate goods and capital machines needed, at a heavy cost to production and for economic development.

But back to Japan: Add a high rate of savings, sustained year after year, coming from an equal post-land-reform income distribution and channels—such as a postal savings system, where post offices across the country were used as consumer banks with the ability to accept deposits, make loans, and provide a variety of other financial services—that made savings easy, in an environment where people could be confident that their savings would not disappear. Ensure that the sellers of machines to the firms that took out loans from these banks charged low prices—so that buyers did not have to pay high prices to domestic machine producers, or higher prices to those lucky enough, and politically well-connected enough, to have scrounged scarce import licenses, and so had foreign-made machines to sell. Tilt the economy's price structure so that machines that embodied modern technological knowledge were cheap and foreign-made and luxurious consumption goods were expensive.

Taking these steps would mean, of course, heavy, hidden taxes on labor, and especially on skilled labor. They would also mean financial repression relative to what "free-market" prices would have been: squeezing returns to savers, and shifting those returns to the industrial companies that accessed the savings, and to those who ended up owning them. And they would mean export surpluses via undervalued exchange rates—subsidies relative to Smithian prices to foreigners who purchased the exports—in the hope that the human- and organizational-capital gains, via learning by doing from producing exports successfully, would outweigh the cost of the implicit subsidies.

The lesson of history throughout the Pacific Rim is that as long as exports earn enough dollars for domestic businesses to obtain access to the global-north-produced machines they need, and the global-north-invented technologies they embody, and as long as the machines go to firms that are efficient and effective, this formula enables a country to advance.

And this is why it is important that subsidies go to companies that successfully export—pass a market-efficiency test, albeit a market-efficiency test applied not in some home free-market economy but among the import-purchasing middle classes of the global north.

Ultimately, the East Asian developmental model is predicated on other nations—cough, the United States of America—being able to absorb exports and run trade deficits because they are operating on a different, open economy model. Could the United States have absorbed everyone's exports, had everyone attempted this? No. The model could only ever have worked for a small handful of countries.

Yet it did work. Consider South Korea, now home to one of the two most efficient high-tech microprocessor-building factory complexes of the world, Samsung. As noted above, no one watching South Korea in the 1950s anticipated that it would become one of the world's fastest-growing economies. At the time, it had just been devastated by a bitter war, during which its capital and major industrial center, Seoul, had changed hands four times. Its savings rate was low. Its exports were low. More than half of its imports in the late 1950s were paid for by US assistance, either in the form of foreign aid or expenditures to support the US military presence in South Korea.

The government of President Syngman Rhee in 1948–1960 sought to control the flow of foreign affairs and imports. It overvalued Korea's currency (so as to charge the United States as much as possible for support of its military), imposed high tariffs, and implemented stringent quantitative import restrictions. The results were slow and erratic growth and continued dependence on the United States. With the takeover of the government by Park Chung-Hee in 1961, everything changed. Park was brutal (although not extraordinarily so by the standards of the twentieth century) but remarkably effective. The shift of Korea's development strategy from one of import substitution to one of export-led industrialization was very rapid. The consequences were astounding. Exports grew from 3 percent of GDP to 40 percent of GDP. The growth rate of income per capita averaged more than 7 percent of GDP for the three decades after 1960.

Even where rapid growth would seem to have been swimming against the regional political-economic tide, it was possible. The shining beacon is Botswana, with an annual real income per capita estimated at $900 in 1960 and $14,000 in 2010. Then it had the highest Human Development Index in sub-Saharan Africa, despite being landlocked, despite being severely affected by HIV/AIDS, and despite being in a regional neighborhood that has done very poorly in terms of economic growth.[20] Its neighbor Zambia's income per capita went from $2,800 in 1960 to $3,500 in 2010, from three times Botswana's to one-fourth of Botswana's. In Botswana, an independent and uncorrupt judicial system, a lack of tariffs on machinery imports (to encourage technology transfer), a banking system that encouraged savings, and a policy of plowing back government revenues into infrastructure investment all helped. So did the luck and the skill of the Tswana chiefs in the late 1800s in managing to guide the British Empire into ruling with a very light hand, which made postindependence state-building very easy. And the fact that Botswana's population was about 80 percent Tswana, as was the leader of the independence movement and the first president of independent Botswana (1966–1980), Seretse Khama, *kgosi* ("king" or "chief") of the Ngwato, one of the eight principal Tswana chieftaincies. Not to mention that Botswana negotiated a 50 percent ownership interest in the country's De Beers mining subsidiary, plus a

15 percent ownership stake in the overall De Beers corporation. Any country, anywhere, could have done it if Botswana could.

RECALL ROBERT ALLEN'S CHECKLIST for successful development: promote markets, build railroads and canals and ports, charter banks, teach children, teach engineers, impose tariffs on commodities, and nurture the creation of communities of engineering practice. Finally, once all those conditions are met, provide, from somewhere, a Big Push, to create expectations that there will be growth. The Pacific Rim added its own special sauces—but nevertheless, the key gap between the Pacific Rim and the rest of the global south was due to its successful implementation of the obvious. Carl von Clausewitz wrote, famously, about war: "Everything is very simple in war, but the simplest thing is difficult. These difficulties accumulate and produce a friction, which no man can imagine exactly who has not seen it."[21] The same has held true of economic development nearly everywhere in the global south.

Moreover, the logic of politics is that of favors performed, wealth redistributed, influence exercised, and taxes collected. That is very different from the logic of economic growth. A state that is still emerging and establishing itself cannot successfully midwife economic development. Only a state that is limited in the amount of damage it can do to the economy, or a state that is secure enough, independent enough, and committed enough to rapid economic growth, can avoid these political survival traps. Therefore, what is needed is either a stringently limited government—one incapable of redistributing resources to favored clients because its economy is so integrated into the global economy and so governed by its norms, laws, and treaties—or a functioning developmental state. Either "neoliberal"-style international market-led development or Pacific Rim–style governance and growth. And attempting the latter is very risky. As economist Lant Pritchett likes to say, "There are few things in the world that are worse than state-led development led by an anti-development state."[22]

That was what too many postindependence Asian and African states, and too many post–World War II Latin American states, turned out to be.

So suppose that a global-south economy does not want to risk trying, and failing, to follow the Pacific Rim model. Is there another approach it could follow? What if you simply cannot create a government bureaucracy whose first goal is development?

For many what remains as the only viable option—and this is a counsel of despair—is "neoliberalism." What this means in practice is less clear than what it means in desired consequence: the goal, at least, is to insulate the economy from the (semi-predatory) government, so that the government's attempts to tilt the distribution of income in favor of the politically powerful are relatively ineffective and so do little harm. Starting in the 1980s, hopes for development did indeed shift in the direction of this "neoliberalism." Because it seemed like the state's interventions were more likely to be destructive than constructive, people who thought themselves wise deemed it better to try to limit the state's involvement in the process of development. Rely instead, they advised, on the world market as a source of demand, and on the requirements for integration into the world market as a source of good-enough governance.

These pressures, taking the post–World War II period as a whole, at least, have been strong enough to counteract the natural tendency for poor countries to learn rapidly about technology and catch up to rich ones. There is no clear reason on the horizon for these pressures to diminish. Optimists hope that the record of economic failure provided by much third world experience in the past generation will lead to the creation of intellectual pressures for reform strong enough to overcome the bias for stagnation. And if ideas truly are the decisive forces making history in the long run, perhaps the optimists are right.

If the optimists are wrong, then we are all in big trouble. Successful handling of global warming and other future global environmental problems, and successful long-run stabilization of human populations, hinges on successful industrialization in the global south and their consequent—rapid—passage through the demographic transition, especially in sub-Saharan Africa and in much of the Islamic world, where it is currently semistalled. "Neoliberalism" in the global south has thus been the strategy of pessimistic optimists. Having grown pessimistic about the ability of developing states to attain enough security, stability, and independence to pursue economic growth, they optimistically expect evidence of economic failure to generate ideas, constituencies, and pressures that will reform states toward economic growth. Pessimism in the short run—but optimism in the long.

13

Inclusion

As we have seen, in the years before the beginning of the long twentieth century, from roughly 1800 to 1870, new developments in technology and organization seemed to be opening the door to a better world, one in which humanity would not be kept desperately poor by the Malthusian trap. As the long twentieth century began, humanity started to walk through that door, along the path to the utopia beyond. But in the following years, 1914–1949 or so, the utopia beyond the door proved elusive as humanity grappled with a world war, a major depression, and another world war. There were also civil and revolutionary wars—and the last of these, China's, which did not come to an end until 1949, brought with it a famine in which between fifty million and one hundred million people died throughout the country. Technology and organization, rather than acting as forces to free and enrich, were increasingly used to kill and oppress.

If one looked only at the ideological challenges, the political mechanisms, and the dilemmas of growth and distribution during this period, one would not have found much of a basis for optimism in the immediate aftermath of World War II.

And yet, after World War II, the world, or at least the global north, picked up its mat and walked—nay, ran—forward toward true utopia. High taxes to fight wars had fallen most heavily upon the rich, who had also seen their wealth substantially reduced by the Great Depression. In the United States, an enormous demand for workers to build capacity for the war had driven up wages—and compressed them, too. The wages of the "unskilled" rose more than the wages of the "skilled," both because the War Labor Board decreed it so and because those running the factories were under immense pressure to get the job done, and it turned out to be not that difficult to teach skills if you really needed to. And in the aftermath of World War II, strong unions everywhere made it economically risky for bosses to claim or boards to approve extraordinary compensation packages for high executives. Growth was faster than ever before, unemployment was low, incomes were not too unequally distributed—at least if you were a white guy who had been born in the United States or some other country of the global north—and the boom-bust business cycle was very moderate. It was closer to material utopia for white guys in the global north than ever before, and rapidly getting closer still.

But still, this was only true for white guys. For everyone else? In most places, for most people, it's true that things were better than in the times of their predecessors. As the Nigerian novelist Chinua Achebe wrote, putting himself in the place of his colonized Igbo ancestors, "The white man had indeed brought a lunatic religion, but he had also built a trading store and for the first time palm-oil and kernel became things of great price, and much money flowed into Umofia."[1] But close to utopia? Not so much. And yet, although huge gaps remained between the white guys who were full citizens of the global north and other guys who were not, the derivative was in the right direction: things did get somewhat better for those who were not.

W. Arthur Lewis was born on the British-ruled island of Saint Lucia in 1915. He was a gifted student who finished high school at the age of fourteen. He wanted to become an engineer, but, as he later wrote, "This seemed pointless since neither the government nor the white firms would employ a black engineer."[2] He decided to go into business administration and won a scholarship that enabled him to become the first African-heritage student at the London School of Economics in 1933. The economists at the LSE recognized immense talent. In 1953 he was promoted to full professor at the University of Manchester and was considered perhaps the leading development economist in the world. In 1959 he was appointed vice chancellor of the University of the West Indies and returned to the Americas. But Lewis did not see his success as in any way validating the system. He was a strident advocate for reparations and always sought to bring the issue of "underdevelopment" to the forefront. Underdevelopment, he said, was not a lack of economic change but rather a form of economic change—one imposed on the global south by how the market economy had globalized.[3]

For a long, long time, reaching back into human history, it was the case that a person could have social power only if he was male, and even then only if he was special—from the right tribe, the right caste, the right lineage, or the right social order, or had enough property, or enough education. This was how people expected it would always be—unless, as Aristotle theorized, humans obtained the fantasy technologies of the Golden Age, by which he meant something akin to utopia. To quote Aristotle, "Chief workmen would not want servants, nor masters slaves," once "every instrument could accomplish its own work, obeying or anticipating the will of others, like the [blacksmithing] statues of Daidalos, or the three-wheeled catering serving-carts of Hephaistos."[4] Until then, Malthusian demographic pressure along with an anemic pace of invention would keep productivity low. If some were to have the leisure to, as John Adams put it, study philosophy, painting, poetry, and music, others—most—would have to be degraded and deprived of social power, and a good chunk of what they produced would be taken from them.

Gross inequality did not mean that status was fixed across generations. For much of Agrarian Age history, in many places, such status was malleable: you or your father could change it—if you were or he was lucky. The centurion stops, turns to the tribune, and says, "This man is a Roman citizen," and the beating that Saint Paul is about to receive is immediately prevented—never mind that he has citizenship because his father did some favor for or paid some bribe to a Roman magistrate, and that none of his ancestors had ever seen Rome.

As time passed, and the Imperial-Commercial Age progressed, Europe increasingly chose violence: the Atlantic slave trade grew, and perhaps seventeen million people were kidnapped from Africa and brought to the Americas to be enslaved and, mostly, to be worked to death or near death. We think life expectancy for a Black slave in the Caribbean before 1800 was perhaps seven years once they arrived and were put to work. Guilt grew in Europe: this was a crime—a very profitable crime—unless there was some reason that Africans *deserved* to be enslaved. W. E. B. Du Bois lamented this history in his 1910 essay "The Souls of White Folk":

> The discovery of personal whiteness among the world's peoples is a very modern thing. . . . Even the sweeter souls of the dominant world as they discourse with me . . . are continually playing above their actual words an obligato of tune and tone, saying:
> "My poor, un-white thing! Weep not nor rage. I know, too well, that the curse of God lies heavy on you. Why? That is not for me to say, but be brave! Do your work in your lowly sphere, praying the good Lord that into heaven above, where all is love, you may, one day, be born—white!"[5]

As a matter of genetic fact, the overwhelming bulk of the human race's genes passed through a very narrow bottleneck some

75,000 years ago, so much so that the overwhelming bulk of us receive the overwhelming bulk of our genes from a few thousands alive then.[6] They are all of our great- (multiply that word by 3,000) grandparents. Do the math, and discover that the number of slots in each of our family trees divided by the number of ancestral people alive back then is a number that begins 153,778,990,270 and then continues with another 888 digits, approximately 1.5×10^{99}. The average person alive 75,000 years ago who is among our collective ancestors—who has any living descendants today—thus fills not only more slots in that generation of each of our ancestral family trees than there are particles in the universe but more than there are particles in a billion billion universes. Which means that if a human from 75,000 years ago has living descendants today, the odds are overwhelming that we are all descended from that individual, and descended through myriads upon myriads upon myriads of lines. Thus all humans are close cousins: there is reputed to be more genetic variation in a typical baboon troop than in the entire human race.

Yes, humans have coevolved with culture and migration. Those of us whose ancestors moved far from the equator are descended only from those among the migrants who developed mutations disrupting their melanin-production genes so that enough sunlight could get through the outer layers of the skin to turn cholesterol into Vitamin D. It looks as though lactose tolerance has evolved six times in the past 6,000 years. Yes, we wish right now that whatever founder effects produced Tay-Sachs disease had not occurred.

Some believe that there are important genetic differences between the sociological group divisions that we draw between different groups of our very close cousins—and that these differences explain other differences in social, political, cultural, and, yes, economic outcomes among genders and ethnicities. As the right-wing economist Thomas Sowell pointed out long ago, to no effect in the corridors of the Hoover Institution, "Progressive"

Anglo-Saxons in 1900 thought it was extremely important to restrict immigration to keep the feeble-minded Jews of Eastern Europe from coming to America.[7]

It is exhausting, indeed debasing, to many, to have to expend effort refuting claims that, for example, Black Americans living in relative poverty today face those circumstances because, as a group, they have inherited genes for dumbness. As a rule, those who are "just asking questions" are not doing so because they wish to learn about inheritance, population genetics, and the intergenerational transmission of inequality. Perversely, any effort to rebut such claims tends to trigger a "where there is smoke, there must be fire" reaction, rather than exposing the emptiness of the idea. It is a hard problem, how to conduct rational public discourse in a twenty-first century in which communications channels such as Facebook and Twitter are run by those whose business model it is to scare and outrage their readers in order to glue their eye-balls to a screen so they can then be sold fake diabetes cures and cryptocurrencies.[8]

Perhaps these views are so persistent because they have such deep roots in US history. Abraham Lincoln—a politician and statesman much more committed to the dignity of labor and to the equality of humanity than most—spoke to the issue in an 1858 campaign speech: "I have no purpose to introduce political and social equality between the white and the black races. There is a physical difference between the two, which, in my judgment, will probably forever forbid their living together upon the footing of perfect equality, and inasmuch as it becomes a necessity that there must be a difference, I, as well as Judge Douglas, am in favor of the race to which I belong having the superior position."[9]

As a matter of economic history, this meant that after World War II, when the global north picked up its mat and ran toward utopia, white men were given a vast head start vis-à-vis all other men and all women. But, for Lincoln, full-throated assertions that he meant to protect white supremacy were, in context, more anticipatory concessive throat clearing than a line in the sand. They were the lead-up to a "but." The core meaning of his speech came later, after the "but." In Lincoln's view, Black Americans deserved—and more importantly, had inalienable rights to—a much better deal than they were getting: "There is no reason in the world why the negro is not entitled to all the natural rights enumerated in the Declaration of Independence, the right to life, liberty, and the pursuit of happiness. . . . In the right to eat the bread, without the leave of anybody else, which his own hand earns, he is my equal and the equal of Judge Douglas, and the equal of every living man."[10] The record then shows that from the white audience of the citizens of Illinois who were seeking entertainment and information about their state's Senate race on that summer Saturday afternoon, there came "Great Applause."

Whatever inequalities might exist in society, the right for you to make somebody else your slave was not one of them, Lincoln was saying. You only had a right to eat what you had earned by the work of your hands. That was part of your rights to life, liberty, and the pursuit of happiness. To keep others from taking the bread that you had earned was the point of government. Moreover, any such government was legitimate only through your consent.

That was the theory. But, as Martin Luther King Jr. would later put it in his famous 1963 "I Have a Dream" speech, the writers of the Declaration of Independence and the United States Constitution had signed a "promissory note" to Black Americans that was still in arrears then, and is still in arrears today.[11] Think of it: one-half of US states currently have election laws crafted to diminish the voting power of Black people and to make it disproportionately burdensome and inconvenient for them to exercise their franchise. And, no, you cannot make a society that keeps Blacks poor and enact policies that make them prefer to vote for Democratic candidates and then claim that there is no racial animus in the disparate impact of vote suppression.[12]

Nevertheless, Lincoln's Emancipation Proclamation was a mighty blow that made visible a glacial creep toward what we now call "inclusion." And throughout the long twentieth century, things have at least started to change. As the century advanced, being a male and being of the right tribe, the right caste, the right lineage, or a member of the right social order became less and less essential for social power.

But having property and education (and the right amounts and kinds of both) remained crucial. Where a person was born continued to be decisive in shaping what their opportunities would be. Throughout the long twentieth century, in other words, "inclusion" continued to be more goal than reality.

In the long twentieth century's social movement toward inclusion, the United States was once more, to a substantial degree, the furnace where the future was being forged. It was not that the United States did better than other countries. But the combination of its global hegemonic power and the larger gap between its aspirations and its reality generated a great deal of high-tension energy. Or so it had been since the United States decided that it would be defined by Thomas Jefferson's declaration—that "all men are created equal" and "endowed . . . with certain unalienable Rights"—rather than Roger B. Taney's—that Black people were "so far inferior, that they had no rights which the white man was bound to respect."[13]

AT THE END OF World War II, all indications were that a combination of de jure and de facto discrimination against Black Americans would continue indefinitely to prevent them from attaining education, climbing out of poverty, and building wealth. The economist and sociologist Gunnar Myrdal entitled his 1944 book on race and America *An American Dilemma*—the dilemma being the inconsistency between an "American creed" of equality of opportunity and the actual position of Blacks in America. There seemed to be no reason why the country could not live with this dilemma indefinitely.

The Republican Party retained a vestigial commitment to Black uplift as part of its belief in "free labor." But the American aspiration to equality managed to coexist with official state-sanctioned discrimination and disenfranchisement for another full century after the Emancipation Proclamation. In the South, Black disenfranchisement was settled policy, overwhelmingly popular among whites. Eight Blacks from the South served in Congress between 1875 and 1877, but then there would be no southern Black representatives from 1901 to 1973, when Barbara Jordan from Texas and Andrew Young from Georgia took office.

In the North, up until the beginning of the first Great Migration in the 1910s, there were too few Blacks in the population for the election of a Black representative to be likely, and so there were none. Even after the migration was underway, there were very few Black congressmen from the North. Indeed, the first northern Black congressman did not take office until 1929, when a Republican, Oscar Stanton De Priest, was elected from a majority-minority district in Southside Chicago. A second Black congressman, Adam Clayton Powell Jr. from Harlem, took office in 1945. Then came Charles Diggs from Michigan in 1955, Robert Nix from Pennsylvania in 1959, Augustus Hawkins from California in 1963, and John Conyers from Michigan in 1965. In short, there were only four Black congressmen, all Democrats, in the last Congress before the passage of the landmark 1965 Voting Rights Act, which finally provided a meaningful set of protections for Black voters.

And yet, today, nearly half of the states have voting restrictions targeted at reducing the share of Black votes. A majority of US Supreme Court justices pretend to believe that these are partisan restrictions imposed by Republican Party legislators to give them an edge over the Democratic Party in the next election, rather than racist restrictions to keep Black men and women down. But considering the ugly reality of American political history even in the later decades of the long twentieth century, this is not that surprising; this was a time, after all, when a Republican Party standard-bearer (Ronald Reagan) referred to diplomats from Tanzania as "monkeys from those African countries," and an economic policy standard-bearer (the University of Chicago's George Stigler) damned Martin Luther King Jr. and other civil rights leaders for their "growing insolence."[14] Plus there is the question that Republican-appointed Supreme Court justices do not ask: If a political party goes all-in to attract bigots, is it then unbigoted to attempt to suppress the votes of those who are repelled by that political strategy?

What is a political party that seeks to widen and reinforce hierarchies and differentials of wealth and income to do in a democracy?[15] It needs to provide at least some potential majority with reasons to vote for it. Such a party can claim that it is superior at generating economic growth: that although it will give you a smaller piece of the economic pie, the pie will be bigger by more than enough to compensate. Sometimes this approach can lead to good governance, particularly in the context of a two-party system in which power alternates as median voters swing back and forth between the priorities of delivering faster growth and providing fairer distributions and less insecurity. But eventually, it requires more than just saying that the conservative policies will grow the economic pie faster—it requires actually delivering on that promise.

Failing that, the party can seek to make economic cleavages and inequalities of wealth less salient. That requires making other issues more salient: in other words, highlighting non-economic political cleavages and exploiting them. It can play the nationalism card: the nation is in danger, under threat, and since defense is more important than opulence, you cannot afford to vote for your lunch-pail interests. Or it can find some enemy not external but internal, against whom a majority of the electorate can be rallied. And since the founding of the United States, political parties have found that the most effective way to deploy this strategy has been to declare rhetorical (and often all-too-deadly real) war against its Black population. Note that it is not always the Republicans—it was, up until the 1940s, the Democrats. Back then, with respect to the American creed of equality of opportunity, the Democrats had an edge on the equality part *among white men*, and the Republicans on the opportunity part. But a large part of making white men feel equal to each other was making them feel superior to Black men.[16] And so a large chunk of the appeal of the Democratic piece of America's "Progressive" moment was its white supremacy.

The damage done during the Progressive Era by the rollback of freedoms for Black Americans has often been underestimated. Emancipation was followed by Reconstruction, which was then rolled back, and that political-economic-societal equilibrium was then further rolled back by Jim Crow, which devastated the then rising Black middle class.

As of 1940, the average Black worker in the United States had three fewer years of education than the average white worker. A substantial majority of white Americans approved of discrimination—in employment, in housing, in education, and in voting. Black men were concentrated in unskilled agricultural labor, primarily in the low-productivity and low-income South; Black women were concentrated in unskilled agriculture and in domestic service. Both were extremely low-paid occupations: Black men and women earned an average weekly wage some 45 percent that of their white counterparts. Black male college graduates earned some $280 a week (in today's dollars); white high school graduates earned some $560 a week. In 1940, some 48 percent of white families fell below today's "poverty line" according to official statistics; meanwhile, some 81 percent of Black families were in poverty.

These disparities, along with a wide variety of other factors, converged to keep Black men and women subordinate. By the later decades of the long twentieth century much had changed. Virtually all whites publicly espoused the principle of equal employment opportunity for Black Americans. Educational attainment by race was almost identical for those finishing school in the late 1980s and 1990s. Black men's average weekly wages were two-thirds those of whites; Black women's average weekly wages were more than 95 percent those of white women's wages, on average.

It is impossible not to credit the change to the wise leadership and skillful use of moral force by the Black community. Civil rights leaders played a weak hand with immense skill and patience and achieved extraordinary long-run success. They are among the greatest of the heroes of the long twentieth century.

Three factors in particular played a major role in bringing about the gains that were realized between 1940 and 1970: the end of formal, legal, state-sanctioned discrimination; the migration of Black Americans from the rural South to the urban North during the Second Great Migration; and the associated shift from low-paid, low-skill agricultural employment to industrial and service industries. The period was accompanied by large increases in the educational levels attained by Black Americans and high rates of employment and productivity growth in the rest of the economy. A fourth very significant factor came in 1964, when Title VII of the Civil Rights Act made employment discrimination illegal. There is every reason to think that without it the economic advancement of Black Americans would have been considerably slower.

If the period from 1940 to 1970 was one of substantial relative advance, the picture after 1970 was more mixed. By the end of the 1980s, at least one in five Black men between the ages of twenty-five and fifty-four in the United States were reporting no annual earnings at all. And even today, real per capita family income for Black Americans is still only some 60 percent of what it is for whites: almost exactly what it had been at the end of the 1960s. The majority of white Americans believe there is no more personal racism—that white animus against Blacks was a thing in previous generations but is no longer. And yet what keeps the relative incomes of Blacks so far down, except for racism? Much of this racism, indeed, is now recognized as "structural racism": the frictions, institutions, and legacies of the past in their current shape of wealth and social network access performing the functions that personal racial animus used to perform.

Most important in stalling progress toward economic equality for Black people, in my judgment, was a general, economy-wide factor: the growth in income inequality as employers' relative demands for less-skilled and less-educated workers diminished. Also important were changes in family structure: a rise in divorce, a rise in births outside of marriage, and the consequent rise in single-parent households (almost inevitably female headed). By the later decades of the twentieth century, the poverty rate for two-parent Black families with children was 12.5 percent. The poverty rate for single-parent Black families with children was 40 percent. And a full half of Black children spent at least half their childhood below the poverty line.

The right-wing explanation for the decline in the number of Black two-parent families—the explanation provided by the likes of Charles Murray[17] and George Gilder[18]—was that more generous welfare payments triggered a collapse by disincentivizing work and removing the material economic benefits of keeping adult couples together. The seminal work out of which Murray and Gilder and similar thinkers constructed their interpretation was a mid-1960s document written by a Johnson administration policy maker, Daniel Patrick Moynihan. But Moynihan's

The Negro Family: The Case for National Action was shaped in part by his own tendency to look inward rather than outward, by memories of his own Irish American family dynamics under material pressure. It was more his own personal psychodrama than an analysis of the circumstances facing Black families. He did see powerful parallels between his own experience and what he imagined to be the experience of Black children growing up in dire circumstances—parallels that he felt called for a national commitment, so that in America's future no child would have to grow up as he had, running with gangs in Hell's Kitchen, Manhattan, or as he saw so many Black children growing up in the 1960s.[19]

Indeed, it is hard to escape the conclusion that Murray and Gilder simply had not done their arithmetic. Welfare and food stamp payments for a mother with three children rose by one-third between 1960 and 1970, but then declined. By the mid-1990s, welfare payments were lower in inflation-adjusted terms than they had been in 1960; real wages were some one-third higher—some 50 percent higher for Black males. Maintaining a two-parent household was, in material terms, a much more advantageous option in the 1990s relative to splitting up and collecting welfare than it had been in the 1950s and 1960s.

A better explanation was that Black families were caught in the backwash of broader, society-wide changes—but were especially vulnerable to them. The tide of inclusion may have carried with it a declining significance of *race*, but the post-1980 future was to bring with it a rising significance of *class* in the coming of a Second Gilded Age, and an explosion of income and wealth inequality even among white guys. To a degree, for Black Americans, the gains in social inclusion came not just too little but at least half a generation too late.

LET US RETURN, FOR a moment, to the immediate post–World War II period. Again, growth was faster than ever before, unemployment was low, incomes were not too unequally distributed—at least if you were a white guy in the global north—and the boom-bust business cycle was very moderate. It was closer to material utopia for white guys than ever before, and rapidly getting closer still. But what about the women?

Plato's Socrates, in the *Republic*, posited that there would be women among the ideal city's Guardians, for the souls of men and women were fundamentally the same. Writing a generation after that, in 340 BCE or so, his pupil Aristotle begged to differ— he thought there were significant differences:

> Although there may be exceptions to the order of nature, the male is by nature fitter for command than the female, just as the elder and full-grown is superior to the younger and more immature. . . . The relation of the male to the female is of this kind, but there the inequality is permanent. . . . The slave has no deliberative faculty at all; the woman has, but it is without authority. . . . The courage and justice of a man and of a woman, are not, as Socrates maintained, the same; the courage of a man is shown in commanding, of a woman in obeying.[20]

We do need to look at the bigger picture. Why male supremacy became so firmly established millennia ago, back in the Agrarian Age, is not obvious. Yes, it was of the utmost importance to have surviving descendants so that someone would be there to take care of you in your old age. Yes, in order to maximize their chances of having surviving descendants to take care of them, it was important for men and women to have a lot of children. Thus the typical woman spent twenty years eating for two: pregnant and breastfeeding. And yes, eating for two is an enormous energy drain, especially in populations near subsistence level (and Agrarian Age populations were near subsistence level). Yes, breastfeeding required women to remain physically close to their children, and this helped enforce a concentration of female labor on activities that made it easy to do so: gardening and other forms of within-and-near-the-dwelling labor, especially textiles.

But, even given all that, men did derive tangible benefits from further oppressing women far above what one might argue were the limitations imposed by necessity in the form of mammalian biology under Malthusian conditions—especially if women could be convinced that they deserved it: "Unto the woman he said, 'I will greatly multiply thy sorrow and thy conception; in sorrow thou shalt bring forth children; and thy desire shall be to thy husband; and he shall rule over thee.'"

But for how long this high patriarchy has been a major piece of human culture is not something that we know. There are at least some signs in our genes of a big change about five thousand years ago: a sudden drop in humanity's "effective" male population—that is, the number of men living then who have descendants now. There was no such drop in humanity's "effective" female population. About five thousand years ago, even as nearly all women who survived past menarche had children, a substantial proportion of men who survived past puberty did not.[21] How much societal pressure was required for it to become more or less the rule for women to share husbands, or to accept a much older one, and for a substantial proportion of men to remain unmarried? What institutions applied this pressure, and how? About three thousand years ago the situation rebalanced: one-to-one in the household again became dominant. Was the origin of high patriarchy responsible for this rebalancing? Is this what we see in Aristotle's statement that "the courage of a man is shown in commanding, of a woman in obeying"? (Do note that Aristotle maintains this conviction over strong disagreement from Socrates—and Plato—for whom the souls of men and women were fundamentally the same.) Or was it present in human societies before?

If I were female, would I see the remarkable change in the position of women as central to history? Would I see the shift from a typical experience in those ancient times—of eight or more pregnancies, twenty years of eating for two, and a one-in-seven chance of dying in childbirth—to the modern experience of one or two pregnancies—along with a much reduced chance of dying in childbirth, depending on where you live—as one of the biggest changes? Is the rise of feminism the biggest news of the long twentieth century? Will historians a thousand or so years hence see it as more consequential than—although interlinked with—the end of Malthusian poverty?

Let us jump back in time for a moment. In 1900, in the United States, paid male workers outnumbered paid female workers by a margin of about four to one. The imbalance was perhaps not quite that high—census procedures undercounted the number of women whose work products were in fact sold on the market, and economists' measures have traditionally undervalued within-the-household production. Nevertheless, the difference was striking. By the end of the century, however, the paid labor force was nearly half female.[22]

In 1900, the bulk of female workers in the census-counted, formally paid segment of the labor force were unmarried. Some 43.5 percent of single women fifteen years old and up were in the officially counted labor force—41.5 percent of white and 60.5 percent of nonwhite women. By contrast, only 3.2 percent of married white women (and 26 percent of married nonwhite women, for a national average of 5.6 percent) participated in the labor force. In 1920 only 4 percent of married white women around the age of thirty worked; by 1980 nearly 60 percent of married white women near thirty worked. Labor force participation by married nonwhite women near thirty rose less, but from a higher base and to a greater level: from approximately 33 percent in 1920 to 72 percent by 1980.

But this gives us an incomplete picture. Consider, for instance, the difference between women born around 1920 and those born around 1960. The earlier cohort reached adulthood around 1940 and were sixty years old in 1980. The labor force participation rate of those who were married rose from roughly 15 percent when they were twenty to approximately 45 percent when they were fifty. Women born forty years later, around 1960, already had a 60 percent labor participation rate (among those who were married) when they were twenty—and every sign is that married women's labor force participation rises with age.

However, the large increase in female labor force participation over the course of the twentieth century, while encouraging, was not accompanied by any rapid closing of the earnings gap between male and female workers. Although various sources report substantial rises in female-relative-to-male wages over the course of the nineteenth century, and some continued gains up until 1930, for most of the twentieth century female wages remained roughly 60 percent of male wages.

One reason female relative earnings failed to rise throughout the middle years of the twentieth century is the rapidity with which women expanded into the labor force. This rapid expansion in labor force participation meant that at any moment a relatively low share of the female labor force had a high level of experience. And because firms pay more for experienced workers—both because experienced workers are more productive and because the promise of regular pay increases along a well-established career track can serve as a powerful way to motivate employees—that relative lack of experience kept women's relative wages low.

A second factor keeping relative female earnings low was the persistence of occupational segregation by sex. Between 1900 and 1960, roughly two-thirds of the female labor force would have had to change occupations in order to produce the same distribution across occupations as the male labor force. Occupational segregation has fallen somewhat since the end of the 1960s, but it is still the case that women are concentrated in occupations that are relatively low paid.

A third factor keeping women's relative earnings low has been their inability to attain the qualifications that employers value. Women back at the start of the twentieth century had little opportunity for formal education. Nor did they have, for the most part, opportunities to gain economically valuable skills through informal education and on-the-job training. By and large, women were employed only in tasks that were relatively easily and quickly learned, and in which the benefits of experience on productivity were slim. The economist Claudia Goldin has estimated that if we compensate for all three factors, we will see that the gap between what women and men with similar experience and education were paid at the start of the twenty-first century was relatively small.

Today the pay gap is less attributable to differences in women's and men's experience, education, and other job-relevant characteristics than to what is apparently simply wage discrimination: paying women less than men because they are women. Goldin traced the emergence of such wage discrimination to the development of the large modern firm, with its personnel department. Before the development of the large, bureaucratic firm, the market provided substantial insulation against discrimination to women. With many small employers, should any one firm begin to discriminate—to pay women less than men for the same work—women would have the opportunity to vote with their feet for some other, less discriminatory employer.

As Goldin wrote, once firms had established personnel departments with centralized human resource policies, they discovered that many women would not remain on the job long enough to take advantage of the regular wage increases that come with efficient, strong performance and loyalty to the firm. Then why reward the atypical woman who did remain on the job with those increases? This is not to say that all pay discrimination has been in service of firms' profit maximizing. Naked prejudice certainly played a role—prejudice on the part of male workers, employers, and customers. Male workers, for example, fearing competition, tried to bar women from their occupations.

From today's perspective, the most surprising thing about the transformation of the role of women in the economy is how long it took. This despite the fact that after World War II, the birth rate had fallen; a large clerical and retail sector, in which physical strength was completely irrelevant, had emerged; and female education had taken hold. Barriers to women's employment persisted, such as jobs that assumed workers must work full time; pervasive discrimination; social attitudes that deemed certain occupations inappropriate for women; and personnel policies that restricted or even prohibited the employment of married women.

In the long run, it took action on the part of the federal government to erode the framework of restrictions and customs that kept women's economic roles from expanding. The action came in the form of the 1964 Civil Rights Act, which prohibited discrimination in employment on the basis of race, color, religion, national origin, or *sex*. When the House Rules Committee chair during the debates over the bill, Howard Smith (D-VA), proposed the amendment adding "sex" to the list of protected categories, he was at least half-joking, and it was not liberal Democrats but southern Democrats and Republicans who approved it, 168–133. Courts decided that the "sex" part of the prohibition could not have been intended to stand on an equal footing with the others, and did not require that possible discrimination be scrutinized as strictly as in cases where race, color, or religion was at issue. Nevertheless, it was subject to more scrutiny than "here: we just thought up this reason." Thus the legal environment mattered.[23] And so Claudia Goldin could conclude her book on the gender gap by pointing to the possibility of a future near death of gender discrimination. Encouraged by "the convergence between men and women in the percentage graduating from college," she wrote that "we can forecast the future by observing the experiences of young cohorts today, and these experiences give us ample ground for optimism."[24]

But surely, even in the Agrarian Age, a shift to a society with less male supremacy would have been a positive-sum change. Women as equal participants in society, rather than just chattels—classified as only a rung above slaves and cattle—could have done, and contributed, much more than they were able to do and contribute under the conditions of male supremacy that existed. Optimistic economists like me have a strong bias toward believing that people in groups will become more inclusive, will find ways to share, will become, collectively, more productive, and then will distribute the fruits of that productivity to make their social order more sustainable. Productivity depends on the division of labor. And if you invite more people into your tent, your division of labor can be finer and hence more productive. But apparently that is not how people saw it in the Agrarian Age or for many years thereafter.

The underpinnings of male supremacy did begin to erode before 1870. But it was over the long twentieth century that these underpinnings dissolved more completely. Reductions in infant mortality, the advancing average age of marriage, and the increasing costs of child-rearing all contributed to a decrease in fertility. The number of years the typical woman spent eating for two fell from twenty down to four as better sanitation, much better nutrition, and more knowledge about disease made many pregnancies less necessary for leaving surviving descendants, and as birth control technology made it easier to plan families. And, after exploding in the Industrial Age, the rate of population growth in the industrial core slowed drastically. The population explosion turned out to be a relatively short-run thing. Humanity appears to be rapidly moving toward zero long-run population growth.

The path of within-the-household technological advance also worked to the benefit of the typical woman over the course of the long twentieth century: dishwashers, dryers, vacuum cleaners, improved chemical cleansing products, other electrical and natural gas appliances, and especially clothes-washing machines—all these made the tasks of keeping the household clean, ordered, and functioning much easier. Maintaining a high-fertility household in the nineteenth century was much more than a full-time job. Doing so in the late twentieth century could become more like a part-time job. Thus a great deal of female labor that had previously been tied to full-time work within the household could now be redirected to other purposes. And, as Betty Friedan wrote in the early 1960s, women who sought something like equal status could find it only if they found "identity . . . in work . . . for which, usually, our society pays."[25] As long as women were confined to separate, domestic occupations that the market did not reward with cash, it was easy for men to denigrate and minimize their labor.

While it is undeniably true that the explosion of wealth begun in 1870 was a multiplier of this century's brutal and barbaric tyrannies, two more enduring tyrannies—racism and sexism—gave ground, slowly, reluctantly, and partially. On the one hand, this progress, even if its speed was deliberate, raised the bar as to how fast humanity should be slouching toward utopia, and how much of a slowdown in progress would generate strong calls for change. On the other hand, status in society is, if not zero-sum, close to zero-sum. How were those whose gender, ethnicity, and caste privileges were being eroded by the tide of inclusion to reconcile themselves with what was *dérogeance*? The answer, for the first post–World War II generation in the global north, was through unprecedented rapid income growth, opportunity, and upward mobility.

14

Thirty Glorious Years
of Social Democracy

History does not repeat itself, but it does rhyme—oddly. As of 1870, the then 1.3 billion people on earth had an average income of about $1,300 of today's dollars per year. By 1938 the population had perhaps doubled from 1870, and the average income had grown a bit more than 2.5-fold. Things were much better. Before 1870, things had been rocky for the world. Remember John Stuart Mill's pessimism, let alone Karl Marx's, about how few of the potential gains from technological advance had been trickling down? Before 1938, things had been rocky for the world in World War I and then again in the Great Depression, and they were about to get rockier still. The world was about to fall into the immense destruction of World War II, along with its more than 50 million deaths, a devastating interruption of the slouching progress upward. Yet 1870–1914 also brought with it an extraordinary era of prosperity, a never-before-seen economic El Dorado, and 1938–1973—for the World War II mobilization brought a powerful spurt of growth to those countries lucky enough not to be battlefields, most notably the United States— was to bring with it another such glorious age.

Thus from 1938 to 1973 the world economy leaped ahead once again—and once again at an unprecedented pace. And the core of the global north, the countries we now call the G-7 (the United States, Canada, Japan, Britain, France, Germany, and Italy) raced forward: not at the 0.7 percent per year pace of 1913–1938, or even the 1.42 percent per year pace of 1870–1913, but—in spite of all the destruction wrought by World War II—at an average pace of 3 percent per year. That means the material wealth of those countries was increasing fast enough to double every twenty-three years—in the space of less than a generation. The G-7 was thus three times as well-off in material terms by 1973 as it had been in 1938.

The poorest of them, Japan, grew the fastest: at a previously unseen rate of 4.7 percent per year—in spite of the extensive damage it sustained during the war, including the atomic bombs that incinerated two Japanese cities in 1945. Canada and Italy grew at rates of more than 3 percent per year. And the G-7 countries were not alone: Mexico, Spain, and many others achieved similar rates of growth.

The French call this period the Thirty Glorious Years: the *Trente Glorieuses*.[1] So much good luck in one package was unexpected. It is still to marvel at—if you are a political economist.

If you are a neoclassical economist, however, you shrug your shoulders. The market economy delivered, as it should, full employment, proper infrastructure, and protection of contracts and private property. Modern science delivered, too, in the form of a host of fundamental technological breakthroughs. Moreover, there was a large backlog of previous discoveries that had been left undeveloped and undeployed during the chaos of the Great Depression. So it was profitable for businesses to provide their industrial research labs with generous funding and then to deploy the labs' new innovations at scale. In doing so, companies were able to build their knowledge and pull previously untrained and unskilled workers from farms and craft workshops into "Fordist" assembly lines.[2] This was, for us neoclassical economists, the normal and natural way things work, or should work, in the Modern Economic Growth Age. Never mind that for economic progress to follow this natural course was, in the long twentieth century, unusual, to say the least.

It was, come to full life and power, Friedrich von Hayek's positive vision of the power of the market. The market giveth, and giveth, and giveth yet more. There were those who questioned Hayek's conclusions. The economist Herbert Simon liked to point out that what Hayek called a "market economy" was not a field of green market exchanges, in which were scattered red dots of small individual firms, but instead red areas of firm command-and-control organization connected by green lines of market exchange. Harvard economist Martin Weitzman liked to point out that there was no deep theoretical reason why providing the information that firms needed via a price target—produce if you can make it for a fully amortized unit cost of less than $X—should be more efficient than via a quantity target—produce Y units.[3] But Hayek's colleague Ronald Coase, at the University of Chicago, pointed out that one of the market economy's great strengths was that it allowed firms to decide whether to use a bureaucratic command-and-control-style system or a system based on transaction costs (of buying and selling) to make decisions: the fact that firms could *choose* was key.[4] Plus the fact that firms were always subject to the discipline of the marketplace, with those that lost money shrinking and vanishing in a way that state-run bureaucracies that lost money did not.[5]

But before Friedrich von Hayek's word could become flesh, and dwell among us, there were three prerequisites. First, Hayek had to be divorced from theories and philosophies such as those of the novelist Ayn Rand. A functional market required *competition*—not monopolies bossed by technological and organizational visionaries.[6]

Second, Hayek had to be blessed by the ideas of John Maynard Keynes. The market economy could only work properly—could only direct resources to their "best" uses—if the spending was there to make enterprise profitable.

John Maynard Keynes had written in 1936, with more than a hint of sarcasm, that his proposals for the "enlargement of the functions of government" that were required in order to adjust "the propensity to consume and the inducement to invest" might seem "a terrific encroachment" on freedom "to a nineteenth-century publicist or . . . contemporary American financier." But, in fact, they were "the condition of the successful functioning of individual initiative." And "if effective demand is deficient," he added, a businessperson was "operating with the odds loaded against him. The game of hazard which he plays is furnished with many zeros, so that the players as a whole will lose." Only "exceptional skill or unusual good fortune" would then allow entrepreneurship and enterprise to be rewarded, and economic growth to continue. But with Keynes's policies in place, "effective demand [would be] adequate, [and] average skill and average good fortune will be enough." In the Thirty Glorious Years, wise business leaders recognized that Keynes and his full-employment policies were not their enemies but their best friends.[7]

Third, Friedrich von Hayek had to be married to Karl Polanyi. One of the foundation stones of Hayek's worldview was that the market economy was the only way to generate growth and prosperity, but that it could never, and should never, be asked to produce fairness and social justice. Fairness and social justice required distributing good things to people who had acted well and deserved them. The market economy distributed things to people lucky enough to control resources that produced things for which the rich had a serious jones.

In Polanyi's worldview, people and communities believed extremely strongly that they had the right to demand certain things—among them stable land-use patterns that they deemed fair, income levels commensurate with their effort and merit, and the ability to keep their jobs, or at least find new ones without too much trouble. But the market economy would deliver those essentials only if they passed a maximum-profitability test. Some violations of Polanyian rights could be overlooked if economic growth was fast enough: I am not getting the slice of the pie I deserve, but at least I am getting a bigger slice than my mother and father got. The fiscal dividend the government received from growing tax revenues could, in a time of rapid economic growth, allow the government to do something to protect and vindicate Polanyian rights as well. A social democratic government needed to enable the market economy in order to generate growth and prosperity. But it also needed to check the market and keep the "market economy" from turning into a "market society" that people might reject, a society where employment was not stable, incomes were not commensurate with what people deserved, and communities were being continually upended and transformed by market fluctuations.

It was a balancing act. In some sense, the balancing act was made more complex by the swiftness of the tide toward greater inclusion. On the one hand, the tide extended not just to gender, race, and ethnicity but also to class: it no longer made as much sense to working-class males that they were in their subordinate place for a good reason. On the other hand, they found themselves losing some part of the deference from others that they had taken as their due and that had softened the perceived slope of the class pyramid. Both of these factors magnified the chances that they would see violations of this expected order—of what they saw as what they deserved—large enough to become calls for action.

But rapid growth in incomes and perceived opportunities for yourself and your children made up for much of the disruption of whatever old-order patterns supported you in what you saw as your proper place in society, the place you thought you deserved. So the global north was able to keep the balance through the

1960s and into the 1970s. And by 1975, the deployed technological capability of humanity stood at nine times what it had been in 1870. The population explosion meant that there were then 4 billion people, compared to 1.3 billion in 1870. But that population explosion, and the pressure it placed on the resource base, merely meant that material productivity was only five times what it had been in 1870—and as of 1975 it was astonishingly unequally distributed across countries, and also unequally (although less so, markedly, than it had been over 1870–1930) distributed within countries.

Things had worked. The Great Depression, in the United States at least, had convinced many that these divorces and marriages had to happen. The Gilded Age oligarchy of the robber barons had failed, and had in fact brought on the Great Depression—how was not quite clear, but, as Franklin Roosevelt put it, there was near consensus that the oligarchs and the plutocratic financiers needed to be cast down "from their high seats in the temple of our civilization."[8] Competition needed to rule. The Great Depression had also convinced the private sector that it needed the help of an active government to manage the economy in order to attain at least an approximation of full employment. Perhaps, more importantly, the Depression convinced the middle class that it had powerful interests in common with the working class—and from then on, both would demand social insurance and full employment from politicians. Adding to all of this, the totalitarian threat from Stalin's Soviet Union played a large role in convincing the nascent North Atlantic alliance to follow America's lead in both security policy and political-economic restructuring. And those were topics on which America had strong ideas.

Between the two world wars, the governments of rich countries had been badly hobbled by their doctrines of orthodoxy and austerity, by their insistence on pure laissez-faire, that the government should simply leave the economy alone. That doctrine had started out as a weapon to dismantle aristocratic mercantilism and then turned into a weapon to fight progressive taxes, social insurance programs, and "socialism" more generally.

We can mark the sea change in ideas that enabled these by looking at American right-wing economist Milton Friedman, who saw himself as—and sold himself as—the apostle of laissez-faire. Right-wingers trying to hold tight to their belief that the market could not fail but could only be failed, claimed that the Great Depression had been caused by government interference with the natural order. Economists such as Lionel Robbins, Joseph Schumpeter, and Friedrich von Hayek claimed that central banks had set interest rates too low in the run-up to 1929. Others claimed that central banks had set interest rates too high. Whatever. What they agreed on was that the central banks of the world had failed to follow a properly "neutral" monetary policy, and so had destabilized what, if left alone, would have been a stable market system. Milton Friedman was chief among them.

But dig into Friedman's thesis that the Great Depression was a failure of *government* and not of *market*, and things become interesting. For how could you tell whether interest rates were too high, too low, or just right, when "just right" was itself fluctuating with every tremor of the market? According to Friedman, too-high interest rates would lead to high unemployment. Too-low interest rates would lead to high inflation. Just-right interest rates—those that corresponded to a "neutral" monetary policy—would keep the macroeconomy balanced and the economy smoothly growing. Thus theory became tautology.[9]

It is an insult to the ghost of the astronomer Claudius Ptolemy, who developed some brilliant insights, to call this exercise Ptolemaic: that is to say, saving the phenomenon by redefining terms and adding complications, rather than admitting that you are looking at things upside down to preserve your intellectual commitments. But this, from Friedman, was positively Ptolemaic. Strip away the camouflage and the underlying message is Keynes's: the government needs to intervene on as large a scale as needed in order to shape the flow of economy-wide spending and keep it stable, and, in doing so successfully, guard the economy against depressions while preserving the benefits of the market system, along with human economic liberty and political and intellectual freedom.

The only substantive difference between Keynes and Friedman was that Friedman thought that central banks could do all this alone, via monetary policy, by keeping interest rates properly "neutral." Keynes thought more would be required: the government would probably need its own spending and taxing incentives to encourage businesses to invest and households to save. But the incentives alone would not be enough: "I conceive," he wrote, "that a somewhat comprehensive socialisation of investment will prove the only means of securing an approximation to full employment, though this need not exclude all manner of compromises and of devices by which public authority will co-operate with private initiative."[10]

And a large majority of people agreed with him. The magnitude of unemployment during the Great Depression had shifted politicians', industrialists', and bankers' beliefs about the key goals of economic policy. Before the Depression, a stable currency and exchange rate were key. But afterward, even the bankers recognized that a high overall level of employment was more important than avoiding inflation: universal bankruptcy and mass unemployment were not only bad for workers but bad for capitalists and bankers.

Thus, entrepreneurs, the owners and managers of industry, and even the bankers found that they gained, not lost, by committing to maintain high employment. High employment meant high-capacity utilization. Rather than seeing tight labor markets erode profits by raising wages, owners saw high demand spread fixed costs out over more commodities, and so increase profitability.

In the United States, the consolidation of the mixed-economy Keynesian social democratic order was straightforward. The United States had always been committed to a market economy. Yet it had also always been committed to a functional and pragmatic government. It had had a Progressive movement that had set out plans for the management of the market economy in the interests of equitable growth at the start of the 1900s. And it was the beneficiary of the fortunate accident that the right-wing party had been in power up until 1932, and hence took the lion's share of the blame for the Depression. All of this together made its path relatively smooth. Roosevelt picked up the reins, and in 1945, when he died, Truman picked them up again. The electorate ratified the New Deal order by giving Truman his own full term in 1948. And in 1953, the new Republican president, Dwight Eisenhower, saw his task not as rolling back his Democratic predecessors' programs but rather as containing the further expansion of what he muttered under his breath was "collectivism."

The 1946 Employment Act declared that it was the "continuing policy and responsibility" of the federal government to "coordinate and utilize all its plans, functions, and resources . . . to foster and promote free competitive enterprise and the general welfare; conditions under which there will be afforded useful employment for those able, willing, and seeking to work; and to promote maximum employment, production, and purchasing power."[11] Laws that establish goals can and do serve as markers of changes in opinions, perceptions, and aims. The largest shift in policy marked by the Employment Act was the post–World War II practice of allowing the government's fiscal automatic stabilizers to function.

We have already noted Eisenhower's letter to his brother Edgar in the 1950s, in which he argued that laissez-faire was dead, and that attempts to resurrect it were simply "stupid." Milton Friedman and Eisenhower saw the same escape hatch that John

Maynard Keynes had seen, and were just as eager to open and crawl through it. Indeed, the government programs that Eisenhower pointed to in his letter and their analogues in other advanced industrial countries have been remarkably successful in uniting political coalitions. As Eisenhower put it, "Should any political party attempt to abolish social security, unemployment insurance, and eliminate labor laws and farm programs, you would not hear of that party again in our political history."[12] Voters, in other words, distrusted politicians who sought to cut these programs back, and tended to find taxes earmarked to support social insurance programs less distasteful than other taxes. Outside of the United States, right-of-center parties have seldom made any serious attempt to take a stand against social democracy.

Eisenhower's vision was a consensus, not in the sense that overwhelming majorities agreed with it in their hearts of hearts, but in the sense that overwhelming majorities believed that it would be impolitic to call for a return to Calvin Coolidge's or Herbert Hoover's America.

The result was big government and then some. Federal spending under Eisenhower was 18 percent of GDP—twice what it had been in peacetime even at the height of the New Deal. And state and local government spending raised total government spending to over 30 percent. In pre–New Deal 1931, federal spending had been just 3.5 percent of GDP, and a full half of all federal employees were in the Post Office. By 1962, the federal government directly employed some 5,354,000 workers. And that was in a nation of some 180 million people. In 2010, that number was down to 4,443,000—with a population of over 300 million. This very large flow of government cash immune to the vagaries of the business cycle enabled vigorous and profitable private initiative. And high taxes, not high borrowings, paid for big government: federal deficits averaged less than 1 percent of GDP from 1950 to 1970.

Although there was no major reshuffling of class and wealth, median incomes steadily rose, creating a strong middle class. Cars, houses, appliances, and good schools had previously been reserved for the top 10 percent—by 1970, they became the property of, or at least within the grasp of, the majority.

Federal government efforts to promote home building and homeownership by making mortgage financing more flexible actually began under Herbert Hoover, who in August 1932 signed the Federal Home Loan Bank Act to provide government credit for mortgages on houses. It set out what was to become the United States' approach to government promotion and assistance for housing. Instead of directly providing housing (which became the norm in Europe), the government would offer substantial support for the financing of the private development and ownership of houses. The Home Owners' Loan Corporation, created around the same time, financed over one million mortgages between August 1933 and August 1935, and set in place what would become the enduring mechanisms of US mortgage financing: long terms, fixed rates, low down payments, and amortization—backstopped by a government guarantee, which was necessary to persuade banks that it was good business to lend at a fixed rate for thirty years to borrowers who always had the option to pay off their loan at any instant.

Single-family houses on lots of even one-fifth or one-tenth of an acre meant automobiles. At scale, the older model, of suburbs connected to urban centers by streetcars or commuter trains, would not work. What took their place were the stupendous, omnipresent circulatory systems of limited-access highways. The National Interstate and Defense Highways Act of 1956 called for forty-one thousand miles of high-speed highways with the federal government paying 90 percent of the costs. Transportation money was even more sharply skewed to the suburbs (and away from the needs of the cities) than Federal Housing Administration insurance: only about 1 percent of federal transportation funding went to mass transit. And two-thirds of the highway lane miles were built within the boundaries of metropolitan areas: the Interstate Highway System should have been named the Suburban Highway System.

Indeed, the migration to the suburbs brought with it a new kind of built-in democratization, a homogenization of consumption patterns. All but the lower ranks—and the Blacker ranks—of American families found their place and felt it to be much the same place: middle-class America. They repeatedly told this to survey takers. Social scientists had difficulty understanding how and why three-fourths of Americans persisted in saying that they were middle class. White middle-class Americans did not: they happily marched, or rather drove, out to take possession of their new suburban homes. Suburban development was an extreme form of segregation by class and, of course, by race. But the divide was not all-important. There was still just one nation—middle-class America—even as some got more than others.

In 1944, with the end of the war in sight, the government was worried about how sixteen million GIs returning home would find jobs. It passed the GI Bill providing, in place of a traditional veterans' bonus, a generous program of support for GIs wishing to go to college—it would keep them out of the labor force for a little while—plus a major mortgage-assistance program for returning soldiers, with the valuable extra kicker of possibly zero down payment.

The post–Great Depression, postwar consensus that was forming in the United States included a place for labor unions, too: they would be an essential part of the marriage of Hayek and Polanyi. In 1919, union membership in the United States had amounted to some five million. Membership fell into a trough of perhaps three million by the time of FDR's inauguration in 1933, grew to nine million by the end of 1941, and took advantage of the tight labor market of World War II to grow to some seventeen million or so by the time Eisenhower was inaugurated in 1953.

From 1933 to 1937, organizing unions became easier—in spite of high unemployment—because of the solid swing of the political system in favor of the increasingly liberal Democrats. The federal government was no longer an anti-, but a pro-union force. The Wagner Act gave workers the right to engage in collective bargaining. A National Labor Relations Board monitored and greatly limited the ability of anti-union employers to punish union organizers and members. Employers in large mass-production industries learned to value the mediation between bosses and employees that unions could provide. And workers learned to value the above-market wages that unions could negotiate.

Along with the 1930s rise and institutional entrenchment of the union movement, there came the great compression of America's wages and salaries. In the late 1920s and 1930s, the top 10 percent, the top 1 percent, and the top 0.01 percent of the US population held 45 percent, 20 percent, and 3 percent of the nation's wealth, respectively. By the 1950s, those shares were down to about 35 percent, 12 percent, and 1 percent. (By 2010 they would be back up, rising to 50 percent, 20 percent, and 5 percent.)[13] To some degree, this was because education had won its race with technology, temporarily making usually poorly paid "unskilled" workers relatively scarce—and hence valued. To some degree, too, it was because closing down immigration had similar effects on the supply of workers with shaky (or no) English. But that this "great compression" is found all across the North Atlantic economies suggests that the political-economic factors played a greater role than the supply-and-demand factors. Unions also contributed to compressing the wage distribution. And minimum wage laws and other regulations played a role, too. Finally, there was the strongly progressive tax system instituted to fight World War II—which disincentivized the wealthy from trying too hard to enrich themselves at the expense of others. If a CEO rewarding himself with a much larger share of the company's total profits incited the ire of the union, it might not have been worthwhile for him to try.

Walter Reuther was born in 1907 in Wheeling, West Virginia, to German immigrant socialist parents.[14] His father took him to visit imprisoned socialist-pacifist Eugene V. Debs during World War I. And he learned "the philosophy of trade unionism," and heard about "the struggles, hopes, and aspirations of working people," every day he spent in his parents' house. At the age of nineteen he left Wheeling to become a mechanic at the Ford Motor Company in Detroit, making the tools that the assembly-line workers would use. In 1932 he was fired from Ford for organizing a rally for Norman Thomas, the Socialist Party candidate for president. He spent 1932 through 1935 traveling the world. During this time, he trained Russian workers in Gorky—Nizhny Novgorod—to work the Model T production-line machines that Ford had sold to Stalin when he replaced the Model T with the Model A in 1927. Back in Detroit, he joined the United Auto Workers (UAW), and in December 1936 he launched a sit-down strike against Ford's brake supplier, Kelsey-Hayes. Thousands of sympathizers came out to block management's attempts to move the machines elsewhere so they could restart production with scabs.

Democrat Frank Murphy had just narrowly defeated incumbent Republican Frank Fitzgerald for the post of Michigan governor. In an earlier decade, the police—or, as in the Pullman strike forty years earlier, the army—would have shown up to enforce the owners' and managers' property rights. Not in 1936. After ten days, under very strong pressure from Ford, which needed those brakes, Kelsey-Hayes gave in. Membership in Reuther's UAW Local 174 grew from two hundred at the start of December 1936 to thirty-five thousand by the end of 1937. In 1937 Reuther and his brothers launched a sit-down strike against General Motors, then the largest corporation in the world, in its production center of

Flint, Michigan. The striking workers gained control of the only plant that made engines for GM's best-selling brand, Chevrolet. This time, the new governor, Murphy, did send in the police, but not to evict the strikers; rather, they were told to "keep the peace."

By 1946 Reuther was head of the UAW, following a strategy of using the union's power not just to win higher wages and better working conditions for its members, but to "fight for the welfare of the public at large . . . as an instrument of social change." The UAW was one; the auto companies were many—the big three, GM, Ford, and Chrysler, and a number of smaller producers that shrank over time. Reuther's tactic was, each year, to threaten to strike one of the three and then to carry through on the threat: the struck company would lose money while it was shut down, and UAW members working for other companies would support the strikers, but the other companies would neither lock out workers nor support their struck competitor with cash. After four post–World War II years of annual strike threats, in 1950 GM CEO Charlie Wilson proposed a five-year no-strike contract. Reuther negotiated not just higher wages but also company-financed health care and retirement programs plus cost-of-living increases. This was the "Treaty of Detroit." It meant that auto-workers now had not just a fair income but also the stability to think about buying a detached house, moving to the suburbs, and commuting in the cars they built: the upper levels of the working class were now middle class.

In 1970, Reuther along with his wife, May, and four others were killed when the plane they were in crashed in the fog on final approach to the Pellston Regional Airport in Michigan. The plane's altimeter had both missing parts and incorrect parts, some of which had been installed upside down. Reuther had previously survived at least two assassination attempts.

The third component of the postwar Keynesian consensus in the United States was the welfare, or social insurance, state. But the United States' social insurance state turned out to be significantly less generous than the typical European iteration. From a Western European perspective, the US version was anemic. Even the conservative Margaret Thatcher in Britain found the absence of state-sponsored medical care in the United States appalling, and even barbarous. And across the board, means-tested social insurance programs in the United States did less to level the playing field than similar European programs did. US efforts to give the poor additional purchasing power in the first post–World War II generation included initiatives such as food stamps to subsidize diet, Aid to Families with Dependent Children to provide single mothers with some cash, and a small and rationed amount of low-quality public housing.

At the same time, social democracy in a broader sense in the United States encompassed a vast array of initiatives and organizations, which included, among many others, the Interstate Highway System, airport construction, air traffic control, the US Coast Guard, the National Park Service, and government support for research and development through agencies such as the National Institute of Standards and Technology, the National Oceanic and Atmospheric Administration, and the National Institutes of Health. It also included the antitrust lawyers of the Department of Justice and the Federal Trade Commission, the financial regulators in the Securities and Exchange Commission, the Office of the Comptroller of the Currency, the Federal Reserve, and the Pension Benefit Guarantee Corporation. And it included a promise by the federal government to insure small bank depositors against bank failures, and big bankers—systemically important financial institutions—against collapse, as well as Social Security and all of its cousins—Supplemental Security Income, Head Start, and the Earned Income Tax Credit. None of these programs would be seen as a proper use of the government by even the weakest-tea sympathizer with libertarianism.

That the Great Depression was a major impetus for America's leftward shift from a laissez-faire system to a more managed, "mixed" economy had an impact on the form of the post–World War II welfare state. In Europe, the mixed economy had a somewhat egalitarian bent: it was to level the income distribution and insure citizens against the market. In the United States, the major welfare state programs were sold as "insurance" in which individuals, on average, got what they paid for. They were not tools to shift the distribution of income. Social Security made payments proportional to earlier contributions. The prolabor Wagner Act framework was of most use to relatively skilled and well-paid workers with secure job attachments who could use the legal machinery to share in their industries' profits. And the degree of progressiveness in the income tax was always limited.

The goals of social democracy were notably different from the high socialist goal of making it the state's responsibility to provide necessities such as food and shelter as entitlements of citizenship, or comradeship, rather than things that had to be earned by the sweat of one's brow. Social democracy instead focused on providing income supports and progressive taxes to redistribute income in a more egalitarian direction. Whereas high socialism's system of public provision could often be inefficient, a system that simply distributed income in a more egalitarian way avoided waste by providing only for those in need, and by harnessing the magical efficiencies of the market to societal goals.

In something like a shotgun marriage, Hayek and Polanyi awkwardly kept house under social democracy for decades—as long as the country was blessed with Keynes's full employment—more inclusively than before, and with sufficient, if wary, cordiality.

IT WAS NOT A given that Western Europe would become more social democratic than the United States in the post–World War

II period. Its internal politics had by and large swung to the right during the Great Depression. And its commitments to both political democracy and market institutions had been weaker than such commitments in the United States for generations. Yet somehow, in total, Western Europe's social safety net and welfare state policies drastically exceeded those of the United States.

And as we have observed in previous chapters, Western Europe's commitment to social democracy paid off: the Western European economies boomed in the 1950s and 1960s. What post–World War II Europe accomplished in six years had taken post–World War I Europe sixteen. The growth rate of the Western European GDP, which had been hovering between 2 and 2.5 percent per year since the beginning of the long twentieth century, accelerated to an astonishing 4.8 percent per year between 1953 and 1973. The boom carried total production per capita to unprecedented levels—and in both France and West Germany, labor productivity had outstripped their pre-1913 trends by 1955.[15]

Part of what drove Europe's rapid growth was its exceptionally high rate of investment, nearly twice as high as it had been in the last decade before World War I.

Another part of what drove the growth was the European labor market, which achieved a remarkable combination of full employment and very little upward pressure on wages in excess of productivity gains.

As economic historian Charles Kindleberger explained, this stability in the labor market was caused by elastic supplies of underemployed labor from rural sectors within the advanced countries and from Europe's southern and eastern fringe. Elastic supplies of labor disciplined labor unions, which otherwise might have pushed aggressively for untenable wages. But the situation was surely also a result of the shadow cast by recent history. Memory of high unemployment and strife between the wars served to moderate labor-market conflict. Conservatives remembered that attempts to roll back interwar welfare states had led to polarization and a lack of stability—and had ultimately set the stage for fascism. Left-wingers, meanwhile, could recall the other side of the same story. Both could reflect on the stagnation of the interwar period and blame it on political deadlock. For all, the better strategy seemed to be to push for productivity improvements first and defer redistributions later.[16]

As the first post–World War II generation turned into the second, and as industries in the industrial core became more and more mechanized, they should have become more and more vulnerable to foreign competition from other, lower-wage countries. If Henry Ford could redesign production so that unskilled assembly-line workers did what skilled craftsmen used to do, what was stopping Ford—or anyone else, for that matter—from redesigning production so that it could be carried out by low-wage workers from outside the North Atlantic region?

Industries did indeed begin to migrate from the rich industrial core to the poor periphery. But in the first post–World War II generation or two, they did so slowly. One reason was added risk of political instability: investors tend to be wary of committing their money in places where it is easy to imagine significant political disruptions. Moreover, there were substantial advantages for a firm in keeping production in the industrial core, near other machines and other factories making similar products. Doing so meant both access to a reliable electric power grid and proximity to the specialists needed to fix the many things that could go wrong with complex machinery.

These factors were an order of magnitude more important for industries in technological flux than they were for industries centered on a settled, relatively unchanging technology. Companies tended to choose locations near the firms that made their machines in large part because of the significant advantages stemming from the interchange and feedback of users and producers—feedback that is especially valuable if designs are still evolving. Doing so also meant being able to take advantage of a well-educated labor force familiar with machinery and able to adapt to using slightly different machines in somewhat different ways. As industries reached technological maturity, their production processes tended to settle into static patterns, and their business models became ones in which sales were made on the basis of the lowest price. It was at this level of maturity that industries and companies tended to migrate to the periphery of the world economy.

BECAUSE SOCIAL DEMOCRACY WAS democracy, people could choose at the ballot box how much income and wealth inequality they were willing to accept. They could vote for more or less progressive taxes. They could opt to either expand or contract the set of public and semipublic goods and of benefits offered to all citizens. And they could expand or contract the benefits offered to the poor. But fundamentally, social democracy as a system was built on the premise that universal redistribution was desirable because all citizens wanted to be insured against the risk of poverty. Incentives for maximizing production were fine, too. However, the trick was the question of how to balance insurance against risk and incentives for production, a matter of both judgment and politics. Wherever it took root, social democracy strove for programs that leaked small amounts of redistributed income, all while aiming for the utilitarian greatest good of the greatest number.

For these reasons, social democracy was a powerful force. But there was a problem. It would in the end, perhaps, bring about the demise of social democracy and the rise of what became known as "neoliberalism": there remained, in the shadows, a memory of the belief that the market economy was not society's servant, but its master—that social democratic attempts to vindicate Polanyian rights would impose a crushing burden that would severely hobble long-run economic growth, and would not produce so-cial justice because universalist provision of benefits would make equals of people who should not be equals.

Perhaps there was, at bottom, a near-innate human aversion to even semicentralized redistributive arrangements that take from some and give to others. Humans, at least we humans, see society as a network of reciprocal gift-exchange relationships. As a general principle, we agree that all of us do much better if we do things for one another rather than requiring that individuals do everything for themselves. We do not always want to be the receiver: it makes us feel small and inadequate. We do not always want to be the giver: that makes us feel exploited and grifted. And as a matter of principle and practice, we tend to disapprove whenever we spy a situation in which somebody else seems to be following a life strategy of always being the receiver.[17]

Moreover, what it means to be a "giver" or a "receiver" is con-tested. Are mothers raising children without a partner performing the hard and incredibly valuable work of raising the next gener-ation, whose Social Security taxes will fund our Social Security checks? Or are they "welfare queens," who are milking a system because it is easier, as their critics confidently declare, than get-ting and holding a job? Is a moneylender a giver when he forgives you half of the interest you owe, but holds you to the principal sum and the other half of the interest?

The logic of social democracy is that we are all equals as cit-izens, and equals should not be treated unequally without good cause. In a market economy, the good cause that justifies inequal-ity is that we need to incentivize economic growth by rewarding skill, industry, and foresight, even if doing so inevitably involves rewarding good luck as well.

But what happens when some citizens think that they—because of birth, education, skin color, religious affiliation, or some other characteristic—are more equal than others? And what of those who, in the case of means-tested programs, seem to be receiving not because they have bad luck, but simply because they never contribute?

These dilemmas can be papered over as long as employment stays high and growth stays strong. But when growth slows and employment becomes less certain, the fear that the "moochers" are taking advantage gains ever-greater sway. And this fear of moochers was a significant part of what prompted the downfall of social democracy and the turn toward neoliberalism.

At the same time that social democracies were striving to treat their citizens equally through redistributive programs, they embarked on another, stranger endeavor. All over the world, in industrialized and developing areas alike, social democratic governments—even the most anticommunist among them—got it into their heads that they should run and operate businesses.

Consider the case of Britain's government under Prime Minister Clement Attlee, Winston Churchill's immediate successor after World War II. In the late 1940s, the Attlee government nationalized the Bank of England, the railways, the airlines, telephones, coal mining, electric power generation, long-distance trucking, iron and steel, and natural gas provision. Officially, management policy did not change once industries were nationalized: commercial profitability remained the official objective (although it was pursued with less vigor, especially when the pursuit of profitability might involve, say, closing plants and factories).

In retrospect, the social democratic insistence on government production of goods and services is puzzling. Governments were not merely demanding, nor distributing, nor regulating prices and quality. They were engaged in *production*. All over the world, the belief that large chunks of productive industry ought to be publicly owned and managed dominated the mid-twentieth century. Even today, in the twenty-first century, there are still immense state-owned and state-managed enterprises: railroads, hospitals, schools, power-generating facilities, steelworks, chemical factories, coal mines, and others.

None of which have ever been part of governments' core competence. Organizations such as hospitals and railroads ought to be run with an eye on efficiency: getting the most produced with the resources available. But the logic that shapes how governments operate is different: it is the logic of the adjustments made in light of conflicting interests. As a result, government-managed enterprises—whether the coal mines of Britain or the telecommunications monopolies of Western Europe or the oil-production monopolies of developing nations—have tended to be inefficient and wasteful.

Some of the organizations and industries being nationalized were ones for which you do not want "efficiency" over all else. There are times when you want "soft" rather than "hard" incentives: a health clinic that is paid by insurance companies should not be replacing antibiotic solutions with colored water in order to decrease its costs. A company running an electricity distribution network should not skimp on maintenance in order to boost its current profits.

But the cases in which "soft" incentives are desirable are not that many: only when consumers are poor judges of quality, or when they are unable to vote with their feet by switching to alternative suppliers. Almost everywhere else the hard material incentives that motivate for-profit enterprise are more appropriate.

So why did social democratic states, all to varying degrees, do it? There seem to have been three main reasons:

The first was an inordinate fear of monopolies. The leaders of these governments believed that economies of scale would ultimately lead to the domination of a single firm in most industries, which would then exploit the public mercilessly unless it was owned by the state. The second was a fear of attendant corruption, or the fear that the monopoly bosses would simply buy off the regulators. And third, the push for nationalization was motivated by a resurgence of the classical Marxist belief that the market was inherently exploitative—and that such exploitation could be avoided by eliminating the private ownership of the means of production.

All of these beliefs seem naïve to us now. If the market is inherently corrupted by exploitation, what do we think of bureaucratic hierarchies? Yes, monopoly is to be feared. Yes, there are grave problems in a world in which much economic life depends on increasing returns to scale for the controlling monopoly. But a publicly managed monopoly is still a monopoly. Ultimately, the efforts on the part of social democracies to operate the "commanding heights" of their economies ended in disappointment, which hurt the long-term political support for the project of social democracy.

This problem, however, was small beer compared to damage that would be wrought by the inflation crises of the 1970s in the United States. For much of that decade, the US rate of inflation bounced between 5 percent and 10 percent annually, an unprecedented pace, as unemployment also reached painful and unsustainable levels. How did it happen?

In the 1960s, the administration of President Lyndon Johnson was unwilling to accept a floor or even an average of around 5 percent or so unemployment, and so set its sights on pushing that number lower. As Johnson economic adviser Walter Heller put it, "The government must step in to provide the essential stability [of the economy] at high levels of employment and growth that the market mechanism, left alone, cannot deliver." The task was no longer just to avoid depressions but to attain *high levels* of employment—and growth.

This ambitious new mission raised an important question: Would it be possible to maintain the balance of supply and demand while pushing the unemployment rate below 5 percent? In other words, could the unemployment rate stay this low without accelerating inflation? By 1969 the answer was reasonably clear: no.

Average nonfarm nominal wage growth in the United States had fluctuated around or below 4 percent per year between the end of the Korean War and the mid-1960s. It had jumped to more than 6 percent in 1968. Moreover, a half decade of slowly rising inflation had led people to begin to pay attention to what was happening. People make all sorts of decisions based on their expectations of what next year's price level will be: decisions about how much to demand, in terms of cash to hold on to and of prices and wages to charge. An episodic excess supply of money can cause *unexpected* inflation. But when people look back on the past half decade or so and see that there has been an excess supply of money during that time, they will expect inflation in the years ahead. This can become doubly damning. The price level will jump in part as expected and in part as unexpected. And the total inflation rate—expected plus unexpected—will accelerate upward.

The sharp rise in inflation came as a surprise to the Johnson administration. Macroeconomist Robert Gordon later reminisced on the analytical framework that had been reliable before and that they had been using, saying it "collapsed with amazing speed after 1967." He and his economist peers, who had recently all obtained their graduate degrees and started their first jobs, "were acutely aware of the timing of this turn of the tide, . . . and almost immediately found our graduate school education incapable of explaining the evolution of the economy."[18]

Economic advisers to both Johnson and, before him, President John F. Kennedy had argued that a substantial reduction in unemployment could be achieved with only a moderate increase in inflation. But expectations of inflation became "unanchored." Prices and wages were not set to an expectation of price stability, or even to a slow upward creep in inflation, but rather to last year's inflation, which had become the new normal. Over the four years from 1965 to 1969, the Federal Reserve accommodated

President Johnson's desire to reduce unemployment by expanding the money supply, to keep interest rates low, and then Vietnam War spending unbalanced by higher taxes overheated the economy further. By 1969, the United States was not a 2 percent but a 5 percent per year inflation economy.

President Richard Nixon took office in 1969, and the economists of the incoming Republican administration planned to ease inflation with only a small increase in unemployment by reducing government spending and encouraging the Federal Reserve to raise interest rates. Their plan only half worked: unemployment did indeed rise—from 3.5 percent to almost 6 percent between 1969 and 1971, but inflation barely budged.

This outcome presented a great mystery. Up until this point, it looked as though the US economy had been sliding back and forth along a stable inflation-unemployment "Phillips curve" (named after economist A. William Phillips). Democratic governments tended to spend more time at the left end of the curve, with relatively low unemployment. Republican governments tended to spend more time at the right end, with relatively low inflation and higher unemployment. But by both absolute standards and historical standards, both inflation and unemployment were low. Nixon's economists had intended to move the economy from the left to the right side of the curve, but now they found that it would not go.

Their attempts to fight inflation by marginally increasing unemployment no longer worked because no one believed that the administration would have the fortitude to continue those efforts for very long. Autoworkers, for example, believed that the government would not allow widespread unemployment in the automobile industry—and would step in to help by pumping up nominal demand, and giving people enough liquidity to buy cars if ever the industry's sales began to drop. This left the United Auto Workers without any incentive to moderate its wage demands—and automobile manufacturers without any incentive to resist those demands: they could simply pass the increased costs on to consumers in higher prices.

This unexpected result of their efforts left Nixon's economists in a difficult situation. One possible "solution" was to create a truly massive recession: to make it painfully clear that even if inflation rose to painful levels, the government would not accommodate, and would keep unemployment high until inflation came down. No president wanted to think about this possibility. It was, in the end, the road the United States took, but largely by accident and after many stopgaps.

Confronted with an unemployment rate of 6 percent, an inflation rate of 5 percent, and a loud chorus of complaints that he had mismanaged the economy, Nixon could see the political winds shifting against him. Arthur Burns, the president's former counselor, newly installed as chair of the Federal Reserve, gloomily predicted that it would take a large recession to reduce inflationary expectations via market mechanisms, and that enacting such a plan would put him out of a job. Congress, he surmised, would vote overwhelmingly to fire a Federal Reserve chair who created such a large recession. To Nixon, the political situation was painfully familiar: back in 1960, as a vice president running for president, he and then Eisenhower aide Arthur Burns had begged their boss, President Eisenhower, not to let unemployment rise during the 1960 election year. Eisenhower had turned them down, and Nixon had narrowly lost the 1960 election to Kennedy.[19]

This time, Nixon decided on a version of "shock therapy": suspend the pegged-but-flexible exchange-rate system put in place back during Bretton Woods (the suspension would eventually become permanent), impose wage and price controls to reduce inflation, and make sure that Arthur Burns, his Fed chair, understood that unemployment needed to be lower and declining as the election of 1972 approached. Nixon's political calculations, however, were not entirely to blame for the upward burst in inflation. Many economists, including Johnson adviser Walter

Heller, believed that Nixon's policies were not nearly stimulative and inflationary enough.

In practice, the supply of money greatly outran demand, and as Nixon's price controls were lifted, inflation accelerated ever upward.

In retrospect, we might wonder if there was any way Nixon could have reduced inflation back to a "normal" rate of 3 percent or so, or at least contained it at less than 6 percent. On a technical level, of course, he could have. It was around the same time that West Germany became the first economy to undertake a "disinflation." The peak of German inflation came in 1971: thereafter the Bundesbank pursued policies that did not tend to accommodate supply shocks or other upward pressures on inflation. By the early 1980s, West German inflation was invisible. Japan began a similar disinflation effort in the mid-1970s, while Britain and France waited until later to begin their disinflations. France's last year of double-digit inflation was 1980; Britain's was 1981.[20]

Given these examples, there were no "technical" obstacles to making the burst of moderate inflation the United States experienced in the late 1960s a quickly reversed anomaly. But Arthur Burns did not dare.

Burns lacked confidence that he could reduce inflation without driving up unemployment to unacceptable levels. In 1959, as president of the American Economic Association, he delivered an annual address that he called "Progress Towards Economic Stability."[21] Burns spent the bulk of his speech detailing how automatic stabilizers and monetary policy based on a better sense of the workings of the banking system had made episodes like the Great Depression of the past extremely unlikely. Toward the end of his talk, he spoke of what he saw as an unresolved problem created by the progress toward economic stability: "a future of secular inflation." Workers had hesitated to demand wage increases in excess of productivity growth during booms when they had the market power to do so because they feared the consequences of being too expensive to their employers in the depressions to come. But what if there were no depressions to come?

Then, after 1972, came the oil shocks. First, world oil prices tripled in response to the Yom Kippur War of 1973, and they tripled again in the wake of the Iranian Revolution of 1979, as the Organization of the Petroleum Exporting Countries (OPEC) realized how much market power it had.

It is possible that the first tripling was a not regretted result of US foreign policy. Back in the early 1970s, Nixon's chief foreign policy adviser, Henry Kissinger, wanted to strengthen the shah of Iran as a possible counterweight to Soviet influence in the Middle East. With the oil price tripled, the shah was indeed immensely strengthened—at the price of enormous economic damage to the industrial West and to the rest of the developing world, which saw its oil bill multiply many times over. It is certain that the economic repercussions of the oil price rise came as a surprise to the Nixon administration—Kissinger always thought economic matters were boring and unimportant, in spite of the fact that the military and diplomatic strength of the United States depended on them. It is most likely that the rise in oil prices struck the administration as not worthy of concern, and certainly not worth the trouble of combatting—it did, after all, strengthen the shah. Few had any conception of the economic damage it might do, and those few were not listened to by the US government.

Because oil was the key energy input in the world economy, the shock of these price increases reverberated throughout the world, and eventually they would lead to the double-digit annual inflation of the late 1970s.

The first of the inflation spikes, the one triggered by the Yom Kippur War oil price increases, sent the world economy into one of the deepest recessions of the post–World War II period, leaving the US economy with high inflation that would eventually lead to another recession in 1980–1982, the deepest of the post–World War II era. Each surge in inflation was preceded by or coincided with a sharp increase in unemployment. And throughout the late 1960s and the 1970s, each cycle was larger than the one before it: in 1971, unemployment peaked at around 6 percent; in 1975, at about 8.5 percent; and in 1982–1983 at nearly 11 percent.

By the time the 1975 recession had hit its worst point, people were ready to try something new. In that year, Senator Hubert Humphrey (D-MN), a former presidential contender, cosponsored a bill with Congressman Augustus Hawkins (D-CA) that would have required the government to reduce unemployment to 3 percent within four years and offer employment to anyone who wanted it at the same "prevailing wage" paid for government construction projects. In its House version, the bill also granted individuals the right to sue in federal court for their Humphrey-Hawkins jobs if the federal government failed to provide them. In early 1976, observers felt the bill had a high probability of passing, though President Gerald Ford, a Republican, was likely to veto it. Indeed, many assumed that Humphrey and Hawkins's primary intention was to bait Ford into vetoing the bill, thereby creating an issue for his challenger, Jimmy Carter, to campaign on during the upcoming 1976 election.

What happened in fact was that the Humphrey-Hawkins bill was watered down, and watered down, and watered down again until it was essentially a set of declarations that the Federal Reserve should try to do good things—completely without teeth as far as shaping actual policy was concerned. Ultimately, Jimmy Carter prevailed in the 1976 election. And the most important long-term effect of the Humphrey-Hawkins bill was, perhaps, to make it difficult in the late 1970s to propose policies to reduce inflation. Any measure that risked at least a temporary rise in unemployment was deemed a nonstarter.

By the end of the 1970s, inflation was perceived to be out of control.

From an economist's perspective, an inflationary episode like what happened in the United States in the 1970s might not seem to matter much. Prices go up. But wages and profits go up as well. In other words, economists might argue, inflation is a zero-sum redistribution. Some lose, but others gain as much. With no strong reason to think that the losers are in any sense more deserving than the gainers, economists might ask, why should anyone, including economists, care very much?

This view is profoundly misguided. To understand why, we need only return to John Maynard Keynes's assessment of the consequences of inflation during and after World War I: "There is no subtler, no surer means of overturning the existing basis of society than to debauch the currency. The process engages all the hidden forces of economic law on the side of destruction, and does it in a manner which not one man in a million is able to diagnose." Keynes was speaking of high inflation: enough to take "all permanent relations between debtors and creditors, which form the ultimate foundation of capitalism," and make them "utterly disordered"—and the inflation of the 1970s, while severe, was nothing of the sort.[22]

But woven through this passage is another effect of inflation: one can usually pretend that there is a logic to the distribution of wealth—that behind a person's prosperity lies some rational basis, whether it is that person's hard work, skill, and farsightedness, or some ancestor's. Inflation—even moderate inflation—strips the mask. There is no rational basis. Rather, "those to whom the system brings windfalls . . . become profiteers," Keynes wrote, and "the process of wealth-getting degenerates into a gamble and a lottery."[23]

And a government that generates such inflation is obviously not competent. By the late 1970s, all critics of social democracy had to do was point at the inflation and ask: Would a well-functioning political-economic system have produced this? And the answer was no.

15

The Neoliberal Turn

History does not repeat itself, but it does rhyme—oddly. The period from 1945 to 1975 was an economic El Dorado that rhymed with the previous years of economic El Dorado, 1870–1914. And the post-1975 breakdown of that second golden age had some rhymes with the failure to stitch the first golden age back together after the end of World War I.

The period after the American Civil War, 1870–1914, the first economic El Dorado, had been an age of a swift jog or even a run along the path toward utopia at a pace previously unseen in any historical era. For the poor majority, it delivered greatly lessened pressures for necessity and material want. For the rich, it brought a near utopia of material abundance: by 1914, life offered, "at a low cost and with the least trouble, conveniences, comforts, and amenities beyond the compass of the richest and most powerful monarchs of other ages." Moreover, civilization's confidence as of 1914 was great. For the well-thinking, any idea that this progressive economic system of rapidly increasing prosperity might break down was, as Keynes put it, "aberrant [and] scandalous."[1] Yet then came World War I, and the failures of economic management after World War I to restore stability, confidence in the system, and the prewar rate of rapidly advancing prosperity. And so things fell apart. The center did not hold.

Here I need to issue a warning: The time since the beginning of the neoliberal turn overlaps my career. In it I have played, in a very small way, the roles of intellectual, commentator, thought leader, technocrat, functionary, and Cassandra. I have been deeply and emotionally engaged throughout, as I have worked to advance policies for good and for ill, and as my engagement has alternately sharpened and blurred my judgment. From this point on this book becomes, in part, an argument I am having with my younger selves and with various voices in my head. The historian's ideal is to see and understand, not advocate and judge. In dealing with post-1980, I try but I do not think I fully succeed.

After World War II, or, to be more precise, 1938–1973 in North America and 1945–1973 in Western Europe, came another economic El Dorado, an age of a swift jog or even a run along the path toward utopia at a pace previously unseen in any historical era—including 1870–1914. For the poor majority, it delivered relief from the pressures of dire necessity and access to considerable amounts of at least the most basic conveniences of life. For the rich, it delivered a cornucopia of material abundance not just beyond the compass but beyond the wild imaginings of the richest and most powerful monarchs of other ages. Social democracy was delivering. Creative destruction might eliminate your job, but there would be another one as good or better because of full employment. And because of rapid productivity growth, your income would certainly be higher than that of the typical person of your accomplishments and position in any previous generation. And if you did not like what your neighborhood was or was becoming, you could buy a car and change your residence to the suburbs without disrupting the other parts of your life—at least if you were a white guy with a family in the global north.

Still, civilization's confidence as of 1973 was great, fears of the ongoing Cold War turning hot notwithstanding. For the well-thinking, any idea that this progressive economic system of rapidly increasing prosperity might break down was once again aberrant and scandalous. In the global north, on average, people in 1973 had between two and four times the material abundance that their parents had had a generation before. In the United States, especially, the talk was about how to deal with the end state seen in Keynes's "Economic Possibilities for Our Grandchildren"— the civilization of material abundance, in which humanity's problem was not how to produce enough to escape from the kingdom of necessity and have some useful conveniences, but rather "how to use . . . freedom from pressing economic cares . . . to live wisely and agreeably and well"[2]—fifty years before Keynes had predicted it might come to pass. Smokestacks and fog were no longer seen as welcome harbingers of prosperity but as nuisances that needed to be squashed so we could have clean air. It was the time of *The Greening of America* and of the expansion of human consciousness. It was a time to question the bourgeois virtues of hard, regular work and thrift in pursuit of material abundance and instead to turn on, tune in, drop out.

And if things did not fall apart, precisely, the center did not hold. There was a sharp neoliberal turn away from the previous order—social democracy—of 1945–1973. By 1979 the cultural and political energy was on the right. Social democracy was broadly seen to have failed, to have overreached itself. A course correction was called for.

Why? In my view, the greatest cause was the extraordinary pace of rising prosperity during the Thirty Glorious Years, which raised the bar that a political-economic order had to surpass in order to generate broad acceptance. People in the global north had come to expect to see incomes relatively equally distributed (for white guys at least), doubling every generation, and they expected economic uncertainty to be very low, particularly with respect to prices and employment—except on the upside. And people then for some reason required that growth in their incomes be at least as fast as they had expected and that it be stable, or else they would seek reform.

Karl Polanyi died in 1964, in Toronto.[3] Had he been more listened to, he could have warned the well-thinking who discoursed in the years of rapid economic growth about how successful management had brought about the end of bitter ideological struggles. People, he would have said—and did say—want their rights respected. While delivering increasing prosperity year by year can substitute for respect to a degree, it is only to a degree. And egalitarian distribution was a sword with at least two edges. People seek to *earn*, or to feel that they have earned, what they receive—not to be given it out of somebody's *grace*, for that is not respectful. Moreover, many people don't want those who are ranked lower than them to be treated as their equals, and may even see this as the greatest of all violations of their Polanyian societal rights.

As generations became accustomed to very rapid growth, the amount of increasing prosperity required to quiet the worries and concerns thrown up by market capitalism's creative destruction grew as well. The bar was raised. The polities and economies of the late 1970s did not clear that bar. And so people looked around, searching for ideas about how to reform.

Say what you like about Benito Mussolini, Vladimir Lenin, and others who proposed all kinds of ideas about how to reform after, and indeed before, World War I, at least they were intellectually creative. Very creative. But the things that were displayed in the shop windows in the marketplaces of ideas in the global north in the late 1970s were rather shopworn. On the left, there were declamations that what was going on behind the Iron and Bamboo Curtains in Brezhnev's Russia and immediate post-Mao China was in fact glorious, and not just glorious—but successful![4] On the right, there were declamations that everything had in fact been about to go fine when Hoover was defeated in 1932, and that the entire New Deal and all of social democracy were big mistakes.

But still, the late 1970s saw the generation of a rough consensus that the global-north political economy needed substantial reform, at the very least: that something in the shop window needed to be purchased.

One very powerful factor contributing to this consensus was that after 1973, in Europe and in the United States and in Japan, there was a very sharp slowdown in the rate of productivity and real income growth.[5] Some of it was a consequence of the decision to shift from an economy that polluted more to an economy that attempted to begin the process of environmental cleanup. Cleanup, however, would take decades to make a real difference in people's lives. Energy diverted away from producing more and into producing cleaner would quickly show up in lower wage increases and profits. And some of it was a consequence of the upward oil price shocks of 1973 and 1979—energy that had been devoted to raising labor productivity was now devoted to figuring out how to produce in a more energy-efficient manner, and how to produce in a flexible manner that could cope with either high or low relative energy prices. Some of it was also due to running out of the backlog stock of undeployed useful ideas that had been discovered and partially developed. Especially in Western Europe and in Japan, the easy days of post–World War II "catch-up" were over. As the postwar baby boom generation entered the workforce, making them fully productive proved a difficult task, and the failure to fully accomplish it was one source of drag.[6] But it is difficult to gauge how much each of these sources contributed to the slowdown. It remains a mystery even today. The important thing was that the social democratic promise of ever-increasing prosperity was not kept in the 1970s.

The irritation of markedly slowed economic growth was amplified by inflation. Not, admittedly, the doubling or septupling inflation of the post–World War I period. Rather, 5 to 10 percent a year. The productivity slowdown meant that if nominal wages were to keep rising at their previous pace, prices would have to rise faster. The decade starting in 1966, of having, almost every year, surprise upward shocks to the rate of growth of money prices on average, convinced businesses, unions, workers, and consumers that (a) inflation needed to be paid attention to, and (b) it was likely to be the same as or a bit more than it had been last year—so you needed (c) to build into your planning the expectation that, over the next year, your wages and other people's wages, and your prices and other people's prices, would rise by at least as much as, and probably more than, they had last year. This then produced *stagflation*. If inflation were to stay constant, then employment would have to fall below full employment to put pressure on workers to accept wage increases lower than they had expected. If the economy were to be at full employment, then the rate of inflation would have to creep upward.

The Organization of the Petroleum Exporting Countries imposed an oil embargo against the United States and the Netherlands in the aftermath of the 1973 Yom Kippur War, and this deranged the oil market. OPEC woke up to its market power, and its maintenance of high oil prices sent the world economy into a major recession.[7] Moreover, high oil prices pushed the world economy to shift its direction, from focusing on raising labor productivity to focusing on energy conservation. That meant that many people's incomes and jobs disappeared—permanently—and that many others' future jobs would fail to appear. And it meant an acceleration of the inflation that had already been in progress before 1973.

The tripling of world oil prices worked its way through the economy like a wave, which then reflected and passed through the economy again and again—not a one-time rise in the price level, but a permanent upward ratchet of the inflation rate. The rising rate of inflation from 1965 to 1973 predisposed people to take last year's inflation as a signal of what next year's inflation would be.[8] And no one in a position to make anti-inflation policy cared enough about stopping inflation, given the likely high cost of doing so in terms of idled factories and unemployed workers. Other goals took precedence: solving the energy crisis, or maintaining a high-pressure economy, or making certain that the current recession did not get any worse.

This inflation was an annoyance that governments found it damnably hard to deal with. The only way to offset these expectations was to scare workers and businesses: to make labor demand weak enough that workers would not dare demand wage increases in accordance with expected inflation, out of the fear that they would lose their jobs, and to make spending in the economy as a whole weak enough that businesses would not dare raise prices in accordance with expected inflation, either. To hold inflation constant required a weak, low-profit, elevated-unemployment economy.

Inflation of 5 to 10 percent per year is not the trillionfold inflation of Weimar Germany. And productivity-growth slowdown is not productivity-growth stop. From 1973 to 2010, worker productivity in the global north grew at an average rate of 1.6 percent per year. That is a significant drop from the 3 percent rate sustained between 1938 and 1973. But from a long-term historical perspective, it was still a lot: 1.6 percent per year is essentially the same as the productivity growth rate over the period 1870–1914, that original economic El Dorado to which economists after 1918 desperately wanted to return.

But after expectations had been set so high by the prosperity of 1945–1973, 1.6 percent didn't look so impressive. Moreover, post-1973 growth was accompanied by rising inequality. At the top, the average pace of real income growth continued at its 1945–1973 pace, 3 percent per year, or even more. For the middle and the working classes of the global north, who were paying for continued steady growth for the upper-middle class and the explosion of plutocrat wealth, it has meant inflation-adjusted paychecks growing at only 0.5 to 1 percent per year. Plus

there were the effects of inclusion: if you were of the "right" ethnicity and gender in 1973, whatever satisfaction you got from
your position in the pyramid leaked away as Blacks and women
got "uppity." And with at least some closing of race, ethnic, and
gender income gaps, white male earnings, especially for those of
relatively low education, had to, on average, lag behind the low-
er-middle and working-class average of 0.5 to 1 percent per year.

Inflation creating at least the appearance of great instability
in incomes, oil shocks producing the first noticeable economic
recessions since World War II, sociological turmoil and income
stagnation—all of this makes some change likely. Still, the neoliberal turn, accomplished in little more than half a decade in the
1970s, was remarkably rapid.

In the United States, the Vietnam War did not help. President Richard Nixon and Henry Kissinger had blocked the ending
of the war in late 1968, promising South Vietnamese president
Nguyễn Văn Thiệu that they would get him a better deal and a
better chance of long-term political survival than Lyndon Johnson's administration was offering.[9] They lied. After an additional
1.5 million Vietnamese and 30,000 American deaths after 1968,
North Vietnam conquered South Vietnam in mid-1975—and
promptly began an ethnic cleansing campaign against Vietnamese
of Chinese ancestral descent. Domestic discontent with the war
was, for Nixon, a political plus: his strategy had always been one
of ramping up culture-war divisions, in the belief that if he could
break the country in two, the larger half would support him.

Yet even with all of the inflation, with the productivity slowdown, and with the quagmire land war in Asia and Nixon's
crimes, things were still very good in terms of the rate of economic growth and the indicia of societal progress, at least compared to what had gone on between the world wars, or even in
any decade between 1870 and 1914. Why, then, did the 1970s
see such a powerful swing against the social democratic political-
economic order that had managed its successful balancing act

since World War II? True, the US death toll in the Vietnam War was high. But inflation, save for the somewhat elevated unemployment level, which turned out to be required to keep it from rising further, was a zero-sum redistribution, with the gainers matching the losers. The productivity slowdown was a disappointment, but it still left wages growing faster than in any previous era of human history.

Those economists who minimized the downside of inflation should have listened more closely to Karl Polanyi. People do not just seek to have good things materially; they like to pretend that there is a logic to the distribution of the good things, and especially its distribution to them in particular—that their prosperity has some rational and deserved basis. Inflation—even the moderate inflation of the 1970s—stripped the mask away.

There were, in right-wing eyes, additional problems with social democracy. Social democratic governments were simply trying to do too many things. Too much of what they were attempting was technocratically stupid, and bound to be unsuccessful, and many of the apparent defects they were trying to repair were not real defects but actually necessary to incentivize good and proper behavior. Reagan's future chief economist (and my brilliant, charismatic, and superb teacher) Martin Feldstein claimed that expansionary policies "adopted in the hope of lowering . . . unemployment" produced inflation: "Retirement benefits were increased without considering the subsequent impact on investment and saving. Regulations were imposed to protect health and safety without evaluating the reduction in productivity," he wrote. Moreover, "unemployment benefits would encourage layoffs," and welfare would "weaken family structures."[10]

Marty, dedicated to trying as hard as he could to nail the empirics right, and devoted to honest academic and scholarly debate, believed all this to the core of his being. We have seen this before. It is the conviction that authority and order are of overwhelming importance, and that "permissiveness" is fatal. It is the opinion that, again in the words of Churchill's private secretary, P. J. Grigg, an economy and polity cannot perpetually "live beyond its means on its wits." It is the idea that the market economy has a logic of its own, and does what it does for reasons that are beyond feeble mortal comprehension, and that need to be respected, or else. It is the belief that believing you can re-arrange and govern the market is *hubris*, and that it will bring about *nemesis*.

Yet Marty's take was also not completely false. Why, in Brit-ain, did social democratic education policy turn out to give chil-dren of doctors and lawyers and landowners the right to go to Oxford for free? Why did social democracies that had nationalized the "commanding heights" of their economies use that power not to accelerate technological progress, and keep employment high, but rather to prop up increasingly obsolete "sunset" industries? When judged by a technocratic logic of efficiency, all politically popular arrangements will turn out to be lacking to some degree. It is the broadness of the discontent and the rapidity of its reemer-gence after a decade that, compared to the Great Recession of 2008, or the COVID-19 plague of 2020–2022, does not appear to have been that large a shock—it is *that* that strikes me as inter-esting. A tripling of global-north living standards between 1938 and 1973 had not brought about utopia. Growth gets interrupted and slowed. And in less than a decade, all of this was felt to indi-cate that social democracy needed to be replaced.

One touchstone, again, is British left-wing historian Eric Hobsbawm. Hobsbawm saw the late 1970s and the subsequent discontent with the social democratic order as justified, writ-ing, "There were good grounds for some of the disillusion with state-managed industries and public administration." He de-nounced the "rigidities, inefficiencies and economic wastages so often sheltering under Golden Age government policies." And he declared that "there was considerable scope for applying the neo-liberal cleansing-agent to the encrusted hull of many a good ship

'Mixed Economy' with beneficial results." He went on with the clincher, saying that neoliberal Thatcherism had been necessary, and that there was a near consensus about this after the fact: "Even the British Left was eventually to admit that some of the ruthless shocks imposed on the British economy by Mrs. Thatcher had probably been necessary."[11]

Hobsbawm was a lifelong communist. To the end of his days, he would continue to stubbornly maintain, while drinking tea with his respectful interviewers, that the murderous careers of Lenin and Stalin (but perhaps not Mao?) had been worth undertaking, because they indeed might, had things turned out differently, have unlocked the gate and opened the road to a true utopia.[12] Yet he also eagerly attended the Church of the Thatcherite Dispensation, where he heard and then himself preached the Lesson: the market giveth, the market taketh away; blessed be the name of the market.

So what was the global north going to purchase in the marketplace of ideas as its reform program? On the left there was very little. Really-existing socialism had proven a bust, yet too much energy on the left was still devoted to explaining away its failures. On the right there were real ideas. Never mind that to the historically minded they seemed to be largely retreads from before 1930. After all, many of the ideas of the New Deal had been retreads from the Progressive Era of the first decade of the 1900s. The right wing's ideas were backed by lots of money. The memory of the Great Depression, and of austerity's failures in the Great Depression, was old and fading. Once again cries for sound finance orthodoxy and austerity—even for the gold standard—were heard. Once again the standard answer—that everything that went wrong was somehow an over-mighty government's fault—was trotted out. It was, after all, for true believers a metaphysical necessity that it was government intervention that had caused the Great Depression to be so deep and to last so long. The market could not fail: it could only be failed.

The fading memory of the Great Depression led to the fading of the middle class's belief, or rather recognition, that they, as well as the working class, needed social insurance. In an environment of economic stability and growth, the successful not only prospered materially but could convince themselves that they prospered morally as well, for they were the authors of their own prosperity—and government existed merely to tax them unfairly and then to give what was rightfully theirs to poorer, deviant people who lacked their industry and their moral worth.

From this point, the right-wing critique spread out to sweep up much more than a faltering economy. For the right wing also embraced a cultural critique, one squarely aimed at the very advances in racial and gender equality sketched above. Social democracy, conservatives declared in a Polanyian backlash, was flawed because it treated unequals equally. Remember University of Chicago economics professor and Nobel laureate George Stigler, who wrote in 1962—before the Civil Rights Act, before the Voting Rights Act, before affirmative action—in his essay "The Problem of the Negro" that, as he saw it, Blacks *deserved* to be poor, to be disliked, and to be treated with disrespect: "The problem is that on average," Stigler wrote, "he lacks a desire to improve himself, and lacks a willingness to discipline himself to this end." And although prejudice might be part of the problem, "the Negro boy," as Stigler put it, "is excluded from more occupations by his own inferiority as a worker": "Lacking education, lacking a tenacity of purpose, lacking a willingness to work hard, he will not be an object of employers' competition." And the "Negro family," he said, was, "on average, a loose, morally lax, group," and brought into neighborhoods "a rapid rise in crime and vandalism." "No statutes, no sermons, no demonstrations," he concluded, would "obtain for the Negro the liking and respect that sober virtues commend."[13]

Social democracy set up a benchmark of treating everyone as equals. Blacks, knowing that American society had dishonored the promissory note they had been passed, demonstrated, protesting that America had written them a bad check. And those demonstrations, "growing in size and insolence," as Stigler characterized them, were a sign of things going wrong. Social democracy was, to Stigler and company, economically inefficient. But it was also, in their eyes, profoundly unfair in its universalistic distribution of benefits. The word "insolence" is truly the tell.

Geopolitical and geo-economic instability comes and goes. The memory of the Great Depression was bound to fade. Could social democracy have held itself together if the inflation rate of the 1970s had not served as a convenient index of the incompetence of "Keynesian" and social democratic governments, and as a focal point for calls for a return to more "orthodox" policies? Or was the deeper logic of the morality play saying that Keynesian social democrats had tried to create prosperity out of thin air, and so had gotten their comeuppance, bound to dominate eventually, somehow, someday? That morality-play version did become generally accepted in the corridors of influence and power. Might social democracy have survived, regrouped, and staggered onward? Here again is a place where a great deal of the course of history might, or might not, have evolved differently had a relatively small number of influential groups of people thought different thoughts. But along this branch of the universe's quantum wave function, at least, the world made a neoliberal turn.

FED CHAIR ARTHUR BURNS HAD ALWAYS BEEN VERY RELUCtant to use tools of tight monetary policy to reduce inflation at the risk of inducing a recession.[14] When Jimmy Carter replaced Burns with G. William Miller, Miller likewise balked; he was uninterested in causing (and likely being blamed for) a significant recession. Inflation continued. So things stood in 1979. Then Jimmy Carter found himself disappointed with the state of his government, as well as of the economy. He decided, suddenly, to fire five cabinet members, including his treasury secretary, Michael Blumenthal.

Carter's aides told him that he couldn't just fire the treasury secretary without naming a replacement—it would look like he was running a disorganized White House. But Carter *was* running a disorganized White House. There was no obvious replacement at hand. To placate his aides, and the press, Carter decided to move G. William Miller over from the Fed to the Treasury.

Carter's aides then told him that he couldn't just leave a vacancy as Fed chair without naming a replacement—it would look like he was running a disorganized White House. But Carter *was* running a disorganized White House. There was no obvious replacement at hand. So Carter grabbed the most senior career Treasury Department and Federal Reserve official—New York Federal Reserve Bank president Paul Volcker—and made him Federal Reserve chair.[15]

As best as I can determine, there was no more than a cursory inquiry into what Volcker's policy preferences might turn out to be.

One thing soon became clear, however: Volcker believed that there was now a mandate to fight inflation even at the cost of inducing a significant recession. And he was ready to use that mandate to bring inflation under control. By raising interest rates high enough and keeping them high long enough, he hoped to convince the economy that things were different, and that inflation would stay below 5 percent per year indefinitely. In 1982 the unemployment rate kissed 11 percent. The United States, and the world, for the first time since the Great Depression, experienced an economic downturn for which the word "recession" seems too mild a description.

Many observers would say that the costs of the Volcker disinflation of the early 1980s were worth paying. After 1984, the United States boasted an economy with relatively stable prices and—up until 2009—relatively moderate unemployment; without Volcker's push, inflation would have likely continued to slowly creep upward over the 1980s, from just under 10 percent to perhaps as high as 20 percent per year. Others insist there must have been a better way. Perhaps inflation could have been brought under control more cheaply if government, business, and labor had been able to strike a deal to restrain nominal wage growth. Or perhaps if the Federal Reserve had done a better job of communicating its expectations and targets. Perhaps "gradualism" rather than "shock therapy" would have worked. Or is "gradualism" inherently noncredible and ineffective, and the shock of a discrete "regime shift" necessary to reanchor expectations?[16]

For those on the right, there is no question that the Volcker disinflation was necessary—indeed, long delayed past its proper time. One of the charges that right-wingers leveled at social democracy was that it led people to expect that life would be easy, that there would be full employment, that jobs would be plentiful. This, in turn, encouraged workers to be insufficiently deferential, and to demand too-high wages, spurring inflation, which kept profits too low to justify investment. And since it promised to reward even those who had not pleased previous employers with jobs, it undermined public virtue.

The government and Federal Reserve needed to impose discipline by focusing on price stability, the right-wingers insisted, and then let the unemployment rate go wherever it needed to go. Government couldn't be a "nanny state" offering everybody a bottle when they cried. Monetary policy needed to be turned over to strongly anti-inflationary policy makers—as Jimmy Carter had already done, half- or unwittingly, in turning the Federal Reserve over to Paul Volcker. And if the Fed was strong enough and disciplined enough, conservatives argued, inflation could be stopped with only a small and temporary rise in unemployment. And, stated and unstated, without upending the conservative cultural hierarchies.

But it was not just in the United States. Union wage demands and strikes in Britain—especially public-sector strikes—convinced the center of the electorate that union power needed to be curbed, and that only the Conservatives would have the necessary resolve. Labour governments just were not working. Margaret Thatcher's Tories promised a restoration of order and discipline, and also promised that they would produce full employment and low inflation, and make Britain work again. In France, newly installed socialist president François Mitterrand turned on a dime and embraced the neoliberal turn to inflation control and orthodox austerity. Volcker disinflation policies in the United States raised unemployment throughout the North Atlantic, putting the project of social democracy in even more of a difficult position, as many social democracies now could not even keep their own commitments to full employment.

Such were the circumstances in which Ronald Reagan and Margaret Thatcher came to power. They would remain at the top of their respective countries' political establishments for much of the 1980s, and their shadows would dominate the thinking of the political right—and the center, and the center-left—in their countries thereafter for much longer.

Yet the curious thing is that the domestic policies of both Reagan and Thatcher were, judged from any rational perspective, unsuccessful. There was a larger than usual gap between their promises and their accomplishments. They sought to raise employment and wages by removing debilitating regulations. They sought to end inflation by stabilizing money. They sought to boost investment, enterprise, and growth by cutting taxes—especially for the rich. And they sought to reduce the size of the government by using their tax cuts to force government spending onto a diet.

The world could have been such that these were all, by and large, good ideas that would have advanced general prosperity.

Many politicians and strategists predicted that Reagan's and Thatcher's policies would be extremely popular and successful. Tax cuts would please electorates. They would also substantially weaken opposition to subsequent spending cuts: any proposal to maintain spending would then necessarily include large budget deficits. Moreover, tax cuts would have the added benefit of tilting income distribution in favor of the rich, correcting the excesses of social democracy by reversing its equal treatment of unequals. The tax cuts would ensure that industry was rewarded and sloth punished. The logics of Stigler et al. would be appeased.

Yet the predicted good things did not happen—except for the end of inflation, enforced at heavy cost in people made unemployed and people made poor by Paul Volcker.[17] And except for the large tax cuts for the rich, which began the process of destabilizing the distribution of income in a way that has led to our Second Gilded Age. Recovery toward full employment was unimpressive both in Western Europe and in the United States. Indeed, unemployment remained scarily high in Western Europe. Rapid wage growth did not resume. Government did not shrink—instead, it dealt with lower tax revenues by running up budget deficits. Investment, enterprise, and growth did not accelerate, in part because the big budget deficits soaked up financing that otherwise could have added to the capital stock. The value of the dollar became excessively high and deranged as a consequence of the large government appetite for finance, and so the market sent a false "shrink and shutdown" signal to American Midwestern manufacturing.[18] The gap between promise and accomplishment was largest in the United States. Thatcher did accomplish her goal of curbing the British union movement. And she had promised less than Reagan had.

The Reagan administration also planned a massive military buildup—an expansion, not a contraction, of the size of the government. How was greater spending to be reconciled with lower taxes and balanced budgets? Policy elites assured each other that their candidate would say a lot of silly things before the election, but that he and his principal advisers understood the important issue. Tax cuts were to be followed by a ruthless attack against programs such as farm subsidies, subsidized student loans, the exemption from taxation of Social Security income, the subsidization of the Southwest's water projects, and so forth. The "weak claims" to the federal government's money would get their just deserts. But those who had weak claims on a technocratic level, and yet benefited from government subsidies, did so because they had, and were good at exercising, political power.

To reduce anxiety, Reagan and his allies increasingly pushed the idea that no spending cuts at all would be required: lifting the hand of regulation from the economy, combined with tax cuts, would spur economic growth enough to quickly reverse the deficits. It would be "morning in America."

No one with a quantitative grasp of the government's budget and its pattern of change ever meant this story to be taken seriously. But the broader administration welcomed its dissemination. In fact, the tax cuts, the expansion of the military budget, and the disarray over spending cuts left the United States with large budget deficits throughout the 1980s. Previous decades had seen one year, or perhaps two, of large budget deficits, and only during deep recessions. But the 1980s saw large budget deficits persist throughout years of prosperity and low unemployment as well. This was a bitter outcome for those who had worked hard to elect a Republican administration because they thought Democrats would impoverish America's future by pursuing short-sighted, antigrowth policies.

After the US economy reattained the neighborhood of full employment in the mid-1980s, the Reagan deficits diverted about 4 percent of national income from investment into consumption spending: instead of flowing out of savers' pockets through banks to companies that would buy and install machines, finance flowed out of savers' pockets through banks into the government, where it funded the tax cuts for the rich, so the rich could then spend their windfalls on luxury consumption. Such large and previously unseen deficits in a near-full employment economy would by themselves typically have inflicted a 0.4 percent per year negative drag on productivity and income growth. Plus there was the substantial indirect harm done to US economic growth by the Reagan deficit cycle. For more than half of the 1980s the US dollar was substantially overvalued as the US budget deficit sucked in capital from outside and raised the exchange rate. When a domestic industry's costs are greater than the prices at which foreign firms can sell, the market is sending the domestic industry a signal that it should shrink: foreigners are producing with more relative efficiency, and the resources used in the domestic industry would be put to better use in some other sector, where domestic producers have more of a comparative advantage. This was the signal that the market system sent to all US manufacturing industries in the 1980s: that they should cut back on investment and shrink. In this case, it was a false signal—sent not by the market's interpretation of the logic of comparative advantage but by the extraordinary short-run demand of cash to borrow from the US government. But firms responded nevertheless. The US sectors producing tradable goods shrank. And some of the ground lost would never be recovered. The Reagan tax cuts hammered manufacturing in the Midwest, starting the creation of what is now known as the "Rust Belt."

Thus the neoliberal turn, in the form it took during the Reagan administration, did not end the slowdown in productivity growth but reinforced it. Moreover, the size of the government relative to the economy was not improved. The technocratic quality of public regulation was not raised. The major effect was to set the distribution of income on a trend of sharply increasing inequality.

The root problem was that the world just did not seem to work as those advocating for the neoliberal turn had predicted.

Back in 1979, a year before Reagan's election, Milton and Rose Friedman wrote their classic book *Free to Choose: A Personal Statement*, in which they set out to defend their brand of small-government libertarianism. In the book, they made three powerful factual claims—claims that seemed true, or maybe true, at the time, but that we now know to be pretty clearly false. And their case for small-government libertarianism rested largely on those claims.[19]

The first claim was that macroeconomic distress is caused by governments, not by the instability of private markets, because the macroeconomic policy required to produce stability with low inflation and full-as-possible employment is straightforward, and easily achieved by a competent government that knows its limits. It is only because governments try to do too much that we experience difficult fluctuations. The second claim was that externalities (such as pollution) were relatively small and better dealt with via contract and tort law than through government regulation. Their third and most important claim was that, in the absence of government-mandated discrimination, the market economy would produce a sufficiently egalitarian distribution of income. The equality of equals would be achieved, and the equality of unequals would be avoided. Slashing the safety net and eliminating all legal barriers to equality of opportunity, the Friedmans argued, would lead to a more equitable outcome than the social democratic approach of monkeying with taxes and subsidies.

Alas, each of these claims turned out to be wrong, a fact that wouldn't become clear to (almost) everyone until the Great Recession began after 2007.

The story as I have told it so far is one of a social democratic system of governance that ran into bad luck in the 1970s. A combination of that bad luck, built-in flaws, and the high expectations for prosperity that had been set during the Thirty

Glorious Years caused it to lose support. This gave right-wingers their opening. But was it really chance and contingency? Or were there structural reasons why the social democratic balancing act would become increasingly hard to maintain as the societal memory of the Great Depression ended and the perceived really-existing socialist threat to the bourgeoisie of the global north declined in intensity?

Neoliberal policies, once enacted, were no more successful than social democratic ones had been—save in reducing inflation. Rapid growth did not resume. Indeed, median incomes declined under Reagan and Thatcher, as the era's meager productivity growth was funneled into the pockets of the rich, and a Second Gilded Age drew near. By the end of the 1980s, it was clear that the neoliberal project of rolling back social democracy had failed to surpass the bar of high expectations set by the Thirty Glorious Years, just as social democracy itself had failed.

But the failure of the neoliberal project to boost income growth in the 1980s did not lead to renewed calls for a further revolution in policy and in political economy. Somehow, the neoliberal project became accepted, conventional wisdom—so much so that in the following decades it gained support from the center-left. It was not Ronald Reagan but Bill Clinton who announced, in one of his State of the Union speeches, that "the era of big government is over."[20] It was not Margaret Thatcher but Barack Obama who called for austerity when the unemployment rate was above 9 percent: "Families across the country are tightening their belts and making tough decisions," he said. "The federal government should do the same."[21] It was Bill Clinton who made his major social-insurance commitment one to "end welfare as we know it."[22] It was Prime Minister Tony Blair, from the Labour Party, who validated Margaret Thatcher's strong allergy to British Labour's union-centered cultural politics.[23] In the United States, Democrats and Republicans fenced over what form partial Social Security privatization would take—Would your private plan be an add-on or a carve-out?[24] Both sides called for the market rather than the government to guide industrial development. US public investment fell from 7 percent to 3 percent of national income. Rather than ramping up the government role via large-scale increases in R&D funding at the back end and guarantees of procurement at the front end, financial deregulation was trusted to create venture capital and other pools of private investment to fund technological revolutions. Not pollution-control mandates but, rather, methods of marketing rights to pollute. Not welfare programs but—notionally, as implementation was always lacking—education programs to eliminate the need for welfare. To do more would be to return to outdated social democratic command-and-control planning initiatives that had supposedly demonstrated their failure.

But social democracy had worked in the 1960s and 1970s. And—except on the inflation-control front—neoliberalism had done no better in the 1980s at generating growth, and a lot worse at generating equitable growth, than social democracy had in the 1970s. What gives?

Centrist and left neoliberals understood themselves as advocates for achieving social democratic ends through more efficient, market-oriented means. Markets—as Friedrich von Hayek had rightly stressed throughout his career—crowdsource the brainstorming and then the implementation of solutions that the market economy sets itself, and the market economy sets itself the task of making things tagged as valuable. Left-neoliberals understood themselves as advocating for this crowdsourcing and the carrot, where it would be more effective.

Besides, there was still Big Government, even if Bill Clinton had thrown rhetorical red meat to working-class white men who felt somehow wounded by inclusion by claiming that Big Government's era was over. There were powerful government interventions and policies that appear to have been powerful boosters of growth: education (especially female secondary education) in accelerating the demographic transition; policies making it easy for domestic producers to acquire industrial core technology (embodied in capital goods or not); administrative simplicity and transparency; transportation and communication infrastructure—all things that made government effective and that only the government could provide. Relying on the market and rightsizing an efficient government could, left-neoliberals hoped, both restore rapid economic growth and attract a durable, centrist governing coalition. Then attention could be turned to trying to reverse the growing perception that treating people equally and generously was unfair, because some people received things they had not merited and did not deserve.

Rightist neoliberalism was much harder edged. A much steeper slope in the distribution of income and wealth was not a bug but a feature. The top 0.01 percent—the job creators, the entrepreneurs—deserved to receive not 1 percent but 5 percent of national income.[25] They deserved to have societal power, in the form of the salience given to their preferences in the market's semiutilitarianism, over the direction of human beings' time and effort that gave them not 100 to 1,000 times but 500 to 250,000 times the national average income.[26] And to tax them even after they died was not only impolitic but immoral: theft. This revived and restored form of pseudo-classical semi-liberalism was earnestly supported by a plutocrat-funded network of think tanks and "astroturf" interest groups. ("Don't tell me that you are speaking for the people," I heard Treasury Secretary Lloyd Bentsen once say. "I am old enough to know the difference between the grassroots and astroturf.") This network's central claim was that social democracy was one huge mistake, and if only the governments of the world got rid of it, we could move swiftly to a utopia. The makers wouldn't have to carry the takers on their backs, and the takers would shape up—and if they did not, they would suffer the consequences, and it would serve them right!

That this did not seem to actually work was not much of an obstacle to belief.

From my perspective, this pattern of empirical failure followed by ideological doubling down was reminiscent of what we are told of religious politics in the Jerusalem-centered Kingdom of Judah late in the First Temple era. The Kingdom of Israel to the north had already been conquered by the Assyrians, its cities leveled, its elite carried off to subjection in Nineveh. The kings of Judah in Jerusalem sought foreign alliances, especially with the only other great power in the neighborhood interested in resisting Assyria, Egypt. The prophets said: No! Trust not in your own swords, and especially not in those of foreign allies who worship strange and false Gods! Trust in YHWH! His strong arm will protect you! And when armies returned defeated, the prophets said: Your problem was that you did not enforce the worship of YHWH strongly enough! You allowed women to dance in the streets making cakes for the Queen of Heaven! Worship YHWH *harder*![27]

And, truth to tell, the neoliberal turn was very successful in restoring the growth rate—and more than restoring the growth rate—of the incomes and wealth of those at the top. The rich had the largest megaphones, and they trumpeted the fact that their incomes were growing rapidly. And those lower down, who voted for candidates and politicians who had turned the wheel and made the neoliberal turn? They were told that if only they were sufficiently worthy, the unleashed market would give to them too, and they more than half believed it.

THE ERA OF THE neoliberal turn did deliver one thing out of what its salesmen had promised: it delivered a rapidly rising share of the rich in the distribution of national income.

We already noted that America's true upper class, the top 0.01 percent of households, went from 100 to 500 times the average in terms of their incomes. The next 0.99 percent, the rest of the top 1 percent, went from 8 to 17 times the average. The next 4 percent, the rest of the top 5 percent, went from 3.25 to 4.25 times the average. The next 5 percent, the rest of the top 10 percent, treaded water in their share of income. And all the niches lower down saw their shares of national income fall.

These are the incomes associated with the ranked slots in the income distribution, not the incomes of tagged individuals or households. And as people age, moreover, their incomes rise. And the pie, per capita, was greater in 2010 than it had been in 1979. In real per capita terms, the measured US income average was nearly twice as much in 2010 as it had been in 1979. And a great many things of substantial use value were available in 2010 really cheaply. That mattered. As a general rule, a standard physical good—a blender, say—sold in the market has an average use-value to consumers of perhaps twice its market value: half of the wealth from production and distribution of a physical good comes from the resources, natural and human, used in production—that is, its cost of production—and half is consumer surplus, which has to do with how much consumers are willing to pay for the product, which is based on getting the good to the right user in the right place at the right time. For information age nonphysical commodities, the ratio may well be greater—perhaps five to one, maybe more.

Rising inequality begs caveats. Such as that 55 percent of US households had home air-conditioning in 1979, rising to 90 percent by 2010. Washing machines rose from 70 percent to 80 percent, and dryers from 50 percent to 80 percent. Five percent of US households had microwave ovens in 1979, and 92 percent had them by 2010. Computers or tablets went from 0 percent to 70 percent, cell phones to more than 95 percent, and smartphones to more than 75 percent.[28] The American working and middle classes were richer in 2010 than their counterparts had been in 1979. In the neoliberal era, the United States was no longer rapidly increasing the educational level attained by the young, no longer aggressively investing in public infrastructure, and no longer keeping the government from partially draining the pool of savings that would have otherwise flowed to finance private investment. Productivity growth was only half the rate it had been during the Thirty Glorious Years. Equitable growth was no longer being delivered. But there was still growth—and growth in typical incomes at a pace that came close to matching that of 1870–1914, and that people over 1913–1938 would have wept to see.

Still, many things that people had taken, and do take, to be indicia of middle-class status—of having made it—such as an easy commute; a detached house in a good neighborhood; the ability to get their children into what they think is a good college, *and then to pay for it*; good-enough employer-sponsored health insurance that won't bankrupt them and allow them to lose their homes to pay for a heart attack—these seemed more difficult to attain in the America of 2010 than they had been, at least in memory, back in 1979. Plus, there was a person's relative status. A successful middle-class American in the age of social democracy could meet American Motors CEO and future Michigan governor and Housing and Urban Development (HUD) secretary George Romney and know that he lived in a normal house—albeit a relatively large one—in Bloomfield Hills, Michigan, and drove a compact car, a Rambler American (admittedly, because American Motors made it). A successful middle-class American in the age of neoliberalism would meet Bain CEO and future Massachusetts governor and US senator (R-UT) Mitt Romney and know that he had seven houses, some of them mansions, scattered around the country and, well, I do not know what models of cars he has driven, but I have been told that the house in La Jolla, California, near the beach, has a car elevator. Even when people have more material wealth at their disposal in absolute terms than their parents did, a proportional gulf that large that is growing that rapidly can make them feel small.

French economist Thomas Piketty popularized an understanding of the striking differences between how the economy had functioned in the global north before World War I and how it functioned after World War II.[29] In the First Gilded Age, before World War I, wealth was predominantly inherited, the rich dominated politics, and economic (as well as race and gender) inequality were extreme. After the upheaval of World War II, everything changed. Income growth accelerated, wealth was predominantly earned (justly or unjustly), politics became dominated by the middle class, and economic inequality was modest (even if race and gender equality remained a long way off). The global north seemed to have entered a new era.

And then things shifted back.

Piketty's central point was that we shouldn't have been surprised. In a capitalist economy, it is normal for a large proportion of the wealth to be inherited. It is normal for its distribution to be highly unequal. It is normal for a plutocratic elite, once formed, to use its political power to shape the economy to its own advantages. And it is normal for this to put a drag on economic growth. Rapid growth like that which occurred between 1945 and 1973, after all, requires creative destruction; and, because it is the plutocrats' wealth that is being destroyed, they are unlikely to encourage it.

Why, then, did the neoliberal era last? It had pointed out that social democracy was no longer delivering the rapid progress toward utopia that it had delivered in the first post–World War II generation. It promised to do better. Yet it did not do better—save for curbing the union movement in Britain, and providing income gains for the rich through tax cuts, as well as through the side effects of wage stagnation, which were truly staggering in magnitude. Why didn't discontent with neoliberalism's failure to deliver cause another turn of the political-economic societal-organizational wheel?

I believe it lasted because Ronald Reagan won the Cold War. Or, rather, I believe it was because soon after Ronald Reagan's presidency came to an end, the Cold War came to an end, and he was given credit for it. And the manifest failure of ideas in the shop window of possibilities weren't uniquely being sold by the right.

Looking back from today, or from the 1990s, or even from the late 1970s, on the phenomenon of really-existing socialism, perhaps the most striking feature is how inevitable the decay and decline of the system was. German sociologist Max Weber did not have to see what happened from 1917 to 1991 to understand how the history of the Bolshevik regime installed by Lenin and his comrades was going to go. He looked back before 1917, at previous history, at episodes in which entrepreneurship and enterprise had been replaced with bureaucracy, and he wrote that wherever "bureaucracy gained the upper hand, as in China and Egypt, it did not disappear": there was going to be no Marxist "withering away" but rather a hypertrophy of a state issuing commands.

German-Polish activist and moral philosopher Rosa Luxemburg, writing in 1918, was even more clear-eyed (and pessimistic):

> Without general elections, without unrestricted freedom of press and assembly, without a free struggle of opinion, life dies out in every public institution. . . . Only the bureaucracy remains. . . . A few dozen party leaders of inexhaustible energy and boundless experience direct and rule. . . . An elite of the working class is invited from time to time to meetings where they are to applaud the speeches of the leaders, and to approve proposed resolutions unanimously—[it is] at bottom, then, a clique affair. . . . Such conditions must inevitably cause a brutalization of public life: attempted assassinations, shooting of hostages, etc.[30]

Both Weber and Luxemburg, however, thought that the bureaucracy would be efficient, even if anti-entrepreneurial. Weber thought really-existing socialism would be regimented and organized. Luxemburg thought it would be brutal and dictatorial. Neither predicted the waste, the bread lines, the irrationality of economic organization, and the centrality of corruption, influence, and networks: *blat*. Neither predicted that when the Iron Curtain fell at the end of the 1980s, it would turn out that the countries where Stalin's (or Ho Chi Minh's, or Kim Il-Sung's, or Fidel Castro's) armies had marched would be but one-fifth as prosperous in material terms as the countries just next door that they had not conquered.

Many outside the USSR—for example, the left-wing Marxist economist Paul Sweezy—had confidently predicted that Leninist socialism and government planning would deliver a more efficient allocation of productive forces and a faster rate of economic growth than any other possible system. Even many who feared the destructive potential of Leninist socialism agreed that the USSR and its satellites were likely to forge ahead in total and per capita production. Paul Samuelson—no Leninist—wrote the leading post–World War II American economics textbook. Up until the late 1960s, its forecasts showed the USSR economy surpassing the US economy in production per head well before 2000. That the Soviet Union might produce superior production and equality, if not prosperity, even if it remained inferior as to freedom and choice, seemed a possibility even into the 1960s.

Yet all this turned out to be wrong. The Soviet Union and its satellites turned out, when the Iron Curtain fell, to be poor indeed. Gross inefficiency in consumer goods allocation turned out to be generated by forces that also produced gross inefficiency in investment allocation, and so the lands that were to be studded with automated factories were not. The Soviet Union had enjoyed some successes. By 1960, it had by and large attained a global-north level of health, education, and life expectancy. In the

1970s it appeared to have created a military at least as strong as that of the United States—but it did so by devoting 40 percent of its national income, rather than the United States' 8 percent, to building it up.

And the economic failures were massive. Increased output was limited, mostly, to steel, machinery, and military equipment. The collectivization of agriculture ended in ruin: we do not know how many died. We think it was in the mid seven figures. It might have been eight figures. And the Soviet growth rate was not impressively high when seen in a world context.

The late Yegor Gaidar, a Soviet economist and politician, liked to tell the story of the failure of Soviet industrialization through the lenses of grain and oil. As he put it, the prominent communist economist Nikolay Bukharin and Soviet official Aleksey Rykov "essentially told Stalin: 'In a peasant country, it is impossible to extract grain by force. There will be civil war.' Stalin answered, 'I will do it nonetheless.'" As of the 1950s, Nikita Khrushchev was dealing with the consequences of the backward, enserfed agricultural sector Stalin had created. As of 1950, he wrote, "In the last fifteen years, we have not increased the collection of grain. Meanwhile, we are experiencing a radical increase of urban population. How can we resolve this problem?" He ultimately decided to throw resources at the problem and undertook large-scale projects to put more land under grain cultivation. In the end, the plan failed. In 1963, the USSR informed its allies that it would no longer be able to ship them grain, and then started buying grain on the world market.[31]

It may be that the collapse of the Soviet economy and the Soviet model was delayed for a decade by the more-than-tripling of world real oil prices during the OPEC decade of the 1970s. According to Gaidar, the beginning of the end came when Saudi Arabia decided at the end of 1985 to resume pumping oil at capacity, and to crash the price of oil, largely to curb the ambitions of Iran's theocrats. This put the Soviet Union in the extremely difficult position of being unable to earn enough to buy grain to feed its massive population. As Gaidar assessed the situation, the Soviets were left without any other option and started borrowing to cover the difference in 1986. But by 1989, when a Soviet effort "to create a consortium of 300 banks to provide a large loan" collapsed, they were forced "to start negotiations directly with Western governments about so-called politically motivated credits."

That was the ultimate revelation of the industrial bankruptcy of the Soviet Union: in a time of low oil prices, the regime could only feed its people by bargaining away political concessions in return for concessionary loans with which to purchase wheat from abroad.

Ronald Reagan and his team had decided to amp up the Cold War in Latin America by hiring soldiers from Argentina's fascist dictatorship to be the core cadres of what they hoped would become a right-wing guerrilla insurgency against the left-wing "Sandinista" government of Nicaragua. The Argentine generals in their junta thought—did high officials in the Reagan administration, such as UN Ambassador Jeane Kirkpatrick, tell them so?—that in return the United States would stay neutral if there was any conflict between Argentina and Britain over the Falkland Islands, which lay three hundred miles off the coast of Argentina, and which Britain had colonized centuries before. So, seeking to boost their domestic political standing via a short, victorious war, the Argentine generals conquered the Falklands. Margaret Thatcher sent the British navy—with ample American logistical support—to retake them. This was the lift beneath her wings to win her reelection as prime minister in 1983. Rather than a failed four-year experiment, neoliberalism thus cemented the neoliberal turn in Britain.

In the United States, the economy came roaring back in time to win reelection for Ronald Reagan in 1984—plus, he was superb at being a head-of-state-type president, even if rather bad and underqualified as a policy-analyst-type president. His wife,

Nancy, persuaded him to see Mikhail Gorbachev as a potential friend in his second term. And it was the end of the Cold War that was the wind beneath neoliberalism's wings in the United States.

The hopes and claims at the start of the neoliberal turn in 1980 had been that the post–World War II golden-age pace of economic growth in the global north could be restored by governments and societies turning (at least partway) to serve the imperatives of the market, rather than the social democratic practice of managing, supplementing, and controlling the market economy. These hopes and claims were dashed. Growth continued, but at a much slower pace than during 1938–1973—albeit at a slightly faster pace than 1870–1914, and a much faster pace than 1914–1938.

Distribution had shifted. Inclusion, especially for women, but also, to some degree, for minorities, meant that the incomes of white men did not keep pace with the average. More important, however, was that the neoliberal turn accomplished its explicit goal of transferring income and wealth to the top of the distribution. The claim had been that thus incentivizing the rich and the superrich would induce them to work harder and unleash waves of entrepreneurial energy. That claim proved false. But the income and wealth was transferred up nevertheless.

This was disturbing to the established male ethnomajority working and middle classes. After 1980 they found the growth in their real incomes to be small and, in their minds, at least, neutralized by the fact that they no longer received the respect from women, minorities, and foreigners—or from the plutocrats growing in wealth and salience in their mental pictures of the world—that was their expectation, and that they saw as their due. Somehow, things had been rigged against them. The rich got richer, the unworthy and minority poor got handouts. Hardworking white men who deserved more of the good things (according to this view) did not get them. Thus a critical mass of the electorate grew to distrust the system—a system that did not seem to be providing them with better lives in the early aughts than their predecessors had seen thirty years earlier—and the system's rulers.

When the Great Recession came along, and when recovery from the Great Recession was delayed and hesitant, the government and the political system barely seemed to care. A reason was that the rich dominated public discourse. And for the rich, there was no crisis. But everyone else—roughly 90 percent of the US population—continued to lose ground. And for them, the economy since 2007 has proved gravely disappointing. They seek an explanation, and something to change, and often, someone to blame. They are right to do so.

16

Reglobalization, Information Technology, and Hyperglobalization

The world began to take the neoliberal turn in the 1970s. The turn was all but complete by 2000. Neoliberalism in its various forms had ascended, and was providing the world's political-economy governance default presumptions and practices.

This ascent is a puzzle. The neoliberal turn had failed to deliver higher investment, greater entrepreneurship, faster productivity growth, or the restoration of middle-class wage and income growth. The new policies had delivered massively greater income and wealth inequality. What was the appeal? The neoliberal order hung on because it took credit for victory in the Cold War, because it took credit for making sure the undeserving didn't get anything they did not deserve, and because the powerful used their megaphones to loudly and repeatedly tell others that they deserved the credit for whatever they claimed neoliberal policies had achieved. And so the hand that had been dealt was played out.

Four forces in particular led to things playing out the way they did. The first was post–World War II *reglobalization*: the reversal of the step backward away from the 1870–1914 globalization that had taken place over the period 1914–1950. The second was a big shift in technology: starting in the mid-1950s, the steel-box shipping container conquered the world. The third was another big shift in technology: the nearly ethereal zeros and ones of information technology conquered the world. The fourth consisted of the neoliberal policies themselves and how they interacted with the other three. Together these four forces turned *reglobalization* into *hyperglobalization*.

It should now be obvious that this chapter's story is not a simple one. Making it even more complex, the story of reglobalization, information technology, and hyperglobalization in the age in which the world took the neoliberal turn has two threads. One thread follows the consequences of reglobalization, the rise of information technology, and then hyperglobalization for the global south. The second focuses on the consequences for the global north. And what bottom line you ultimately draw—Was it great, good, or something else?—very much depends on whether your patron saint is Hayek or Polanyi.

Global south countries that managed to use neoliberal ideas to make their own societies less corrupt (and that escaped being hammered by any blowback consequences of neoliberal policies in the global north) found themselves able to use, rather than be used by, the global world market. For the first time since 1870, these economies were no longer forced to diverge from the trajectory of the global north, growing relatively poorer even as they grew absolutely richer. From 1990 on, in very broad strokes, the global south began to see real income growth faster than the global north.[1] And so it looked as if the market's workings might in fact be for the benefit of humankind.

For global-north countries, there were gains from increasing world trade and the spread of information technology. But these gains wound up concentrated among those at the top of global-north societies, further enriching the rich. Having a union job in a factory in the same region as the corporate headquarters no longer meant that you got a healthy share of that concentrating wealth. Re- and hyperglobalization plus infotech in the context of the neoliberal turn meant that bosses and engineers now found that they could put their factories elsewhere in the world. The greatly accelerated flow of information meant they no longer needed to drive to the factory to see what was going on, manage it, and improve it. Elegies for Polanyian rights were sounded in regions of the global north that for the first time experienced the deindustrialization that the global south had been experiencing since before 1870.

But elegiac hillbillies were just one piece of the global north: one theme of squares in a more complicated quilted arrangement. Infotech's realization of critical mass at the start of the 1990s meant that the global north attained productivity growth equivalent to that of the Thirty Glorious Years for a decade and a half. And while the workings of the Second Gilded Age kept that productivity growth from fully trickling down to wages, it also meant that the violation of people's expectations and Polanyian rights was likewise quilted—here, but not there, and not in equal measure. One result was profound changes in the underpinnings of how political economic decisions were made.

As late as 2007, neoliberals at the top were able to congratulate themselves, believing that things were going not unreasonably well, and that they would continue to go not unreasonably well.[2] Productivity growth seemed back, and, they told themselves, when the income distribution stabilized, broad-based waves of growth would resume and pockets of populist discontent would ebb. At the top it looked, again, as if the market's workings might actually be for the benefit of humankind.

But that belief missed much of what was really going on underneath. After 2007, the financial crisis and the Great Recession, subjects a chapter away, were both thoroughgoing disasters in their own right. Useful to know for this chapter, however, is that these disasters would pull back the curtain to reveal that neo-liberal hubris had truly brought forth nemesis.

POST–WORLD WAR II REGLOBALIZATION was history rhyming the post-1870 pattern: the establishment of an international economic order under a hegemon plus a transportation technology revolution, once again advancing globalization at a rapid pace. But after 1870, Britain-as-hegemon had gone it alone, laying down a pattern in splendid isolation to which others had to accommodate themselves. The United States after World War II built institutions, and so the post–World War II era became a great time for new global cooperative organizations. On the political side, of course, there was the UN—the United Nations—with its Security Council, its General Assembly, and all of its branches.

On the economic side, there would be three more organizations. Or at least that was the plan—only two and a half actually came into existence. The newly dominant United States wagered that international trade would soon become an enabler of both international peace and domestic prosperity. Western Europe joined in on this wager, most prominently with the creation in the mid-1950s of the European Coal and Steel Community for free trade in those commodities, an initiative that grew into today's European Union. And at the 1944 Bretton Woods Conference, Harry Dexter White from the United States and John Maynard Keynes from Britain designed a system to try to make increased globalization work for good.

The three planned organizations to promote global economic cooperation were the World Bank, the International Monetary Fund (IMF), and—the one that failed to fully come into existence—the International Trade Organization (ITO). The World Bank began as what was called the International Bank for

Reconstruction and Development and was created for the dual purpose of financing reconstruction in the wake of the war's destruction and developing those parts of the world that had not yet grasped the productive opportunities of industrial technology. The IMF was created to manage the values of currencies and the net flow of financial resources across borders, to enable countries that needed to reset the terms on which they traded, and to coerce certain countries into living up to their economic obligations. And the planned-for ITO was going to negotiate mutually beneficial reductions in tariffs and referee trading disputes.

But while the Truman administration pushed the UN, the World Bank, and the IMF through the US Congress, it decided at the end of 1950 that ratifying the ITO would be one international organization too many. It was, the administration decided, too much to ask of Congress. By that time, the tides had shifted against the ethos of open-handed international cooperation that had dominated in the immediate postwar years; the long twilight struggle between the free world and global communism known as the Cold War was beginning. The demise of the ITO was a result. And so, instead of an organization with teeth intended to enforce resolutions to trade disputes, there was to be an agreement—a General Agreement on Tariffs and Trade (GATT), under the aegis of which multiple rounds of multilateral tariff reductions would be negotiated over decades. Thus even at the start of this reglobalization push, there were countercurrents, of which this was the chief: while the ITO would have required countries and sectors and classes to eat whatever the market set before them in response to automatic tariff reductions, the GATT required that a domestic political coalition be put together in every signatory country before a GATT tariff-reduction round could be completed and come into effect.

Such coalitions were put together. Eight rounds of tariff reductions were negotiated and implemented between 1947 and

1994: Geneva (completed in 1947), Annecy (1949), Torquay (1950–1951), Geneva II (1956), Geneva III (1962, more commonly called the Dillon Round, as it was proposed by C. Douglas Dillon when he was undersecretary of state for Republican president Eisenhower and concluded by C. Douglas Dillon when he was secretary of the treasury for Democratic president Kennedy), the Kennedy (Memorial) Round (1967), the Tokyo Round (1979), and the Uruguay Round (1994). By the 1990s each round was taking nearly a decade to negotiate, with nearly a decade of exhaustion between rounds.

But that was only part of the story. Improvements in domestic production had raced ahead of productivity improvements in long-distance transportation from 1914 to 1950. Then the paces reversed, with revolutions in ocean transport, the most impressive of which was the coming of containerization.[3]

The cargo container: it is 20 or 40 feet long, 8.5 or 9.5 feet high, and 8 feet wide. It carries up to 29 tons in its 2,000 cubic feet of recommended available space—goods worth roughly $500,000 (or more) when sold at retail. It can be transported in a month anywhere in the world where there are suitable harbors, railways, locomotives, flatcars, truck tractors, and roads. It can be moved carrying nonfragile, nonperishable goods from any modern factory with a loading dock to any modern warehouse anywhere in the world for perhaps 1 percent of the goods' retail value. Before 1960, costs of international transoceanic shipment for most commodities could easily amount to 15 percent of retail value. Back in the 1950s, the city of San Francisco held eight hundred thousand people, and fifty thousand of them were longshoremen, at least part time. By 1980 there were less than one-fifth as many.

When my family bought a German-made washing machine from a warehouse store in San Leandro, California, just on the south side of the city of Oakland as we here in Berkeley are on the north side, it cost us eight times as much to get the machine from the warehouse to our basement as it had cost to get it from the factory where it was made, in Schorndorf, to the warehouse.

And so reglobalization proceeded during the Thirty Glorious Years after World War II. A great deal of the force for expansion came from the political-economic side, especially as the United States came to see access to its markets as an important tool in fighting the Cold War. And then the virtuous trade circle set in: rising productivity drove demand for goods ever higher, and so expanded capacity was met by expanded demand. By 1975 world trade as a share of global economic activity was back to its 1914 peak of 25 percent—about one-eighth of what a typical region spent on goods and services was for imported goods and services, and about one-eighth of a typical region's earnings came from exporting goods and services.

This virtuous circle was strongest by far in the global north. That 1800–1914 had concentrated industry and knowledge about industry in the global north's industrial districts had consequences, since ideas creation builds on the ideas stock. Previous global-north industrialization accelerated global-north growth, while previous global-south deindustrialization held back global-south growth. The generation of new ideas, after all, depends on the density and magnitude of the stock of already deployed ideas in use in the region. The global north's industrial districts thus drove growth forward. This virtuous circle was much less evident in the global south, which, remember, had been relatively deindustrialized by the workings of the earlier wave of globalization.

Without vibrant manufacturing districts and deep and dense communities of engineering practice of its own, how could the global south benefit from this reglobalization? The only way was by further entrenching itself into its slot in the world division of labor. That meant taking advantage of the valuable resources it owned, such as minerals and tropical agricultural products, where relative prices continued to decline. And so, while the global south did get richer during the post–World War II decade of reglobalization, it got richer more slowly, and the relative income gap continued to grow up to at least 1990.

In the first post–World War II generation, in a nutshell, you could understand who benefited from reglobalization by talking of the "frown curve." At the start, the left side, the frown curve is low: there is relatively little wealth to be gained by providing raw materials, as elastic supply and inelastic demand means that primary-product producers, who as a group work hard to increase their productivity, can do little more than to reduce the prices at which they can sell as productivity increases; and thus there is relatively little wealth to be gained in design, as competitors can quickly reverse-engineer something that's already in existence and visible. There is, however, a great deal of wealth to be gained in the middle, where the frown curve is high. There, the know-how and the know-what of the industrial districts of the global north brought about the enormous efficiencies of mid- and late-1900s mass production. And there is relatively little wealth to be gained at the end, the right side, where the frown curve is once again low: marketing and distribution—matching commodities to the particular needs of individuals, or at least convincing individuals it is worth paying you to do so—is also not where the bulk of the action is.

But the story of reglobalization via political economy and containerization is only the first third of the story of this chapter. In the 1980s there was another huge technological shift gathering force that would have powerful influences on world trade and far beyond: information technology. There came a true revolution in the cost of transporting not goods but bits, not material objects but *information*. The communication and data global internet—and the massive fiberoptic submarine and subsurface cables, plus the narrowcast and broadcast transmitters, receivers, and satellites, on which it rides—transformed the world again starting in the 1990s.

I HAVE NOT WRITTEN much in this book about precisely how new technologies have advanced human collective powers over nature, about how they allowed us to organize ourselves in new ways, and what they were and did. I have simply written about their rate of growth: for example, the 2 percent per year in ideas growth after 1870. To have focused on what they were and what they did would have been a very different book, one that needs more of an engineer and less of a political economist. Let me hasten to add that that different book, competently executed, would be a great book about things of vital, perhaps overwhelming, importance. My late teacher David Landes's *The Unbound Prometheus* accomplished this task for Europe from 1750 to 1965, and it remains a classic. And Robert Gordon has written a new classic covering the United States since 1870 in the same vein.[4]

But right here and now it is, I think, appropriate to bring some features of these technologies to center stage. Consider the idea of General Purpose Technologies (GPTs): those technologies where advances change, if not everything, nearly everything, as they ramify across sector upon sector.[5] Steam power in the early 1800s was the first. Early machine tools—embodying in their design and construction so much technological knowledge about how to shape materials—in the mid-1800s were the second. Then after 1870 came telecommunications, materials science, organic chemistry, internal combustion engines, the assembly line, subsequent machine-tool generations, and electricity—the technologies the flowering of which make up Robert Gordon's "one big wave" of technological advance, and which he sees as transforming the global north over the period 1870–1980 and then ebbing. Starting in the 1950s and reaching critical mass in the 1990s, there came another GPT: microelectronics. Electrons were now made to dance not in the service of providing power but rather to assist and amplify calculation—and communication. And it turned out that microelectronics as microcontrollers could allow the construction of materials that could perform much better and that were cheaper and lighter than relying on dumb matter arranged in ways that linked mechanically.[6]

Take the quartz components of common sand. Purify and liquefy them by heating them to more than 1,700°C (3,100°F). Add carbon to pull the oxygen atoms out of the quartz, leaving behind pure molten liquid silicon. Cool the silicon, and, just before it solidifies, drop a small seed crystal into it. Then pull up the seed crystal and the surrounding silicon attaching itself to it.

If you have done this right, you will then have a monocrystalline silicon cylinder. Slice it finely and thinly into "wafers." These wafers of pure silicon crystal do not conduct electricity. Why not? Because of a silicon atom's fourteen electrons, ten cannot move to become currents because they are locked to the nucleus in what chemists call their 1s and 2sp "orbitals." ("Orbital" is a misnomer: they do not really "orbit." Niels Bohr a century and more ago thought they did, but he did not have it right. Erwin Schrödinger put him straight.) Only the outermost four electrons, in the 3sp orbitals, might ever get energized and then move around to become electric currents. But in pure silicon they cannot ever do so because they are locked between their atom's nucleus and the nuclei of its four neighbors in the crystal. Enough energy to knock them out of the 3sp orbitals and into the "conduction band" orbitals would break the crystal.

But suppose you were to replace a few of the silicon atoms in the crystal—1 in every 10,000 atoms is more than enough—with phosphorus atoms, which have not fourteen but fifteen electrons each. Fourteen of each phosphorus atom's electrons will act like the silicon atom's electrons: locked into place, tightly bound in their 1s and 2sp orbitals to their home nucleus, and the outer four bound in their 3sp orbital to both their home nucleus and to the four neighboring nuclei. But the fifteenth electron cannot fit. It finds a higher energy orbital state, in which it is only loosely bound to any one nucleus. It can and does move about in response to small gradients in the local electric field. And so the region of your silicon crystal that you have "doped" with phosphorus becomes a conductor of electricity. But if you were to do something that pulled those fifteenth electrons away to someplace else, that region would then also become a nonconductive insulator like the rest of the crystal. A doped region of a silicon crystal is thus like the on-off switch on your wall that controls your ceiling light. By applying or removing small voltages of electrical current and electromagnetic pressure, we can flip that switch on and off as we choose, and so let the current flow or not as we choose.

Right now, in the semiconductor fabricators of the Taiwan Semiconductor Manufacturing Company (TSMC), the machines that it has bought (from ASML Holding in the Netherlands and Applied Materials in Silicon Valley) and installed and programmed are carving thirteen billion such semiconductor solid-state switches with attached current and control paths onto a piece of a wafer that will become a crystal silicon "chip" about two-fifths of an inch wide and two-fifths of an inch tall. TSMC's marketing materials imply that the smallest of the carved features is only twenty-five silicon atoms wide. (In actual fact, the features are more like ten times that size.) If the thirteen billion component switches of this small chip of crystal rock made from sand were carved correctly, and it passes its tests, which require that its current pathways switch on and off accurately and synchronously 3.2 billion times a second, the chip will wind up at the heart of a machine like the one connected to the keyboard on which were typed these words. It will be an Apple M1 microprocessor, a very large-scale integration (VLSI) circuit made up of these tiny switches of doped silicon crystal, which we call *transistors*.

William Shockley, John Bardeen, and Walter Brattain are the three credited with building the first transistor at Bell Telephone Laboratories in 1947. Dawon Kahng and Mohamed Atalla are credited with building the first metal-oxide semiconductor field effect transistor. Jay Last's group, building on the ideas of Robert Noyce and Jean Hoerni of Fairchild Semiconductor, built the first operational solid-state integrated circuit made up of more than one transistor. By 1964 General Microelectronics was making and selling a 120-transistor integrated circuit. Previous vacuum-tube electronic switching elements were four inches long—one hundred millimeters. Transistors in 1964 were packed one-twenty-fifth of an inch, one millimeter apart: they were one hundred times smaller, enabling ten thousand times as much computation power to be packed into the same space, with orders of magnitude less power consumption.

Gordon Moore, then also working at Fairchild Semiconductor, observed in 1965 that the number of solid-state microelectronic transistors in frontier integrated circuits had grown from one to one hundred in the seven years since 1958. He made a bold and highly speculative prediction that we could look forward to a future of "component-crammed equipment," projecting that in 1975, which was just ten years away, a one-hundred-square-millimeter silicon chip would hold sixty-five thousand components. That would allow for "electronic techniques more generally available throughout all of society, performing many functions that presently are done inadequately by other techniques or not done at all," he said. He predicted "home computers—or at least terminals connected to a central computer, automatic controls for automobiles, and personal portable communications." He said there would be "integrated circuits in digital filters [to] separate channels on multiplex equipment," and forecast advances in telephone circuits and data processing. "Computers will be more powerful, and will be organized in completely different ways," he concluded.[7]

By 1971, integrated-circuit semiconductor fabricators had taken four steps downward to a finer process for inscribing patterns on the crystal. The first microprocessor, the Intel 4004, packed twenty thousand transistors into a square millimeter—features were two hundred microns, two hundred millionths of a meter, apart. By 2016 the feature-plus-separation distance was down to two hundred nanometers, two hundred billionths of a meter. (And by 2021, there would be a further shrinkage, by more than half, and the feature-plus-separation distances would be only ninety nanometers—450 silicon atoms—across). Back in 1979, to execute one MIPS—a million instructions per second—required one watt of power. By 2015, one watt could drive more than one million MIPS. As components became smaller, they became faster. Halve the size of the feature, and you can run it twice as fast—up to a point. Before 1986, microprocessor speed quadrupled every seven years. Then, with the coming of the simplicity of reduced instruction sets, came seventeen years in which each quadrupling of speed took three years rather than seven. Then, after 2003, the quadrupling time went back to seven years, until further speed improvements hit a wall in around 2013.

But the packing of more and more smaller and smaller transistors into VLSI chips continued through what I can only call Deep Magic, albeit at a slower pace than with the original "Moore's Law." I can read that the ASML TWINSCAN NXE:3400C machine uses extreme ultraviolet light with a wavelength of 13.5 nanometers and think: that machine is keeping itself aligned and carving twenty million lines with its lasers into the silicon crystal of a three-hundred-millimeter (twelve-inch) wafer without erring in positioning any one of those lines by as much as one-thirty-thousandth of a human hair. And I cannot grasp how this could possibly be done, regularly and reliably, for a variable cost of only $50 per microprocessor.[8]

At its most rapid pace during the information-technology revolution, the company at the heart of the innovation economy, microprocessor designer and manufacturer Intel, was tick-tocking—tick, improving the microarchitectural details of its microprocessors so programs could run faster; tock, improving the fine resolution of its manufacturing so that it could make the features, and thus the entire microprocessor, smaller—and completing a full cycle in under three years. With microprocessors doubling in speed every two years, and with the information-technology sector taking full advantage, measured economy-wide productivity growth after 1995 rose again—coming close to its golden-age immediate post–World War II pace—until the Great Recession disruption came at the end of 2007. The wealth created was spread widely and diffused among users, who gained remarkable capabilities to learn, communicate, and be entertained at an astonishingly low price, and the technoprinces of Silicon Valley and those who assisted them. There were economic disruptions: losers. There were half a million women in the United States staffing telephone switchboards in phone companies and at reception desks in 1960. There are less than two thousand today. But, for the most part, and on the domestic level, the coming of information technology to critical mass changed the tasks that had to be done in order to make up the occupation, rather than destroying occupations themselves.

As infotech spread through the economy, the nature of work changed. We East African plains apes have long had strong backs and thighs with which to move heavy objects, nimble fingers to do fine work, mouths and ears with which to communicate, and brains with which to think and manipulate symbols. Starting with the domestication of the horse and continuing with the steam engine, the place of backs and thighs in human work had been greatly reduced by 1870, but there was still plenty of fine manipulation to do. With the coming of electricity and its machinery, human fingers began to be replaced by machines also, but there was still a huge amount of complex design to be done, along with brainstorming and routine accounting and informing, all work to be done by brains, mouths, and ears. Every machine required a microcontroller, and the human brain was by far the best one available. So technology had so far complemented labor rather than substituting for it: more machines and more information technology made human beings more valuable and more productive, rather than less so. But to many, the new work seemed less like the type of thing that a high-status master craftsman might do and more like the tasks required of a servant—either of the customer, or of the increasingly autonomous-looking machine itself.

On the international scale, information technology plus ongoing reglobalization turned, in the 1990s when infotech reached critical mass, into hyperglobalization.[9]

The international economist Richard Baldwin put his finger on the pulse of what he calls the "second unbundling": that of intra-firm communication. With the coming of the internet, it was no longer necessary for a firm's sophisticated industrial division of labor to be geographically concentrated. You no longer had to be able to walk or drive to your supplier's offices and factories to show them how what they had was not quite what you needed. You could, first, in the 1980s, draw a picture and send a fax. Then, in the 1990s, you could send an email. By the late 2000s you could send multimegabyte data files around the globe.

And for those—many—cases in which words-on-paper or words-and-pictures-on-screen were not enough? After 1990, increasingly, you could hop onto an overnight transoceanic nonstop jet. The word is that Apple Computer had fifty first-class seats a day back and forth between San Francisco and China in the months before the coming of the COVID-19 plague. And for those cases in which the limits of the division of labor were not so much the communication of knowledge but the face-to-face, looking-in-the-eye establishment of trust and its limits? The transoceanic airplane flight worked there as well.

Thus, after 1990, manufacturing, which had been increasingly concentrating itself in the global north since 1800, began to spread out away from the global north at tremendous speed. Not just better—but revolutionarily and superlatively better—communications made it possible to spread out what had been regional concentrations of firms into globe-spanning value chains. The extraordinary wage gaps that a century of economic divergence had created between global north and global south made all of this immensely profitable. In the space of a generation, with the spreading-out of production into globe-spanning value-chain networks, much of global manufacturing became both high tech and low wage.

As Baldwin put it, the logic of global production after 1990 was increasingly driven by the "smile curve": low in the middle, high at the beginning and the end. Great value was earned at the beginning by providing raw materials and resources and, more important, *industrial design*. Little value was added in the middle by increasingly routinized manufacturing and assembly. And great value was added at the end by marketing, branding, and distribution—providing information (and misinformation) to consumers about what they might want from the enormous variety of types and qualities of goods that could be churned out from the expanding capacity of factories. And it was, again, a quilt. Very good things happened in selected places. Other places, nearby in culture, political allegiances, and attitudes, got left behind—either their industries that they drew on for relatively high-value and high-income niches in the world's division of good things packed up and moved away, or they never arrived.

Although I have said that this "second unbundling" process transferred manufacturing to the global south, that is not quite right. High-tech global manufacturing went to Korea, so much so that Korea is now a full member of the global north, alongside Japan, as well as Taiwan. It went, above all, to parts of China—but specifically to the growth-pole megacities of the Pearl River Delta, Shanghai, and Beijing, and secondarily to the coasts, but not to the interior. It also went to India—but overwhelmingly to Maharashtra and Karnataka, not to Uttar Pradesh. It went to Indonesia, Thailand, and Malaysia, and is now going to Vietnam. It went to Poland, next door to the manufacturing powerhouse of Germany, whose firms found enormous benefits in spreading out their value chains to make use of the low-wage labor found next door. It went to Mexico, but much less so than those of us who had high hopes for the North American Free Trade Agreement (NAFTA) in the early 1990s expected. Elsewhere? By and large, not. It is a quilt. The opportunity to grasp a substantial place in global value-chain production networks opened only to a few in the global south. Firms had to invite local producers to join their value networks. And while knowledge can be broadcast via the internet, trust still requires face-to-face interaction. It may have been the transoceanic nonstop jet flight and the international hotel chains that were the key link in this second unbundling.

The ongoing contests over who would benefit and how much produced enormous gains for the world. More than 80 percent of the world's population lived on less than US$2 per day in 1870. That fraction was down to 72 percent by 1914, 64 percent by 1950, and 40 percent by 1984. That extreme fraction was down to 9 percent by 2010—in large part because of the spillovers from hyperglobalization.

But half the world's population still lived on less than US$6 per day. It was not the case that the whole world was flat. Lack the necessary infrastructure for containers, transport vehicles, and forklifts, and you were still far away from the global trading system that carried high-end German manufactured washing machines from Westphalian factories to California warehouses for just a penny a pound, and far from the global trade network. If your electricity is unreliable, so that you can't count on being able to pump diesel into a truck tractor; if the volume of your production is too small to fill two thousand cubic feet of space; if the money to fix your roads was embezzled; if your courts function so badly that few outsiders are confident that what you say is theirs really is theirs; if nobody has yet noticed what your workers can produce; if your entrepreneurs cannot build organizations at container-scale without attracting politically well-connected extortionists—then you are not attached to the network. Attaching to the global trade network is an immense opportunity, but it requires that everything, or nearly everything—infrastructure, scale, public administration, governance, and foreign knowledge of your production capabilities—be working just right. And to fully participate in hyperglobalization, a region needs the international airline connections and the hotels required by the firms that orchestrate globally distributed value chains to incorporate them.

Still, by 2010 the world's deployed technological capability stood at more than twenty times what it had been in 1870, and more than twice what it had been in 1975. Yes, the population explosion had continued—the world was on a track that could lead to a stable population of between nine and ten billion after 2050—but in many places the forces slowing population growth were not yet that visible. And, yes, the population explosion meant that resources were scarce: thus average productivity was not twenty but nine times what it had been in 1870. And, yes, the creation had been accompanied by a lot of creative destruction, and many people felt that the market had taken away from them, or that it had not given them their fair share, while giving an overabundance, in undeserved measure, to others.

THIS LAST, ESPECIALLY. WHILE hyperglobalization may have meant the arrival of much manufacturing production in parts of the global south, it also meant the departure of a large share of manufacturing production from the global north. This did not mean that manufacturing production in the global north fell—with total production increasing, a smaller share of the total was still a larger absolute amount. It did mean that the share of jobs in manufacturing in the global north declined—relatively slowly at first, but more precipitously as the end of the twentieth century neared.

In the decades after 1970, it was primarily the so-called less-skilled manufacturing jobs that decreased as a share of employment in the global north. Along with this shrinkage, general demand for lesser-skilled workers—well proxied as those without college educations—also decreased. This drop in demand manifested differently in different parts of the global north. In Western Europe, it showed up as a rise in unemployment (especially among men), while in the United States it manifested as falling real wages for "lesser-skilled" workers (again, especially men).

Both the left and the right reacted to these developments by claiming they were primarily the result of hyperglobalization—especially increasing imports from developing economies. And yet that could not have been the case. Consider, for example, the United States over the years from 1970 to 1990, when the argument that imports were costing Americans good jobs first became influential. Over the course of those two decades, imports increased from about 6 percent of GDP to 12 percent. But the relative average wage of a country selling imports to the United States rose from 60 percent to 80 percent of the US level. Each typical import, therefore, came from a country where the relative income gap was only half as large, and so the pressure put on America by the fact that imports came from countries with lower wages remained about the same.

Individual regions' employment levels were decimated by competition from elsewhere, yes. But that had always been the case since 1870, and before—it was the creative destruction of the growing market economy at work. Those in the crosshairs of "the market taketh away" regarded this instability as a violation of their Polanyian rights. But for losers there were gainers, and—at least before 1980—this did not bring about any pronounced class skew within the global north.

Consider the career of my grandfather, William Walcott Lord, who was born in New England early in the twentieth century. When the Lord Brothers Leather Company, in Brockton, Massachusetts, faced imminent bankruptcy during the Great Depression in 1933, he and his brothers relocated to South Paris, Maine, where wages were lower. The Brockton workers were out of a job and had few prospects for finding a new one, given the widespread destruction of relatively high-paying blue-collar factory jobs across southern New England. But in the aggregate statistics, their loss was offset by a bonanza for the rural workers of South Paris, who went from slaving away in near-subsistence agriculture to holding seemingly steady jobs in a shoe factory (until that shoe factory became uneconomic to run in 1946, with competition from the Carolinas and the end of the World War II boom).

We tend to think of the post–World War II period as a time of relative stability, but in fact large numbers of manufacturing and construction jobs were churning in this way—not disappearing, but moving en masse from one region to another. In 1943, 38 percent of the US nonfarm labor force was in manufacturing, owing to high demand for bombs and tanks at the time. After the war, that number decreased to around 30 percent. Had the United States been a normal postwar industrial powerhouse like Germany or Japan, technological innovation would have continued to bring it down over the course of 1950–1990 to around 17 percent as of 1990. But Ronald Reagan's decision to run big budget deficits and turn the United States from a country that saved more than it invested to one that invested more than it saved led it to decline even further, down to 13 percent as of 1990.

Then, in the final part of the long twentieth century, from 1990 to 2010, the relative wage of the country from which the average nonoil import came to the United States fell sharply. This was driven largely by China, which was contributing an ever-larger share of manufactured imports even as its wages remained extremely low. Yet the pace of decline in US manufacturing employment did not accelerate. And the share of jobs that were regarded as suitable for blue-collar men—in manufacturing, construction, distribution, and transportation—held steady. American consumers bought Chinese manufactures, and an assembly-line job that had been in Dayton, Ohio, moved to Shenzhen. But there were distribution jobs moving the goods from Long Beach to their final destination. And dollars earned by Chinese manufacturers were recycled through China's financial system and invested in the United States, where they funded housing construction. Blue-collar manufacturing assembly-line jobs shrank in relative numbers. Blue-collar distribution and blue-collar construction jobs rose in relative numbers.

Meanwhile, rapidly increasing manufacturing productivity and incompetent macroeconomic management drove the blue-collar job share down even further. Hyperglobalization's principal effect was to cause not a decline in blue-collar jobs but a roll of the wheel from one type of blue-collar job to another—from assembly-line production to truck-driving and pallet-moving distribution, plus, for a while, construction. And yet it was hyperglobalization that entered the public sphere as the principal cause of blue-collar economic distress in the world's richest economies.

Why is this?

Harvard University economist Dani Rodrik has observed that as trade barriers decline, the benefits of increased trade diminish: that is, more and more trade is required to generate a smaller and smaller reward for participants. The volume of trade thus becomes very large relative to the net gains—and as jobs move at a faster pace, even if they're being replaced, there's still a greater number of people caught up in the churn. It's not hard to see why they might blame globalization for their plight. Moreover, some demographic groups have been particularly susceptible. The shift in US employment from assembly-line manufacturing to construction, services, and caretaking had very little impact on the overall distribution of income. But it did have a large effect on the distribution by gender: the jobs closing down were overwhelmingly male jobs, and those opening up were not. Moreover, the jobs that were closing down—whether by trade, technology, regional shift, or otherwise—were those that had historically been good paths to upward mobility for those with less education, paths from which minorities, especially Blacks, had been excluded by segregation before. To those groups whose jobs were closing down or who were seeing gates slam shut for paths that previous generations had used for upward mobility, it's no wonder that globalization seemed like a plausible explanation for their misfortune.[10]

Furthermore, China's economic rise coincided with a period when the United States and other industrialized countries were struggling to reach full employment. Successful economic readjustments do not happen when bankruptcies force labor and capital out of low-productivity, low-demand industries, but rather when booms pull labor and capital into high-productivity, high-demand industries. That the "China shock" hit a shaky economy made it much more likely that it would be substantially destructive.

So if hyperglobalization has not impoverished the workers of major industrial economies, what has it done? The question can be sharpened by thinking back to the pre–World War I Belle Époque. In pre–World War I Britain, industry after industry saw its share of exports decline as competition from German and American producers picked up. My wheat-farming great grandparents in Illinois, whose prices hinged on European demand for grain, would have been astonished to have been told that they were not part of an integrated economy.

So what is the difference? Are financial flows stronger or more important today? Probably not. Is trade stronger and more important? Maybe: world trade as a share of world product is a bit larger. But the net embodied factor content of trade as a share of world product appears smaller, and that is presumably what matters most for trade's effect on, say, unskilled workers' wages. Trade is just swapping: what you had produced before at home you now import, and you pay for it by producing something else. Trade affects wages because that shift in production from "what you had produced before" to the "something else" changes the supply-and-demand balance for different kinds of workers with different skills. But if the workers who had produced the "what . . . before" have the same skills as the workers who now produce the "something else," it is hard to see where a big effect on average wages could come from.

Has international labor migration become a more important factor? Certainly not: between 1850 and 1920, one in every ten people in the world moved from one continent to another. Post–World War II, post-1973, or even post-1990 world population flows are a far smaller share of world population than in the old days.

So what is different? Why did "globalization" become such a powerful red cape to elicit rage at the end of the long twentieth century?

One possibility that I favor: back before the Belle Époque, what you could transfer across national boundaries was pretty much limited to commodities and securities. You could really only transfer something if you could pack it in a crate or an envelope and send it across the sea (or over the telegraph lines). International transactions that required more in the form of cross-border linkages were very hard to accomplish. Think of the Ford Motor Company's early post–World War I attempts to transfer its assembly-line productivity to Britain; of British and Japanese attempts to use Lancashire-manufactured textile machinery to achieve high productivity in factories in India or China; or of the frantic attempts of British investors—who had never imagined how easily Jay Gould would be able to buy the courts of New York—to extract bond coupons and dividends from the Erie Railroad that their debenture and share certificates said they "owned." Goods and payments flowed across borders. Control was exercised within countries by countries' own nationals.

But in hyperglobalization, the breadth of cross-national links, especially people in other countries controlling what goes on in yours, has vastly increased. Back then you could not effectively exercise corporate control across national borders. Now you can. Back then you could not transfer forms of organization to achieve home-country productivity in foreign production operations. Now you can. Back then you could not integrate design and specification in one country with production in another. Now you can. In this environment, transnational or multinational corporations are going to be a good candidate for someone to blame.

And with the coming of the Great Recession after 2007, there was going to be a great deal of demand for somebody to blame.

17

Great Recession and Anemic Recovery

As of the spring of 2007, the well-thinking, at least in the United States, did not recognize that the long twentieth century of American exceptionalism—indeed, of North Atlantic dominance—was already over.

The heart of the innovation economy, microprocessor designer and manufacturer Intel, was still ticktocking, with the microprocessors at the heart of the information sector doubling in speed and computational power every three years, and with the information-technology sector taking full advantage of that. Measured economy-wide productivity growth over the preceding decade was close to its golden-age post–World War II pace.[1] Inflation high enough and recessions deep enough to be major disturbances had last been seen twenty-five years before: this was the "Great Moderation" of the business cycle.[2] Plus the neoliberal turn appeared to have delivered benefits in the global south: its growth had been the fastest ever.

Yes, there had been a generation of rapidly growing income and wealth inequality. But voters did not seem to care much. Tax cuts, the lion's share of which went to the rich, were enacted more often than reversed. Center-left parties believed they had to make concessions to the right to be electorally competitive. Right-wing parties by and large did not feel they had to make concessions to the left. Unhappiness with the neoliberal turn was not showing itself in solid, long-lasting majorities for parties that wanted to soften—let alone possibly reverse—at least parts of it. And center-left parties in the North Atlantic remained conflicted: ideas and interests both sang the sirens' song that left-neoliberalism might work, that market mechanisms might be used to attain social democratic ends, and that a reinvigorated economic growth rate would make the political lift to reverse the coming of the Second Gilded Age easier.

The well-thinking should have known better. The deep structural supports were breaking. In 1993, then US congressman Newt Gingrich (R-GA) and press lord Rupert Murdoch had begun the process of constructing, around the globe, via direct-mail, cable television, and eventually internet, an easily grifted right-wing base that would freely open their pocketbooks because they were easily convinced that center-left political adversaries were not just wrong but evil and immoral—running pedophile rings out of pizza parlors.[3] The center-left kept hoping for political detente: its leaders kept saying that they saw not red (right wing) and blue (left wing) but purple.[4] But the right said nope: were they to dial down the urgency, the base's eyeballs would no longer be so glued to their screens for the selling of ads, and their pocketbooks would no longer be so open.

In 2003, the era in which the United States was the trusted leader of the global-north "Western alliance" came to an end. At the end of the 1980s, after the end of the Cold War, the George H.W. Bush administration had reassured the nations of the world that US military supremacy was benign, because the US military would be deployed only in support of an overwhelming majority vote of a country's people, or according to the will of the UN Security Council. The Clinton administration had changed this to "according to the will of the NATO alliance"; and then the George W. Bush administration had changed it to "more or less at random, according to false and misleadingly interpreted intelligence, against countries that do not possess nuclear weapons." Countries took note.

In 2007 the era in which high-tech advances gave measured global-north productivity growth a materially significant boost was at an end. The ticktock ran into a so-far insuperable technological barrier: before 2007, shrink a component to half its size and you could run it twice as fast without generating too much heat to be dissipated; after 2007, this "Dennard scaling" began to break down because of increased current leakages at extremely small sizes.

Moreover, the focus shifted from providing information to capturing attention—and capturing attention in ways that played on human psychological weaknesses and biases. The commodity-economy market had served the interests of the rich and so raised their utility, a goal that at least a utilitarian philosopher could approve. The attention-economy market threatened simply to grab their attention in ways that might or might not raise even their utility.

Plus, there had been a sequence of financial crises—Mexico in 1994, East Asia in 1997–1998, Argentina in 1998–2002—that had not been handled well, either in the run-up or the workout. Japan had been mired in, if not depression, at least stagnation, with inadequate total spending for fifteen years. Yet among policy makers the dominant feeling was that financial regulation should not be tightened to guard against overleverage, and against bubbles that might threaten to cause crisis and depression, but rather loosened. The Clinton administration had refused to regulate derivative markets when they were small, on the grounds that business-model and asset-type experimentation was needed in finance, in order to figure out ways to make investors as a group more comfortable with their risk-bearing role.

When derivative markets became large and incomprehensible in the 2000s, the George W. Bush administration doubled down on deregulation. And the Federal Reserve—with the honorable exception of the wise Board of Governors member Ned Gramlich—agreed. The Fed, after all, had stopped any serious depression from happening after the stock market crash of 1987, after the S&L overleverage crash of 1990, and after the Mexican financial crisis of 1994, the East Asian crisis of 1997, the Russian state and Long-Term Capital Management hedge-fund bankruptcies of 1998, the dot-com crash of 2000, and the 2001 terrorist attacks.

Surely all this lent confidence that the Federal Reserve could handle whatever shocks the finance sector could throw at it. In a world that still had a very large gap between average returns on safe and risky assets, was it not worthwhile to encourage financial experimentation, to explore what mechanisms might induce more risk-bearing on the part of investors, even if it led to some cowboy-finance excesses?[5]

"It is only when the tide goes out," long-term investor Warren Buffett always likes to say, "that you discover who has been swimming naked."[6] Central banks' confidence that they could manage whatever problems arose, and center-right governments' enthusiasm for financial nonregulation, meant that a relatively small shock to the global financial system came appallingly close to delivering a repeat of the Great Depression in the years after 2007, and did deliver a lost half decade as far as global north economic progress was concerned.

By 2007, very few of the great and good in the global north expected any serious risk of a major financial crisis and threatening depression. The last such *in the global north* had been in the Great Depression itself. Since the 1930s, the memory of the financial losses had kept financiers and investors from borrowing and leveraging on a scale that would make systems vulnerable to a chain of bankruptcies—and thus to a mass panic followed by a rush to sell at fire-sale prices all the financial assets suddenly deemed risky. Not until those who remembered, or whose immediate mentors had remembered, the Great Depression had retired would that leash on the financial system be slipped.

As a result, economic crises had in fact been very rare in the global north in the years after World War II. Governments that prioritized full employment kept recessions modest to stave off the losses that might trigger the initial bankruptcies that would potentially set off such a downward spiral. One of the two substantial postwar recessions in the global north, in 1974–1975, was caused by war, a tumultuous Middle East, and disruptions in the oil market. The second substantial global-north recession, from 1979 to 1982, was deliberately self-inflicted: the price paid for Volcker's Fed breaking the inflationary spiral of prices that had arisen in the 1970s.

Yes, Western Europe had a stubbornly high rate of unemployment for decades after 1982, but in the judgment of the neoliberal consensus, it was because Western Europe was still too social democratic for the market system to work properly.[7] And, yes, Japan fell into a permanent deflationary crisis after 1990, but the consensus had long been that Japan was a special case, that it was a self-inflicted problem, and that more general lessons should not be drawn from it.[8] Both within the US government and among the public, confidence remained that the neoliberal turn had been the right call, that the foundations of prosperity were sound, and that risks were low and could be easily managed. And as of 2007 there was no inflation, no war in the Middle East of large-enough scale to trigger any prolonged supply shortage. In any event the dominance of Middle Eastern oil in the energy sector of the economy had been greatly attenuated.

There were Cassandras. In 2005, at the US Federal Reserve system's annual conference in Wyoming, held in the shadow of the Grand Tetons, economist and future Reserve Bank of India governor Raghuram Rajan presented a paper warning not so much of a chain-of-bankruptcies crisis and a potential depression as of "uncertainty" in the sense of University of Chicago economist Frank Knight.[9] The financial system had grown so opaque that nobody knew what the systemic risks were, and nobody could even calculate reasonable probabilities. Everyone commenting on Rajan's paper said they had enjoyed reading it. Almost everyone (there was one exception, economist and former Fed vice chair Alan Blinder) also subjected Rajan to "unremitting attack." Rajan, they said, was being Chicken Little. Things were at least as robust and as sound as ever before. Not only was there no need to worry, Rajan's worrying was to be lamented.

They were, of course, grotesquely wrong. The emergence and rapid growth of financial derivatives meant that nobody could now tell where any losses that flowed into the financial system would ultimately come to rest. That meant that, should a crisis come, everyone would have to regard all their counterparties with great suspicion, as institutions that might be insolvent and might not pay. It was the equivalent of painting the windshield of a car black. And so the world economy drove into a wall, with those at the wheel only belatedly hoping the air bags would deploy and prove adequate.

Axel Weber, who had been at the helm of Germany's central bank, the Deutsche Bundesbank, in the mid-2000s, told a rueful story in 2013.[10] There was a bank, the Deutsche Bank, that had for nearly 150 years been one of the world's largest commercial banks, with a wide scope of business interests. Since "Deutsche Bundesbank" sounded like "Deutsche Bank," he wound up by accident on a panel alongside a number of CEOs of large commercial banks. At the panel, they talked about what marvelously profitable things they were doing with derivatives: buying mortgages, bundling them together, chopping up the financial flows from them into pieces they judged risky and pieces they judged safe, and then selling them off—the risky pieces to those investors willing to run risks for higher return, the safe pieces to those willing to sacrifice return for safety. Profit! They reassured the audience: yes, this strategy would work only as long as their financial modeling was good enough to actually determine which tranches of the financial flows were risky and which were safe. But the commercial banks' stockholders should not worry: they sold off *all* of the derivative financial instruments they created.

Then, at the panel, Axel Weber got up and said that as the German central bank was one of their regulators, he could see that while the twenty largest commercial banks were the largest creators and sellers and suppliers of securitization products, they were also the largest buyers. He told them: "As a system [you] have not diversified." Each individual bank was not exposed to the risk that its own financial models were wrong. It had, after all, sold off all of the financial instruments it had created using its models. The risk that the models were wrong thus lay on the purchasers. But some of those—many of those—assets were being purchased by the other major banks. Each of them gave its own models some scrutiny. But each of them did not give the models of the banks whose created securities they were buying any scrutiny, for the assets they were buying were rated AAA.

They were not set up, bureaucratically, to wonder: Are these things we are buying really ultra-high-quality AAA? We know that when we create derivative securities, we play games in order to get them the AAA seal of approval.

The banking industry, Axel Weber said, "was not aware at the time that while its treasury department was reporting that it bought all these [high-yielding] products its credit department was reporting that it had sold off all the risk."[11] Indeed, Bob Rubin—who took over as head of Citigroup in November 2007, just in time to be in charge when all the chickens came home to roost—confessed that month that the previous July was the first time he had ever heard of a feature of Citigroup-created securities, called a "liquidity put," that was going to wind up costing Citigroup perhaps $20 billion.[12]

Now comes the rueful part: Axel Weber said he had viewed this as an issue that was potentially important for bank CEOs and bank stockholders who did not understand how risky banks' portfolios of assets actually were. He did not view it as any of his business as a central banker, however, as a potential source of *systemic* risk, or as a problem that might give rise to a serious depression. It was a reasonable calculation. It is reasonable to suppose that, had the Great Recession been avoided, the total unexpected losses of those holding mortgage-backed derivative securities would have been only $500 billion. In a world economy with $80 trillion in assets, that should not have been a big deal. The dot-com crash of 2000 had carried with it $4 trillion in losses, yet had not brought the financial economy near to a serious crisis. Plus, Weber had shared the great confidence that central banks could handle whatever shocks the financial system might throw at them. Recall that during US Federal Reserve chair Alan Greenspan's eighteen-year tenure (1987–2005), the US financial system avoided a serious depression despite a string of five major financial crises. And behind it all was the confident neoliberal consensus that markets were smarter than governments: that the market had a wisdom and a will, and knew what it was doing.

All this was hubris, overweening self-confidence. And it bred nemesis, or retributive comeuppance. But because the former is heady fun and the latter unpleasant, few have had the patience to linger over the better lessons. After 2009, neoliberal technocrats were unable to explain why they had been so sanguine. The evidence of an impending crisis had been visible. There had been crises in Mexico in 1994–1995, East Asia in 1997–1998, Russia in 1998, and then Brazil, Turkey, and Argentina. All of them knew that a chain-of-bankruptcies crisis might have a catastrophic outcome—that countries hit by financial crisis suffered not only a short-run depression but often a sharp and sometimes longer-run slowdown in growth as well. Global current account imbalances, unusually low interest rates, and bubble-like asset prices—they were there to see.[13] And yet in the wake of the neoliberal turn, financial markets were more lightly regulated than ever. The principal fear was always that an overly intrusive government might hobble the market.

After the crisis, many argued that both the Great Recession and the housing bubble of the mid-2000s that preceded it had been inevitable—or in some sense necessary. "We should have a recession. People who spend their lives pounding nails in Nevada need something else to do," said University of Chicago economist John Cochrane in November 2008.[14] He was but one of many trained professional economists who really should have known better, but who adhered to this Hayekian line: there could not be a big depression unless the economy somehow needed to generate one, and so when they saw a depression coming they looked around for the need. The case seemed very plausible, for it fell into the template of hubris and nemesis. Housing prices had been too high, housing construction had been too rapid, and housing stock had grown to excess. Housing construction needed to be drastically cut back. Workers in the construction sector would be put out of work, but they would then also have an incentive to find other jobs in sectors where their work would be socially useful.

In point of fact, Cochrane was 100 percent wrong. By November 2008 there was no sense in which construction employment "needed" to fall. It had managed to make its adjustment from its boom-bubble 2005 high back to normal and even subnormal levels in 2006 and 2007 without a recession. By November 2008, employment in construction nationwide—and in Nevada—was well below its normal and average share of the US workforce. Rather than having to be pushed into unemployment, adjustment had already taken place. It had taken place via workers being pulled into export and investment manufacturing—without a recession.

You simply do not need a recession for structural adjustment to take place. Indeed, it is hard to see how pushing people out of low-productivity occupations into the zero productivity of unemployment is a constructive "adjustment" when the alternative of having high demand to pull them out of low- and into high-productivity occupations is available.

But the attraction of "the market giveth, the market taketh away; blessed be the name of the market" is very strong. Economies do need, sometimes, structural adjustment to rebalance workers to where future demand will be. There are, sometimes, big depressions. Therefore, said Hayek and Schumpeter—and a host of others as well, from Andrew Mellon and Herbert Hoover and John Cochrane and Eugene Fama to even Karl Marx—big depressions are this adjustment.

The story was very tempting. And telling the story that way pushed blame back from those in charge of the world economy from 2005 on to other, earlier policy makers no longer on the scene. So they pushed the chain of argument backward: Why was the housing stock too high? Because construction had been too rapid. Why was construction too rapid? Because housing prices were too high. Why were prices too high? Because of too-low interest rates and too-available financing. Why were interest rates so low and financing so readily available? That question had several different answers.

After the dot-com bubble burst in 2000, investors were left with fewer productive places in which to put their savings. At the same time, the industrializing countries of Asia were running large trade surpluses with the North Atlantic and accumulating large stockpiles of cash, with which they hoped to buy assets (primarily bonds) in North Atlantic economies (primarily the United States). For China, especially, this became a development strategy: maintain full employment in Shanghai by (indirectly) lending America's consumers the renminbi they need to keep their purchases up. The result was what future Federal Reserve chair

Ben Bernanke called a "global savings glut," or an excess demand for savings vehicles worldwide.[15]

This glut threatened to turn the small global economic downturn of 2000–2002 into a big downturn. To fend that off, the number of bonds being issued by businesses needed to be ramped up to satisfy the worldwide demand for savings vehicles. Globally, central banks responded to the savings glut by flooding the world with liquidity—buying bonds for cash and promising to continue such easy money policies in the future. The intent was to lower interest rates and therefore the cost of capital to firms, thereby motivating firms to scale up their operations and build future capacity. To some degree this worked: corporate investment did rise. But it had unintended and severe consequences: lower interest rates generated a mortgage and a financial engineering boom, which generated a housing boom, which returned the United States and the other global-north economies to full employment.[16]

Home prices, however, rose much more than they should have, given how low mortgage rates were. To understand why, we need to understand the drastic changes made to mortgage financing and financial engineering during the 2000s. By now the litany is familiar: the old model of banking, in which banks held on to the loans they made, was replaced by the practice of originate and distribute. Mortgage originators—firms that in many cases had no traditional banking business—made loans to buy houses, then quickly sold those loans off to other firms. These firms then repackaged the loans by pooling them and selling shares of these pools. Rating agencies were then willing to bestow their seal of approval, the AAA rating, on the more senior of these securities, those that had first claim on interest and principal repayment.

In the United States, housing prices would ultimately shoot up by 75 percent between 1997 and 2005, but the bubble wasn't limited to the States. Throughout the North Atlantic region, real estate prices soared, more than doubling in Britain and nearly doubling in Spain. Everyone ignored the risks, and the bubble continued to inflate. And when the bust came, much of that claimed-AAA paper turned out to be worth less than twenty-five cents on the dollar.

Everyone agreed that there were lessons to be learned in all of this, but specifying exactly what those lessons were required identifying the correct underlying problems—and there was far less agreement about that.

For some, the problem was overregulation: the Federal Reserve and other government agencies had been forcing banks to lend to financially unsound and unworthy—read, minority—buyers because of things like the Community Reinvestment Act. It was impious interference with the market, the last ebbing remnants of social democracy in government interfering to give lazy and unproductive minorities *good things they did not deserve*, that had broken the system and caused the catastrophe. Except there was never a shred of evidence supporting this argument. But that did not matter for its advocates: they had faith that the market could not fail unless it was perverted by social democracy, and faith is assurance and certainty about things that we do not see.

Others, along similar but less racist lines, felt the problem was that the US government simply had no business subsidizing housing lending in the first place. For this there *was* a convincing rationale, but the overall assessment was still faulty. Programs that provided subsidies to mortgage lenders and borrowers, such as the Federal National Mortgage Association (FNMA, or "Fannie Mae"), did drive up prices. But during the 2000s, Fannie Mae played no role in the additional jump in prices, for its price pressure was there at the start and did not grow during the housing boom. The lending that allowed buyers to purchase houses at higher and higher prices was primarily made by private specialized mortgage lenders such as the infamously bankrupt Countrywide, not Fannie Mae or any other government-sponsored enterprise.

Another theory was that the problem was the Federal Reserve's insistence on keeping interest rates so low. The Federal Reserve did reduce the overnight rate on loans between banks, from 6.5 percent per year in 2000 to 1 percent per year in 2003. But the European Central Bank (ECB) reduced interest rates by only half as much as the Federal Reserve did, so, according to this theory, we would expect Europe to have experienced a smaller bubble. Europe's housing bubbles, however, were, if anything, larger than those in the United States. Overlooking this inconvenient fact, many argued that the Federal Reserve should have started raising interest rates in the spring of 2002, a year before the unemployment rate peak of the early 2000s, rather than waiting until the year after. But keeping interest rates 2.5 percentage points below the optimal path for two years only pushed up warranted housing values by 5 percent—much too little to drive any significant amount of overbuilding or any significant part of the spike in housing prices.

A final explanation of what drove the housing bubble was that it was not too much regulation, but too little. Down-payment requirements and the standards by which creditworthy home buyers were matched to homes they could afford were rendered a joke. This was a fair assessment but requires a caveat: it doesn't explain the jump-the-rail moment in 2008. By 2005, establishment concern about financial stability had shifted from America's enormous trade deficit with Asia to its surging property markets, which had unmistakably become a bubble. Could an obviously overheating market be cooled without sending the United States, and its main trading partners around the world, into an economic tailspin?

The answer was that it could be and it was.

Mark this, for it is important: the whole premise that the Great Recession was in some way a necessary adjustment after the housing boom is wrong. Housing prices had begun to fall early in 2005. By the end of 2007, the massive migration of workers into the housing sector had been reversed, and housing construction fell back below its average share of total economic activity. Had Cochrane said there were too many people pounding nails in Nevada in late 2005, he would have been correct—although the claim that a recession was "needed" would still have been false. But by 2008, the claim that there were too many people pounding nails in Nevada was simply and completely false—and obviously so to anyone who even glanced at Bureau of Labor Statistics counts of workers employed in construction. For by early 2008 the US economy had already found other things to occupy all the extra construction workers, and a recession wasn't necessary to accomplish this. In a properly dynamic economy, the reallocation of workers from shrinking to growing sectors takes place because of incentives and need not involve unemployment benefits: workers are happy to leave their current jobs and move into growing sectors if those industries can offer them higher wages.

The idea that the Great Recession was inevitable, or in some sense necessary, or even wise, given the housing boom, fits our narrative expectations of transgression and retribution, of hubris and nemesis. And there was hubris. And there was nemesis. There is something exculpatory to faith in a market that gives, takes, and is blessed either way. What is given and what taken is never the acolytes' fault. And it was for those with the purest faith in a Hayekian market that the Great Recession was declared inevitable, or in some sense necessary, or even wise. For them, the housing boom fit a narrative expectation of transgression and retribution, of hubris and nemesis.

But it did not take that form.

Understanding the form that nemesis took in the global north after 2007 requires patience. The simple, short path of blameless faith in a wiser-than-thou market is insufficient. Understanding requires a reminder of the root causes of high-unemployment recessions and depressions. It is then possible to see why the particular chain-of-bankruptcies type of downturn that was the Great Recession of 2007–2009 came as such a surprise.

Recall what was cutting-edge macroeconomic theory back in 1829, when John Stuart Mill pointed out that a "general glut"— an excess supply of produced commodities and workers, not in one sector but pretty much everywhere in the economy—emerged whenever there was an excess demand for whatever served that economy as *cash*. That is to say, assets that everyone was confident would hold their value and that were "liquid," in the sense that people would be eager to accept them in payment for commodities or to discharge debts.[17]

Cash in an economy is very special because it serves as a means of payment. If you have a demand for anything else, you satisfy that demand by going out and buying more of it. But if you have a demand for cash, you can either sell stuff (for cash, naturally), or you can stop buying stuff. Keep your cash income the same and reduce your cash outflow, and your normal cash inflows will pile up. Your demand for cash will be satisfied. Simple.[18]

This principle is at the root of high-unemployment recessions and depressions. This way of satisfying your demand for cash by buying less works for individuals, but it cannot work for the entire economy. One person's cash inflows are another's cash outflows, after all. When everyone tries to push their cash outflow below their cash inflow, each individual's cash inflow drops along with their outflow. The excess demand for cash remains unsatisfied. All that happens is that the total sum of incomes in the economy amounts to less, and so people buy less stuff and fewer people are employed.

Such an excess demand for cash can happen in three different ways:

The first I call a *monetarist depression*. A good example is the United States during 1982. Paul Volcker's Federal Reserve had sought to reduce inflation by reducing the total flow of spending in the economy. It did so by selling bonds to banks and investors, requiring as payment that banks reduce their balances in their Federal Reserve accounts. This left the banks with less cash than they would have preferred to have in their reserve account balances. In order to build those balances back up, they reduced their spending, which meant giving out fewer loans to businesses. Because of this, fewer businesses opened or expanded—and ultimately, unemployment kissed 11 percent by the time I graduated from college in the summer of 1982.

You can tell when the economy is in a monetarist depression because the interest rates that bonds pay are high. Here's how that happens. When many players in the economy are trying to build up their liquid cash balances by selling bonds, bond prices go down. To induce purchases, the interest rates that bonds pay are high. Consider that from the summer of 1979 to the fall of 1981 the interest rate on the US government's ten-year Treasury bond rose from 8.8 percent per year to 15.8 percent per year. That was the Federal Reserve setting the Volcker disinflation, and its associated monetarist depression, in motion.

The cure for a monetarist depression is straightforward: have the central bank increase the economy's money stock. When Volcker's Federal Reserve decided that spending had fallen enough to bring inflation under control, it bought back bonds for cash. Voilà. The excess demand for cash in the economy evaporated almost overnight, and over 1983–1985 the economy roared back with very rapid growth in production and employment.

A second scenario that triggers excess demand for cash is what I call a *Keynesian depression*. People in general divide their cash outflows into three streams: cash spent on goods and services, cash for paying taxes, and cash for buying investments. One way that people can invest their cash is in business-issued stocks, which raise the money a business uses to fund growth. But suppose businesses get fearful, are depressed, and decide not to issue stock in order to expand their operations. Then the price of the other financial investment vehicles the economy is creating will go up, and the rate of profit offered on them will go down—they will become very much like cash, save that they will also be risky should the company that backs them dry up and blow away.

In such circumstances, people will decide that they would rather hold extra cash instead of expensive and dubious investment vehicles. These decisions, in turn, will lead to an economy-wide excess demand for cash. With it comes the "general glut" of commodities, idle factories, and the high unemployment of a depression. The depressed state of the world economy during the 2020–2022 coronavirus pandemic—not the initial panic shutdown, but later—was such a Keynesian depression. People were willing to pay for financial investment vehicles, and so bond and stock prices were high and bond yields and stock earnings yields were low. But businesses were waiting for the pandemic to pass before they would begin to expand again. And so people demanded excess cash to hold as a substitute for normal financial investment vehicles.

The central bank cannot cure a Keynesian depression by increasing the money stock. The way the central bank increases the money stock is by buying bonds for cash. But in so doing, it gives firms cash to hold while taking other financial investment vehicles off of the private sector's balance sheet. The one neutralizes the other: the shortage of total financial investment vehicles—cash held plus others—remains. The cure for a Keynesian depression is for the government to either incentivize businesses to expand, and in so doing create the financial investment vehicles the economy lacks, or sell its own bonds and then return the cash to the private sector by spending it, to satisfy the demand for financial investment vehicles. The latter translates into a larger-than-usual deficit, for the government then needs to spend the cash it has earned in order to keep it circulating in the economy.

But what happened over 2007–2009 was neither a monetarist depression nor a Keynesian depression. It was, rather, what I call a *Minskyite depression*, after St. Louis economist Hyman Minsky.[19]

In this type of downturn, what there is a shortage of—what there is an excess demand for—is *safe stores of value*: assets that are either cash or can be quickly turned into cash at little or no discount to their face value. Safe is the operative word.[20] Over 2007–2009, the world was not short of means-of-payment cash or financial investment vehicles. You could buy risky savings vehicles—private debt that was not AAA rated, and the stocks of companies that faced some market and growth risk—for an absolute song. And central banks, in their attempts to stem the onrushing downturn, worked hard to make the world absolutely awash in cash. But over 2007–2009 a great many "safe" assets that had been issued by investment banks as AAA rated turned out not to be so safe. And people scrambled to sell them and shift their portfolios into cash instead.

Where did this safe-asset shortage come from? It emerged in the second half of 2007. Too many financiers had bet too heavily on a continued boom in housing prices, leveraging themselves precariously. Thus the real estate bust created a crisis of confidence in much of the world's financial system and eventually paralyzed crucial parts of it. Signs of strain had already begun appearing in the late summer of 2007. The Federal Reserve reacted by standing ready to provide liquidity at normal market rates to institutions that found themselves momentarily embarrassed. But it showed little willingness to take broader action—to substantially ease monetary conditions or begin acting as a lender of last resort. It feared encouraging more imprudent lending in the future.

At the end of 2007, Federal Reserve vice chair Donald Kohn was nervous. "We should not hold the economy hostage to teach a small segment of the population a lesson," he warned.[21] But his view was a minority one back then, and so it remained until it was too late. And that is why the Great Recession of 2007–2009 came as such a surprise.

In March 2008 I myself had reasoned that the problem was manageable.[22] Perhaps five million houses had been built in the desert between Los Angeles and Albuquerque that should never have been built. On average, each carried $100,000 in mortgage debt that would never be paid and that somebody would have to eat. So, I figured, there was a $500 billion financial loss from the housing crash that holders of financial securities would have to bear, one way or another. But, the dot-com crash involved an even greater financial loss—and the dot-com crash only pushed unemployment up by about 1.5 percent. The housing crisis, I concluded, was unlikely to have large effects on the economy. But the market reasoned differently.

As a large swath of those with money who move financial markets saw things, there were $500 billion in known losses somewhere. But maybe that was just the tip of an iceberg. Maybe the trained professionals who had told us that owning tranches of millions of houses between Los Angeles and Albuquerque was safe had lied, or were profoundly misinformed. The desire on the part of investors to dump risky assets—at any price—and buy safer ones—at any price—became an imperative.

The desire on the part of the Fed and the Treasury to prevent Wall Street from profiting from the crisis drove their decisions in September 2008. Previously, equity shareholders had been severely punished when their firms were judged too big to fail—the shareholders of Bear Stearns, AIG, Fannie Mae, and Freddie Mac essentially had all their wealth confiscated. But this was not true of bondholders and counterparties, who were paid in full.

The Fed and Treasury feared that a bad lesson was being taught. To unteach that lesson required, at some point, allowing a bank to fail. Hubris, after all, needed its comeuppance. And so they decided to let the Lehman Brothers investment bank collapse in an uncontrolled bankruptcy without oversight, supervision, or guarantees. In retrospect, this was the major mistake.

All hell broke loose. Investors dumped assets they had thought were safe only to discover an extremely limited supply of truly safe assets. Panic selling set in as investors urgently sought to avoid being the ones left holding on to unsellable risky assets. The result was that financial losses were magnified by a factor of forty: what would have been a $500 billion destruction of wealth became the destruction of somewhere between $60 trillion and $80 trillion. During the winter of 2008–2009, borrowing costs for almost everyone except governments soared, and the world economy looked dangerously close to a complete meltdown.

How do you cure such a safe-asset shortage?

What will not work is the central bank expanding the money supply via its so-called open-market operations—in other words, buying bonds for cash. Yes, this provides cash, a safe asset, but only by taking another safe asset, short-term government bonds, off the table. The result is a continued shortage of safe assets. What will also not work is incentivizing businesses to expand by issuing stock. There is no shortage of risky assets to hold, just a shortage of safe assets. Stocks don't meet the need.

There are, however, a number of things that can be done. In fact, a standard playbook has been in existence ever since the British journalist Walter Bagehot, the editor of *The Economist*, wrote his book about financial crises, *Lombard Street*, in the 1870s. Call it the Bagehot-Minsky playbook.[23] In a Minskyite depression, such as the one that followed the collapse of Lehman Brothers, a government's best bet is to immediately combat the shortage of safe assets by *lending freely* on collateral that is *good in normal times*, but to do so at a *penalty rate*. The "lending freely" part means to create enough safe assets that they are no longer in short supply. The "good in normal times" part means to try to distinguish institutions that are in trouble and face bankruptcy only because of the financial crisis from institutions that are permanently insolvent and need to be put into receivership. The "penalty rate" part means to discourage opportunistic financiers from exploiting the situation.

A number of the things that could be done were tried over 2007–2009. Central banks took risk off of the private sector's balance sheet and put it onto their own by buying up long-term risky assets for cash, and so increasing the supply of safe assets. This *quantitative easing* was a good idea, but central banks suffered from sticker shock. They balked at spending what was needed, and so this effort was only marginally effective. Governments also increased the supply of safe assets by running bigger deficits, issuing bonds, and using the resulting purchasing power to put people to work directly. This strategy was generally effective, but worked only in cases where the government's debts were perceived as safe assets.

Governments also offered loan guarantees and asset swaps, transforming unsafe savings vehicles into safe ones—by far the cheapest and most effective method of combatting a Minskyite depression. However, to do this effectively, governments needed expertise in pricing these guarantees and swaps. Too high, and no one would buy them and the economy would crash. Too low, and financiers would take the government—and the public—to the cleaners. Moreover, such loan guarantees and asset swaps treat unequals equally: those who have been financially imprudent and bear some responsibility for the crisis get bailed out along with those whose only fault was getting caught in the unexpected financial whirlwind.

The safest play for governments would have been to boost purchases and let the short-run deficit go where it needed to go to preserve full employment. That's what China did, starting its massive fiscal-stimulus and job-creation policies in the middle of 2008. Only China's government grasped that the key task was to do whatever it took to keep the flow of spending through the economy high enough to avoid mass unemployment. And only China avoided the Great Recession. The proof? China continued to grow. The United States and Europe did not.

The most imprudent play was to assume that things would not get worse. Yet that is what the governments of the global north and their central banks did. Spending and employment collapsed.

The US unemployment rate would ultimately rise to a peak of 10 percent in late 2009, and would not even begin to recover until 2012. In fact, US unemployment could have risen much higher. According to the economists Alan Blinder and Mark Zandi, if the government had followed the cold-turkey policies advocated by Republicans during the early years of the Obama administration, unemployment would have been driven to 16 percent, about halfway between the actual peak and the peak unemployment rate of the Great Depression.[24]

In September 2008, I had been confident that the world's governments were capable of keeping the world economy out of a deep and long depression. By March 2009 it was clear that I had been wrong and that they had failed. The problem was not that economists who were reality based were unsure about what to do and how to apply the Bagehot-Minsky playbook—the problem was that assembling the political coalition to do it was judged impossible. Put differently, governments and politicians found there was no political will to dole out nemesis in useful measure to hubris in ways that would provide a net benefit to the recovering economy. And so many governments, instead of taking drastic and immediate action, decided simply to wait and see what would happen.

In Blinder and Zandi's judgment—and mine—the alphabet soup of interventions by the Federal Reserve to guarantee loans, expand the money supply, and take risk off of the private sector's balance sheet was quite effective. The TARP and the TALF and the HAMP and the Federal Reserve's quantitative-easing policies and extra deficit spending via the ARRA—and all the other government interventions—together accomplished 6 of the 10 percentage-point reduction-in-unemployment-relative-to-where-it-would-otherwise-have-been job that the government should have carried out when the crisis hit.[25] That is three-fifths of the job—and a glass three-fifths full is not empty. On the other hand, the glass remained two-fifths empty. And forecasts in 2011 that the restoration of full employment would take a long time turned out to be accurate. There was no "bounce back" rapid recovery. Indeed, for the first four years of the recovery, workers' ability to find jobs barely improved.

Recall the Bagehot-Minsky playbook: *lend freely* at a *penalty rate* on collateral that is *good in normal times*. Policy makers did rush in. Financial institutions were bailed out at taxpayer expense. Guarantees were extended to restore confidence—Ireland, for example, took the extraordinary step of guaranteeing all Irish bank debt. Central banks and government agencies stepped in as "lenders of last resort," providing credit where banks could or would not. These measures were successful in stemming the panic—by the early summer of 2009, most measures of financial stress had subsided to more or less normal levels, and the world economy ended its headlong plunge. But that was just the "lend freely" part. Governments neglected to implement the "good in normal times" part of the Bagehot-Minsky playbook. Not even too-big-to-fail Citigroup was put into receivership. Worse still, governments completely ignored the "penalty rate" part: bankers and investors, even or perhaps especially those whose actions had created the systemic risks that caused the crisis, profited handsomely.

Financial bailouts are always unfair because they reward those who made bad bets on risky assets. But the alternative would be a policy that destroys the web of finance—and thus a policy that shuts down dynamism in the real economy. A crash in prices of risky financial assets sends a message: shut down risky production activities and don't undertake any new activities that might be risky. That is a recipe for a deep, prolonged depression. The political problems that spring from financial bailouts can be finessed. The fallout from a major depression cannot. Thus, financial rescue operations that benefit even the unworthy can be accepted if they are seen as benefiting all. In 2007–2009, for instance, teaching a few thousand feckless financiers not to overspeculate was ultimately far less important than securing the jobs of millions of Americans and tens of millions around the globe.

When vice presidential candidate Jack Kemp attacked Vice President Al Gore in 1996 for the Clinton administration's decision to bail out Mexico's feckless government during the 1994–1995 financial crisis, Gore responded that they had charged Mexico a penalty rate and so the United States had made $1.5 billion on the deal.[26] In 1997–1998, Clinton's treasury secretary, Robert Rubin, and IMF managing director Michel Camdessus were attacked for committing public money to bail out New York banks that had loaned to feckless East Asian countries. They responded that they had "bailed in" the banks, rather than bailing them out, by requiring them to cough up additional money to support South Korea's economy, and that everyone had benefited massively because a global recession was avoided. In 2009, however, the US government could say none of these things. What was readily apparent, however, was that bankers continued to receive bonuses even as the real economy continued to shed jobs.

Perhaps there was a rationale. Perhaps policy makers recognized that assembling a political coalition in the United States or in Western Europe to do what China was doing—have the government borrow and spend on the scale needed to preserve or promote a rapid return to full employment—was not going to happen. Given that reality, policy makers would have realized that the only way to generate enough spending and investing to drive a rapid recovery was to restore the confidence of businesses and investors. And decapitating banks and deposing bank executives, placing banks into receivership, and confiscating bonuses would do the opposite.

But I think the most likely explanation is that policy makers simply did not understand the situation—nor did they understand the Bagehot-Minsky playbook.

In any event, the situation was on its face outrageous: bankers were getting bailed out while unemployment hit 10 percent and huge numbers of people faced foreclosure. If policy makers had focused more on the "penalty rate" part of the Bagehot-Minsky playbook, they might at least have moderated that perception of unfairness—and potentially built more of a political base for further action. But they did not, and so there was very little public trust in governments to take the steps necessary to spur recovery.

But this is not the only reason the much-touted effort to restore the "confidence" of financiers and investors failed to produce much of a recovery after 2009. The global north's economy was still hamstrung with too much risky debt.

At the macro level, the story of the post-2008 decade is almost always understood as a failure of economic analysis and communication. We economists supposedly failed to convey to politicians and bureaucrats what needed to be done because we hadn't analyzed the situation fully and properly in real time. But many of us did understand.

For example, consider Greece: When the Greek debt crisis erupted in 2010, it seemed to me that the lessons of history were so obvious that the path to a resolution would be straightforward. The logic was clear. Had Greece not been a member of the euro zone, its best option would have been to default, restructure its debt, and depreciate its currency. But because the European Union did not want Greece to exit the euro zone (which would have been a major setback for Europe as a political project), it made sense that it would offer Greece enough aid, debt forgiveness, and assistance with payments to offset any advantages it might gain by exiting the monetary union. But this did not come to pass. Instead, Greece's creditors unexpectedly chose to tighten the screws. As a result, Greece is likely much worse off today than it would have been had it abandoned the euro in 2010. Iceland, which was hit by a financial crisis in 2008, provides the counterfactual. Whereas Greece remained mired in depression, Iceland—not in the euro zone—recovered, and recovered quickly.

In the United States, as well, policy makers lifted their foot off the gas pedal in the early 2010s. Future historians will find least comprehensible the unwillingness of governments at that moment to borrow and spend. Starting in the mid-2000s, there came an era of what the economist Larry Summers has named "secular stagnation": a time of very low interest rates on safe bonds, driven by a shortage of risk-bearing capacity and a hunger for safe assets on the part of insecure private investors.[27] As long as these circumstances held, governments could truly borrow for free. By now most economists agree that in such situations, governments should take advantage and borrow. I always found it hard to believe—and still do—that anybody could or can take exception to this.[28]

And yet, at the start of 2010, in his State of the Union Address, President Barack Obama said that "just as families and companies have had to be cautious about spending, government must tighten its belt as well." And he called for a federal spending freeze, making clear that he would pursue it at all costs, saying, "If I have to enforce this freeze by veto, I will." Watching, my first reaction was that issuing a veto threat against his two chief lieutenants, House Speaker Nancy Pelosi and Senate Majority Leader Harry Reid, was a unique way of building intraparty comity.[29] It was a previously unheard-of way of maintaining a functioning governing coalition. In the space of a moment, it changed the policy discussion from "What should we do?" to "I am the boss!" Here we reached the limits of my mental horizons as a neoliberal, as a technocrat, and as a mainstream neoclassical economist. The global economy was suffering from a *grand mal* seizure of slack demand and high unemployment. We knew the cures. Yet we seemed determined to inflict further suffering on the patient.

Obama's former economic policy staffers say that he was the global north's most rational and best-behaved ruling politician in the first half of the 2010s. And they are right. But it is nevertheless disturbing that Obama's address—delivered when the

US unemployment rate was still 9.7 percent—went so strongly against John Maynard Keynes's 1937 observation that "the boom, not the slump, is the right time for austerity at the Treasury."[30] The arithmetic always seemed clear to me. Starting in 2009, the US government could borrow for thirty years at a real interest rate of 1 percent per year—or less. Given this, an additional $500 billion in infrastructure spending would yield enormous benefits to the government and the country—at no cost. Investors would have effectively been willing to pay the United States to be the custodian of their wealth because they were so desperate to hold safe assets. Yet Obama seemed completely uninterested.

He was not alone. In the summer of 2011, Federal Reserve chair Ben Bernanke offered a rosy assessment: "We expect a moderate recovery to continue and indeed to strengthen," he proclaimed, because "households also have made some progress in repairing their balance sheets—saving more, borrowing less, and reducing their burdens of interest payments and debt." Moreover, deflation in commodity prices would "help increase household purchasing power." And perhaps most promising of all, he continued, "the growth fundamentals of the United States do not appear to have been permanently altered by the shocks of the past four years."[31] But at that very moment state and local budget cutting had slowed America's pace of investment in human capital and infrastructure, bringing the country's long-term growth trajectory down by a third percentage point on top of the two it had already suffered.

After the Great Depression of the 1930s, the vast wave of investment in industrial capacity during World War II made up the shortfall of the lost decade. As a result, the Depression did not cast a shadow on future growth. There was no analogous set of floodlights deployed to erase the shadow that was cast by 2008–2010. On the contrary, the shadow lengthened with each passing day of stalled recovery. And whereas Franklin Roosevelt had inspired confidence that full employment would be rapidly reattained, because reattaining it was the government's highest priority, in the early 2010s the public was rightfully skeptical of the government's commitment to reattaining full employment. The result was a half-lost decade of economic growth in the United States, when the magnitude of the downturn and the sluggishness of the recovery are both taken into account, and in much of Western Europe, a full lost decade.

Contrast this with China, where it was certainly not the case that blessed be the market whatever it happened to do. China in 2007 and after knew not so much that the market was made for man, but that the market was made for the purpose of serving the goals of the Chinese Communist Party. One of those goals was maintaining full employment. And so full employment was maintained. Were "ghost cities" built and lots of people put to work building infrastructure that would decay and degrade before anybody could use it? Yes. Were unstable financial structures constructed that would not be fully accepted by banks without government arm-twisting? Yes. But those costs were trivial relative to the damage avoided by maintaining full employment and growth through what was, elsewhere, the Great Recession. During the Great Recession, China gained from five to ten extra years in its race to catch up to the global north.

We can begin to theorize explanations for such irrationality. Some highly capable and competent economists, such as Carmen M. Reinhart and Kenneth Rogoff, saw the dangers of the financial crisis but greatly exaggerated the risks of public spending to boost employment in its aftermath.[32] Other highly capable and competent economists, including Federal Reserve chair Bernanke, understood the importance of keeping interest rates low but overestimated the effectiveness of additional monetary-policy tools such as quantitative easing.[33] Still others, perhaps less capable and competent, like me, understood that expansionary monetary policies would not be enough but, because we had looked at global imbalances the wrong way, missed the principal source of risk—US financial misregulation—and found ourselves still trying to catch up to the situation in order to give accurate policy advice in real time.[34]

In hindsight, technocrats' errors of judgment and failures of communication seem to me a large part of how events unfolded so disastrously—if we economists had spoken up sooner about what we knew about depressions and their cure, had been more convincing on the issues where we were right, and had been better at recognizing where we were wrong, the situation today might be considerably better. Columbia University historian Adam Tooze has little use for such a group-action contingency narrative; for him, the calamity of the post-2008 decade was a result of deep historical currents. Financial deregulation and tax cuts for the rich became idols for the right—to a greater extent even than they already were.[35] The fallout from the George W. Bush administration's ill-advised war against Iraq effectively squandered America's credibility to lead the North Atlantic through the crisis years. And the Republican Party began to suffer its nervous breakdown, eventually embracing a brutish, race-baiting reality-TV star.

Yet where Tooze sees tides and structures, I see contingency and bad luck. I think back to the Great Depression: to, in Japan, Takahashi Korekiyo's rapid devaluation and reflation; to, in Germany, the economic success of reflation (which was ultimately absolutely catastrophic because it cemented the hold of Adolf Hitler's Nazi regime); and to, in the United States, FDR's New Deal. All had much weaker hands to play than Barack Obama and his administration in the United States and their counterparts in Europe had in 2009. All had much better excuses for not grokking the essentials of the situation. All reacted better.

There is a striking contrast between the two US presidents Roosevelt and Obama that reinforces my confidence in the view that it was contingent luck and choice rather than structural necessity. Obama could see what was coming. Indeed, he warned against it. Back in 2004, when he was still a rising star in the

Democratic Party, Obama had warned that failing to build a "purple America" that supported the working and middle classes would lead to nativism and political breakdown. In the Great Depression, Roosevelt knew what to do to address problems of such magnitude. "The country needs . . . bold persistent experimentation," he said in 1932, at the height of the Great Depression. "It is common sense to take a method and try it; if it fails, admit it frankly and try another. But above all, try something."[36] Obama was unwilling to follow in Roosevelt's footsteps.

Had the Obama administration been more aggressive, would things have been very different? Professional economists could not convince those in power of what needed to be done because those in power were operating in a context of political breakdown and lost American credibility. With policy-making having been subjected to the malign influence of a rising plutocracy, economists calling for "bold persistent experimentation" were swimming against the tide—even though well-founded economic theories justified precisely that course of action.

But then, nobody expected very much from Roosevelt, who in the 1920s was considered a second-class intellect who had jumped up beyond his station because of his family's wealth and his uncle Teddy's reputation.[37]

Fed policy makers still insist that they did the best they could, considering the fiscal headwinds at the time. Obama administration policy makers pat themselves on the back for preventing a second Great Depression and say they did the best they could, given the recalcitrant Republican majority in the House of Representatives that came to power after the 2010 midterms and promptly turned off the spigot of fiscal stimulus. And somehow, these Obama officials fail to mention that their boss had already turned it off with his talk of how "the government must tighten its belt as well."[38]

Right-leaning economists, for their part, still busy themselves arguing that the Obama administration's fiscal policies and Fed

chair Bernanke's monetary policies were dangerously inflationary. If we are to believe them, we should consider ourselves lucky
to have escaped an economically disastrous fate like Zimbabwe's
hyperinflation.[39]

In the 2050s, when economic historians compare the "Great
Recession" that started in 2007 with the Great Depression that
started in 1929, they will surely praise early twenty-first-century
policy makers for keeping the later one from becoming a repeat
of the earlier one. On the other hand, these future historians
will be left profoundly puzzled by our failure to remember the
lessons of 1933. The forceful policies of the New Deal era laid
the foundations for the rapid and equitable growth of the long
postwar boom. In the face of such a precedent, how could we
have failed to see the benefits of a more aggressive stance?

From 1980 on, left-neoliberals had, when they were at the
wheel, made the neoliberal turn, believing that market-incentive-
utilizing policies were often a much better road to social democratic ends than directives and commands and controls from
on high were. Markets, after all—when properly managed to
preserve competition and correct for Pigouvian externalities—
were extraordinarily effective at crowdsourcing solutions, and
so using the brainpower of all humanity as an anthology intelligence. And excessive reliance on command-and-control would
be highly inefficient, and you could not ask voters to be generous to those whom the market economy did not give opportunity unless growth was rapid. From 1980 on, right-neoliberals
had, when they were at the wheel, made the neoliberal turn as
well, believing that the apparent success of social democracy in
rapid growth from 1945–1973 had been borrowed from the
past and from the future, and that only renewed submission to
the logic of the market could produce fast growth again. And
if that free-market growth produced a greatly unequal income
and wealth distribution? Then that was good, because that was
what was deserved.

As of 2007, dogmatic neoliberals could still explain the situation away. Hyperglobalization and neoliberalism looked to have been superior to the previous era of too much state-led development led by antidevelopmental states in the global south. The high income and wealth inequality of the Second Gilded Age could be sold as a feature rather than a bug for those who wished to buy it. The information-technology revolution—and a visible future biotechnology revolution—could be sold as a permanent return to the golden-age growth pace. The Great Moderation of the business cycle—low inflation without periodic shocks of high unemployment—looked to prove the excellence and competence of neoliberal technocrats. And voters were, if not happy, unwilling to provide majorities for politicians with positions far to the left or far to the right of the neoliberal center.

By 2016 it was clear that 2007–2010 had not been a simple backfire, after which forward motion resumed as normal. It was even clear that things had fallen apart even before 2007: it was simply that people had not noticed. The analogy that comes to mind is of the old Warner Bros. "Road Runner" cartoons, in which the Road Runner's hapless and helpless nemesis Wile E. Coyote often runs off of cliffs but remains suspended in midair until he looks down and recognizes his predicament—only then does he plummet into the canyon.

Back at the end of Chapter 2 I noted that US income per capita growth was only 0.6 percent per year over the decade from 2006 to 2016, contrasted with 2.1 percent per year (driven by information technology, albeit unequally distributed) over 1976–2006 and 3.4 percent per year over 1946–1976. In Western Europe the 2006–2016 falloff was worse: 0.6 percent per year in Britain, 0.3 percent per year in France, –0.9 percent per year in Italy, and 1.1 percent per year in Germany.

Whatever you had thought of neoliberalism in 2007, its creation of an intellectual and policy-making climate that produced this massively subpar response to a relatively small macroeconomic shock, that brought on first the Great Recession and then an anemic recovery, weighed very heavily in the negative in the balance. And this poor performance had been purchased at the price of a strengthening and intensification of income and wealth inequality.

People noticed. But this did not produce, among global-north electorates, solid, long-lasting majorities for politicians to the left of left-neoliberalism, who wanted to soften and possibly reverse at least parts of the neoliberal turn. Instead, voters increasingly began looking for somebody to blame, and for some leader who would punish whoever the scapegoats turned out to be. Plus, the United States was no longer leading. The politics of opposition had transformed itself into an agenda where job number one was to make the president of the opposing party a failure. "What are you in America going to do to fix your broken system?" senior Chinese Communist Party cadre and IMF deputy managing director Min Zhu asked me in 2015. I had no answer.

As I noted early in Chapter 15, the time since the beginning of the neoliberal turn overlaps my career, and so memories of my personal engagement alternately sharpen and blur my judgment. I have a hard time believing that I can even approach the historian's ideal of telling the narratives *wie es eigentlich gewesen*, as they essentially came to pass, or viewing things *sine ira et studio*, without anger or bias, seeing and understanding rather than advocating and judging.[40]

The way to bet, however, is that I personally cannot but overestimate the degree to which bad luck and bad choices by powerful and crucial individuals produced the rather sorry state of the global north as of 2010.

I do now think that bad luck and bad choices—hanging chads in ballots in Florida voting machines in 2000, George H.W. Bush giving the astonishingly unqualified-for-the-job George W. Bush his Rolodex and his full support, and what followed that—plus the weaknesses and errors of neoliberalism are what cracked the system from 2000 to 2007. I do now think that things were so badly cracked as of 2007 that the shattering of the system by 2010 was likely, if not inevitable. With skill and luck, could things have been glued back together? In the United States, the Obama administration, the leaders of the Republican Party, and the American people were not up to the job, as 2016 showed. In Western Europe things were worse.

But others see not contingency but necessity. They see not choice but structure in what I call the end of the long twentieth century. They agree that the years after 2000 saw the end of the era in which what we call the global north, and especially the United States, were—in a more good than bad way—the furnaces where the future was being forged.

And I also think that future historians' judgment will probably be in accord with theirs, rather than mine.

CONCLUSION

Are We Still Slouching Towards Utopia?

I n 1870 a major shift took place for humanity. With the coming of the industrial research lab, the modern corporation, and truly cheap ocean and land transport and communication, we went from a world in which economic patterns formed a semistable backdrop of grinding mass poverty to one where the economy was constantly revolutionizing itself, entering into states of increasing prosperity via the discovery, development, and deployment of new technologies. This Schumpeterian process of creative destruction doubled humanity's potential productive power in each generation. And in the years that followed, the foundations and underpinnings of society were repeatedly shaken and fractured. Long centuries like the one from 1870 to 2010 are, obviously, made up of many, many moments. The twentieth century's important moments were set in motion by this creative destruction and the corresponding shaking and fracturing. Here are two moments I see as important. Both come from about the long twentieth century's midpoint:

The first moment occurred in 1930 when John Maynard Keynes gave his speech "Economic Possibilities for Our Grandchildren" (quoted in Chapter 7), in which he concluded that economic problems were not humanity's most "permanent problem," but that instead, once our economic problems were solved, the real difficulty would be "how to use . . . freedom from pressing economic cares . . . to live wisely and agreeably and well." I will address the significance of these comments later in this conclusion.

The second important moment was nearly contemporaneous. It was when Franklin Delano Roosevelt took hold of the US government, broke the gridlock in US politics, and started to experiment with ways to solve the economic problem of the Great Depression.

The day after his inauguration in March 1933, FDR forbade the export of gold and declared a bank holiday. Within four days the House and Senate had convened, and the House unanimously passed Roosevelt's first bill, a banking reform bill called the Emergency Banking Act that arranged for the reopening of solvent banks, as well as the reorganization of other banks, and gave Roosevelt complete control over gold movements. The second bill Roosevelt submitted to Congress also passed immediately. It was the Economy Act, cutting federal spending and bringing the budget closer to balance. The third was the Beer and Wine Revenue Act, a precursor to an end to Prohibition—the repeal of the constitutional amendment banning the sale of alcohol. On March 29 he called on Congress to regulate financial markets. On March 30 Congress established Roosevelt's Civilian Conservation Corps. On April 19 Roosevelt took the United States off of the gold standard. On May 12 Congress passed Roosevelt's Agricultural Adjustment Act. On May 18 Roosevelt signed the Tennessee Valley Authority Act creating the first large government-owned utility corporation in the United States. Also on May 18, he submitted to Congress the centerpiece of his first hundred days: the National Industrial Recovery Act (NIRA). All factions within the newly constituted administration won something in the legislation: Businesses won the ability to collude—

to draft "codes of conduct" that would make it easy to maintain relatively high prices, and to "plan" to match capacity to demand. Socialist-leaning planners won the requirement that the government—through the National Recovery Administration (NRA)—approve the industry-drafted plans. Labor won the right to collective bargaining and the right to have minimum wages and maximum hours incorporated into the industry-level plans. Spenders won some $3.3 billion in public works.

And so the First New Deal entailed a strong "corporatist" program of joint government-industry planning, collusive regulation, and cooperation; strong regulation of commodity prices for the farm sector and other permanent federal benefits; a program of building and operating utilities; huge amounts of other public works spending; meaningful federal regulation of financial markets; insurance for small depositors' bank deposits along with mortgage relief and unemployment relief; a commitment to lowering working hours and raising wages (resulting in the National Labor Relations Act of 1935, or Wagner Act); and a promise to lower tariffs (fulfilled in the Reciprocal Tariff Act of 1935).

The NIRA, plus the devaluation of the dollar, did break the back of expectations of future deflation. The creation of deposit insurance and the reform of the banking system did make savers willing to trust their money to the banks again and began the re-expansion of the money supply. Corporatism and farm subsidies did spread the pain. Taking budget balance off the agenda helped. Promising unemployment and mortgage relief helped. Promising public works spending helped. All these policy moves kept things from getting worse. They certainly made things somewhat better immediately and substantially better soon thereafter.

But aside from devaluation, monetary expansion, an end to expectations of deflation, and an end to pressure for more fiscal contraction, what was the effect of the rest of Roosevelt's "first one hundred days"? It is not clear whether the balance sheet of the rest of that period is positive or negative. A full-fledged policy of monetary inflation and mammoth fiscal deficits that might have pulled the country out of the Great Depression quickly—that did pull Hitler's Germany out of the Great Depression quickly—was not really tried. Consumers complained that the National Recovery Administration raised prices. Workers complained that it gave them insufficient voice. Businessmen complained that the government was telling them what to do. Progressives complained that the NRA created monopoly. Spenders worried that collusion among businesses raised prices, reduced production, and increased unemployment. Hoover and his ilk declared that if FDR had only done as Hoover had been doing, everything would have been better sooner.

In the face of such criticism Roosevelt kept trying different things. If business-labor-government "corporatism" did not work—and was blocked by the mostly Republican-appointed Supreme Court—perhaps a safety net would. The most enduring and powerful accomplishment of the New Deal was to be the Social Security Act of 1935, which provided federal cash assistance for widows, orphans, children without fathers in the home, and the disabled and established a near-universal system of federally funded old-age pensions. If pushing up the dollar price of gold did not work well enough, perhaps strengthening the union movement would: the Wagner Act set down a new set of rules for labor-management conflict and strengthened the union movement, paving the way for a wave of unionization in the United States that survived for half a century. Massive public works and public employment programs restored some self-esteem to workers and transferred money to households without private-sector jobs—but at the probable price of some delay in recovery, as firms and workers saw higher taxes.

Other policies were tried: Antitrust policy and the breaking-up of utility monopolies. A more progressive income tax. A hesitant embrace of deficit spending—not just as an unavoidable temporary evil but as a positive good. As the decade came to an end, Roosevelt's concerns necessarily shifted to the forthcoming war in Europe and to the Japanese invasion of China. Dr. New Deal was replaced by Dr. Win the War. In the end the programs of the Second New Deal probably did little to cure the Great Depression in the United States.[1] But they did turn the United States into a modest European-style social democracy.

Much followed of consequence. That Franklin Roosevelt was center-left rather than center-right, that the length of the Great Depression meant that institutions were shaped by it in a durable sense, and that the United States was the world's rising superpower, and the only major power not crippled to some degree by World War II—all these factors made a huge difference. After World War II, the United States had the power and the will to shape the world outside the Iron Curtain. It did so. And that meant the world was to be reshaped in a New Deal rather than a reactionary or fascist mode.

Keynes and Roosevelt are useful reminders that the fact of individuals acting in particular ways at precise moments, not just thinking thoughts but finding themselves with opportunities to make those thoughts influential, matters profoundly. Even in grand narratives.

MANY—MOST PROMINENTLY British communist historian Eric Hobsbawm[2]—take Lenin's Bolshevik coup and Stalin's subsequent construction of really-existing socialism as the axis on which twentieth-century history turns. Under this interpretation, the main thread of twentieth-century history covers the period 1917–1990 and recounts the three-cornered struggle of liberal quasi-democratic capitalism, fascism, and really-existing socialism. Perhaps this story is an epic: the good guys win. But for Hobsbawm, this story is tragic: really-existing socialism was humanity's last best hope; though crippled by the circumstances of its birth, still it grew strong enough to rescue the world from fascism, but then it decayed, and its dissolution closed off the true road to a socialist utopia. In short, the bad—but not the worst—guys win.

I do not take this view.

In some sense, I am more optimistic. I see the build-out of technology and organization and the development of better ways to manage modern economies as more important things to focus on than faction fights within the post-1917 Kremlin. But as nearly everyone in the world today is keenly aware, the struggle for human liberty and prosperity has not been decisively and permanently won.

Thus I see the history of the long twentieth century as primarily the history of four things—technology-fueled growth, globalization, an exceptional America, and confidence that humanity could at least *slouch* toward utopia as governments solved political-economic problems. And even that slouch was going to be done at uneven, unequal, and unfair rates, depending on skin tone and gender. Still, twice in that long century, 1870–1914 and 1945–1975, something every preceding generation would have called near utopia came nearer, rapidly. But these generation-long episodes of economic El Dorados were not sustained. Individuals, ideas, and opportunities help explain why.

Before 1870, only wild optimists had any confidence that humanity might have a path to utopia—and even for them, the path was a rugged road requiring massive transformations of human society and psychology.

One such utopian was Karl Marx. He and his close associate Friedrich Engels, writing in 1848, theorized that they were in the midst of what they called the *bourgeois epoch*—a time when private property and market exchange served as fundamental organizing principles in human society, creating powerful incentives for scientific research and engineering development and spurring business investment to deploy marvels of technology to amplify human productivity beyond previous imaginings. Marx and Engels saw the interrelated phenomena that defined this bourgeois epoch as both Redeemer and Satan. They were Redeemer insofar as they created the possibility of a wealthy society in which people could, cooperatively, do what they wanted to live full lives. But at the same time, their Satanic workings kept impoverished and even further impoverished the overwhelming majority of humanity, and would in the end force them into a more bitter state of slavery than before. For Marx the path to utopia required the descent of humanity into an industrial inferno, for only that could trigger it to call forth the descent from Heaven of a New Jerusalem, in the form of a communist revolution and the total overthrow of the existing order of society. But to believe that that path was there, and that humanity was certain to walk it—that required great confidence that things hoped for had solid substance, and that things not seen were truly in evidence.[3]

Another relative optimist, John Stuart Mill, anticipated a lesser utopia that would require less of an overthrow. Mill was an ardent believer in freedom, individual initiative, science, and technology—but he was also deeply fearful of the Malthusian dilemma. The inventions of science and the deployment of technology would create fortunes for the rich and expand the numbers of comforts of the middle class, but the great majority of humanity would remain working class and continue to live lives of drudgery and imprisonment. Mill saw only one out: government would have to control human fertility via mandatory birth control.[4] Then all could be well.

But Marx's and Mill's rather odd optimisms made them somewhat outliers in their day, not in that their optimisms were odd but in that they were optimistic at all. Back in 1870, there was great reason to doubt that social equality, individual liberty, political democracy, and general, let alone abundant, prosperity lay in humanity's future. The United States had just narrowly survived a bloody civil war that had killed 750,000 men, one-twelfth of its adult white male population. Typical standards of living were still gravely impoverished. Most people were stunted, by our standards, and often hungry and illiterate.

Did Marx and Mill see the trends of their day more clearly than others? Or were they simply lucky in seeing something of the magnitude of forthcoming material wealth and the possibilities that material wealth might deliver for humanity? Humanity had been shaking the portcullis before 1870. And in 1870 a few major changes broke the lock. The coming of the industrial research lab, of the modern corporation, and of globalization opened up, for the first time in human history, the opportunity to solve our problems of material want. Moreover, at that moment, humanity was lucky enough to have an about-to-be-global market economy. As the genius Friedrich von Hayek keenly observed, the market economy crowdsources—incentivizes and coordinates—solutions to the problems that it sets itself. After 1870 it could solve the problem of providing those with control over valuable property resources with an abundance of the necessities, conveniences, and luxuries they wanted and believed they needed.

Thus the trail to human material abundance, and to utopia, became visible and walkable—or runnable. And everything else should have followed from that. Much has. By 1914 the prevailing pessimism of 1870 appeared old-fashioned, if not completely wrong. The intervening years had truly been, for the world, an extraordinary episode in the economic progress of humanity. And there was every reason to think it would continue: it seemed we could look forward to a genuine utopia of abundance, a future in which further scientific discoveries would be developed in the world's industrial research laboratories and then spread worldwide into the globalized economy by modern corporations.

But then World War I came. And afterward it was clear that what the optimistic had regarded as aberrant and scandalous was the rule, and that deep trouble could not be avoided. People were not satisfied with what the market economy offered them. Governments proved incapable of managing economies to preserve stability and guarantee year-to-year growth. Sometimes populations with democracy threw it away to authoritarian demagogues. Other times, the rich and the top military professionals of the world decided that domination was in fact worth trying. Technology and organization enabled tyrannies of unprecedented magnitude, and economic disparities—both between and within countries—grew and grew. The demographic transition to low fertility and low population growth was rapid, but not rapid enough to prevent the twentieth-century population explosion, with its additional stresses on and transformations of societal order.

Throughout this process, the global south was falling further and further behind—growing, on average, but not catching up, as decade upon decade saw it with less manufacturing and thus less in relative terms of an engineering and science community on which to build up its economy's productive-knowledge stock. Outside of two charmed circles—the group of Marshall Plan aid recipients, and those clinging to the Pacific Rim of Asia—the global south did not even begin to right itself, in the sense of starting to grow faster than the global north, and thereby even taking the first step toward catching up, rather than falling further behind, until more than a decade after the 1979 neoliberal turn. Those that did worst were unlucky enough to be ensorcelled by the spell of Lenin and thus took the really-existing socialist road from 1917 to 1990.

The global north was lucky enough to refind after World War II what it thought was the path to utopia. The pace of economic growth during the Thirty Glorious Years that followed made, by its end in the 1970s, people dizzy with success: expecting more and tremendously upset at what seem in retrospect to be relatively minor speedbumps and roadblocks. But mere rapid growth did not satisfy those of a right-wing temperament, who felt that a prosperity that was shared too equally was unfair and degrading. And mere rapid growth did not satisfy those of a left-wing temperament, either, for they felt that the problems that the market, even tweaked and managed by social democrats, solved did not produce even a partial version of the utopia they sought. And so the world took its neoliberal turn. But the neoliberal policy prescriptions did not produce a slouching toward utopia that was more rapid in any sense.

From 1870 to 2010 was 140 years. Who back in 1870, poor as humanity was then, would have thought that by 2010 humanity would have the ability to provide each person with more material resources than could have been imagined in 1870? And who would have thought that with those resources humanity would be unable to use them to build a close approximation to a true utopia?

Recall that, back at the beginning of this book and of the long twentieth century, Edward Bellamy had thought that the power to dial up any one of four live orchestras and put it on the speakerphone would carry us to "the limit of human felicity." There was only one person in Britain in the early 1600s who could watch a theatrical entertainment about witches in his home: King James I—and that was only if Shakespeare and company currently had *Macbeth* in repertory. There was one thing that Nathan Mayer Rothschild, the richest man in the first half of the 1800s, wanted in 1836: a dose of antibiotics, so that he would not die in his fifties of an infected abscess. Today we can not only thereby produce the sorts of things that were produced in 1870 with remarkably less human effort but easily produce conveniences (that we now regard as necessities), former luxuries (that we now regard as conveniences), and things that previously could not have been produced at any price. Does saying that we are more than ten times richer than our 1870 predecessors really capture that sea change in a satisfactory way?

Yet we found as of 2010 that we had not run to the utopian trail's end. Moreover, for us the end of the utopian trail was no longer visible, even if we had previously thought that it was.

Driving it all, always in the background and often in the foreground, were the industrial research labs discovering and developing things, the large corporations developing and deploying them, and the globalized market economy coordinating it all. But in some ways the market economy was more problem than solution. It recognized only property rights, and people wanted Polanyian rights: rights to a community that gave them support, to an income that gave them the resources they deserved, and to economic stability that gave them consistent work. And for all the economic progress that was achieved during the long twentieth century, its history teaches us that material wealth is of limited use in building utopia. It is an essential prerequisite but far from sufficient. And this is where Keynes's comment about the most permanent problem being how "to live wisely and agreeably and well" comes in once again. His speech was an important moment because he perfectly expressed what the essential difficulty has proved to be.

Of the four freedoms that Franklin Roosevelt thought ought to be every person's birthright—freedom of speech, freedom of worship, freedom from want, and freedom from fear[5]—only freedom from want is secured by material wealth. The others remain to be secured by other means. What the market taketh and giveth can, and often is, overshadowed by hopes and fears arising out of other wants and needs.

The shotgun marriage of Friedrich von Hayek and Karl Polanyi, blessed by John Maynard Keynes, that helped raise the post–World War II North Atlantic developmental social democracy was as good as we have so far gotten. But it failed its own sustainability test, partly because a single generation of rapid growth raised the bar high, and partly because Polanyian rights required stability, the treating of equals equally, and the treating of perceived unequals unequally in ways that neither the Hayekian-Schumpeterian market economy of creative destruction nor the

Polanyian social democratic society of universal egalitarian social insurance rights could ever deliver.

In the decades around 2000, there were four developments that together brought to an end the time span of the long twentieth century, and that together might mark the end of humanity's time slouching toward utopia. The first came in 1990, when the highly innovative and productive industries of Germany and Japan successfully challenged the United States' technological edge, undermining the underpinnings of American exceptionalism. The second was 2001, when forms of fanatic religious violence that we all thought had been in retreat for centuries flamed up again, and pundits scratched their chins and opined about a "war of civilizations"—but there was no such thing. The third was the Great Recession, which began in 2008, when it became clear that we had forgotten the Keynesian lessons of the 1930s and lacked either the capacity or the will to do what was necessary. The fourth was the world's failure during the period from roughly 1989 (when the science became clear) to the present to act decisively to combat global warming. History after the confluence of these events looks notably distinct from history before, as if it requires a new and different grand narrative to make sense of it.

That the long twentieth century was over by 2010 and would not be revivified was confirmed by the rupture that came next, on November 8, 2016, when Donald Trump won that year's presidential election. In that moment, it became clear that each of the four defining developments of the long twentieth century could not be restored. Economic growth in the North Atlantic had slipped substantially—if not all the way to the pre-1870 slower pace, a substantial part of the way. Globalization was definitely in reverse: it had few public advocates, and many enemies.

Plus, people elsewhere—rightly—no longer saw the United States as an exceptional country, or the US government as a trustworthy leader on the world stage. Those judgments were massively strengthened when more than the counted 345,323

Americans died in the COVID-19 pandemic in 2020 alone, as the only virus-containment reaction the Trump administration could muster was to spin in circles and whisper *sotto voce* that the deaths weren't their fault, for how could they have been expected to anticipate an unleashed Chinese bioweapon? Science and technology produced marvels in terms of the extremely rapid and successful development of powerful vaccines. US-led global governance, however, proved inept by failing to vaccinate the world before the pandemic spread widely and developed new variants.

In addition, confidence in the future was also, if not gone, greatly attenuated. The threat of global warming was the Devil of Malthus taking, if not yet flesh, at least a form of shadow. The only place where confidence in the future was strong was among the cadres of the Chinese Communist Party, who saw themselves leading humanity forward holding high the banner of Socialism with Chinese Characteristics and guided by Mao Zedong–Deng Xiaoping–Xi Jinping Thought. But to all outside, that seemed more like corrupt authoritarian state surveillance capitalism with Chinese characteristics (although paying lip service, and perhaps someday more, to egalitarian-utopian "common prosperity" aspirations). So China's ascendance seemed to outsiders unlikely to promise forward steps on the path to utopia. Instead, it seemed to signal a return—albeit at a much higher level of general prosperity—to history's Wheel of Fortune, to a cycle of rulers and ruled, the strong grabbing what they wished and the weak suffering what they must.

To the extent that the Trump administration had a worldview, it was one of suspicion, premised on the idea that internal and external enemies, especially nonwhite and non-English-speaking people, were taking advantage of America's values of freedom and opportunity. To the extent that there were policies, they consisted of, first and most of all, tax cuts for the rich. Second, there was climate change denial. Third, there were random regulatory rollbacks, largely uninformed by technocratic calculation of benefits and costs. And, behind everything, cruelty—which often seemed to be the sole point.[6] And then there were raving denunciations of the administration's own public health officials, whom Trump nevertheless did not seek to replace: "But Fauci's a disaster. If I listened to him we'd have 500,000 deaths"; "Dr. Fauci and Dr. Birx . . . [are] self-promoters trying to reinvent history to cover for their bad instincts and faulty recommendations, which I fortunately almost always overturned"; and—after a rally crowd chanted "Fire Fauci!"—"Don't tell anybody, but let me wait until a little bit after the election. I appreciate the advice, I appreciate it!"[7] The plague was, in the end, to kill more than one million Americans, spreading across the country during the last year of his presidency in 2020 and concentrated in regions where local election-winning politicians pledged allegiance to Donald Trump thereafter. It killed only one-fourth as large a fraction of the population in Canada.

With the 2016 presidential election, even as Americans divided into two opposing camps that agreed on virtually nothing, nearly everyone shared a sense that the nation was in big trouble. Depending on who you asked, Donald Trump was either a symptom of this decline or its only potential "Flight 93" cure.[8] Either case saw a transformation to a very different America. Either it had already happened, and had brought the story of American exceptionalism to an end, or it was necessary to make an America that had lost its compass great again. And the United States was not alone in its unhappy circumstances. Both America and the world faced a constellation of new and worsening problems that seemed certain to challenge, and perhaps to threaten, civilization's many accomplishments over the course of the long twentieth century.

President Trump did not just put a period to the long twentieth century's exhaustion but served as a reminder that pessimism, fear, and panic can animate individuals, ideas, and events as readily as optimism, hope, and confidence.

What went wrong? Well, Hayek and his followers were not only Dr. Jekyll–side geniuses but also Mr. Hyde–side idiots. They thought the market could do the whole job and commanded humanity to believe in "the market giveth, the market taketh away; blessed be the name of the market." But humanity objected: the market manifestly did not do the job, and the job that the market economy did do was rejected and marked "return to sender."

Throughout the long twentieth century, many others—Karl Polanyi, John Maynard Keynes, Benito Mussolini, Vladimir Lenin, and many others—tried to think up solutions. They dissented from "the market giveth . . ." constructively and destructively, demanding that the market do less, or do something different, and that other institutions do more. Perhaps the closest humanity got to a successful "something different" was the shotgun marriage of Hayek and Polanyi, blessed by Keynes, in the form of post–World War II global north developmental-state social democracy. But that social democratic institutional setup had failed its own sustainability test. And while subsequent neoliberalism fulfilled many of the promises it had made to the global-north elite, it was in no wise progress toward any desirable utopia.

Thus the world found itself in a position analogous to the one that John Maynard Keynes had described in 1924, when he critiqued Leon Trotsky's assumption "that the moral and intellectual problems of the transformation of society have already been solved—that a plan exists, and that nothing remains except to put it into operation." Because, Keynes said, this was not true: "We lack more than usual a coherent scheme of progress, a tangible ideal. All the political parties alike have their origins in past ideas and not in new ideas—and none more conspicuously so than the Marxists. It is not necessary to debate the subtleties of what justifies a man in promoting his gospel by force; for no one has a gospel. The next move is with the head, and fists must wait."[9]

Economic improvement, attained by slouch or gallop, matters. The attainment of more than enough—more than enough calories, shelter, clothing, material goods—matters. Once attained, even pessimists are reluctant to give them up. And certain thoughts, once thought, are hard to forget. This is an unsung benefit of the quantitative index of the global value of useful human knowledge. It compounds. Among these thoughts are "the market giveth, the market taketh; blessed be the name of the market"; and, equally, "the market is made for man, not man for the market"; and also, I would add: because often demand creates supply, governments must manage, and manage competently, at times with a heavy touch.

Humans' ideas and visions of utopia have been widely disparate: the Holy Kingdom of the Heavens brought down to earth; the harmonious and natural leisured life of Arcadia; the luxurious sensual pleasures and ecstasies of Sybaris; the disciplined excellence of Sparta; the cacophonous free speech and action of Athens; the collective purpose and good order of Rome and its Pax. Material scarcity, it was largely agreed, kept and would keep those (except for the theological ones) out of humanity's permanent grasp. The golden age was almost always seen as in the past, or at least in some distant and semimythical elsewhere, where resources were much more abundant, not in any likely future.[10]

It was in 1870 that things began to change. As early as 1919, Keynes had emphasized that humanity had already attained the power to produce "conveniences, comforts, and amenities beyond the compass of the richest and most powerful monarchs of other ages," even though the enjoyment of such was still confined to an upper class.[11] Aristotle in 350 BCE had his asides about how it was fantasy to imagine that the authority of masters and the bondage of slaves could be superseded, for that would require humans to have the godlike powers to make and then command servitors—the robot blacksmiths of Daidalos and the self-aware, self-propelled serving vessels that Hephaistos made for the gods' banquets on Mount Olympos.[12] We humans had, as of 2010, wildly outstripped their dreams and imaginings.

Is there anybody in any previous century who would not be amazed and incredulous at seeing humanity's technological and organizational powers as of 2010? Yet they would then go on to the next question: Why, with such godlike powers to command nature and organize ourselves, have we done so little to build a truly human world, to approach within sight of any of our utopias?

By 2010 distrust in America's hegemonic role had been cemented by Middle Eastern misadventures. Discontent had grown with exploding income and wealth inequality that few associated with any boost to economic growth. The Great Recession of 2008–2010 had revealed the emptiness of claims that the neoliberal technocrats had finally gotten the problems of economic management right. The political institutions of the global north did not even begin to grapple with the problem of global warming. The underlying engine of productivity growth had begun to stall. And the great and good of the global north were about to fail to prioritize a rapid restoration of full employment, and to fail to understand and manage the discontents that would bring neofascist and fascist-adjacent politicians to prominence worldwide in the 2010s.

Thus the long twentieth century's story was over.

Perhaps it did not have to end then, in 2010. Perhaps the bright future that many of us had envisioned during the Clinton administration—the idea that if its policies could be continued, they would start to work to restore rapid equitable growth as the information-technology boom roared ahead—was always illusory. Or perhaps the opportunity could have been grasped, had chance and contingency turned out otherwise. Perhaps if in 2008 the United States had elected an FDR, he (or she) could have worked a miracle—as the original FDR had unexpectedly done in 1933 and after. Perhaps even in 2016 the dry bones of the long twentieth century's pattern of rapid productivity growth, governments that could manage the creative-destruction transformations that such growth brought to the world, and American exceptionalism could have been made to live again.

But it turned out that post-2010 America would instead elect Donald Trump, and Western Europe would do little better, ending possibilities of revivification.

A new story, which needs a new grand narrative that we do not yet know, has begun.

Acknowledgments

My debts in writing this book are vast: my wife, Ann Marie Marciarille, and children, Michael and Gianna, have made the long process of writing it a very joyous one. My development editor, Thomas Lebien, and my editor at Basic, Brian Distelberg, have been essential: much of this book might be better framed as a Platonic dialogue with them, and it would not exist without them. My intellectual debts are so great, and there are very many who deserve to be thanked (without implicating any of them in the many, many mistakes I am sure I have committed in this book). But let me cheat and thank only ten more. First of all, let me thank Andrei Shleifer and Larry Summers: whenever I have been able to think thoughts worth recording and disseminating, more often than not my train of thought has begun with "What would Larry say here?" or "What would Andrei think about this?" Then there is the huge amount of my intellectual formation that springs from the Committee on Degrees in Social Studies, most importantly Jeff Weintraub and Shannon Stimson. The senior faculty of the Harvard Economic History Seminar must also belong: Peter Temin, Jeffrey Williamson, Claudia Goldin, and the late David Landes. Paul Krugman has been an immense influence, albeit mostly at a distance: the person who I think comes closest to wearing the mantle of John Maynard Keynes in our generation. For the tenth, let me cheat again: my colleagues at the University of California at Berkeley, the finest collection of colleagues anywhere in economics at the end of the twentieth century, and—collectively, for the whole is much greater than the sum of its parts—the best teachers I can imagine. And to all those I have not mentioned, be assured that I try hard to remember my intellectual debts, and to at least pay them forward.

Notes

A few words about notes:

I have limited the endnotes in this volume to direct quotations, close paraphrases, markers for where my thought and knowledge has been predominantly shaped by a single source, and places where I think a reference for "what to read next to go more deeply" is appropriate.

I have done so even though I am well aware that they are grossly inadequate. Nearly every single paragraph needs to be substantially buttressed, for each certainly could be—and, I hope, will be—fiercely disputed by at least one person of great intelligence and knowledge. Moreover, where I am swimming with (or against) a current, I have not dropped a note to any of the people who make up that current, save where I think I can recommend a best entry point into the literature. And even where I think I am original . . . put it this way: Keynes wrote of the madmen in authority who thought they were hearing voices in the air when actually academic scribblers had insinuated themselves into their minds. Machiavelli wrote of how his books were his friends who he spoke to, and they answered—as he spun up from black marks on white pages sub-Turing instantiations of the minds of the authors which he then ran on his wetware. Even where I think that I am most original, I am almost surely simply repeating something that my internal model of some wiser person's mind has said to me in my internal dialogue.

So there should for justice's sake be many more notes. But there are stringent limits to how effective lengthy footnotes can possibly be. And there are even more stringent limits to how effective endnotes can be.

So this book also has a supporting- and contradicting-arguments website at https://braddelong.substack.com/s/slouching-towards -utopia-long-notes. Come on over, and read and comment, please.

Introduction: My Grand Narrative

1. Steven Usselman, "Research and Development in the United States Since 1900: An Interpretive History," Economic History Workshop, Yale University, November 11, 2013, https://economics.yale.edu/sites/default/files/usselman _paper.pdf; Thomas P. Hughes, *American Genesis: A Century of Invention and Technological Enthusiasm, 1870–1970*, Chicago: University of Chicago Press, 2004; Alfred Chandler, *The Visible Hand: The Managerial Revolution in American Business*, Cambridge, MA: Harvard University Press, 1977.

2. Eric Hobsbawm, *Age of Extremes: The Short Twentieth Century, 1914– 1991*, London: Michael Joseph, 1984.

3. Also seeing a "long" twentieth century as most useful is the keen-sighted and learned Ivan Berend in *An Economic History of Twentieth-Century Europe: Economic Regimes from Laissez-Faire to Globalization*, Cambridge: Cambridge University Press, 2006.

4. Friedrich A. von Hayek, "The Use of Knowledge in Society," *American Economic Review* 35, no. 4 (September 1945): 519–530.

5. Hans Rosling et al., Gapminder, http://gapminder.org; "Globalization over Five Centuries, World," Our World in Data, https://ourworldindata .org/grapher/globalization-over-5-centuries?country=~OWID_WRL.

6. Karl Marx and Friedrich Engels, *Manifesto of the Communist Party*, London: Communist League, 1848; Jonathan Sperber, *Karl Marx: A Nineteenth-Century Life*, New York: Liveright, 2013; Marshall Berman, *All That Is Solid Melts into Air: The Experience of Modernity*, New York: Verso, 1983.

7. Friedrich A. von Hayek, "The Pretence of Knowledge," Nobel Prize Lecture, 1974, www.nobelprize.org/prizes/economic-sciences/1974/hayek/lecture.

8. Karl Polanyi, *The Great Transformation*, New York: Farrar and Rinehart, 1944.

9. Takashi Negishi, "Welfare Economics and Existence of an Equilibrium for a Competitive Economy," *Metroeconomica* 12, no. 2–3 (June 1960): 92–97.

10. Friedrich A. von Hayek, *The Mirage of Social Justice: Law, Legislation, and Liberty*, vol. 2, London: Routledge and Kegan Paul, 1976.

11. Arthur Cecil Pigou, "Welfare and Economic Welfare," in *The Economics of Welfare*, London: Routledge, 1920, 3–22.

12. Ludwig Wittgenstein, *Tractatus Logico-Philosophicus*, London: Kegan Paul, Trench, Trubner, 1921, 89; Jean-François Lyotard, *The Postmodern Condition: A Report on Knowledge*, Minneapolis: University of Minnesota Press, 1984; William Flesch, *Comeuppance: Costly Signaling, Altruistic Punishment, and Other Biological Components of Fiction*, Cambridge, MA: Harvard University Press, 2007.

13. Greg Clark, *A Farewell to Alms: A Brief Economic History of the World*, Princeton, NJ: Princeton University Press, 2007.

14. John Stuart Mill, *Principles of Political Economy, with Some of Their Applications to Social Philosophy*, London: Longmans, Green, Reader, and Dyer, 1873, 516.

15. Edward Bellamy, *Looking Backward, 2000–1887*, Boston: Ticknor, 1888; Edward Bellamy, "How I Came to Write *Looking Backward*," *The Nationalist* (May 1889).

16. Bellamy, *Looking Backward*, 152–158.

17. "Utopia," Oxford Reference, www.oxfordreference.com/view/10.1093/oi/authority.20110803115009560.

18. This was Berlin's favorite Kant quotation. See, for example, Isaiah Berlin, "The Pursuit of the Ideal," Turin: Senator Giovanni Agnelli International Prize Lecture, 1988, https://isaiah-berlin.wolfson.ox.ac.uk/sites/www3.berlin.wolf.ox.ac.uk/files/2018-09/Bib.196%20-%20Pursuit%20of%20the%20Ideal%20by%20Isaiah%20Berlin_1.pdf; Henry Hardy, "Editor's Preface," in Isaiah Berlin, *The Crooked Timber of Humanity: Essays in the History of Ideas*, London: John Murray, 1990.

19. G. W. F. Hegel as quoted by John Ganz, "The Politics of Cultural Despair," Substack, April 20, 2021, https://johnganz.substack.com/p/the-politics-of-cultural-despair. @Ronald00Address reports that it is from G. W. F. Hegel, Letter to [Karl Ludwig von] Knebel, August 30, 1807, NexusMods, www.nexusmods.com/cyberpunk2077/images/15600, quoted in Walter Benjamin,

On the Concept of History, 1940, translated by Dennis Redmond, August 4, 2001, Internet Archive Wayback Machine, https://web.archive.org/web/2012 0710213703/http://members.efn.org/~dredmond/Theses_on_History.PDF.

20. Madeleine Albright, *Fascism: A Warning*, New York: HarperCollins, 2018.

21. Fred Block, "Introduction," in Karl Polanyi, *Great Transformation*.

22. See Charles I. Jones, "Paul Romer: Ideas, Nonrivalry, and Endogenous Growth," *Scandinavian Journal of Economics* 121, no. 3 (2019): 859–883.

23. Clark, *Farewell*, 91–96.

24. Simon Kuznets, *Modern Economic Growth: Rate, Structure, and Spread*, New Haven, CT: Yale University Press, 1966.

25. Edward Shorter and Lawrence Shorter, *A History of Women's Bodies*, New York: Basic Books, 1982. Consider that one in seven of the queens and heiresses apparent of England between William I of Normandy and Victoria of Hanover died in childbed.

26. Mill, *Principles*, 516.

27. Opposed, drawing a line in the sand between good "negative liberty" and not-so-good "positive liberty," is Isaiah Berlin, "Two Concepts of Liberty," in *Four Essays on Liberty*, Oxford: Oxford University Press, 1969. Mill did not buy that pig in a poke.

28. Mill, *Principles*, 516.

29. William Stanley Jevons, *The Coal Question: An Enquiry Concerning the Progress of the Nation, and the Probable Exhaustion of Our Coal-Mines*, London: Macmillan, 1865.

30. Marx and Engels, *Manifesto*, 17.

31. Friedrich Engels, "Outlines of a Critique of Political Economy," *German-French Yearbooks*, 1844.

32. Karl Marx, *Critique of the Gotha Program*, in *Marx/Engels Selected Works*, vol. 3, Moscow: Progress Publishers, 1970 [1875], 13–30, available at Marxists Internet Archive, www.marxists.org/archive/marx/works/1875/gotha.

33. Richard Easterlin, *Growth Triumphant: The Twenty-First Century in Historical Perspective*, Ann Arbor: University of Michigan, 2009, 154.

34. Easterlin, *Growth Triumphant*, 154.

35. Thomas Robert Malthus, *First Essay on Population*, London: Macmillan, 1926 [1798], Internet Archive, https://archive.org/details/b31355250. The phrase "Malthus had disclosed a Devil" is from John Maynard Keynes, *The Economic Consequences of the Peace*, London: Macmillan, 1919, 8.

1. Globalizing the World

1. Thomas Robert Malthus, *An Essay on the Principle of Population, as It Affects the Future Improvement of Society*, London: J. Johnson, 1798.

2. Gregory Clark, "The Condition of the Working Class in England, 1209–2004," *Journal of Political Economy* 113, no. 6 (December 2005): 1307–1340, http://faculty.econ.ucdavis.edu/faculty/gclark/papers/wage%20-%20jpe%20-2004.pdf.

3. John Maynard Keynes, *The Economic Consequences of the Peace*, London: Macmillan, 1919, 8.

4. Consider the contrast between the material culture available to support the lifestyle of, say, Thomas Jefferson in 1800 and that available in the days of Gilgamesh five thousand years earlier. Alexander Heidel, trans. and ed., *The Gilgamesh Epic and Old Testament Parallels*, Chicago: University of Chicago Press, 1946; Robert Silverberg, ed., *Gilgamesh the King*, New York: Arbor House, 1984; George W. Boudreau and Margaretta Markle Lovell, eds., *A Material World: Culture, Society, and the Life of Things in Early Anglo-America*, University Park, PA: Pennsylvania State University Press, 2019.

5. Quoted to me by Trevon Logan.

6. I owe my persuasion on this point—that Industrial Revolution–era Britain's unique path before 1870 was more of a "globalization" phenomenon than a "technorevolution" phenomenon—to Gregory Clark, "The Secret History of the Industrial Revolution," October 2001, http://faculty.econ.ucdavis.edu/faculty/gclark/papers/secret2001.pdf.

7. William Stanley Jevons, *The Coal Question: An Enquiry Concerning the Progress of the Nation, and the Probable Exhaustion of Our Coal-Mines*, London: Macmillan, 1865.

8. Rudyard Kipling, "Recessional," first published in *The Times* (London), July 17, 1897, reprinted at Poetry Foundation, www.poetryfoundation.org/poems/46780/recessional.

9. Keynes, *Economic Consequences*, 8.

10. Anton Howes, "Is Innovation in Human Nature?," *Medium*, October 21, 2016, https://medium.com/@antonhowes/is-innovation-in-human-nature-48c2578e27ba#.v54zq0ogx.

11. "Globalization over Five Centuries, World," Our World in Data, https://ourworldindata.org/grapher/globalization-over-5-centuries?country=~OWID_WRL, piecing together estimates from many authorities.

12. W. Arthur Lewis, *The Evolution of the International Economic Order*, Princeton, NJ: Princeton University Press, 1978, 14.

13. Henry David Thoreau, *Walden; or, a Life in the Woods*, Boston: Ticknor and Fields, 1854, 58–59.

14. Mark Chirnside, *Oceanic: White Star's "Ship of the Century"*, Cheltenham: History Press, 2019, 72.

15. Elisabeth Kehoe, *Fortune's Daughters: The Extravagant Lives of the Jerome Sisters—Jennie Churchill, Clara Frewen and Leonie Leslie*, Boston: Atlantic, 2011, 71.

16. For the story of Gandhi, by far the best thing I have read is the three-volume set by Ramachandra Gupta, *Gandhi Before India*, New York: Alfred A. Knopf, 2013; *Gandhi: The Years That Changed the World, 1914–1948*, New York: Random House, 2018; *India After Gandhi: The History of the World's Largest Democracy*, London: Pan Macmillan, 2011.

17. Benjamin Yang, *Deng: A Political Biography*, London: Routledge, 2016, 22–46.

18. Jeffrey Williamson, "Globalization and Inequality, Past and Present," *World Bank Observer* 12, no. 2 (August 1997): 117–135, https://documents1.worldbank.org/curated/en/502441468161647699/pdf/766050JRN0WBRO00Box374378B00PUBLIC0.pdf.

19. Steven Dowrick and J. Bradford DeLong, "Globalization and Convergence," in *Globalization in Historical Perspective*, ed. Michael D. Bordo, Alan M. Taylor, and Jeffrey G. Williamson, National Bureau of Economic Research (NBER) Conference Report, Chicago: University of Chicago Press, 2003, 191–226, available at NBER, www.nber.org/system/files/chapters/c9589/c9589.pdf.

20. Neal Stephenson, "Mother Earth, Motherboard," *Wired*, December 1, 1996, www.wired.com/1996/12/ffglass.

21. Keven H. O'Rourke and Jeffrey G. Williamson, *Globalization and History: The Evolution of a Nineteenth-Century Atlantic Economy*, Cambridge, MA: MIT Press, 1999.

22. "Globalization over Five Centuries."

23. Richard Baldwin, *The Great Convergence: Information Technology and the New Globalization*, Cambridge, MA: Harvard University Press, 2016, 5.

24. Robert Allen, *Global Economic History: A Very Short Introduction*, Oxford: Oxford University Press, 2011, 6–8.

25. Robert Fogel, *Railroads and American Economic Growth: Essays in Econometric History*, Baltimore: Johns Hopkins University Press, 1964, 39.

26. Wladimir S. Woytinsky and Emma S. Woytinsky, *World Commerce and Governments: Trends and Outlook*, New York: Twentieth Century Fund, 1955, 179.

27. Keynes, *Economic Consequences*, 32.

28. Elizabeth Longford, *Wellington: The Years of the Sword*, London: Weidenfeld and Nicolson, 1969.

29. Thoreau, *Walden*.

30. Vincent P. Carosso and Rose C. Carosso, *The Morgans: Private International Bankers, 1854–1913*, Cambridge, MA: Harvard University Press, 1987, 133–200.

31. W. Arthur Lewis, *Growth and Fluctuations, 1870–1913*, London: G. Allen and Unwin, 1978, 20.

32. Laura Panza and Jeffrey G. Williamson, "Did Muhammad Ali Foster Industrialization in Early Nineteenth-Century Egypt?," *Economic History Review* 68, no. 1 (February 2015): 79–100; David S. Landes, "Bankers and Pashas: International Finance and Imperialism in the Egypt of the 1860's" (PhD diss., Harvard University, 1953).

33. Stephen S. Cohen and J. Bradford DeLong, *Concrete Economics: The Hamiltonian Approach to Economic Policy*, Boston: Harvard Business Review Press, 2016; John Stuart Mill, *Principles of Political Economy, with Some of Their Applications to Social Philosophy*, London: Longmans, Green, Reader, and Dyer, 1873, 556.

34. AnnaLee Saxenian, *Regional Advantage: Culture and Competition in Silicon Valley and Route 128*, Cambridge, MA: Harvard University Press, 1996, 32–34.

35. Allen, *Global Economic History*, 7.

36. Allen, *Global Economic History*, 41–42; Lewis, *Evolution*; Joel Mokyr, *The British Industrial Revolution: An Economic Perspective*, New York: Routledge, 2018 [1999]; Edgar J. Dosman, *The Life and Times of Raul Prebisch, 1901–1986*, Montreal: McGill-Queen's University Press, 2008.

2. Revving Up the Engine
of Technology-Driven Growth

1. Kenneth Whyte, *Hoover: An Extraordinary Life in Extraordinary Times*, New York: Alfred A. Knopf, 2017; Herbert Hoover, *The Memoirs of Herbert Hoover*, vol. 1, *Years of Adventure, 1874–1920*; vol. 2, *The Cabinet and the Presidency, 1920–1933*; vol. 3, *The Great Depression, 1929–1941*, New York: Macmillan, 1951–1953; Rose Wilder Lane, *The Making of Herbert Hoover*, New York: Century, 1920.

2. Ellsworth Carlson, *The Kaiping Mines*, Cambridge, MA: Harvard University Press, 1957.

3. On global economic leadership, see W. Arthur Lewis, *Growth and Fluctuations, 1870–1913*, London: G. Allen and Unwin, 1978, 94–113.

4. Jack Goldstone, "Efflorescences and Economic Growth in World History: Rethinking the 'Rise of the West' and the Industrial Revolution," *Journal of World History* 13, no. 2 (September 2002): 323–389.

5. Lewis, *Growth*, 14.

6. "Globalization over Five Centuries, World," Our World in Data, https://ourworldindata.org/grapher/globalization-over-5-centuries?country =~OWID_WRL.

7. Ragin in the older tales before Wagner. See Stephan Grundy, *Rhinegold*, New York: Bantam, 1994, 47–63, 332–333.

8. For the technological history from 1700 to 1945, the best thing, for me at least, remains David Landes, *The Unbound Prometheus*, Cambridge: Cambridge University Press, 1969.

9. Robert Gordon, *The Rise and Fall of American Growth: The U.S. Standard of Living Since the Civil War*, Princeton, NJ: Princeton University Press, 2017, 61.

10. Donald Sassoon, *One Hundred Years of Socialism: The West European Left in the Twentieth Century*, New York: New Press, 1996, xxxiii. Note that Sassoon does not especially like this transformation of the revolutionary idea into a celebration of the wonders of technology.

11. Thomas Piketty, *Capital in the Twenty-First Century*, Cambridge, MA: Harvard University Press, 2014, 24; Mark Twain and Charles Dudley Warner, *The Gilded Age: A Novel of Today*, Boone, IA: Library of America, 2002 [1873].

12. On the lives of America's industrial working class around 1900, see Margaret Frances Byington, *Homestead: The Households of a Mill Town*, New York: Charities Publication Committee, 1910.

13. Nicola Tesla, *My Inventions: The Autobiography of Nicola Tesla*, New York: Hart Bros., 1982 [1919]; Marc Seifer, *Wizard: The Life and Times of Nikola Tesla*, Toronto: Citadel Press, 2011.

14. Margaret Cheney, *Tesla: Man Out of Time*, New York: Simon and Schuster, 2001, 56.

15. Nikola Tesla, "My Early Life," *Electrical Experimenter*, 1919, reprinted by David Major at Medium, January 4, 2017, https://medium.com/@dlmajor/my-early-life-by-nikola-tesla-7b55945ee114.

16. Paul David, "Heroes, Herds, and Hysteresis in Technological History: Thomas Edison and the 'Battle of the Systems' Reconsidered," *Industrial and Corporate Change* 1, no. 1 (1992): 125–180; Landes, *Unbound Prometheus*, 284–289.

17. For the atmosphere, see Graham Moore, *The Last Days of Night: A Novel*, New York: Random House, 2016.

18. Quentin Skrabec, *George Westinghouse: Gentle Genius*, New York: Algora, 2007, 7–23.

19. David Glantz, *Operation Barbarossa: Hitler's Invasion of Russia, 1941*, Cheltenham, UK: History Press, 2011, 19–22.

20. Irwin Collier believes G.H.M. to be Gilbert Holland Montague. Irwin Collier, "Harvard(?) Professor's Standard of Living, 1905," Economics in the Rear-View Mirror, 2017, www.irwincollier.com/harvard-professors-standard-of-living-1905; "Gilbert Holland Mongague, 1880–1961," Internet Archive Wayback Machine, https://web.archive.org/web/20040310032941/http://www.montaguemillennium.com/familyresearch/h_1961_gilbert.htm.

21. G.H.M., "What Should College Professors Be Paid?," *Atlantic Monthly* 95, no. 5 (May 1905): 647–650.

22. Byington, *Homestead*.

23. Ray Ginger, *Age of Excess: American Life from the End of Reconstruction to World War I*, New York: Macmillan, 1965, 95.

24. J. R. Habakkuk, *American and British Technology in the Nineteenth Century: The Search for Labour-Saving Inventions*, Cambridge: Cambridge University Press, 1962.

25. Claudia D. Goldin and Lawrence F. Katz, *The Race Between Education and Technology*, Cambridge, MA: Harvard University Press, 2008; Claudia Goldin, "The Human Capital Century and American Leadership: Virtues of the Past," National Bureau of Economic Research (NBER) working paper 8239, *Journal of Economic History* 61, no. 2 (June 2001): 263–292, available at NBER, www.nber.org/papers/w8239.

26. Leon Trotsky, *My Life: An Attempt at an Autobiography*, New York: Charles Scribner's Sons, 1930.

27. Joseph Schumpeter, *Capitalism, Socialism, and Democracy*, New York: Harper and Bros., 1942, 83.

3. Democratizing the Global North

1. Alexander Hamilton, John Jay, and James Madison, *The Federalist Papers, New York Packet, Independent Journal, Daily Advertiser*, collected with nos. 78–85 added, in *The Federalist: A Collection of Essays, Written in Favour of the New Constitution, as Agreed upon by the Federal Convention, September 17, 1787*, New York: J. and A. McLean, 1787–1788, no. 10. For full text online, see Library of Congress, https://guides.loc.gov /federalist-papers/full-text.

2. Thomas Jefferson, Letter to George Washington, May 23, 1792, in Noble Cunningham, *Jefferson vs. Hamilton: Confrontations That Shaped a Nation*, Boston: Bedford / St. Martins, 2000, 79.

3. Munro Price, *The Perilous Crown*, New York: Pan Macmillan, 2010, 308, 351–360.

4. Daniel Ziblatt, *Conservative Parties and the Birth of Democracy*, Cambridge: Cambridge University Press, 2017, 109.

5. Ellis A. Wasson, "The Spirit of Reform, 1832 and 1867," *Albion: A Quarterly Journal Concerned with British Studies* 12, no. 2 (Summer 1980): 164–174.

6. John W. Dean, *The Rehnquist Choice: The Untold Story of the Nixon Appointment That Redefined the Supreme Court*, New York: Free Press, 2001, 160, 312.

7. Friedrich A. von Hayek, *The Constitution of Liberty*, Chicago: University of Chicago Press, 1960, 148.

8. Hayek, *Constitution*, 286.

9. Friedrich A. von Hayek, *The Road to Serfdom*, London: Routledge, 1944, 124.

10. Friedrich A. von Hayek, *Law, Legislation and Liberty: The Political Order of a Free People*, Chicago: University of Chicago Press, 1979, 172.

11. Isaiah Berlin, *The Hedgehog and the Fox: An Essay on Tolstoy's View of History*, London: Weidenfeld and Nicolson, 1953, 1.

12. Karl Polanyi, *The Great Transformation*, New York: Farrar and Rinehart, 1944, 84.

13. Note that before Karl Marx settled on "bourgeois" as his label for all that he hated and loved about the industrial-market economy he saw coming to be, he had used the word "Jewish" in his writings instead. See Jonathan Sperber, *Karl Marx: A Nineteenth-Century Life*, New York: Liveright, 2013, 133.

14. Polanyi, *Great Transformation*, 144, 153–162.

15. William Cronon, *Nature's Metropolis: Chicago and the Great West*, New York: W. W. Norton, 1992.

16. Ray Ginger, *The Age of Excess: The United States from 1877 to 1914*, New York: Macmillan, 1965; Ray Ginger, *Altgeld's America: The Lincoln Ideal Versus Changing Realities*, Chicago: Quadrangle Books, 1958.

17. John Peter Altgeld, *Our Penal Machinery and Its Victims*, Chicago: A. C. McClurg and Company, 1886.

18. Clarence Darrow, *The Story of My Life*, New York: Scribner's, 1932, 66.

19. US Constitution, Art. IV §4.

20. Allan Nevins, *Grover Cleveland: A Study in Courage*, New York: Dodd, Mean, 1930, 691.

21. Ginger, *Age of Excess*, 359.

22. Darrow, *My Life*, 93.

23. Clarence Darrow, *Closing Arguments: Clarence Darrow on Religion, Law, and Society*, Columbus: Ohio University Press, 2005, 202.

24. W. E. B. Du Bois, "My Evolving Program for Negro Freedom," in *What the Negro Wants*, ed. Rayford W. Logan, Chapel Hill: University of North Carolina Press, 1944, 36.

25. Booker T. Washington, *Up from Slavery: An Autobiography*, London: George Harrap, 1934 [1901], 137.

26. Annette Gordon-Reed, "The Color Line: W. E. B. Du Bois's Exhibit at the 1900 Paris Exposition," *New York Review of Books*, August 19, 2021, www.nybooks.com/articles/2021/08/19/du-bois-color-line-paris-exposition.

27. W. E. B. Du Bois, *The Souls of Black Folk*, Chicago: A. C. McClurg, 1903, n.p.

28. Alexis de Tocqueville, *Souvenirs*, Paris: Calmann Lévy, 1893 [1850–1852], n.p.

29. Jean-François de La Harpe, *Cours de Littérature Ancienne et Moderne*, Paris: Didot Frères, 1840, n.p.

30. William L. Shirer, *The Collapse of the Third Republic: An Inquiry into the Fall of France in 1940*, New York: Pocket Books, 1971, 33–39.

31. Donald Sassoon, *One Hundred Years of Socialism: The West European Left in the Twentieth Century*, New York: New Press, 1996, 5–25.

32. John Maynard Keynes, *The End of Laissez-Faire*, London: Hogarth Press, 1926, n.p.

33. Andrew Carnegie, "Wealth," *North American Review* 148, no. 391 (June 1889): n.p., available from Robert Bannister at Swarthmore College, June 27, 1995, www.swarthmore.edu/SocSci/rbannis1/AIH19th/Carnegie .html.

34. Winston S. Churchill, *The World Crisis*, vol. 1, New York: Charles Scribner's Sons, 1923, 33.

35. Arthur Conan Doyle, *His Last Bow: Some Reminiscences of Sherlock Holmes*, New York: George H. Doran, 1917, 307–308.

36. John Maynard Keynes, *The Economic Consequences of the Peace*, London: Macmillan, 1919, 22.

4. Global Empires

1. Bernal Díaz del Castillo, *The History of the Conquest of New Spain*, Albuquerque: University of New Mexico Press, 2008 [1568].

2. David Abernethy, *The Dynamics of Global Dominance: European Overseas Empires, 1415–1980*, New Haven, CT: Yale University Press, 2000, 242–248.

3. Eric Williams, *Capitalism and Slavery*, Chapel Hill: University of North Carolina Press, 1944; Nathan Nunn and Leonard Wantchekon, "The Slave Trade and the Origins of Mistrust in Africa," *American Economic Review* 101, no. 7 (December 2011): 3221–3252, available at American Economic Association, www.aeaweb.org/articles?id=10.1257/aer.101.7.3221.

4. Winston Churchill, *The River War: An Historical Account of the Reconquest of the Sudan*, London: Longmans, Green, 1899, n.p.

5. L. A. Knight, "The Royal Titles Act and India," *Historical Journal* 11, no. 3 (1968): 488–507.

6. Karl Marx, "British Rule in India," *New-York Daily Tribune*, June 25, 1853, available at Marxists Internet Archive, www.marxists.org/archive/marx

/works/1853/06/25.htm; Karl Marx, "The Future Results of British Rule in India," *New-York Daily Tribune*, July 22, 1853, available at Marxists Internet Archive, www.marxists.org/archive/marx/410.htm.

7. Dugald Stewart, *Account of the Life and Writings of Adam Smith, LL.D.*, Edinburgh: Transactions of the Royal Society of Edinburgh, 1794, available at my website at https://delong.typepad.com/files/stewart.pdf.

8. Mancur Olson, *The Rise and Decline of Nations: Economic Growth, Stagflation, and Social Rigidities*, New Haven, CT: Yale University Press, 1982, 179.

9. Afaf Lutfi al-Sayyid Marsot, *A Short History of Modern Egypt*, Cambridge: Cambridge University Press, 1985, 48–68.

10. Laura Panza and Jeffrey G. Williamson, "Did Muhammad Ali Foster Industrialization in Early 19th Century Egypt?," *Economic History Review* 68 (2015): 79–100.

11. David Landes, "Bankers and Pashas: International Finance and Imperialism in the Egypt of the 1860's" (PhD diss., Harvard University, 1953).

12. Alicia E. Neve Little, *Li Hung-Chang: His Life and Times*, London: Cassell and Company, 1903; Jonathan Spence, *The Search for Modern China*, New York: W. W. Norton, 1990.

13. Ellsworth Carlson, *The Kaiping Mines*, Cambridge, MA: Harvard University Press, 1957.

14. Robert Allen, *The British Industrial Revolution in Global Perspective*, Cambridge: Cambridge University Press, 2009.

15. A. L. Sadler, *The Maker of Modern Japan: The Life of Tokugawa Ieyasu*, London: Routledge, 1937; Conrad D. Totman, *The Collapse of the Tokugawa Bakufu: 1862–1868*, Honolulu: University Press of Hawaii, 1980.

16. Robert Allen, *Global Economic History: A Very Short Introduction*, Oxford: Oxford University Press, 2013, 118–119.

17. Totman, *Collapse of the Tokugawa Bakufu*; Jerry Kamm Fisher, *The Meirokusha*, Charlottesville: University of Virginia Press, 1974.

18. John P. Tang, "Railroad Expansion and Industrialization: Evidence from Meiji Japan," *Journal of Economic History* 74, no. 3 (September 2014): 863–886; George Allen, *A Short Economic History of Modern Japan, 1867–1937*, London: Allen and Unwin, 1972, 32–62, 81–99.

19. Myung Soo Cha, "Did Takahashi Korekiyo Rescue Japan from the Great Depression?," *Journal of Economic History* 63, no. 1 (March 2003): 127–144; Dick Nanto and Shinji Takagi, "Korekiyo Takahashi and Japan's Recovery from the Great Depression," *American Economic Review* 75, no. 2 (May 1985): 369–374; Richard J. Smethurst, *From Foot Soldier to Finance Minister: Takahashi Korekiyo, Japan's Keynes*, Cambridge, MA: Harvard University Asia Center, 2007.

20. Kozo Yamamura, "Success Illgotten? The Role of Meiji Militarism in Japan's Technological Progress," *Journal of Economic History* 37, no. 1 (March 1977): 113–135.

21. Rudyard Kipling, "White Man's Burden," *The Times*, February 4, 1899, reprinted at Wikipedia, https://en.wikipedia.org/wiki/The_White_Man%27s _Burden.

22. Joseph Schumpeter, "The Sociology of Imperialisms," 1918, in *Imperialism and Social Classes: Two Essays by Joseph Schumpeter*, Cleveland: Meridian Books, 2007.

23. John Hobson, *Imperialism: A Study*, London: James Nisbet, 1902.

24. Norman Angell, *Europe's Optical Illusion*, Hamilton, Kent, UK: Simpkin, Marshall, 1908.

5. World War I

1. Norman Angell, *Peace Theories and the Balkan War*, London: Horace Marshall and Son, 1912, 124.

2. "Otto von Bismarck," Social Security Administration, n.d., www.ssa .gov/history/ottob.html; Otto von Bismarck, "Bismarck's Reichstag Speech on the Law for Workers' Compensation (March 15, 1884)," German Historical Institute, German History in Documents and Images, https://german historydocs.ghi-dc.org/sub_document.cfm?document_id=1809.

3. Thomas Pakenham, *The Boer War*, New York: HarperCollins, 1992.

4. George Dangerfield, *The Strange Death of Liberal England*, London: Harrison Smith and Robert Haas, 1935.

5. Max Weber, *The National State and Economic Policy*, Freiburg, 1895, quoted in Wolfgang J. Mommsen and Jürgen Osterhammel, *Max Weber and His Contemporaries*, London: Routledge, 1987, 36.

6. Max Weber, *The Sociology of Religion*, excerpted in Max Weber, Hans Heinrich Gerth, and C. Wright Mills, eds., *From Max Weber: Essays in Sociology*, London: Routledge and Kegan Paul, 1948, 280.

7. Robert Forczyk, *Erich von Manstein: Leadership, Strategy, Conflict*, Oxford: Osprey Publishing, 2010.

8. Christopher Clark, *The Sleepwalkers: How Europe Went to War in 1914*, London: Allen Lane, 2012; David Mackenzie, *The "Black Hand" on Trial: Salonika 1917*, New York: Columbia University Press, 1995; W. A. Dolph Owings, *The Sarajevo Trial*, Chapel Hill, NC: Documentary Publications, 1984.

9. Arno Mayer, *The Persistence of the Old Regime: Europe to the Great War*, New York: Pantheon Books, 1981.

10. Robert Citino, *The German Way of War: From the Thirty Years' War to the Third Reich*, Lawrence: University Press of Kansas, 2005.

11. Niall Ferguson, *The Pity of War*, London: Penguin, 1998, xxxix.

12. Adam Tooze, *The Deluge: The Great War, America and the Remaking of the Global Order*, New York: Penguin Random House, 2014.

13. Walther Rathenau, *To Germany's Youth*, Berlin: S. Fischer, 1918, 9.

14. Hugo Haase, "Social Democratic Party Statement on the Outbreak of the War," August 4, 1914, quoted in "The Socialists Support the War (August 4, 1914)," German Historical Institute, German History in Documents and Images, https://germanhistorydocs.ghi-dc.org/sub_document .cfm?document_id=816&language=english.

15. Michael Howard, *The First World War*, Oxford: Oxford University Press, 2002. Much shorter is Michael Howard, *The First World War: A Very Short Introduction*, Oxford: Oxford University Press, 2007.

16. John Maynard Keynes, *The Economic Consequences of the Peace*, London: Macmillan, 1919, 7.

17. Robert Skidelsky, *John Maynard Keynes, 1883–1946: Economist, Philosopher, Statesman*, New York: Penguin, 2005.

6. Roaring Twenties

1. As proposed by the Soviet Union's general secretary, Mikhail Gorbachev, in his address "Europe as a Common Home," July 6, 1989, transcript at Roy Rosenzweig Center for History and New Media, formerly the Center for History and New Media, George Mason University, https://chnm.gmu .edu/1989/archive/files/gorbachev-speech-7-6-89_e3ccb87237.pdf.

2. Joseph Schumpeter, *Capitalism, Socialism, and Democracy*, New York: Taylor and Francis, 2013 [1942].

3. Karl Popper, *The Open Society and Its Enemies*, New York: Taylor and Francis, 2012 [1945].

4. Peter Drucker, *Management: Tasks, Responsibilities, Practices*, New York: HarperCollins, 1993 [1973]; Alasdair Macintyre, *After Virtue: A Study in Moral Theory*, South Bend, IN: University of Notre Dame Press, 1981.

5. A very good introduction to this idea as applied to science and technology is Chapter 5 of Partha Dasgupta, *Economics: A Very Short Introduction*, Oxford: Oxford University Press, 2007, 90–99.

6. Charles Kindleberger, *The World in Depression, 1929–1939*, Berkeley: University of California Press, 1973, 291–292.

7. Margaret MacMillan, *Paris 1919: Six Months That Changed the World*, New York: Random House, 2001.

8. Laura Spinney, *Pale Rider: The Spanish Flu of 1918 and How It Changed the World*, New York: PublicAffairs, 2017.

9. Wladimir S. Woytinsky, *Stormy Passage: A Personal History Through Two Russian Revolutions to Democracy and Freedom, 1905–1960*, New York: Vanguard, 1961.

10. Woodrow Wilson, "Address of the President of the United States to the Senate," January 22, 1917, posted at University of Michigan–Dearborn, Personal Pages, www-personal.umd.umich.edu/~ppennock/doc-Wilsonpeace.htm.

11. John Maynard Keynes, *The Economic Consequences of the Peace*, London: Macmillan, 1919, 37–55.

12. Keynes, *Economic Consequences*, 3.

13. Keynes, *Economic Consequences*, 3–4.

14. Jan Christiaan Smuts, *Selections from the Smuts Papers*, vol. 4, *November 1918–August 1919*, Cambridge: Cambridge University Press, 1966, 152–153.

15. George H. Nash, *The Life of Herbert Hoover: The Humanitarian, 1914–1917*, New York: W. W. Norton, 1988; George H. Nash, *The Life of Herbert Hoover: Master of Emergencies, 1917–1918*, New York: W. W. Norton, 1996; Kendrick A. Clements, *The Life of Herbert Hoover: Imperfect Visionary, 1918–1928*, New York: Palgrave Macmillan, 2010.

16. Keynes, *Economic Consequences*, 268.

17. Keynes, *Economic Consequences*, 149.

18. Christian Seidl, "The Bauer-Schumpeter Controversy on Socialization," *History of Economic Ideas* 2, no. 2 (1994): 53, quoting Joseph Schumpeter's 1917 "Die Krise des Steuerstaates," itself reprinted in Joseph Schumpeter, "Die Krise des Steuerstaates," *Aufsätze zur Soziologie*, Tübingen: J. C. B. Mohr (Paul Siebeck), 1953.

19. Joe Weisenthal, Tracy Alloway, and Zach Carter, "The Real Story of Weimar Hyperinflation," Bloomberg, *Odd Lots Podcast*, April 15, 2021, www.bloomberg.com/news/articles/2021-04-15/zach-carter-on-the-real-story-of-weimar-hyperinflation; Sally Marks, "The Myths of Reparations," *Central European History* 11, no. 3 (2008): 231–255.

20. Barry J. Eichengreen, *Golden Fetters: The Gold Standard and the Great Depression*, New York: Oxford University Press, 1992. The phrase "golden fetters," as in, "It was not disaster which had befallen us, but a happy release; that the snapping of our golden fetters restored to us the control over our fortunes," comes from John Maynard Keynes, "Two Years Off Gold: How Far Are We from Prosperity Now?," *Daily Mail*, September 19, 1933, reprinted in John Maynard Keynes, *The Collected Writings of John Maynard Keynes*,

vol. 21, *Activities, 1931–1939: World Crises and Policies in Britain and America*, Cambridge: Cambridge University Press, 1982, 285.

21. Robert Skidelsky, *John Maynard Keynes, 1883–1946: Economist, Philosopher, Statesman*, New York: Penguin, 2005, 217–249.

22. Skidelsky, *Keynes*; P. J. Grigg, *Prejudice and Judgment*, London: Jonathan Cape, 1948, 183. I do not find Grigg reliable, for reasons I go into in my notes on this chapter on my website at https://braddelong.substack.com/p /chapter-vi-roaring-twenties.

23. Eichengreen, *Golden Fetters*, 153–186.

24. Paul Krugman, "Notes on Globalization and Slowbalization," November 2020, The Graduate Center, City University of New York, www.gc .cuny.edu/CUNY_GC/media/LISCenter/pkrugman/Notes-on-globalization -and-slowbalization.pdf.

25. Kevin H. O'Rourke, "Globalization in Historical Perspective," in *Globalization and Unemployment*, ed. H. Wagner, Berlin: Springer-Verlag, 2000.

26. William C. Widenor, *Henry Cabot Lodge and the Search for an American Foreign Policy*, Berkeley: University of California Press, 1980; Henry Cabot Lodge, "Lynch Law and Unrestricted Immigration," *North American Review* 152, no. 414 (May 1891): 602–612. Woodrow Wilson firmly believed that the typical immigrant had become a threat to America by the 1880s. Woodrow Wilson, *Division and Reunion, 1829–1889*, London: Longmans, Green, 1893, 297.

27. Eric S. Yellin, "How the Black Middle Class Was Attacked by Woodrow Wilson's Administration," *The Conversation*, February 8, 2016, https:// theconversation.com/how-the-black-middle-class-was-attacked-by-woodrow -wilsons-administration-52200; Franklin Delano Roosevelt, "Cover Memorandum," August 7, 1916, reprinted in "Roosevelt Exposed as Rabid Jim Crower by Navy Order," *Chicago Defender*, October 15, 1932, 1, available at Internet Archive Wayback Machine, web.archive.org/web/20110104185404 /http://j-bradford-delong.net/2007_images/20070728_Roosevelt_memo.pdf.

28. J. H. Habakkuk, *American and British Technology in the Nineteenth Century: The Search for Labour Saving Inventions*, Cambridge: Cambridge University Press, 1962; David A. Hounshell, *From the American System to Mass Production: The Development of Manufacturing Technology in the United States, 1850–1920*, Wilmington: University of Delaware Press, 1978.

29. Paul A. David, "The Dynamo and the Computer: An Historical Perspective on the Modern Productivity Paradox," *American Economic Review* 80, no. 2 (May 1990): 355–361.

30. Daniel Raff, "Wage Determination Theory and the Five-Dollar Day at Ford: A Detailed Examination" (PhD diss., Massachusetts Institute of

Technology, 1987); Daniel M.G. Raff and Lawrence H. Summers, "Did Henry Ford Pay Efficiency Wages?," *Journal of Labor Economics* 5, no. 4, pt. 2 (October 1987): S57–S86.

31. "Theodore N. Vail on Public Utilities and Public Policies," *Public Service Management* 14, no. 6 (June 1913): 208.

32. Alfred P. Sloan, *My Years with General Motors*, New York: Doubleday, 1964; Peter F. Drucker, *The Concept of the Corporation*, New York: John Day, 1946.

33. Aldous Huxley, *Brave New World*, New York: Random House, 2008 [1932].

34. O. M. W. Sprague, *History of Crises Under the National Banking System*, Washington, DC: Government Printing Office, 1910, archived at Federal Reserve Archival System for Economic Research (FRASER), https://fraser.stlouisfed.org/files/docs/historical/nmc/nmc_538_1910.pdf; Elmus Wicker, *Banking Panics of the Gilded Age*, Cambridge: Cambridge University Press, 2000.

35. Nash, *Master of Emergencies*; Clements, *Imperfect Visionary*.

36. Calvin Coolidge, "Sixth Annual Message," 1928, American Presidency Project, University of California, Santa Barbara, www.presidency.ucsb.edu/documents/sixth-annual-message-5.

37. Calvin Coolidge, "Address to the American Society of Newspaper Editors, Washington, D.C.," January 17, 1925, American Presidency Project, University of California, Santa Barbara, www.presidency.ucsb.edu/documents/address-the-american-society-newspaper-editors-washington-dc.

38. Edward A. Filene, "The New Capitalism," *Annals of the American Academy of Political and Social Science* 149, no. 1 (May 1930): 3–11.

39. "Fisher Sees Stocks Permanently High," *New York Times*, October 16, 1929, https://timesmachine.nytimes.com/timesmachine/1929/10/16/96000134.html.

40. J. Bradford DeLong and Andrei Shleifer, "Closed-End Fund Discounts: A Yardstick of Small-Investor Sentiment," *Journal of Portfolio Management* 18, no. 2 (Winter 1992): 46–53.

41. Eichengreen, *Golden Fetters*, 222–256.

42. Douglas Irwin, "Who Anticipated the Great Depression? Gustav Cassel Versus Keynes and Hayek on the Interwar Gold Standard," *Journal of Money, Credit, and Banking* 46, no. 1 (February 2014): 199–227, https://cpb-us-e1.wpmucdn.com/sites.dartmouth.edu/dist/c/1993/files/2021/01/jmcb.12102.pdf.

43. John Kenneth Galbraith, *The Great Crash, 1929*, Boston: Houghton Mifflin, 1955.

7. The Great Depression

1. Jean-Baptiste Say, *A Treatise on Political Economy*, Philadelphia: Gregg and Elliot, 1843 [1803].

2. John Stuart Mill, *Essays on Some Unsettled Questions in Political Economy*, London: John W. Parker, 1844 [1829]; John Maynard Keynes, *The General Theory of Employment, Interest and Money*, London: Macmillan, 1936; William Baumol, "Retrospectives: Say's Law," *Journal of Economic Perspectives* 13, no. 1 (Winter 1999): 195–204, available at American Economic Association, https://pubs.aeaweb.org/doi/pdfplus/10.1257/jep.13.1.195.

3. Karl Marx, *Theories of Surplus Value*, Moscow: Progress Publishers, 1971 [1861–1863], chap. 17, n.p., available at Marxists Internet Archive, www.marxists.org/archive/marx/works/1863/theories-surplus-value/ch17.htm.

4. Thomas Robert Malthus, *Principles of Political Economy Considered with a View Toward Their Practical Application*, 2nd ed., London: W. Pickering, 1836 [1820]; Mill, *Unsettled Questions*.

5. This powerful and crucial point is best expressed by Nick Rowe. See "Why Is Macroeconomics So Hard to Teach?," *Economist*, August 9, 2018, www.economist.com/finance-and-economics/2018/08/09/why-is-macroeconomics-so-hard-to-teach.

6. Jean-Baptiste Say, *Cours Complet d'Economie Politique Pratique*, Paris: Chez Rapilly, 1828–1830.

7. E. M. Forster, *Marianne Thornton: A Domestic Biography, 1797–1887*, New York: Harcourt Brace Jovanovich, 1973 [1902], 109–123.

8. Quoted in Walter Bagehot, *Lombard Street: A Description of the Money Market*, London: Henry S. King, 1873, 53.

9. John Kenneth Galbraith, *The Great Crash 1929*, Boston: Houghton Mifflin, 1955.

10. Barry J. Eichengreen, *Golden Fetters: The Gold Standard and the Great Depression*, New York: Oxford University Press, 1992, 258–316.

11. George Orwell, *The Road to Wigan Pier*, London: Left Book Club, 1937.

12. Eichengreen, *Golden Fetters*, 256–268.

13. Joseph Schumpeter, "Depressions," in Douglass V. Brown, Edward Chamberlin, Seymour E. Harris, Wassily W. Leontief, Edward S. Mason, Joseph A. Schumpeter, and Overton H. Taylor, *The Economics of the Recovery Program*, New York: McGraw-Hill, 1934, 16.

14. Friedrich A. von Hayek, "Prices and Production," 1931, in Friedrich A. von Hayek, *Prices and Production and Other Works*, Auburn, AL: Ludwig von Mises Institute, 2008, 275.

15. Schumpeter, "Depressions," 16.

16. Herbert Hoover, *The Memoirs of Herbert Hoover*, vol. 3, *The Great Depression, 1929–1941*, New York: Macmillan, 1953, 30.

17. Mill, *Unsettled Questions*, n.p.

18. Bagehot, *Lombard Street*; Robert Peel, "Letter of 1844," in *British Parliamentary Papers*, 1847, vol. 2, xxix, quoted in Charles Kindleberger, *A Financial History of Western Europe*, London: George Allen and Unwin, 1984, 90.

19. Ralph G. Hawtrey, *A Century of Bank Rate*, London: Taylor and Francis, 1995 [1938], 145.

20. John Maynard Keynes, "The Great Slump of 1930," *Nation and Athenaeum*, December 20 and 27, 1930, n.p.

21. John Maynard Keynes, *The Economic Consequences of the Peace*, London: Macmillan, 1919, 251.

22. Barry Eichengreen and Jeffrey Sachs, "Exchange Rates and Economic Recovery in the 1930s," National Bureau of Economic Research (NBER) working paper 1498, *Journal of Economic History* 45, no. 4 (December 1985): 925–946, available at NBER, www.nber.org/papers/w1498.

23. Franklin Delano Roosevelt, "First Inaugural Address," March 4, 1933, American Presidency Project, University of California, Santa Barbara, www.presidency.ucsb.edu/documents/inaugural-address-8.

24. P. J. Grigg, *Prejudice and Judgment*, London: Jonathan Cape, 1948, 7.

25. Jacob Viner, "Review: Mr. Keynes on the Causes of Unemployment," *Quarterly Journal of Economics* 51, no. 1 (November 1936): 147–167.

26. Keynes, *General Theory*, chap. 24, n.p.

27. Margaret Weir and Theda Skocpol, "State Structures and Social Keynesianism: Responses to the Great Depression in Sweden and the United States," *International Journal of Comparative Sociology* 24, nos. 1–2 (January 1983).

28. Richard J. Smethurst, *From Foot Soldier to Finance Minister: Takahashi Korekiyo*, Cambridge, MA: Harvard University Asia Center, 2007.

29. Hjalmar Horace Greeley Schacht, *Confessions of "the Old Wizard": Autobiography*, Boston: Houghton Mifflin, 1956.

30. Nico Voigtlaender and Hans-Joachim Voth, "Highway to Hitler," National Bureau of Economic Research (NBER) working paper 20150, issue date May 2014, revised January 2021, available at NBER, www.nber.org/papers/w20150.

31. Adolf Hitler, *Mein Kampf*, Baltimore: Pimlico, 1992 [1925]; Adolf Hitler, *Hitler's Second Book*, New York: Enigma Books, 2006.

32. Eichengreen, *Golden Fetters*, 411.

33. "Statement of J. Bradford DeLong, Professor of Economics, University of California at Berkeley," in "Lessons from the New Deal: Hearing Before

the Subcommittee on Economic Policy of the Committee of Banking, Housing, and Urban Affairs, United States Senate, One Hundred Eleventh Congress, First Session, on What Lessons Can Congress Learn from the New Deal That Can Help Drive Our Economy Today," March 31, 2009, Washington, DC: Government Printing Office, 2009, 21–22, 53–60, available at US Government Publishing Office website, www.govinfo.gov/content/pkg/CHRG -111shrg53161/html/CHRG-111shrg53161.htm.

34. Peter Temin, *Lessons from the Great Depression*, Cambridge, MA: MIT Press, 1991.

35. William L. Shirer, *The Collapse of the Third Republic: An Inquiry into the Fall of France in 1940*, New York: Pocket Books, 1971, 294.

36. Orwell, *Wigan Pier*, 78.

37. Orwell, *Wigan Pier*, 40–42.

38. Franklin Delano Roosevelt, "Address Accepting the Presidential Nomination at the Democratic National Convention in Chicago," July 2, 1932, American Presidency Project, University of California, Santa Barbara, www .presidency.ucsb.edu/documents/address-accepting-the-presidential-nomination -the-democratic-national-convention-chicago-1.

39. Ellis Hawley, *The New Deal and the Problem of Monopoly, 1934–1938: A Study in Economic Schizophrenia*, Madison: University of Wisconsin Press, 1958.

40. Vaclav Smil, *Creating the Twentieth Century: Technical Innovations of 1867–1914 and Their Lasting Impact*, Oxford: Oxford University Press, 2005; Vaclav Smil, *Transforming the Twentieth Century: Technical Innovations and Their Consequences*, Oxford: Oxford University Press, 2006.

41. Dwight D. Eisenhower, Letter to Edgar Newton Eisenhower, November 8, 1954, available at Teaching American History, https://teachingamerican history.org/library/document/letter-to-edgar-newton-eisenhower.

42. John Maynard Keynes, *Essays in Persuasion*, London: Macmillan, 1933, 326–329.

8. Really-Existing Socialism

1. Giuseppe Tomasi di Lampedusa, *The Leopard*, New York: Random House, 1960 [1958], 40.

2. Joseph Weydemeyer, "Dictatorship of the Proletariat," *Turn-Zeitung*, January 1, 1852, available at Libcom, https://libcom.org/files/Joseph%20 Weydemeyer%20-%20The%20Dictatorship%20of%20the%20Proletariat %20(article%20published%20in%20New%20York,%201852).pdf. There are definite similarities with Friedrich A. von Hayek's concept of a "Lykourgan moment," in which one saves freedom in the long run by means of authoritarian violence in the short run. Margaret Thatcher, Letter to Friedrich von

Hayek, February 17, 1982. For a transcript and digitized image of the letter, see Corey Robin, "Margaret Thatcher's Democracy Lessons," Jacobin, n.d., https://jacobinmag.com/2013/07/margaret-thatcher-democracy-lessons.

3. Then again, not only Lenin, but also Cromwell, and even Caesar himself, had problems with the "temporary" nature of the dictatorship.

4. Karl Marx, "Wage Labour and Capital," *Neue Rheinische Zeitung*, April 5–8, 11, 1849 [1847], chap. 9, available at Marxists Internet Archive, www.marxists.org/archive/marx/works/1847/wage-labour.

5. Karl Marx and Friedrich Engels, *Manifesto of the Communist Party*, London: Communist League, 1848, n.p.

6. George Boyer, "The Historical Background of the Communist Manifesto," *Journal of Economic Perspectives* 12, no. 4 (Fall 1998): 151–174.

7. Eric Hobsbawm, *Age of Extremes: The Short Twentieth Century, 1914–1991*, London: Michael Joseph, 1984, 379.

8. Evan Mawdsley, *The Russian Civil War*, New York: Simon and Schuster, 2009.

9. Peter Boettke, *Calculation and Coordination: Essays on Socialism and Transitional Political Economy*, New York: Routledge, 2001, 312, quoting Vladimir Lenin, "Theses for an Appeal to the International Socialist Committee and All Socialist Parties" [1931], in *Lenin Collected Works*, vol. 23, Moscow: Progress Publishers, 1964, 206–216, available at Marxists Internet Archive, www.marxists.org/archive/lenin/works/1916/dec/25.htm.

10. Edmund Wilson, *To the Finland Station: A Study in the Writing and Acting of History*, Garden City, NY: Doubleday, 1955 [1940], 384–385.

11. A central point of Michael Polanyi, "Planning and Spontaneous Order," *Manchester School of Economics and Social Studies* 16, no. 3 (1948): 237–268.

12. Vladimir Lenin, *Testament*, November 1922, in *Lenin Collected Works*, vol. 36, Moscow: Progress Publishers, 1966, 594–596, available at History Guide: Lectures on Twentieth Century Europe, www.historyguide.org/europe/testament.html.

13. Adolf Hitler, *Mein Kampf*, Baltimore: Pimlico, 1992 [1925].

14. Bertholt Brecht, "The Solution," June 1953, reprinted at Internet Poem, https://internetpoem.com/bertolt-brecht/the-solution-poem.

15. Timothy Snyder, *Bloodlands: Europe Between Hitler and Stalin*, New York: Basic Books, 2010, 21–87.

9. Fascism and Nazism

1. Aleksandr Solzhenitsyn, *The Gulag Archipelago*, vol. 1, New York: Harper and Row, 1976, 79. He was thinking of the Boshevikii and the Communist Party of the Soviet Union. But the truth, I think, applies equally well to really-existing socialism and its fraternal twin, fascism.

2. Andrew Carnegie, "Wealth," *North American Review* 148, no. 391 (June 1889): n.p., available from Robert Bannister at Swarthmore College, June 27, 1995, www.swarthmore.edu/SocSci/rbannis1/AIH19th/Carnegie.html.

3. Benito Mussolini, "The Doctrine of Fascism," first published in *Enciclopedia Italiana di Scienzek Lettere ed Arti*, vol. 14, Rome: Instituto Giovanni Treccani, 1932, available at San José State University faculty webpage of Andrew Wood at https://sjsu.edu/faculty/wooda/2B-HUM/Readings/The-Doctrine-of-Fascism.pdf; Antonio Scurati, *M: Son of the Century*, New York: HarperCollins, 2021; R. J. B. Bosworth, *Mussolini's Italy: Life Under the Fascist Dictatorship, 1915–1945*, New York: Penguin, 2005.

4. Leon Trotsky, "Political Profiles: Victor Adler," *Kievskaya Mysl*, no. 191 (July 13, 1913), available at Marxists Internet Archive, www.marxists.org/archive/trotsky/profiles/victoradler.htm.

5. Jasper Ridley, *Mussolini: A Biography*, New York: St. Martin's Press, 1998, 64.

6. George Orwell, "In Front of Your Nose," *London Tribune*, March 22, 1946, reprinted at Orwell Foundation, www.orwellfoundation.com/the-orwell-foundation/orwell/essays-and-other-works/in-front-of-your-nose.

7. John Lukacs, *A Short History of the Twentieth Century*, Cambridge, MA: Belknap Press of Harvard University Press, 2013; Francis Fukuyama, *The End of History and the Last Man*, New York: Free Press, 1992.

8. The best thing I have read about people's reactions to the figure of Hitler—then and since—is Ron Rosenbaum, *Explaining Hitler: The Search for the Origins of His Evil*, New York: Random House, 1998.

9. I still like, as a general history of Nazism more than any other, William L. Shirer, *The Rise and Fall of the Third Reich: A History of Nazi Germany*, New York: Simon and Schuster, 1960, for reasons that are well expressed by Ron Rosenbaum, "Revisiting the Rise and Fall of the Third Reich," *Smithsonian*, February 2012, www.smithsonianmag.com/history/revisiting-the-rise-and-fall-of-the-third-reich-20231221. You can read the raw material of what makes Shirer so special in William L. Shirer, *Berlin Diary*, New York: Knopf, 1941.

10. Adolf Hitler, *Mein Kampf*, Baltimore: Pimlico, 1992 [1925], 298.

11. Hitler, *Mein Kampf*, 121.

12. Hitler, *Mein Kampf*, 119.

13. Hitler, *Mein Kampf*, 500.

14. See David Ceserani, *Final Solution: The Fate of the Jews, 1933–49*, New York: Pan Macmillan, 2017; Christopher Browning, *Ordinary Men: Reserve Police Battalion 101 and the Final Solution in Poland*, New York: Harper Perennial, 1993. Worth watching, in my opinion at least, is *Conspiracy*, directed by Frank Pierson, written by Loring Mandel, featuring Kenneth Branagh (BBC and HBO Films, 2001).

15. Leo Strauss, Letter to Karl Löwith, May 19, 1933, in Leo Strauss, *Gesammelte Schriften, Bd. 3: Hobbes' politische Wissenschaft und zugehörige Schriften, Briefe*, ed. Heinrich Meier, Stuttgart: Metzler Verlag, 2001, 624–625, translation by Scott Horton at Balkinization, https://balkin.blogspot.com/2006/07/letter_16.html.

16. Ludwig von Mises, *Liberalism: The Classical Tradition*, Jena, Germany: Gustav Fischer Verlag, 1927, 51.

17. Margaret Thatcher, Letter to Friedrich von Hayek, February 17, 1982, transcript and digitized image available at Corey Robin, "Margaret Thatcher's Democracy Lessons," Jacobin, n.d., https://jacobinmag.com/2013/07/margaret-thatcher-democracy-lessons.

18. Hitler, *Mein Kampf*.

19. George Orwell, *Homage to Catalonia*, London: Seeker and Warburg, 1938, 34.

20. Hermann Rauschning, *The Voice of Destruction*, New York: Pelican, 1940, 192.

21. Eric Hobsbawm, *Age of Extremes: The Short Twentieth Century, 1914–1991*, London: Michael Joseph, 1984, 76.

22. Anton Antonov-Ovseenko, *The Time of Stalin—Portrait of a Tyranny*, New York: Harper and Row, 1981, 165. The supposed chain of transmission is from witness Klement Voroshilov to Anastas Mikoyan.

23. Rosa Luxemburg, *The Russian Revolution*, New York: Workers' Age Publishers, 1940 [1918], 34.

24. Janek Wasserman, *The Marginal Revolutionaries: How Austrian Economists Fought the War of Ideas*, New Haven, CT: Yale University Press, 1919, 98.

25. Eric Phipps, *Our Man in Berlin: The Diary of Sir Eric Phipps, 1933–1937*, Basingstoke, UK: Palgrave Macmillan, 2008, 31.

10. World War II

1. William L. Shirer, *The Rise and Fall of the Third Reich: A History of Nazi Germany*, New York: Simon and Schuster, 1960, 197.

2. Eric Phipps, *Our Man in Berlin: The Diary of Sir Eric Phipps, 1933–1937*, Basingstoke, UK: Palgrave Macmillan, 2008, 31.

3. Of all the "I told you so" accounts ever written, the gold medal has to go to Winston S. Churchill, *The Gathering Storm*, Boston: Houghton Mifflin, 1948, which is excellent, but only with the necessary corrective: David Reynolds, *In Command of History: Churchill Fighting and Writing the Second World War*, New York: Random House, 2005.

4. I have always thought that Winston S. Churchill was right in seeing the Dardanelles campaign in Turkey as a vastly preferable use of British resources than sending young men "to chew barbed wire in Flanders." Winston

S. Churchill to Herbert Henry Asquith, December 29, 1914, Churchill Papers, 26/1; quoted by W. Mark Hamilton, "Disaster in the Dardanelles: The History of the History," International Churchill Society, November 10, 2015, https://winstonchurchill.org/publications/finest-hour/finest-hour-169 /disaster-in-the-dardanelles-the-history-of-the-history.

5. David Faber, *Munich: The Appeasement Crisis*, London: Pocket Books, 2008.

6. Neville Chamberlain, "Peace for Our Time," speech, September 30, 1938, transcript at EuroDocs, https://eudocs.lib.byu.edu/index.php/Neville _Chamberlain%27s_%22Peace_For_Our_Time%22_speech.

7. Martin Gilbert, ed., *Winston S. Churchill, Companion*, vol. 5, pt. 3, *The Coming of War, 1936–1939*, London: Heinemann, 1982.

8. "The End of Czecho-Slovakia: A Day-to-Day Diary," *Bulletin of International News* 16, no. 6 (March 25, 1939): 23–39.

9. Winston S. Churchill, "The Russian Enigma," BBC, October 1, 1939, transcript at Churchill Society, www.churchill-society-london.org.uk/Rusn Enig.html.

10. For World War II, the briefest possible book I can recommend is Gerhard Weinberg, *World War II: A Very Short Introduction*, Oxford: Oxford University Press, 2014. To go deeper, see Gerhard Weinberg, *A World at Arms: A Global History of World War II*, Cambridge: Cambridge University Press, 1994; R. J. Overy, *Why the Allies Won*, London: Pimlico, 1996.

11. I feel the book needs at least one nonreference footnote: of course Wernher von Braun had a long life as other than a Nazi slavemaster and terror weapon builder after he came to the United States in 1945, but do mark me down as still astonished that there is a Wernher von Braun Center in downtown Huntsville, Alabama, for "conferences, conventions, concerts, Broadway performances, ballets, symphonies, a full range of sporting events and so much more!" See www.vonbrauncenter.com/about-us.

12. David Glantz, *Barbarossa: Hitler's Invasion of Russia, 1941*, Stroud, UK: Tempus Books, 2001.

13. Ernest May, *Strange Victory: Hitler's Conquest of France*, New York: Hill and Wang, 2000, 410.

14. William L. Shirer, *The Collapse of the Third Republic: An Inquiry into the Fall of France in 1940*, New York: Pocket Books, 1971, 690.

15. Shirer, *Collapse*, 691. The commander of the French Sixth Army, General Robert-Auguste Touchon, in whose area the Fourth Armored Division was operating, wrote in his reports of the division striking a "vigorous blow," noting that as a result it had "slowed down the [attacking] panzers." Jean Lacouture, *De Gaulle: The Rebel: 1890–1944*, trans. Patrick O'Brian, New York: Norton, 1990 [1984], 182.

16. Charles de Gaulle, "The Appeal of June 18," BBC, June 18, 1940, Internet Archive Wayback Machine, https://web.archive.org/web/20130423194941/http://www.france.fr/en/institutions-and-values/appeal-18-june.

17. Winston S. Churchill, *Their Finest Hour*, Boston: Houghton Mifflin, 1949, 59.

18. Churchill, *Their Finest Hour*.

19. One of the most astonishing and extraordinary accomplishments of the entire twentieth century—and one about which I know much, much too little.

11. The Cold War of Hostile Yet Coexisting Systems

1. Ron Rosenbaum, *How the End Begins: The Road to a Nuclear World War III*, New York: Simon and Schuster, 2011.

2. Nikita S. Khrushchev, "On Peaceful Coexistence," *Foreign Affairs* 38, no. 1 (October 1959): 1–18.

3. "We Will Bury You," *Time*, November 26, 1956, Internet Archive Wayback Machine, https://web.archive.org/web/20070124152821/http://www.time.com/time/magazine/article/0,9171,867329,00.html.

4. The next thing I think you should read on the Cold War is John Lewis Gaddis, *The Cold War: A New History*, New York: Penguin, 2005, and then his *We Now Know: Rethinking Cold War History*, Oxford: Clarendon Press, 1997, and *The United States and the Origins of the Cold War*, New York: Columbia University Press, 1972.

5. Vladimir Lenin, *Imperialism: The Highest Stage of Capitalism*, London: Lawrence and Wishart, 1948 [1916].

6. Paul Sweezy, *The Theory of Capitalist Development*, New York: Monthly Review Press, 1942, 361.

7. Charles Maier, *In Search of Stability: Explorations in Historical Political Economy*, Cambridge: Cambridge University Press, 1987, 153.

8. J. Bradford DeLong and Barry Eichengreen, "The Marshall Plan: History's Most Successful Structural Adjustment Program," in *Postwar Economic Reconstruction and Its Lessons for the East Today*, ed. Rüdiger Dornbusch, Willem Nolling, and Richard Layard, Cambridge, MA: MIT Press, 2003, 189–230.

9. Richard Strout, TRB (column), *New Republic*, May 5, 1947.

10. As reported by Clark Clifford. Forrest C. Pogue, *George C. Marshall: Statesman, 1945–1959*, Lexington, MA: Plunkett Lake Press, 2020 [1963], 236.

11. See Barry Eichengreen and Marc Uzan, "The Marshall Plan: Economic Effects and Implications for Eastern Europe and the Former USSR," *Economic Policy* 7, no. 14 (1992): 13–75.

12. Paul Krugman, "The Conscience of a Liberal," *New York Times*, November 30, 2010, https://krugman.blogs.nytimes.com/2010/11; Étienne Davignon, "Address," in *Jean Monnet: Proceedings of Centenary Symposium Organized by the Commission of the European Communities, Brussels, 10 November 1988*, Luxembourg: Office for Official Publications of the European Communities, 1989, 36, available at Archive of European Integration, University of Pittsburgh, http://aei-dev.library.pitt.edu/52373/1/A7287.pdf.

13. Dean Acheson, "Speech on the Far East," January 12, 1950, available at Teaching American History, https://teachingamericanhistory.org/document /speech-on-the-far-east.

14. Max Hastings, *The Korean War*, New York: Simon and Schuster, 1987.

15. John Foster Dulles, "The Evolution of Foreign Policy," Council on Foreign Relations, New York, January 12, 1954, reprinted in archives of *Air Force Magazine*, www.airforcemag.com/PDF/MagazineArchive/Documents /2013/September%202013/0913keeperfull.pdf.

16. George F. Kennan, "Sources of Soviet Conduct," *Foreign Affairs* 25, no. 4 (July 1947): 566–582.

17. "We Will Bury You"; "False Claim: Nikita Khrushchev 1959 Quote to the United Nations General Assembly," Reuters, May 11, 2020, www .reuters.com/article/uk-factcheck-khrushchev-1959-quote/false-claim-nikita -khrushchev-1959-quote-to-the-united-nations-general-assembly-idUSKBN 22N25D.

18. Dwight D. Eisenhower, Letter to Edgar Newton Eisenhower, November 8, 1954, available at Teaching American History, https://teachingamerican history.org/library/document/letter-to-edgar-newton-eisenhower.

12. False (and True) Starts to Economic Development in the Global South

1. W. Arthur Lewis, *Growth and Fluctuations, 1870–1913*, London: G. Allen and Unwin, 1978, 215–219.

2. Lant Pritchett, "Divergence, Bigtime," *Journal of Economic Perspectives* 11, no. 3 (Summer 1997): 3–17.

3. Robert Allen, *Global Economic History: A Very Short Introduction*, Oxford: Oxford University Press, 2013, 131–144.

4. Stanley Engerman and Kenneth Sokoloff, "Institutions, Factor Endowments, and Paths of Development in the New World," *Journal of Economic Perspectives* 14, no. 3 (Summer 2020): 217–232, available at American Economic Association, www.aeaweb.org/articles?id=10.1257/jep.14.3.217; Rafael La Porta, Florencio Lopez-de-Silanes, and Andrei Shleifer, "The Economic Consequences of Legal Origins," *Journal of Economic Literature* 46, no. 2 (June 2008): 285–332.

5. Harold Macmillan, "Winds of Change," BBC, February 3, 1960, www .bbc.co.uk/archive/tour-of-south-africa—rt-hon-macmillan/zv6gt39.

6. Ashutosh Varshney, "The Wonder of Indian Democracy," *East Asia Forum Quarterly*, February 29, 2012, www.eastasiaforum.org/2012/02/29 /the-wonder-of-indian-democracy.

7. Robert Bates, *Markets and States in Tropical Africa: The Political Basis of Agricultural Policies*, Berkeley: University of California Press, 1981, 1.

8. Nathan Nunn, "Long Term Effects of Africa's Slave Trades," *Quarterly Journal of Economics* 123, no. 1 (February 2008): 139–176.

9. Abubakar Tafawa Balewa, *Shaihu Umar*, Princeton, NJ: Markus Weiner Publishers, 1989 [1934]; see also discussion at Aaron Bady (@zunguzungu), Twitter, May 9, 2021, https://twitter.com/zunguzungu/status/139146383631 4607618.

10. Niccolò Machiavelli, *The Prince*, 1513.

11. Bates, *Markets and States*, 131.

12. Carlos Diaz-Alejandro, *Essays on the Economic History of the Argentine Republic*, New Haven, CT: Yale University Press, 1970; Gerardo della Paolera and Alan M. Taylor, *A New Economic History of Argentina*, Cambridge: Cambridge University Press, 2011.

13. Paul H. Lewis, *Guerrillas and Generals: The "Dirty War" in Argentina*, Westport, CT: Praeger, 2002. Lewis's fundamental view is that "what lay at the bottom of Argentina's . . . decline was the refusal of its entrenched elites . . . to accept the age of mass politics" (p. 4).

14. J. Bradford DeLong and Barry Eichengreen, "The Marshall Plan: History's Most Successful Structural Adjustment Program," in *Postwar Economic Reconstruction and Its Lessons for the East Today*, ed. Rüdiger Dornbusch, Willem Nolling, and Richard Layard, Cambridge, MA: MIT Press, 2003.

15. Said Amir Arjomand, *The Turban for the Crown: The Islamic Revolution in Iran*, Oxford: Oxford University Press, 1988.

16. Roderick MacFarquhar, ed., *The Politics of China: Sixty Years of the People's Republic of China*, Cambridge: Cambridge University Press, 2011.

17. Roderick MacFarquhar and Michael Schoenhals, *Mao's Last Revolution*, Cambridge, MA: Belknap Press of Harvard University Press, 2006.

18. Victor Shih, *Coalitions of the Weak: Mao and Deng's Power Strategy*, forthcoming.

19. Joe Studwell, *How Asia Works: Success and Failure in the World's Most Dynamic Region*, New York: Grove Press, 2013.

20. Ellen Hillbom and Jutta Bolt, *Botswana—A Modern Economic History: An African Diamond in the Rough*, Basingstoke, UK: Palgrave Macmillan, 2018.

21. Carl von Clausewitz, *On War*, Princeton, NJ: Princeton University Press, 1976 [1832].

22. Pritchett, "Divergence, Bigtime."

13. Inclusion

1. Chinua Achebe, *Things Fall Apart*, New York: Anchor Books, 1958, 178.

2. W. Arthur Lewis, "Biographical," in *Nobel Lectures: Economics, 1969–1980*, ed. Assar Lindbeck, Singapore: World Scientific Publishing Company, 1992 [1979], 395, reprinted at NobelPrize.org, www.nobelprize.org/prizes /economic-sciences/1979/lewis/biographical.

3. W. Arthur Lewis, *The Evolution of the International Economic Order*, Princeton, NJ: Princeton University Press, 1978.

4. Aristotle, *Politics*, trans. B. Jowett, Oxford: Clarendon Press, 1885 [350 BCE], 6.

5. W. E. B. Du Bois, "The Souls of White Folk," *The Collected Works of Du Bois*, e-artnow, 2018 [1903], n.p.

6. Doug Jones, "Toba? Or the Sperm Whale Effect?," *Logarithmic History*, August 6, 2017, https://logarithmichistory.wordpress.com/2017/08/05 /toba-or-the-sperm-whale-effect-2.

7. Thomas Sowell and Lynn D. Collins, *Essays and Data on American Ethnic Groups*, Washington, DC: Urban Institute, 1978, 208.

8. Sheera Frenkel and Cecilia Kang, *An Ugly Truth: Inside Facebook's Battle for Domination*, New York: HarperCollins, 2021. In my view, those who think that authors like Richard Herrnstein and Charles Murray are just "asking questions" and "presenting data" (see Richard Herrnstein and Charles Murray, *The Bell Curve: Intelligence and Class Structure in American Life*, New York: Simon and Schuster, 1994), which then lead them to assert that there are important and fundamental genetically driven racial differences in intelligence, should reflect. They should reflect that Charles Murray burned a cross to try to terrify the two Black families living in the Midwestern suburb where he grew up—and then has the cheek to claim that "there wouldn't have been a racist thought in our simple-minded minds. That's how unaware we were." See Jason DeParle, "Daring Research or 'Social Science Pornography'? Charles Murray," *New York Times*, October 9, 1994, https:// timesmachine.nytimes.com/timesmachine/1994/10/09/397547.html. They should reflect on the sources of their own gullibility, and on the sources of their need to believe that Blacks are relatively poor in America today not because of past and present discrimination but because of unchangeable elements of nature.

9. Abraham Lincoln and Stephen Douglas, "First Debate: Ottawa, Illinois," August 21, 1858, National Park Service, www.nps.gov/liho/learn /historyculture/debate1.htm.

10. Lincoln and Douglas, "First Debate."

11. Martin Luther King Jr., "I Have a Dream Today," August 28, 1963.

12. Republican campaign tactician Lee Atwater said back in 1981, in an interview with Alexander P. Lamis, that the Republican Party was not a racist organization because if it were, suppressing the Black vote and reversing the Voting Rights Act "would have been a central part of keeping the South [electing Republicans]." But now, he continued, "they don't have to do that. All you gotta do to keep the South is for Reagan to run in place on the issues . . . fiscal conservatism, balancing the budget, cutting taxes—you know that old cluster—[and] being tough with national defense." Atwater was thus very hopeful. He may or may not have been right in 1981. But the litmus test he proposed strongly suggests that he would be wrong about America's Republican Party now. Lee Atwater, "Southern Strategy Interview," 1981, posted on YouTube in three parts by "john smith," August 3, 2013, www.youtube.com/watch?v=yeHFMIdDuNQ, www.youtube.com/watch?v=btW831W0o34, and www.youtube.com/watch?v=dxmh5vXyhzA.

13. Continental Congress, Declaration of Independence, July 4, 1776, transcript at National Archives, www.archives.gov/founding-docs/declaration-transcript; Roger B. Taney, Dred Scott v. Sandford, 60 U.S. 393 (1856), Justia, https://supreme.justia.com/cases/federal/us/60/393; Harry V. Jaffa, *Crisis of the House Divided: An Interpretation of the Issues in the Lincoln-Douglas Debates*, Seattle: University of Washington Press, 1973; Harry V. Jaffa, *Storm over the Constitution*, New York: Lexington Books, 1999.

14. Tim Naftali, "Ronald Reagan's Long-Hidden Racist Conversation with Richard Nixon," *Atlantic*, July 30, 2019, www.theatlantic.com/ideas/archive/2019/07/ronald-reagans-racist-conversation-richard-nixon/595102; George Stigler, "The Problem of the Negro," *New Guard* 5 (December 1965): 11–12.

15. Dan Ziblatt, *Conservative Parties and the Birth of Democracy*, Cambridge: Cambridge University Press, 2017.

16. Edmund S. Morgan, *American Slavery, American Freedom: The Ordeal of Colonial Virginia*, New York: W. W. Norton, 1975.

17. Charles Murray, *Losing Ground: American Social Policy, 1950–1980*, New York: Basic Books, 1984.

18. George Gilder, *Wealth and Poverty*, New York: ICS Press, 1981.

19. Daniel Patrick Moynihan, *The Negro Family: The Case for National Action*, Office of Policy Planning and Research, US Department of Labor, March 1965, full text at US Department of Labor, www.dol.gov/general/aboutdol/history/webid-moynihan.

20. Aristotle, *Politics*, 24.

21. Doug Jones, "The Patriarchal Age," *Logarithmic History*, September 27, 2015, https://logarithmichistory.wordpress.com/2015/09/27/the-patriarchal-age; Monika Karmin, Lauri Saag, Mário Vicente, Melissa A. Wilson

Sayres, Mari Järve, Ulvi Gerst Talas, Siiri Rootsi, et al., "A Recent Bottleneck of Y Chromosome Diversity Coincides with a Global Change in Culture," *Genome Research* 25, no. 4 (April 2015): 459–466.

22. Claudia Goldin, *Understanding the Gender Gap: An Economic History of American Women*, New York: Oxford University Press, 1990.

23. Louis Menand, "How Women Got in on the Civil Rights Act," *New Yorker*, July 21, 2014, www.newyorker.com/magazine/2014/07/21/sex-amendment.

24. Goldin, *Understanding the Gender Gap*, 217.

25. Betty Friedan, *The Feminine Mystique*, New York: W. W. Norton, 1963, 474.

14. Thirty Glorious Years of Social Democracy

1. Jean Fourastié, *Les Trente Glorieuses: Ou, la Révolution Invisible de 1946 à 1975*, Paris: Hachette Littérature, 1997 [1949].

2. Antonio Gramsci, "Americanism and Fordism," in *Selections from the Prison Notebooks of Antonio Gramsci*, London: Lawrence and Wishart, 1971 [1934], 277–320; Charles S. Maier, "Between Taylorism and Technocracy: European Ideologies and the Vision of Industrial Productivity in the 1920s," *Journal of Contemporary History* 5, no. 2 (1970): 27–61.

3. Martin Weitzman, "Prices Versus Quantities," *Review of Economic Studies* 41, no. 4 (October 1974): 477–491.

4. Ronald Coase, "The Nature of the Firm," *Economica* 4, no. 16 (1937): 386–405.

5. Janos Kornai, *The Economics of Shortage*, Amsterdam: North-Holland, 1979.

6. Consider Chicago School of Economics cofounder Henry Simons, with his belief that the trust-busting Federal Trade Commission ought to be the most important and most activist arm of the government. Henry Simons, *Economic Policy for a Free Society*, Chicago: University of Chicago Press, 1948.

7. John Maynard Keynes, *The General Theory of Employment, Interest and Money*, London: Macmillan, 1936, chap. 24.

8. Franklin Delano Roosevelt, "First Inaugural Address," March 4, 1933, American Presidency Project, University of California, Santa Barbara, www.presidency.ucsb.edu/documents/inaugural-address-8.

9. For a while in his career, Friedman relied on historical correlations for his claim that a "neutral" monetary policy could be made automatic. But as Charles Goodhart had warned him, the historical correlations broke down as soon as central banks started to try to rely on them as control mechanisms. See C. A. E. Goodhart, "Problems of Monetary Management: The UK Experience," in *Monetary Theory and Practice: The UK Experience*, London: Palgrave

Macmillan, 1984, 91–121. Friedman then took refuge in a "'neutral' is whatever works" position. See Timothy B. Lee, "Milton Friedman Would Be Pushing for Easy Money Today," *Forbes*, June 1, 2012, www.forbes.com/sites/timothylee/2012/06/01/milton-friedman-would-be-pushing-for-easy-money-today/?sh=76b918545b16.

10. Keynes, *General Theory*, chap. 24.

11. Employment Act of 1946, 15 U.S.C. § 1021, archived at Federal Reserve Archival System for Economic Research (FRASER), https://fraser.stlouisfed.org/title/employment-act-1946-1099; J. Bradford De Long, "Keynesianism, Pennsylvania Avenue Style: Some Economic Consequences of the Employment Act of 1946," *Journal of Economic Perspectives* 10, no. 3 (Fall 1996): 41–53.

12. Dwight D. Eisenhower, Letter to Edgar Newton Eisenhower, November 8, 1954, available at Teaching American History, https://teachingamericanhistory.org/library/document/letter-to-edgar-newton-eisenhower.

13. Thomas Piketty and Emmanual Saez, "Income Inequality in the United States," *Quarterly Journal of Economics* 118, no. 1 (February 2003): 1–39, https://eml.berkeley.edu/~saez/pikettyqje.pdf.

14. Nelson Lichtenstein, *The Most Dangerous Man in Detroit: Walter Reuther and the Fate of American Labor*, New York: Basic Books, 1995.

15. J. Bradford DeLong and Barry Eichengreen, "The Marshall Plan: History's Most Successful Structural Adjustment Program," in *Postwar Economic Reconstruction and Its Lessons for the East Today*, ed. Rüdiger Dornbusch, Willem Nolling, and Richard Layard, Cambridge, MA: MIT Press, 2003.

16. Charles Kindleberger, *Europe's Postwar Growth: The Role of Labor Supply*, Cambridge, MA: Harvard University, Center for International Affairs, 1967; Barry Eichengreen, *The European Economy Since 1945: Coordinated Capitalism and Beyond*, Princeton, NJ: Princeton University Press, 1947.

17. Marcel Mauss, *The Gift: The Form and Reason for Exchange in Archaic Societies*, New York: Routledge, 1990 [1950].

18 Robert Gordon, "Postwar Macroeconomics: The Evolution of Events and Ideas," National Bureau of Economic Research (NBER) working paper 459, issue date March 1980, available at NBER, www.nber.org/system/files/working_papers/w0459/w0459.pdf.

19. Richard Nixon, *Six Crises*, New York: Doubleday, 1962.

20. Paul Volcker and Toyoo Gyohten, *Changing Fortunes: The World's Money and the Threat to American Leadership*, New York: Random House, 1992.

21. Arthur Burns, "Progress Towards Economic Stability," *American Economic Review* 50, no. 3 (March 1960): 1–19.

22. John Maynard Keynes, *The Economic Consequences of the Peace*, London: Macmillan, 1919, 220.

23. Keynes, *Economic Consequences*, 235–236.

15. The Neoliberal Turn

1. John Maynard Keynes, *The Economic Consequences of the Peace*, London: Macmillan, 1919, 22.

2. John Maynard Keynes, "Economic Possibilities for Our Grandchildren," reprinted in John Maynard Keynes, *The Collected Writings of John Maynard Keynes*, vol. 9, *Essays in Persuasion*, Cambridge: Cambridge University Press, 2013, 328.

3. Gareth Dale, *Karl Polanyi: A Life on the Left*, New York: Columbia University Press, 2016. Also very much worth reading is Tim Rogan, *The Moral Economists: R. H. Tawney, Karl Polanyi, E. P. Thompson, and the Critique of Capitalism*, Princeton, NJ: Princeton University Press, 2017.

4. Joan Robinson, *The Cultural Revolution in China*, New York: Penguin, 1967; Jan Myrdal, *Report from a Chinese Village*, New York: Pantheon Books, 1965.

5. Robert Gordon, *The Rise and Fall of American Growth: The U.S. Standard of Living Since the Civil War*, Princeton, NJ: Princeton University Press, 2017.

6. William Nordhaus, *Retrospectives on the 1970s Productivity Slowdown*, Cambridge, MA: National Bureau of Economic Research, 2004.

7. The extent to which Nixon and Kissinger approved of the oil price tripling (because, trying to play eleven-dimensional chess, they thought that higher oil prices would benefit the United States by giving the Iranian shah, Mohammed Reza Pahlavi, money with which to purchase weapons and annoy the Soviet Union) is something I have never been able to run down satisfactorily. Then treasury secretary William Simon thought it was the dominant consideration, and a horrible mistake. V. H. Oppenheim, "See the Past: We Pushed Them," *Foreign Policy* 25 (Winter 1976–1977): 24–57; David M. Wight, *Oil Money: Middle East Petrodollars and the Transformation of US Empire*, Ithaca, NY: Cornell University Press, 2021.

8. Jonathon Hazell, Juan Herreño, Emi Nakamura, and Jón Steinsson, "The Slope of the Phillips Curve: Evidence from U.S. States," National Bureau of Economic Research (NBER) working paper 28005, issue date October 2020, revised May 2021, available at NBER, www.nber.org/papers/w28005; Olivier Blanchard, "The U.S. Phillips Curve: Back to the 60s?," Peterson Institute for International Economics, January 2016, www.piie.com/publications/pb/pb16-1.pdf.

9. John A. Farrell, *Richard Nixon: The Life*, New York: Doubleday, 2017.

10. Martin Feldstein, "Introduction," in *The American Economy in Transition*, ed. Martin Feldstein, Chicago: University of Chicago Press, 1980, 1–8; Albert O. Hirschman, *The Rhetoric of Reaction: Perversity, Futility, Jeopardy*, Cambridge, MA: Belknap Press of Harvard University Press, 1991.

11. Eric Hobsbawm, *Age of Extremes: The Short Twentieth Century, 1914–1991*, London: Michael Joseph, 1984, 460.

12. See Eric Hobsbawm's interview with Michael Ignatieff, "The Late Show—Eric Hobsbawm—Age of Extremes (24 October 1994)," YouTube, posted by "tw19751," November 6, 2012, www.youtube.com/watch?v=Nnd 2Pu9NNPw; Sarah Lyall, "A Communist Life with No Apologies," *New York Times*, August 23, 2003, www.nytimes.com/2003/08/23/books/a-communist -life-with-no-apology.html.

13. George Stigler, "The Problem of the Negro," *New Guard* 5 (December 1965): 11–12, available at Digressions and Impressions, website of Eric Schliesser, https://digressionsnimpressions.typepad.com/digressionsimpres sions/2020/06/stiglerracism.html.

14. Paul Volcker and Toyoo Gyohten, *Changing Fortunes: The World's Money and the Threat to American Leadership*, New York: Random House, 1992. Volcker recounts telling Burns "with some exasperation," when Burns was Fed chair: "Arthur . . . you better go home and tighten money." See also Arthur Burns, "Progress Towards Economic Stability," *American Economic Review* 50, no. 3 (March 1960): 1–19.

15. Stuart Eizenstat, "Economists and White House Decisions," *Journal of Economic Perspectives* 6, no. 3 (Summer 1992): 65–71.

16. Barrie Wigmore and Peter Temin, "The End of One Big Deflation," MIT Department of Economics working paper 503, 1988, https://dspace .mit.edu/bitstream/handle/1721.1/63586/endofonebigdefla00temi.pdf; Thomas Sargent, "Stopping Moderate Inflations: The Methods of Poincaré and Thatcher," Federal Reserve Bank of Minneapolis, working paper W, May 1981, JSTOR, www.jstor.org/stable/10.2307/community.28111603; Laurence Ball, "The Genesis of Inflation and the Costs of Disinflation," *Journal of Money, Credit and Banking* 23, no. 3, Part 2: Price Stability (August 1991): 439–452.

17. Laurence Ball, "What Determines the Sacrifice Ratio?," in *Monetary Policy*, ed. N. Gregory Mankiw, Chicago: University of Chicago Press, 1994, 155–194.

18. Martin Feldstein, "The Dollar and the Trade Deficit in the 1980s: A Personal View," National Bureau of Economic Research (NBER) working paper 4325, issue date April 1993, available at NBER, www.nber.org/system /files/working_papers/w4325/w4325.pdf.

19. Milton Friedman and Rose Friedman, *Free to Choose: A Personal Statement*, New York: Avon, 1979.

20. Bill Clinton, "Address Before a Joint Session of the Congress on the State of the Union," January 23, 1996, American Presidency Project, University of California, Santa Barbara, www.presidency.ucsb.edu/documents /address-before-joint-session-the-congress-the-state-the-union-10.

21. Barack Obama, "Address Before a Joint Session of the Congress on the State of the Union," January 27, 2010, American Presidency Project, University of California, Santa Barbara, www.presidency.ucsb.edu/documents /address-before-joint-session-the-congress-the-state-the-union-17.

22. Martín Carcasson, "Ending Welfare as We Know It: President Clinton and the Rhetorical Transformation of the Anti-Welfare Culture," *Rhetoric and Public Affairs* 9, no. 4 (Winter 2006): 655–692.

23. Alwyn W. Turner, *A Classless Society: Britain in the 1990s*, London: Aurum Press, 2013.

24. J. Bradford DeLong, "Private Accounts: Add-on, Not Carve-Out," *Grasping Reality*, May 3, 2005, https://delong.typepad.com/sdj/2005/05 /private_account.html.

25. Thomas Piketty and Emmanuel Saez, "Income Inequality in the United States, 1913–1998," *Quarterly Journal of Economics* 118, no. 1 (February 2003): 1–39, https://eml.berkeley.edu/~saez/pikettyqje.pdf.

26. Takashi Negishi, "Welfare Economics and Existence of an Equilibrium for a Competitive Economy," *Metroeconomica* 12 (June 1960): 92–97.

27. Jeremiah 7:18.

28. "Globalization over Five Centuries, World," Our World in Data, https://ourworldindata.org/grapher/globalization-over-5-centuries?country= ~OWID_WRL.

29. Thomas Piketty, *Capital in the Twenty-First Century*, Cambridge, MA: Harvard University Press, 2014.

30. Rosa Luxemburg, *The Russian Revolution*, New York: Workers' Age Publishers, 1940 [1918].

31. Yegor Gaidar, "The Soviet Collapse: Grain and Oil," American Enterprise Institute for Public Policy Research, April 2007, www.aei.org/wp-content /uploads/2011/10/20070419_Gaidar.pdf.

16. Reglobalization, Information Technology, and Hyperglobalization

1. Michael Kremer, Jack Willis, and Yang You, "Converging to Convergence," in *NBER Macroeconomics Annual 2021*, vol. 36, ed. Martin S. Eichenbaum and Erik Hurst, Chicago: University of Chicago Press, 2021, available at National Bureau of Economic Research, www.nber.org/books-and-chapters /nber-macroeconomics-annual-2021-volume-36/converging-convergence.

2. Alan S. Blinder and Janet Louise Yellen, *The Fabulous Decade: Macroeconomic Lessons from the 1990s*, New York: Century Foundation, 2001; Dale W. Jorgenson, Mun S. Ho, and Kevin J. Stiroh, "A Retrospective Look at

the U.S. Productivity Growth Resurgence," *Journal of Economic Perspectives* 22, no. 1 (Winter 2008): 3–24, available at American Economic Association, https://pubs.aeaweb.org/doi/pdfplus/10.1257/jep.22.1.3.

3. Marc Levinson, *The Box: How the Shipping Container Made the World Smaller and the World Economy Bigger*, Princeton, NJ: Princeton University Press, 2008.

4. David S. Landes, *The Unbound Prometheus: Technological Change and Industrial Development in Western Europe from 1750 to the Present*, Cambridge, UK: Cambridge University Press, 1969; Robert S. Gordon, *The Rise and Fall of American Growth: The U.S Standard of Living since the Civil War*, Princeton, NJ: Princeton University Press, 2016.

5. Elhanan Helpman, *General Purpose Technologies and Economic Growth*, Cambridge, MA: MIT Press, 1998.

6. Paul E. Ceruzzi, *Computing: A Concise History*, Cambridge, MA: MIT Press, 2012.

7. Gordon Moore, "Cramming More Components onto Integrated Circuits," *Electronics* 38, no. 8 (April 1965), available at Intel, https://newsroom.intel.com/wp-content/uploads/sites/11/2018/05/moores-law-electronics.pdf.

8. "EUV Lithography Systems: TwinScan NXE:3400," ASML, www.asml.com/en/products/euv-lithography-systems/twinscan-nxe3400c.

9. Richard Baldwin, *The Great Convergence: Information Technology and the New Globalization*, Cambridge, MA: Harvard University Press, 2016.

10. Dani Rodrik, *Has Globalization Gone Too Far?*, Washington, DC: Institute for International Economics, 1997; David Autor, "Work of the Past, Work of the Future," *American Economic Association Papers and Proceedings* 109 (2019): 1–32; J. Bradford DeLong, "NAFTA and Other Trade Deals Have Not Gutted American Manufacturing—Period," *Vox*, January 24, 2017, www.vox.com/the-big-idea/2017/1/24/14363148/trade-deals-nafta-wto-china-job-loss-trump.

17. Great Recession and Anemic Recovery

1. John Fernald, "Productivity and Potential Output Before, During, and After the Great Recession," National Bureau of Economic Research (NBER) working paper 20248, issue date June 2014, available at NBER, www.nber.org/papers/w20248.

2. James H. Stock and Mark W. Watson, "Has the Business Cycle Changed, and Why?," *NBER Macroeconomics Annual* 17 (2002): 159–230, available at National Bureau of Economic Research, www.nber.org/system/files/chapters/c11075/c11075.pdf.

3. Amanda Robb, "Anatomy of a Fake News Scandal," *Rolling Stone*, November 16, 2017, www.rollingstone.com/feature/anatomy-of-a-fake-news-scandal -125877.

4. Barack Obama, "2004 Democratic National Convention Speech," *PBS NewsHour*, July 27, 2004, www.pbs.org/newshour/show/barack-obamas-key note-address-at-the-2004-democratic-national-convention.

5. J. Bradford DeLong, "This Time, It Is Not Different: The Persistent Concerns of Financial Macroeconomics," in *Rethinking the Financial Crisis*, ed. Alan Blinder, Andrew Lo, and Robert Solow, New York: Russell Sage Foundation, 2012.

6. Warren Buffett, Berkshire-Hathaway chairman's letter, February 28, 2002, Berkshire-Hathaway, www.berkshirehathaway.com/2001ar/2001letter .html.

7. Olivier Blanchard and Lawrence Summers, "Hysteresis and the European Unemployment Problem," National Bureau of Economic Research (NBER) working paper 1950, *NBER Macroeconomics Annual* 1 (1986): 15–78, available at NBER, www.nber.org/papers/w1950.

8. The rough consensus is represented by Ben Bernanke, "Japanese Monetary Policy: A Case of Self-Induced Paralysis?," Princeton University, December 1999, www.princeton.edu/~pkrugman/bernanke_paralysis.pdf; Kenneth Rogoff, "Comment on Krugman," *Brookings Papers on Economic Activity* 2 (1998): 194–199, www.brookings.edu/wp-content/uploads/1998/06/1998b _bpea_krugman_dominquez_rogoff.pdf.

9. Raghuram Rajan, "Has Financial Development Made the World Riskier?," in *The Greenspan Era: Lesson for the Future*, Kansas City: Federal Reserve Bank of Kansas City, 2005, 313–369, www.kansascityfed.org/docu ments/3326/PDF-Rajan2005.pdf. The most prominent other Cassandra was Paul Krugman. See his essay "It's Baaack: Japan's Slump and the Return of the Liquidity Trap," *Brookings Papers on Economic Activity* 199, no. 2 (1998): 137–187; and his book *The Return of Depression Economics*, New York: Norton, 1999.

10. "What Should Economists and Policymakers Learn from the Financial Crisis?," London School of Economics, March 25, 2013, www.lse.ac.uk /lse-player?id=1856.

11. "What Should Economists and Policymakers Learn . . . ?"

12. Carol Loomis, "Robert Rubin on the Job He Never Wanted," *Fortune*, November 26, 2007, available at Boston University Economics Department, www.bu.edu/econ/files/2011/01/Loomis.pdf.

13. See, for example, Chris Giles, "Harvard President Warns on Global Imbalances," *Financial Times*, January 28, 2006, www.ft.com/content/f925

a9e0-9035-11da-9e7e-0000779e2340; Maurice Obstfeld and Kenneth Rogoff, "The Unsustainable U.S. Current Account Position Revisited," in *G7 Current Account Imbalances: Sustainability and Adjustment*, ed. Richard Clarida, Chicago: University of Chicago Press, 2007, 339–375, available at National Bureau of Economic Research, www.nber.org/system/files/chapters /c0127/c0127.pdf.

14. Keynote address to the Center for Research in Security Prices (CRSP) Forum, Gleacher Center, University of Chicago, quoted in John Lippert, "Friedman Would Be Roiled as Chicago Disciples Rue Repudiation," *Bloomberg*, December 23, 2008, available at "John Lippert on the Chicago School," *Brad DeLong's Egregious Moderation*, blog, December 30, 2008.

15. Brad Setser, "Bernanke's Global Savings Glut," Council on Foreign Relations, May 21, 2005, www.cfr.org/blog/bernankes-global-savings-glut.

16. The best overview is, I believe, Barry J. Eichengreen, *Hall of Mirrors: The Great Depression, the Great Recession, and the Uses—and Misuses—of History*, New York: Oxford University Press, 2015.

17. John Stuart Mill, *Essays on Some Unsettled Questions in Political Economy*, London: John W. Parker, 1844 [1829].

18. Nick Rowe, "Money Stocks and Flows," Worthwhile Canadian Initiative, September 11, 2016, https://worthwhile.typepad.com/worthwhile _canadian_initi/2016/09/money-stocks-and-flows.html.

19. Hyman Minsky, *Stabilizing an Unstable Economy*, New Haven, CT: Yale University Press, 1986; Charles P. Kindleberger, *Manias, Panics, and Crashes: A History of Financial Crises*, New York: Basic Books, 1978.

20. J. Bradford DeLong, "John Stewart Mill vs. the European Central Bank," Project Syndicate, July 29, 2010, www.project-syndicate.org/commen tary/john-stewart-mill-vs—the-european-central-bank; Ricardo J. Caballero, Emmanuel Farhi, and Pierre-Olivier Gourinchas, "The Safe Assets Shortage Conundrum," *Journal of Economic Perspectives* 31, no. 3 (Summer 2017): 29–46, available at American Economic Association, https://pubs.aeaweb.org/doi /pdfplus/10.1257/jep.31.3.29.

21. Donald Kohn, "Financial Markets and Central Banking," Board of Governors of the Federal Reserve System, November 28, 2007, www.federa lreserve.gov/newsevents/speech/kohn20071128a.htm.

22. For my views at the time as the Great Recession developed, see J. Bradford DeLong, "Battered ~~but not~~ and Beaten," GitHub, October 29, 2010, https://github.com/braddelong/public-files/blob/master/2010-10-29 -battered-and-beaten.pdf.

23. Walter Bagehot, *Lombard Street: A Description of the Money Market*, London: Henry S. King, 1873.

24. Alan Blinder and Mark Zandi, "The Financial Crisis: Lessons for the Next One," Center on Budget and Policy Priorities, October 15, 2015, www.cbpp.org/sites/default/files/atoms/files/10-15-15pf.pdf.

25. The acronyms are for the Troubled Asset Relief Program, the Term-Asset Backed Security Loan Facility, the Home Affordable Modification Program, and the American Recovery and Reinvestment Act.

26. "Gore vs. Kemp: The 1996 Vice-Presidential Debate," YouTube, posted by PBS NewsHour, September 26, 2020, www.youtube.com/watch?v=HZCcSTz1qLo.

27. Lawrence Summers, "The Age of Secular Stagnation," *Foreign Affairs*, March/April 2016, www.foreignaffairs.com/articles/united-states/2016-02-15/age-secular-stagnation.

28. See Olivier J. Blanchard, "Public Debt and Low Interest Rates," American Economic Association, January 4, 2019, www.aeaweb.org/webcasts/2019/aea-presidential-address-public-debt-and-low-interest-rates.

29. Barack Obama, "Remarks by the President in State of the Union Address," White House, President Barack Obama, January 27, 2010, https://obamawhitehouse.archives.gov/the-press-office/remarks-president-state-union-address.

30. John Maynard Keynes, "How to Avoid a Slump," *The Times*, January 12–14, 1937, reprinted in John Maynard Keynes, *Collected Writings of John Maynard Keynes*, vol. 21, *Activities, 1931–1939: World Crises and Policies in Britain and America*, Cambridge: Cambridge University Press, 1982, 390.

31. Ben Bernanke, "The Near- and Longer-Term Prospects for the U.S. Economy," August 26, 2011, archived at Federal Reserve Archival System for Economic Research (FRASER), https://fraser.stlouisfed.org/title/statements-speeches-ben-s-bernanke-453/near-longer-term-prospects-us-economy-9116; Cf. J. Bradford DeLong, "Ben Bernanke's Dream World," Project Syndicate, August 30, 2011, www.project-syndicate.org/commentary/ben-bernanke-s-dream-world.

32. Josh Bivens, "The Reinhart and Rogoff Magical 90 Percent Threshold Loses Its Magic?," Economic Policy Institute, April 16, 2013, www.epi.org/blog/reinhart-rogoff-magical-90-percent-threshold.

33. Ben Bernanke, "Japanese Monetary Policy: A Case of Self-Induced Paralysis?," Princeton University, December 1999, 14–15, www.princeton.edu/~pkrugman/bernanke_paralysis.pdf.

34. J. Bradford DeLong, "Understanding the Lesser Depression" (incomplete draft), *Grasping Reality*, August 2011, https://delong.typepad.com/delong_long_form/2011/09/understanding-the-lesser-depression-incomplete-draft.html.

35. Adam Tooze, *Crashed: How a Decade of Financial Crises Changed the World*, New York: Penguin, 2018.

36. "Franklin Delano Roosevelt Speeches: Oglethorpe University Address. The New Deal," May 22, 1932, Pepperdine School of Public Policy, https://publicpolicy.pepperdine.edu/academics/research/faculty-research/new-deal/roosevelt-speeches/fr052232.htm.

37. Geoffrey Ward, *A First-Class Temperament: The Emergence of Franklin Roosevelt, 1905–1928*, New York: Vintage, 2014, xv; Randy Roberts, "FDR in the House of Mirrors," *Reviews in American History* 18, no. 1 (March 1990): 82–88.

38. Obama, 2010 State of the Union Address.

39. Cliff Asness et al., "Open Letter to Ben Bernanke," *Wall Street Journal*, November 15, 2010, www.wsj.com/articles/BL-REB-12460.

40. Leopold von Ranke, "Preface: Histories of the Latin and Germanic Nations from 1494–1514," excerpted in Fritz Stern, *The Varieties of History*, Cleveland, OH: Meridian Books, 1956, 57; Max Weber, *From Max Weber: Essays in Sociology*, ed. and trans. C. Wright Mills and Hans Heinrich Gerth, New York: Oxford University Press, 1946, 95.

Conclusion: Are We Still Slouching Towards Utopia?

1. John Maynard Keynes wrote two important letters to Roosevelt in the 1930s, both pleading for him to be more Keynesian: to spend less energy on social democratic structural reform and more on simply returning to full employment. See John Maynard Keynes, "An Open Letter to President Roosevelt," *New York Times*, December 31, 1933, www.nytimes.com/1933/12/31/archives/from-keynes-to-roosevelt-our-recovery-plan-assayed-the-british.html; John Maynard Keynes to President Franklin Roosevelt, February 1, 1938, facsimile on my website at https://delong.typepad.com/19380201-keynes-to-roosevelt.pdf.

2. Eric Hobsbawm, *Age of Extremes: The Short Twentieth Century, 1914–1991*, London: Michael Joseph, 1984.

3. Hebrews 11:1.

4. John Stuart Mill, *Principles of Political Economy, with Some of Their Applications to Social Philosophy*, London: Longmans, Green, Reader, and Dyer, 1873, 455. In Mill's view, the uneducated working class could not be judicious, and yet only after utopia had been approached would the resources per capita exist to properly educate the working class.

5. "Transcript of President Franklin Roosevelt's Annual Message (Four Freedoms) to Congress," January 6, 1941, Our Documents, www.ourdocuments.gov/doc.php?flash=false&doc=70&page=transcript.

6. Adam Serwer, *The Cruelty Is the Point: The Past, Present, and Future of Trump's America*, New York: One World Books, 2021.

7. Will Steakin, "Trump Dismisses Pandemic, Rips Fauci as 'Disaster' in Campaign All-Staff Call," ABC News, October 19, 2020, https://abc news.go.com/Politics/trump-dismisses-pandemic-rips-fauci-disaster-cam paign-staff/story?id=73697476; Benjamin Din, "Trump Lashes Out at Fauci and Birx After CNN Documentary," *Politico*, March 29, 2021, www.politico .com/news/2021/03/29/trump-fauci-birx-cnn-documentary-478422; "'Fire Fauci' Chant Erupts at Trump Rally as Tensions Simmer," YouTube, posted by "Bloomberg Quicktake: Now," November 2, 2020, www.youtube.com /watch?v=nWBqeTXKdTQ.

8. See Publius Decius Mus, "The Flight 93 Election," *Claremont Review of Books*, September 5, 2016, https://claremontreviewofbooks.com/digital/the -flight-93-election.

9. John Maynard Keynes, *Essays in Biography*, London: Macmillan, 1933, reprinted in John Maynard Keynes, *Collected Writings*, vol. 10, Cambridge: Cambridge University Press, 2013, 66–67.

10. Francis Bacon and Tomasso Campanella, *New Atlantis and City of the Sun: Two Classic Utopias*, New York: Dover, 2018.

11. John Maynard Keynes, *The Economic Consequences of the Peace*, London: Macmillan, 1919, 9, 12.

12. Aristotle, *Politics*, trans. Ernest Barker, Oxford: Oxford University Press, 2009 [350 BCE], 14, Bekker sections 1253b–1254a.

Index

AC induction motors, 70–72
Achebe, Chinua, 374
Acheson, Dean, 296, 325–326
Adams, John, 375
Addams, Jane, 103
adjusted yield factor, 201
Adler, Victor, 262
Afghanistan, 129
Africa, 344–346
Age of Extremes, The
    (Hobsbawm), 280
agriculture
  in 1914, 73
  collectivization of, behind the
    Iron Curtain, 255, 360, 456
  importation of plants and, 46
  plantation, 56
Aguiyi-Ironsi, Johnson, 348
Aid to Families with Dependent
    Children (AFDC), 410
AIG, 503
Albright, Madeleine, 12
Alfonso XIII, 172
Ali, Muhammed, 121–122

Allen, Robert, 57, 133, 135–136,
    341, 370
Allende, Salvador, 278, 333–334
alternating current, 68–70, 71
Altgeld, John Peter, 97–99,
    100–102
American Civil War, 122, 152
American Dilemma, An Myrdal,
    380–381
American Economic Association,
    422
American exceptionalism, 78–79,
    107, 330, 530
American Federation of Labor,
    97
American Institute of Electrical
    Engineers, 71
American Railway Union,
    99–100
American Recovery and
    Reinvestment Act (ARRA),
    506
American system of manufactures,
    192–193

American Telephone and
    Telegraph, 196
An Jung-geun, 135
anarchists, 191
Angell, Norman, 139, 141–142
anthology intelligence, 52–53
antisemitism, 191, 275–276
antitrust policies, 522
appeasement, strategies of,
    283–287
Ardennes Forest, 300
Argentina, 318, 352–355, 457
aristocracy, 154–155
Aristotle, 375, 387, 388,
    534–535
Arkhilokhos, 93
Asiatic flu, 171
assembly lines, 193–195
Atatürk, Mustafa Kemal, 173
Atkins, Edwin F., 72
Atlanta compromise, 105
Atlantic, Battle of the, 308
atomic bomb, 308
Attala, Mohamed, 472
attention-economy market, 487
Attlee, Clement, 416
austerity measures, 187, 213,
    221, 447, 510–511
Austria, 1938 German annexation
    of (Anschluss), 286
Austrian Republic, 181, 183
Austro-Hungarian Empire,
    151–152, 160–161, 167,
    172, 173, 180
Austro-Prussian War (1866), 152
automobiles, 405–406

baby boom generation, 431
Bagehot, Walter, 504

Bagehot-Minsky playbook,
    504–507, 508–509
Baker, George F., 72
Baldwin, Richard, 47–48, 475,
    476
Balewa, Abubakar Tafawa, 343,
    347–348
Balkan Wars (early twentieth
    century), 152
Bandung Conference, 334
Bank of England, 186, 189, 197,
    208–209, 224, 416
banking crises in 1930s, 210–211
Bardeen, John, 472
barriers, lack of, 37–38
Batchelor, Chris, 67
Bates, Robert, 345, 351
Bauer, Otto, 181
Bear Stearns, 503
Beer and Wine Revenue Act
    (1933), 520
Bell Telephone Laboratories, 472
Bellamy, Edward, 9–10, 528
Bentsen, Lloyd, 449
Berlin, Isaiah, 10–11, 93
Bernanke, Ben, 208, 495, 511,
    512, 515
Bessemer, Henry, 64
Bessemer-Mushet process, 64
Bewick Moreing, 60
birth rates, 393
Birx, Deborah, 532
Bismarck, Otto von, 153
Black Plague, 28
Blair, Tony, 447
Bland, Richard P., 101
blat, 248
Blinder, Alan, 490, 506
Blum, Léon, 225

Blumenthal, Michael, 440
boarders, 74–75
Boer War, 138, 144–147
Bohr, Niels, 470
Bolsheviks, 81
bonds, 178–179, 180, 185, 201
Bosch, Carl, 158
Bosnians, 152
Botswana, 369–370
Bouisson, Fernand, 225
Boulanger, Georges Ernest
    Jean-Marie, 108
bourgeois epoch, 524–525
bourgeoisie, 238–239
Boxer Rebellion, 126
Brandeis, Louis, 191
Brattain, Walter, 472
Braun, Wernher von, 292
Brave New World (Huxley), 195,
    196
Brecht, Bertolt, 253
Bretton Woods Conference, 323,
    421, 464
Brezhnev, Leonid, 334
Briand, Aristide, 224
Bridges, Harry, 231
Britain/British Empire
    1870 income levels in, 340
    after World War II, 319
    Boer War and, 144–147
    domination of, 128–130
    Egypt and, 123
    as example, 131–132
    gold standard and, 186–189
    during Great Depression,
        224
    India and, 119–121
    inflation in, 422
    Kaiping mine and, 126–127

    lead-up to World War II and,
        283–289
    war production and, 307–308
    World War I and, 153,
        156–157
    World War II and, 291–292,
        297–298
    zenith of, 115
British Canal Panic (1825), 207,
    208
British East India Company,
    119
British Industrial Revolution,
    30–32
Bronstein, David and Anna,
    79–80
Bronstein, Lev Davidovich
    (Leon Trotsky), 79–81
Brunel, Isambard Kingdom, 53
Brüning, Heinrich, 217
Bryan, William Jennings,
    101–102, 103
Buckner, Simon Bolivar, 101
Buffett, Warren, 488
Bukharin, Nikolai, 250, 456
Buller, Redvers, 145
Burghardt, Othello and Sarah
    Lampman, 104
Burns, Arthur, 421, 422–423,
    439
Bush, George H. W., 486, 517
Bush, George W., 487, 488, 513,
    517

Cambodia, 335
Camdessus, Michel, 508
Canada, 396
Canal Crisis of 1825, 208–209
capital, free flow of, 130–131

capitalism
  creative destruction and, 82
  failures of, 265–267
  imperialism and, 313–314
  Marx on, 239–240
caravels, 61–62
cargo containers, 466–467
Carlson, Ellsworth, 126
Carnegie, Andrew, 260
Carter, Jimmy, 424, 439–440
cash, demand for, 499–501
cast iron, 64
Castro, Fidel, 336
Caucasus oils fields, 304–305
Čermák, Anton, 35
Chamberlain, Joseph, 145
Chamberlain, Neville, 287, 288,
  291–292, 302
Chang Li "Yenmao," 125–127
Chautemps, Camille, 224
Chi Shihehang, 125
Chiang Kai-shek, 315, 316, 366
Chicago, pre-World War I,
  96–98
Chicago World's Fair, 71
childbirth and child care, 18,
  27–28, 75, 387–388
China
  CCP in, 43, 359–363, 531
  empire and, 116–117,
    123–128
  First Sino-Japanese War and,
    134–135
  Great Recession and, 505,
    512
  Japan and, 296
  modernization and, 134
  second unbundling and,
    476–477
  US trade and, 481
  World War II and, 294
Chinese Communist Party
  (CCP), 43, 359–362, 531
Chinese People's Liberation
  Army, 327
Chrysler, 409
Churchill, Winston Spencer
  German battle fleet and, 113,
    153
  parents of, 41–42
  on Soviet Union, 290
  value of pound and, 187–188
  World War II and, 285, 287,
    291–292, 302–303, 308
Citigroup, 491, 507
Civil Rights Act (1964), 384, 392
civil rights movement, 384
Civilian Conservation Corps, 520
Cixi, Empress Dowager, 124, 126
Clark, Greg, 28–29
Clark Field, Philippines, 297
class, inclusion and, 399. *see also*
  income inequality; middle
  class, growth of
Clausewitz, Carl von, 370
clearing house certificates, 197
Clemenceau, Georges, 170, 174
Cleveland, Grover, 97, 98–100,
  197
Clinton, Bill, 447, 448, 486–487,
  508
Clive, Robert, 119
closed-end investment funds,
  201–202
coal production, 318–319
Coal Question, The (Jevons), 33
Coase, Ronald, 397
Cochrane, John, 221, 493, 498

Cold War, 311–312, 325, 334–337, 454, 457–458, 467

Colfax Massacre, 89

Collapse of the Third Republic, The (Shirer), 301–302

collectivization of agriculture, 255, 360, 456

command economy, 158

commodity demand, 54

communication
globalization of, 37
increase in speed of, 51–53

Community Reinvestment Act, 496

comparative advantage, 49–50

computer chips, 470–471

concentration camps, 146

consumer goods, rise in ownership of, 451–452

containerization, 466–467

containment, 320, 329–331

Conyers, John, 381

Cooke and Company, Jay, 197

Coolidge, Calvin, 198–199, 215

Cornwallis-West, George, 41

corporations/corporatism, 1, 3, 17–18, 35, 267

corruption, fear of, 417

cosmopolitanism, 166

cotton famine, 122

cotton industry, 37

Cotton States and International Exposition, 104–105

Council of Ministers (France), 262

Countrywide, 496

COVID-19 pandemic, 171, 530–532

Cranford, Alfred, 105

Cranford, Mattie, 105

Crimean War (1853–1856), 152

Critique of the Gotha Program (Marx), 21

Croats, 151–152

Cross, Lillian, 35

Cuban missile crisis, 335–336

Cultural Revolution, 361–362

currency depreciation, 187, 220. *see also* inflation

currency-to-deposits ratio, 211

Czechoslovakia, 286–287, 316

Czolgosz, Leon, 190

Daladier, Édouard, 224–225, 287, 291–292

Dark Age, 61

Darrow, Clarence, 99, 102–103

De Beers, 369–370

de Gaulle, Charles, 300, 302

De Priest, Oscar Stanton, 381

Debs, Eugene V., 99–100, 103, 104, 408

decentralization, 168

decolonization and independence, 326, 334, 341–344

deficits
New Deal and, 522
under Reagan, 444–445

deflation, 187, 211, 217, 318

deindustrialization, 463, 467

democracy
Hayek and, 92
Madison on, 85–86
representative, 226, 238, 278, 343–344
see also social democracy

Democratic National Convention (1896), 101
Deng Pufang, 361
Deng Xiaoping, 43, 361–363
Dennard scaling, 487
depressions, government's cures for, 207–208
deregulation, 488
derivative markets, 487–488, 490–492
Deutsche Bank, 490
Deutsche Bundesbank, 490
dictatorship of the proletariat, 237
Diderot, Denis, 108
Diggs, Charles, 381
Dillon, C. Douglas, 466
direct current, 68–70, 71
disability insurance, 184
discrimination
    Civil Rights Act and, 392
    illegality of, 384
    wage, 391–392
disinflation, 422, 440–442
Disraeli, Benjamin, 112
distrust, culture of, 346
dot-com bubble, 494, 503
double movement, 94, 96
Doumergue, Gaston, 225
Doyle, Arthur Conan, 113
Drexel, Anthony, 53
Drexler, Anton, 272–273
Drucker, Peter, 167–168
Du Bois, W. E. B., 104, 105–106, 191, 376
dual administration, 243
Dubček, Alexander, 334
Dulles, Allen, 329–330
Dzerzhinsky, Feliks, 246, 250, 253

East, Rupert, 347
East Asian Pacific Rim, 364–365, 527
East India Company, 52
Easterlin, Richard, 22
Ebert, Friedrich, 160, 173
Economic Consequences of the Peace, The (Keynes), 175, 177, 188
Economic Cooperation Administration, 322
"Economic Possibilities for Our Grandchildren" (Keynes), 429, 519–520
economic versus political economic, 85
Economy Act (1933), 520
Edison, Thomas Alva, 35, 66, 67–68, 69–70, 71–72
Edison Machine Works, 67
education
    in America, 78
    Talented Tenth and, 106
egalitarianism, 92
Egypt, 121–123
Eichengreen, Barry J., 223–224, 321
Eiffel, Gustave, 65
eight-hour workday, 97
Eisenhower, Dwight D., 231–232, 333, 403–404, 421
Eisenhower, Edgar, 333, 403
El Alamein, Battle of, 308
electricity/electrification, 68–71, 199
Emancipation Proclamation, 380
Emergency Banking Act (1933), 520
Employment Act (1946), 403

energy consumption, in 1914
    Britain, 34
Engels, Friedrich, 20–21, 112,
    237, 524–525
engineering practice, community
    of, 130
Essay on the Principle of Population
    (Malthus), 27–28
eugenicists, 103
European Central Bank (ECB),
    497
European Coal and Steel
    Community, 323, 325,
    464
European Economic Community,
    325
European Union, 323, 325, 464
Europe's Optical Illusion (Angell),
    141

Fairchild Semiconductor, 472
Falkland Islands, 457
family structure, changes in, 385
fanatic religious violence, 530
Fannie Mae (Federal National
    Mortgage Association;
    FNMA), 496, 503
fascism, 167, 227, 237, 261–262,
    264–269, 277–279, 281–282,
    313
Fauci, Anthony, 532
fecundity, technology and, 8–9
Federal Home Loan Bank Act
    (1932), 405
Federal Housing Administration,
    405
Federal National Mortgage
    Association (FNMA; Fannie
    Mae), 496, 503

Federal Reserve
    in 1920s, 200
    establishment of, 198
    Great Depression and,
        202–203, 209, 213–214
    Great Recession and, 488,
        496–497, 502, 506
    inflation and, 419–420, 421,
        440, 441–442, 499–500
Federalist Papers, 85, 86
Feldstein, Martin, 435–436
financial asset prices, 200–202
financial bailouts, 507–509
financial crises of late twentieth
    century, 487, 488, 492
financial deregulation, 448
First Sino-Japanese War, 134
first unbundling, 47–48
fiscal theory of the price level,
    179–180, 184
Fisher, Irving, 201
Fitzgerald, Frank, 408
Five-Year Plans, 254, 256
Flandin, Pierre-Étienne, 225
flying shuttle, 36
Fogel, Robert, 31, 49
food stamps, 410
food supply
    population growth and, 29–30
    under war communism, 245
Ford, Gerald, 424
Ford, Henry, 55, 193–196, 200,
    413
Ford Motor Company, 408, 409,
    483–484
France
    after the French Revolution,
        108–109
    after World War II, 319

France (*continued*)
  gold standard and, 202
  during Great Depression,
    224–225
  inflation in, 183, 422
  lead-up to World War II and,
    283–289
  post–World War I Germany
    and, 183
  Russia and, 131
  worker movement in, 107–108
  World War I and, 153, 157
  World War II and, 291–292,
    300–302
Franco, Francisco, 227, 279, 313
Franco-Austrian War (1859), 152
Franco-Prussian War (1870), 152
Franz Ferdinand, Archduke, 152
Franz Joseph, 152, 153
Freddie Mac, 503
Fredendall, Lloyd, 303–304
Free Silver movement, 100–101
Free to Choose (Friedman and
  Friedman), 446
French Revolution, 65, 108, 259,
  344
Friedan, Betty, 394
Friedman, Milton, 203, 208, 212,
  401–402, 403–404, 446
Friedman, Rose, 446
frown curve, 468

G-7, 396
Gaidar, Yegor, 456–457
Gallagher, Edmund Edward, 40
Gallatin, Albert, 215
Gamelin, Maurice, 302–303
Gandhi, Mohandas Karamchand,
  42

Gatacre, William, 145
Gattopardo, Il (Lampedusa), 236
gender, occupational segregation
  and, 390–391. *see also*
  women
General Agreement on Tariffs
  and Trade (GATT), 324,
  465
General Electric, 66, 70
General Microelectronics, 472
General Motors, 196, 408–409
General Purpose Technologies
  (GPTs), 469–470
genetic variation, lack of in
  human race, 377
German Workers' Party, 272
Germany
  after World War I, 174–176,
    270
  after World War II, 319
  demilitarized zone in, 285–286
  Great Depression and, 223,
    283
  industry in, 530
  inflation in, 181, 182–183, 422
  rearmament and, 283
  reparations demanded from,
    181–182
  Soviet Union and, 252
  war economy of, 244–245
  war production and, 307–308
  World War I and, 153–154,
    155–157, 158–160
  World War II and, 297–310
  World War II personnel losses
    and, 306–307
G.H.M., 73–74
GI Bill, 406
Gilder, George, 385–386

Gill, José F., 40–41
Gillett, M. C., 176
Ginger, Ray, 76
Gingrich, Newt, 486
global north
  economic crises in, 489
  hyperglobalization and,
    478–479
  manufacturing and, 130
  see also individual countries
global savings glut, 495
global south
  falling behind of, 527
  income levels in, 340–341
  neoliberalism and, 371–372,
    462, 485
  population growth in, 348
  reglobalization and, 467–468
  see also individual countries
global warming, 530, 531
globalization
  as accelerant, 36
  decrease in transportation costs
    and, 47–49
  emergence of, 1, 3, 17–18
  epidemics and, 171–172
  hyperglobalization, 462–463,
    475–484
  impact of, 24
  population growth and, 51
  reglobalization, 461–463, 464,
    467–468
Godwin, William, 27
gold standard, 100–101, 185–
    189, 197, 202, 212, 214,
    219–220, 223–225, 295,
    520
Goldin, Claudia, 391, 392–393
Gompers, Samuel, 97

goods famine, 254
Gorbachev, Mikhail, 458
Gordon, Robert, 63, 65, 419, 469
Gore, Al, 508
Gorky, Maxim, 246
government, republic as form of,
    85–86
governments
  enterprises managed by,
    416–418
  market economy and, 24
  priorities of, 349–350
  see also democracy; *individual*
    countries
Gowon, Yakuba, 348
grain famine, 254
Gramlich, Ned, 488
Grant, Ulysses S., 104
Great Depression
  bankruptcies during, 211
  fading memory of, 437–438
  as failure of economic order,
    235–236
  Germany and, 182, 223, 270,
    283
  Japan and, 135, 222–223, 295
  lack of action from central
    banks and, 209
  lead-up to, 202–203, 213
  lessons learned from, 400
  reactions to, 213–218, 223–225,
    226–229
  reasons for, 212–213
  reasons for length of,
    219–220
  recovery from, 511
  right-wingers on, 401
  Roosevelt and, 520–523
  Scandinavia and, 222

Great Depression (*continued*)
shift to "mixed" economy and, 411
slide into, 210–212
unemployment during, 209–210, 213, 225–226, 402
United States' recovery from, 227–233
Great Eastern, SS, 52
Great Illusion, The (Angell), 141
Great Leap Forward, 360–361
Great Migrations, 381, 384
Great Mississippi Flood, 198
Great Purge (1930s), 257–258
Great Recession, 1, 82, 446, 459, 463–464, 493, 502–508, 510–515, 530
Great Transformation, The (Polanyi), 94
Greece, 509
Greenspan, Alan, 492
Grey, Earl, 87, 112
Grigg, P. J., 187, 220, 436
growth rate
acceleration of in 1870, 3
after 1973, 433
in early 2000s, 516
of G-7 countries, 396
impact of, 4–5
in post-World War II Europe, 412
Guadalcanal, Battle of, 308
Guangxu, Emperor, 124
guerrilla insurgency, 146
Guizot, François, 86–87

Haase, Hugo, 159–160, 262
Haber, Fritz, 158–159
Haber-Bosch process, 158–159
Halifax, Lord, 288
Hall, Clara, 41
Hamilton, Alexander, 56, 86
HAMP, 506
Harding, Warren G., 103, 185, 198, 215
Harland and Wolff shipyard, 39
Harman, Jeremiah, 208
Harriman, E. H., 197
Hastings, Warren, 119
Hawkins, Augustus, 381, 424
Hawtrey, R. G., 218
Hayek, Friedrich August von
on depressions, 214
on fascism, 278
on Great Depression, 202–203, 401
Keynes and, 398
on market economy, 2, 5, 168, 526
philosophy of, 90–94, 142–143
Polanyi and, 398–399
questioning of, 397
social justice and, 6, 13
Hayes, Rutherford B., 105
Haymarket Square, 97–98
heavy plows, 61–62
"hedonic treadmill," 22–23
Heeresgruppe Sud (Army Group South), 148
Hegel, G. W. F., 12
hegemon, 169, 218, 220, 322
Heller, Walter, 418, 421–422
Herriot, Édouard, 224
highways, 405–406
Hindenberg, Paul von, 149

Hitler, Adolf
  after World War I, 270–271,
    313
  Great Depression and, 223,
    227
  Haber and, 159
  horsepower and, 73
  lead-up to World War II and,
    283–291
  Malthus and, 273–274
  Mussolini and, 279
  oil fields and, 304–305
  platform of, 282
  rearmament and, 283
  reflation and, 513
  rise of, 272–273
  Stalin and, 289–292
  suicide of, 308
  World War I and, 271–272
  World War II and, 148, 252,
    276–277, 291–294
HIV/AIDS, 171
Hobart, Garret, 101
Hobsbawm, Eric, 2, 242, 280,
  436–437, 523
Hobson, John, 138–139
Hoerni, Jean, 472
Home Owners' Loan
  Corporation, 405
Homestead, Pennsylvania,
  75–77
Hong Kong, 362
Hoover, Herbert
  Belgium grain shipments and,
    176–177
  globalization of, 59–60
  gold standard and, 236
  Great Depression and, 212,
    215–216, 228–229

  housing policy and, 405
  importance of, 143
  industrialization and, 198
  Kaiping mine and, 126–127
  Roosevelt and, 522
  World War II and, 314
horse collars, 61–62
Hose, Sam, 105–106
housing
  bubble in, 493–494, 495–498,
    502–503
  decrease in immigration and,
    192
  policy regarding, 405
Howes, Anton, 36
Hu Yaobang, 363
Hull-House, 103
Human Development Index,
  369
Humphrey, Hubert, 424
Humphrey-Hawkins bill, 424
Huntziger, Charles, 300, 301
Huxley, Aldous, 195, 196
hyperglobalization, 462–463,
  475–484
hyperinflation, 180, 182–183,
  185

"I Have a Dream" speech (King),
  379
Iceland, 509
ideology, 259–260, 281,
  358–359
Illinois and Michigan Canal,
  96–97
Imperial-Commercial Age, 117
Imperial-Commercial Revolution,
  16, 62
imperialism, 53–54, 57, 313–314

income inequality
  after World War II, 374
  gender and, 390–392
  neoliberalism and, 445,
    449–453, 458
  race and, 383–385
income levels
  in 1870, 340
  after World War II, 319
  average increase in, 3–4
income tax, 101
India, 119–121, 343, 477
Indonesia, 335, 477
indoor plumbing, 63, 75
induction motors, 70–72
industrial design, 476
industrial research labs, 1, 3,
    17–18, 35–36, 70–71,
    158–159
Industrial Revolution, 16, 19,
    29–32
Industrial Workers of the World,
    194
Industrial-Commercial
    Revolution, 30
industry, technological transitions
    in, 413–414
inequality
  in early twentieth century,
    73–75
  extent of, 13
  in market economy, 415
  see also income inequality; race
inevitable immiseration, doctrine
    of, 239–240
infant mortality, 75
inflation
  in 1970s, 418–425, 432–433,
    439–442

gold standard and, 202
  hyperinflation, 180, 182–183,
    185
  post–World War I, 177–179,
    181–186
  unemployment and, 418–421,
    424, 431–433
  during World War I, 294
influenza epidemics, 171–172
information technology, 462–463,
    468–474, 485
Insull, Samuel, 199
integrated-circuit semiconductors,
    471–473
Intel, 473–474, 485
interchangeable parts, 193
interest rates
  on bonds, 500
  Friedman on, 401–402
  during Great Depression, 217
  housing bubble and, 497
International Bank for
    Reconstruction and
    Development, 464–465.
    see also World Bank
International Monetary Fund
    (IMF), 323, 464–465
international trade
  before 1700, 36–37
  after World War II, 323–324
  comparative advantage and,
    49–50
  decrease in transportation costs
    and, 47–49
  hyperglobalization and,
    481–484
  labor division and, 45–46
  United States and, 323–324
  see also tariffs

International Trade Organization (ITO), 323, 464–465
International Workers' Day, 97
inventions, changes in, 61–62
Iran, 333, 355–358
Iranian Revolution, 423
iron-hulled, steam-powered, screw-propellered steamships, 39–40
Ismail (of Egypt), 122
isolationism, 170, 189–192, 315
Italy, 396
Itō Hirobumi, 133–134, 135

Jackson, Andrew, 198
Jackson, Lidian, 39
James I, 528
Japan
  after World War II, 364–367, 396
  asset freeze and, 296–297
  bombing of, 308
  China and, 124, 296
  deflationary crisis in, 489
  empire and, 132–136
  First Sino-Japanese War and, 134–135
  Great Depression and, 222–223, 295
  industry/industrialization in, 294–295, 530
  inflation in, 422
  World War I and, 294
  World War II and, 294–298
Jefferson, Thomas, 86, 380
Jerome, Jennie, 41
Jerome, Leonard, 41
Jevons, William Stanley, 20, 33
Jim Crow, 383

John the Theologian, 241
Johnson, Lyndon, 418, 419–420, 434
Jordan, Barbara, 381
June Days uprising, 107–108

Kahng, Dawon, 472
Kaiping mine, 125–127
Kamenev, Lev, 241
Kant, Immanuel, 10
Karl I, 173
Kasserine Pass, 303–304
Kay, John, 36
Kelsey-Hayes, 408
Kemp, Jack, 508
Kennan, George, 330, 333
Kennedy, John F., 336, 419
Kerensky, Aleksandr, 172–173
Keynes, John Maynard
  after World War I, 177–178, 187–188
  on austerity, 511
  Bretton Woods Conference and, 323, 464
  on destruction of trust, 185
  Friedman and, 401–402, 403–404
  on Great Depression, 218–219, 221–222
  Hayek and, 398
  Hayek and Polanyi and, 168
  on inflation, 425
  on living wisely and well, 232–233, 429, 519–520, 529
  on Malthus, 29
  as marker, 7
  on post-Civil War period, 427
  on pre-World War I period, 34, 50, 114

Keynes, John Maynard
(*continued*)
  social Darwinism and, 112
  Trotsky and, 533
  World War I and, 162–163,
    174–176
Keynesian depression, 500–501
"khaki election," 146
Khama, Seretse, 369
khedive (viceroy) or Egypt, 55
Khmer Rouge, 335
Khomeini, Ayatollah Ruhollah,
    357–358
Khrushchev, Nikita Sergeyevich,
    311–312, 331, 335–336,
    456
Kido Takayoshi, 133
Kim Il-Sung, 325–326
Kindleberger, Charlie, 169, 412
King, Martin Luther, Jr., 379,
    382
Kipling, Rudyard, 33, 137
Kirkpatrick, Jeane, 457
Kissinger, Henry, 423, 434
kleptocracy, 349
Knight, Frank, 490
Kohn, Donald, 502
Korea, 135, 476
Korean War, 325–328, 364
Kosygin, Aleksei, 305
Kremer, Michael, 349
Krestinsky, Nikolai, 241
Ku Klux Klan, 191
kulaks, 254–255, 258
Kuznets, Simon, 17

labor force/market
  elastic supplies of, 412
  gender differences in, 389–390

literate, 130
  stability in, 412
laissez-faire, 231–232, 260,
    400–401, 403
Lampedusa, Giuseppe Tomasi di,
    236
land reform, in Iran, 356
Landes, David, 469
language, national borders and,
    284
Last, Jay, 472
Latin America, 344, 366–367
Laval, Pierre, 224
League of Nations, 170, 181
legions, 61–62
Lehman Brothers, 503
Lend-Lease supplies, 305
Lenin, Vladimir
  after World War I, 131
  as axis point, 523
  on capitalism, 313–314
  command economy and, 158
  impact of path of, 282
  Keynes on, 178
  as marker, 7
  Russian Civil War and,
    242–244, 246
  Russian Revolution and,
    172–173
  socialism and, 167, 237–238,
    241
  Soviet Union and, 247
  Stalin and, 253
  succession planning of,
    249–250
  Trotsky and, 81
  World War I and, 262
"Lenin's Testament," 249–250
Leuchtenburg, William, 228

leveraged buyout (LBO), 181
Lewis, W. Arthur, 54, 57, 62–63, 339, 374–375
Li Hongzhang, 123–125, 127, 128, 134, 143
libertarianism, 446
Liebknecht, Karl, 173, 262
life expectancy
  in 1870, 32
  in 1914, 73
  in Agrarian Age, 16
  for Black slave in 1800, 376
  in post–World War I Russia, 247
  in pre–World War I Russia, 32
  in Soviet Union, 251, 455
Lin Biao, 361
Lincoln, Abraham, 52, 378–380
"liquidationist" doctrine, 218
liquidity, depressions and, 216
List Regiment, 271–272
literacy
  in 1914, 73
  in Japan, 133
  labor force and, 130
Liu Shaoqi, 361
Lloyd George, David, 170, 174, 287
Lodge, Henry Cabot, 170, 190–191, 192, 195
Lombard Street (Bagehot), 504
London Economic Conference, 223–224
"long twentieth century"
  consequences of, 11
  defining, 1–2
  economics as most consequential thread of, 7–8
  reasons for focus on, 2

Looking Backward, 2000–1887 (Bellamy), 9–10
Lord, William Walcott, 480
Lord Brothers Leather Company, 480
Louis XVI, King, 108
Louis-Philippe, King, 87
Luxemburg, Rosa, 173, 262, 282, 454–455
Lykourgan moment, 92
lynchings, 104–106

MacArthur, Douglas, 327
Machiavelli, Niccolò, 350
"MAD" strategies, 333
Madison, James, 85–86
Mafeking Night party, 137–138
Magnitogorsk, 256
Mahdist regime, 118
make-or-buy decisions, 249
Malaysia, 477
Malthus, Thomas Robert, 25, 27–29, 206, 273–274
Manchuria, 296
Manhattan Project, 308
Manstein, Fritz Erich Georg Eduard von, 148–149
Mao Zedong, 315, 316, 327, 360–362
market economy
  absence of fairness in, 90–91
  after World War II, 317–320
  competition and, 397
  crowdsourcing of, 2
  deficiencies of, 331–332
  governments and, 24
  Hayek and, 90–94
  inequality in, 415
  neoliberalism and, 448

market economy (*continued*)
  Polanyi and, 94–96
  property rights and, 6, 13, 92, 95
  in Soviet Union, 248
  start of changes in, 2–3
  technological diffusion and, 56–57
Marshall, George C., 321
Marshall Plan, 319, 320–322, 324, 328, 527
Marx, Karl, 20–21, 112, 119–120, 206–207, 237–241, 254, 315, 395, 524–525
mass production, 193–197
massive retaliation, US policy of, 329
material interests, 148
Mather, Robert, 72
May, Ernest, 300
Mayr, Karl, 272, 273
McCormick Harvesting Machine Company, 97, 193
McGinnis, Lydia, 40
McKinley, William, 101–102, 190
Meckel, Jakob, 134
Mehmed VI, 173
Meiji Restoration, 133–134, 365, 366
Mein Kampf (Hitler), 273, 274
Mellon, Andrew, 215–216
Methuen, Lord, 145, 146
microelectronics, 470
microprocessors, 473–474, 485
middle class, growth of, 406, 409
Midway, Battle of, 308
migration
  in 1914, 73
  free, 130–131
  globalization and, 37–38, 40–45
  post–World War I, 171
  resistance to in United States, 190–192, 212–213
  technological diffusion and, 57
  United States and, 46–47, 77
  urban, 256–257
  wages and, 44–45
military expansion, 443–444
Mill, John Stuart, 8–9, 19–21, 29, 57, 205–207, 216, 395, 499, 525
Miller, G. William, 439–440
Min Zhu, 517
mining, 124–127
Minsky, Hyman, 501–502
Minskyite depression, 501–502, 504–505
Mises, Ludwig von, 277–278
Mitterand, François, 442
modern economic growth, era of, 17
Mogul Empire, 119
Mokyr, Joel, 57–58
monetarist depression, 499–500
money, excess demand for, 206–207
monopolies
  breaking up of, 522
  fear of, 417–418
Moore, Gordon, 472
Morgan, J. Pierpont, 53, 72, 197
Mori Arinori, 133
mortgages, 405, 495–497. *see also* derivative markets; housing
Mossaddegh, Mohammad, 333

Moynihan, Daniel Patrick, 385–386
Muhammed, Murtala, 348
Muhammed Ali of Egypt, 55
Murdoch, Rupert, 486
Murphy, Frank, 408, 409
Murray, Charles, 385–386
Mushet, Robert, 64
muskets, 61–62
Mussolini, Benito, 7, 167, 262, 263–264, 266–268, 279, 313
Myrdal, Gunnar, 380–381

Nabeshima Naomasa, 133
National Democratic Party, 101
National Industrial Recovery Act (NIRA; 1933), 230, 520
National Interstate and Defense Highways Act (1956), 405–406
National Labor Relations Act (Wagner Act; 1935), 231, 407, 411, 521, 522
National Labor Relations Board, 407
National Recovery Administration (NRA), 521, 522
National Socialist German Workers' Party (Nazis), 270, 272–273, 276, 278–279
"National State and Economic Policy, The" (Weber), 147
National Telephone Company of Hungary, 67
nationalism
    definition of, 147–148
    economic, 318
        income inequality and, 382–383
    post–World War I, 174
    in pre–World War I Germany, 148–150
    socialism and, 316
    World War I and, 154, 160
nationalization of industry, 416–418
natural resources, 48–49, 54, 77
Nazi Army Group Center, 307
Nazis. *see* National Socialist German Workers' Party (Nazis)
"necessity, realm of," 12
Negro Family, The (Moynihan), 386
Nehru, Jawaharlal, 334
neoliberalism
    Cold War and, 454–458, 461
    context for turn to, 427–431, 436–438
    failures of, 445–447
    global south and, 371–372, 462, 485
    income inequality and, 449–453, 458
    left versus right, 448–449
    politics and, 515–517
    social democracy and, 414–415, 416, 448–449
    turn to, 439–446
net military transactions, 328
New Deal, 228–231, 333, 403, 513, 520–521
New Economic Policy, 248
Nguyễn Văn Thiệu, 434
Nicaragua, 457
Nicholas II, 152, 154, 172

Nigeria, 343, 347–348
Nix, Robert, 381
Nixon, Richard, 420–422, 434
nonaligned nations, 334–335
North American Aerospace
    Defense Command
    (NORAD), 336
North Atlantic Free Trade
    Agreement (NAFTA), 477
North Atlantic Treaty
    Organization (NATO),
    320–321, 324–325,
    328–330, 336
North Korea, 327
Northern Pacific Railroad, 197
Northern People's Congress
    (Nigeria), 347
Noyce, Robert, 472
nuclear weaponry, 329, 333,
    335–336
Nunn, Nathan, 345
Nzeogwu, Chukwuma Kaduna,
    347–348

Obama, Barack, 447, 510–511,
    513–515
occupational segregation by sex,
    390–391
Oceanic, RMS, 39–40
oil embargo, 432
oil prices, 356, 423, 431, 432,
    456
Ōkubo Toshimichi, 133
Ōkuma Shigenobu, 134
Olney, Richard, 100
Omdurman, Battle of, 118
On the Origin of Species (Darwin),
    112
Operation Bagration, 307

Operation Mars, 305–306
Operation Uranus, 306, 308
Orange Free State, 145–146
Ordzhonikidze, Sergo, 250, 253
Organisation for Economic Co-
    operation and Development
    (OECD), 363–364
Organization of the Petroleum
    Exporting Countries
    (OPEC), 423, 432
O-ring theory, 349
Orwell, George, 212, 225–226,
    279
Ottoman Empire, fall of, 173
*Our Penal Machinery and Its
    Victims* (Altgeld), 98

Pacific Rim development model,
    364–368, 370
Pahlavi, Mohammed Reza, 333
Paine, Thomas, 108
Palmer, John M., 101, 103
Panic of 1893, 101
Panic of 1901, 197
Panic of 1907, 197
Paris Peace Conference, 176
Park Chung-Hee, 366, 369
Patton, George, 314, 315
Paul-Boncour, Joseph, 224
Peace Theories and the Balkan War
    (Angell), 141
peaceful coexistence, 312, 329,
    333–334
Pearl Harbor, 294, 297
Pelosi, Nancy, 510
Peng Dehuai, 361
Perkins, Frances, 103, 230–231
permanent employment system,
    295

permissiveness, 92

Perón, Juan, 279, 353–354

personnel departments, wage
    discrimination and, 391–392

Pétain, Philippe, 313

Petrov, Stanislav, 336

Philippines, 132

Phillips, A. William, 420

"Phillips curve," 420

Phipps, Eric, 282, 284

Piketty, Thomas, 453

Pinochet, Augusto, 278, 334

plantation agriculture, 56

Plato, 387

Poland, 183, 288–289, 291, 477

Polanyi, Karl, 6, 7, 13, 90,
    94–95, 142–143, 168, 281,
    398–399

Polanyi, Michael, 168

political economic, the, 85

politics, in 2010s, 12

Popolo d'Italia, Il, 264

Popper, Karl, 167

population growth
    changes in, 16
    in China, 44–45
    curtailing, 20
    decrease in rate of, 393
    explosion of, 527
    food supply and, 29–30
    in global south, 348
    globalization and, 51
    Hitler and, 274–276
    Industrial Revolution and,
        30–32
    Malthus on, 27–28
    sustaining, 14
    technology and, 34
    in United States, 46–47

Populists, 199

Portugal, 116–117

"positive check," 27–28

poverty rates
    changes in, 11
    in early twentieth century, 73,
        76
    extreme, 345
    family structure and, 385
    population growth and, 348
    racial inequality in, 383–384

Powell, Adam Clayton, Jr., 381

Prebisch, Raul, 58

Preobrazhensky, Yevgeni, 254

"preventative check," 28

price controls, 244, 317–318

price level, fiscal theory of the,
    179–180, 184

primitive accumulation, 254

Principles of Political Economy
    (Mill), 19

printing, 61

priorities of governments,
    349–350

Pritchett, Lant, 370–371

"Problem of the Negro, The"
    (Stigler), 438

product differentiation,
    196–197

"Progress Towards Economic
    Stability" (Burns), 422–423

Progressivism/Progressive Era,
    200, 383

Prohibition, 520

property rights
    Great Depression and, 235
    under Lenin, 243–244
    market economy and, 6, 13,
        92, 95

prosperity, political participation
and, 86–88
protagonists, 142–144
protectionism, 364–366
Province of the Transvaal,
144–146
Prussia, 156
Prusso-Austro-Danish War
(1864), 152
Ptolemy, Claudius, 401
public goods, 169
Pullman Company, 200
Pullman Strike, 99–100
Pyatakov, Georgy, 250

Qing dynasty, 123–126, 128
quantitative easing, 505, 506, 512

race
income inequality and,
383–385
inequality and, 376–384, 438
lynchings and, 104–106
voting rights and, 89, 381–382
radio, 70, 72
railroad, 38–39, 49, 50, 61
Rajan, Raghuram, 489–490
Rand, Ayn, 397
Rathenau, Walther, 159, 244
rationing, 244–245, 317
Rauschning, Hermann, 279
Reagan, Nancy, 457–458
Reagan, Ronald, 382, 442–445,
447, 454, 457–458, 480
real wages, changes in, 28–29,
34–35, 44–45, 50, 183, 386,
479
Reciprocal Tariff Act (1935), 521

Reconstruction, 383
Red Army, 148
reflation, 220–221, 224
reglobalization, 461–463, 464,
467–468
Rehnquist, William, 89
Reichstag fire, 270–271
Reid, Harry, 510
Reinhardt, Georg-Hans, 301
Reinhart, Carmen M., 512
representative democracy, 226,
238, 278, 343–344
Republic (Plato), 387
republic, as form of government,
85–86
Republican Party National
Convention, 52
reserves-to-deposits ratio, 211
resource scarcity, 3, 8, 13
Reuther, Walter, 408–409
Reynaud, Paul, 302
Reza Shah Pahlavi, 355–358
Richardson, Florence Wyman,
88, 89
Road to Wagon Pier, The (Orwell),
212
Robbins, Lionel, 202–203, 401
Roberts, Lord, 146
Robinson, Joan, 129
Rodrik, Dani, 481
Rogoff, Kenneth, 512
Rommel, Erwin, 301
Romney, George, 452
Romney, Mitt, 452
Roosevelt, Franklin Delano
on birthright freedoms, 529
Čermák and, 35
Churchill and, 42

Great Depression and,
227–229, 400, 511–512,
520–523
growth rate and, 403
Inaugural Address of, 220
Japan and, 296
Obama and, 513–514
Perkins and, 103
World War I and, 191
World War II and, 320
Roosevelt, Theodore, 87, 191
Rothschild, Nathan Mayer, 528
rubber, 46
Rubin, Bob, 491
Rubin, Robert, 508
Ruhr Valley, 183
Russia
France and, 131
Hitler and, 275
inflation in, 183
population level in, 246
post–World War I, 172–173
before Revolution, 242
World War I and, 153–154
see also Soviet Union
Russian
Civil War in, 81, 173, 243,
246
Revolution in, 81, 242
Russo-Japanese War (1905), 152
Rust Belt, 445
Rykov, Aleksey, 456

Saigō Takamori, 133
Salisbury, Lord, 146
Samsung, 368
Samuelson, Paul, 455
Sandinistas, 457

Sarraut, Albert, 224–225
Sassoon, Donald, 65
savings vehicles, demand for, 495
Say, Jean-Baptiste, 205–206, 207
"Say's Law," 205–206
Scandinavia
during Great Depression, 222
social democracy in, 222,
226–227
Schrödinger, Erwin, 470
Schumpeter, Joseph, 82, 137–138,
167, 180–181, 214–215, 401
Schwartz, Anna, 212
scissors crisis, 254–255
Scopes Monkey Trial, 103
sea control, 117
Second Anglo-Maratha War, 51
Second Bank of the United
States, 198
second industrial revolution, 63
Second International, 262–263
second unbundling, 475–477
secret police, 246
secular stagnation, 510
segregation, 191
Selim III the Reformer, 121
Sepoy Mutiny, 119
Serbian nationalism, 151–152
Sewall, Arthur, 101
Shaihu Umar (Balewa), 347
Shimonoseki, Treaty of, 124
Shirer, William L., 301–302
Shockley, William, 472
"short twentieth century," 2
Siemens-Martin process, 64
silicon, 470–471
Silva, Maria Rosa, 40–41
Simon, Herbert, 397

Singer, 193
Siraj ud-Dowla, Mirza
    Mohammad, 119
Skidelsky, Robert, 188
slavery/slave trade, 36, 117,
    345–347, 376
Sloan, Alfred P., 196
smile curve, 476
Smith, Adam, 120–121
Smith, Al, 198
Smith, Howard, 392
Smuts, Jan Christian, 176
social Darwinism, 103,
    112–114, 260
social democracy
    discontent with, 435–436,
        438–439, 446–447
    elections and, 414
    inequality in, 415
    inflation and, 418
    nationalization of industry and,
        416–418
    neoliberalism and, 415–416,
        448–449
    in Scandinavia, 226–227
    socialism and, 222
Social Democratic Party of
    Germany (SPD), 159–160,
    173
social insurance, 409–411,
    447
social justice, market economy
    and, 6–7
Social Party of Germany, 173
Social Security Act (1935), 231,
    522
socialism
    attempts to implement,
        237–238

expectations for after World
    War II, 316
fascism and, 279
with a human face, 334
ideal of, 238–241
as intangible, 237
Mussolini and, 264
really-existing, 241–242,
    247–248, 260–261, 279–
    282, 316–317, 360–361,
    454–455
in Soviet Union, 167, 314,
    445–457
World War I and, 262–263
Socialist Party of Germany,
    110–111, 270, 273
socialization, 181
"soft" incentives, 417
Solzhenitsyn, Alexander, 259–260
"Souls of White Folk, The"
    (Du Bois), 376
South Korea, 366, 368–369
Soviet Union
    after World War II, 314,
        316–317
    containment and, 320,
        329–331
    Germany's attack on, 252
    impact of socialism on,
        455–457
    industrialization in, 254–257
    lead-up to World War II and,
        289–291
    recovery of, 251–252
    urban migration in, 256–257
    World War II and, 292,
        293–294, 305–306, 307
    see also Cold War; Russia
Sowell, Thomas, 377–378

Spaak, Paul-Henri, 324–325
Spain, 116–117, 132
Spanish Civil War, 227
Spanish flu epidemic, 151,
    171–172
Spartacus League, 173
Spencer-Churchill, John
    Winston, 41
Spencer-Churchill, Randolph, 41
stagflation, 432
Stalin, Joseph
  after Lenin's death, 251
  after World War II, 314, 315
  agriculture and, 456
  as axis point, 523
  China and, 360
  Cold War and, 316
  death of, 327, 328
  Hitler and, 289–292
  Korea and, 325–326
  Lenin and, 250, 253
  scissors crisis and, 254–255
  socialism and, 227, 238, 241
  Trotsky and, 81
  unification against threat from,
    324–325
  World War II and, 252, 293
Stalingrad, 304–306, 307, 308
Stanford, Leland, 42, 50
Statue of Liberty, 65
steam engines, 61
steam-driven machinery, 130
steamships, 39–40
Steeg, Théodore, 224
steel, 63–64
Stewart, Dugald, 120–121
Stigler, George, 382, 438–439
stock market crash (1929), 210
Strange Victory (May), 300

Strauss, Leo, 277
strikes, 408–409
Strout, Richard, 320
structural racism, 385
submarine telegraph cables, 53
suburbs, migration to, 406
Sudetenland, 286–287
Suharto, 335
Sukarno, 334, 335
Summers, Larry, 510
Sun Yat-sen, 128
supply and demand, 205–207
Sweezy, Paul, 315–316, 455
Syngman Rhee, 368

Taiping Rebellion, 123
Taiwan, 362, 366
Taiwan Semiconductor
    Manufacturing Company
    (TSMC), 471
Takahashi Korekiyo, 135,
    222–223, 513
Talented Tenth, 106, 191
TALF, 506
Taney, Roger B., 380
Tang Tingshu, 125
Tardieu, André, 224
tariffs, 136, 154, 171, 323–324,
    465–466
TARP, 506
taxes, 101, 207, 407–408, 411,
    442–445, 485–486, 522,
    531
Taylor, A. J. .P., 316, 324
technology
  acceleration of capabilities of,
    34–35, 60–65
  communication speed and, 53
  fecundity and, 8–9

technology (*continued*)
impact of progress in, 13–15
pace of diffusion of, 55–57
population growth and, 34
shifts in, 462, 469–470
wealth explosion and, 24
see also information technology
telegraph, 52–53
Tennessee Valley Authority Act
(1933), 520
Tesla, Nikola, 35, 66–68, 69–73,
143
Tesla Electric Light and
Manufacturing, 70
textile industry, 37, 49, 54–55,
61
Thailand, 477
Thatcher, Margaret, 278, 410,
437, 442–443, 447, 457
Thirty Glorious Years, 396, 398,
429, 446–447, 527
Thomas, Norman, 408
Thomas-Gilchrist process, 64
Thoreau, Henry David, 38, 39,
52
Title VII, Civil Rights Act, 384
Tocqueville, Alexis de, 107–108
Tojo, Hideki, 313
Tokugawa Ieyasu, 132
Tokugawa Shogunate, 132
Tokyo earthquake (1923), 294
tolkachi (barter agents), 248
Tongzhi, Emperor, 124
Tooze, Adam, 513
Totenritt, 158
transformers, 69
transistors, 471–472
transportation
decrease in costs of, 38, 47–49

funding for, 405–406
globalization of, 37
improvements in, 466–467
railroad, 38–39, 49, 50
steamships, 39–40
Transvaal, Province of the,
144–146
Treaty of Detroit, 409
triangle trade, 37
Trotsky, Leon (Lev Davidovich
Bronstein), 79–81, 241, 243,
246, 250, 252, 253, 254,
533
Truman, Harry S, 227, 316–317,
320–321, 323, 327, 403,
465
Truman Doctrine, 320
Trump, Donald, 530–532, 536
Turkey, 173
tyrannies, 24

Unbound Prometheus, The
(Landes), 469
unbundling
first, 47–48
second, 475–477
unemployment
deflation and, 187
depressions and, 209–210
gold standard and, 188–189
during Great Depression,
209–210, 213, 225–226, 402
Great Recession and, 221, 506,
508–509
imperialism and, 138
inflation and, 418–421, 424,
431–433
in post-World War I Germany,
270

unemployment insurance, 184
union movement, 231
Union Pacific, 49
unions, 374, 406–409, 442, 522
United Auto Workers (UAW),
    408–409, 420
United Nations, 313, 326, 464
United States
    after World War I, 169–171,
        197–203
    anti-immigration stance of,
        190–192, 212–213
    challenging of, 530
    Cold War and, 325
    defense perimeter of, 325–326
    emergence of as superpower, 18
    freezing of Japan's assets by,
        296–297
    gold standard and, 202
    income levels in, 340–341
    international trade and,
        323–324
    isolationism and, 189–192
    Korean War and, 327–328
    loss of status of, 530–532
    manufacturing and, 192–197
    national security spending in,
        328
    rising inequality in, 199–200
    social democracy in, 403–405,
        410–411
    social insurance of, 409–410
    transportation funding in,
        405–406
    unions in, 406–409
    war production and, 307–308
    World War II and, 294,
        297–298, 299–300,
        303–304, 523

    see also Cold War; Great
        Depression; *individual
        presidents*
Unity Building, 98
universal suffrage, 88
Urban League, 89
urban migration, 256–257
U.S. Steel, 75–76
Usher, Abbott Payson, 31
utilities, 199
utopia, definition of, 10
Uzan, Marc, 321

"V" series of weapons, 292
Vail, Theodore N., 196
Vandenberg, Arthur, 321
Versailles, Treaty of, 170, 181,
    283, 284–285
Vietnam War, 434–435
Viner, Jacob, 221
Vistula, 149–150
Viviani, René, 262
Volcker, Paul, 440–442, 443,
    489, 499–500
Volta, Alessandro, 68–69
voting rights, 18, 86–89, 105,
    184, 379, 381–382
Voting Rights Act (1965), 89,
    381

wages
    changes in real, 28–29, 34–35,
        44–45, 50, 183, 386, 479
    compression of distribution of,
        407
    migration and, 44–45
    in terms of calories, 18
    in United States, 419
    see also income inequality

Index

Wagner Act (1935), 231, 407, 411, 521, 522
war communism, 243–246
War Labor Board, 374
war of the currents, 71
Washington, Booker T., 105, 106, 191
water mills, 61
wealth, explosion of, 23–24
wealth tax, 181
weaving, 36
Weber, Axel, 490–492
Weber, Max, 147–148, 150, 282, 454–455
Weimar Republic, 182
Weitzman, Martin, 397
welfare capitalism, 200
welfare payments, 386
welfare state, 409–411, 447
Wellesley, Arthur, 51–52
Wellesley, Richard, 51
Western Europe
  interwar years in, 412–413
  social democracy in, 411–412
  welfare state and, 411–412
  see also individual countries
Western Wheel Works, 193
Westinghouse, George, 70–72
Westinghouse Electric and Manufacturing Company, 71
Weydemeyer, Joseph, 237
White, Harry Dexter, 323, 464
"White Revolution," 356
white supremacism, 104–107
Whitney, Eli, 192–193
Wilhelm II, 152–153, 154, 173, 263
Wilson, Charlie, 409
Wilson, Paul, 230

Wilson, Woodrow, 103–104, 107, 170, 174, 190, 191, 198
windmills, 61
Winthrop, John, 330
Wittgenstein, Ludwig, 8
women, 387–394
Workers' Party of Marxist Unification, 279
World Bank, 323, 464–465
World War I
  American advantage and, 79
  aristocracy and, 154–155
  conditions after, 165–167, 169, 172–176
  impact of, 144, 151, 153–154, 161–163, 526–527
  lead-up to, 113–114, 151–153
  research labs and, 158–159
  resources needed during, 157–158
  start of, 155–156
  United States after, 169–171
World War II
  Britain and, 291–292, 297–298
  China and, 294
  conditions after, 310
  deaths caused by, 298
  France and, 291–292, 300–302
  German personnel losses during, 306–307
  Germany and, 297–310
  Japan and, 294–298
  lead-up to, 283–288
  Soviet Union and, 292, 293–294, 305–306, 307
  start of, 276–277

United States and, 294,
297–298, 299–300,
303–304, 523
wrought iron, 63–64

Xi Zhongzun, 363
Xiang Army, 123

Yamagata Aritomo, 133
Yom Kippur War, 423, 432
Young, Andrew, 381
Young Majors, 347–348

Ypres, First Battle of, 271
Ypres, Second Battle of, 159
Yuan Shikai, 128

zaibatsu, 295
Zambia, 369
Zandi, Mark, 506
Zangara, Giuseppe, 35
Zeng Guofan, 123
Zhao Ziyang, 363
Zhou Enlai, 43
Zinoviev, Gregory, 280

BASIC
BOOKS

Basic Books UK is a dynamic imprint from John Murray Press that seeks to inform, challenge and inspire its readers. It brings together authoritative and original voices from around the world to make a culturally rich and broad range of ideas accessible to everyone.

RECENT AND FORTHCOMING TITLES BY BASIC BOOKS UK

The Nowhere Office by Julia Hobsbawm

Free Speech by Jacob Mchangama

Hidden Games by Moshe Hoffman and Erez Yoeli

The Ceiling Outside by Noga Arikha

Before We Were Trans by Kit Heyam

Slouching Towards Utopia by J. Bradford DeLong

African Europeans by Olivette Otele

How to Be Good by Massimo Pigliucci

The Mongol Storm by Nicholas Morton

For Profit by William Magnuson

Escape from Model Land by Erica Thompson

Truth and Repair by Judith L. Herman

Queens of a Fallen World by Kate Cooper

Elixir by Theresa Levitt

Power and Progress by Daron Acemoglu and Simon Johnson

1923 by Mark Jones

Credible by Amanda Goodall

The Master Builder by Alfonso Martinez Arias

A Theory of Everyone by Michael Muthukrishna

Justinian by Peter Sarris

The Women Who Made Modern Economics by Rachel Reeves

Starborn by Roberto Trotta